Public Sector Reform Using Information Technologies:

Transforming Policy Into Practice

Thanos Papadopoulos
University of Southampton, UK

Panagiotis Kanellis
Ernst & Young, Greece

Information Science
REFERENCE

Senior Editorial Director:	Kristin Klinger
Director of Book Publications:	Julia Mosemann
Editorial Director:	Lindsay Johnston
Acquisitions Editor:	Erika Carter
Development Editor:	Michael Killian
Production Editor:	Sean Woznicki
Typesetter:	Christen Croley
Print Coordinator:	Jamie Snavely
Cover Design:	Nick Newcomer

Published in the United States of America by
Information Science Reference (an imprint of IGI Global)
701 E. Chocolate Avenue
Hershey PA 17033
Tel: 717-533-8845
Fax: 717-533-8661
E-mail: cust@igi-global.com
Web site: http://www.igi-global.com

Library of Congress Cataloging-in-Publication Data

Public sector reform using information technologies: transforming policy into practice / Thanos Papadopoulos and Panagiotis Kanellis, editors.

p. cm.

Includes bibliographical references and index.

Summary: "This book offers an analytical, interdisciplinary examination of electronic governance implementation from theoretical and practical perspectives, for researchers in fields like computer science, information systems, and sociology, and practitioners in policy formulation, implementation, and IT and systems deployment"--Provided by publisher.

ISBN 978-1-60960-839-2 (hardcover) -- ISBN 978-1-60960-840-8 (ebook) -- ISBN 978-1-60960-841-5 (print & perpetual access) 1. Online social networks. 2. Internet in public administration. 3. Public administration--Technological innovations. I. Papadopoulos, Thanos. II. Kanellis, Panagiotis, 1967-

HM742.P83 2012

352.3'80285--dc22

2011011411

British Cataloguing in Publication Data

A Cataloguing in Publication record for this book is available from the British Library.

Table of Contents

Detailed Table of Contents

As part of ongoing research about the transformative impact of information technology (IT) on politics and government, this chapter outlines developments over the last four years in the use of IT in the federal government of Canada and the Province of Ontario. Areas discussed include online political campaigning, politicization of government's online presence, advocacy websites, online service delivery, and public consultation. While Canada and Ontario were previously considered to be at the leading edge and have made progress over the last four years, the 2008 Obama election campaign as well as online consultation and service delivery initiatives undertaken in the first year of the Obama Administration strongly suggest that the United States Government has surpassed Canada.

IT based public sector reforms takes place within a contested policy and socio-economic context but one that often appears non-controversial since the pursuit of development is generally desirable. In this chapter we explore this context from two discursive perspectives, the dominant international ICT development dialogue associated with western institutions, and from postcolonial theory that emanates from reflections on the postcolonial condition found in most developing countries. They are presented as representing a contrived and an actual context respectively that give rise to policy-practice gaps. The discussion brings out the limitations of developmentalism when conceptualizing IT innovations and change in postcolonial developing countries, and suggests an approach that factors in postcolonial theory in bridging these gaps. This would strengthen existing innovative approaches and provide new analytical perspectives that factor in history, time, global geo-political structures, and the submerged potentially destabilizing voices in former colonies. Future research directions towards post-development and their challenges are also highlighted.

Management is what makes e-Government successful by coordinating the use of corporate resources, managing relationships and empowering strategic alliances. However, current e-Government methodologies and models used are only tailored to specific requirements. This restrains the ability to compare cases and draw valuable conclusions as to how to improve e-Government and its performance measurements. Therefore, the authors are attempting to address the issues faced by surveying the models consisting of effective practices in e-Government and information technology integration management and support. The study provides in depth overview of the current status of e-government models and links with emerging information technology.

The objective of the chapter is to discuss how information technology can mitigate constraints to policy implementations stemming from a highly contested context. Main recommendations have been drawn by discussing main challenges met by Kenya in the restructuring of its health information systems as demanded by health sector reforms. The discussion will focus on how information technology can be used to limit the drawbacks of a highly contested policy context, mediate between global and local interests, and mitigate resistance to change. The chapter concludes with main recommendations on how to extend research on the implications of software designs in implementing public sector reforms and other policies in developing countries.

The use of information technologies in government as a strategy for public sector reform has increased in the last few years. Governments around the world are attempting to obtain the benefits of what is now called "electronic government." However, information technologies are only one component of what should be a much more complex reform strategy involving changes in organizational characteristics, institutional arrangements, and contextual factors. Based on a survey of public servants from the federal Mexican government and using institutional theory as the analytical lenses, this chapter presents descriptive results about the characteristics, objectives, results, and success of inter-organizational electronic government initiatives. Overall, the projects were considered successful and some of these aspects could be considered important for administrative reform efforts. The areas identified with the greatest success were (1) improvement in the quality of service, (2) creation of a more transparent government, and (3) creation of the necessary infrastructure for the use of information technologies. In contrast, the areas with room for improvement were (1) fostering citizen participation, (2) cost reduction, and (3) increased agency productivity.

This chapter highlights the research findings of a longitudinal study of online privacy and security practices among global municipalities conducted in 2005 and 2007. As cities worldwide implement sophisticated e-government platforms to increasingly provide services online, many barriers still inhibit the adoption of such strategies by the citizen users, and one such factor is the availability of a comprehensive privacy policy. The survey examines cities throughout the world based upon their population size, the total number of individuals using the Internet and the percentage of individuals using the Internet. Specifically, we examined if the website has a privacy or security policy, does the website utilize digital signatures and if the website has a policy addressing the use of "cookies" to track users. Overall, results indicate that cities are increasingly emphasizing on providing privacy and security policies with major improvements in 2007, along with significant changes in the top ranking cities in when compared to the 2005 study.

One of the cornerstones of Democracy is the participation of citizens in decisions that affect their lives. This participation, traditionally, is exercised: a) through national elections and the body of representatives, and b) through binding procedures such as referendums. However, there are decisions that affect citizens' everyday lives that require more frequent, day to day participation. Information and Communication Technologies (ICT) can create fast and secure communication channels, enabling politicians and citizens to engage in a mutually rewarding interaction leading to the development eDemocracy. However, lack of trust either between politicians and citizens or lack of trust of citizens towards ICT can raise barriers to this opportunity. In this chapter we discuss the issue of trust among government, citizens, and ICT. Our view is that it is nowadays possible to, at least, handle effectively the citizen-ICT facet of trust and provide the drivers for the convergence of eGoverment and eDemocracy realizing the concept of eGovernance. As a case study we present our experiences from the design and implementation of an eVoting system, which has the same strong relationship with eGovernance as traditional elections have with Governance.

This work presents the specific case of Turkey for public sector transformation by e-Government services development. The Turkish case will be presented with an aim to provide interesting and useful information for practitioners as well as academicians in the field of e-government and public transformation, and a focus on central government examples and policy orientations affecting daily lives of citizens. The rationale and perspective of the paper reflects practitioners' viewpoint, and assumes that the experiences of Turkey case will have echoes on other places, as the experienced and discussed issues have common characteristics with other cases. This practitioner analysis paper is then based on the co-authors' personal involvement in and reflections on the various aspects of the Turkish case, while the paper is written mostly as a result on secondary research.These reflective analyses are embedded within background information about e-Government development in Turkey, presented together with academic perspective of transformational government. E-Government Gateway, MERNIS, UYAP, e-tax projects in Turkey are specifically highlighted. A discussion of policy orientations that affect daily lives of citizens follows, and suggestions for future work and directions are also provided. The discussion especially underlines the shared service and citizen-oriented approach to e-Government service development with implications for process integration and improvement, if not yet for thorough transformation. It is hoped that the reflections and directions with respect to Turkish case presented in this work provides useful guidelines for new e-Government initiatives in Turkey and all around the world.

In recent years, ICT innovation is explicitly linked to deep structural reforms in public administrations. In this chapter, I examine the role of context, during the establishment of a minimal and accountable government apparatus, using the concept of 'negotiation space' as my theoretical lens. The process of imbricating ICT innovation within the local context is viewed as a clash between local institutions and the ones carried by new information technologies. This clash is empirically examined in the case of TAXIS, the flagship information technology project of the Greek government in the mid 1990s. TAXIS's implementation has been strongly supported by both the political system and Greek society. Nevertheless, ICT innovation did not triggered radical changes in taxation. Instead, it was infused by strongly engrained political practices which resulted in the implementation of an information system functional yet unable to support radical tax reform.

Information and communications technologies are emerging as important drivers of reform in the public sector. This chapter explores both enabling and constraining aspects of the role that ICTs can play in

Foreword

Electronic Government should counter, either in an active or in a passive manner, the profound, economic, social, or cultural changes that are taking place. It goes without saying that any change initiative becomes a major challenge especially if the stakes and the costs, either on monetary or political terms, are set too high. In an almost deterministic fashion, there is no choice; the way governments work, the way they offer services, and how they are monitored and controlled must be revisited and - in many cases - designed from scratch.

The Editors of this book hold posts in both academia and industry and exhibit significant experience and profound sensitivity to the practical issues involved in such initiatives, something that is clearly reflected in the structure and content of this book. Strategy and planning, implementation, and the required infrastructures are three of the main, if not the only, pillars of successful electronic government. The book chapters provide the analysis that an informed reader would require, in a manner that theoretical and practical issues are bridged in a seamless way. It should be stressed that the success of electronic government will be judged by the citizens through the implemented electronic services. Furthermore, the multinational character of the book is highlighted. Public transformation is not required only in certain parts of the world, something clearly indicated by the book.

Public Sector Reform Using Information Technologies: Transforming Policy into Practice offers informative and sometimes provocative insights on thinking about, designing, and implementing electronic government. This triggers really useful discussions on a variety of topics making clear that public sector transformation is necessary and important but at the same time really challenging to achieve.

Stefanos Gritzalis
Hellenic Ministry of Interior, Decentralisation and E-Government &
University of the Aegean, Greece

Stefanos Gritzalis *is a Professor at the Department of Information and Communication Systems Engineering, University of the Aegean, Greece and the Director of the Laboratory of Information and Communication Systems Security (Info-Sec-Lab). He also serves as the Special Secretary for the Administrative Reform at the Greek Ministry of Interior, Decentralization and Electronic Government. He holds a BSc in Physics, an MSc in Electronic Automation, and a PhD in Information and Communications Security from the Dept. of Informatics and Telecommunications, University of Athens, Greece. He has been involved in several national and EU funded R&D projects. His published scientific work includes 30 books or book chapters, 90 journals, and more than 120 international refereed conference and workshop papers. The focus of these publications is on information and communications security and privacy. His most highly cited papers have more than 1000 citations. He has acted as Guest*

Editor in 22 journal special issues, and has been involved in more than 30 international conferences and workshops as General Chair or Program Committee Chair. He has served on more than 230 Program Committees of international conferences and workshops. He is an Editor-in-Chief or Editor or Editorial Board member for 15 journals and a Reviewer for more than 40 journals. He has supervised 10 PhD dissertations. He was an elected Member of the Board (Secretary General, Treasurer) of the Greek Computer Society. His professional experience includes senior consulting and researcher positions in a number of private and public institutions. He is a Member of the ACM, the IEEE, and the IEEE Communications Society "Communications and Information Security Technical Committee."

Preface

As entities, governments are formed to serve and promote the will of the people. In following the utilitarian principles that were set almost two centuries ago, the modern government sees itself as a coordinating mechanism that plans, decides, and acts for the welfare of its citizens. It is controlled by the rules of democracy, which confer authority upon it and give it power, whilst at the same time scrutinizing it for the way it defines its mission and operationalizes its strategy. Efficient, effective, and accountable are the words that describe to a large extent any successful organization, and any government as such should aspire to those.

Governments reinvent themselves. They have no other choice as they are pushed by forces that are beyond the control of any single politician or groups of policy makers operating within the geographic boundaries that define single countries. This is one world we all live in and if the notion of one proves difficult to be perceived by the intellect alone then one has to look at his next door neighbour. Neither the possible difference in the colour of the skin and religious beliefs nor differences in food taste, dress code, or mannerisms will negate the fact that this is your fellow citizen. And it doesn't really matter whether the name of the country where this fellowship exists is United States, India, or Singapore.

And as I look at my different next-door neighbour as my fellow citizen, I look at the country that I share geographical boundaries with and compare the things that for some reason I've been cut off from, the things that I could also experience and enjoy but I cannot. These may be many and of varied forms, some I can demand and some I cannot, but in a democracy I can certainly contest my rights to the fundamentals and I will judge my government according to its ability or inability to deliver those.

What those fundamentals can be? For example, I don't want to be cut off from the accumulated wisdom of my country and from the world of learning. Could a national digital library be the answer? At this very moment, the Dutch are set to digitize every book and newspaper published in printed form from 1470 to the present day. The French announced the same, committing themselves by reserving 750 million Euros to the process. Developed countries aim for inclusion and not exclusion. They offer superior services to their citizens striving at the same time to be efficient and effective. They are the ones that the citizens of this one world will choose to live in and make them prosper in turn. For that, countries have to build competencies and remain competitive in this global pallete, serving the needs of their citizens as a corporation protects its most precious assets or take care of the needs of its customer base who keeps it alive.

Fight for inclusivity, offer superior service and reduce administrative burden to the bare minimum at the same time. This is the call, and the means to achieve the results are without doubt numerous. This book's focal point is the technology as one of the means - or tool - and the aspects around its mobilization for this purpose. There is enough collective wisdom available and lessons learned from countries around the world that pioneered electronic government solutions and transformed the ways services reach their citizenship. At the bottom is change, and change is never easy to achieve. Everybody learns in the process; both the supplier of the service and the consumer of it, provided there is the will from both sides.

Anybody who had the experience to be a stakeholder in such an initiative and lived to tell the tale so to speak can certify of the polymorphous nature and extent of the challenge. There are many things to consider here but if you focus on just one, namely the scale of such projects, the above becomes clear. Many have succeeded and many have failed. Singapore is hailed as one of the countries that has a digital government. Success is also evident in Scandinavia where countries there can also offer countless best practices and how-to's to the uninitiated. But failure is also evident and –because of scale again– when it happens, it becomes front page news that plagues governments for the rest of their service. Consider the negative publicity (and the extent of it) that surrounded the failed attempts of the British government to modernize the country's National Health System (NHS).

To this collective wisdom of the one world, then, this books aims to contribute. It is a multinational book in the sense that the authors of the chapters truly bring in a global perspective to the interested reader; for example, European, American, African, and Australian views are all fused forming a prism of multi-dimensionality of our attempts to reform the public sector using information technology (IT) across the globe. It is divided into three main sections, namely (a) E-Government & Public Sector Transformation Issues and Strategies, (b) Applied E-Government, and (c) Infrastructure for E-Government.

Professor Sandford Borins from the University of Toronto opens the first section by putting Canada and the United States side by side in the race for the coveted title of a 'Digital State' and tries to pick the winner. It is an interesting perspective on what it takes to be a digital leader from two developed economies judged accordingly to how well they fare in aspects such as channel choice, information technology procurement and organizational integration. The chapter by James M. Njihia of the University of Nairobi provides the contrast as the setting changes to post - colonial developing countries with the author exploring policy and socio-economic contexts for IT based public sector reform. Like Borins he seeks to understand by examining the difference between the 'contrived context', i.e. the context that is implied by a given approach, such as the dominant developmental models of progress within which public sector reform initiatives are usually framed, and the 'actual context', what actually exists in the proposed implementation domain, with or without the proposed IT based reform initiative. In the same vein but from a different and wider angle, Angelopoulos, Kitsios, and Moustakis argue that current approaches and methodologies in use are too specific and as a result we are restrained when we try to compare cases and draw valuable conclusions as to how to measure the performance and improve e-government initiatives. They go on to summarise the state of research to-date on the design of a model for e-government integration management and identify the most common dimensions which can be applied for measuring e-government management in the context of its use.

If an integrated model is what Angelopoulos et. al. are concerned with, Roberta Bernardi's contribution, which follows next, discusses how highly contested contexts can, in a sense, be modified by IT in limiting the drawbacks, mediating between global and local interests, and mitigating resistance to change. Frameworks are needed as reality abstractions and those two studies may be complementary to each other; one providing the lens, the other the real world. The two chapters that follow, the first by Luna-Reyes and Gil-Garcia from Mexico and the second by Manoharan and Fudge from the U.S. remind us that delivering an e-government system which is actually utilized and put to effective use by its stakeholders is by no means an easy task. The former wisely remind us that IT is only one component of what should be a much more complex reform strategy involving changes in organizational characteristics, institutional arrangements, and contextual factors. The latter report the results from a longitudinal study of online privacy and security practices among global municipalities they conducted in 2005 and 2007. What they found carries weight as it shows that IT on its own may not be worth much but when it is utilized to mitigate privacy issues or fears which restrict the widespread use of e-services by citizens across the globe, then success may ensue. Their results indicate that cities place increased emphasis on providing privacy and security policies with major improvements in 2007, along with significant changes in the top ranking cities when compared to the 2005 study.

Two contributions from Greece close this section. Manolopoulos, Sofotassios, Spirakis, and Stamatiou continue on the topic of trust but this time in the context of a far more ambitious scale. The freedom to choose and the exercise to vote are two cornerstones of democracy and the authors argue that although the technology may exist to make voting virtual and democracy itself an e-democracy, the lack of trust either between politicians and citizens or lack of trust of citizens towards IT can raise barriers to this opportunity. These issues are examined and discussed at length and the authors project a positive view that it is possible to overcome barriers and to proceed to practical implementations. They share their experience derived from the design and implementation of an e-voting system, which, they claim, could replace the traditional way elections are being conducted. Florou and Gouscos touch on sustainability, which is a national and European strategic objective, and set to examine how education through technology can strengthen social cohesion which is an essential condition for security and sustainable development. They support the view that Communities of Practice can utilize current social media technologies to such an extent so as to achieve the desired levels of cohesion offering in the long run the ability to remodel the public sphere, strengthen public consultation, promote proposals from the citizens and promote the policy of sustainability itself.

The second section of the book begins with a contribution which continues on the theme of education. This time the context is set by the Greek Ministry of Education and Garofalakis, Koskeris, Michail, and Oikonomou from the University of Patras present a Government Resource Management System. One of the key issues for governments worldwide is to run efficiently and efficiency means the reduction of the administrative burden to the lowest level possible. In this particular case, the challenge faced by the Greek Ministry was the management of several educational units and a large number of teachers spread around the globe whose purpose is to provide education opportunities for students with Greek origin. The authors describe the as-is situation and state of affairs concluding that the tools employed were primitive and largely ineffective. To address and transform this situation, they describe how an integrated Web-based solution was designed, developed, and applied together with the ensuing benefits from its implementation.

The new forms of interaction between citizens and governments made possible by the emergence of new technologies and the ways these can be conceptualised and developed is the subject of the two contributions which follow. Loukis, Xenakis, and Soto-Acosta correctly observe the rush of the governments across the globe to reform and improve their communication and interaction with citizens on important public policies issues through electronic channels. In doing so they feel it is highly important to develop and systematically evaluate IT and communication tools which can facilitate and support high quality interaction and consultation. In this respect they evaluate the use of a structured e-forum tool through a pilot on new legislation, which constitutes arguably the most important, complex, and extensively debated component of every public policy. Both advantages and limitations are extensively discussed. In turn, Purian, Ahituv, and Ein-Dor all from Tel-Aviv University draw attention to a single but important fact: as should be expected, there is heterogeneity of users in the public sphere. How do you accommodate it? They go on to propose a new citizen-view model, which takes heterogeneity into account according to three knowledge categories of participation. According to the authors, the knowledge level should not characterize the inputs but should instead refer to the knowledge level of the user in a specific context. In other words, since similar inputs may be perceived differently by different users in different contexts, the categories might be set according to the value that each user produces from the input. And so it follows that we cannot ignore but need to address and actively observe differences in demands, qualifications and aspirations if we want to be successful in enhancing collaboration of individuals.

Dicle Yurdakul Şahin and Deniz Türsel Eliiyi from Izmir University of Economics take the mobilization of IT to a different level, namely as a national strategic weapon with which a country's capability can be transformed and enhanced so as to increase its competitive position. In particular, they focus upon Turkey's pubic logistics systems and the authors review exemplary implementations of such systems around the world and pinpoint the specific benefits to be gained in terms of efficient operation and improved performance, profitability, customer satisfaction and social welfare. Unfortunately, they conclude, Turkey has not been able to reap the benefits of its geographical strategic position due to the unsuccessful and late attempts in implementing IT and transforming its logistics systems. From the same country, Balci and Medeni provide an overview on a series of attempts to transform the public sector by the development of E-Government services. Projects such as the E-Government Gateway, T-VOHSU (Turkish Project for measuring satisfaction from provision of citizen-oriented e-Government services), CEES (citizen-oriented evaluation of e-Government services), and UbiPOL (Ubiquitous Participation Platform for Policy Making) are discussed and reflected upon whilst the directions from the lessons learned that are provided by the authors offer useful guidelines for new e-government initiatives not only for Turkey but for the rest of the world also.

This section of the book closes with contributions by Elpida Prasopoulou from the Athens University of Economics and Business and Nick Letch from the University of Western Australia. Both underline the importance of the context. Prasopoulou explores theoretically the infusion of a local context with Information & Communication Technologies (ICT) innovation as a clash between the old and the new. She then empirically examines the nature and dynamics of this clash in a case setting, that of TAXIS, which constituted the flagship Information Technology project of the Greek government in the mid 1990s. Although TAXIS's implementation has been strongly supported by both the political system and Greek society, ICT innovation did not trigger radical changes in taxation. Instead, it was held back by strongly ingrained political practices, which resulted in the implementation of a functional Information System, yet was unable to support radical tax reform. Letch explores both enabling and constraining aspects of the role that ICTs can play in transforming the development and delivery of public policy, placing emphasis on two issues: (a) the reduction in the flexibility of decision making that frequently accompanies ICT-based initiatives, and (b) the critical role of knowledge embedded in networks of stakeholders in policy development and delivery, examining them in the setting of an Australian public sector agency.

The last section of the book has a strong technical focus on the infrastructures needed over which public sector services will be transformed and carried to the citizens. The section opens a contribution by Kubo, Akebe, and Nakagawa from Japan. As the authors note, Japan is a mature country regarding e-transformation, showing steady progress since 2001 when the e-Japan strategy was announced. However, the paradox is that although the use of ICT has spread, there is little system satisfaction among the citizens of Japan. Using a 5-stage maturity model the authors survey local government authorities aiming to explain this dissatisfaction paradox and come up with a number of interesting results unifying and expanding the maturity model with a management model. Bouras, Ganos, and Kapoulas, all from the University of Patras, Greece, inform us that broadband infrastructure is just a commodity, and local governments had better understand this. Under this prism the objective of the local governments is the creation of an open competitive environment, in which access and services are offered by many providers, thereby reducing the cost of services for citizens and businesses, while developing advanced, high-quality services. The authors go on to delineate five scenarios for broadband business models and illustrate their points by using a case study of a Greek inter-municipal broadband company (IBC) as the medium.

Stamati, Karantjias, and Martakos next present a case of implementing an innovative Local Government Access Framework - LGAF, deployed for the Central Union of Municipalities and Communities of Greece. The LGAF integrates almost two hundred and fifty government services in many different domains of the public administration, implementing peak XML technologies, worldwide standards, and specifications. The authors provide insights to critical success design factors that should be taken into account in order for the provided services to gain end-users' acceptance and allow the coordination and alignment of business processes and information architectures that span both intra- and inter- public organizational boundaries.

As the previous authors discuss intra- and inter- coordination, Muhammad Kamal from Brunel University, UK, takes this issue a bit further focusing on the importance of integration technologies and noticing that local governments have been slow in adopting cost-effective integration solutions to significantly expand the capabilities of their conventionally inflexible information systems. Kamal investigates what does and what should instead influence the decision making process for EAI adoption in local governments following a qualitative case study approach. Arifoğlu, Afacan, and Er, all from METU Informatics Institute in Turkey examine and analyze the aspects and factors related to Public Internet Access Points (PIAPs) by studying over 21 PIAP implementations in the world. They offer sound practical advice related to implementation issues by addressing such questions as what could be the potential PIAP types and how to create or increase public demand for PIAPs. The section concludes with a contribution by Stylios, Christodoulakis, Besharat, Vonitsanou, Kotrotsos, Kompouri, and Stamou, who explore text and data mining techniques for empowering e-government applications and services for citizen benefit. Stimulated by the need to transform e-government services to e-inclusion applications, they suggest the utilization of data mining techniques for processing the governmental data so as to extract and associate information fragments with real citizen needs and thus enables the encapsulation of the latter in future governmental decisions. This contribution can be seen as a fitting epilogue to the book as a whole; it deals with aspects any public transformation initiative should strive to cover, namely increase added value and enable citizen participation, enhance quality of life and cut off administrative burden to the bare minimum.

We believe that the book provides an interesting and informative ride for the interested reader in electronic government and public transformation. It offers a truly multinational perspective and the contributions through the issues they unearth, the successes, as well as the failures they discuss, prove that whoever is, or will be engaged in this topic, whether a practitioner or an academic, can be sure that (s)he is in for a challenging ride. Most importantly, however, the book reminds us that we should never forget that these projects and initiatives have a serious purpose, i.e. to increase the life quality level of our fellow citizens whilst promoting inclusion and the principles of democracy. To this, we need all the help we can get and we believe that in this book one can find many a valuable lesson to learn.

Thanos Papadopoulos
University of Southampton, UK

Panagiotis Kanellis
Ernst & Young, Greece

July 2011

Section 1

E-Government & Public Sector Transformation Issues and Strategies

Chapter 1
Which Digital State is Now at the Leading Edge?
Contrasting Canada and the United States

Sandford Borins
University of Toronto, Canada

ABSTRACT

As part of ongoing research about the transformative impact of Information Technology (IT) on politics and government, this chapter outlines developments over the last four years in the use of IT in the federal government of Canada and the Province of Ontario. Areas discussed include online political campaigning, politicization of government's online presence, advocacy websites, online service delivery, and public consultation. While Canada and Ontario were previously considered to be at the leading edge and have made progress over the last four years, the 2008 Obama election campaign as well as online consultation and service delivery initiatives undertaken in the first year of the Obama Administration strongly suggest that the United States Government has surpassed Canada.

INTRODUCTION

In our book *Digital State at the Leading Edge*, published in January 2007, my co-authors and I explored whether information technology (IT) is indeed transforming politics and government (Borins et al., 2007). The book attempted to transcend the bifurcation between research on the impact of IT on politics and research on the impact of IT on service delivery that characterizes the field by considering both areas of impact in an integrated conceptual and empirical framework. As a transformation necessarily unfolds over time, we did this by means of longitudinal research about the impact of IT between 2000 and 2005 upon the federal government of Canada and the government of

DOI: 10.4018/978-1-60960-839-2.ch001

the Province of Ontario, two widely considered to be at the leading edge. (For comparative purposes, the book also included chapters about the US and UK.) The transformation we were tracking was not in the essence of politics (seeking office and exercising power) or government (implementing policy and delivering service) but rather in how people understand and perform these activities. Our research ended with the federal election of January 2006. The purpose of this chapter is to report on how the evolution of the relationship between IT, politics and government in the last four years – a considerable period of time for rapidly-changing technology – focusing on the Canadian and Ontario governments, but continuing to pay attention to the US and UK.

The primary basis for the claim – incorporated in the book's title – that the Government of Canada was at the leading edge was that it was consistently ranked first in the annual surveys of e-government maturity conducted in the early years of the previous decade by Accenture. Accenture was particularly impressed by Canada's Government On-Line initiative to put all major government services online and integrate them by user needs rather than departmental affiliation (Borins, 2007, p.37). The e-government literature has identified integrated online service as the penultimate step in the transformation of government, and interactive online democracy as its culmination (West 2005). I consider this notion of a sequence of developmental steps to be deeply flawed because it leads researchers to look first at online services and only later at online democracy initiatives emanating from the public service. As this chapter will show, initiatives in online democracy are more likely to emanate from the political world as the consequence of practices in online campaigning, and may occur well before online government services have been fully developed. This chapter – as reflected in its title – argues that Canada has fallen behind the United States because the Obama Administration has begun to apply to the work of governing the leading edge digital politics techniques developed by the Obama campaign. Whether or not the United States Government is now *the* leading edge requires comparisons with governments other than Canada's, something beyond the scope of this chapter.

The research for *Digital State at the Leading Edge* involved two surveys of federal and Ontario legislators, interviews of public servants in the IT area, and comprehensive tracking of party websites during several election campaigns. It was generously supported by grants of $333,000 Canadian (210,000 GBP at current exchange rates) from the Social Sciences and Humanities Research Council of Canada between 2002 and 2007. The research methodology for this chapter was more informal because it was conducted after the funding for the project expired. In April 2007, I began a weekly blog focusing on the impact of technology on politics and government (www.sandfordborins.com). I observed the use of IT in political campaigning in the 2007 Ontario election, 2008 federal election, and 2008 US primaries and federal election, paying considerable attention to the ways candidates and activists used social media such as YouTube and Facebook. Finally, I did considerable reading about IT, particularly in the newspapers of record in Canada (*The Globe and Mail*) and the US (*The New York Times*). During the last four years, these two newspapers have been paying growing attention to IT issues, as well as expanding their online editions, which have become increasingly important to their readership. It is not uncommon to see hundreds of comments, some by well-known party activists, on lead articles by 6 a.m., just as the print version is being delivered. These observations were validated by a recent Pew Research Center survey that noted that the US population's use of the Internet as the primary source of news increased dramatically from 24 percent in 2007 to 40 percent in 2008, thus for the first time surpassing newspapers, which held constant at 35 percent (Mindlin, 2009).

This chapter begins by reviewing the conclusions reached in *Digital State at the Leading Edge* about the nature and extent of IT-based transformation in government as of early 2006. The chapter then presents evidence from the last four years that bears upon those conclusions. It starts with politics, focusing first on Barack Obama's successful campaign for the presidency, which now represents the global leading edge of online campaigning, before moving to the Canadian federal and Ontario campaigns. Shifting from politics per se to the interface between politics and government, it discusses evidence of the politicization of the online presence of Canadian governments, coupling this with a related phenomenon: the establishment of advocacy websites for government priorities. The chapter also deals with the use of digital technology within the public service, and includes an overview of the state of online service delivery, as well as recent Web 2.0 initiatives undertaken by public servants. The chapter concludes with some speculation about the likely impact of IT on government in the near future.

AN INCOMPLETE TRANSFORMATION

The over-arching conclusion reached in *Digital State at the Leading Edge* was that the IT-based transformation was incomplete, with more evidence of material change in some areas than in others (Borins et al., 2007, pp. 357-69). We begin where the difference has been most striking. Government workplaces now fully incorporate, and public servants use, up-to-date IT. There has been a reduction in the ranks of clerical employees, with a concomitant increase in the ranks of the IT organization. Technology has heightened immediacy as an increasing proportion of public servants, especially senior managers, use BlackBerries or other personal digital assistants, with the consequence that politicians and public servants are constantly accessible to each other, the media, and citizens generally. Government websites are now the means of choice for the communication and accessing of government information. Citizens are making use of both official government information posted online and other information generated by or about politicians and available online in unanticipated ways, some of which have proven to be acutely embarrassing to governments and individual politicians.

The transformation is less complete in the area of service delivery and organizational restructuring. Service delivery by online transactions has grown rapidly, but the older media, particularly the telephone, remain popular. IT has the potential to restructure government based on integrated service delivery at the front end, joined-up policy making in the middle, and integrated procurement and support service at the back end. Restructuring initiatives such as Service Canada and ServiceOntario have made some progress in that direction, but it is a reflection of their relative immaturity, that more needs doing in front-end integration and shared services. The organizational home and political reporting relationships of these initiatives are still unclear; Service Canada, for example, remains a component of Human Resources and Skills Development Canada (HRSDC), though it could well lay claim to status as a department.

Management consultants selling IT-based solutions to government have emphasized its potential to affect enormous cost savings. Advocates within government have predicted transformative effects stemming from these savings. In reality, the impact of such savings is felt primarily on the twenty percent of government spending accounted for by overhead costs. What is more, such savings are always at risk of being undercut by cost overruns on the complex IT projects on which they depend.

THE NEW PRIMACY OF ONLINE POLITICS

In the course of conducting the research for *Digital State at the Leading Edge*, several CIOs and politicians who were early adopters of IT were interviewed, and they often complained that most politicians, in their personal lives, were on the backward side of the digital divide and did not understand the potential impact of IT on government or politics. In the light of developments over the last four years, these statements now appear ironic, to the point that one might say to CIOs seeking more attention from politicians, "be careful what you wish for." Indeed, the two surveys of politicians' use of IT reported in *Digital State at the Leading Edge* showed increasing use of technology to the point that by 2005, over 90 percent of federal and Ontario legislators were using email and the Internet daily, and a majority of both groups described themselves as either very competent or at least confident in their use of technology (Borins et al, 2007, pp. 234-47). More and more legislators carry BlackBerries and use them constantly to stay in touch with their parliamentary and constituency offices, their colleagues, and the bureaucracy (MacLeod, 2008).

That IT is becoming increasingly important in political campaigning should not be surprising. Political campaigning is, in its essence, cut-throat competition; unlike the economic marketplace, politics is not focused on winning market share, but is winner-take-all. Political campaigns, because they involve long hours, little or no pay, commitment to a cause, and the prospect of rapid advancement if they are victorious, attract a disproportionate number of young adult participants (Harfoush, 2009, Tapscott, 2009). They have brought their IT-driven culture to politics, thus rapidly increasing the technological sophistication of campaigning in particular.

This perspective on the use of IT in campaigning is clearly evident in Conservative Party strategist Tom Flanagan's book *Harper's Team: Behind the Scenes in the Conservative Rise to Power*. Flanagan (2007) describes a number of episodes including the development of a sophisticated electoral data base (the Constituency Information Management System) now used effectively for direct-mail fund-raising, website development, the growth of the "Blogging Tories," and the use of the BlackBerry for immediate contact with the media. He thus generalizes from these experiences: "We are living in the biggest, fastest-moving communications revolution in human history. Each election campaign features new technologies. We [Conservatives] must be at the forefront in adapting new technologies to politics." (Flanagan, 2007, pp. 288-9) To paraphrase Bill Clinton's 1992 campaign: It's the technology, stupid.

THE OBAMA PHENOMENON

The prospect of a little-known first term senator defeating a much better-known candidate who had the support of the party establishment, and then being elected president, was very unlikely. But, in retrospect, it is clear that Barack Obama was able to capitalize on his own formidable strengths: rhetorical skill with large audiences, experience in community organizing, an ability to connect with younger voters, and a deep understanding of technology's transformative potential. The question for those interested in the digital state is what part online technology played in Obama's improbable but resounding election victory.

Consider, first, the magnitude of the Obama campaign's achievements. It raised nearly $750 million from 4 million donors, 550,000 of whom were contributing for the first time (Luo, 2008). It built huge online communities on www.mybarackobama.com, Facebook, and Myspace. The ultimate achievement, of course, was his election victory. From the digital state perspective, the most important aspect of that victory was his strength among Net Generation voters (defined as those between the ages of 18 and 29), who are the most active online. Their turnout increased from 48 to 52 percent, and while John Kerry's margin over George Bush among this group in 2004 was 9 percent, Obama's margin soared to a landslide-scale 34 percentage points (Tufts University Center for

Information and Research on Civic Learning and Engagement, 2008).

The Obama online campaign is now the true leading edge of the application of the online technology to politics. *Digital State at the Leading Edge* developed four key concepts for analyzing digital politics and government, and these can clearly be applied to the Obama campaign: digital leadership, procurement, organizational integration, and channel choice (Borins et al, 2007, pp. 14-36). I will explain them briefly. Digital leadership recognizes that innovations are driven by early adapters and thus focuses on those politicians and public servants who, perhaps because of their own technological expertise, play that role. While computer hardware has become increasingly commoditized, the large specialized software systems governments require pose major procurement challenges and run a high risk of failure. IT has the potential to restructure government along the lines of integrated front-line service delivery organizations at the user interface, integrated policy-making units in the middle, and integrated procurement at the back end. Whether the potential of this model to enhance service delivery and policy capacity while reducing cost will be realized depends on factors such as the willingness of politicians and public servants to restructure organizations of long standing and the willingness of the public to have their data shared across organizational boundaries. Finally, channel choice refers to choices by citizens about which channels (for example, online, telephone, or in-person) to use for services as well as choices by government about the availability, price, and other characteristics of services delivered through these alternative channels.

The Obama campaign's digital leadership began with the candidate himself, who is a technically-sophisticated BlackBerry user (or even addict). He saw the political potential of the Internet, stating "one of my fundamental beliefs from my days as a community organizer is that real change comes from the bottom up. And there's no more powerful tool for grass roots organizing than the Internet" (Stelter, 2008). As Obama was launching his campaign, he sought out IT industry leaders, for example, Netscape founder Marc Andreessen, for their insights into how online technology could support his community organizing approach (Carr, 2008).

Digital leadership leads to procurement, the second key analytic concept. What matters here is whom the Obama campaign used for its online services and here, too, Obama's choice was fortuitous. Obama hired Blue State Digital (www.bluestatedigital.com) a web development company founded in 2004 by four Net Generation members of Howard Dean's presidential campaign. The firm's mission is to use online tools to mobilize support for progressive candidates, causes, and products (Lowry, 2008). The contractors at Blue State Digital set out to advance the techniques used in the Dean campaign, taking advantage of the latest technological developments. Within the campaign organization, Joe Rospars, the Director of New Media, had worked with Howard Dean's campaign in 2004, and Chris Hughes, the Director of Online Organizing, was a co-founder of Facebook (Harfoush, 2009). The website www.mybarackobama.com was modeled on Facebook (which was launched in 2005), but with the goal of providing online support for activities such as personal fund-raising, calling voters, and hosting meetings or parties.

The concept of organizational integration has a slightly different meaning in this context than in government departments, for which it was used in *Digital State at the Leading Edge*. Here it means integration of the various components of the election campaign. Drawing on his rhetorical ability, Obama often spoke at large rallies. To get a ticket, supporters were asked to provide their email address, zip code, and telephone number. From this minimal but critical personal information, the Obama campaign built up huge email and telephone banks, creating a flexible and invaluable data arsenal.

The final concept is channel choice. The Obama campaign operated on all channels, both traditional and online. Candidate speeches at large rallies is a political tradition in both the US and Canada, though, as will be discussed in the next section, Canadian campaigns have forsaken it for speeches to small groups of party faithful intended to produce thirty-second video clips and sound-bites. Ultimately, the Obama campaign involved huge amounts of face-to-face activity: participation in caucuses in the states that held them, meetings, and door-to-door canvassing. The online operation supported these activities by giving volunteers information and by fund-raising. Those who signed up for www.barackobama.com (which I did) received repeated messages detailing the broad outlines of the campaign's rhetoric, new videos available online, and appeals for frequent small donations. The online campaign was also waged in a wide variety of media, including www.mybarackobama.com, Facebook, MySpace, Twitter, LinkedIn, and a YouTube channel with hundreds of videos.

The Obama campaign showed how to integrate the entire online package both internally and with traditional face-to-face community organizing and campaigning. It had its roots in the Howard Dean campaign of 2004, but went far beyond the Dean campaign in two respects. First, Obama was a much more convincing orator. Second, the Dean campaign used online technology for its own sake, for example in its plethora of meetups and online blogs, while the Obama campaign focused its use of online resources on mobilizing support for and participation in traditional face-to-face politics. In contrast to Obama's integrated online vision, the 2007 Ontario and 2008 federal campaigns show that in Canada all the pieces are there, but they still do not add up to a coherent whole – or a digital vision.

THE 2007 ONTARIO AND 2008 FEDERAL CAMPAIGNS ONLINE

None of the party leaders in the Ontario or federal campaigns adopted a mass mobilization approach comparable to President Obama's campaign. Instead of taking their message to the masses, their preferred platforms are speeches in small rooms to the party faithful. The standard format is for the leader to speak in front of visual props and representative individuals (police, firefighters, nurses, teachers) reflecting the theme of the speech. The objective of such a speech is to produce short clips that network television could use or that could be posted online. It was not ever thus in Canadian politics, and indeed the tradition into the seventies was for party leaders to speak in large venues open to all, including hecklers. The rubric that comes to mind for appearances by Canadian politicians now is "boy in the bubble," to signify the desire to keep tight control over the event, avoiding anything that could disrupt the intended message. A second great difference between the Obama campaign and Canadian campaigns is that Obama caught on with young adults in a way that no Canadian party leader since Pierre Trudeau at the height of Trudeaumania in 1968 has done, with the consequence that Canadian campaigns have not reflected as clearly the online behaviour of young adults.

Canadian party websites contain considerable content similar to American party websites such as information about the leader, the platform, and the party and lots of video, in particular advertisements that have aired on television. The material about the leader was generally intended to humanize him or her, for example by emphasizing his/her childhood and youth, family, and leisure interests. The parties often hive off separate sites to attack their rivals' policies and in particular their leaders' capability. The attack sites often appear to be aimed at younger voters with ironic and irreverent features the Net Generation is assumed to prefer. Where the websites fall far short of the Obama campaign is in the area of citizen engagement. Available activities are limited to joining the party, donating money, getting a sign, or volunteering for the local constituency organization. The most advanced was the federal Conservatives' "My Campaign" page, which provided text for letters to the editor of local newspapers and scripts for calls to local talk radio.

Despite the limitations of the party websites, there was considerable online activity in the federal and Ontario elections, much of it initiated by citizens, rather than party leaders' campaigns. It occurred in a number of areas, and reveals some of the changes the Internet and related technologies have generated in the world of election campaigning.

In the federal campaign there was a great deal of online vetting of local candidates by rival party organizations and citizen journalists, with the result that discoveries of embarrassing information online compelled several candidates to be dropped by the national party. This illustrates that, while individuals may control their own websites, they cannot control the information about them posted elsewhere. The level of scrutiny has dramatically increased from that undertaken in the pre-Internet era and, not surprisingly, skeletons are being found in the online closets of more candidates.

A second area of online politics involves the use of YouTube. Founded in early 2005, YouTube first came to political prominence with a video in the 2006 Virginia senatorial campaign showing Republican incumbent George Allen referring to a cameraman hired by the Democrats by the racial epithet "macaca." The video, downloaded 500,000 during the campaign, contributed significantly to Allen's unexpected defeat.

Since then, YouTube has come to serve a variety of political functions, including parties using it as an alternative channel for their advertising, parties and citizens using it to post candidates' gaffes (which reinforces the tendency discussed above of Canadian parties to run "boy in the bubble" campaigns), and citizens using it to advocate on behalf of candidates or causes. Two recent Canadian instances include Quebec singer Michel Rivard's *Culture en Peril* video attacking the Harper government's cuts to arts funding and a televised interview in which federal Liberal leader Stephane Dion stumbled answering a question about how he would handle the economic slowdown. *Culture en Peril*, with one million views in three weeks, and the Dion interview, with 300,000, both went viral, the former contributing to the Conservatives' failure to improve their showing in Quebec in the 2008 election compared to 2006, and the latter contributing to the damaging and ultimately fatal perception of Stephane Dion as a weak leader.

The widespread use of YouTube in both the American and Canadian election campaigns gives rise to the hypothesis that it has become the current political killer app (that is, a software application so popular that it transforms online political discourse). YouTube poses significant advantages: anyone, whether highly organized political parties or individuals working at home, can post at no charge. Anyone can watch, as it has no membership requirement. It is easy for individuals to email YouTube videos or post them on other websites, hence facilitating their viral spread. When journalists refer to YouTube videos, they need not publish or display a complicated URL, but need only refer to the creator or subject of the video: the reader can readily find it using YouTube's internal search engine. Finally, the developers of YouTube were proactive in contacting the presidential candidates in the primaries about how they could use it and in forging a partnership with CNN for candidate debates, in which questions were submitted on YouTube and posed to candidates on CNN (Heffernan, 2008).

A third online aspect of the federal and Ontario elections consists of a variety of activities that could be referred to under the rubric of citizen engagement. These include issue-oriented websites, such as those supporting and opposing proportional representation in the Ontario referendum on electoral reform; political blogs, such as those linked to the blog consolidator www.bloggingtories.ca; and citizen initiatives, such as the Facebook group Fair Vote Canada that facilitated strategic voting by supporters of the Liberals, Greens, or New Democrats designed to block a Conservatives majority.

While no Canadian campaign was comparable to Obama's, there was still considerable online activity in the federal and Ontario campaigns. What is difficult to determine is how significant it all was. The Canadian government does not require the detailed month-to-month campaign donation reports that presidential candidates must file, and Canada has nothing comparable to www.techpresident.com, which tracks statistics such as YouTube views and Facebook supporters for the candidates, and hosts discussion of online politics. There is also no data available about party website traffic or donations made online. The one longitudinal indicator that could be accessed was the Canada Election Study which in 2004 and again in 2008 asked voters what was their main source of election information. In 2004, 55 percent said television, 21 percent newspapers, 12 percent radio, and 3 percent the Internet. In 2008, this had changed to 55 percent television, 19 percent newspapers, 8 percent radio, and 8 percent the Internet. This does show Internet use beginning to cut into radio and newspaper.[1] Clearly, this is an area where more longitudinal information would be valuable.

POLITICIZING GOVERNMENT'S ONLINE PRESENCE

Tom Flanagan's advice to the Conservatives – It's the technology, stupid – raises the question of how IT-savvy politicians will use the government portal when they come to power. They will likely view the portal as an important opportunity to sell their political message to the voters. During the Chretien and Martin governments (1993 – 2003) the Government of Canada home page (www.gc.ca/home or www.canada.ca/home) emphasized service delivery, with most space given to the links to three service gateways (service to Canadians, service to business, service to non-Canadians), and only a small postage-stamp sized link in the top left corner to the prime minister's page. In April 2006, the Harper Government unveiled a totally revamped three-column home page, with news about the government, usually featuring the prime minister, in the dominant central column; a right sidebar with links to government priorities; and a left sidebar with a variety of links, including three small ones to the service gateways. The home page is bold, forceful, brightly coloured and, not surprisingly, contains considerably more Conservative blue than Liberal red. The Service Canada site (www.servicecanada.ca) provides an interesting contrast. It emphasizes connectedness by presenting services in terms of recipients rather than providers, and has an inclusive and friendly look and feel. As discussed in *Digital State at the Leading Edge*, the Service Canada site is a descendant of the Gateways and Clusters project, which utilized collaborative inter-departmental work teams with a higher than expected proportion of women (Borins et al, 2007, pp.42-57, 282-4). If the Canada site is Mars, then the Service Canada site is Venus.

The Conservative rebranding of the Canada site is not unique. Former British Prime Minister Tony Blair, while a masterful communicator through traditional media, had little facility with new media, and the prime minister's site (www.number10.gov.uk) during his government paid as much attention to the history of Number 10 Downing Street and former prime ministers, in particular Winston Churchill, as it did to the current prime minister. A little over a year after Gordon Brown succeeded Blair, the Number 10 website was revamped to emphasize the current prime minister, his policies, and news about him, and the historical material was relegated to a link at the lower right corner. Brown's successor, David Cameron, has maintained this structure on the

Number 10 website, but with an increased emphasis on interactivity and links to social media.

Some governments, such as those of the US and UK, have both a political portal (www.whitehouse.gov and www.number10.gov.uk, respectively) and a service portal (www.usa.gov and www.directgov.gov.uk, respectively). To an extent, the Canadian government is evolving in that direction, with the Canada portal and the prime minister's home page looking very similar, and three service portals, the most prominent of which is Service Canada's. In the provinces, the standard URL for a portal is http://www.gov.[name].ca/ where the province's abbreviated name falls in the middle. The question then arises of how much of any province's portal is used for political purposes (news stories with photos of the premier, political priorities, policy initiatives) and how much for governmental purposes such as links to services and departments or travel information for visitors. During summer 2007, a research assistant measured political content, so defined, versus governmental content for the federal government and the provinces and territories. Using the crude metric of surface area on the computer screen, considerable variation was observed, from 62 percent political content for the province of British Columbia, 48 percent for the federal government, to less than 20 percent political content for several provinces.

In addition to the sharing of space on the portal there are other issues that have emerged concerning the limits of political use of the government's property in cyberspace, with politicians demanding more, and public servants quietly resisting. Practices that have been worked out between politicians and public servants represent what in the online world is called netiquette. Basic elements include the understanding between politicians and public servants that the content of the government portal is frozen when an election campaign begins, so that the sitting government loses the advantage of incumbency[2]; material created at the political level for the government website (for example, a premier's video-blog) may not be transferred to the governing party's website (though there is nothing to stop it from linking to the government website); and a new government may not use the government website to criticize its defeated successor (say under the rubric of correcting the misguided policies of the past). The Harper Government, controversially, posted links to its 2007 Speech from the Throne on frequently-visited government services sites such as the Environment Canada weather site (www.weatheroffice.gc.ca) ; it did not do so for the November 2008 Throne Speech.

ADVOCACY WEBSITES

Exhortation has long been one of government's policy instruments. Increasingly, governments have been turning to the Internet as a vehicle for it. *Digital State at the Leading Edge* profiled Steven Green, manager of creative services and new media in the Ontario Cabinet Office, who described one of his major functions as the development of "eye candy" websites (Borins et al, 2007, pp. 280-1). By this, he meant Ontario government websites using leading edge technology and attractive graphics to communicate the government's messages to citizens. A research assistant surveyed the federal government and provincial government portals for such sites in summer 2007. The sites are generally linked to tabs on the right sidebar of the governmental portals. At that time, the topics of such sites included public services and lifestyle information for youth (5 cases), healthy lifestyles (4), combating domestic violence (2), economic opportunities (2), the environment (1), and medical wait-times (1). In February 2010 the federal government portal was revisited to observe its most recent advocacy websites. These were the Economic Action Plan (programs responding to the recession), the H1N1 virus, the earthquake in Haiti, armed forces recruitment, and the Vancouver Winter Olympics.

Looking at these sites together, a number of patterns appear. The sites are often, as Green says, "eye candy," making use of video and eye-catching graphics. This is particularly the case with sites aimed at the Net Generation. Most of these sites are on "transmit" rather than "receive": they provide information for all visitors but do not disaggregate information locally, provide transactions, or permit dialogue. The sites are likely not too expensive to develop and can readily be contracted out. When the sites go live, they are often accompanied by a launch intended to attract mainstream media attention to show that, by creating a website, a government is taking action about a problem. The launch might also be accompanied by television or print advertising intended to drive viewers or readers to the site. Thus, if exhortation is a policy instrument, then governments will take credit for using it. In some cases, though, government's urge to take credit might be at odds with the desired impact; the Ontario government's teen anti-smoking site, www.stupid.ca, in an attempt to be cool, downplays its origins.

A final concern with advocacy sites is their evolution. After being developed outside the government, a site may start out with a grand launch supported by a marketing campaign and linked to a button on the portal. Over time, government priorities change, and its button on the portal will give way to buttons for the latest priorities. If an older eye-candy site is not to die, it must be kept current and must have an institutional home. It is therefore likely it will migrate back to some departmental site, and give up its distinct look and feel and high online profile in exchange for regular updating.

ONLINE SERVICE DELIVERY

In *Digital State at the Leading Edge,* we discussed Government On-Line, the initiative of the Chretien and Martin governments to increase the availability and quality of online delivery of major federal government services (Borins et al., 2007, pp 42-57.). The program involved providing online information and transactional capability for 135 federal services, organized by three gateways and 31 clusters. It also included the creation of the Secure Channel for transmission of financial and personal data between government and individuals. Government On-Line reached its mandated sunset date on March 31, 2006, which turned out to coincide with the election of the Harper Government.

An ongoing legacy of Government On-Line was the creation in February 2005 of Service Canada, an agency reporting to the Minister of Human Resources and Skills Development Canada (HRSDC), with the responsibility of providing integrated services to Canadians through the in-person, telephone, and Internet channels. Thus, it was given responsibility for the federal government's 23 call centres as well as the management of what was the service to Canadians gateway on the Canada site. At approximately the same time, the Government of Ontario established ServiceOntario, also an integrated service delivery agency.

One way of measuring progress in online service delivery is the biennial Citizen's First survey undertaken by the Institute for Citizen-Centred Service on behalf of a consortium of agencies at all levels of government. The most recent survey, Citizens First 5, interviewed 6700 Canadians in fall 2007. It found a dramatic increase in the use of the online channel between 2003 and 2008, with the percentage indicating that they used the Internet in a recent service experience rising from 30 to 47 percent and the percentage using email rising from 8 to 13 percent. In contrast, telephone use stayed constant at 55 percent and in-person service at government offices at 48 percent. These percentages sum to more than 100 percent, and indeed 59 percent used two or more channels to receive service. Thus, the growing use of the Internet and email has complemented rather than displaced the other channels. The Internet has become the dominant channel for securing information and forms but service is often completed through one or more of the other channels. In terms of service quality, the Internet did very well, but telephone, while the most popular, continued to be the most problematic, with low satisfaction rates due to busy lines, lengthy waiting times, and trouble with automated systems (Kernaghan, 2008).

Service Canada has now been in existence for almost five years. It has grown to include 22,000 employees at over 600 points of service throughout the country, and its 1-800-O-Canada call centre takes 55 million calls and the Service Canada website receives 22 million visits annually. By applying IT, it achieved savings of $300 million in its first year through streamlining, for example consolidating 23 call centres, and reducing benefit payments made in error due to fraud. It has put in place performance standards and league tables for all its service centres and call centres. It has established a number of partnerships, for example, an agreement with Service Ontario by which parents registering a newborn can receive both a provincial birth certificate and federal Social Insurance Number within two weeks (Kernaghan, 2008).

Despite the progress Service Canada has made, improving service delivery does not appear to be one of the major interests of the Harper Government. Service Canada still has a somewhat anomalous and unresolved existence within HRSDC. It is understandable that it started its life within HRSDC, its first major client. But as Service Canada has begun to deliver services on behalf of an increasing number of departments, there is a rationale for making it a free-standing department or agency. Service Canada undertook one major advertising campaign, in spring 2007, using unexpended funds at the end of the fiscal year. The campaign has not been repeated. The e-pass, the electronic certificate developed by the Secure Channel initiative to support data exchanges and transactional services, is now readily available but it has not been supported by an awareness campaign. It would appear that the Harper Government is satisfied if Service Canada is running smoothly, but has made no attempt to invest in it in a way that would lead to displaying it as a major accomplishment.

A final concern of the Harper Government is that enhancements in online service delivery would require investments in large IT systems. Such investments carry the risk of cost overruns and delays, failures which can be embarrassing to the minister(s) responsible. The Conservatives are also familiar with the large project syndrome, having experienced it with their own Constituency Information Management System (Flanagan, 2007).

The most dramatic recent instance of the large project syndrome concerns Ontario's decade-long attempt to develop a system of electronic health records. After media reports of conflict-of-interest and inflated costs in consulting contracts, the Auditor-General of Ontario (2009) did a comprehensive audit of the $1 billion the province has spent on eHealth since 2002. He identified a host of problems, including poor strategic planning, delayed development of software applications resulting in underutilization of infrastructure, excessive reliance on consultants, and procurement deficiencies such as sole-sourcing and conflict-of-interest. The audit led to the forced resignations – tantamount to dismissals by Ontario Premier Dalton McGuinty–of the CEO and Chair of the Board of Directors of the eHealth agency as well as the Deputy Minister and Minister of Health. The dismissals of the deputy minister, the top public servant in the department, and the minister of the largest department in the provincial government vividly illustrate the risks to the careers of senior public servants and politicians resulting from failures in managing large IT projects.

FROM E-CONSULTATION TO WEB 2.0

Digital State at the Leading Edge chronicled the federal and Ontario government's early attempts at e-consultation. The federal government initially focused on regulatory issues, while the McGuinty Government in the first year of its mandate (2003-04) consulted on a wide range of issues. The federal government built a low key consultation portal, www.consultingcanadians.gc.ca, while Ontario's McGuinty Government launched a relatively high profile portal, but then scrapped it when turning from consultation to implementation in the middle of its mandate (Borins er al, 2007, pp. 253-76). The federal government's portal is still active, though it is not linked to high profile portals such as the Canada or Service Canada sites and, at time of writing, hosts only 10 mainly technical consultations.

The last four years have seen rapid growth in the popularity of social networking sites and wikis. As discussed above, politicians have embraced them enthusiastically as a way of spreading their message, particularly to Net Generation voters. In addition, citizens' groups have used them to mobilize support on issues that matter intensely to them. On November 16, 2008, the Ontario Government introduced a number of restrictions on young drivers. Within a few days, a Facebook opposition group – Young Drivers against New Ontario Laws – was formed and it quickly grew to 150,000 members. On December 8, a mere three weeks later, the government rescinded its most offensive proposals (Campbell, 2008).

The question governments are pondering is how to respond to spontaneous citizen, especially Net Generation, use of social networking sites for policy discussion. Unlike the politicians, the bureaucracy has been wary of these sites. The Ontario government, seeing Facebook as a potential distraction from work, has blocked public servants accessing it. In addition, there is a likely bias in the public service against involvement by public servants with such sites even in their private lives. Having a high online profile, especially one that is controversial, is seen by some public servants as inconsistent with the traditional anonymity and non-partisanship of the career public service. Despite the official position, public servants seem to be coming to the realization that social networking sites cannot be ignored, especially if they are where the citizens are. The federal Department of Foreign Affairs and International Trade – which is among the most liberal in terms of staff Internet use policy – has developed its own YouTube Channel and Facebook groups. Several departments have developed internally-oriented wikis for staff dialogue. Two notable ones are GCPEDIA, developed by the Treasury Board Secretariat's Chief Information Officer Branch and intended for the entire public service, which has approximately 1600 users, and the Natural Resources Canada wiki, which is used by approximately 2000 of its 5000 person staff (Pilieci, 2008).

The overall impression is of a public service that is now groping for answers about how to fit into Web 2.0. For example, the Ontario Cabinet, including Premier McGuinty, saw the Net Generation response to the proposed driver's license restrictions as a wake-up call. Consultation under the government's rules on its tame e-consultation sites may work for highly organized groups such as regulated industries, but not for the large communities that form quickly about controversial topics. How does a government analyze, evaluate, and respond to something like the 15,000 wall posts on Young Drivers Against New Ontario Laws? Canadian governments appear to be on the verge of lifting their bans on public servants visiting social networking sites, but they are still wary of the outspoken commentary found on them. Public servants are establishing wikis for internal use, but are not yet opening them up to the public. The advent of social networking sites in the last four years clearly has the potential to transform public consultation, but the politicians and public servants involved in policy-making are not yet as ready to jump into the unpredictable and fundamentally uncontrollable world of social networking as avidly as politicians seeking office.

CONCLUSION: LOOKING BACK AND FORWARD

Looking back over the last four years, there have been a number of very significant developments in the ongoing IT-based transformation of politics and government in Canada.

- The increased use of social networking sites (YouTube, Facebook, MySpace, twitter, Wikipedia), led by but not restricted to the Net Generation, in political campaigning and in citizen-initiated policy dialogue
- The more aggressive use by politicians of government websites for political messaging
- The increased use of advocacy websites
- The greater use by citizens of the online channel for the delivery of public services, even in the absence of high profile government initiatives in that area
- Governments' growing experiences with integrated service delivery agencies or ministries.

Clearly, Canada's digital state has advanced significantly in the last four years, with the growth of social networking technologies as an important driver of change.

The four basic concepts of digital leadership, channel choice, IT procurement, and organizational integration – applied earlier in this chapter to the Obama campaign – can also be applied to the current situation in Canada. The Harper Government has shown digital leadership in the sense of energetically exploiting government websites for political messaging, and some provincial governments, most notably British Columbia, have done likewise. From the standpoint of channel choice, it is clear that the growing political involvement of the Net Generation is leading to more utilization of the online channel, particularly in terms of leading edge social networking sites, but also in terms of more popularity for online media and government services. Under procurement, we note that advocacy websites are reasonably compact IT projects with high political salience that can readily be outsourced. On the other hand, large IT projects, which often must be outsourced, still raise political concerns in terms of the likelihood of politically embarrassing cost overruns or delays. The final concept, organizational integration, comes into play in the growth of integrated service delivery organizations such as Service Canada, but it also speaks to their efforts to enable users to integrate the various services available to them, for example through information shared among government services accessible on the Secure Channel.

In as swiftly-changing an area as this, prediction, especially for the long term, is difficult, so we will focus only on some evolving issues, best considered as open questions.

The use of Web 2.0 social networking sites for policy dialogue, particularly by the Net Generation, will continue to grow. The overnight growth to 150,000 members of a Facebook group opposing Ontario's proposed law changes for young drivers demonstrates how quickly that constituency can mobilize when its interests are challenged. While Canadian politicians have used social networking sites without a great deal of popular response (as measured by the membership of their Facebook groups), some public servants have been denied access to Facebook, on the grounds it would be a distraction. Net generation public servants, where encouraged by their senior managers, are experimenting with social networking approaches such as departmental Facebook groups and internal wikis. While the online component of public consultations was, in the past, handled by government websites, the public service is likely to turn to popular private sector social networking sites as part of its consultation and outreach initiatives.

The Harper and McGuinty Governments might provide an interesting contrast, in that the former has exerted tight central control over its message, while the latter has often encouraged open public dialogue as an important component of policy development.

What can we expect for the future development of integrated service delivery agencies such as Service Canada and ServiceOntario? In his recent study, Kernaghan mentioned a number of unresolved issues (Kernaghan, 2008). Will governments require that departments transfer their service delivery operations to these organizations, or will they be contestable, in that departments can retain their own service delivery operations unless the government-wide service agency can do it better? Will the service agencies remain as operations within a particular ministry, as is now most commonly the case? Or will they become ministries in their own right? Will they be able to co-operate across jurisdictional boundaries (both geographically and by level of government) to offer truly seamless service? Will they be able to put in place identity management and authentication systems that protect users' privacy, thereby convincing them to agree to share their data across programs?

A radically different alternative to governmental integrated service delivery agencies such as Service Canada would be a Web 2.0 approach (Chang & Kannan, 2008). Government would attempt to meet citizens wherever they are online, and make extensive use of intermediaries. The intermediaries could be social networking sites or entrepreneurs who could combine government content and transactions with private sector content to develop business models that meet user needs. Examples of the latter could include banks acting as intermediaries for government financial transactions such as taxation and benefits in combination with their own financial services, or travel agents integrating their services with government online health and travel advisory services. The same questions that were posed about Web 2.0 consultation are relevant here. Governments have built their own websites to combine messaging about services, policy, and politics. Intermediary-developed services would likely undercut the cyberspace identity governments have worked so hard and spent so much to build since the dawn of the Internet age. A second consideration is whether intermediary-delivered services would meet the same standards of privacy and confidentiality that governments have developed on their own websites.

In the United States, Barack Obama's two months as President-elect and first year as President show that he has moved from leading edge digital politics to leading edge digital governance. At the personal level, he resolved the security issues posed by continuing to use his BlackBerry to keep in contact with his closest friends and associates (Baker, 2009). His organization created the first-ever website for the office of the President-elect with the revealing URL www.change.gov and it hosted a popular consultation process to develop a citizens' briefing book for the incoming Administration. When Obama became President, the official website www.whitehouse.gov was completely revamped. The most dramatic change was the establishment of a series of blogs about major initiatives, with frequent posts by White House staff or other administration officials, often leading to public consultations hosted on other governmental websites. In effect, www.whitehouse.gov has become the Obama Administration's consultation portal at the highest possible level. President Obama transformed the traditional Saturday morning radio broadcast by posting it as a video on YouTube. The Obama Administration has taken a major step to involve intermediaries in the development of public services by making numerous government databases available at www.data.gov and, through its Open Government Directive, requiring all departments and agencies to make available at least three new high-value databases. Finally, the Obama campaign organization, renamed Organizing for

America, has effectively taken over the Democratic National Committee, the machinery of the Democratic Party. Organizing for America continues to contact its 13-million person email list, for example urging supporters to lobby in support of the Administration's legislative proposals for health care reform and reform of the financial sector (Bai, 2010).

The Harper Government is using online technology to forcefully transmit its message. The Obama Administration, while no less forceful about its chosen message of change, is using technology to give citizens a greater opportunity to shape that change. Ultimately, that is the basis for the conclusion that it has surpassed Canada as a leading edge digital government. Academic observers of digital politics and government in the United States and Canada will continue to have much to comment upon and analyze.

REFERENCES

Auditor General of Ontario. (2009). *Special report: Ontario's electronic health records initiative.* Retrieved February 15, 2010, from http:// www.auditor.on.ca/ en/ reports_en/ ehealth_en.pdf

Bai, M. (2010, June 13). Democrat in chief? *The New York Times.*

Baker, P. (2009, February 1). New symbol of elite access: Email to the chief. *The New York Times.*

Borins, S., Kernaghan, K., Brown, D., & Bontis, N. 6, P., Thompson, F. (2007). *Digital state at the leading edge.* Toronto, Canada: University of Toronto Press.

Campbell, M. (2008, December 9). Ontario drops plans to limit passengers in teens' cars. *The Globe and Mail.*

Carr, D. (2008, November 10). Obama's personal linkedin. *The New York Times.*

Chang, A., & Kannan, P. (2008). *Leveraging Web 2.0 in government.* Arlington, VA: IBM Center for the Business of Government.

Flanagan, T. (2007). *Harper's team: Behind the scenes in the Conservatives' rise to power.* Montreal, Canada: McGill Queen's University Press.

Harfoush, R. (2009). *Yes we did: An inside look at how social media built the Obama brand.* Berkeley, CA: New Riders.

Heffernan, V. (2008, November 16). Clicking and choosing: The election according to YouTube. *The New York Times Magazine.*

Kernaghan, K. (2008). *Integrating service delivery: Barriers and benchmarks.* Toronto, Canada: Institute for Citizen-Centred Service.

Lowry, T. (2008, June 24). Obama's secret digital weapon. *Business Week.*

Luo, M. (2008, December 5). Obama hauls in $ 750 million for campaign, with plenty left to spend. *The New York Times.*

MacLeod, H. (2008, June 2). Call them Crack-Berries: MPs addicted to their little BlackBerries. *The Hill Times.*

Mindlin, A. (2009, January 5). Web passes papers as a news source. *The New York Times.*

Pilieci, V. (2008, October 29). Government creates own version of Wikipedia. *The Ottawa Citizen.*

Tapscott, D. (2009). *Grown up digital: how the net generation is changing your world.* New York, NY: McGraw-Hill.

Tufts University Center for Information and Research on Civic Learning and Engagement. (2008). Young voters in the 2008 presidential election. Retrieved February 12, 2010, from www.civicyouth.org

West, D. (2005). *Digital government: Technology and public sector performance*. Princeton, NJ: Princeton University Press.

KEY TERMS AND DEFINITIONS

Advocacy Website: Government websites intended to encourage certain behaviours among citizens (for example healthy lifestyle choices).

Digital Leadership: Politicians and public servants who are early adopters on information technology.

Government On-Line: Government of Canada initiative between 2002 and 2006 to put all major government services online and integrate them by user needs.

Net Generation: People between the ages of 18 and 29 who are the most active online and most sophisticated users of information technologies.

Online Campaigning: Use of the online channel (for example Internet, email, social networking) for political campaigning.

Secure Channel: Government of Canada initiative to develop an electronic certificate to support citizens using online transactional services.

Service Canada: Government of Canada agency with the responsibility of providing integrated multi-channel service.

ENDNOTES

1 The 2004 data are in Borins et al. (2007, pp. 190-1). The sample size was 4220. Unpublished data for the 2008 Canada Election Study were provided by its research director, Professor Elisabeth Gidengil. The sample size was 2354.

2 This can be considered the online extension of the practice of the public service ceasing its role in policy-making during election campaigns.

Chapter 2
Policy and Socio-Economic Contexts for IT Based Public Sector Reform in Postcolonial Developing Countries:
The Contrived vs. the Actual

James M. Njihia
University of Nairobi, Kenya

ABSTRACT

IT based public sector reforms takes place within a contested policy and socio-economic context but one that often appears non-controversial since the pursuit of development is generally desirable. In this chapter we explore this context from two discursive perspectives, the dominant international ICT development dialogue associated with western institutions, and from postcolonial theory that emanates from reflections on the postcolonial condition found in most developing countries. They are presented as representing a contrived and an actual context respectively that give rise to policy-practice gaps. The discussion brings out the limitations of developmentalism when conceptualizing IT innovations and change in postcolonial developing countries, and suggests an approach that factors in postcolonial theory in bridging these gaps. This would strengthen existing innovative approaches and provide new analytical perspectives that factor in history, time, global geo-political structures, and the submerged potentially destabilizing voices in former colonies. Future research directions towards post-development and their challenges are also highlighted.

DOI: 10.4018/978-1-60960-839-2.ch002

INTRODUCTION

This chapter contributes to the expansion of contextual approaches by drawing contrasts between *contrived* and *actual* contexts in developing countries. By contrived I mean contexts that are implied by a given approach, in particular, the dominant developmental models of progress within which public sector reform initiatives are usually framed. The actual [context] would refer to what actually exists in the proposed implementation domain, with or without the proposed information technology (IT) based reform initiative. The distinction between the contrived and actual contexts as defined may also be framed within the philosophical debate between forms of idealism and realism (Weber, 2004). However I use the terms in their everyday sense similar to Heeks' (2002b) notion of western design context vs. developing country usage context in his discussion of IT project failure in developing countries. The contrived context differs from Heeks' pragmatic definition of a western design context; it is more general as that implied by predominant paradigms informing international development policy and aid efforts for information and communication technologies (ICT). The actual context is taken as that implied by postcolonial theory, and is proposed as a better reflection of developing country contextual realities.

Postcolonial theory is associated with post-structuralism and critical social science theories in western philosophy. Although it is well known in the liberal arts, its possible practical implications for development policy are less well understood. We shall attempt to show how such a perspective may be used to bridge the policy-practice gap in IT based public sector reform initiatives. First we introduce IT based public sector reform and E-Government adoption in developing countries, and then highlight key issues in the international development and policy context. Dominant development policy paradigms are then contrasted to the postcolonial theory perspective in undertaking IT based reforms. We include examples of current research where such a perspective has been adopted as an improvement when transforming policy into practice, though inadvertently.

The arguments presented would apply to countries that were once territories colonized by European powers mainly in Africa, Asia and Latin America, collectively termed the tricontinental countries (Young, 2001). Over the last decade the term developing country has taken on new meaning with the rise of emerging economies e.g. China and Brazil as important players in the global economy and geo-politics. Some Asian countries are now classified as developed, middle income, or newly industrialized economies (NICs). This does not preclude their inclusion because it will be shown that the manner of their 'development' was because they selectively appropriated the idea and domesticated it strategically, which lends support to the postcolonial thesis and proposals in this chapter.

BACKGROUND

There is near universal consensus on the efficaciousness of adopting ICTs in the whole world including developing countries (Avgerou, 2003). ICT *for* development (ICT4D) and E-Governance are widely championed by international development agencies as important avenues out of poverty for faster integration into the global economy. It is frequently cited as a major opportunity for them (Mansell, 2002) and in the public sector, E-Government is associated with good governance (CAFRAD, NEPAD, & UNDESA, 2003; Grindle, 2004). In the year 2000 the G8 leaders adopted the Charter on the Global information Society and established a public-private partnership, the Digital Opportunity Task Force (DOT Force), to champion ICT globally. This resulted in a report that put ICT at the heart of development (Digital-Opportunity-Initiative, 2001). ICT was thus recognized as an *enabler* of development beyond the traditional conception of ICT initiatives as stand alone infrastructure projects, now they would be evaluated in the context of broader development goals. ICTs were also underlined as a major contributor to fighting poverty, and to achieving the UN Millennium Development Goals. With such high level attention, the pursuit of ICT4D and E-Government becomes imperative for national legitimacy in the international arena (Mansell & Wehn, 1998b; Stoltzfus, 2005).

IT-Based Public Sector Reforms in Developing Countries: Policy and Practice

Public Sector IT services cover delivering citizen services, services to business, industry, e-communication and document processing, and empowering citizens through access to information. Services may be availed online by departments, through conveniently located service centers or through a portal (Bhatnagar, 2002), and today through mobile phones, termed M-Government (Cilingir & Kushchu, 2004). E-Governance hardware and software solutions are available from vendors covering a whole range of requirements. In many cases it calls for distributed system solutions to overcome integration problems of legacy systems, and of existing stand alone applications (silos) for each government department (Bannister, 2001). Realizing this in practice is much more difficult and is context dependent. It is a context characterized by competing international and local discourses around the idea of development and the role of ICTs in its realization.

Public sector reform in developing countries has revolved around the drive towards better governance measured in terms of efficiency, transparency and accountability. This is also the presumptive aim of IT based public sector reform projects that are normally implemented as part of broader New Public Management (NPM) reforms. Such are today touted as key towards the attainment of desirable performance levels in government services (Heeks, 2001). There is strong external pressure for such reforms from international financial agencies (Ciborra & Navarra, 2005). As internet use grows in the world, increased global normative pressure will continue to drive E-Government growth and change (Wong & Welch, 2004). However it is apparent in the literature that a gap exists between policies and practices that compromise their effectiveness. At worst ICTs would be a "fatal distraction" that detracts from more important concerns for developing countries (Adesina, 2006).

According to Polidano (1999) NPM is more rhetoric than reality in these countries. Outcomes are contingent upon local factors and general national characteristics. Similarly Wong and Welch (2004) found that accountability was dependent on national characteristics and type of bureaucracy rather than technology adoption. Accountability gaps are maintained across nations even as the overall level of technology use rises. Accordingly, interactivity and transparency may represent different dimensions of accountability such that it is possible to have greater interaction through technology without a corresponding change in transparency. The case of E-Government adoption illustrates the contingent nature of efforts to translate ICT policy into practice in public sector reforms.

E-Government Adoption

Carter and Bélanger (2005) used the Technology Adoption Model and found that perceived ease of use, compatibility and trustworthiness were significant indicators of citizens' intention to use state E-Government services in the United States. Qualitative evaluations are more common in developing countries. They shed light on the human, institutional and social factors that influence E-Government adoption. First and most significant is political and E-Government project championship and leadership. Successful projects in Jordan and India were directly attributable to the political and national leaders with strong interest and belief in the benefits of E-Government (Al-Qirim, 2007; Krishna & Walsham, 2005). The governing religious movement slowed the pace of E-Government adoption in Iran due to concerns about citizen's access to the internet (Sharifia & Zareib, 2004). Kumar (2006) investigated the failure of village internet based services in Tamil Nadu state in India and found that they lost political and institutional sustainability. The project leadership failed to manage people, managerial, cultural and structural factors that would ensure continued support. Related to this is user demand as an important driver for E-Government adoption in developing countries (Mansell & Wehn, 1998).

Strong project management skills and the involvement of multiple partners also contribute to success (Bhatnagar, 2002; Ciborra & Navarra, 2005; Krishna & Walsham, 2005). Some of these partners are private sector groups, vendors and consultants that bring in specialized technical skills, and for long term strategic visioning. But public-private partnerships are no substitute for bad government; they still require effective governance to work. Training and cultivating departmental ownership for the initiative are crucial to pull through required business process redesign and administrative improvements. E-Government systems tend to reduce opportunities for rent-seeking by first-line clerical officers and will likely meet stiff resistance; again if not done well they may create new loop-holes (Bhatnagar, 2002; Ciborra & Navarra, 2005).

Long term sustainability requires integration into public budgetary systems and the development of local human resource capacities. This was cited as a potential problem in Jordan where there was great reliance on foreign sources that would exacerbate structural constraints (Ciborra & Navarra, 2005). Kimaro and Nhampossa (2005) term Mozambique's Ministry of Health as a 'ministry of projects' because it is simply a collection of fragmented donor policies and projects, a recipe for un-sustainability.

E-Government adoption in developing countries as this survey indicates is contingent upon multiple factors that vary across nations. An adaptive learning approach together with persistence has been recommended from a successful example (Krishna & Walsham, 2005). Iran adopted an adaptive implementation model to cater for its unique mode of governance, and national and social characteristics (Sharifia & Zareib, 2004). Local interpretations and reactions to policy issues arising from global pressures towards better governance and external players such as donors will also influence E-Government adoption. (These emerging approaches are summarized towards the end when discussing the implications of post-colonial theory for conceptualizing IT reforms)

Indeed the poor record of success especially in public sector IT developing countries has inspired research programs on failure avoidance and risk reduction (Heeks, 2000, 2001, 2002a, 2003; Sahay & Avgerou, 2002). Developing countries can ill afford policy-practice gaps in IT based public sector reforms in the form of failed projects, and thus merit greater attention by researchers. A better understanding of their policy and socio-economic contexts is a good starting point.

UNDERSTANDING THE POLICY AND SOCIO-ECONOMIC CONTEXT FOR IT BASED PUBLIC SECTOR REFORM

We may illuminate the gap in IT based public sector reform policy and practice by tracing backwards to that observed between research and its influence on policy (Carden, 2009). Today there is a trend towards better linking research to policy through an emergent field termed *policy dialogue* (Dhunpath & Paterson, 2004). It is an intermediate sphere where interaction between interest groups such as academia, politicians, civil society, private sector, and government may lead to shared interests founded on research finding their way into policy. Understanding the international development policy dialogue in ICT4D and technology transfer also requires an appreciation of associated discourses.

According to Carden (2009) "The record shows there are no universal 'best practices' for influencing policy with research. Every circumstance is different. Every situation presents its own complications of need and choice, danger and advantage for researchers and for policymakers." In practice, it tends to reflect existing power relations, for example between richer and poorer countries, where the former have many advantages in any dialogue. Secondly, Carden (2009) notes that any researcher that seeks to influence policy must count themselves as part of the policy process. Discourses by definition serve to obscure the role of power in knowledge creation (Avgerou, 2003). The use of particular types of research e.g. 'objective', for policy making, may simply be an avenue for powerful groups to have their way as they are usually founded on some discourse or paradigm that is not open to discussion. These are well illustrated in discourses of ICT and poverty, the digital-divide and 'development' as an idea, that inform much of policy research for IT based public sector reform. I term this a *contrived* context because it is a discursive environment only vaguely founded on developing country realities. Its real object is the interests of powerful players a particular discourse favors, and hence the policy-practice gaps.

Postcolonial theory on the other hand derives from experiences under colonialism by most developing countries that some consider as failed projects of colonialism (Dawson, 2004). It is a large and diverse body of knowledge with competing schools, ranging from post-modern/post-structural orientations to Marxian, critical theory, nationalists, and essentialists. Postcolonial theory suffers from its very founding as a dependent discourse defined by alterity, by that which it is not, i.e. the west as former colonial master (Mbembé, 2001). Debates amongst postcolonial writers are as heated and divisive as those in western philosophy (Dirlik, 1994). This is not surprising since postcolonial writers are often first trained in the western canon before applying these to their own contexts and life experiences. Potentially it may therefore offer nothing new.

However it does in one important sense, in that behind the western metaphors and structures to frame arguments there is a voice no matter how indistinct of the previously submerged. Using it is also an invitation to stop and listen by those engaged in reforms in former colonies, instead of assuming some generally accepted composite universal voice of the international policy dialogue. Resistance does not always have to be 'violent'; it could be covert over a lengthy period. This sense is well captured in Bhaba's (1994) notions of colonial ambivalence and mimicry. He explains how the ambivalence of mimicry by colonized subjects produces something almost the same, but not quite, in efforts to be like the colonizer. This is said to be profoundly disturbing to the colonial project. As imperfect resemblances they have their own presence though partial, as though the colonial project spread by producing the possibility of its own failure through the excess difference. Postcolonial theory explores such manifestations of similarity and difference. Thus it acts as a catalyst to go beyond the dominant international development discourse that as we shall see, is historically associated with colonialism, and to some extent is its heir.

Secondly, postcolonial theory forces development policy to confront history. It shall be argued that modern development planning is a-historical and ignores structural-historical forces that define and constrain policy contexts in ways that are generally disadvantageous to developing countries. Important research themes and paradigms restrict themselves to the immediate period or abstract theoretical formulations, locking out geo-politics. For example the reasons behind official policy (paradigm) change by dominant players in aid policy are rarely queried officially by bureaucrats in developing counties. A robust evaluation would deepen understanding of policy and socio-economic contexts and possibly narrow the policy-practice gap in IT based public sector reforms.

The Contrived: International ICT for Development Dialogue and Discourses

Contributions to Olsson and Wohlgemuth (2003) indicate that development policy dialogue favors richer nations (Edgren, 2003). It has not been successful in Africa where in the 1990s development policy was increasingly made to 'please donors' thus increasing aid dependency (Heijden, 2003). Over the 1990s technologically advanced countries formulated national ICT policies and strategies to guide its exploitation. By the start of the new millennium, tricontinental countries joined in with assistance from western countries, international development agencies, and international civil society organizations with different policy emphases. Because this information revolution took place at a time of rapid change in development policy, the ICT4D policy dialogue process ought to be understood in the context of broader reforms in addition to its immediate technical computing and telecommunications aspects. Two discourses are especially important to shaping, and possibly sustaining inequalities in the developed-developing country ICT4D policy dialogue: ICT and *poverty*; and the *digital-divide*. They illustrate the complexity of making sense of ICT *for* development in a world with many players, groups and interests, and that may be the genesis of policy-practice gaps.

ICT and Poverty

The 'war on poverty' spearheaded by the World Bank is the most visible and arguably successful discursive strategy in development practice. According to Escobar (1995) it led to a massive expansion of its 'poverty fighting' strategies and lending programmes, accompanied paradoxically by an increase in poverty. Escobar (1995) and like minded critics attribute this paradox to the absence of any real intention to do anything about poverty except as part of discursive strategies that perpetuate dominant power relations and resource distribution patterns. ICTs would then be construed as only the latest fashionable 'weapon' against poverty. McNamara's (2003) recent review of ICT4D global practices for the World Bank backed *InfoDev* ICT4D program acknowledged that poverty-ICT links were complex, requiring a multifaceted approach.

'Poverty fighting' involves the promotion of intermediate advocacy groups between citizen and state that raise the demand for good governance. Ultimately they reduce the role of central governments as they pursue 'alternative' non-government solutions (McNamara, 2003). Therefore while the Bank legally can only deal with governments, at the same time it may come across as undermining their legitimacy through such advocacy. Digital ICT internetworks and personal networks are central to facilitating these links.

Advocacy for the poor is divided between the dominant perspective of leading development agencies, and of left leaning social activists and movements. Pithouse (2003) compares a World Bank report *Voices of the Poor* on poverty to a contemporaneous report by a social activist, Ashwin Desai *We are the Poors*, which evaluates poverty in post-apartheid South Africa. He finds that the Bank's report presents the poor as victims and persons incapable of agency that can only be saved within the Bank's neoliberal vision. Desai's analysis is from a historical perspective to arrive at different left leaning conclusions.

Not all development agencies agree on approaches to poverty, but ever since the High Level Ministerial Forum on Aid Effectiveness in Paris the major agencies work together to coordinate policies and aid disbursement (Paris-HLF, 2005). This gives the Bank greater control over development activities and its version of what poverty is and how to fight it will likely continue to set the agenda even for ICTs.

The Digital-Divide

Aid and development agencies exist to address perceived material and ideational disparities across nations. An exemplar today is the *digital-divide* in knowledge and capabilities to use ICTs, and in infrastructure. It is often liked to poverty eradication to inform global ICT policy formulation (McNamara, 2003). However its role as discursive strategy is ambivalent in the construction of power asymmetries as it may be presented positively or negatively. It may be presented as easier to transcend than industrialization through technology leapfrogging, as evidenced with the rapid uptake of mobile and wireless communications in Africa (Wijkman & Afifi, 2002). Conversely, the rush to close the divide also provides an entry point for the west to lock up developing countries into quasi-monopoly providers of ICT services (Wade, 2004). This would be a serious long-term difficulty under the current global trade regime that appears to favor trans-national corporations (TNCs) over the poor and nation-states (Pithouse, 2003).

Presentation modalities and interpretations of the notion digital-divide in positive or negative terms (utopian vs. dystopian visions in Younis (2005)) are subject to human or institutional goals, interests, norms, and values. Castell's (2000b) global informational network economy spatializes inclusion and exclusion creating horizontal global categories. Useful social analysis would go beyond the nation state to economic and social class, ethnic, gender, age, and location differences among others. Accordingly the rich in poorer countries are hardly excluded while the poor in richer countries are marginalized.

Evidence shows that successful and beneficent transition to an information based society requires judicious management of relationships with global capital. Today India is often cited as an ICT success story, but it mandates that 51% of all foreign direct investment (FDI) in ICTs be locally owned against the logic of neo-liberalism and globalization (Mowlana, 1997). According to Wade (2004), ICTs and globalization would reinforce existing patterns of dependency if we 'bridge the divide' without giving attention to existing and potential ideological and structural pathologies in global power relations. It is instructive that since the early 1950s the realist (power oriented) paradigm other than idealist (traditional western liberal democratic values) has dominated in the field of international relations (Mowlana, 1997). The digital-divide as discourse may therefore be used positively to generate innovative interventions, or negatively to sustain historical power and resource distribution differences. Linkage with poverty multiplies the complexity of discourse and policy making in IT based public sector reform.

To better make sense of this complex policy environment for ICTs and development, we shall re-examine the underlying idea of 'development' as a contested concept, and how information systems researchers and policy makers interpret it for developing countries.

Development

Development has been the most notable policy goal over the years for tricontinental countries, many of which gained independence from European nations after the Second World War. Like the agrarian (1000 BC – 1800s) and industrial (1800 – 1950) revolutions, Mowlana (1997) holds that the information revolution (1960 – present) is similarly transformative. ICTs have a central place in the pursuit of development since ICT discourse is strongly associated with the linear time-based modernity discourse, while ICT implementation is associated with modernization (Mowlana, 1997). ICT also reflexively shapes development discourse when instrumentally linked to knowledge as power (M. Thompson, 2004).

Wallerstein (2004) explains that the original meaning of the term 'development' was "to exploit, draw profit from" the colonies by European powers. After World War II it took on new meaning as the present development phenomenon founded on economic principles to assist newly independent tricontinental countries attain industrialization and higher standards of living. It became the ideology of *developmentalism* when the new states came to believe that they could develop themselves through appropriate policy choices (Wallerstein, 2004). The International Bank for Reconstruction and Development (IBRD), better known as the World Bank[1], was started to help reconstruct Europe after the war. Later it found new purpose spearheading 'development' across the globe. Together with the International Monetary Fund (IMF) and World Trade Organization (WTO) (collectively termed International Financial Institutions (IFIs)) they wield enormous power over 'developing' nation-states, and their ideological orientation at any time greatly influences global development policies (Broad, 2006).

According to Dow and Dow (2005) the preferred model of development has generally been modernist in outlook based on rational models of economic growth. Rostow's (1960) liberal capitalist development model with five stages from traditional subsistence to modern consumer societies is widely cited. Policy emphasis in the form of development paradigms has changed over the years ranging from modernization to structural adjustment in 1980 (Emmerij, 2005). With the rise of liberalism (small government, macro-economic stability, free markets, termed the Washington Consensus) in the late 70s in the west (Britain's Margaret Thatcher and US' Ronald Reagan), neoliberal positive economics came to dominate development analysis (Fine, Lapavitsas, & Pincus, 2001a; Friedman, 1966). For the tricontinental countries it culminated in the Berg Report of 1981 *Accelerated development for Africa: an Agenda for Africa* that instituted it as the solution to 'developing' through Structural Adjustment Programmes (SAPs). 'Aid' disbursements to developing countries henceforth were made conditional upon sticking to highly specified IMF and World Bank policy and structural reforms, targeted towards market liberalization and the privatization of state enterprises.

"The World Bank in its 1980 World Development Report 'officially' signalled the end of the long-running definition of development as nationally managed economic growth. Henceforth, 'development' would measure the extent of participation in and integration with the world market. The notion of 'reform' was also rewritten to erase any connotation of income redistribution or agrarian reform, to signify the extent to which market mechanisms should be given free rein". (Munck, 2000)

SAPs effectively reversed the drive to industry by again encouraging primary commodity exports on the basis of the neoliberal argument of comparative advantage (Pender, 2001). 'Good governance' was added to aid conditionality in the late 1990s. Critics have presented the resultant scenario as the vain pursuit of theoretical ideal states designed by WB/IMF 'experts' for aid recipient countries (Grindle, 2004; Mbembé, 2001). Funded public ICT initiatives would be required to meet new standards for *transparency* and *accountability* as part of the good governance agenda adopted by leading development agencies (Ciborra & Navarra, 2005; World-Bank, 2005). ICTs importance to monitoring and control for better governance make them an important rallying point for developmentalism.

By the 1990s there was a major crisis of confidence in WB/IMF policies. The record in transforming economies from dependence on primary products to industry was mixed with only a few Asian countries attaining a newly industrialized country (NIC) status by the 1990s. A Bank report *The East Asian Miracle* of 1993 undermined its own free market policy prescriptions when it acknowledged the positive effects of some active state intervention in the market (Pender, 2001). This was a shift from neoliberal orthodoxy towards the emerging New Institutional Economics that considers the role of institutions and social norms in economic theory (Cameron, 2004).

Acceptance in principle that markets can fail paved the way for reform minded President James Wolfensson and Chief Economist Joseph Stiglitz to make fundamental changes to its vision for development in a globalizing capitalist world. Subsequent ideological battles within the Bank resulted in measured policy changes to accommodate criticism over SAP failures and the Asian currency crisis of the late 1990s (Wade, 2002).[2] Wolfensson and Stiglitz integrated the ideas of social capital and neoliberal economic growth into the *Comprehensive Development Framework* (CDF) as the new vision for development (Stiglitz, 1998; World-Bank, 2004).

"The Comprehensive Development Framework, then, is precisely what it says it is—a blueprint for a complete set of social and governmental relations and institutions, founded on macroeconomic discipline and extending across a range of economic and social policies without parallel in the depth and intensity of intervention they implied in the affairs of supposedly sovereign states". (Cammack, 2004)

CDF is presented as a set of four principles that embody values desirable to the Bank: Long-term, holistic vision, Country ownership, Country-led partnership, and Results focus (World-Bank, 2004). In line with this vision, the bank strategically incorporates civil society and the private sector in the drive towards participatory development processes to increase 'social capital'. The major policy implication arising for developing countries was a new requirement to develop *Poverty Reduction Strategy Papers* (PRSPs) that operationalize the principles of CDF.[3] As policy tools PRSPs were a great improvement over SAPs in sensitivity to development contexts. They may however embody a fundamental contradiction between country sovereignty and the bank's supervisory role. It is required they be developed in a participatory process and country owned, but to also provide a policy matrix 'summary management tool' for ongoing WB/IMF supervision (Cammack, 2004). According to Cammack (2004) country ownership, is necessary for governments to implement the strategy and to legitimate it vis-à-vis the citizenship and the international community.

Critiques of Development

Development and its associated institutions that Hancock (2004) pejoratively terms 'Development Incorporated' have been criticized in the popular press as perpetuating rather than reducing poverty and inequality (Caufield, 1998; Hancock, 2004; Rivero, 2001). I shall outline some critiques of development relevant to this study, political economy, constructivism, and postcolonial studies. Both political economy and constructivism critiques stay within established frames of reference in development studies. In contrast, postcolonial literary studies constitute critical reviews and interpretations of the post-independence settlement. They explicate emergent identities and cultures to touch on and problematize received epistemologies and ontologies. Some critique development from its 'exteriority' by posing positions outside of modernity (Dussel, 2002). We shall first consider critiques from political economy and constructivism.

Distributional and equity issues from a Marxian and historical political economy perspective have for long constituted the most important critiques of developmentalism (Leys, 1975; Rodney, 1972; Rupert, 2000). Under colonialism and neocolonialism, European nations are said to have systematically underdeveloped today's poor countries (Rodney, 1972). Wallenstein's (1991) sociological critique of capitalism is closely associated with the Latin American dependency school (Ruccio & Simon, 1992). Both use a system theoretic approach to conceptualize the capitalist economy as a World System in historical time to explain the continuity of economic imbalances. His most innovative extension beyond western episteme was the notion derived from Gunnar Myrdal that capitalism requires and generates an 'understratum' in the form of reserve labor in third world countries to cushion the capitalist system from normal ups and downs and afford it flexibility.[4] Development under liberal capitalism would thereby be more of an illusion sustained through developmentalism as discourse. Evidence from state led Asian 'tiger' economies and Japan supports interventionist states that curb large corporations so that producers keep the surplus (Pender, 2001; Wallerstein, 1991).

An additional and increasingly important source of criticism is campaigns by anti-globalization Non-governmental and civil society organizations. Official development assistance from developed to developing countries has had to contend with determined campaigns like the *Jubilee 2000* and *50 Years is Enough* that seek debt forgiveness and are calling for IFIs to be abolished.

Critics also take issue with the concept of social capital as employed in the new CDF approach to development. Fine (2001) accuses the bank of selective appropriation of social capital literature by relying on James Coleman's *functional* definition and Gary Becker's extensions to all spheres of human life as 'economics colonizes sociology' (Archer & Tritter, 2000). Pierre Bourdieu's more critical, contextual and ultimately Marxian take on social capital is ignored. Fine further expounds on the non-trivial measurement problems arising from social capital model specification, multicollinearity, multiple variables, and linearity assumptions. Similar criticisms on the limits of the underpinning Rational Choice Theory are leveled by contributors to the compilation in Archer and Tritter (2000).

IFI's appear to have difficulties when dealing with criticism of the core tenets of neo-liberalism as Toussaint's (2004) exposition of a speech by then IMF First Managing Director Anne Kueger illustrates (Krueger, 2003). In a rather simple and straightforward but damning analysis, he finds her defense of globalization and corporate interests in the name of helping the poor as simply untrue, and in many cases self-contradictory. The seemingly credible charges of intellectual dishonesty leveled at the World Bank by Fine (2001) and the IMF by Toussaint (2004) raise serious questions of an ideological nature. It would appear as has been proposed that paradigm maintenance in development policy by IFIs and by extension the US Treasury, supersedes all other concerns (Broad, 2006; Wade, 2002).

Yet what appears as neoliberal intransigence on development policy stems from a different perception of inequality by classical and neoliberal economists. Inequality is not a 'problem' in classical liberal thinking, rather it is said to arise from natural differences in endowment (Mises, 1985). Inequality is desirable in capitalist systems for it provides incentive for enterprise. Communist and socialist policies that equate persons materially are assumed to kill incentive for human enterprise or creativity. The rise of neo-liberalism was accompanied by the regression of Keynesian economics in the west that advocated government management of the economy. It is this more extreme version associated with Ludwig von Mises, Frederick von Hayek and Milton Friedman and the Chicago School of economics (Friedman, 1966) that Margaret Thatcher and Ronald Reagan took up in the 1980s to shape IFI's economic and development policies. The collapse of communism and China's enthusiastic embrace of capitalism have strengthened their hand. Therefore the gulf between neo-liberal economics and those advocating for some form of redistribution is primarily *ideological* and *ethical*. Each position embodies certain values that would lead onto different approaches to development.

Constructivism has been the traditional alternative to positivism. But it has come in for some criticism in international relations though its advocates are associated with progressive liberal ideas in economics, human rights, and minority rights (gender, racial etc.) advocacy. In ICT and public sector reforms in developing countries it is associated with civil society and non-governmental organizations that have had significant influence on global ICT policy particularly on equity and the drive for universal access (Mueller, Kuerbis,

& Pagé, 2007). Landolt (2004) discusses three constructivist texts on international relations that analyze the diffusion of the western liberal norm, including how poverty fighting became a moral requirement for richer nations and institutions such as the World Bank. She finds that they tend to censor material factors during explanation in order to demonstrate that 'norms matter' on the belief that social factors determine material interests. Excluding or downplaying the possibility of structural influence from material interests and power relations on norm diffusion keeps their findings firmly within the boundaries of the neoliberal agenda of minimal government and free markets. She proposes the inclusion of both social *and* material factors in analyzing norm diffusion in international relations. Such norms would include ideas of good governance that provide rationale for IT based public sector reforms.

Landolt (2004) further argues that constructivists focus on elite socialization at a global level, downplaying domestic material factors and political processes. Another consequence is to obscure ongoing North-South struggles over the international distribution of wealth, and that influence norm diffusion. Consequently she concludes that constructivists cannot fully explain instances of successful norm diffusion. The high level role played by civil society and NGOs at the World Summit on the Information Society (WSIS) forums was a significant change in strategy that resulted in their active involvement in ICT policy formulation across the globe (Munyua, 2005). This was a recognition that change would only come from active engagement with material and political processes, lending support to Landolt's (2004) critique.

The international context within which IT based public sector reform initiatives take place is a contested intellectual and ideological sphere. IFIs and networks of bilateral and donor relationships are influential in determining what counts as important to developing countries when undertaking IT based reforms. Universal policy goals as has been the practice may not be appropriate, but poorer developing countries usually comply due to their weak bargaining power. Of those Asian countries that did 'develop', it was because they struck a different own path (Clark, 2000). Evidently, undertaking IT based public sector reforms in such a policy context would likely lead to 'failed' projects for reasons largely outside the control of their managers. Their goals and objectives, hence evaluation, would have to be revised to meet changing development paradigms.

Earlier we saw that E-Government adoption is contingent upon multiple factors in different countries. Despite this ICT initiatives continue and information systems researchers have come up with novel ways to address complex policy contexts and realities. Instances of success or failure are not easily explained by the policy adopted. In the next section we introduce postcolonial theory that relooks at the situation, incorporating issues specific to postcolonial developing countries, people, and history, in relation to the relatively enduring structure of international relations.

The Actual: A Postcolonial Theory Perspective on Development and IT-Based Public Sector Reform Contexts

Arguably the mission to 'save' and 'civilize' others has been the western world's conscience for several centuries through the beneficial intermingling of religious, commercial and imperial interests (Coquery-Vidrovitch, 1988; Thiongo, 1996). The postcolonial critique of development draws from 'third world' literary writers and postmodern philosophers to provide alternative visions of 'development'. Academic disciplines and industries today flourish around the ideas 'postcolonial' and 'development' where ICT4D may be located. Given that postcolonial theory is a large diverse body of knowledge, I have concentrated on development related papers and well known writers whose work frames the field.

The practical focus of this chapter means that those selected have a structural, critical theory, and possibly Marxian bias as we are interested in transforming policy into practice, in other words, praxis. Certain genres like the post-modern leaning ones are useful in generating fresh insights, but are in greater danger of vitiating analysis by dwelling on philosophical and linguistic technicalities, rather than agency and material aspects of policy making (Appiah, 1991; Mbembé, 2001; Weate, 2003). Those with a nationalist or essentialist focus are more easily identified as captive discourses because they tend to be reactive rather than generative. Postcolonial theory as research lens is slippery but its advantages may outweigh the disadvantages given the material reality of poorly performing IT reform projects.

Firstly, a pertinent question would be, 'On whose behalf are the proponents of development speaking or acting?' Spivak's (1988) famous question 'Can the *subaltern* speak?' is a fundamental one.[5] 'Third-world' writers prefer to read it through historiography, closer to Antonio Gramsci's original Marxist class based appropriation of the term 'subaltern' (Chakrabarty, 2000). It may be rephrased as: Does the subaltern in the tricontinental countries have voice in ICTs and public sector reforms? It is a contemporary one as these seek to redefine their relations with global institutions of governance to recover agency and begin participating in history. This aspiration is captured in the case of Africa:

"The African continent and its people occupy a 'subaltern' position in global politics where voices from the African continent remain on the peripheries of global governance. Since the Human Rights Council is envisaged to be a forum for dialogue on thematic issues on all human rights, Africans need to seize the opportunity to be heard, rather than remaining as a problem to be solved... It calls for the African continent to transcend its current 'subaltern position' in international relations and make its voice heard within global governance". (Ndlovu-Gatsheni, 2007:3)

Why do the tricontinental countries lack voice on the international arena decades after attaining independence? The postcolonial critique of development links the large body of postcolonial literary writings to actual development policy in addressing this question. Sylvester (1999) illustrates in one sentence from Appiah (1991) the everyday nature of the development studies/postcolonial literary critique dilemma:

"Despite the overwhelming reality of economic decline; despite unimaginable poverty; despite wars, malnutrition, disease, and political instability, African cultural productivity grows apace: popular literatures, oral narrative and poetry, dance, drama, music, and visual art all thrive'. Remove the word 'despite', and end the sentence after 'instability', and one has a capsule statement of the types of issues that occupy development studies. Put 'despite' back in, and fast-forward to the second half of the sentence beginning with the word 'African', and some sources of postcolonial studies' interest in the 'Third World' are highlighted".

Both fields ought to be considered together since "development studies does not tend to listen to subalterns and postcolonial studies does not tend to concern itself with whether the subaltern is eating" (Sylvester, 1999); an eloquent expression of the schism Sumner and Tribe (2004) identified in the epistemology and ontology of development studies. Today, there is a move to bring the two closer and operationalize long dormant critiques and reformulations where development meets postcolonial discourse (Sylvester, 1999).

Against the modernity development paradigm, postcolonial critics argue that policies founded on putatively objective development economics conveniently elide colonial and imperial history in political economy discourse to institutionalize neocolonialism (Biccum, 2002; Matthews, 2004). These tend to rely on quantification and 'objective' analysis, such as the case of social capital at the World Bank, which impoverishes policy analysis. In effect it considers the problem outside of time and history, while sustaining the dominant discourse of linear progressive development. This would explain the division between the World Bank and the United Nations Development Programme (UNDP) on the importance of ICTs in development (Patterson & Wilson, 2000). To the World Bank the ICT glass in developing countries was half full, but half empty to the UNDP, because of their different interests. IT based reforms sponsored by the two institutions are likely to differ significantly. Patterson and Wilson (2000) found little empirical evidence or logic in utopian claims for ICT and equity, but also very little real research in the important area of E-Equity. Such misunderstandings and poorly researched concepts may find their way into policy under the umbrella of a dominant discourse. Postcolonial theory's response to such misrepresentation has so far been confined to literary fields, but it is now "interrupting the discourse of development" (Biccum, 2002; Escobar, 1995; Munck, 2000; Nustad, 2001).

Escobar's (1995) pioneering Foucaldian deconstruction study of 'development' showed that as an institutionalized and professionalized practice, it invents its own problems, disciplines, and study programs dedicated to the 'Third World', essentially for its own self perpetuation through powerful discursive strategies. He shows how in the case of women in development it proceeds as discursive formation, professionalization and institutionalization. In the long run human subjects (such as poor or peasant women – Spivak's (1988)*subalterns*) become invisible and are disempowered in the de-politicized discursive space. The rise of civil society and NGOs in the area of information rights has led to their incorporation in the policy making process. Their involvement lends credibility to the process and may lead to more sensitive policies as in the case of universal access, and easier implementation amongst marginalized groups. However, this may not apply in the case of the World Bank's CDF where their involvement appears instrumental towards meeting the aims of the New Washington Consensus (Fine, Lapavitsas, & Pincus, 2001b).

ICT and poverty and digital-divide discourses may be better understood when we factor in material and structural factors that would explain observed differences. McNamara's (2003) findings that poverty is complex or that ICTs can exercabate existing disparities when examined in the light of history and time are not surprising, others have arrived at the same conclusions (Pithouse, 2003; Wade, 2004). The question is whether they do more harm than good for developing countries if as it appears they serve the interests of the powerful.

From the differing perspectives presented above, we may conceive the dominant international ICT and development discourse as generating a *contrived context* within which various discourses thrive, but whose principal concern is divorced from immediate developing country material and sociological realities. This would be a diversion from the *actual context*, as implied by postcolonial theory and its critique of development. The latter highlights the centrality of international power relations, postcolonial subject agency (and hence capacity to participate in reform initiatives), the importance of history in conceptualizing societal change, and the complexity of postcolonial societies and identities. Postcolonial concepts such as hybridity, ambivalence, and mimicry would need reevaluation to help developing countries negotiate integration into a globalizing world (Bhabha, 1994; Pieterse, 1995). The enduring search for human freedoms and emancipation would continue to have voice on the international ICT and development dialogue (Freire, 1972; Ndlovu-Gatsheni, 2007).

Implications of Postcolonial Theory and Critique to IT-Based Public Sector Reforms

Earlier on it was noted that E-Government adoption was a contingent phenomena with gaps in policy and practice. Information systems researchers have identified three related issues that stand out in the literature as important directions in developing country information systems research: 1) local adaptation and cultivation; 2) balancing standardization vs. localization of technology; and 3) the importance of IT artifact conceptualization (Njihia, 2008). These would be key considerations in research, during project conception and design, and to outcomes in terms of success, failure and sustainability. Each is discussed briefly, then further below we undertake a comparative evaluation from the postcolonial and developmental positions in ICT policy and practice, and their implications for IT based public sector reforms.

Local adaptation and cultivation: IS projects are in most cases designed in developed countries for implementation in developing countries. Theoretical and empirical studies have indicated the need for local improvisation or adaptation for higher chances of success (Heeks, 2002b). Corea (2007) introduces the notion of 'artfulness' in IT innovation to overcome the problem of IT artifact concretization in one context and its realization in another non-isomorphic context. Local adaptation requires local shaping of new cultures implicit in a proposed ICT initiative (Kimaro & Nhampossa, 2005). Part of this requires that local users be incorporated in the development process, and their capacity be enhanced for effective adaptation.

A related finding is preference for a cultivation approach to information systems development (Braa & Hedberg, 2002; Kimaro & Nhampossa, 2005). Design would be considered rather as the cultivation of networks and infrastructures starting from the installed base. An extensive case of what amounts to cultivation is Rensburg et al.(2008) description of gradual shift in research focus from technology as in the case of failed telecenters, to creating networks of community based ICT-enabled sustainable micro-enterprises.

Balancing standardization vs localization of technology: The need for local adaptation of existing technologies creates an associated problem of balancing standardization and localization when operations cut across regions and countries. Too much standardization means the technology may not work well locally, while too much adaptation leads to higher costs and may lead to pockets of unwieldy and incompatible systems. Braa and Hedberg (2002) and Thompson (2002) suggest a cultivation approach to negotiate these tensions.

Importance of IT artifact conceptualization: At the heart of all ICT in development is an implicit or explicit conception of the 'IT artifact'. According to Corea (2007) this has varied from the very technical that tended to overstate the potential impacts of technology on society, to socio-technical models where it is understood in the context of its realization. His proposal is for an artifact and behavior that facilitates a learning approach to IT innovation for social development. Sein and Harindramath's (2004) proposal is ultimately concerned with outcomes in terms of human development, of which they are silent on what is desirable as development paradigm.

The three issues lean towards constructivism rather than a linear model of development, evidently to address its weaknesses. This implies that to a large extent researchers have already come to terms with the linear developmental model, as the trend towards interpretivism and critical research in developing countries shows (Sahay & Avgerou, 2002; Walsham, Robey, & Sahay, 2007), and the increasing acceptance of case studies and interpretive research in top rated journals (Chen & Hirschheim, 2004). The postcolonial critique would however suggest that they are ameliorative rather than transformative of the problem situation. They do not question the north-south division, the unbalanced international ICT dialogue, or that technology innovation is presumed to originate in the west. As earlier seen in the critiques of development, constructivism evades important historical and structural factors that would explain change. None addresses the problematic conceptualization of development or the need to 'interrupt the discourse of development' (Biccum, 2002) except marginally.

Studies earlier reviewed on E-Government adoption identified project championship, a political leadership with interest in technology, strong project management skills, integration within established budgetary systems, partnerships with donors and privates sector groups, and garnering broad-based support for sustainability as important factors for success. The design of IT based reform programs that factor in these concerns requires an historic-institutional perspective of governance systems, and the socio-political environment in developing countries. A postcolonial reading would also include critical non-official perspectives that the domestic ruling class may not favor, and that may be held by a significant populace. Frequently these are the sources of political and institutional instability that negatively affect IT reform projects.

Factoring in history and structural factors may lead to better reform program design because it would entail first understanding why present donor relations are so. It could mitigate the problem of programs designed to 'please donors' (Heijden, 2003) that leads to almost certain policy-practice gaps. During the recent financial crisis, the World Bank and IMF were conspicuously absent as western nations went against free market arguments they had forced on developing countries through SAPs, and recapitalized or nationalized banks to save their financial systems from collapse (Cho, Irwin, & Whoriskey, 2008; Muñoz, Macdonald, & Mollenkamp, 2009). Such instances of shifting ideology and ambiguity of donor interests require careful evaluation before tricontinental countries commit to a given partnership. Postcolonial theory provides the rationale for such queries given the continued dominance in international relations by former colonial powers, now organized around bodies such as the European Union and the Organization for Economic Cooperation and Development (OECD). The same argument would apply to emerging developing countries such as China, Brazil and South Africa, now wealthy or influential enough to play the role of potential benefactor.

Contemporary postcolonial writers have drawn attention to the still colonized minds, violence, kleptomania, and kaleidoscopic, yet vibrant nature that characterize life in the postcolony (Mbembé, 2001; Thiongo, 1996). Reform efforts that fail to give these sufficient efforts are likely to have insignificant or even detrimental impacts. For instance Letch & Carroll (2008) cite an E-Government project that brought efficiencies to traffic management and driver licensing, but that also led to greater exclusion for marginalized Aboriginal communities. An externally sourced integrated software package imposed its own cultural logic on the Maldives Customs Service in a form of neo-colonialism (Adam & Myers, 2003). Recent suggestions for ICT policy making in developing countries give attention to history and the interplay of material factors. Gillwald's (2002) institutional historical approach with periodization to produce an integrated national holistic policy. Ram´ırez (2007) proposes a new sociotechnical, holistic, multiple perspectives, with multiple stakeholders, paradigm for adaptive ICT policymaking for rural communities. It relies on a metaphor of "reading how the system responds" rather than linear analysis.

A comparative survey with experiences in the west indicates that governance systems tend to display self similarity, the same issues arise on a different scale in different contexts. Policy-practice gaps have been cited in Europe especially with regard to the preferred managerial model that seeks to transfer private sector practices into government, in contrast to the putative aims of E-Government towards consultative models of governance and citizen participation (Chadwick & May, 2003). Policy-practice gaps are cited in education and the possibility of increased social exclusion for young or marginalized persons and communities (Phipps, 2000 ; Tondeur, Braak, & Valcke, 2007). Researchers have also observed differences in appropriation of the NPM model across the US and European countries. Scandinavian countries emphasize democratic accountability and cooperation while Britain and the US are managerial, giving greater weight to models such as Business Process Reengineering and Total Quality Management (Navarra & Cornford, 2003; Rhodes, 1999).

Though similar, these IT reform policy-practice gaps differ from those in developing countries in that these countries are dealing with their own situations relatively freely and independently, hence the diversity of appropriation. Developing country policy-practice gaps are founded externally. Their inadequate capacity and weak participation in the international ICT and development policy dialogue means that their policy-practice gaps can only be understood with reference to external forces. Hence the two regions are addressing similar problems but from very different perspectives and scales.

Postcolonial theory and an historical approach to development provide a fruitful alternative and additional starting point to theorizing IT based public sector reforms. It may contribute to providing a legitimating framework for the idea of development and its meaning to information systems researchers and policy makers in developing countries. Policy may then be more easily transformed into practice, or at least reduced to a manageable own problem as in Europe.

FUTURE RESEARCH DIRECTIONS

Realizing the challenge of the postcolonial critique in IT based public sector reform requires that alternatives to development or alternative development are first explored. The third key research issue in developing countries implies that IT artifact conceptualization is inseparable from our value systems as far as human development is concerned. We may thus understand Walsham's (2005) 'polemic' reflecting on the difficulties of conceptualizing development and its purposes for information systems research (ISR). He discusses global inequalities, ideology, discourses, gender, and the problem of the excluded fourth world of 'failed humanity' in Castells (2000a). More importantly, what development could mean, including personal transformation to become a Gandhi or a Mandela, all in the context of critical ISR. He proposes a reconsideration of the goals of development towards broader aims of humanity's growth and development to make a better world with ICT. This is a difficult challenge that would change almost every area of critical ISR, its teaching and dissemination.

Along these lines and as a reaction to modernity and developmentalism, there have been many calls for alternatives *to* development, *post*-development, or for substantive reforms. But coming up with alternatives that are not in some way related to, or that simply reflect, western frames of reference is challenging (Matthews, 2004; Pieterse, 1998; Ziai, 2004). The search for authentic originary traditional forms not 'contaminated' with coloniality and modernity is a difficult one to say the least. Mudimbe's (1988) *The Invention of Africa* demonstrates the difficulty of defining present Africa apart from colonialism and its accompanying army of anthropologists and ethnographers, many of them amateurs, upon whose representations, whether good or bad, the present must be read. As he states in another paper *Globalization and African Identity*:

"All utopias of a unitary field of knowledge have become suspect. Diversity is not only a fundamental component of life but a major perspective on both our identities and our knowledge. We are, all of us, métis. Thus a fundamental element of our present situation and our major difficulties is a need to negotiate universalization and particularization." (Mudimbe, 2003)

This is only one position and may have overstated the case. But it demonstrates the dilemma and centrality of identity in the postcolony when conceptualizing 'development' and its possibilities. Earlier it was indicated that the value of postcolonial discourses lies in the questions they pose rather than the answers they provide. They enrich the international development dialogue with hints of previously submerged voices, and more importantly draw attention to socio-political change in time and history. The complex discursive and political environment within which IT based public sector reforms are conceptualized ought to factor in the ongoing search for firm postcolonial national and individual identities. Researchers ought therefore to be cognizant of contemporary debates, and of "turning points in development thinking" at which 'development' takes on new meanings (Emmerij, 2005).

CONCLUSION

Our consideration of the policy and socio-economic context for ICTs and international development indicates that discursive practices embedded within development institutions shape trends and practices in IT based public sector reform. Models of development have changed over the years from modernization to structural adjustment programs, neoliberal free market policies, and the new institutional economics today. Their record of success is varied, with strong criticisms from Marxian, dependency school, global system theorists, and postcolonial studies. Western countries and IFIs are very influential and even determine development policy in line with their interests, presently aligned with neo-liberal and new institutional economics. It would appear that differences in development paradigms arise from ideology and ethical differences because their proponents subscribe to different value systems, which later manifest as policy-practice gaps.

Development discourse has material implications for powerful interest groups in global trade for the supply of ICT technology and services to 'emerging markets'. The digital-divide and poverty were examined as two powerful discursive strategies that shape, and that may sustain inequalities between developing and developed countries. Broader policy objectives implicit in IT based public sector reforms such as accountability and transparency are related to global normative pressures, while their realization is dependent on the national and bureaucratic character rather than technology adoption (Wong & Welch, 2004). Therefore success in IT based public sector reforms such as E-Government adoption and sustainability depends on multiple factors that vary across nations. Postcolonial theory gives impetus to existing institutional and historic-structural approaches that may lead to more actionable policies. These would include a reevaluation of the purpose and function of donors in projects, and give more attention to underlying domestic forces that give rise to institutional and political instability in IT project environments.

Alternatives to development and post-development from the postcolonial/postmodern critiques relook at development beyond the modernity paradigm, widely criticized in the literature for its linearity assumptions and inattention to history (Biccum, 2002). It was observed that conceiving forms outside of received western frames of reference is a difficult challenge. Emerging approaches that integrate structural and contextual aspects, and postcolonial theory, were highlighted as pointers to new research and policy directions. Any new forms and meanings of development arising from these would have to address concretely history, complex postcolonial subject identities, and agency. We may then begin to address the *actual* rather than the *contrived* policy and socio-economic context to bridge existing policy-practice gaps in IT based public sector reforms in postcolonial developing countries.

REFERENCES

Adam, M. S., & Myers, M. D. (2003). Have you got anything to declare? Neo-colonialism, Information Systems, and the imposition of customs and duties in a third world country. In M. Korpela, R. Montealegre & A. Poulymenakou (Eds.), *Proceedings of the International Federation of Information Processing, IFIP 9.4 and 8.2 Joint Conference on Organizational Information Systems in the Context of Globalization* (pp. 101-116). Dordrecht, The Netherlands: Kluwer.

Adesina, J. O. (2006). When is 'techno-talk' a fatal distraction? ICT in contemporary development discourse on Africa. *Africa Development. Afrique et Developpement, 31*(3), 118–151.

Al-Qirim, N. (2007). The adoption and diffusion of e-commerce in developing countries: The case of an NGO in Jordan. *Information Technology for Development, 13*(2), 107–131. doi:10.1002/itdj.20053

Appiah, K. A. (1991). Is the post- in postmodernism the post- in postcolonial? *Critical Inquiry, 17*(2), 336–357. doi:10.1086/448586

Archer, M. S., & Tritter, J. Q. (Eds.). (2000). *Rational choice theory: Resisting colonization*. London, UK & New York, NY: Routledge.

Avgerou, C. (2003). The link between ICT and economic growth in the discourse of development. In Korpela, M., Momtealegre, R., & Poulymenakou, A. (Eds.), *Organizational Information Systems in the context of globalization* (pp. 373–386). Boston, MA: Kluwer.

Bannister, F. (2001). Dismantling the silos: Extracting value from IT investments in public administration. *Information Systems Journal, 11*, 65–84. doi:10.1046/j.1365-2575.2001.00094.x

Bhabha, H. K. (1994). *The location of culture*. London, UK & New York, NY: Routledge.

Bhatnagar, S. (2002). E-government: Lessons from implementation in developing countries. *Regional Development Dialogue, 24*(Autumn).

Biccum, A. R. (2002). Interrupting the discourse of development: On a collision course with postcolonial theory. *Culture, Theory and Critique, 43*(1), 33–50. doi:10.1080/14735780210162094

Braa, J., & Hedberg, C. (2002). The struggle for district-based health Information Systems in South Africa. *The Information Society, 18*, 113–127. doi:10.1080/01972240290075048

Broad, R. (2006). Research, knowledge, and the art of paradigm maintenance: The World Bank's Development Economics Vice-Presidency (DEC). *Review of International Political Economy, 13*(3), 387–419. doi:10.1080/09692290600769260

Cafrad. Nepad, & Undesa. (2003). Plan of action for the implementation of the e-Africa Initiative for Good Governance. *e-Africa 2003: Expert Consultative Meeting on Building e-governance capacity in African Countries*. Tangier, Morocco.

Cameron, J. D. (2004). The World Bank and the new institutional economics: Contradictions and implications for development policy in Latin America. *Latin American Perspectives, 31*, 97–103. doi:10.1177/0094582X0403100408

Cammack, P. (2004). What the World Bank means by poverty reduction, and why it matters. *New Political Economy, 9*(2), 189–211. doi:10.1080/1356346042000218069

Carden, F. (2009). *Knowledge to policy: Making the most of development research. Los Angeles, CA/ London, UK/ New Delhi, India/ Singapore*. Washinton, DC: Sage.

Carter, L., & Bélanger, F. (2005). The utilization of e-government services: Citizen trust, innovation and acceptance factors. *Information Systems Journal, 15*, 5–25. doi:10.1111/j.1365-2575.2005.00183.x

Castells, M. (2000a). *End of millennium* (2nd ed.). Malden, MA: Blackwell Publishers.

Castells, M. (2000b). *The rise of the network society* (2nd ed.). Oxford, UK/ Malden, MA: Blackwell.

Caufield, C. (1998). *Masters of illusion: The World Bank and the poverty of nations*. London, UK: Pan.

Chadwick, A., & May, C. (2003). Interaction between states and citizens in the age of the Internet: E-government in the United States, Britain, and the European Union. *Governance: An International Journal of Policy, Administration, and Institutions*, *16*(2), 271–300.

Chakrabarty, D. (2000). Subaltern studies and postcolonial historiography. *Nepantla: Views From South*, *1*(1), 9–31.

Chen, W., & Hirschheim, R. (2004). A paradigmatic and methodological examination of Information Systems research from 1991 to 2001. *Information Systems Journal*, *14*, 197–235. doi:10.1111/j.1365-2575.2004.00173.x

Cho, D., Irwin, N., & Whoriskey, P. (2008, October 14). U.S. forces nine major banks to accept partial nationalization. *Washington Post*.

Ciborra, C., & Navarra, D. D. (2005). Good governance, development theory, and aid policy: Risks and challenges of e-government in Jordan. *Information Technology for Development*, *11*(2), 141–159. doi:10.1002/itdj.20008

Cilingir, D., & Kushchu, I. (2004). *E-government and m-government: Concurrent leaps by Turkey*. Mobile Government Lab (mGovLab). Retrieved May 9, 2009, from http://www.mgovlab.org

Clark, C. (2000). *Theories of development and the Taiwan experience: Success and challenge from incongruity*. Paper presented at the Annual Meeting of the American Political Science Association, August 31 - September 3, 2000.

Coquery-Vidrovitch, C. (1988). *Africa: Endurance and change south of the Sahara*. University of California Press.

Corea, S. (2007). Promoting development through Information Technology innovation: The IT artifact, artfulness, and articulation. *Information Technology for Development*, *13*(1), 49–69. doi:10.1002/itdj.20036

Dawson, A. (2004). "To remember too much is indeed a form of madness": Caryl Phillips's *The Nature of Blood* and the modalities of European racism. *Postcolonial Studies*, *7*(1), 83–101. doi:10.1080/1368879042000210612

Dhunpath, R., & Paterson, A. (2004). The interface between research and policy dialogue: Substantive or symbolic? *Journal of Education*, *33*, 125–146.

Digital-Opportunity-Initiative. (2001). *Creating a development dynamic: Final report of the Digital Opportunity Initiative: Accenture, Markle Foundation*. UNDP.

Dirlik, A. (1994). The postcolonial aura: Third world criticism in the age of globalization. *Critical Inquiry*, *20*(2), 328–356. doi:10.1086/448714

Dow, A. C., & Dow, S. C. (2005). The application of development economics: General principles and context specificity. *Cambridge Journal of Economics*, *29*, 1129–1143. doi:10.1093/cje/bei072

Dussel, E. (2002). World-system and trans-modernity. *Nepantla: Views from South*, *3*(2), 221–244.

Edgren, G. (2003). The unequal dialogue. In Olsson, J., & Wohlgemuth, L. (Eds.), *Dialogue in pursuit of development* (pp. 23–38). Expert Group in Development Studies.

Emmerij, L. (2005). *Turning points in development thinking and practice*. Paper presented at the WIDER Jubilee Conference on WIDER Thinking Ahead: The Future of Development Economics.

Escobar, A. (1995). *Encountering development: The making and unmaking of the Third World.* Princeton, NJ: Princeton University Press.

Fine, B. (2001). The social capital of the World Bank. In Fine, B., Lapavitsas, C., & Pincus, J. (Eds.), *Development policy in the twenty-first century: Beyond the post-Washington consensus* (pp. 136–154). London, UK: Routledge.

Fine, B., Lapavitsas, C., & Pincus, J. (2001a). Preface. In Fine, B., Lapavitsas, C., & Pincus, J. (Eds.), *Development policy in the twenty-first century: Beyond the post-Washington consensus* (pp. x–xvi). London, UK: Routledge.

Fine, B., Lapavitsas, C., & Pincus, J. (Eds.). (2001b). *Development policy in the twenty-first century: Beyond the post-Washington consensus.* London, UK: Routledge.

Freire, P. (1972). *Pedagogy of the oppressed.* Penguin Books.

Friedman, M. (1966). The methodology of positive economics. In M. Friedman (Ed.), *Essays in positive economics* (pp. 3-16, 30-43). Chicago, IL: Univ. of Chicago Press.

Gillwald, A. (2002). Experimenting with institutional arrangements for communications policy and regulation: The case of telecommunications and broadcasting in South Africa. *The Southern African Journal of Information and Communication, 2*(1).

Grindle, M. S. (2004). Good enough governance: Poverty reduction and reform in developing countries. *Governance, 17*(4), 525–548. doi:10.1111/j.0952-1895.2004.00256.x

Hancock, G. (2004). *Lords of poverty.* Nairobi, Kenya: Camerapix Publishers International.

Heeks, R. (2000). The approach of senior public officials to information technology related reform: Lessons from India. *Public Administration and Development, 20*, 197–205. doi:10.1002/1099-162X(200008)20:3<197::AID-PAD109>3.0.CO;2-6

Heeks, R. (2001). *Reinventing government in the information age: International practice in IT-enabled public sector reform.* London, UK/New York, NY: Routledge.

Heeks, R. (2002a). E-government in Africa: Promise and practice. *Information Polity, 7*, 97–114.

Heeks, R. (2002b). Information Systems and developing countries: Failure, success, and local improvisations. *The Information Society, 18*, 101–112. doi:10.1080/01972240290075039

Heeks, R. (2003). Most e-government-for-development projects fail: How can risks be reduced? In Heeks, R. (Ed.), *iGovernment working paper series.* Manchester, UK: Institute for Development Policy and Management, University of Manchester.

Heijden, H. d. (2003). Making the policy dialogue more effective: What the development co-operation record suggests. In Olsson, J., & Wohlgemuth, L. (Eds.), *Dialogue in pursuit of development* (pp. 78–106). Expert Group in Development Studies.

Kimaro, H. C., & Nhampossa, J. L. (2005). Analyzing the problem of unsustainable health Information Systems in less-developed economies: Case studies from Tanzania and Mozambique. *Information Technology for Development, 11*(3), 273–298. doi:10.1002/itdj.20016

Krishna, S., & Walsham, G. (2005). Implementing public Information Systems in developing countries: Learning from a success story. *Information Technology for Development, 11*(2), 123–140. doi:10.1002/itdj.20007

Krueger, A. O. (2003). *Address on globalization at the Seventh St. Petersburg International Economic Forum*. IMF External Relations Dept.

Kumar, R. (2006). Impact and sustainability of e-government services in developing countries: Lessons learned from Tamil Nadu, India. *The Information Society*, *22*, 1–12. doi:10.1080/01972240500388149

Landolt, L. K. (2004). (Mis)constructing the third world? Constructivist analysis of norm diffusion. *Third World Quarterly*, *25*(3), 579–591. doi:10.1080/0143659042000191447

Letch, N., & Carroll, J. (2008). Excluded again: Implications of integrated e-government systems for those at the margins. *Information Technology & People*, *21*(3), 283–299. doi:10.1108/09593840810896037

Leys, C. (1975). *Underdevelopment in Kenya: The political economy of neo-colonialism, 1964-1971*. Heinemann.

Mansell, R. (2002). Constructing the knowledge base for knowledge-driven development. *Journal of Knowledge Management*, *6*(4), 317–329. doi:10.1108/13673270210440839

Mansell, R., & Wehn, U. (1998). *Information Technology for sustainable development*. SPRU Research and Oxford University Press.

Mansell, R., & Wehn, U. (1998b). *Information Technology for sustainable development: Friend or foe? Developing countries and the international governance system*. SPRU Research and Oxford University Press.

Matthews, S. (2004). Post-development theory and the question of alternatives: A view from Africa. *Third World Quarterly*, *25*(2), 373–384. doi:10.1080/0143659042000174860

Mbembé, J. A. (2001). *On the postcolony*. University of California Press.

McNamara, K. S. (2003). *Information and Communication Technologies, poverty and development: Learning from experience*. Paper presented at the infoDev Annual Symposium, December 9-10, 2003.

Mises, L. v. (1985). *Liberalism in the classical tradition*. New York, NY /San Francisco, CA: The Foundation for Economic Education, Inc./ Cobden Press.

Mowlana, H. (1997). *Global information and world communication: New frontiers in international relations* (2nd ed.). Sage Publications.

Mudimbe, V. Y. (1988). *The invention of Africa: Gnosis, philosophy, and the order of knowledge*. Bloomington & Indianapolis, IN/London, UK: Indiana University Press/James Currey.

Mudimbe, V. Y. (2003). Globalization and African identity. *CR (East Lansing, Mich.)*, *3*(2), 205–218.

Mueller, M. L., Kuerbis, B. N., & Pagé, C. (2007). Democratizing global communication? Global civil society and the campaign for communication rights in the information society. *International Journal of Communication*, *1*, 267–296.

Munck, R. (2000). Deconstructing development discourses: Of impasses, alternatives and politics. In Munck, R., & O'Hearn, D. (Eds.), *Critical development theory: Contributions to a new paradigm*. London, UK: Zed Books.

Muñoz, S. S., Macdonald, A., & Mollenkamp, C. (2009). U.K., U.S. expand bank rescue bids. *The Wall Street Journal*.

Munyua, A. W. (2005). New generation of policy development: The case of multi-stakeholder ICT policy process in Kenya. *Information Technology in Developing Countries*, *15*(1), 2–9.

Navarra, D., & Cornford, T. (2003). *A policy making view of e-government innovations in public governance.* Paper presented at the 9th Americas Conference on Information Systems (AMCIS 2003), Tampa, FL, USA

Ndlovu-Gatsheni, S. J. (2007). *Giving Africa voice within global governance: Oral history, human rights and the United Nations (UN) Human Rights Council.* Leiden, The Netherlands: African Studies Centre.

Njihia, J. M. (2008). *ICT for Development reconsidered: A critical realist approach to the strategic context in Kenya's transition to e-governance.* Unpublished PhD thesis University of Warwick, Coventry, UK.

Nustad, K. G. (2001). Development: The devil we know? *Third World Quarterly, 22*(4), 479–489. doi:10.1080/01436590120071731

Olsson, J., & Wohlgemuth, L. (Eds.). (2003). *Dialogue in pursuit of development.* Expert Group in Development Studies.

Paris-HLF. (2005). *Paris Declaration on Aid Effectiveness, Ownership, Harmonization, Alignment, Results and Mutual Accountability.* High-Level Forum on Aid Effectiveness. Retrieved March 6, 2010, from http://www.aidharmonization.org/secondary-pages/Paris2005

Patterson, R., & Wilson, E. J. (2000). New IT and social inequality: Resetting the research and policy agenda. *The Information Society, 16,* 77–86. doi:10.1080/019722400128347

Pender, J. (2001). From structural adjustment to comprehensive development framework: Conditionality transformed? *Third World Quarterly, 22*(3), 397–411. doi:10.1080/01436590120061679

Phipps, L. (2000). New communications technologies: A conduit for social inclusion. *Information Communication and Society, 3*(1), 39–68. doi:10.1080/136911800359419

Pieterse, J. N. (1995). Globalization as hybridization. In Featherstone, M., Lash, S., & Robertson, R. (Eds.), *Global modernities* (pp. 45–68). London, UK: Sage Publications.

Pieterse, J. N. (1998). My paradigm or yours? Alternative development, post-development, reflexive development. *Development and Change, 29,* 343–373. doi:10.1111/1467-7660.00081

Pithouse, R. (2003). Producing the poor: The World Bank's new discourse of domination. *African Sociological Review, 7*(2), 118–148.

Polidano, C. (1999). The new public management in developing countries. *IDPM Public Policy and Management Working Papers* (vol. 13). Manchester, UK: University of Manchester.

Ramirez, R. (2007). Appreciating the contribution of broadband ICT with rural and remote communities: Stepping stones toward an alternative paradigm. *The Information Society, 23,* 85–94. doi:10.1080/01972240701224044

Rensburg, J. R. V., Veldsman, A., & Jenkins, M. (2008). From technologists to social enterprise developers: Our journey as ICT for Development practitioners in Southern Africa: View from practice. *Information Technology for Development, 14*(1), 76–89. doi:10.1002/itdj.20088

Rhodes, R. A. W. (1999). Traditions and public sector reform: Comparing Britain and Denmark. *Scandinavian Political Studies, 22*(4), 341–370. doi:10.1111/1467-9477.00023

Rivero, O. d. (2001). *The myth of development: Non-viable economies of the 21st century.* Zed.

Rodney, W. (1972). *How Europe underdeveloped Africa.* London, UK: Bogle-L'Ouverture Publications.

Rostow, W. W. (1960). *The stages of economic growth: A non-Communist Manifesto.* Cambridge, UK: Cambridge University Press.

Ruccio, D. F., & Simon, L. H. (1992). Perspectives on underdevelopment. In C. K. Wiber & K. P. Jameson (Eds.), *The political economy of development and underdevelopment* (5 ed., pp. 119-150). New York, NY: McGraw Hill.

Rupert, M. (2000). *Ideologies of globalization: Contending visions of a new world order*. London, UK / New York, NY: Routledge.

Sahay, S., & Avgerou, C. (2002). Introducing the special issue on Information and Communication Technologies in developing countries. *The Information Society*, *18*, 73–76. doi:10.1080/01972240290075002

Schwartz, N. D. (2003, June 23). Down and out in white-collar America, professionals have never had a tougher time finding a job. It's not just the economy; the rules of the game are changing. *Fortune*.

Sein, M. K., & Harindramath, G. (2004). Conceptualizing the ICT artifact: Towards understanding the role of ICT in national development. *The Information Society*, *20*, 15–24. doi:10.1080/01972240490269942

Sharifia, H., & Zareib, B. (2004). An adaptive approach for implementing e-government in I.R. Iran. *Journal of Government Information*, *30*, 600–619. doi:10.1016/j.jgi.2004.10.005

Spivak, G. C. (1988). Can the subaltern speak? In Nelson, C., & Grossberg, L. (Eds.), *Marxism and the interpretation of culture* (pp. 271–313). Chicago, IL: University of Illinois Press.

Spivak, G. C. (2005). Scattered speculations on the subaltern and the popular. *Postcolonial Studies*, *8*(4), 475–486. doi:10.1080/13688790500375132

Stiglitz, J. E. (1998). *Towards a new paradigm for development: Strategies, policies, and processes.* Paper presented at the 9th Raul Prebisch Lecture, UNCTAD, Geneva.

Stoltzfus, K. (2005). Motivations for implementing e-government: An investigation of the global phenomenon. In *Proceedings of the 2005 National Conference on Digital Government Research* (Vol. 89, pp. 333–338). Atlanta, GA: ACM International Conference Proceeding Series.

Sumner, A., & Tribe, M. (2004). *The nature of epistemology and methodology in development studies: What do we mean by rigour?* Paper presented at the The nature of Development Studies, DSA Annual Conference, Bridging Research and Policy, Church House, London.

Sylvester, C. (1999). Development studies and postcolonial studies: Disparate tales of the third world. *Third World Quarterly*, *20*(4), 703–721. doi:10.1080/01436599913514

Thiongo, N. W. (1996). *Decolonizing the mind: The politics of language in African literature*. Nairobi, Kenya: East African Educational Publishers.

Thompson, M. (2004). Discourse, development & the digital divide: ICT & the World Bank. *Review of African Political Economy*, *31*, 103–123. doi:10.1080/0305624042000258441

Thompson, M. P. A. (2002). Cultivating meaning: Interpretive fine-tuning of a South African health Information System. *Information and Organization*, *12*(3), 183–211. doi:10.1016/S1471-7727(01)00016-1

Tondeur, J., Braak, J. v., & Valcke, M. (2007). Curricula and the use of ICT in education: Two worlds apart? *British Journal of Educational Technology*, *38*(6), 962–976. doi:10.1111/j.1467-8535.2006.00680.x

Toussaint, É. (2004). *Anne Krueger, the white knight of globalisation*. Committee for the Abolition of Third World Debt. Retrieved March 7, 2010, from http:// www.cadtm.org/ Anne-Krueger-the-White-Knight-of

Wade, R. H. (2001). US hegemony and the World Bank: The fight over people and ideas. *Review of International Political Economy*, *9*(2), 215–243. doi:10.1080/09692290110126092

Wade, R. H. (2004). Bridging the digital divide: New route to development or new form of dependency? In Avgerou, C., Ciborra, C., & Land, F. (Eds.), *The social study of information and communication technology: Innovation, actors and contexts* (pp. 185–206). Oxford University Press.

Wallerstein, I. M. (1991). *Unthinking social science: The limits of nineteenth-century paradigms*. Cambridge, MA: Polity Press.

Wallerstein, I. M. (2004, October). *After developmentalism and globalization, what?* Paper presented at the Keynote address at conference, Development Challenges for the 21st Century, Cornell University, Ithaca, NY.

Walsham, G. (2005). Development, global futures and IS research: A polemic. *The Journal of Strategic Information Systems*, *14*, 5–15. doi:10.1016/j.jsis.2004.11.009

Walsham, G., Robey, D., & Sahay, S. (2007). Foreward: Special issue on Information Systems in developing countries. *Management Information Systems Quarterly*, *31*(2), 317–326.

Weate, J. (2003). Achille Mbembe and the postcolony: Going beyond the text. *Research in African Literature*, *34*(4), 27–41. doi:10.2979/RAL.2003.34.4.27

Weber, R. (2004). The rhetoric of positivism versus interpretivism: A personal view. *Management Information Systems Quarterly*, *28*(1), iii–xii.

Wijkman, A., & Afifi, M. (2002). Technology leapfrogging and the digital divide [Electronic Version]. *ICT Regulation Toolkit*, 124-143. Retrieved May 15, 2007, from http:// www.ictregulationtoolkit.org/ en/ Document.1996.html

Wong, W., & Welch, E. (2004). Does e-government promote accountability? A comparative analysis of website openness and government accountability. *An International Journal of Policy, Administration, and Institutions*, *17*(2), 275–297.

World-Bank. (2004). *Supporting development programs effectively - Applying the comprehensive development framework principles: A staff guide*. Washington, DC: World Bank.

World-Bank. (2005). *E-government* (vol. 8/9). Washington, DC: World Bank Group.

Young, R. (2001). *Postcolonialism: An historical introduction*. Oxford, UK: Blackwell.

Younis, R. A. (2005). Integral reality, digital cultures, digital divides. *Postcolonial Studies*, *8*(2), 219–226. doi:10.1080/13688790500196744

Ziai, A. (2004). The ambivalence of post-development: Between reactionary populism and radical democracy. *Third World Quarterly*, *25*(6), 1045–1060. doi:10.1080/0143659042000256887

ADDITIONAL READING

Adedeji, A. (2002). *From the Lagos Plan of Action to the New Partnership for African Development and from the Final Act of Lagos to the Constitutive Act: Wither Africa?* Paper presented at the African Forum for Envisioning Africa.

Ahluwalia, P. (2005). Out of Africa: post-structuralism's colonial roots. *Postcolonial Studies*, *8*(2), 137–154. doi:10.1080/13688790500153554

Angell, I. O., & Ilharco, F. M. (2004). Solution is the problem: a story of transitions and opportunities. In Avgerou, C., Ciborra, C., & Land, F. (Eds.), *The social study of information and communication technology: innovation, actors and contexts* (pp. 38–61). Oxford University Press.

Appiah, K. A. (1992). *In My Father's House: Africa in the Philosophy of Culture*. New York: Oxford University Press.

Ashcroft, B., Griffiths, G., & Tiffin, H. (2002). *The Empire writes back: theory and practice in post-colonial literatures* (2nd ed.). London, New York: Routledge.

Avgerou, C. (2000). Recognising Alternative Rationalities in the Deployment of Information Systems. *The Electronic Journal on Information Systems in Developing Countries*, *3*(7), 1–15.

Avgerou, C., & Madon, S. (2004). Framing IS studies: understanding the social context of IS innovation. In Avgerou, C., Ciborra, C., & Land, F. (Eds.), *The social study of information and communication technology: innovation, actors and contexts* (pp. 162–184). Oxford University Press.

Berman, B. J., & Tettey, W. J. (2001). African States, Bureaucratic Culture and Computer Fixes. *Public Administration and Development*, *21*, 1–13. doi:10.1002/pad.166

Castells, M. (2004). *The power of identity* (2nd ed.). Oxford, U.K.: Blackwell.

Césaire, A. (1972). *Discourse on colonialism*. New York, NY: Monthly Review Press.

Ciborra, C. (2004). *The labyrinths of information: challenging the wisdom of systems*. Oxford University Press.

Cornwall, A., & Brock, K. (2005). What do Buzzwords do for Development Policy? A critical look at 'participation', 'empowerment' and 'poverty reduction'. *Third World Quarterly*, *26*(7), 1043–1060. doi:10.1080/01436590500235603

Dussel, E. D. (2003). The "World System": Europe as "Center" and Its "Periphery" beyond Eurocentricism. In Mendieta, E. (Ed.), *Beyond philosophy: ethics, history, Marxism, and liberation theology* (pp. 53–81). Rowman & Littlefield Publishers.

Fanon, F. (1967). *The wretched of the earth*. Penguin.

Fanon, F. (1986). *Black skin, white masks*. Pluto.

Freire, P. (1972). *Pedagogy of the Oppressed*. Penguin Books.

Gilroy, P. (1993). *The black Atlantic: modernity and double consciousness*. London, New York: Verso.

Godin, B. (2004). The New Economy: what the concept owes to the OECD. *Research Policy*, *33*, 679–690. doi:10.1016/j.respol.2003.10.006

Hancock, G. (2004). *Lords of Poverty*. Nairobi: Camerapix Publishers International.

Hirschheim, R., & Klein, H. K. (1989). Four paradigms of information systems development. *Communications of the ACM*, *32*, 1199–1216. doi:10.1145/67933.67937

Kallinikos, J. (2004). Farewell to constructivism: technology and context embedded action. In Avgerou, C., Ciborra, C., & Land, F. (Eds.), *The social study of information and communication technology: innovation, actors and contexts* (pp. 140–161). Oxford University Press.

Kock, N., Gray, P., Hoving, R., Klein, H., Myers, M., & Rockart, J. (2002). IS Research Relevance Revisited: Subtle Accomplishment, Unfulfilled Promise, or Serial Hypocrisy? *Communications of the Association for Information Systems (Volume,)* *8*, 330-346.

Laderchi, C. R., Saith, R., & Stewart, F. (2003). Does it Matter that we do not Agree on the Definition of Poverty? A Comparison of Four Approaches. *Oxford Development Studies*, *31*(3), 243–274. doi:10.1080/1360081032000111698

Ladson-Billings, G. (2003). Radicalized Discourses and Ethnic Epistemologies. In Denzin, N. K., & Lincoln, Y. S. (Eds.), *The Landscape of Qualitative Research* (2nd ed., pp. 398–432). Sage.

Lawson, T. (1997). *Economics and reality*. London, New York: Routledge.

López, A. J. (Ed.). (2005). *Postcolonial whiteness: a critical reader on race and empire*. Albany: State University of New York Press.

Mezzadra, S., & Rahola, F. (2006). The Postcolonial Condition: A Few Notes on the Quality of Historical Time in the Global Present. *Postcolonial Text, 2*(1), Retrived March 6, 2010, from http://journals.sfu.ca/pocol/index.php/pct/article/viewArticle/2393.

Mignolo, W. D. (2002). The Geopolitics of Knowledge and the Colonial Difference. *The South Atlantic Quarterly, 101*(1), 57–96. doi:10.1215/00382876-101-1-57

Miller, L. (Ed.). (1997). *From the heart: voices of the American Indian / edited and with narrative by Lee Miller*. London: Pimlico.

Mingers, J. (2003). A classification of the philosophical assumptions of management science methods. *The Journal of the Operational Research Society, 54*, 559–570. doi:10.1057/palgrave.jors.2601436

Mingers, J. (2004c). Real-izing information systems: critical realism as an underpinning philosophy for information systems. *Information and Organization, 14*, 87–103. doi:10.1016/j.infoandorg.2003.06.001

Morgan, J. (2003). The global power of orthodox economics. *Journal of Critical Realism, 1*(2), 7–34.

Walsham, G., & Sahay, S. (2006). Research on Information Systems in Developing Countries: Current Landscape and Future Prospects. *Information Technology for Development, 12*(1), 7–24. doi:10.1002/itdj.20020

Wilson, E. J. (2004). *The information revolution and developing countries*. Cambridge, MA: MIT Press.

KEY TERMS AND DEFINITIONS

Development: The idea that planned initiatives undertaken by or under the direction of a government can lead to a better quality of life for its population.

Discourse: A nexus of power and knowledge that acts as a legitimating framework for ideas acceptable to those in power, while delegitimizing or suppressing undesirable ones. The effect is to conceal the operation of power in the generation of such knowledge.

E-Government: The use of information and communications technology systems in the management of government functions, and in communicating and providing access to government services to citizens and organizations.

ICT for Development: Information and communications technology systems when used as part of an initiative aimed at bringing about development. It may comprise mainly ICTs, or their use in a supporting role.

New Public Management: An intellectual and policy practice movement that started in the 1980s to bring about a private sector mindset to public sector management in place of traditional bureaucracies. Its key characteristics are market discipline in decision-making, operational efficiency and effectiveness, and the use of measures to gauge performance against set targets.

Postcolonial: The condition or period that follows a period of colonization for a given country, and is usually used in reference to countries in Africa, Asia and Latin America that emerged after gaining independence from European and western powers.

Postcolonial Theory: The diverse set of ideas and concepts from literary and social science studies in the period preceding and following independence, to interpret or better understand the postcolonial condition, state, and its people, in the context of an existing world order. Some are closely associated with Marxist ideas and the post-structural movement in European philosophy, while others originate in postcolonial countries.

ENDNOTES

1 The World Bank Group comprises IBRD and International Development Association (IDA). IDA gives concessional loans to eligible developing countries that are the main form of 'aid'.

2 These battles finally led to Joseph Stiglitz's firing in 2000 and the resignation of Ravi Kanbur, appointed by Stiglitz to head the World Development Report 2000, both apparently at the instigation of the US treasury. (Wade, 2002)

3 PRSPs are also used by the WB/IMF to assess whether countries qualify for the Highly Indebted Poor Countries Initiative (HIPC) for debt forgiveness program that emerged at about the same time.

4 This 'understratum' may be expanding in the west and developing regions as a 'fourth world' of 'failed humanity' while multinational corporate profits hit record levels. See Castells (2000a) and also Schwartz (2003)

5 Gayatri Spivak is often noted for her opaque poststructuralist writing style. In Spivak (2005), she reflects: "*I think* disapprovingly on the subaltern's entry into history" for to her 'Subalternity is a position without identity'.

Chapter 3
Transformation of Management in the Public Sector:
Exploring the Strategic Frameworks of E-Government

Spyros Angelopoulos
The University of Warwick, UK

Fotis Kitsios
University of Macedonia, Greece

Vasilis Moustakis
Technical University of Crete, Greece

ABSTRACT

Management is what makes e-government successful by coordinating the use of corporate resources, managing relationships, and empowering strategic alliances. However, current e-government methodologies and models used are only tailored to specific requirements. This restrains the ability to compare cases and draw valuable conclusions as to how to improve e-government and its performance measurements. Therefore, the authors are attempting to address the issues faced by surveying the models consisting of effective practices in e-government and Information Technology integration management and support. The study provides in depth overview of the current status of e-government models and links with emerging Information Technology.

DOI: 10.4018/978-1-60960-839-2.ch003

INTRODUCTION

E-government projects have a breadth of impact that extends far beyond the agency concerned and where benefits often expand beyond the agency owning the aforementioned project. These projects utilize technology to accomplish reform by fostering transparency, eliminating distance and other divides, and empowering people to participate in the political processes that affect their lives (CDT, 2002). The usability, the lower cost of communication channels, the function of electronic services as well as the increased participation of citizens, can enable the creation of a socio-economic environment, which could satisfy both the administration and the citizen (Tahinakis et al, 2006).

During the previous years very few academic studies have concentrated on this area, which means that the knowledge of new service development (NSD) in the public sector has not advanced very far. The majority of NSD research has concentrated on the financial service sector, but so far there has been no important research on NSD in the public sector. This study leads to a literature review of current strategic and managerial frameworks for e-government implementation. The overall aim of the research project is to conduct a critical analysis of well-established e-government models and strategic frameworks.

DEFINING E-GOVERNMENT

Despite the fact that e-government has emerged as a popular catch phrase in public administration (Yildiz, 2007), it still remains one of those concepts that mean a lot of different things to a lot of different groups (Grant & Chau, 2005). The goal of e-government is to make government services more accessible, more citizen-focused, more relevant to citizens as well as more responsive to their needs and expectations. E-government comprises the use of Information and Communication Technologies (ICT) in delivering public services to citizens and businesses. It entails the transformation of public services available to citizens using new organizational processes as well as new technological trends (Gunter, 2006). Furthermore, it is regarded as a player with a significant role in enabling greater citizen involvement in civic and democratic matters in the sense of direct democracy as the one practiced in the city-states of ancient Greece (Angelopoulos et al. 2010; Angelopoulos, 2010). E-government is also designed to facilitate a more integrated mode of government, while it encapsulates the relationships between governments, their customers and their suppliers by the use of electronic means (Means & Schneider, 2000).

Until now, researchers have not been able to come up with a universally accepted definition in order to describe the e-government concept (Halchin, 2004). The United Nations and the American Society for Public Administration (2002) defines e-government as the utilization of the World Wide Web for the delivery of government information as well as services to citizens. Jaeger (2003), believes that it may also include the use of other ICT in addition to the World Wide Web, such as databases, networking, discussion support, multimedia, automation, tracking and tracing, and personal identification technologies. However, Doty and Erdelez, (2002) propose that e-government should enable an open government with transparency as well as responsiveness. E-government is the use of technology, especially web-based applications in order to enhance access to and efficiently deliver government information and services (Brown & Brudney, 2001).

Balutis (2001) classifies the development of e-government into four phases. These four phases include information dissemination, forms-only, end-to-end electronic transactions, and transforming government. According to this classification, information dissemination is the least-developed and fundamental phase, describing a stage in which information is simply provided online. In the second, forms-only phase, users can download forms in a digital format. The third, end-to-end electronic transactions involve allowing citizens to commence their transaction digitally and ultimately ending their transaction in the same way. The transaction is hence characterized as being entirely executed digitally (Lau et al. 2007). The fourth phase in the development of e-government is its final goal, in which the government provides all services and information online. In this way, e-government acts as a stand-in for traditional forms of government services, as citizens can simply log onto the Internet to meet their needs.

What is also lacking in the treatment of the subject is a more in-depth analysis of the political nature of the e-government process, and a deeper recognition of complex political and institutional environments (Yildiz, 2007). According to the World Bank (2004), e-government refers to the use by government agencies of information technologies that have the ability to transform relations with citizens, businesses, and other arms of government. Lastly, according to the Center for Democracy and Technology (2002), "e-government is the use of ICT in order to transform government by making it more accessible, effective and accountable". However, e-government is not about the use of technology or technological innovation for its own sake. Certain technologies do not fundamentally define what e-government is and will be (Yildiz, 2007).

BARRIERS IN IMPLEMENTATION OF E-GOVERNMENT

Fundamental changes have occurred in the structure of most countries' economies, with services becoming the major sector of economic activity (OECD, 2000) and therefore, meeting the challenges of an unstable and unsettled environment is not easy. E-government requires strong political leadership in order to succeed (CDT, 2002). Obviously, there are several economical and political reasons underpinning this move. The utilization of ICT in the public sector does not constitute a panacea, however, it has been a means to manage the limitations of bounded-rationality and provide the infrastructure for better decision-making (Simon, 1976).

In light of the discussion presented above, the most significant limitation of the e-government concept is that there is still no standard definition of it. This difficulty stems from many reasons, such as the fact that it is a concept defined by the objective of the activity, rather than by the specific technology used, provider of the service/information, or clear-cut activities of the related actors.

Many barriers such as the high cost or the low security can impede its implementation and adoption. The integration of various Information Technology (IT) applications and components inside and outside the organizational boundary remains costly and time-consuming due to the heterogeneity of the computing environments involved in public-sector organizations (Themistocleous & Irani, 2002). Bonham et al. (2001), Bourn (2002), Dillon and Pelgrin (2002), McClure (2000) and the National Research Council (2002) agree that governments face a shortage of technical infrastructure. The above-said shortage presents a significant barrier in the development of the capabilities of government organizations to provide online services and transactions. They also agree that unreliable IT infrastructure in public sector organizations will certainly degrade the e-government performance.

A frequently cited barrier in literature seems to be the need for security and privacy in an e-government strategy (Daniels, 2002; James, 2000; Joshi & Ghafoor, 2001; Lambrinoudakis & Gritzalis, 2003; Layne & Lee, 2001; Bonham et al, 2001; Gefen & Pavlou, 2002). The shortage of IT skills is also a barrier, which contends many challenges regarding the efficiency of a public administration to provide innovative e-government services (Chen & Gant, 2001; Heeks, 2001; Ho, 2002; Moon, 2002). Finally, a major barrier to the adoption and implementation of e-government is funding (Bonham, Seifert & Thorson, 2001; Heeks, 2001; Ho, 2002), which also relates to the business procedure of government, management strategy, and organizational culture (Lenk & Traunmuller, 2000; McClure, 2000).

Organizational barriers relate to structural issues such as fragmentation, poor relations and communication between the functional departments, and an acceptance of the strategic benefits of new initiatives by the senior management (Aichholzer & Schmutzer, 2000; Fletcher & Wright, 1995). Moon (2002) concludes that, to enhance the effectiveness of e-government practices, public-sector organizations would need to progress toward a higher level of e-government development, which will require a greater number of highly trained technical staff.

CURRENT STATUS OF STRATEGIC E-GOVERNMENT FRAMEWORKS LITERATURE

E-government studies until now, limit themselves by researching the outcomes and outputs of e-government projects. However, understanding the political process behind e-government development is vital for overcoming both definitional and analytical limitations (Yildiz, 2007). In the recent years, many attempts have been made by different research teams around the globe to describe e-government architecture frameworks, in many aspects of the digital side of public services, such as the financial, ethical, strategic, legal, semantic, security, implementation, evaluation as well as interoperability. The most significant frameworks in the area of e-government, categorized according to the fore-mentioned architectures, are being presented in Table 1.

Management is what makes e-government successful by coordinating the use of corporate resources, managing relationships and empowering strategic alliances. However, current e-government methodologies and models used are only tailored to specific requirements. This greatly restrains the ability to compare cases and draw valuable conclusions on how to improve e-government and its performance measurements. Therefore, the authors are attempting to address the issues faced by proposing a model consisting of effective practices in e-government IT integration management and IT support. Moreover, an attempt is being made for a description of current status of strategic frameworks for e-government literature.

Research in strategic frameworks for e-government implementation begun in 2000 with the Central IT Unit study at United Kingdom. Four years later, in 2004, three new strategic frameworks published by Ebrahim & Irani, Lambert et al as well as Mittal et al. The following year, 2005, Scholl publishes one more study. A year later, Affisco & Soliman as well as Mahapatra & Perumal publish their work on strategic frameworks and the literature continues until Flak et al. investigate the insights from 48 Norwegian Government Funded Projects in 2007 (See also Table 2).

The UK Central IT Unit (2000) framework tries to achieve a segmentation of the public e-services market, which assists in focusing efforts at profitable customers, or alternatively aiming products at subtly different demand characteristics. According to their study, major issues obstructing the development of e-government at present include:

- How to address security and privacy concerns.
- Determining which services to integrate.
- Deciding whether to outsource the service delivery either entirely or through public-private partnerships.

It is received wisdom that e-government services are targeted at one of four broad constituencies, namely: businesses, citizens, other governments as well as employees. It is more

Table 1. E-government frameworks literature

Architecture	Year	Author
financial	2007	Johnson
ethical	2004	Mullen & Horner
	2001	Bannister & Lalor
strategic	2000	UK Central IT Unit
	2006	Affisco & Soliman
	2004	Ebrahim & Irani
	2006	Mahapatra & Perumal
	2005	Scholl
	2004	Mittal et. al,
	2004	Abie et al
	2007	Flak et al
	2004	Lambert et al
legal	2005	Giraldo
	2006	Teswanich et. Al
semantic	2004	Lenk & Traunmüller
	2001	Fernandes, et. Al
	2005	Stojanovic & Stojanovic
	2006	Herborn & Wimmer
	2007	Goudos et al
	2006	Abecker et al
	2004	Caituiro-Monge & Rodríguez-Martinez
	2005	Belanger et al
	2006	Mauher & V.Smokvina
	2007	Crichton et al
	2005	Frederic & Michel
	2007	Alkhatib et al
	2008	Chun
	2005	ECS
security	2005	Belanger & Hiller
	2002	Rieke
	2003	Makedon et. Al
	2004	Kalloniatis
	2003	Caloyannides
	2003	GovTalk
	2003	Lambrinoudakis et. Al
	2003	Sharma & Gupta
	2004	Abie, et. Al

continued on following page

Table 1. Continued

Architecture	Year	Author
implementation	2002	Di Maio et al
	2006	Chen et al
	2005	Evans & Yen
evaluation	2003	Gupta & Jana
	2005	Castellano et al
	2004	Banerjee & Chau
	2005	Montagna
	2005	Williams & Fedorowicz
	2004	Oyomno
	2006	Codagnone & Boccardelli
	2004	Chircu
	2004	Al-Omari & Al-Omari
	2003	Bui et al
	2007	Kumar et al
	2005	Ebrahim & Irani
interoperability	2004	European Commission
	2004	Gijarro
	2000	UK Crown
	2005	Neumann & Benda
	2005	Antovski & Gusev
	2007	Charalabidis et al
	2005	Guijarro
	2005	Sundar & Garg
	2005	Mukherjee & Biswas
	2006	Diedrich et al

Table 2. Strategic e-government frameworks literature

Author	Year	Research
UK Central IT Unit	2000	e-Government, a strategic framework for public services in the information age.
Ebrahim & Irani	2004	A Strategic Framework for E-government Adoption in Public Sector Organisations.
Lambert et al	2004	A Framework for Experience Management in e-Government: The Pellucid Project.
Mittal et al	2004	A framework for e-Governance solutions.
Scholl	2005	The mobility paradigm in electronic government theory and practice: A strategic framework.
Affisco & Soliman	2006	E-government: a strategic operations management framework for service delivery.
Mahapatra & Perumal	2006	e-governance in India: a strategic framework.
Flak et al	2007	An Exploratory Approach for Benefits Management in e-Government: Insights from 48 Norwegian Government Funded Projects.

than obvious that e-services in the public sector generally apply to all four constituents, but at least citizen and subject services. The most common examples of e-government services are:

- Exchanges of information and payment to obtain some permission.
- To register for a service.
- To claim a benefit giving and receiving of money or information.
- Regulation and procurement.

These four constituents must be able access the service, if the infrastructure for the delivery of these services is not available, then constituents will not be able to access them.

Although different researchers propose different solutions for strategic frameworks and e-government implementation, most share three fundamental statements (Ebrahim & Irani 2005; Tambouris & Wimmer 2004; Traunmuller & Wimmer 2004):

- Involvement of citizens in the development process
- Proposal of a holistic approach
- A focus on work-processes

As a first step in a holistic approach it is recommended that governments should group the citizens according to their life situation (Tambouris & Wimmer 2004; Traunmuller & Wimmer 2004). Also, significant social, organisational and technical challenges will need to be understood well and overcome in those efforts that strive to achieve governmental transformation (Affisco & Soliman, 2006).

Organizational mobility is increasingly commonplace in public organizations, and presents both opportunities and challenges: opportunities for improving working practices through the introduction of new perspectives, and challenges arising from the constant loss of experience and the learning curve of the newly arrived staff. Experience management is a special kind of knowledge management, focusing on the dissemination of specific knowledge situated in a particular problem-solving context (Bergmann, 2002). The experience management model in Lambert et al. (2004) framework, exploits these experience-sharing concepts. The main benefits expected from the Pellucid project (Lambert *et al*, 2004) are the improvement in efficiency and effectiveness due to the reduction of time spent, and leveraging of experience due to the movement of staff among different roles. The main purpose of this project was to enhance employees' performance by giving them access to the required knowledge by the activity they are performing at the time they are actually performing this specific activity.

The cost of e-government implementation has always been a significant barrier and that is the reason why solutions which promise to lower the cost of developing; deploying and managing e-government projects really deserve researchers' focus. Mittal et al. (2004) study a framework that simplifies the procedures of developing, deploying, as well as managing complex, integrated, and standards-compliant e-government solutions. Their framework enables development, configuration, integration, and management of solutions at a higher semantic level. Furthermore, it provides commonly used services. Some of these services are:

- Access to citizen and property records.
- Access control and authentication services.
- Public key infrastructure.
- Support for digital signatures.

In this framework, the solution components as well as data models are described at a higher semantic level. They are constructed with customisation points that can be programmed through a policy administration interface, which is fairly intuitive and intended for solution managers who may not be well versed in application development. The ability to manage solutions at a higher semantic level enables participants who are not familiar with programming to customise solutions in order to address specific needs of the different national, state, and local governments. This also embraces the ability to build custom user interfaces for multiple local languages used in governmental transactions as well as to customise workflows in order to comply with the organisational structure and policies to manage access to and retention of government records.

Scholl (2005) discusses a phase model of strategic choice that constitutes an addition in the field of organizational development and transformation induced by mobile technology diffusion. He contributes to the understanding of mobile technology diffusion in government by identifying and assessing the influential forces and the direction in this process. Scholl's study presents a parsimonious phase model of the diffusion process. He identifies the various classes of fully mobile wirelessly connected applications and uses, while discusses specific challenges in the implementation process. Finally, he presents a framework of alternative strategic approaches to fully mobile wirelessly connected diffusion, and maps the fully mobile wirelessly connected application classes to the strategic approaches as well as to the diffusion stages. By doing so, he develops an understanding of phase-related strategic choices and presents testable propositions regarding the assumed distribution of approaches over the phases. Finally, he proposes a business-information and user-need-oriented principle to guide the various strategic approaches under consideration, which may also be of utility to practitioners in the field.

While in some cases the implementations are conducted meritoriously, they are effort-centered rather than being result-centric. Mahapatra & Perumal (2004) provide a strategic framework for the implementation of e-governance projects in the Indian context, to achieve a result-centric implementation by presenting and analyzing the components of good e-government:

- Stakeholder Analysis
- Organizational Structure
- Project Management
- Process Streamlining
- Technological Feasibility and Up-gradation

Mahapatra and Perumal present a workable strategic framework to provide a roadmap for the projects to be sustainable in long-term. Their study concentrates on stake-holders, environment, technology enablers, internal processes as well as delivery mechanisms along with the factors that should be taken care of for scaling-up of the e-government projects and making it self-sustainable.

E-services in the public sector address the digital divide for citizens and businesses through multiple access channels and have been successful in creating a government without walls, doors and civil servant work shifts. With these in mind, Flak et al. (2007) described and summarized a Norwegian approach to benefits management particularly targeting e-government efforts. Forty-eight government-funded projects have implemented the approach and insights from these projects are used to provide empirical insights on the usefulness of the process. Flak et al. (2007) present rich insights from a large number of projects employing a benefits management approach and thus respond to the lack of empirical studies on benefits management in the e-government domain. The results provide extensive insights in terms of hindrances for benefits realization, examples of qualitative benefits as well as some indications of quantitative benefits.

CONCLUSION

Defining a model is a complex and multi-faceted issue made even more difficult in the context of e-government management. This paper has summarised the state of research on the design of a model for e-government integration management to date as well as the most common dimensions, which can be applied to measure the concept of management in this context. Understanding e-government from the point of view of the customer/citizen/public, however, also implies understanding the IT processes of the council prior to applying metrics to assess service quality.

This study does not try to stand out either as a review or as a synthetic summary of past literature concerning managerial and strategic frameworks for e-government implementation, rather, its main objective has been an in-depth overview of the current status of e-government phenomenon. E-government is considered to be one of the key contributors to the development of an information society. However, the application of ICT in e-government should not be considered as an end in itself.

It has already been clear that a competitive telecommunications market as well as an environment conducive for e-government will enable e-government to become an affordable channel for citizens and businesses to interact with government as long as legal frameworks provide the legitimacy and guarantees needed to secure and protect electronic transactions and data exchanges. In cases that telecommunications infrastructure is already available or affordable, as a result of competition, e-government applications are quickly embraced and its projects are more likely to lead to success. Governments all around the world have seen the rapid evolution of e-government when there is an integrated approach to planning and implementation of public sector reform.

As an addition to the current status of e-government, future works need to give an answer to the dilemma, which derived from this study, whether e-government is really a tool for decentralization and democratization or the result of a sociotechnical process towards a new model of public administration. A scientifically documented answer will certainly boost the evolution of e-government. Finally, in an attempt to focus on the changes in business process that are needed inside governmental institutions in order e-government to be successfully implemented, a second recommendation for future work resides on the need for a holistic model which can embrace the back-office, the front-office as well as the real citizens' needs.

REFERENCES

Abecker, A., Sheth, A., Mentzas, G., & Stojanovic, L. (2006). *Semantic Web meets e-government. Stanford University*. AAAI Press.

Abie, H., Foyn, B., Bing, J., Blobel, B., Pharow, P., & Delgado, J. (2004). The need for a digital rights nanagement framework for the next generation of e-government services. [Inderscience Publishers]. *International Journal of Electronic Government*, *1*(1), 8–28. doi:10.1504/EG.2004.004134

Affisco, J., & Soliman, K. (2006). E-government: A strategic operations management framework for service delivery. *Business Process Management Journal*, *12*(1), 13–21. doi:10.1108/14637150610643724

Aichholzer, G., & Schmutzer, R. (2000). *Organisational challenges to the development of electronic government*. IEEE Computer Society, London, paper presented at 11th International Workshop on Database and Expert Systems Applications.

Al-Omari, A., & Al-Omari, H. (2004). *A framework model for assessment of e-government readiness*. IMTC 2004 - Information Technology Conference Amman, Jordan.

Aldrich, J., Bertot, J. C., & McClure, C. R. (2002). E-government: Initiatives, developments, and issues. *Government Information Quarterly*, *19*, 349–355. doi:10.1016/S0740-624X(02)00130-2

Alkhatib, G., Bataineh, E., Fraihat, H., & Maamar, Z. (2007). An intelligent integrated e-government framework: The case of Jordan. *Proceedings of the 7th European Conference on E-Government*.

Angelopoulos, S. (2010). *Ancient Greek values as a paradigm for e-government*. Athens Dialogues. Democracy and Politeia. EUNIC Papers. Available at: http:// athensdialogues.chs.harvard.edu/ cgi-bin/ WebObjects/ athensdialogues.woa/ wa/ dist?dis=86.

Angelopoulos, S., Kitsios, F., & Babulak, E. (2008). (in press). From e to u: Towards an innovative digital era. *Heterogeneous Next Generation Networking: Innovations and Platform*. doi:10.4018/978-1-60566-108-7.ch019

Angelopoulos, S., Kitsios, F., & Papadopoulos, T. (2010). New service development in e-government: identifying critical success factors. *Transforming Government: People, Process and Policy*, *4*(1), 95–118.

Antovski, L., & Gusev, M. (2005). *M-government framework*. EURO mGOV 2005, Brighton, UK, (pp. 36-44).

Balutis, A. (2001). E-government 2001a, part I: Understanding the challenge and evolving strategies. *Public Management*, *30*, 33.

Banerjee, P., & Chau, P. Y. K. (2004). An evaluative framework for analysing e-government convergence capability in developing countries. *Electronic Government*, *1*(1), 29–48. doi:10.1504/EG.2004.004135

Bannister, F., & Lalor, S. (2001). Public service values: Towards an ethical framework for e-government, In *Proc. European Conference on e-Government*, Trinity College Dublin. Reading, UK: MCIL.

Belanger, F., Carter, L. D., & Schaupp, L. C. (2005). U-government: A framework for the evolution of e-government. *Electronic Government, an International Journal*, *2*(4), 426-445.

Belanger, F., & Hiller, J. (2005). A framework for e-government: Privacy implications. *Business Process Management Journal*, , 11.

Bergmann, R. (2002). *Experience management. Lecture Notes in Artificial Intelligence Series, 2432*. Springer.

Bonham, G. M., Seifert, J. W., & Thorson, S. J. (2001). *The transformational potential of e-government: The role of political leadership*. European Consortium for Political Research, which was held at the University of Kent at Canterbury, U.K.

Bourn, J. (2002). *Better public services through e-government*. London: The National Audit Office.

Brown, M. M., & Brudney, J. L. (2001). *Achieving advanced electronic government services: An examination of obstacles and implications from an international perspective*. Paper presented at the National Public Management Research Conference, Bloomington, IN.

Bui, T. X., Sankaran, S., & Sebastian, I. M. (2003). A framework for measuring national e-readiness. *International Journal of Electronic Business*, *1*(1), 3–22. doi:10.1504/IJEB.2003.002162

Caituiro-Monge, H., & Rodríguez-Martinez, M. (2004). *Net traveler: A framework for autonomic Web services collaboration, orchestration and choreography in e-government Information Systems. ICWS* (pp. 2–10). San Diego, California: IEEE.

Caloyannides, M. (2003). US e-government authentication framework and programs. *IT Professional*, *5*(3), 16–21. doi:10.1109/MITP.2003.1202230

Castellano, M., Pastore, N., Arcieri, F., Summo, V., & Bellone de Grecis, G. (2005). An e-government cooperative framework for government agencies. *Proc. of 38th Intern. Conf. on System Sciences, Hawaii*, *5*(5), 121c.

Center for Democracy and Technology (CDT). (2002). E-government handbook for developing countries. *CDT Policy Post*, *8*(26).

Central, I. T. Unit. (2000). *E-government: A strategic framework for public services in the Information Age*. UK Cabinet Office, London.

Charalabidis, Y., Lampathaki, F., & Stassis, A. (2007). *A second-generation e-government interoperability framework. 5th Eastern European e|Gov Days 2007 in Prague*. Austrian Computer Society.

Chen, Y., & Gant, J. (2001). Transforming local e-government services: The use of application service providers. *Government Information Quarterly, 18*(4), 343–355. doi:10.1016/S0740-624X(01)00090-9

Chen, Y. N., Chen, H. M., Huang, W., & Ching, R. K. H. (2006). E-government strategies in developed and developing countries: An implementation framework and case study. *Journal of Global Information Management, 14*(1), 23–46. doi:10.4018/jgim.2006010102

Chircu, A. M. (2004). *E-government value assessment: Towards a multidimmensional framework*. Retrieved from http:// www.informatik.umu.se/ ~qron/ Chircu.doc

Chun, A. H. W. (2008, Spring). An AI framework for the automatic assessment of e-government forms. *AI Magazine*.

Codagnone, C., & Boccardelli, P. (2006). *Measurement framework final version*. E-Government Economics Project. Rome, Italy: eGEP Consortium. Retrieved from http:// 82.187.13.175/ eGEP/ Static/ Contents/ final/ D.2.4_Measurement_Framework_final_version.pdf

Crichton, C., Davies, J., Gibbons, J., Harris, S., & Shukla, A. (2007). Semantic frameworks for e-government. *Proceedings of the 1st International Conference on Theory and Practice of Electronic Governance*. WORKSHOP SESSION: Formal engineering methods for electronic governance, (pp. 30-39). Macao, China.

Crown, U. K. (2000). *E-government interoperability framework* (e-GIF). Office of the e-Envoy. Retrieved from http:// www.uk-online.gov.uk

Daniels, M. (2002). *E-government strategy: Simplified delivery of services to citizens*. Washington, DC: Office of Management and Budget.

Di Maio, A., Baum, C., Keller, B., Kreizman, G., Pretali, M., & Seabrook, D. (2002). *Framework for e-government strategy assessment: Strategic analysis report*. 8 March 2002. Stamford, Connecticut: Gartner, pl. 2

Diedrich, E., Schmidt, D., & Wimmer, M. (2006). A three dimensional framework to realize interoperability in public administrations. *Proceeding of the Workshop on Semantic Web for eGovernment*. Workshop at the 3rd European Semantic Web Conference 12 June 2006, Budva, Serbia & Montenegro.

Dillon, J., & Pelgrin, W. (2002). *E-government / commerce in New York State*. New York, NY: Office of Technology.

Doty, P., & Erdelez, S. (2002). Information micro-practices in Texas rural courts: Methods and issues for e-government. *Government Information Quarterly, 19*, 369–387. doi:10.1016/S0740-624X(02)00121-1

Duffy, D. (2000). *Q&A: Balancing the role of e-government: Interview with Mike Hernon, vice president of e-government for New York City based Gov Works*. Retrieved from http:// www.cnn.com/ 2000/ TECH/ computing/ 11/ 13/ qna.egov.idg

Ebrahim, Z., & Irani, Z. (2005). E-government adoption: Architecture and barriers. [Emerald Group Publishing Limited.]. *Business Process Management Journal, 11*(5), 589–611. doi:10.1108/14637150510619902

European Commission. (2004). *European interoperability framework for pan-European e-government services.* IDA working document, version 2.4, Brussels.

European Committee for standardization. (2005). *EU e-government metadata framework* (ecs). Retrieved from ftp:// ftp.cenorm.be/ PUBLIC/ CWAs/ e-Europe/ MMI-DC/ cwa15245-00-2005-Apr.pdf

Evans, D., & Yen, D. C. (2005). E-government: An analysis for implementation: Framework for understanding cultural and social impact. *Government Information Quarterly, 14*, 3–6.

Fernandes, D., Gorr, W., & Krishnan, R. (2001). *Servicenet: An agent-based framework for one-stop e-government services.* Americas Conference on Information Systems.

Flak, L. S., Eikebrokk, T. R., & Dertz, W. (2007). An exploratory approach for benefits management in e-government: Insights from 48 Norwegian government funded projects. *Proceedings of the 41st Annual Hawaii International Conference on System Sciences*, (p. 210).

Fletcher, K., & Wright, G. (1995). Organizational, strategic and technical barriers to successful implementation of database marketing. *International Journal of Information Management, 15*(2), 115–126. doi:10.1016/0268-4012(95)00005-R

Frederic, C., & Michel, L. (2005). *A semantical reasoning framework for e-government of French national retirement system.* Retrieved from http:// www.imu.iccs.gr/ sweg/ papers/ Comte+Leclere.pdf

Gefen, D., & Pavlou, P. (2002). *E-government adoption.* Paper presented at Americas Conference on Information Systems.

Gijarro, L. (2004). *Analysis of the interoperability frameworks in e-government initiatives.* EGOV'04

Giraldo, R. L. (2005). *Public policy and the new regulatory framework on electronic government procurement in Colombia.* AR: Revista de Derecho Informático, ISSN 1681-5726, vol. 88.

Goudos, S., Loutas, N., Peristeras, V., & Tarabanis, K. (2007). Public administration domain ontology for a Semantic Web services e-government framework. *Proceedings of 2007 IEEE SCC*, (pp. 270-277).

GovTalk. (2003). *Smart cards: Enabling e-government.* Draft Policy Framework. Retrieved from www.govtalk.gov.uk

Grant, G., & Chau, D. (2005). Developing a generic framework for e-government. *Journal of Global Information Management, 13*(1), 1–30. doi:10.4018/jgim.2005010101

Guijarro, L. (2005), Policy and practice in standards selection for e-government interoperability frameworks. In *Proc. of EGOV 2005 Conference*, (pp. 163–173). Copenhaguen (Denmark)

Gunter, B. (2006). Advances in e-democracy: overview. [Emerald Group Publishing Limited. Great Britain.]. *Aslib Proceedings, 58*(5), 361–370. doi:10.1108/00012530610692320

Gupta, M. P., & Jana, D. (2003). E-government evaluation: A framework and case study. *Government Information Quarterly, 20*(4), 365–387. doi:10.1016/j.giq.2003.08.002

Halchin, L. E. (2004). Electronic government: Government capability and terrorist resource. *Government Information Quarterly, 21*, 406–419. doi:10.1016/j.giq.2004.08.002

Heeks, R. (2001). *Understanding e-governance for development.* The University of Manchester, Institute for Development, Policy and Management Information Systems, Technology and Government: Working Papers Series, Number 12/2001. Retrieved from http:// idpm.man.ac.uk/ idpm/ igov11abs.htm

Heeks, R. (2008). *Success and failure in e-government projects*. Retrieved on January 28, 2008, from http:// www.egov4dev.org/ success/ definitions.shtml

Herborn, T., & Wimmer, M. A. (2006). Process ontologies facilitating interoperability in e-government: A methodological framework. In K. Hinkelmann, D. Karagiannis, N. Stojanovic, & G. Wagner (Eds.), *Proceeding of the Workshop on Semantics for Business Process Management at the 3rd European Semantic Web Conference 2006*, Budva, Montenegro, June 2006, (pp. 76–89).

Ho, A. T.-K. (2002). Reinventing local governments and the e-government initiative. *Public Administration Review*, *62*(4), 434–444. doi:10.1111/0033-3352.00197

Hwang, S. D., Choi, Y., & Myeong, S. H. (1999). Electronic government in South Korea: Conceptual problems. *Government Information Quarterly*, *16*(3), 277–285. doi:10.1016/S0740-624X(99)80028-8

Jaeger, P. T. (2003). The endless wire: E-government as a global phenomenon. *Government Information Quarterly*, *20*(4), 323–331. doi:10.1016/j.giq.2003.08.003

James, G. (2000). Empowering bureaucrats. *MC Technology Marketing Intelligence*, *20*(12), 62–68.

Johne, A., & Storey, C. (1998). New service development: A review of the literature and annotated bibliography. *European Journal of Marketing*, *32*(3-4), 184–251. doi:10.1108/03090569810204526

Joshi, J., & Ghafoor, A. (2001). Digital government security infrastructure design challenges. *IEEE Computer*, *34*(1), 66–72.

Kalloniatis, C. (2004). Security requirements engineering for e-government applications: Analysis of current frameworks. *Proceedings of the Electronic Government: Third International Conference, EGOV 2004*, Zaragoza, Spain. (LNCS 3183, p. 66). Springer-Verlag.

Kumar, (2007). Factors for successful e-government adoption: A conceptual framework. *Electronic. Journal of E-Government*, *5*(1), 63–76.

Lambert, S. C., Arenas, A. E., Delaitre, S., Mena Raposo, J., Ferrentino, P., Majewska, M., et al. Procopio, V. (2004). A framework for experience management in e-government: The Pellucid Project. In F. Bannister (Ed.), *Electronic Journal of e-Government, 2*(3), 167-176. Academic Conferences Limited.

Lambrinoudakis, C., Gritzalis, S., Dridi, F., & Pernul, G. (2003). Security requirements for e-government services: A methodological approach for developing a common PKI-based security policy. *Computer Communications*, *26*(16), 1873–1883. doi:10.1016/S0140-3664(03)00082-3

Lau, T. Y., Aboulhoson, M., Lin, C., & Atkin, D. J. (2007). Adoption of e-government in three Latin American countries: Argentina, Brazil and Mexico. *Telecommunications Policy*, *32*(2), 88–100. doi:10.1016/j.telpol.2007.07.007

Layne, K., & Lee, J. (2001). Developing fully functional e-government: A four-stage model. *Government Information Quarterly*, *18*(2), 122–136. doi:10.1016/S0740-624X(01)00066-1

Lenk, K., & Traunmüller, R. (2000). A framework for electronic government. *Proceedings of the 11th International Workshop on Database and Expert Systems Applications*, (pp. 340-345).

Mahapatra, R., & Perumal, S. (2006). E-governance in India: A strategic framework. *International Journal for Infonomics: Special issue on measuring e-business for development*.

Makedon, F., Sudborough, C., Baiter, B., Pantziou, G., & Conalis-Kontos, M. (2003). *A safe information sharing framework for e-government communication*. Retrieved from http:// www.ists.dartmouth.edu/ library/ sis0903.pdf.2003

Martin, C. R., & Horne, D. A. (1995). Level of success inputs for service innovations in the same firm. *International Journal of Service Industry Management*, *6*(4), 40–56. doi:10.1108/09564239510096894

Mauher, M., & Smokvina, V. (2006). *Digital to intelligent local government transition framework*. Proceedings MIPRO 2006, (vol. 5, p. 47). Opatija-Croatia.

McClure, D. L. (2000). *Government online: Strategies and challenges*. Retrieved February 3, 2005, from http:// www.house.gov/ reform/ gmit/ hearings/ 2000hearings/ 000522dm.htm

Means, G., & Schneider, D. (2000). *Meta-capitalism: The e-business revolution and the design of 21st century companies and markets*. New York, NY: John Wiley & Sons Inc.

Mittal, P. A., Kumar, M., Mohania, M. K., Nair, M., Batra, N., & Roy, P. … Yagnik, L. (2004). A framework for e-governance solutions. IBM Journal of Research and Development, 48(5/6). IBM Research in Asia. Retrieved from www.research.ibm.com/ journal

Montagna, J. M. (2005). A framework for the assessment and analysis of electronic government proposals. *Electronic Commerce Research and Applications*, *4*(3), 204–219. doi:10.1016/j.elerap.2005.01.003

Moon, M. J. (2002). The evolution of e-government among municipalities: Rhetoric or reality. *Public Administration Review*, *62*(4), 424–433. doi:10.1111/0033-3352.00196

Mukherjee, A., & Biswas, A. (2005). Simple implementation framework for m-government services. In *Proceedings of the International Conference on Mobile Business* (ICMG'05). IEEE, (pp. 288-293).

Mullen, H., & Horner, D. S. (2004). Ethical problems for e-government: An evaluative framework. *Electronic. Journal of E-Government*, *2*(3), 187–196.

National Research Council. (2002). *Information Technology research, innovation, and e-government*. Washington, DC: National Academy Press.

Neumann, L., & Benda, P. (2005). Open ICT e-government architecture as an interoperability framework, *Proceedings, 5th European Conference on E-Government*, University of Antwerp, Belgium, (pp. 585-598).

OECD. (2000). *Annual report 2000*. Retrieved February 3, 2005, from http:// www.oecd.org/ dataoecd/ 30/ 59/ 1842666.pdf

Oyomno, G. (2004). Towards a framework for assessing the maturity of government capabilities for e-government. [LINK Centre.]. *The Southern African Journal of Information and Communication*, *4*, 77–97.

Papadomichelaki, X., Magoutas, B., Halaris, C., Apostolou, D., & Mentzas, G. (2006). *Designing government services, A review of quality dimensions in e-government services. Lecture Notes in Computer Science*. Berlin / Heidelberg, Germany: Springer.

Rieke, R. (2002). *Projects CASENET and SKe - A framework for secure e-government*. In Telecities 2002 Winter Conference, Siena, Italy, Dec. 2002. Retrieved from http:// www.comune.siena.it/ telecities/ program.html

Scholl, H. J. (2005). *The mobility paradigm in electronic government theory and practice: A strategic framework*. Paper presented at Euro Mobile Government (Euro mGov), Brighton, UK.

Sharma, S. K., & Gupta, J. N. D. (2003). Building blocks of an e-government – A framework. *Journal of Electronic Commerce in Organizations*, *1*(4), 34–48. doi:10.4018/jeco.2003100103

Simon, H. A. (1976). *Administrative behavior* (3rd ed.). New York, NY: The Free Press.

Stojanovic, N., & Stojanovic, L. (2005). A change-aware framework for the knowledge management in e-government. In K. V. Andersen, Å Grönlund, R. Traunmüller, & M. Wimmer (Eds.), *Electronic Government - Workshop and Poster Proceedings of the Fourth International EGOV Conference 2005*, Denmark, (pp. 3-10). ISBN 3-85487-830-3

Sundar, D. K., & Garg, S. (2005). *M-governance: A framework for Indian urban local bodies*. Paper presented at the Euro mGov 2005: The First European Mobile Government Conference, Brighton, UK.

Tahinakis, P., Mylonakis, J., & Protogeros, N. (2006). The contribution of e-government to the modernisation of the Hellenic taxation system. *Electronic Government, an International Journal*, *3*(2), 139-57.

Tambouris, E., & Wimmer, M. (2004). Online one-stop government: A single point of access to public services. In Huang, W. (Ed.), *Electronic government strategies and implementation* (pp. 115–139). Hershey, PA: Idea Group Publishing. doi:10.4018/978-1-59140-348-7.ch006

Teswanich, W., Anutariya, C., & Wuwongse, V. (2006). A knowledge management system framework for governmental regulating processes. *Electronic Government, an International Journal*, *3*(1), 56-73.

Themistocleous, M., & Irani, Z. (2002). (in press). Evaluating enterprise application integration technologies: A novel frame of references. *European Journal of Operational Research*.

Torres, L., Pina, V., & Acerete, B. (2005). E-government developments on delivering public services among EU cities. *Government Information Quarterly*, *22*, 217–238. doi:10.1016/j.giq.2005.02.004

Traunmuller, R., & Wimmer, M. (2004). E-government - A roadmap for progress. *Digital Communities in a Networked Society: E-Commerce, E-Business and E-Govemment: The Third IFIP Conference on E-Commerce*. Hingham, MA: Kluwer Academic Publishers.

United Nations & American Society for Public Administration (ASPA). (2002). *Benchmarking e-government: A global perspective*. New York, NY: U.N. Publications.

Williams, C. B., & Fedorowicz, J. (2005). A framework for analysing cross-boundary e-government projects: The CapWin example. *Proceedings of the 2005 National Conference on Digital Government Research*, May 15-18, 2005, Atlanta, Georgia.

World Bank. (2004). *E-government: A definition of e-government*. Retrieved February 3, 2005 from www.worldbank.org

Yildiz, M. (2007). E-government research: Reviewing the literature, limitations, and ways forward. *Government Information Quarterly*, *24*, 646–665. doi:10.1016/j.giq.2007.01.002

Chapter 4
Information Technology and Resistance to Public Sector Reforms:
A Case Study in Kenya

Roberta Bernardi
University of Warwick, UK

ABSTRACT

The objective of the chapter is to discuss how Information Technology can mitigate constraints to policy implementations stemming from a highly contested context. Main recommendations have been drawn by discussing main challenges met by Kenya in the restructuring of its health Information Systems as demanded by health sector reforms. The discussion will focus on how Information Technology can be used to limit the drawbacks of a highly contested policy context, mediate between global and local interests, and mitigate resistance to change. The chapter concludes with main recommendations on how to extend research on the implications of software designs in implementing public sector reforms and other policies in developing countries.

INTRODUCTION

Main research on government information technology has recognised the lack of a causal link between IT and organisational outcomes in public organisations (Kraemer & Dedrick, 1997). It has been acknowledged that contextual factors play a crucial role in conditioning IT implementations and usage (Fountain, 2001). This is particularly true in contexts of developing countries for a number of reasons.

Firstly, IT innovation processes are usually part of public sector reforms involving not only

DOI: 10.4018/978-1-60960-839-2.ch004

national policy actors but also international policy actors such as the World Bank.

Secondly, most developing countries, particularly in Africa, are characterised by poor human capital in the IT sector. In such a context it is difficult to find a satisfactory level of confidence with information technology tools, particularly from public managers and policy makers. This can have a negative influence on the level of commitment of policy makers to IT innovation.

Finally, processes of re-structuration and innovation of public administrations in most developing countries are usually based on reform models and IT designs imported from abroad. Software applications, in particular, may have assumptions embedded in their design (Kirkpatrick, 2004) that do not match those of users in the local context.

All these contextual issues affecting IT innovations in the public administrations of most developing countries cannot be easily changed. In particular, the complexity of multi-agency and multi-interests contexts which can be found in the public sector of most developing countries makes it difficult to arrange for successful change programmes that can align IT systems with organisational structures (Heeks, 2005).

These considerations point to the need to look closer at the way information technology in Governments of developing countries can actually be leveraged to mitigate constraints posed by certain contextual factors. Therefore, besides looking at contextual issues challenging IT implementations and usage in the context of public sector reforms in developing countries, this chapter aims to discuss about bottom-up approaches through which information technology can be used to overcome these same contextual difficulties.

More specifically, the objective of this chapter is to provide researchers and practitioners with directions on major issues that should be looked at to better understand how information technology can actually be used to mediate between different actors' interests and assumptions and other institutional factors affecting innovation processes of public administrations in a developing context.

Main arguments on this topic will be drawn by illustrating the experience of the Ministry of Health in Kenya in the restructuring of its health information systems as part of its health sector reforms.

The main rationale of the chapter is to better analyse knowledge on contextual limitations and enablers of IT innovation in a specific public sector context and to see how this knowledge can be used as a feedback to information technology investments in similar developing contexts.

The discussion of the role of information technology in mediating contextual circumstances will be mainly focused on the case of health sector reforms and the restructuring of health information systems in Kenya. Yet, main arguments and recommendations developed in the chapter discussion can also be applicable to similar cases and situations of public and health sector reforms in other African and developing countries.

BACKGROUND

Information technology has assumed a strategic role in the implementation of recent managerialist public sector reforms such as the rationalisation and decentralisation of management structures and performance-based accountability (Osborne & Gaebler, 1992). However, some studies have drawn attention to the failure of IT initiatives. Such a failure has been linked to the top-down approach of IT-led public sector reforms and New Public Management recipes (Ciborra, 2005; Ciborra & Navarra, 2005), which do not account for constraints posed by the existing institutional setting. In particular, the disaggregation tendencies of new public management matched with the inconsistencies of foreign development programmes (Dunleavy, Margetts, Bastow, & Tinkler, 2006; Therkildsen, 2006) have contributed, in most cases, to the fragmentation of information systems (Kimaro & Nhampossa, 2005), increasing rather than reducing complexity (Bellamy & Taylor, 1992). Most of times IT solutions are conceived and implemented by foreign consultants who protect the software source code from local customisations (Ciborra, 2005). In addition, a lack of local financial (Sander, Bell, & Rice, 2005) and human capacity (Higgo, 2003) often contributes to the discontinuance of IT systems.

Contrary to a top-down technology-centred approach, the sustainability of IT systems in developing countries has been related to other socio-political factors involving the inclusion of local stakeholders' prerogatives in the system design and implementation (Krishna & Walsham, 2005). An effective utilization and institutionalisation of an IT system have been attributed to the participation of local actors in the implementation process. This should include users' creative adaptation of global IT products to their local context along with change management capacity (Macome, 2008). If, on the one hand, the type of approach to IT implementation clearly influences its sustainable usage, on the other hand, less is known about the processes that shape and direct its usage and its transforming implications.

In this regard, major studies carried out in developed countries have found a lack of a linear causal relationship between information technology and organisational change (Kraemer & Dedrick, 1997). For example, there have been cases where integrated information systems and network technology seems to have supplanted bureaucracies with centralised structures (Bovens, Zouridis, & Tilburg, 2002; Dunleavy et al., 2006). Likewise, electronic information exchange has not always been successful in converting traditional hierarchical structures of public administrations into flatter forms of organisations (Bretschneider, 2003; Kraemer & King, 2006).

Other studies have found little evidence that IT has caused a major impact on the underlying structures of the public sector (e.g. redistribution of values and power, alteration in interaction patterns). IT impact is mostly associated with the efficiency and rationality of behaviour by units of the public administration (Danziger & Andersen, 2002).

Likewise, recent research in most African and developing countries has evidenced that health information systems reforms have not led to expected organisational change (e.g. Kimaro & Sahay, 2007). These reforms are usually sponsored by international partners (Lambo & Sambo, 2003) to decentralise and integrate health management and information systems to improve health care delivery (Kimaro & Nhampossa, 2005).

On the one hand, decentralisation is meant to devolve decision making power to the lower levels (e.g. districts and health care providers) to improve the cost-effectiveness and accessibility of service for the local communities (WHO, 1978; Kimaro & Sahay, 2007). On the other hand, integration aims to reverse the trend of donor-driven verticalisation of health programmes (e.g. HIV/AIDS, malaria, etc.) to rationalize resources and increase value for money (Chilundo & Aanestad, 2004). Yet, available studies show that goals of decentralisation and integration are rarely achieved (e.g. Kimaro & Sahay, 2007; Smith, Madon, Anifalaie, Lazarro-Malecela, & Michael, 2008). In most cases, in fact, the health sector scenario is still characterised by weak district health management systems (Odhiambo-Otieno, 2005) storing information in vertical programmes' data bases that are not accessible by district managers (Chilundo & Aanestad, 2004).

In particular, most of the challenges to restructure management information systems and implement new public management health sector reforms are mainly linked to the institutional complexity of African health sector contexts (e.g. Chilundo & Aanestad, 2004). These are in fact characterised by the divide between imported reforms and IT designs at the macro level and expectations and actions of implementers at the micro-level (Heeks, 2006; Madon, Sahay, & Sudan, 2007).

Another reason can been found in divergent interpretations of the value of health information by information system users. Hence, the urgency on data management under the managerialist perspective of improved health planning and management may not be shared by people in charge of data collection on the ground. These are mainly health workers who, constrained by a "resource-deprived environment", prioritise assistance to patients rather than ensuring timely and accurate data reporting (Chilundo & Aanestad, 2004).

Thus, main assumptions embedded in health sector reforms and IT system designs imposed from the top do not often reflect the reality of resource deprivation and poor information culture of a bureaucratic context. It is such a context that characterises routines and practices of most information systems users in the health sector of most African countries (Kimaro & Sahay, 2007).

Hence, the understanding of a lack of continuity between IT-enabled reforms and their implementation needs to take a deeper account of the institutional context. In particular, the public sector context has often been represented as the ground where tensions between competing institutional logics are usually highly accentuated and may involve resistances to IT-led reform programmes (Currie & Guah, 2007).

Fountain (2001) refers to "technology enactment" as the process by which organisational forms, both affecting and being affected by existing institutional arrangements, influence the adoption of information technology. The "enacted technology" can send feedback that creates changes directly in the organisation and indirectly in policy institutions (Fountain, 2001). In this regard of thought, previous studies have stressed the importance of the social context in influencing the usage of information technology artefacts and their consequent processes of organisational and institutional change, in particular, in the context of developing countries (Avgerou, 2000; Walsham, 2005). One of the major assumptions driving this perspective within studies of information technology and organisational change is that the institutional environment both shapes and is shaped by users' enactments of IT (Orlikowski & Barley, 2001).

Avgerou (2003) argues that innovation is not only the outcome of the rational decisions of what type of business process or organisational change we want to implement and what type of technology is more suitable to achieve a certain purpose. In addition to this, there is a need to take into account how users make sense of an IT artefact and innovation process within a specific social context made of peculiar economic conditions, policy interventions, political priorities, managerial, professional and social values (Avgerou, 2003).

According to Ciborra (1999) IS innovation is not the result of a linear implementation of formally and rationally pre-planned information systems designs, but it stems from the spontaneous interpretations and enactments of an IT system as organisational actors draw from their past experience to develop their understanding of the current situation and respond with an adequate competent behaviour (Ciborra, 1999).

Although research has identified the contradictions between policy-making and implementation contexts (e.g. Chilundo & Aanestad, 2004; Smith et al., 2008) as one of the major causes of failed implementations of health information system reforms, there is still a lack of a more systemic understanding of the major sources of these tensions.

Drawing on the experience of the Ministry of Health in Kenya in the restructuring of its health information systems, this chapter argues that three main aspects are important to understand contextual tensions between policy discourses and actions: i. different levels of legitimacy of reforms between different policy actors at macro level; ii. the role of professionals in catalysing processes of innovation; iii. the influence of software designs in either enabling or constraining processes of innovation.

This chapter will discuss these issues by focusing on opportunities and threats that they represent in relation to IT-enabled change in the context of health sector reforms in countries like Kenya. The discussion will aim to elaborate a few recommendations on how information technology could be used to mediate the restructuring of health information systems in support of health sector reforms.

INFORMATION TECHNOLOGY AND PUBLIC SECTOR REFORMS

The Case of Health Management Information Systems in Kenya

Kenya, like other African countries, shares a long history of global health sector reforms bearing implications for its health management and information systems. Kenya was committed to the decentralisation of health planning and management since the adoption of the "District Focus for Rural Development Strategy" in 1983. The strategy complied with the main principles of decentralisation of the health service agreed in the Alma Ata Declaration on Primary Health Care of 1978 (WHO, 1978). In 1994 the decentralisation and integration of health management information systems were among the main objectives of the National Health Policy (Ministry of Health, 1994). Following the Paris Declaration on Aid Effectiveness in 2005, the country also adopted a Sector-Wide Approach (SWAp) (Mwega, 2009) to aid coordination in the health sector through one plan, one monitoring and evaluation framework, and one resource envelope. This last reform put more emphasis on the integration of health management information systems particularly after the set up of national health sector planning and monitoring systems envisaged in the Second National Health Sector Strategy Plan (2005-2010) (Ministry of Health, 2005).

However, the case study of three health information systems – the central Division of Health Management Information Systems HMIS, the Kenya Expanded Programme of Immunisation (KEPI), and the Programme of HIV/AIDS – I conducted at the Ministry of Health in Kenya has confirmed the fragmented scenario of health management and information systems found in other African countries (e.g. Chilundo & Aanestad, 2004). This suggests that the country has not yet been fully successful in implementing health sector reforms advocated by international policies. Data for the case study were obtained from a set of thirty-eight interviews and around five thousand pages of documents collected during a fieldwork in Kenya in 2008. These three cases illustrated below will then be discussed by focusing on the role of information technology in narrowing down the divide between policy and action.

Division of Health Management Information Systems (HMIS)

Since its establishment in the 70s the Division of Health Management Information Systems (HMIS) has suffered from poor political attention, donor support, and shrinking budgets from the Ministry of Health. Under these circumstances, it was very hard for the Division to support health facility and district offices with data collection tools and human resources for the supply of timely and complete data reports from the field.

In the area of computerisation, the Ministry of Health's engagement was even less. This was true not only in terms of insufficient IT investments but, most importantly, in terms of institutionalisation of information technology. As a matter of fact, until the Government approved the e-Government strategy in 2005, the Ministry did not have common IT governance and policy guidelines. Under these circumstances, most IT investments were part of isolated and uncoordinated donor partners' projects both within national and district health information offices. This contributed further to an uneven development of information systems undermining the decentralization and integration of health management information systems as envisaged in the reforms.

In the early 90s, with donor assistance, HMIS adopted Clarion, a warranty-free programming tool for the development of Data Base Management Systems. Most of the interviewed users referred to Clarion as an unfriendly and cumbersome system. This was because Clarion-developed applications were complex and with little flexibility (Grafton & Permaloff, 1991, p. 229) and HMIS lacked the necessary programming skills to adapt query and reporting capabilities of the system to its users' requirements.

It is in this context that HMIS starts putting forward new plans of computerisation for the decentralisation and integration of health management information systems through networked systems. The first plan of computerisation in this sense appeared in 2000. Yet, management in HMIS took divergent approaches to the computerisation of their systems depending on different pressures of donor partners. Thus, one manager in charge of the division soon after 2002 was committed to an incremental approach to the deployment of a computerised system to the districts of a few provinces without taking a longer term vision of the computer requirements for the decentralisation of the health information system country-wide. The system was funded by DANIDA (Danish International Development Agency), which, at the time, was supporting health service delivery including medicines procurements and supplies to health facilities. The Agency was thus keen on investing in district health management information systems to increase the monitoring and planning capacity of health facilities at districts, particularly, in relation to planning of medicines consumption and usage (Danish International Development Agency [DANIDA], 2006, p. 46). In particular, DANIDA decided to focus on local projects because of poor Government's commitment to the strengthening of health management systems (Gallachi, 2000, p. 6).

Yet, when the new manager took over in 2006, new reforms and a new aid scenario imposed different choices. In particular, soon after the presidential elections of 2002 DANIDA acknowledged increased commitment of the Ministry of Health in the implementation of its projects. This encouraged the Agency to scale up its support to HMIS country-wide supporting donor coordination and aid harmonisation as envisaged in the Paris Declaration on Aid Effectiveness (DANIDA, 2006, p. 15). Hence, the Division had to show its ability to provide information for monitoring and planning of the health sector as envisaged in the Second National Health Sector Strategy Plan. Monitoring demands coming from other grant programmes such as the Global Fund to fight AIDS, Tuberculosis, and Malaria were also putting pressure on the division. Such pressures led to prioritise the decentralisation of data entry practices, whereby computerised districts were expected to enter data into a central data base to speed up reporting to the central level and accelerate data transfer from the field to the centre. This put in second place the need to improve data consumption at implementation level to empower local health planning and management putting on hold the strengthening of district health management information systems.

Kenya Expanded Programme on Immunisation (KEPI)

The Kenya Expanded Programme on Immunisation (KEPI) started in 1980 as part of a ten-year project funded by the Danish International Development Agency (DANIDA). At the time monitoring of immunisation activities was under the responsibility of HMIS. Yet, the Programme recognised the deficiencies of HMIS in providing timely and accurate immunisation data. Based on these circumstances, the Programme decided to verticalise its information systems so that immunisation data were sent directly from the districts to the Programme's management unit.

Despite the gradual decline in donor funding following the end of DANIDA's project in 1989 and competing health priorities such as HIV/AIDS (WHO/Africa, 1994), the programme has been engaged in the strengthening of its information systems since the early 1990s. Like in the case of HMIS, pressures at policy level were relevant in influencing the action of the Programme's managers. In fact, it was clear how commitment to the strengthening of disease surveillance and routine immunisation information systems was driven by the Programme's awareness of the importance of accounting for funding and results in a period when donor funding was already scarce.

Until 2000, KEPI was relying on CEIS, a Computerised Epidemiological Information System. CEIS was a dos-based and centralised IT system donated by donors used to handle immunisation and surveillance data for immunisable diseases and generate reports on immunisation and disease incidence rates. Due to its stand-alone architecture, it only provided a centralised and single-user environment for data entry and report generation. Data officers that were using it at the time complained that the system had no few limitations in data processing including frequent crashes with considerable loss of data. Another problem related with CEIS was a lack of IT capacity and the need to rely on inconsistent support from the World Health Organisation.

Soon after CEIS broke down around 2000, the start of new funding from the Global Alliance of Vaccines and Immunisation (GAVI) in 2001 induced donor partners to scale up their support to immunisation. This offered KEPI the opportunity to computerise the provincial offices with a new computerised information system, EPI-Info. EPI-Info is a public domain (free-of-charge) statistical epidemiological software application developed by the US Centres for Disease Control (Harbage & Dean, 1999). A Windows- and Web-based software, EPI-Info allows users with no programming skills to easily build and customise data based management systems (Ma et al., 2008). In 2004 EPI-Info was installed on a server connecting computers at the national level and on separate machines at the provincial offices. The result was the decentralisation of data entry to the provinces, which would send their data reports to the Programme's data management unit at national level. The restructuring of the Programme's information systems was also possible thanks to the pressures from the Programme manager, who convinced the eight provincial offices to be in charge of data entry and supervision at the districts and health facilities in order to ease data workload at the national level. In particular, this was achieved by enforcing policy guidelines or standard operating procedures for data management.

Yet, even in this case, the approach chosen for the strengthening of KEPI's information systems suggests that the main interest was to speed up data reporting from the periphery to the centre rather than empowering local usage of data for planning and management.

National HIV/AIDS Control Programme (NASCOP)

The Kenya National Programme of HIV/AIDS was born with the support of the World Health Organisation's "Global Programme on AIDS". Yet, differently from KEPI, NASCOP's mission had a higher importance for the Government, which resisted the diffusion of HIV/AIDS information in order to preserve the tourism industry (Schoepf, 2004). In addition, official reports stated that lack of transparency and accountability by the Government administration urged donor partners to channel funds directly to projects implemented at the district level by-passing NASCOP (Government of Kenya, 1997).

Under these circumstances, the Programme's activities and information systems received very little support, at least, until the end of 1990s when Arap Moi publicly declared HIV/AIDS as a national threat and announced a national policy on HIV/AIDS (National AIDS Control Council [NACC],

2000). A more favourable political climate released the development of NASCOP's information systems from the Government's hold. Yet, this did not lead to increased public expenditure on HIV/AIDS. An exponential increase in donor funding to HIV/AIDS followed instead, leading to the creation of a series of sub-programmes (e.g. Anti-Retroviral Treatment, Voluntary Counselling and Testing, etc.), each one with its own information system and software applications for statistical analysis.

Following the start of multi-million grant programmes such as the US President's Emergency Plan for AIDS Relief (PEPFAR) and the Global Fund to fight AIDS, Tuberculosis, and Malaria in 2003, the demand for comprehensive and timely data to account for grant funding increased emphasising the need to integrate data reporting systems.

Major support to the strengthening of NASCOP's information systems came from PEPFAR by sponsoring the US Centres for Disease Control's (CDC) technical assistance (President's Emergency Plan for AIDS Relief [PEPFAR], 2004, p. 513) in integrating its sub-programmes data collection tools into a single form and providing the Programme with additional data clerks for data collection at the districts and data analysis at the national level. This eased the workload at the districts and accelerated the transfer of data reports to the national data centre where data were keyed into computers. It can be argued that CDC wanted to streamline data reporting from the districts to the national level to meet the accountability needs of PEPFAR which had to report on funded activities to the US Congress.

In addition, Programme and information officers were very much aware of the value of information for attracting and securing donor money. A couple of them stated that decentralising data entry to computerised districts could not guarantee data validation. It can be argued that pressures from donor partners and their increased interest in HIV/AIDS data contributed to increase the value that information officers attributed to data validity and proprietary information. By doing so they actually supported the centralisation of and verticalisation of the Programme's information systems. This clashed with the integration and decentralisation of information systems expected in the health sector reforms. In particular, information systems were mainly serving monitoring and accountability needs of the national programme management and donor partners and not planning needs at implementation level.

Contextual Challenges to IT Innovation

The case study of health information systems in Kenya has shown how reforms of decentralisation and integration of information systems were not implemented as expected. By contrast, users of the three divisions were still depending on centralised and fragmented information systems. In such a scenario, health data served programme management mainly at national level in contrast with little usage of data for health planning and management at implementation level. This confirms what found in other African countries (e.g. Chilundo & Aanestad, 2004; Smith et al., 2008). However, the case study has focused with more detail on the major factors underpinning tensions between policies and their enactments in relation to the restructuring of health information systems in Kenya (Table 1): i. incompatible political agendas and accountability systems under which national policy makers and international donor partners operate; ii. the role of local actors, in this case health records information officers and medical management, in influencing processes of innovation; iii. the role of imported software designs and their technical complexity in influencing organisation members' engagement in processes of change.

Contested Policy-Making Context

The case study in Kenya has evidenced how decentralisation and integration of health man-

Table 1. Main factors underpinning differences in the restructuring of HIS between the three divisions

	Political pressure	Local improvisation	Software flexibility
HMIS	Low	Low	Low
KEPI	Moderate	Moderate	Moderate
NASCOP	High	Low	N.a.

agement information systems did not receive adequate support from major policy actors. Poor enforcement of these reforms was mainly linked to centralised control and lack of a culture of information characterising the Government administration. In addition, the lack of a systemic approach by donor-driven health management projects led to the uneven development of health information systems country-wide.

One lesson that can be drawn from the case study is that the political value attributed to health information by national governments can negatively affect their support to the strengthening of health information systems. The case study has actually shown how Government's desire of control over health information was in the case of HIV/AIDS a source of political resistance to the strengthening of health information systems.

Faced with little engagement by national governments, IT innovation processes are mostly influenced by donor partners (Heeks, 2005). This was the case of the restructuring of health information systems in Kenya as illustrated in the case study. Yet, whereas health reforms in Kenya envisaged the strengthening of health information systems to benefit planning and management country-wide, donor partners were interested in supporting information systems only to satisfy their monitoring and accountability needs. It can be argued that different approaches to the restructuring of health information systems depended, in part, to differences in aid policies and accountability mechanisms between countries and international donor agencies. For example, district health care projects funded by DANIDA were more focused on the strengthening of district health management and information systems. On the contrary, grant programmes like PEPFAR prioritised country monitoring and evaluation of HIV/AIDS interventions.

Based on the examples presented in the case study, it can be argued that politics of international aid and national governments are still relevant in posing limitations to the vision, sustainability and scalability of IT investments in a crucial sector for development such as health management information systems. This was acknowledged in past research by emphasising the limitations of the piece-meal approach of donor partners (Kimaro & Nhampossa, 2005) and the challenges that the "design-reality gap" can bring to the successful implementation of e-Government projects and health information systems (Heeks, 2005, 2006). Yet, this case study has actually brought to light the complexity of political and structural elements challenging policy reforms and IT innovations in the health sector. The first objective of this chapter is to question what role information technology should have in order to mitigate the shortcomings of a highly contested policy context for the implementation of public sector reforms.

The Influence of Local Actors

The case study showed how pressures from donor funding prevailed over the action of local organisational actors in determining the restructuring of health information systems. In all three cases, pressures from donor funding led to a sort of distorted interpretation and enactments of the reforms by local actors as well. This led to prioritise fast data transfer from the lower levels so that data were used for programme management only at the central level and not for health planning and management at implementation level.

Whereas in relation to HMIS the adaptation to donors' needs could be viewed as resignation because of very little support received, in the case of NASCOP such adaptation was seen more as opening a new window of opportunities. This was reflected in the way Programme's needs overlapped with those of donor partners.

The case of KEPI has also shown how less conditional donor funding functioned as a change enabler by giving local actors more flexibility in the way they leveraged information technology to decentralise data entry to the provinces. Not only was this possible thanks to less constraining pressures from donor funding, but the right commitment and vision from management were also influential for this positive outcome. Yet, even management in KEPI viewed the implementation of a new computerised information system at the provinces as a means to satisfy information demands by donor partners and the monitoring needs of the Ministry of Health. Despite reforms of integration and decentralisation, the need to strengthen planning and management capacity at the lower levels or integrate with HMIS was not a priority.

These findings raise questions about the role of local actors and, in particular, skilled professionals and managers, in bending IT innovation to the local needs of the public service. One could argue that poor Government's commitment makes it difficult for local actors to champion public sector reforms and innovation. Yet, as highlighted in past research, local managers and highly skilled professionals should also be able to mediate between global and local needs leading to local improvisations of imported IT solutions and health information systems designs (Heeks, 2006).

The second objective of this chapter is to discuss whether and how information technology can be used by local actors to adapt global practices to their context.

Implications of Software Designs

The case study has shown how the complexity of legacy systems such as Clarion and CEIS was amplified by a user context characterised by low IT capacity. This can be considered as one factor inhibiting innovation by local actors.

Less complex systems like EPI-Info, on the contrary, facilitated the computerisation of health information systems in KEPI. Yet, the networking capacity of EPI-Info was not fully exploited to the advantage of a full integration and decentralisation of health management and information systems. Neither integration nor the strengthening of districts' planning and management capacity were actually one of the major priorities of KEPI.

Based on these examples it can be argued that the capabilities of IT systems played a determinant role in either enabling or constraining change. IT can enable change as far as assumptions embedded in its design are aligned with those dominating a local context (Heeks, 2005, 2006). At the same time legacy systems that carry assumptions resisting change can further constrain positive pressures towards innovation (Brodie, 1992).

These findings confirm the lack of a linear relationship between IT systems and change in public organisations (e.g. Danziger & Andersen, 2002). The level of alignment of IT designs with assumptions characterising the local public sector context conditions the direction and extent of change of an IT system. Based on this argument, IT cannot have an incisive role in challenging institutionalised structures and practices unless they are accompanied by strong restructuration programmes (Barley, 1990; Avgerou, 2003).

These conclusions bring attention on the problem of how effective top-down change management programmes can be realised in a highly contested context like Kenya. In fact, one can argue that in a policy context characterised by divergent interests between various actors (e.g. national decision makers and donor partners), it can be particularly hard to achieve the necessary political commitment to the implementation of IT-enabled change programmes. This is not impossible to achieve, but it may require a long consensus-building process that would not fit within the timeframe of most donor-driven programmes.

The last objective of this chapter is to discuss whether and how information technology can be used to mitigate contextual limitations to change.

The Role of IT in Narrowing Down the Policy-Action Gap

The case study illustrated in this chapter has raised three main issues. First of all, IT innovation in the public sector can be particularly difficult to achieve due to a highly complex and fragmented policy context characterised by divergent political agendas.

Secondly, political pressures from the top have a strong influence on local improvisations of innovation leading to the alignment between global and local interests. Yet, the case study has also shown that less invasive political pressures at macro level can leave management with more choice of how health information systems should be restructured.

Finally, technical capabilities of imported IT systems have been found to influence innovation processes undertaken by local actors putting into question the efficacy of top-down IT-driven innovation programmes in a highly contested context like the public sector of most developing countries.

These conclusions focus the attention on how information technology can be used to mediate contextual constraints characterising the gap between innovation policies and their implementation in a public sector setting similar to Kenya.

With this regard, we can draw the following recommendations: i. information technology should be used to interface between different accountability systems at policy level; ii. information technology can facilitate local actors in contextualising processes of innovation; iii. the nature and type of software applications need to be thought carefully when we think of using information technology to implement public sector reforms in a specific developing context.

Can Information Technology be Used to Mediate Between Global and Local Interests?

The experience of health information systems in Kenya has shown that one of the major challenges to the strengthening of health information systems in Kenya was a lack of harmonisation of funding mechanisms. In most developing countries, including Kenya, the process required to implement the joint-funding mechanisms is still ongoing and recent research has evidenced the persistence of low and inconsistent contribution from most donor partners, who are still funding individual projects (Biesma et al., 2009).

One of the reasons for poor donor coordination is the need for donor-funded projects to be accountable to the donor country and not the local beneficiaries of the project. As evidenced by the case study, the pressure from donor funding can induce local actors to internalise the accountability needs of donor partners. In this situation, local actors mediating between the design of global IT solutions and projects and the local context (Heeks, 2006) can become the carriers of global interests. Hence, instead of striving for a balance between global and local interests (Heeks & Stanforth, 2007), the former are usually privileged whereas the interests of the local beneficiaries of IT-enabled public sector reforms become a second priority. This is because most of times the survival and emancipation of local mediators depend on the demands and needs of single donor funders. In such circumstances, global actors, such as donor partners, remedy to the lack of direct "power over" local actors by leveraging local mediators to acquire the "power to" pursue their interests (Heeks & Stanforth, 2007).

In this chapter the political nature of poor donor aid coordination and its downside on IT innovation processes within the public sector of developing countries are acknowledged. Yet, it is also believed that information technology can be leveraged to mitigate such downsides. Taking the area of health information systems as an example, one could look at the possibility to integrate and computerise existing manual information systems into a modular health management information system. Different modules would generate different data reports meeting the monitoring demands of different stakeholders at policy and programmatic levels. These would not only include national health programmes but donor funded programmes and grants as well. Each development partner would be responsible for the development and maintenance of its own module. Monitoring reports should be linked to targets of annual strategic plans. This would allow development partners to identify the extent of contribution of external funded activities to the national health sector strategies.

Making donor partners users of a country computerised health information system could increase their commitment to a sustainable and scalable health information system countrywide. Higher and continuous ICT investments could facilitate the computerisation of data entry points where health workers or managers in charge of different health services (e.g. immunisation, disease surveillance, HIV/AIDS anti-retroviral treatments, etc.) could enter data directly into a central data base. This would release the hands of health workers from the task of filling in many data collection forms, whereas district managers could consume data directly for their planning and management needs.

Similar IT solutions could be adopted in other sectors of the public administration of developing countries and could be a way to increase the balance between global interests of international actors and the interests and development needs of local stakeholders.

Can Information Technology Enable Innovation by Local Actors?

Despite recognising the pressure of global actors in conditioning the action of local innovators, the story of the three health information systems presented in this chapter has also evidenced differences in bottom-up pressures and their impact on IT innovations. In particular, the case study has shown how less conditional pressures from policy-makers and international agencies can create a venue for local improvisations.

Focusing on the role of information technology, a close analysis of the different technical capabilities of IT solutions illustrated in the case study has highlighted how software designs matter in either constraining or enabling local improvisations.

With this respect, the case study has shown how different software applications had different implications in influencing local users' action towards change. There were instances where ICT transfers were mostly aiming at donor needs or involved legacy systems embedding wrong assumptions about the local context (e.g. Lee, Ko, Jang, & Heeks, 2008) as happened, for example, with Clarion. Lacking resources to invest in new IT solutions, new users' requirements arising over time could not be met by existing legacy systems (Brodie, 1992). Thus, the inflexibility of legacy systems and a lack of local capacity to innovate hampered local processes of "reciprocations" between software design and reality (Heeks, 2005) widening the "design-reality gap" (Heeks, 2006).

In contrast, the case study has also brought to knowledge positive cases of ICT transfer as experienced by KEPI with EPI-Info. Conceived as a global software application, EPI-Info had the necessary flexibility and sustainability to meet expectations of change and information requirements from both donor partners and local actors. That is why it was successful to enable change, at least within the limits of the users' expectations at that time.

These considerations support the argument that software design matters in enabling emergent adaptation of IT solutions to contextual changes of users' requirements across time. In particular, in highly politicised contexts such as those of the public administrations in developing countries, it is worth looking at whether and how certain software designs can influence local IS users assumptions of change triggering emergent realities of innovation. In the specific case of the decentralisation of health management in Kenya, for example, it would be worth looking at whether computerisation of districts' information offices could bring much more active utilisation of information for problem solving and decision making by local health managers and administrators than non-computerised districts.

Therefore, besides supporting demand-driven approaches to IT innovations in the public sector of developing countries (Lee et al., 2008), there is also the necessity to look at those IT applications that can bridge between donors' and recipients' needs. This could be seen as a transitory approach while developing countries struggle to develop an endogenous IT industry and harness open-source software opportunities.

Can Information Technology be Used to Mitigate Resistance to Change?

One conclusion drawn from the case study is that in a context like Kenya it can be difficult to use information technology for the top-down re-engineering of the public service (e.g. Osborne and Gaebler, 1992). There are too many contradictory factors that would lead to unpredictable situations and make this approach fail. In such a context, starting an organisation change programme can be more challenging. This is particularly true in a situation where, like in the Ministry of Health, you may have coordination problems between different programmes or divisions that, based on their requirements, adopt different IT systems. Most of times, adapting an IT system to the local context in order to achieve specific change outcomes would require institutional or policy change at a higher level. For example, using IT to decentralise health planning and management can succeed only if budgets are decentralised and district health management teams are granted major financial autonomy.

This can be difficult to achieve, particularly, in developing countries where at macro level one has to deal with national policy makers but also with other institutional partners like donors. Thus, a change management process becomes more complex and prone to failure because it requires compromising between different actors and priorities and harmonising different IT systems.

These circumstances impose the need for "technochange solutions" that take into account possible sources of resistance to change to better understand how it can be prevented (Markus, 2004). Focusing on information technology, in a context where there are different political interests, IT solutions should be chosen by looking at their potential of mitigating resistance to change by key stakeholders, in particular, by mediating between competing institutional pressures. In this regard, Heeks (2005) talks about "reality-supporting applications", i.e. software applications that contain "shallow inscriptions", in other words, more generic and less strict assumptions about the local context so that they can provide users with more freedom for local improvisations and accommodation within their context (Heeks, 2005).

Taking the example of health information systems in Kenya, the model of a centralised and integrated health information system sponsored by HMIS was evidently resisted by other health programmes. This would suggest reconsidering how the integration and decentralisation of health information systems should be carried on. One way of doing it could be to take into account resistance from major local actors. In the particular case of Kenya, it was evident that the reluctance of programme managers and officers to loose their control over their data and information systems could pose serious constraints to integration. Having data officers on the ground enter data directly into a central data base is a good solution. However, programme managers should be promoted as the main holders of these data and they should be the ones made responsible for ensuring that such data are correctly entered into a central data base. Based on this approach, information technology could lead to better integration and coordination of monitoring and evaluation across programmes without challenging their autonomy. In this respect, the role of HMIS would be to provide policy and implementation guidelines and coordinate the process of data integration and monitoring and evaluation led by single programmes.

This example shows how an IT solution like a data base embedding few assumptions about local data ownership could prevent resistance to integration. Thus, investing in simple IT solutions that embody less strict assumptions about the local context could facilitate innovation in highly contested contexts characterising the public sector in most developing countries.

FUTURE RESEARCH DIRECTIONS

The chapter has discussed how information technology could be used to reduce the divide between policy-making and policy implementations in highly contested contexts. One major recommendation that can be drawn from this discussion is that there is need for further research that raises a more systemic understanding of how different software designs influence innovation in the Governments of developing countries.

In a couple of instances the case study presented in this chapter has shown how imported legacy systems can negatively influence innovation. It can be argued that increased usability of software tools together with higher exposure to web-based technologies can actually decrease resistance to software tools. This is something that has been suggested by other studies (Heeks, 2005) but that needs to be tested more systematically particularly in the public administrations of developing countries. The more technologies are studied focusing on their technical capabilities, in particular, by including open-source software, the higher will be the understanding of implications of software designs in influencing change.

Implications of different software designs should be made with respect to specific institutional settings. This can help assess the sustainability of certain IT solutions with respect to specific characteristics of the institutional environment. This is particularly relevant for the case of open-source software applications in order to understand major institutional and environmental factors affecting their sustainability. More generally, deeper investigation of the characteristics of various types of software applications and their effect within different institutional contexts can provide feedback to software designs to guarantee more successful endogenous IT innovation processes in the public sector of developing countries.

CONCLUSION

The chapter has raised a set of considerations and recommendations on how information technology can mitigate constraints to policy implementations stemming from a highly contested context. The discussion focused on the challenges that the Ministry of Health in Kenya had to face in the restructuring of its health information systems. Based on this, the chapter has put forward a set of recommendations on how information technology could be used to mitigate contextual limitations in the decentralisation and integration of health information systems.

More specifically, the chapter has brought attention to a series of contextual challenges that can hamper the usage of ICT for reforming and transforming the public sector. These challenges mainly stem from conflicting interests among different stakeholders raising resistance to reforms. Similar accounts of resistance to top-down IT-enabled reforms have been found in European countries as well (Currie & Guah, 2007). Yet, in a developing context the involvement of many international partners and the presence of a resource-deprived environment increase the difficulties in finding a compromise between incompatible political agendas of international and local actors. On the contrary, in such a context, political pressures at the top can enforce global interests and priorities on local actors challenging bottom-up drivers to local improvisations of IT innovation. Under these circumstances, public sector reforms in developing countries are less likely to address the development needs of most disadvantaged citizens.

In consideration of the challenges of a highly contested political context, the chapter has developed a series of recommendations on how information technology could be used to mitigate contextual constraints to innovation and reforms in developing countries. Firstly, information technology should be used to interface between different political agendas. Secondly, IT solutions should be chosen with regard to their potential of bridging between global and local interests. Finally, IT solutions should be chosen by looking at their potential of mitigating resistance to change by key stakeholders. In this regard, one main suggestion has been to focus on IT solutions that embed fewer and less strict assumptions on the local contexts in order to enable local improvisations in IT innovation.

Thus, with respect to a European context, aligning interests between multiple stakeholders in a developing country can be more difficult given that, most of times, actors involved in public sector reforms are from different countries, each of them, supporting different political agendas. Hence, there is need for future research to look at more flexible IT solutions that can meet less resistance within the context of usage and, in particular, mediate between global and local interests in public sector reforms of developing countries. This research can give feedback to the development of more sustainable IT innovation in the public sector of developing countries.

REFERENCES

Avgerou, C. (2000). Recognising alternative rationalities in the deployment of Information Systems. *The Electronic Journal on Information Systems in Developing Countries*, *7*(3), 1–15.

Avgerou, C. (2003). New socio-technical perspectives of IS innovation in organisations. In C. Avgerou & R. L. La Rovere (Eds.), *Information Systems and the economics of innovation* (pp. 141-161). Cheltenham, UK & Northhampton, MA: Edward Elgar Pub.

Barley, S. R. (1990). The alignment of technology and structure through roles and networks. *Administrative Science Quarterly*, *35*, 61–103. doi:10.2307/2393551

Bellamy, C. A., & Taylor, J. A. (1992). Informatization and new public management: A new agenda for public administration. *Public Policy and Administration*, *7*(3), 29–41. doi:10.1177/095207679200700303

Biesma, R. G., Brugha, R., Harmer, A., Walsh, A., Spicer, N., & Walt, G. (2009). The effects of global health initiatives on country health systems: A review of the evidence from HIV/AIDS control. *Health Policy and Planning*, *24*, 239–252. doi:10.1093/heapol/czp025

Bovens, M., Zouridis, S., & Tilburg, U. (2002). From street-level to system-level bureaucracies: How information and communication technology is transforming administrative discretion and constitutional control. *Public Administration Review*, *62*(2), 174–184. doi:10.1111/0033-3352.00168

Bretschneider, S. (2003). Information Technology, e-government, and institutional change. *Public Administration Review*, *63*(6), 738–741. doi:10.1111/1540-6210.00337

Brodie, M. L. (1992). The promise of distributed computing and the challenges of legacy Information Systems. In P. M. D. Gray & R. J. Lucas, (Eds.), *Advanced database systems: Proceedings of the 10th British National Conference on Databases* (pp. 1-28). New York, NY & Heidelburg, Germany: Springer-Verlag.

Chilundo, B., & Aanestad, M. (2004). Negotiating multiple rationalities in the process of integrating the Information Systems of disease-specific health programmes. *Electronic Journal on Information Systems in Developing Countries*, *20*(2), 1–28.

Ciborra, C. (1999). A theory of Information Systems based on improvisation. In Currie, W., & Galliers, B. (Eds.), *Rethinking management Information Systems* (pp. 136–155). Oxford, UK: Oxford University Press.

Ciborra, C. (2005). Interpreting e-government and development: Efficiency, transparency or governance at a distance? *Information Technology & People*, *18*(3), 260–279. doi:10.1108/09593840510615879

Ciborra, C., & Navarra, D. D. (2005). Good governance, development theory, and aid policy: Risks and challenges of e-government in Jordan. *Information Technology for Development*, *11*(2), 141–159. doi:10.1002/itdj.20008

Currie, W., & Guah, M. W. (2007). Conflicting institutional logics: A national programme for IT in the organisational field of healthcare. *Journal of Information Technology*, *22*, 235–247. doi:10.1057/palgrave.jit.2000102

Danish International Development Agency. (2006, November). Health sector programme support to Kenya. [Copenhagen, Denmark: Danish International Development Agency, Ministry of Foreign Affairs.]. *Phase*, *II*, 2006–2011.

Danziger, J. N., & Andersen, K. V. (2002). The impacts of Information Technology on public administration: An analysis of empirical research from the Golden Age of transformation. *International Journal of Public Administration*, *25*(5), 591–627. doi:10.1081/PAD-120003292

Dunleavy, P., Margetts, H., Bastow, S., & Tinkler, J. (2005). New public management is dead-Long live digital-era governance. *Journal of Public Administration: Research and Theory*, *16*(3), 467–494. doi:10.1093/jopart/mui057

Fountain, J. E. (2001). *Building the virtual state: Information Technology and institutional change*. Washington, DC: Brookings Institution Press.

Gallachi, A. (2000). *Project completion report. Ministry of Health, Kenya Health sector support programme, 1995-1998*. Copenhagen, Denmark: Danish International Development Agency, Ministry of Foreign Affairs.

Government of Kenya. (1997). *Sessional paper no. 4 of 1997 on AIDS in Kenya*. Nairobi, Kenya: Government Printer, Republic of Kenya.

Grafton, C., & Permaloff, A. (1991). Inexpensive database management software. *Political Science and Politics*, *24*(2), 226–231. doi:10.2307/419939

Harbage, B., & Dean, A. G. (1999). Distribution of Epi Info software: An evaluation using the Internet. *American Journal of Preventive Medicine*, *16*(4), 314–317. doi:10.1016/S0749-3797(98)00101-9

Heeks, R. (1999). E-government as a carrier of context. *Journal of Public Policy*, *25*(1), 51–74. doi:10.1017/S0143814X05000206

Heeks, R. (2006). Health Information Systems: Failure, success. *International Journal of Medical Informatics*, *75*, 125–137. doi:10.1016/j.ijmedinf.2005.07.024

Heeks, R., & Stanforth, C. (2007). Understanding e-government project: Trajectories from an actor-network perspective. *European Journal of Information Systems*, *16*, 165–177. doi:10.1057/palgrave.ejis.3000676

Higgo, H. A. (2003). Implementing an Information System in a large LDC bureaucracy: The case of the Sudanese Ministry of Finance. *Electronic Journal of Information Systems in Developing Countries*, *14*(3), 1–13.

Kimaro, H. C., & Nhampossa, J. L. (2005). Analyzing the problem of unsustainable health Information Systems in less-developed economies: Case studies from Tanzania and Mozambique. *Information Technology for Development*, *11*(3), 273–298. doi:10.1002/itdj.20016

Kimaro, H. C., & Sahay, S. (2007). An institutional perspective on the process of decentralisation of health Information Systems: A case study from Tanzania. *Information Technology for Development*, *13*(4), 363–390. doi:10.1002/itdj.20066

Kirkpatrick, G. (2004). *Critical technology: A social theory of personal computing*. Aldershot, UK & Burlington, VT: Ashgate Publishing.

Kraemer, K. L., & Dedrick, J. (1997). Computing and public organizations. *Journal of Public Administration: Research and Theory*, *7*(1), 89–112.

Kraemer, K. L., & King, J. L. (2006). Information Technology and administrative reform: Will the time after e-government be different? *International Journal of Electronic Government Research*, *2*(1), 1–20. doi:10.4018/jegr.2006010101

Krishna, S., & Walsham, G. (2005). Implementing public Information Systems in developing countries: Learning from a success story. *Information Technology for Development*, *11*(2), 123–140. doi:10.1002/itdj.20007

Lambo, E., & Sambo, L. G. (2003). Health sector reform in sub-Saharan Africa: A synthesis of country experiences. *East African Medical Journal*, *80*(6), 1–20.

Lee, H., Ko, K., Jang, S., & Heeks, R. (2008). Analysing South Korea's ICT for development and aid programme. *The Electronic Journal on Information Systems in Developing Countries*, *35*(2), 1–15.

Ma, J., Otten, M., Kamadjeu, R., Mir, R., Rosencrans, L., & McLaughlin, S. (2008). New frontiers for health Information Systems using Epi Info in developing countries: Structured application framework for Epi Info (SAFE). *International Journal of Medical Informatics*, *77*(4), 219–225. doi:10.1016/j.ijmedinf.2007.02.001

Macome, E. (2008). On implementation of an Information System in the Mozambican context: The EDM case viewed through ANT lenses. *Information Technology for Development*, *14*(2), 154–170. doi:10.1002/itdj.20063

Madon, S., Sahay, S., & Sudan, R. (2007). E-hovernment policy and health Information Systems implementation in Andhra Pradesh, India: Need for articulation of linkages between the macro and the micro. *The Information Society*, *23*, 327–344. doi:10.1080/01972240701572764

Markus, L. (2004). Technochange management: Using IT to drive organisational change. *Journal of Information Technology*, *19*, 4–20. doi:10.1057/palgrave.jit.2000002

Ministry of Health. (1994). *National health policy framework*. Nairobi, Kenya: Ministry of Health, Republic of Kenya.

Ministry of Health. (2005). *The second national health sector strategic plan 2005-2010 (NHSS II)*. Nairobi, Kenya: Ministry of Health, Republic of Kenya.

Mwega, F. M. (2009). *A case study of aid effectiveness in Kenya: Volatility and fragmentation of foreign aid, with a focus on health.* Wolfensohn Center for Development Working Papers no. 8, Washington, DC: The Brookings Institution.

National AIDS Control Council. (2000). *The Kenya national HIV/AIDS strategic plan 2000-2005.* Nairobi, Kenya: National AIDS Control Council, Republic of Kenya.

Odhiambo-Otieno, G. W. (2005). Evaluation of existing district health management Information Systems. A case study of the district health systems in Kenya. *International Journal of Medical Informatics, 74*, 733–744. doi:10.1016/j.ijmedinf.2005.05.007

Orlikowski, W. J., & Barley, S. R. (2001). Technology and institutions: What can research on Information Technology and research on organizations learn from each other? *Management Information Systems Quarterly, 25*(2), 145–165. doi:10.2307/3250927

Osborne, D., & Gaebler, T. (1992). *Reinventing government: How the entrepreneurial spirit is transforming the public sector*. Reading, MA: Addison-Wesley.

President's Emergency Plan for AIDS Relief. (2004). *Kenya FY 2004. Country Operational Plan (COP). 31 March 2004. Office of U.S. Global AIDS Coordinator and the Bureau of Public Affairs*. Washington, DC: U.S. State Department.

Sander, J. I., Bell, P. J. B., & Rice, S. D. (2005). MIS sustainability in Sub-Saharan Africa: Three case studies from The Gambia. *International Journal of Education and Development using Information and Communication Technology, 1*(3), 135-159.

Schoepf, B. G. (2004). AIDS. History and struggles over meaning. In Kalipeni, E., Craddock, S., Oppong, J. R., & Ghosh, J. (Eds.), *HIV/AIDS in Africa: Beyond epidemiology* (pp. 15–28). Oxford, UK & Malden, MA: Blackwell Publishing.

Smith, M., Madon, S., Anifalaie, A., Lazarro-Malecela, M., & Michael, E. (2008). Integrated health Information Systems in Tanzania: Experience and challenges. *Electronic Journal on Information Systems in Developing Countries, 33*(1), 1–21.

Therkildsen, O. (2006). Elusive public sector reforms in East and Southern Africa. In Bangura, Y., & Larbi, G. A. (Eds.), *Public sector reform in developing countries* (pp. 19–26). New York, NY: Palgrave MacMillan.

Walsham, G. (2005). Development, global futures and IS research: A polemic. *The Journal of Strategic Information Systems, 14*(1), 5–15. doi:10.1016/j.jsis.2004.11.009

WHO. (1978). *Alma Alta Declaration.* Geneva, Switzerland: World Health Organisation.

WHO/Africa. (1994). *Halting the decline in vaccine coverage. EPI Bulletin 001, June 1994.* Brazzaville, Congo: World Health Organisation, Regional Office for Africa.

ADDITIONAL READING

Avgerou, C. (2000). IT and organizational change: an institutionalist perspective. *Information Technology & People, 13*(4), 234–262. doi:10.1108/09593840010359464

Bangura, Y., & Larbi, G. A. (2006). Introduction: Globalisation and Public Sector Reform. In Bangura, Y., & Larbi, G. A. (Eds.), *Public Sector Reform in Developing Countries* (pp. 1–22). New York: Palgrave MacMillan.

Bellamy, C., & Taylor, J. A. (1994). Reinventing Government in the Information Age. *Public Money and Management, 14*(3).

Bozeman, B., & Pandey, S. K. (2004). Public Management Decision Making: Effects of Decision Content. *Public Administration Review, 64*(5), 553–564. doi:10.1111/j.1540-6210.2004.00403.x

Braa, J., & Muquinge, H. (2007). Building collaborative networks in Africa on Health Information Systems and Open Source Software Development - Experiences from the HISP/BEANISH Network. Retrieved August 10, 2010, from http://citeseerx.ist.psu.edu/viewdoc/download?doi=10.1.1.131.8950&rep=rep1&type=pdf

Brewer, G. A., Hicklin, A. K., & Walker, R. M. (2006, December). *Layers of Red Tape: Using Multilevel Modelling to Study the Effects of Red Tape, Management, and the Environment on Performance*. Paper presented at the Conference on "Determinants of Performance in Public Organizations II", 7-9th December 2006, University of Hong Kong, Hong Kong.

Bridgman, T., & Willmott, H. (2006). Institutions and Technology: Frameworks for Understanding Organisational Change. *The Journal of Applied Behavioral Science, 42*(1), 110–126. doi:10.1177/0021886305284990

Dada, D. (2006). The failure of e-government in developing countries: a literature review. *Electronic Journal of Information Systems in Developing Countries, 26*(7), 1–10.

Heeks, R. (2002). Information Systems and Developing Countries: Failure, Success, and Local Improvisations. *The Information Society, 18*(2), 101–112. doi:10.1080/01972240290075039

Heeks, R., & Bailur, S. (2006). Analysing eGovernment Research: Perspectives, Philosophies, Theories, Methods, and Practice. *iGovernment Working Paper Series*, Paper No. 16.

Heeks, R., & Bhatnagar, S. (2001). Understanding success and failure in information age reform. In Heeks, R. (Ed.), *Re-inventing Government in the information age: International practice in IT-enabled public sector reform* (pp. 49–74). London, New York: Routledge.

Hood, C. (2000). Paradoxes of public-sector managerialism, old public management and public service bargains. *International Public Management Journal, 3*(1), 1–22. doi:10.1016/S1096-7494(00)00032-5

Hope, K. R. (2001). The new public management: context and practice in Africa. *International Public Management Journal, 4*, 119–134. doi:10.1016/S1096-7494(01)00053-8

Jacucci, E., Shaw, V., & Braa, J. (2006). Standardization of health information systems in South Africa: The challenge of local sustainability. *Information Technology for Development, 12*(3), 225–239. doi:10.1002/itdj.20044

Krishna, S., & Walsham, G. (2005). Implementing public information systems in developing countries: Learning from a success story. *Information Technology for Development, 11*(2), 123–140. doi:10.1002/itdj.20007

Mutahaba, G., & Kiragu, K. (2002). Lessons of International and African Perspectives on Public Service Reform: Examples from Five African Countries. *Africa Development. Afrique et Developpement, 27*(3-4), 48–75.

Olowu, D. (2006). Decentralisation Policies and Practices under Structural Adjustment and Democratisation in Africa. In Bangura, Y., & Larbi, G. A. (Eds.), *Public Sector Reform in Developing Countries* (pp. 228–254). New York: Palgrave MacMillan.

Olsen, J. P. (2004). Maybe it is time to rediscover bureaucracy. *Journal of Public Administration: Research and Theory, 16*(1), 1–24. doi:10.1093/jopart/mui027

Piotti, B., Chilundo, B., & Sahay, S. (2006). An Institutional Perspective on Health Sector Reforms and the Process of Reframing Health Information Systems: Case Study From Mozambique. *The Journal of Applied Behavioral Science*, *42*(1), 91–109. doi:10.1177/0021886305285127

Rocheleau, B., & Liangfu, W. (2002). Public Versus Private Information Systems. *American Review of Public Administration*, *32*(4), 379–397. doi:10.1177/027507402237866

Weber, M. (1946). *The theory of social and economic organization. Translated from the German*. Glencoe, Ill.: Free Press & The Falcon's Wing Press.

KEY TERMS AND DEFINITIONS

Accountability: In the context of aid policies and the public sector, a series of policies, mechanisms, and actions meant to prove how money has been spent to achieve a set of predefined targets and objectives.

Decentralisation: In the context of health management information systems, the delegation of data entry and analysis to district health officers and health facilities for local planning and management of the health service delivery.

Health Management Information System: A manual or computerised system designed to manage epidemiological and health management data.

Integration: In the context of health management information systems, the integration of vertical health information systems through the merge of data reporting forms and the creation of common standards for the interoperability and exchange of data sets across systems.

Legacy System: An old, obsolete system still in use.

New Public Management: Public sector reforms applying a managerialist and market philosophy to public management.

Sector Wide Approach: In the context of international development, an approach that envisages development partners' coordination and national ownership of aid programmes.

Chapter 5
Government and Inter-Organizational Collaboration as Strategies for Administrative Reform in Mexico

Luis F. Luna-Reyes
Universidad de las Americas-Puebla, Mexico

J. Ramon Gil-Garcia
Centro de Investigación y Docencia Económicas, Mexico

ABSTRACT

The use of Information Technologies in government as a strategy for public sector reform has increased in the last few years. Governments around the world are attempting to obtain the benefits of what is now called "electronic government." However, Information Technologies are only one component of what should be a much more complex reform strategy involving changes in organizational characteristics, institutional arrangements, and contextual factors. Based on a survey of public servants from the federal Mexican government and using institutional theory as the analytical lense, this chapter presents descriptive results about the characteristics, objectives, results, and success of inter-organizational electronic government initiatives. Overall, the projects were considered successful, and some of these aspects could be considered important for administrative reform efforts. The areas identified with the greatest success were (1) improvement in the quality of service, (2) creation of a more transparent government, and (3) creation of the necessary infrastructure for the use of Information Technologies. In contrast, the areas with room for improvement were (1) fostering citizen participation, (2) cost reduction, and (3) increased agency productivity.

DOI: 10.4018/978-1-60960-839-2.ch005

INTRODUCTION

Countries around the world have envisioned information technology (IT) applications in government, or e-government, as powerful tools for public sector reform and organizational transformation. In fact, there is a long tradition of research analyzing the effects of IT on organizational change (Checkland & Holwell, 1998; Cherns, 1977; Fountain, 2001; March, 1981; Orlikowski, 1992, 1996). Although it is common for managers and policy makers to believe that IT *per se* will change organizational performance, most recent research in this area recognizes complex and dynamic interactions among technology, organizational practices, and institutional arrangements. To better understand the effectiveness of e-government programs as public reform strategies and tools, it is necessary to understand not only IT, but also organizational and institutional configurations.

Therefore, theoretical approaches that overemphasize or only pay attention to the technology-related aspects of electronic government offer partial and limited understanding of this phenomenon. In recent years, researchers have developed and used integrative and comprehensive theoretical lenses for e-government research (Fountain & Gil-Garcia, 2006; Orlikowski & Iacono, 2001). One of these lenses is institutional theory, which has been identified as a powerful way to study information systems in general and electronic government in particular for several years and from diverse disciplines (Hassan & Gil-Garcia, 2008). Fountain (2001) proposes a comprehensive and integrative theory based on the more general institutional tradition developed in disciplines such as economics (North, 1999; Rutherford, 1999), political science (Peters, 2001), or sociology (Brinton & Nee, 1998). This chapter uses the technology enactment framework (Fountain, 2001) in order to understand public managers' perceptions about collaboration in terms of organizational, institutional, and contextual factors, as well as the technology-related characteristics and substantive results of inter-organizational e-government initiatives as strategies for administrative reform in Mexico.

The chapter constitutes a summary of questionnaire responses from participants in inter-organizational IT projects in the Mexican federal government during President Fox's Administration (2000-2006). The questionnaire was pursued as part of a research project on e-government and inter-organizational collaboration. The main goal of this research was to better understand the difficulties and potential impacts of IT projects that integrate government processes across multiple agencies to offer informational or transactional services. Many of these initiatives in Mexico have been motivated by both the availability of new information technologies and international trends associated with new public management (NPM). Most of these projects started as part of two important initiatives in Mexico: the e-Mexico program and the Good Government Agenda.

The chapter is organized in five sections, including the foregoing introduction. Section two provides the historical and theoretical background of the chapter, including a brief explanation of institutional theory and its importance for the study of electronic government initiatives. Section three briefly described the research design and methods used to conduct a survey to public servants from the federal Mexican government. Section four presents the main results of the survey, highlighting different aspects of the respondents and their initiatives such as project success, project results, and organizational and institutional factors. Finally, section five provides some concluding remarks and suggests ideas for future research in this area. This final section also includes some general recommendations to guide reconfigurations of institutional frameworks and improvements in organizational structures and processes.

INSTITUTIONAL THEORY, E-GOVERNMENT, AND ADMINISTRATIVE REFORM

Information technologies have the potential to significantly transform government (Fountain, 2001, 2004). However, the government transformation process did not begin in the last 10 to 15 years, when practitioners and researchers started to refer to the use of IT in the public sector as electronic government or e-government. This process actually has its roots in the introduction of IT in government in the 50s, when government agencies started to automate big and repetitive tasks through the use of mainframe computers (Andersen & Dawes, 1991). The 80s came with the introduction of personal computers—greatly reduced in size and cost—which promoted more extended use of computers in public agencies. In the late 90s, the Internet and the spread of computer networks have brought new opportunities and challenges to governments and public managers (J. R. Gil-Garcia & Luna-Reyes, 2008).

Although it could be argued that challenges and developments in the last years are more important than IT challenges and developments in the 50s, it would be over-simplistic to think that such challenges are only the result of technological developments (J. R. Gil-Garcia & Luna-Reyes, 2008). Many other movements in the managerial, organizational, and institutional areas have been developing over the years, resulting in the current e-government phenomenon (Arellano Gault, 2004; Bogdanor, 2005; Gascó, 2004; Grönlund & Horan, 2005; Homburg, 2008). Re-engineering constitutes one such movement, which in public administration takes the form of the trends in new public management or joined-up government. On the other hand, new organizational forms such as networks have begun to substitute hierarchies and bureaucracies to solve complex social problems (Goldsmith & Eggers, 2004). Electronic commerce and other business and contextual trends push citizens to ask government for the same levels of service that they obtain from private companies, and governments around the world are looking for stronger links with citizens and other constituencies. Electronic government is perceived as a strategy to support these trends and goals, but it should be understood in a more integrative way.

Institutional theory provides a powerful framework to understand e-government applications, taking into consideration not only the technology, but also the context, organizational forms, and institutional arrangements in which they are embedded, providing a comprehensive and integrative theoretical lens (Luis F. Luna-Reyes, Gil-Garcia, & Estrada-Marroquín, 2008; Luis F. Luna-Reyes, Hernández-García, & Gil-Garcia, 2009). According to North (1999), "Institutions are the rules of the game in a society, or more formally, they are humanly conceived obligations, which configure human interaction" (p. 3). Institutions have also been understood as the joint group of rules, application mechanisms, and organizations that reinforce each other (Scheela & Van Dinh, 2004). Barley and Tolbert (1997) state that institutions represent obligations created by the options that individuals and groups have, but these obligations are subject to change over time. They define institutions as shared and typified rules with identified categories of social actors, as well as their appropriate activities and relationships. Institutions can also be seen as guidelines that have been created by society and the individuals who are part of that society (Giddens, 1979, 1984). Current institutional approaches recognize the interplay between social structures (macro) and the actions and interactions among individual actors (micro). Therefore, the basic principle of institutional theory is that individual actions and organizations are shaped by institutions, which, at the same time, are either reproduced or modified through the collective action of individuals and organizations (Brinton & Nee, 1998; Giddens, 1984; Scott, 2001).

Figure 1. Technology enactment framework (Adapted from Fountain, 2001)

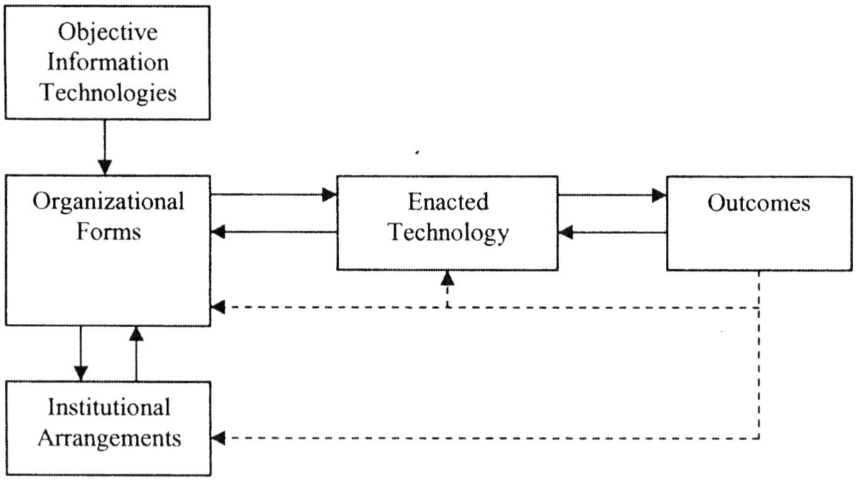

Researchers have used institutional approaches to understand a great variety of phenomena in multiple disciplines, including economics (North, 1999; Rutherford, 1999), political science (Peters, 2001), sociology (Brinton & Nee, 1998), and organizational research (Bansal, 2005; Powell & DiMaggio, 1991; Scott, 2001). Institutional theory has been useful in understanding organizational change by identifying relevant aspects of the context in which information technologies are designed, implemented, and used (Bennett, Bouma, & Ciccozzi, 2004; Fountain, 2008; Hassan & Gil-Garcia, 2008; Schellong, 2007). Based on the institutional tradition and as an attempt to explicitly include the role of technology in a comprehensive approach, Fountain (1995, 2001) developed the technology enactment framework (see Figure 1). The technology enactment framework explains the effects of organizational forms and institutional arrangements on the technology used by government agencies and its ultimate outcomes (Fountain, 1995, 2001; J. Ramon Gil-Garcia, 2006).

Fountain (2004) mentions that "two of the most important influences on the enacted technology are organizations and networks" (p. 6), providing examples of information technologies implemented in comparable organizational contexts, but with very different results. She proposes that the interactions among organizational characteristics, networks, and institutions may explain some of these differences. She also argues that the embeddedness of actors in social, cultural, cognitive, and institutional structures influences the design, perception, implementation, and use of information technologies. Each project is embedded in a certain organizational environment and is affected by specific institutional arrangements. As a result, each organization uses technology differently and obtains different performance, costs, and results (Dawes, 2002; Fountain, 2001). Therefore, organizational characteristics and institutional arrangements have a clear impact on the enacted technology and its outcomes (Fountain, 2001; J. Ramon Gil-Garcia, 2006; Luis F. Luna-Reyes, et al., 2009).

Fountain (2001) proposes an analytical distinction between objective technology and enacted technology. Objective technology is described in terms of its capacity and functionality; it is the hardware, software, telecommunications, and other material characteristics, independently of how people use them (Fountain, 2004). In contrast, enacted technology refers to how users perceive and act upon objective technologies. In this instance, the enacted technology could be conceived as a subset of the objective technology (Puron Cid & Gil-Garcia, 2004). However, social actors can also enact new uses that were not included as part of the original technology's design and functionality (Fountain, 2001; Orlikowski, 2000). Therefore, technology enactment is flexible and fluid and can be observed as it develops over time through interactions among social actors and between actors and technologies (J. Ramon Gil-Garcia, 2006; Orlikowski, 2000). Thus, the enacted technology is affected by social, cultural, cognitive, structural, and political factors, but it also affects these factors in a recursive relationship (Fountain, 2001, 2004). Social actors draw upon institutional arrangements and, therefore, the enacted technology is affected by institutions, organizational characteristics, and environmental conditions (Fountain, 2004; Luis Felipe Luna-Reyes, Gil-García, & Cruz, 2006).

RESEARCH DESIGN AND METHODS

The research reported here is part of a multi-method project developed in three stages. The first stage involved a series of interviews with project managers of interorganizational projects in the Mexican federal government. The second stage encompassed a survey of participants in the projects identified during the first stage. The third stage consisted of conducting three case studies, including additional interviews with participants in some projects and document research. Specifically, this chapter reports on the results of the survey conducted during the second stage of research in summer of 2006. This section of the chapter then includes a brief description of the sample, the data collection instruments, and the procedures followed in the research to gather empirical evidence.

Sampling

The study uses a purposive sample of public managers involved in well-known interorganizational IT projects. An initial sample of projects was identified during the first stage of the research. They were selected using the Internet as a search tool and by asking the project managers interviewed for additional projects to be included, following a snow ball sampling approach. In this way, 13 government agencies were identified as involved in interorganizational projects at the federal level (National Bank for Savings and Financial Services, Ministry of Public Administration, Ministry of Transportation, Ministry of Health, Federal Institute for Access to Information, Mexican Institute for Social Security, INFOTEC, Ministry of Justice, Internal Revenue Service, Ministry of Education, President's Internet Office, Ministry of Economy, and Ministry of Finance). The survey database was created by compiling names and e-mail addresses of project participants from the agencies' web pages or from lists provided by the project managers interviewed. The database included 1,216 employees from federal agencies who participate in 13 interorganizational projects. Therefore, although the population is unknown, which may limit the generalizability of the results, this approach establishes a robust and diverse sampling framework for this research.

Survey Instrument

A survey instrument was adapted and re-designed from Fountain's original instrument (Fountain, McKinnon, & Park, 2003). The instrument included questions that sought to understand the effects of institutional arrangements and organizational forms on interorganizational IT projects. The original instrument was first translated into Spanish and adapted to the Mexican context by the researchers. Then, to ensure content validity and comparability, the instrument was reviewed by two expert translators and four government officials in a two-stage process. Following their recommendations, the research team made adjustments and changes to the survey instrument for both content and format. The final instrument had 35 questions[1]; 30 questions with structured responses and 5 open ended questions. Questions were associated with institutional arrangements, organizational forms, enacted technology, and project results. Other questions in the survey were related to respondents' demographics and previous experience and background. The questionnaire was administered electronically and was open for reply from May 17 to June 12, 2006. After an initial invitation, we sent a total of three e-mail reminders.

INTERORGANIZATIONAL E-GOVERNMENT IN MEXICO

This section of the chapter includes a descriptive summary of questionnaire responses from participants in inter-organizational IT projects in the Mexican federal government. Most of these projects were initiated during President Fox's Administration as a result of Presidential interest and support for this kind of project. In this way, we start this section with a brief overview of the main projects and directives from President Fox's Administration, followed by the descriptive analysis of the survey, which is organized in terms of the main components of the technology enactment framework.

THE E-MEXICO PROGRAM AND THE GOOD GOVERNMENT AGENDA

In 2000, President Fox started a very ambitious program to promote the Mexican Digital Society and the use of information and communication technologies (ICTs) to improve government services. One important component of the program designed to promote a digital society was the e-Mexico system and was housed at the Ministry of Communications and Transportation.

The e-Mexico system was an "umbrella" initiative at the center of the Mexican strategy to develop government services and applications for all member of the society. The mission of e-Mexico was to "be an agent of change in the country, integrating efforts from diverse public and private actors in the elimination of the digital divide and other socio-economic differences among Mexicans, through a system with technical and social components to offer basic services on education, health, commercial interchange, and government services, being at the same time leaders in Mexican technological development" (e-México, 2003). The main rationale of e-Mexico was the widely accepted belief that ICTs offer national economies with opportunities to grow, to develop, and to create sustainable competitive advantages. Moreover, the e-Mexico initiative was looking to coordinate government actions to promote economic development, improve transparency and democracy through the use of IT. Another important driver of the project was the global trend of IT applications in government as a tool to promote the "new public management."

Additionally, the President's Office for Innovation developed the Good Government Agenda in 2002 as a set of policies to transform federal government management and services (Luis F. Luna-Reyes, Gil-Garcia, & Cruz, 2007). One of the six main components in this presidential agenda was the use of IT in government or electronic government as a strategy for administrative reform. The e-Mexico initiative particularly aligned with the Good Government Agenda's goal to create a digital government to facilitate access to government information and services anytime and anywhere (Luis F. Luna-Reyes, et al., 2007). Moreover, the establishment of the Law for Transparency and Access to the Information in 2002 was an important institutional change supporting electronic government projects during this same period.

Following, we present the results of the survey of public managers involved in inter-organizational e-government initiatives in the Mexican federal government. The results are organized in terms of the main conceptual components of the technology enactment framework: outcomes, enacted technology, organizational forms, and institutional arrangements. Prior to presenting this conceptually driven structure, the next section provides some basic characteristics of the respondents and their respective projects.

CHARACTERISTICS OF THE RESPONDENTS AND THEIR PROJECTS

Before describing some of the main variables associated with the technology enactment theory, we start with a brief description of survey respondents and their projects to provide the reader with more specific contextual details. Figure 2 shows the projects or agencies represented by the individuals who responded to the survey. The projects or agencies with the greatest number of responses were the SAT (Federal Tax Administration) with 66 respondents and the SISI (Access to Public Information System) with 60 respondents. The distribution reflects the projects that had the largest number of participants, in accordance with the distribution in the database of the original 1177 persons that were invited to participate in the study. Some projects had a low response rate due to problems accessing the survey website through their agency's Internet connection. It is important to clarify that the respondents associated with the SISI were not only personnel employed at the IFAI (Federal Institute for Access to Public Information), but were also individuals working at liaison units at other agencies of the Mexican federal government.

The governmental projects that on average involved the most agencies (or organizations) were E-Health (230 organizations), followed by E-Mexico (116) and the SISI (83). Projects that did not involve more than 3 areas or institutions include the Mexican Institute for Social Security (IMSS), the Institute for Industry Information and Documentation (INFOTEC), the Bank for National Savings and Financial Services (BANSEFI), E-Economy, and E-Learning. This number may be used as an indicator of the complexity of each of the projects considered in the study. The questionnaire also directly asked participants to rate the complexity of their projects and the average grade was 8.01 on a scale of 1 to 10. The most common grade was 8.0, with 30% of all respondents assigning this level of complexity to their projects. Forty six percent (46%) of the respondents assigned a grade of 9 or 10 and 14% assigned a grade of 6 or less.

Regarding the number of hours per week dedicated to the project, which may be considered as an indicator of the number of individuals who are working full-time on the project, E-Mexico had an average of 47 hours per person per week and MIIT (Justice System) had an average of 40 hours. Other projects with averages around 30 hours per week are E-Learning, E-Health, IMSS, the Tax Revenue System (SAT) and the Presidency Information System (SIP). In contrast, some agencies and projects had a relatively low average number of hours per week such as the SISI, E-Economy, or E-Government.

Participants in the projects included in this study have considerable experience in the field of IT. In fact, 55% of the respondents reported having education or experience in this area. Participants also had training in the areas of policy and program development. Thirty one percent (31%) of the participants reported having education or experience in the area of policy development and 24% in the area of program development. These percentages show that not only do individuals involved in the projects have experience and expertise in IT, but they also understand the procedures and problems of the public sector. About one fourth of the project participants also have experience in other fields or areas of government. Some of the areas respondents mentioned most frequently were

Figure 2. Projects in which questionnaire respondents are employed (278 total responses)

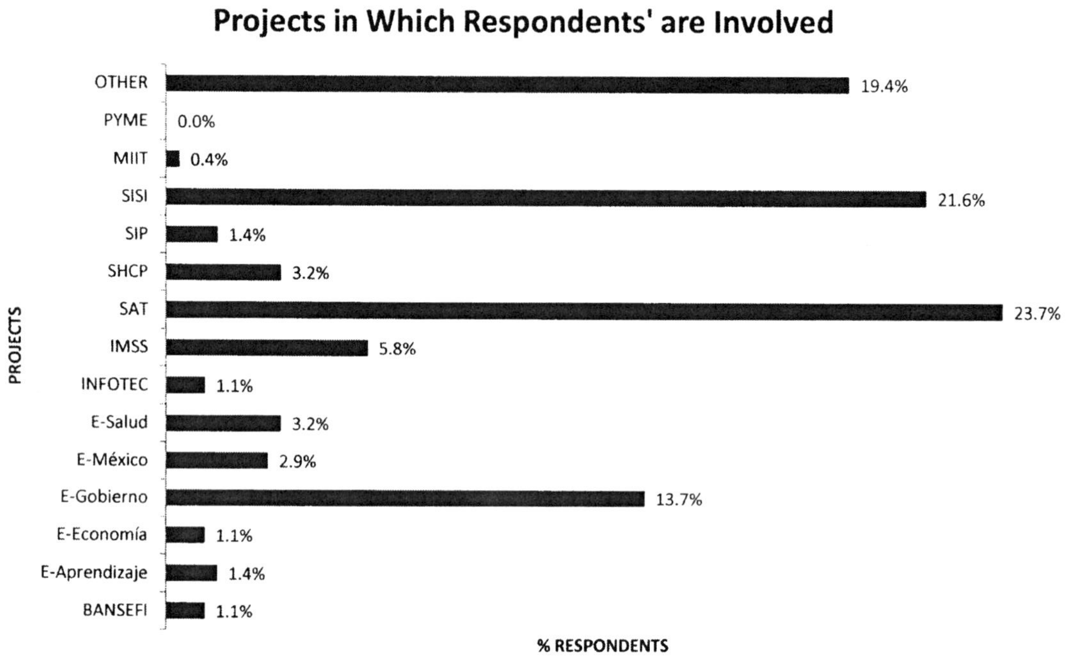

accounting, audits and control, public administration, law, and project management.

In terms of participant work experience within the federal government, the distribution is skewed, with the majority reporting ten years or less of government work experience. Although the distribution of the general work experience of the participants is also skewed, in this case the majority have between 10 and 20 years of work experience. Twenty four percent (24%) of respondents have between 10 and 15 years of general work experience and 21% have between 15 and 20 years. About 12% have more than 30 years of general work experience. The average general work experience is 19 years and the average government work experience is 11 years. Finally, Figure 3 describes the educational level of participants in the projects considered in this research. More than half of the respondents have at least a bachelor's degree (57%), while 35% have a master's degree and 5% hold a doctoral degree.

Project Outcomes

An important component of the technology enactment framework consists of the outcomes of using technology in organizations. In this section we present some information related to project outcomes. First, we present survey responses related to goal and performance measurement definitions, continuing with an assessment of project success in general and some specific outcomes.

Figure 4 presents respondents' perceptions about three aspects considered important to project success: clarity in defining goals, clarity in defining performance measurements, and the feasibility of achieving the project goals. The majority of participants reported that both the project goals and its performance measurements were clearly defined and reachable. In fact, 88% of the respondents agreed or totally agreed that the goals were clearly defined and about 76% felt that performance measurements were clearly defined.

Figure 3. Educational level of the participants (278 total responses)

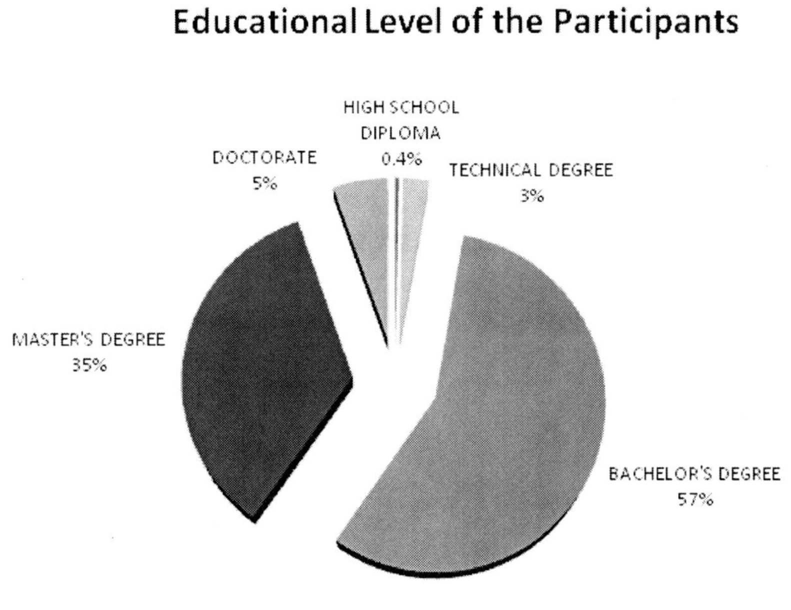

In addition, more than 80% of the respondents thought that achieving the project goals was very feasible. In contrast, about 10% of the respondents felt there was no clarity in the definition of the project goals and performance measurements and a similar percentage felt that achieving the project goals was not feasible.

The projects included in the study considered a diversity of success indicators or measurements. The most important measures of success, among the projects and agencies that responded to the questionnaire, are improving the quality of services to clients (65% of respondents), the creation of a more transparent government (62%), increasing confidence in government (60%), reducing costs (55%), reducing response times (54%), and increasing productivity (51%). It is interesting to note that the measure of success used least frequently is the adoption of systems by potential users. Achieving target dates as a measure of success and improving program effectiveness fell in the midlevel of importance.

Additionally, this question provided the opportunity for respondents to comment freely about the measurements or criteria for success used to evaluate the progress of their projects. Listed below are some of the procedures mentioned most often in this section of the questionnaire.

- Some projects used the increase in the number of agencies that adopted the system (diffusion of the technology) as a success criterion.
- One variation of the above indicator concentrates on the transfer of knowledge and technology, i.e., making it easier for other agencies or organizations to incorporate the technological platform used by the project into their own operations.
- Other respondents considered indicators that reflect the level of usage. That is, how many users connect to, or how many requests are handled by the system or website. Indicators like this complement other measures of effectiveness such as waiting time for system response.
- Some agencies included both the level of client satisfaction and the increase in de-

Figure 4. Goals and indicators in projects (the total number of responses is shown on the graphic between parentheses)

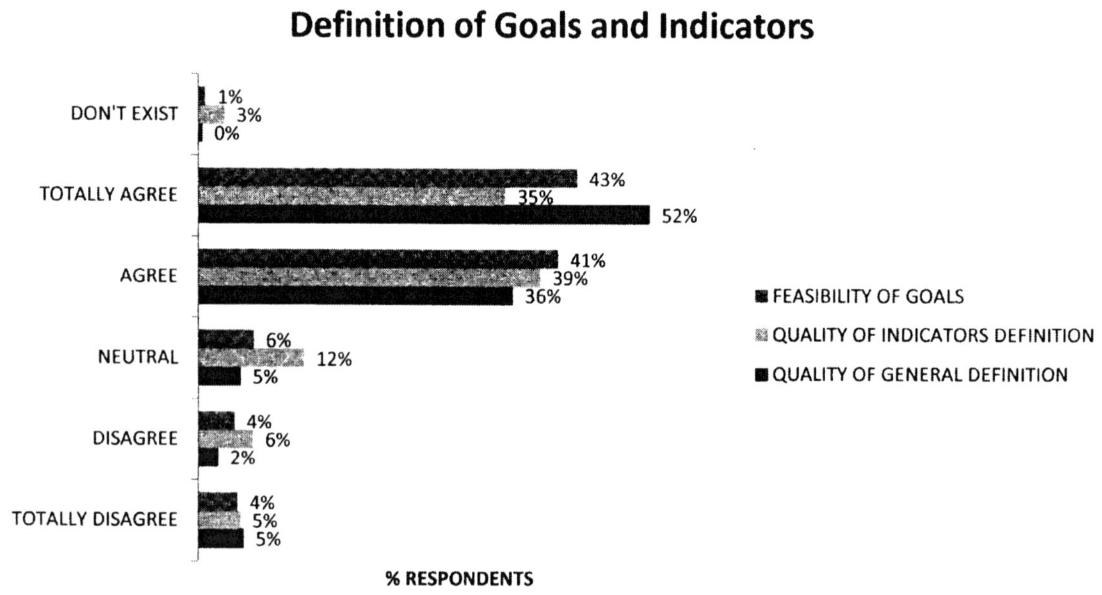

mand for use of IT in e-government services as indicators of success.

- The success of some projects was measured as a function of the support they received from the states, measuring the number of state administrations that adopted their systems.
- In some cases, indicators measure Mexico's progress toward providing society with access to information and services. Some examples are the number of Internet users, the number of fixed and mobile telephone lines, etc.
- Some comments pointed to the use of flow charts that helped in tracking the agency's progress towards meeting goals in terms of time and content.

Regarding the perceived success of the inter-organizational projects included in the study, the general impression of the participants was very positive. Practically all of the participating projects fall in the middle of the distribution with middle to high ratings of success. Projects were most frequently given a score of 9 and the average was 8.3.

Complementing the general perception of success, the questionnaire contained questions that evaluated distinct measures of success. All the participants' responses presented the same distribution as the question that explored the general perception of success. The averages and the standard deviations for each of the evaluated measures of project success are presented in Table 1. As mentioned previously, all of the projects surveyed are seen as successful in terms of these measures. The measures that yielded the highest scores were offering higher quality service, creating a more transparent government, and creating the necessary infrastructure to use ICT. The aspects that require more work include promoting citizen participation, reducing costs, and increasing the productivity of government agencies.

It is interesting that success in creating the necessary infrastructure is ranked higher than success in cost reduction or increasing productivity, despite being a moderately important measure of success in relationship to its level of use by the

Table 1. Measures of success for e-government projects

Measure of success	n	Mean	Standard deviation
General perception	254	8.31	1.34
Offer higher quality service	248	8.75	1.40
Create a more transparent government	248	8.65	1.64
Create the necessary infrastructure to utilize communication and information technologies	246	8.57	1.72
Create a legal and regulatory environment that promotes the use of communication and information technologies in government	245	8.22	1.91
Promote more effective government policies and programs	247	8.19	1.72
Increase agency productivity	245	8.17	1.82
Reduce agency costs	246	7.85	2.13
Promote citizen participation	246	7.83	2.15

projects or agencies that responded to the questionnaire. Cost reduction and increased productivity, while not the most important measures of success, are certainly located in the second tier of importance.

With the national Good Government Agenda, one public sector priority was providing high quality services to citizens. Also related to this agenda is the theme of transparency, mainly in relation to services and access to public information that citizens did not have access to in previous years. The third most successful category, creation of infrastructure, reflects the focus of efforts in recent years to update the existing infrastructure in government agencies and departments.

Moreover, the majority of project participants consider the work they are doing in their project to be important. Eighty percent (80%) of survey participants assigned a grade of 9 or 10 (on a scale from 1 to 10) to their project in terms of importance, and the mean was 9.1. The majority of participants also feel that the current administration has had a major impact on raising the importance of the projects. Many of the study participants are aware that the most important project results will not be seen in the short term but will, over time, yield better communication between society and government.

Enacted Technology

Two key components of the technology enactment framework are the objective and the enacted technology. The objective information technologies constitute the functionalities and characteristics of technology itself, such as computers, servers or the Internet. Some of the questions in the survey were oriented to capture technology enactments in Mexican federal government by exploring the quality of some system features. In this section we present respondents' assessments of these features.

The participants perceived the information systems developed or used in the projects to be of high quality. Seventy percent (70%) of respondents gave a grade of 9 or 10 to the general quality of the systems and the average was 8.78 in a scale from 1 to 10. The majority of the respondents are also satisfied with the results of their projects.

In addition to the evaluation of the general quality of their projects, respondents were asked about their perception of the quality of the information systems in terms of specific features such as ease of use, usefulness, privacy, and security. The average grades for each of these features fell in the range of 8.3 to 8.97 on a scale of 1 to 10 (see Table 2). The three highest scoring features were the usefulness, security and privacy of the system. The lower scoring areas were personalization, ease of use, and the quantity of functions or

Table 2. Quality dimensions for e-government project

Quality dimension	n	Average	Standard deviation
General impression	247	8.78	1.10
Usefulness	249	8.97	1.23
Security	244	8.85	1.27
Privacy	243	8.78	1.41
Information provided by the system	248	8.66	1.33
System operations or functions	246	8.53	1.24
Ease of use	249	8.44	1.31
Personalization	247	8.30	1.59

operations offered by the system. Practically all the quality features had a very similar response distribution, with most respondents assigning grades of 8, 9 and 10. The quality of information provided by the system fell in the middle of the different dimensions due to its average score. Despite that outcome, the quality of information provided by each agency's system plays a very important role in the development of these projects or technological programs, since information reliability facilitates the improvements in efficiencies, ultimately producing greater benefits.

Technology enactments in the agencies included in the survey place an emphasis on usefulness, security and privacy, while personalization, ease of use and system functionalities play a secondary role. In some sense, this particular enactment may be related to simple applications with very specific purposes rather than complex and highly customizable systems. This approach might also be related to the high levels of perceived success of projects.

Organizational Forms and Institutional Arrangements

Some survey questions were related to organizational forms and institutional arrangements as related to the projects in which respondents were collaborating. Some questions attempted to capture organizational factors such as effort recognition or the adequacy of resources, and other questions explored networking and collaboration as important organizational forms. Finally some questions explored the adequacy of institutional arrangements such as laws, regulations, and congressional support. This section of the chapter includes a description of respondents' answers to these questions.

Eighty two percent (82%) of all the respondents are responsible for a specific assignment or area of their project, but only 64% of these people reported that their supervisor recognized and very much appreciated their work efforts. An additional 26% believed their work was recognized, but to a lesser extent than desired and 10% felt that their work in the project was not recognized or appreciated to the extent they desired from their superiors. However, almost 95% of the respondents considered their involvement in the project to be beneficial or very beneficial to their professional careers.

The first two rows in Table 3 present the respondents' perceptions of the adequacy of financial and human resources to bring the project to a successful conclusion. Although slightly more than half of the respondents still believe that their project has the necessary human resources, only about 12% of them are totally convinced of this affirmation and almost 43% are in agreement but to a lesser degree. Almost 26% disagree to some

Table 3. Organizational practices and project collaboration

Dimension	Mean	Standard dev.	Totally disagree	Disagree	Neutral	Agree	Totally agree	n
Adequacy of human resources	3.3	1.11	5.5%	21.4%	18.5%	42.9%	11.8%	238
Adequacy of financial resources	3.5	1.03	3.0%	16.5%	19.4%	45.6%	15.6%	237
Perceived difficulty of interorganizational collaboration	2.9	0.98	8.9%	19.6%	44.3%	23.0%	4.3%	235
Government culture has changed to promote interorganizational projects	3.8	0.87	1.3%	6.3%	21.0%	51.3%	20.2%	238
Government integration and standardization may deteriorate performance	2.2	1.20	37.3%	30.5%	16.3%	10.3%	5.6%	233

extent with the affirmation and 18% maintained a neutral position. On a scale of 1 to 5, the perception of the adequacy of human resources tends to have a neutral position, with a mean of 3.3. Perceptions related to the adequacy of financial resources maintained a similar distribution with slightly fewer respondents in disagreement, improving also in terms of the mean (3.5).

The last three rows in Table 3 present the respondents' perceptions concerning three related aspects. The first aspect is the perceived difficulty of working on a project that requires coordination and collaboration with different agencies. The second seeks to describe the respondents' perceptions concerning the diffusion of such interdepartmental or inter-governmental projects in the coming years. Finally, the third seeks to describe respondents' evaluation of the potential benefits that might be attained through these types of initiatives.

With regard to the difficulty of projects that involve different agencies, the respondents' opinions were distributed symmetrically. Slightly less than half the respondents (44.3%) took a neutral position, which suggests that these types of projects present a level of difficulty similar to other projects in which the respondents have participated. The view of the remaining half of the respondents was divided. About one quarter of the respondents felt these projects were more difficult, while the other quarter saw them as less difficult.

In the qualitative part of this question, the respondents were in agreement that the implementation of the technology in the separate agencies has improved both the internal and external communication. In fact, the external communication is considered a key factor in enabling improvements in the execution of those projects that involve two or more agencies. The respondents are in agreement that the impact of technological projects involving multiple agencies is greater than those projects that involve a single agency.

Nonetheless, the respondents also commented on the existence of certain factors, such as inequality in the standards of each agency, policies, resistance to change, the transparency of information access for citizens, bureaucracy, and private interests, among others, that make collaboration difficult between agencies. Under these circumstances, teamwork is much more difficult and it takes longer to complete the projects than was planned. Similarly, the project's objectives are not fully accomplished.

Although the respondents' opinions concerning project difficulty did not align well, they showed greater accord about the idea that standardization and integration between agencies will be beneficial for governmental performance. About one third have reservations about the expected benefits of the projects (taking a neutral position or agreeing that performance will deteriorate) but the remainder feel that government performance will be improved through the use of the systems they are working on. Finally, almost three-fourths of the respondents (71%) feel that the culture of the government is changing and moving towards the promotion of these types of projects. Only 20% are completely in agreement with this change in governmental culture, while 21% take no position and about 7% believe that the cultural change is still to come.

Inter-departmental or inter-governmental projects, like those included in this investigation, should have a high degree of interaction between the participants, not only because they require communication between agencies or departments, but also because of the complexity of the projects. Table 4 shows a summary of the levels of interaction between working groups of the different areas that participate in the development and execution of the projects. As can be seen in the table, there are different levels of interaction among the members. Face to face meetings are principally held either monthly or weekly, although there is frequent interaction via electronic means among project participants, either daily or several times a week. The availability of electronic communication has had a major impact on the projects, since it is one of the most commonly used means of interaction among project members. The majority of these weekly or daily interactions occur only among some members of the team, rather than with all members.

Another interesting characteristic that emerges in the table is that the majority of projects are developed with a high degree of independence from supervisory organs. Slightly less than half the projects (44%) perform their work with complete independence from supervisory organs and an additional 36% have regular meetings with supervisory organs only once a month. Only the remaining 20% of projects have more frequent periodic meetings with oversight organizations such as the Ministry of Finance.

The last two figures attempt to capture some institutional arrangements related to Mexican ICT projects. Figure 5 shows the respondents' perceptions concerning the adequacy of current legislation to support ICT initiatives that involve sharing information between multiple agencies. Approximately half of the respondents show a certain level of agreement concerning the adequacy of current legislation to support the development of conjoint projects. One third of the respondents took a neutral position, while 20% felt that the legal framework does not support the development of these types of initiatives.

Table 4. Interactions between project team members

Type of Meeting	Never	Monthly	Several times per month	Weekly	Several times per week	Daily
All or Almost All of the Members Face to Face	9.7%	25.9%	18.5%	23.6%	13.4%	8.8%
All or Almost All of the Members by Electronic Media	16.3%	12.5%	18.3%	11.1%	21.2%	20.7%
Some Members Face to Face	6.9%	17.6%	16.7%	15.7%	26.0%	17.2%
Some Members by Electronic Media	13.3%	14.3%	18.2%	8.9%	25.6%	19.7%
With Representatives of Supervisory Organisms in Person or Using Technology	44.0%	36.1%	11.1%	4.6%	2.3%	1.9%

In considering the level of Congressional support given to initiatives that involve more than one governmental department or agency, the respondents were more divided in their opinions (see Figure 5). Slightly less than half of the respondents (42%) took a neutral position. The remainder of respondents was divided between those that felt Congress supports such initiatives and those that believe Congressional support is lacking. The distribution is skewed towards the belief that Congress supports ICT initiatives involving various agencies. Slightly more than one third of respondents (35%) believe that Congress supports these initiatives, whereas slightly less than one quarter (23%) believes that additional Congressional support is needed.

Finally, the respondents acknowledged that their own institutions recognized the importance of applying information technologies in general and, in particular, were supportive of their specific project (Figure 6). The average score for perceived approval of the use ICT was 9.01 and the average score for perceived support of the respondent's specific project was 8.83, both on a scale of 1 to 10 with 10 representing the highest level of support.

FINAL COMMENTS

This chapter provides a descriptive summary of the responses to questionnaires completed by participants from inter-organizational information technology (IT) projects in the Mexican federal government. It is important to clarify that these results are mainly descriptive and represent a preliminary treatment of the survey data. Other papers from this project will perform deeper analyses of some particular and more specific aspects. The responses reflect the opinions of 282 government officials participating in 13 inter-organizational digital government projects, collected during the summer of 2006. It is clear that ICT tools and inter-organizational collaboration could play a very important role in government reform. In fact, ICT tools and systems in the Mexican federal government have a significant impact, according to survey respondents, on offering quality services, creating a more transparent government, creating the necessary infrastructure to use ICT, creating a legal and regulatory environment that promotes the use of ICT, promoting more effective government policies and programs, increasing productivity, and reducing costs. However, ICT tools and infrastructure should be used strategi-

Figure 5. Adequacy of current legislation (234 total responses)

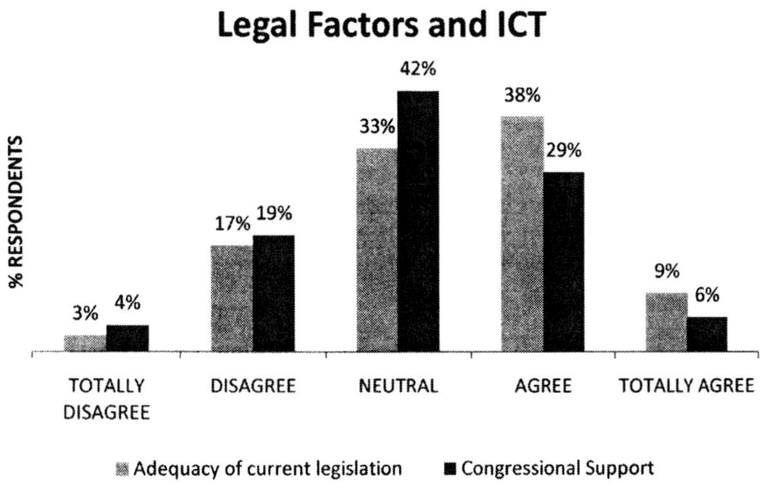

Figure 6. Institutional support of ICT and specific projects

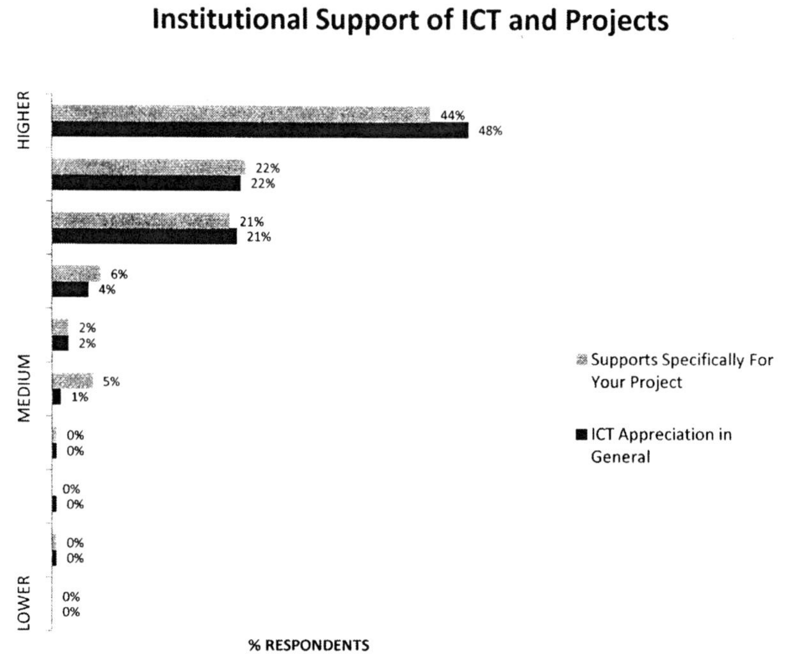

cally and always aligned with the main objectives and goals of government organizations.

In contrast with the promised improvements, e-government applications have encountered important challenges in both their design and implementation. Additionally, the impact of e-government applications is influenced by organizational factors, characteristics of the institutional framework, and important contextual variables such as the political, economic, and social national contexts. Our knowledge of such impacts is still limited, but the descriptive findings presented in this chapter could help to develop a better understanding of this type of initiative. It is important to clarify that for this case the Mexican context was an influential factor in the use of e-government and inter-organizational collaboration for administrative reform. Therefore, some of the findings could apply to any other national context, but others are more specific to developing countries, the Latin American region, or Mexico, as a particular political, economic, and social context. These final comments are also organized in terms of the main conceptual components of the technology enactment framework: outcomes, enacted technology, organizational forms, and institutional arrangements.

Outcomes

Organizational outcomes are the final results of a government IT initiative. They are directly affected by the characteristics of the technology in use (or enacted technology) and indirectly influenced by organizational forms and institutional arrangements. In the survey, these outcomes were measured as different potential benefits from the IT initiatives. Five measures of success were used most often in the projects: improved quality of client services (65% included this as an important measure), creating a more transparent government (63%), increasing confidence in government (60%), reducing costs (55%), and reducing response times (54%). Some measures of success that were not included in the quantitative part of the research, but that were mentioned by respondents in the qualitative section, are associated with the rate of adoption of the systems by government agencies or citizens and measures of the intensity of system usage or user satisfaction. It was also mentioned that success could be measured by the achievement of goals associated with the projects.

In general, the survey participants considered the projects successful. On a scale of 1 to 10, the projects had an average score of 8.31. The areas in which the projects demonstrated greatest success were improvement in the quality of service (average 8.75), the creation of a more transparent government (average 8.65), and the creation of necessary infrastructure for the use of information technologies (average 8.57). The areas with room for improvement are fostering citizen participation, cost reduction, and increasing agency productivity. The success of the projects can also be seen in the fact that about three fourths of the respondents (77%) consider their participation in the project as beneficial to their own career.

Enacted Technology

As mentioned in the literature review, the enacted technology could be understood as the actual characteristics of the information systems in terms of hardware, software, usability, security, etc. The survey measured this concept using several aspects of the quality or functionality of the information technologies used in the initiatives. The evaluation scores for project quality were principally distributed across medium and high levels. The quality criteria for which the projects scored highest were usefulness (average 8.97 on a scale of 10 points), security (average 8.85), and privacy (average 8.78). Those criteria where room for improvement exists include personalization (average 8.30), ease of use (average 8.44) and the level of functionality of the system (average 8.53). In contrast with the quality scores, the perception of project success and optimism regarding the possibility of achieving project goals, only 55% of respondents considered that the project had sufficient human resources to reach a successful conclusion whereas 62% felt that there were adequate financial resources to complete them. Opinions were also divided with respect to the recognition received for working on the project. Sixty eight percent (68%) of the public servants that responded to the survey felt that the recognition they had received for their work on the project was positive.

Organizational Forms and Institutional Arrangements

Organizational forms and institutional arrangements are different characteristics of the organization and the institutional environment in which the e-government initiatives are embedded. In the survey, they were measured using a set of characteristics of the agency responsible for the IT initiative, the institutional and legal environment, and some cultural aspects of the Mexican public administration. Seventy one percent (71%) of the respondents thought the culture of government is changing and moving towards the realization of inter-organizational projects and 67% believe that these types of projects will have a positive effect on government performance. Nonetheless, differences in standards between agencies, political factors, resistance to change, the bureaucratic system, and efforts to serve individual interests on the part of some agencies are cited among the main barriers to capitalizing on the benefits. The area in which a clear division was shown in respondents' opinions is associated with legislation and congressional support for inter-organizational initiatives. Only 47% of respondents felt that current legislation supports IT initiatives involving more than one agency and only 31% believe that Congress supports this type of initiatives.

Respondents also identified the following as being some best practices in the development of inter-organizational IT projects: carefully defining needs and formulating a detailed plan, dividing project development into clearly defined phases, clearly and precisely defining goals, especially those that are shared by different agencies, forming working groups and defining responsibilities, empowering group leaders to make decisions, assuring efficient communication between participants, and continuously monitoring and reviewing progress benchmarks.

The majority of the respondents felt that the administration of President Fox had an important positive impact on the development of ICT projects due to his government's favorable position about technology as a facilitator of governmental reform. Although many respondents felt that the most important results from digital government will not be visible in the short term, they believe that the advances made in recent years are very important – increasing the transparency, the efficiency and improving the quality of the information requested by citizens. Furthermore, during recent years, both a quantitative and a qualitative increase have been noted in the use of government information, thus promoting better communication between the government and society.

Finally, it is important to mention that the interests of each agency, as well as the way in which mutual benefits are negotiated, are very important factors affecting the success of digital government projects that involve more than one agency. Also, it is important to point out that the development of IT applications in digital government initiatives responds to specific problems. Therefore, benchmarks to measure the success of such projects should include observations concerning progress towards solving the initial social problem, in addition to the degree of government transformation achieved. Overall, it is clear that organizational and institutional factors were considered as important influences on the characteristics and success of inter-organizational e-government initiatives as strategies for administrative reform in Mexico. Future research should identify and assess the specific effects and weights of different organizational practices and characteristics, as well as different institutional arrangements on the quality and results of this type of initiatives.

ACKNOWLEDGMENT

The authors would like to thank the valuable contributions of Víctor Manuel Morán, Mireya Estrada, and Cinthia Betiny Cruz in the development and administration of the survey. The authors are also thankful to Jane E. Fountain for her helpful guidance and suggestions throughout the design and development of this study. Any mistakes or omissions are the sole responsibility of the authors. This work was partially supported by the National Council of Science and Technology (CONACYT-Mexico) under grant SEP-2004-C01-46507 and by the National Science Foundation (NSF) under Grant No. 0131923 and Grant No. 0630239. The views, conclusions, and recommendations expressed in this paper are those of the authors alone and do not necessarily reflect the views of CONACYT or NSF.

REFERENCES

Andersen, D., & Dawes, S. (1991). *Government information management: A primer and casebook*. Englewood Cliffs, NJ: Prentice Hall.

Arellano Gault, D. (2004). *Mas allá de la Reinvención del Gobierno: Fundamentos de la Nueva Gestión Pública y Presupuestos por Resultados en América Latina*. Mexico: Centro de Investigación y Docencia Económicas y Miguel Angel Porrúa.

Bansal, P. (2005). Evolving sustainably: A longitudinal study of corporate sustainable development. *Strategic Management Journal*, *26*(3), 197–218. doi:10.1002/smj.441

Barley, S. R., & Tolbert, P. S. (1997). Institutionalization and structuration: Studying the links between action and institution. *Organization Studies*, *18*(1), 93–117. doi:10.1177/017084069701800106

Bennett, M., Bouma, J. J., & Ciccozzi, E. (2004). An institutional perspective on the transfer of accounting knowledge: a case study. *Accounting Education*, *13*(3), 329–346. doi:10.1080/0963928042000273807

Bogdanor, V. (Ed.). (2005). *Joined-up government*. New York, NY: Oxford University Press.

Brinton, M. C., & Nee, V. (1998). *The new institutionalism in sociology*. Stanford, CA: Stanford University Press.

Checkland, P., & Holwell, S. (1998). *Information, systems and Information Systems-Making sense of the field*. Chichester, UK: John Wiley & Sons.

Cherns, A. B. (1977). Can behavioral science help design organizations? *Organizational Dynamics*, *5*(4), 44–64. doi:10.1016/0090-2616(77)90039-0

Dawes, S. (2002). Government and technology: User, not regulator. *Journal of Public Administration: Research and Theory*, *12*(4), 627–631.

e-México. (2003). *Resumen ejecutivo del sistema nacional e-México*. Retrieved January, 2006, from http://www.emexico.gob.mx/wb2/eMex/eMex_Resumen_ejecutivo_del_Sistema_Nacional_eMexic

Fountain, J. E. (1995). *Enacting technology: An institutional perspective*. Cambridge, MA: John F. Kennedy School of Government, Harvard University.

Fountain, J. E. (2001). *Building the virtual state. Information Technology and institutional change*. Washington, DC: Brookings Institution Press.

Fountain, J. E. (2004). *Prospects for the virtual state*. Working papers. Retrieved May, 2006, from http://www.j.u-tokyo.ac.jp/coeps/pdf/040710.pdf

Fountain, J. E. (2008). Bureaucratic reform and e-government in the United States: An institutional perspective. In Chadwick, A., & Howard, P. N. (Eds.), *The handbook of Internet politics*. New York, NY: Routledge.

Fountain, J. E., & Gil-Garcia, J. R. (2006). *Comparing integrative models of technology and structure in government*. Paper presented at the 2006 APPAM Fall Conference "Tax and Spend: Designing, Implementing, Managing and Evaluating Effective Redistributional Policies", Madison, WI.

Fountain, J. E., McKinnon, R., & Park, E. (2003). E-government cross-agency and intergovernmental initiatives research project: Web survey results. Boston, MA: Working Papers Series, National Center for Digital Government, John F. Kennedy School of Government, Harvard University.

Gascó, M. (2004). E-Gobierno en Bolivia y Paraguay. In Araya Dujisin, R., & Porrúa Vigon, M. A. (Eds.), *América Latina Puntogob: Casos y tendencias en gobierno electrónico* (pp. 125–150). Santiago, Chile: FLACSO-Chile/ AICD-OEA.

Giddens, A. (1979). *Central problems in social theory. Action, structure and contradiction in social analysis*. Berkeley/Los Angeles, CA: University of California Press.

Giddens, A. (1984). *The constitution of society*. Berkeley/ Los Angeles, CA: University of California Press.

Gil-Garcia, J. R. (2006, January 4-7, 2006). *Enacting state websites: A mixed method study exploring e-government success in multi-organizational settings*. Paper presented at the 39th Hawaii International Conference on System Sciences (HICSS).

Gil-Garcia, J. R., & Luna-Reyes, L. F. (2008). A brief introduction to electronic government: Definition, applications and stages. *Revista de Administración Pública RAP 116*, *43*(2), 221-241.

Goldsmith, S., & Eggers, W. D. (2004). *Governing by network: The new shape of the public sector.* Washington, DC: Brookings Institution Press.

Grönlund, Å., & Horan, T. A. (2005). Introducing e-gov: History, definitions and issues. *Communications of the AIS*, *15*(39), 713–729.

Hassan, S., & Gil-Garcia, J. R. (2008). Institutional theory and e-government research. In Garson, G. D., & Khosrow-Pour, M. (Eds.), *Handbook of research on public Information Technology* (pp. 349–360). Hershey, PA: IGI Global. doi:10.4018/978-1-59904-857-4.ch034

Homburg, V. (2008). *Understanding e-government: Information Systems in public administration*. Abingdon, UK: Routledge.

Luna-Reyes, L. F., Gil-García, J. R., & Cruz, C. B. (2006, August 4-6). *Collaborative digital government in Mexico: Some lessons from federal Web-based inter-organizational information integration initiatives.* Paper presented at the 12th Americas Conference on Information Systems, Acapulco, Mexico.

Luna-Reyes, L. F., Gil-Garcia, J. R., & Cruz, C. B. (2007). E-Mexico: Collaborative structures in Mexican public administration. *International Journal of Cases on E-Commerce*, *3*(2), 57–74.

Luna-Reyes, L. F., Gil-Garcia, J. R., & Estrada-Marroquín, M. (2008). The impact of institutions on interorganizational IT projects in the Mexican federal government. *International Journal of Electronic Government Research*, *4*(2), 27–42. doi:10.4018/jegr.2008040103

Luna-Reyes, L. F., Hernández-García, J. M., & Gil-Garcia, J. R. (2009). Hacia un Modelo de los Determinantes de Éxito de los Portales de Gobierno Estatal en México. *Gestión y Política Pública*, *XVIII*(2), 307–340.

March, J. G. (1981). Footnotes to organizational change. *Administrative Science Quarterly*, *26*(4), 563–577. doi:10.2307/2392340

North, D. C. (1999). *Institutions, institutional change, and economic performance*. New York, NY: Cambridge University Press.

Orlikowski, W. J. (1992). The duality of technology: Rethinking the concept of technology in organizations. *Organization Science*, *3*(3), 398–427. doi:10.1287/orsc.3.3.398

Orlikowski, W. J. (1996). Improvising organizational transformation over time: A situated change perspective. *Information Systems Research*, *7*(1), 63–92. doi:10.1287/isre.7.1.63

Orlikowski, W. J. (2000). Using technology and constituting structures: A practice lens for studying technology in organizations. *Organization Science*, *11*(4), 404–428. doi:10.1287/orsc.11.4.404.14600

Orlikowski, W. J., & Iacono, C. S. (2001). Research commentary: Desperately seeking the "IT" in IT research--A call to theorizing the IT artifact. *Information Systems Research*, *12*(2), 121–134. doi:10.1287/isre.12.2.121.9700

Peters, B. G. (2001). *Institutional theory in political science. The new institutionalism*. London, UK: Continuum.

Powell, W. W., & DiMaggio, P. J. (1991). *The new institutionalism in organizational analysis*. Chicago, IL: University of Chicago Press.

Puron Cid, G., & Gil-Garcia, J. R. (2004). Enacting e-budgeting in Mexico. *Public Finance and Management*, *4*(2), 182–217.

Rutherford, M. (1999). *Institutions in economics. The old and the new institutionalism*. New York, NY: Cambridge University Press.

Scheela, W., & Van Dinh, N. (2004). Venture capital in a transition economy: The case of Vietnam. *Venture Capital - An International Journal of Entrepreneurial Finance, 6*(4), 333-350.

Schellong, A. (2007). Extending the technology enactment framework. Boston, MA: Harvard University, Kennedy School of Government, Program on Networked Governance, Working Paper No. PNG07-003.

Scott, W. R. (2001). *Institutions and organizations* (2nd ed.). Thousand Oaks, CA: Sage.

ADDITIONAL READING

Andersen, D., & Dawes, S. (1991). *Government Information Management. A Primer and Casebook*. Englewood Cliffs, NJ: Prentice Hall.

Dawes, S. (1996). Interagency Information Sharing: Expected Benefits, Manageable Risks. *Journal of Policy Analysis and Management, 15*(3), 377–394. doi:10.1002/(SICI)1520-6688(199622)15:3<377::AID-PAM3>3.0.CO;2-F

Dawes, S., Cresswell, A. M., & Pardo, T. A. (2009). From "Need to Know" to "Need to Share": Tangled Problems, Information Boundaries, and the Building of Public Sector Knowledge Networks. *Public Administration Review, 69*(3), 392–402. doi:10.1111/j.1540-6210.2009.01987_2.x

Dawes, S., & Pardo, T. (2003). Building Collaborative Digital Government Systems: Systemic Constraints and Effective Practices. In McIver, W. J., & Elmagarmid, A. K. (Eds.), *Advances in Digital Government: Technology, Human Factors, and Policy* (pp. 259–273). Boston, MA: Kluwer Academic Publishers.

DeSanctis, G., & Poole, M. S. (1994). Capturing the Complexity in Advanced Technology Use: Adaptive Structuration Theory. *Organization Science, 5*(2), 121–147. doi:10.1287/orsc.5.2.121

Fountain, J. E. (2001). *Building the Virtual State. Information Technology and Institutional Change*. Washington, D.C.: Brookings Institution Press.

Fountain, J. E. (2008). Bureaucratic Reform and E-Government in the United States: An Institutional Perspective. In Chadwick, A., & Howard, P. N. (Eds.), *The Handbook of Internet Politics*. New York: Routledge.

Fountain, J. E., & Gil-Garcia, J. R. (2006). *Comparing Integrative Models of Technology and Structure in Government*. Paper presented at the 2006 APPAM Fall Conference "Tax and Spend: Designing, Implementing, Managing and Evaluating Effective Redistributional Policies", Madison, WI.

Gil-Garcia, J. R., & Luna-Reyes, L. F. (2008). A Brief Introduction to Electronic Government: Definition, Applications and Stages. *Revista de Administración Pública RAP 116, 43*(2), 221-241.

Goldsmith, S., & Eggers, W. D. (2004). *Governing by Network: The New Shape of the Public Sector*. Wuashington, D. C.: Brookings Institution Press.

Grönlund, Å., & Horan, T. A. (2005). Introducing e-gov: History, definitions and issues. *Communications of the AIS, 15*(39), 713–729.

Hassan, S., & Gil-Garcia, J. R. (2008). Institutional Theory and e-Government Research. In Garson, G. D., & Khosrow-Pour, M. (Eds.), *Handbook of Research on Public Information Technology* (pp. 349–360). Hershey, PA: IGI Global. doi:10.4018/978-1-59904-857-4.ch034

Luna-Reyes, L. F., Black, L. J., Cresswell, A. M., & Pardo, T. A. (2008). Knowledge-sharing and Trust in Collaborative Requirements Analysis. *System Dynamics Review*, *24*(3), 265–297. doi:10.1002/sdr.404

Luna-Reyes, L. F., Gil-Garcia, J. R., & Cruz, C. B. (2007). E-Mexico: Collaborative Structures in Mexican Public Administration. *International Journal of Cases on E-commerce*, *3*(2), 57–74.

Luna-Reyes, L. F., Gil-Garcia, J. R., & Estrada-Marroquín, M. (2008). The Impact of Institutions on Interorganizational IT Projects in the Mexican Federal Government. *International Journal of Electronic Government Research*, *4*(2), 27–42. doi:10.4018/jegr.2008040103

Luna-Reyes, L. F., Hernández-García, J. M., & Gil-Garcia, J. R. (2009). Hacia un Modelo de los Determinantes de Éxito de los Portales de Gobierno Estatal en México. *Gestión y Política Pública*, *XVIII*(2), 307–340.

North, D. C. (1999). *Institutions, Institutional Change, and Economic Performance*. New York: Cambridge University Press.

Orlikowski, W. (2002). Knowing in Practice: Enacting a Collective Capability in Distributed Organizing. *Organization Science*, *13*(3), 249–273. doi:10.1287/orsc.13.3.249.2776

Orlikowski, W. J. (1992). The duality of technology: Rethinking the concept of technology in organizations. *Organization Science*, *3*(3), 398–427. doi:10.1287/orsc.3.3.398

Orlikowski, W. J. (2000). Using Technology and Constituting Structures: A practice lens for studying technology in organizations. *Organization Science*, *11*(4), 404–428. doi:10.1287/orsc.11.4.404.14600

Pardo, T. A., Gil-Garcia, J. R., & Luna-Reyes, L. F. (2008). *Collaborative Governance and Cross-Boundary Information Sharing: Envisioning a Networked and IT-Enabled Public Administration*. Paper presented at the Minnowbrook III, Lake Placid, NY.

Peters, B. G. (2001). *Institutional theory in political science. The 'new' institutionalism*. London: Continuum.

Powell, W. W., & DiMaggio, P. J. (1991). *The New Institutionalism in organizational analysis*. Chicago, IL: University of Chicago Press.

Puron Cid, G., & Gil-Garcia, J. R. (2004). Enacting E-Budgeting in Mexico. *Public Finance and Management*, *4*(2), 182–217.

Scott, W. R. (2001). *Institutions and organizations* (2nd ed.). Thousand Oaks, CA: Sage.

KEY TERMS AND DEFINITIONS

Electronic Government: refers to the selection and use of information and communication technologies to support government action, to improve government relationships with citizens and to create public value.

Enacted Technology: can be considered as a subset of objective technologies, and refers to ways in which users perceive and act upon those objective technologies.

Institutional Arrangements: are represented by procedures, habits, patterns, and regulations that serve as guidelines and constraints for action

Institutions: Institutions are understood as rules or guidelines to action created by society and the individuals who are part of it.

Objective Technology: represents technology capacities and functionality such as hardware, software, telecommunications, and other material characteristics, independently of how people use them.

Organizational Forms: refer to collaboration structures such as networks, as well as to organizational characteristics such as systems of goals, recognition, processes or resources.

Technology Enactment Framework: constitutes an institutional view to explain the selection, implementation and use of technologies in the public sector.

ENDNOTES

1 The Spanish version of the survey can be obtained from the authors.

Chapter 6
An Examination of Global Municipal Government Privacy and Security Policies

Aroon Manoharan
Kent State University, USA

Marc Fudge
California State University, USA

ABSTRACT

This chapter highlights the research findings of a longitudinal study of online privacy and security practices among global municipalities conducted in 2005 and 2007. As cities worldwide implement sophisticated e-government platforms to increasingly provide services online, many barriers still inhibit the adoption of such strategies by the citizen users, and one such factor is the availability of a comprehensive privacy policy. The survey examines cities throughout the world based upon their population size, the total number of individuals using the Internet, and the percentage of individuals using the Internet. Specifically, we examined if the website has a privacy or security policy, does the website utilize digital signatures and if the website has a policy addressing the use of cookies to track users. Overall, results indicate that cities are increasingly emphasizing on privacy and security policies with major improvements in 2007, along with significant changes in the top ranking cities in when compared to the 2005 study.

DOI: 10.4018/978-1-60960-839-2.ch006

INTRODUCTION

During the early stages of e-government, many public administrators, theorists and web-developers commonly subscribed to the belief that, "if it is built they will come." This phrase simply suggests that well-designed and sophisticated e-government platforms will attract more users and increase citizen engagement and participation with government. It has become clear, however, that there are still barriers prohibiting citizen use of government websites. It is therefore important, that a careful examination of issues that inhibit e-government adoption by municipalities and use by their constituents are analyzed. The focus of this chapter is to examine privacy and security practices and policies within municipal governments around the world between the years 2005 and 2007. Specifically, what have been the trends, in terms of Internet privacy and security policy, among municipalities throughout the world? What privacy and security features have increased or decreased during this time period? Have municipal websites increased their focus on these issues to improve citizen engagement or monitor their behavior?

Our analysis examines the security and privacy of municipal websites in two key areas, privacy policies and authentication of users. In examining municipal privacy policies, we determine whether such a policy is available on every page that accepts data, and whether or not the word "privacy" is used in the link to such a statement. We are also interested if privacy policies identify the agencies collecting the information, and whether the policy identifies exactly what data is being collected on the site.

Next we check whether the website explicitly explains the intended use of data collected on the site, whether the privacy policy addresses its use by or sale to outside or third-party organizations, and if the site offers a user option to decline disclosure of personal information to third parties, including other municipal agencies, state and local government offices, or private sector businesses. We also examine privacy policies to determine whether third party agencies or organizations are governed by the same privacy policies as the municipal website and if users have the ability to review personal data records and contest inaccurate or incomplete information. Finally, we address managerial measures that limit access of data and assure that it is not used for unauthorized purposes. The use of encryption in the transmission of data, as well as the storage of personal information on secure servers, is also examined. In assessing how or whether municipalities use their websites to authenticate users, we examine whether public or private information is accessible through a restricted area that requires a password and or registration.

This chapter will utilize data compiled from the 2005 and 2007 Digital Governance in Municipalities Worldwide Surveys. The survey examines cities throughout the world based upon their population size, the total number of individuals using the Internet and the percentage of individuals using the Internet. The survey has been conducted every two years since 2003 and measures a total of 98 performance indicators including 20 privacy and security indicators. Privacy and security questions include whether the website has a privacy or security policy, does the website utilize digital signatures and if the website has a policy addressing the use of "cookies" to track users.

In examining privacy and security policies of local government websites along with factors affecting implementation, this research takes a new approach to assess municipal government Internet privacy and security issues. While a recent survey of municipal managers found that privacy and security issues were not significant barriers to e-government adoption (Schwester 2009), we are particularly concerned whether public agencies might use their websites to monitor citizens or create profiles based on information they access online. For example, many websites use cookies or Web beacons to customize their sites for users; however, that technology can also be used to monitor Internet habits and profile website visitors. Many citizens possess a general distrust of government and therefore are apprehensive to utilize government websites, especially in light of concerns over their privacy and security. Thus, we examine municipal privacy policies to determine if they addressed the use of cookies or web beacons. An additional concern was the impact of the digital divide if public records were available only through the Internet or if municipalities insist on charging a fee for access to public records. Hence, our analysis specifically addresses online access to public databases by determining whether public information like property tax assessments or private information like court documents were available to municipal website users.

BACKGROUND

Online Privacy Trends

Prior to September 11, 2001 one of the most pressing policy issues regarding online security and privacy was whether online privacy could be protected through self-regulation (Culnan, 2000). Now, over 9 years later, the topic is still a key issue, especially as the use of information and communication technologies (ICT's) have increased immensely. Despite the reliance upon the use of ICT by citizens and governments to communicate, conduct transactions, and explore innovative technological mechanisms to enhance governance, the absence of comprehensive national policies to protect user privacy and security online is puzzling. Currently, there is no federal legislation in the United States, and most other countries, specifying the notification of personal information collection required by organizations on their websites (Baumer, et al, 2004).

Topics regarding online privacy and security generally center on designing architecture for ubiquitous computing or securing user information when combinations of web services are used to create new applications, or mashups. Electronic voting is a common topic in e-governance. E-voting allows citizens to cast their ballots from anywhere, negating the requirement of traveling to a specific location (Riera & Brown, 2003). An often-cited benefit of e-voting is that geographic independence of voters will increase participation. Security and voter privacy issues are the most common factors impeding the implementation of remote electronic voting (Riera & Brown, 2003). Although no successful cyber attacks occurred during the 2004 or 2008 U.S. Presidential Elections, there is a persistent fear that online security and privacy policies will become relaxed, thus increasing the chances of cyber attacks in the future (Garson, 2006).

To address the concern over online privacy and security, federal agencies have begun to take proactive steps and implement online privacy policies. The U.S. Federal Information and Security Management (FISM) Act of 2002 requires each federal agency to develop, document, and implement an agency-wide program to provide information security for the information and information systems that support the operation of the agency. This legislation includes information provided or managed by another agency, contractor, or other source (NIST, 2002). FISM provided guidelines federal agencies should follow to secure online privacy. According to Dizard (2006) the fiscal year (FY) 2005 Office of Management and Budget report on agency compliance with the Federal Information Security Management (FISM) Act of 2002 found the percentage of systems certified and accredited as meeting security standards had risen 85 percent. This represented a 77 percent increase from FY 2004.

Another common topic of discussion within e-governance is cyber trust. To this end, research has been conducted on the development of privacy enhancement technologies that will inevitably improve citizen trust in government. Dutton et al. (2005) suggest several studies indicating that lack of trust is the main constraint inhibiting citizens from conducting government transactions. "Those who use the Internet more, and in more ways, are also more likely to be exposed to more negative experiences" (Dutton, 16).

While each of these topics are important and may lead to increased citizen engagement and improved government performance, they do not address an underlying issue of consternation among citizens: online privacy policies and their enforcement on government websites. It seems as if a great deal of emphasis is placed upon security systems that organizations or individuals can use to enhance their privacy while searching for information or conducting business online. However, there is less emphasis upon regulations or laws that the government can implement to safeguard online activity by citizens.

Bannister (2005) states one of the major objectives in e-government is integration, vertical or horizontal, where government and citizen engagement are enhanced. However, as ease-of-access to information increases and government implements strategies to provide integration of information across all levels of government, privacy issues become essential.

The U.S. Federal Trade Commission only provides general oversight of online privacy policies and regulates online privacy for children 13 years old and younger, under the Children's Online Privacy Protection Act (COPPA). Under COPPA legislation, the operator of any website or online service marketed towards children or any operator that is knowingly collecting information from a child must obtain parental consent for collection, use or disclosure of information. Also, the website must contain a description of the specific types of personal information collected from the child by that operator.

Whereas COPPA legislation is important, we argue that similar legislation regarding online privacy and security be extended to all citizens.

Typically, innovation in government occurs at the municipal level, however, it is unclear whether municipal governments across the world are implementing the most simple and basic forms of security measures, such as stating a privacy policy on their websites. At this point, discussing the significance of online security should be preceded by an explanation of privacy, its importance and how they impact citizens' trust in government.

Although information and communication technologies have changed the way information is gathered, the right to privacy is still a basic principle in democratic states. Privacy, according to Westin (1967) can be viewed as a person's ability to control the circumstances under which personal, identifiable information is acquired.

Informational privacy is defined as the right to privacy of one's personal information. This includes information about a person's actions and the deliberate invasion of privacy by the government (Bannister, 2005). According to Haag, et al. (2007) an invasion of privacy occurs when a person or entity obtains information about others without their permission. Security and privacy is a major concern when implementing web applications and is further exacerbated within the public sector because many citizens already distrust government. Between October 2003 and September 2004, approximately 9 million people in the United States were victims of identity theft (Haag et al., 2007). All organizations, in particular government organizations, have a responsibility to protect their clients from invasion of privacy.

Bannister (2005) classifies invasion of privacy into four categories: watching; intercepting; reading; and interpreting. Watching is defined as the "physical observation and monitoring of what people are doing" (Bannister, p. 68). Even in circumstances when citizens are receptive to innovative uses of ICT requiring them to trust government with personal and private information, the government may be ill equipped to meet their needs. As Snijkers (2004) stated, when the quality of shared information or the share agreement itself is not adhered to, collaboration is adversely affected. "Real improvements in public services can only be reached if different administrations from different levels of government collaborate, share information and integrate processes" (Snijkers, p. 214). Attaining this level of service will provide citizens with greater confidence that the information they provide on government websites is secure and will not be used in a negative manner, thus impacting the outcome of a fair and democratic process towards representation.

A central point concerning this research is an examination of the absence of a specific government policy. U.S. law, according to Baumer (2004) does not require websites to offer users the opportunity to consent to the collection of personally, identifiable information (PII). Instead Fair Information Practices (FIPs) are utilized. FIPs are global principles that "fairly balance the need for business to collect and use personal information with the legitimate privacy interests of consumers to be able to exercise control over the disclosure and subsequent uses of their personal information" (Milne and Culnan, p. 345). According to Milne and Culnan (2002) the U.S. definition of FIPs is based upon five guidelines set forth by the Organization of Economic Cooperation and Development (OECD). The five guidelines are notice, choice, access, security/integrity and enforcement/redress. Each of these guidelines or principles is important, but they address online activity amongst consumers and do not specifically deal with protecting privacy of citizens when they conduct business online with government.

Milne and Culnan (2002) conducted a longitudinal analysis, in the years 1998, 1999 and 2000 of online privacy notices and the fair information practices of the top 100 most popular consumer websites. Their study did not examine municipal or state government websites. As a result of the study, they found that the percentage of websites that posted privacy policies increased from 48.3 percent in 1998 to 76.6 percent in 2000. Similarly, disclosure statements that tell users what personal information is collected on the website increased from 49.7 percent in 1998 to 73.5 percent in 2000. This represented an increase of over 20 percent in three years.

More recently, Schuele (2005) conducted a content analysis of municipal government websites. The research evaluated the 100 most populated municipalities in the U.S., based on the 2000 U.S. Census and found that 67 municipalities displayed a privacy policy online. A follow-up survey was sent to the 33 municipalities that did not provide an online policy statement. One city responded that they do not have a privacy policy statement online because it is not legally required, (Schuele, 2005). The results of this study indicated that legislation may be the most effective way to ensure that online communication between citizens and government becomes private and secure. Moreover, legislation can be developed to improve the level and sophistication of online privacy policies that currently exist. For example, in the EU, online service providers must obtain consent from citizens prior to making personally identifiable information available on websites. The 2002 EU Information Directive states:

Any further processing of such data which the provider of publicly available electronic communications services may want to perform, for marketing of electronic services for the provision of added services, may only be allowed if the subscriber has agreed to this on the basis of accurate and full information given by the providers of the publicly available electronic communications services about the types of further processing it intends to perform and about the subscriber's right not to give or to withdraw his/her consent. (EU, 2002)

In general, the standard for online privacy protection in the U.S. is much lower than it is in the European Union (Baumer, 2004). EU laws also require that people be notified when personally identifiable information is collected about them (such as "cookies"). Additionally, organizations attempting to use personally identifiable information for purposes other than transactions must obtain permission from users. Finally, websites and online service providers must grant users access to personally identifiable information and allow them to modify incorrect information (Baumer, 2004).

Bannister (2005) suggests that at the center of any discussion of citizen privacy regarding the state are questions regarding individual and societal risk. First, how real is the risk? Second, what defines a comprehensive risk policy regarding informational privacy when the actual risk is unclear? (Bannister, 2005) Both questions seem to indicate the approach governments in the U.S. have taken, as there has not been a substantive policy regarding online privacy and security. Two critical questions that must be asked at this point are how serious is this topic to government and how much do governments value the trust citizens' place on their actions? In the U.S there are many laws in place to describe the type of data the government can acquire the extent and nature of the data it can accumulate, along with access to data law or policy. As Bannister (2005) states however, it is much more difficult to find a description of when privacy policy or law can be breached.

Discussion regarding online privacy policies should also include two key components: accessibility and content. Jensen and Potts (2004) note that unless privacy policies are readily accessible and can easily be located, they essentially serve little purpose. Another important aspect of online privacy policies deals with the content of the information provided. Specifically, is the content easy to understand by the majority of people who utilize the Internet? To measure readability, Jensen and Potts (2004) utilized the Flesch Reading Ease Score (FRES), which rates text on a 100-point scale. The higher the score, the easier it is to read the text. Currently many computer programs, including Microsoft Word, use FRES to calculate a grade-level score. "The Flesch Grade Level (FGL) determines the U.S. grade school equivalency level of text, and is also based on the average number of syllables and sentence length" (Jensen & Potts, p. 475). In their research, of the 64 policies examined, only 6 percent were accessible to people who had less than or equal to a high school education. This represents over 28 percent of the Internet population in the U.S. Remarkably, 54 percent of the policies examined were beyond the grasp of a person with less than 14 years of education or 56 percent of the Internet population. Finally, 13 percent of the policies examined require someone with post-graduate education, which represents only 15 percent of the population. After online privacy policies are developed it becomes vital that they are written so the majority of citizens who access the Internet are able to fully understand their meanings and implications. Koh et al. (2006) suggest that public-sector projects that utilize ICT's actually increases pressure by citizens on government to continue implementing new and innovative technologies that will improve efficiency and effectiveness. If this is indeed the case then online privacy and security policies are even more important and further research is necessary to assess what is currently being done across the world. International studies are critical contributions to the overall literature on digital governance.

The paper is based on two international surveys conducted in the 2005 and 2007 that evaluated the status of digital governance in large municipalities in the top 100 most wired nations across the world. Overall, the surveys examined five different categories - security, usability, content of websites, the type of online services currently being offered, and citizen response and participation through websites established by city governments. This paper focuses on the results of the two in the area of privacy and security and analyzes the emphasis placed by municipal governments on privacy policies when introducing e-government.

Table 1. E-governance performance measures

Privacy/ Security	
1-2. A privacy or security statement/policy 3-6. Data collection 7. Option to have personal information used 8. Third party disclosures 9. Ability to review personal data records 10. Managerial measures 11. Use of encryption	12. Secure server 13. Use of "cookies" or "Web Beacons" 14. Notification of privacy policy 15. Contact or e-mail address for inquiries 16. Public information through a restricted area 17. Access to nonpublic information for employees 18. Use of digital signatures

RESEARCH METHODOLOGY

This study focused on cities throughout the world selected on the basis on their population size, the total number of Internet users and the percentage of Internet users. The top 100 municipalities were selected using data from the International Telecommunication Union (ITU), an organization affiliated with the United Nations (UN). For the 2007 survey, 86 of the 100 cities selected were found to have official municipal websites and were evaluated between August 2007 and December 2007. For the previous 2005 survey, 81 of the 100 cities were found to have official websites, which increased to 86 for the 2007 survey. This represents a significant increase in the adoption of official websites among municipalities across the world.

The survey instrument of the 2007 and 2005 survey of municipal websites consisted of five components: privacy and security, usability, content, services and citizen participation. For each of those five components, our research utilized 18-20 measures, and each measure was coded on a scale of four-points (0, 1, 2, 3) or a dichotomy of two-points (0, 3 or 0, 1). For the purpose of reliability, each municipal website was assessed in the native language by two evaluators, and in cases of significant variation of 10%, the websites were analyzed a third time. The performance measures in the category of privacy and the description of scale are provided in Table 1 and Table 2.

The analysis examined the privacy and security of global municipal websites in terms of availability of privacy policies and authentication of users. When examining municipal privacy policies, we examined the availability of privacy policy on every page that accepted data, and if the word "privacy" was used in the link to such a statement. Additionally, we also determined if privacy policies identified the agencies collecting the information, as well as what data was being collected on the site and the purpose of the data.

Table 2. E-governance scale

Scale	Description
0	Information about a given topic does not exist on the website
1	Information about a given topic exists on the website (including links to other information and e-mail addresses)
2	Downloadable items are available on the website (forms, audio, video, and other one-way transactions, popup boxes)
3	Services, transactions, or interactions can take place completely online (credit card transactions, applications for permits, searchable databases, use of cookies, digital signatures, restricted access)

FINDINGS AND DISCUSSION

Based on the evaluation of 86 municipal websites during 2007, the top 20 cities in privacy and security are provided in Table 3. Seoul, Helsinki, London, Tokyo and Singapore are top ranked cities with regard to privacy and security. Similar to the 2005 survey, Seoul recorded the highest score in the 2007 survey while the other cities are new to the top five rankings. Helsinki ranked second with a score of 15.60 in 2007, a significant increase from 51st in 2005. London which was ranked 27th in 2005 with a score of 4.80, has also improved to second overall with a score of 15.60 in 2007. The city of Tokyo has improved from 8th with a score of 12.00 in 2005 to 4th overall with a score of 14.41, and Singapore improved from 14th in 2005 to the 5th position in 2007 with a score of 14.0. The average score for all cities evaluated in 2007 is 4.49, an increase from a score of 4.17 in 2005. Overall, it was found that 26 cities selected for evaluation did not provide privacy policies; this represents a significant decrease from the 31 cities without privacy policies in 2005. Many cities are yet to recognize the importance of a privacy and security policy, in their transition to e-governance. Table 3 shows the overall scores of the top 20 ranked municipalities.

Table 4 represents the average score of municipalities by continent. The highest ranked continent was Oceania with a score with 9.20 points, which decreased from 12.00 in 2005. The table also presents the data separated by average scores of cities belonging to OECD and non-OECD member countries. Cities in OECD countries recorded an average of 7.74, while cities in non-member countries scored only 2.84, indicating that cities in economically advanced countries continue to have more emphasis on privacy and security policy than cities in less developed countries.

Overall, cities are gradually realizing the significance of privacy and security policies on their websites based on the comparison between the results of the 2007 and 2005 surveys. All cities evaluated in Oceania, 56 percent of cities in Europe, 52 percent of cities in Asia, and 43 percent of cities in North America have developed a privacy or security statement/policy in 2007. Comparatively in 2005, only 47 percent cities in Europe, 29 percent of cities in Asia, and 38 percent of the North American cities had developed privacy policies in 2005. Finally, only 22 percent of cities in South America and 20 percent of the cities in Africa have developed privacy statements for their websites in 2007.The overall percentage for cities that have a privacy or security policy online is 47 percent, a significant increase from 37 percent in 2005, with Asian cities accounting for much of the increase.

With regard to the use of encryption in the transmission of data, the percentage of cities that provide this facility has increased to 26 percent in 2007 from 21 percent in 2005. Among the continents, all the Oceanic cities continue to enable this feature in 2007 and 2005, while the percentage of European cities increased marginally from 24 percent in 2005 to 25 percent in 2007. However the percentage of cities in Asia has doubled overall from 17 percent to 36 percent along with a significant increase in North American cities from 25 percent in 2005 to 29 percent in 2007. Additionally, all cities evaluated in Oceania, 31 percent of cities in Europe, and 28 percent of cities in North America and Asia have a policy addressing the use of "cookies" or "web beacons" to track users. The overall percentage for cities that have a policy addressing the use of "cookies" or "web beacons" to track users is 27 percent, also an increase from 23 percent in 2005. The most notable change was among the South American cities with 11 percent offering this facility, while none of the cities offered such features in 2005. Another important feature in terms of website privacy is the availability of digital signatures to authenticate the users. Only 9 percent of all utilized this feature in 2005, which increased to 20 percent in 2007. The most significant increases were re-

Table 3. Results in privacy and security (2007)

Rank	City	Country	Score
1	Seoul	South Korea	17.60
2	Helsinki	Finland	15.60
2	London	UK	15.60
4	Tokyo	Japan	14.41
5	Singapore	Singapore	14.00
6	Madrid	Spain	12.80
7	Hong Kong	Hong Kong	12.40
7	Mumbai	India	12.40
9	Almaty	Kazakhstan	12.00
10	New York	USA	11.60
10	Lima	Peru	11.60
10	Dubai	UAE	11.60
13	Bangkok	Thailand	11.20
13	Berlin	Germany	11.20
13	Bratislava	Slovakia	11.20
13	Vienna	Austria	10.40
17	Rome	Italy	10.00
17	Amsterdam	Netherlands	10.00
19	Prague	Czech	9.60
19	Dublin	Ireland	9.60
19	Sydney	Australia	9.60
22	Shanghai	China	9.20
23	Auckland	New Zealand	8.80
24	Ho Chi Minh	Vietnam	8.40
25	Muscat	Oman	7.68
26	Zurich	Switzerland	7.20
26	Istanbul	Turkey	7.20
28	Sofia	Bulgaria	5.60
28	Toronto	Canada	5.60
30	Brussels	Belgium	5.20
30	Luxembourg City	Luxembourg	5.20
32	Minsk	Belarus	4.80
33	Tehran	Iran	4.40
33	Paris	France	4.40
33	Moscow	Russia	4.40
36	Buenos Aires	Argentina	4.00
37	**Jakarta**	**Indonesia**	**3.60**
37	Kuala Lumpur	Malaysia	3.60

continued on following page

Table 3. Continued

Rank	City	Country	Score
37	Copenhagen	Denmark	3.60
37	Warsaw	Poland	3.60
37	Bucharest	Romania	3.60
42	Jerusalem	Israel	2.80
43	Riga	Latvia	2.40
43	Vilnius	Lithuania	2.40
45	Sarajevo	Bosnia and Herzegovina	2.00
46	Amman	Jordan	1.60
46	Zagreb	Croatia	1.60
46	Athens	Greece	1.60
46	Mexico City	Mexico	1.60
50	Kuwait City	Kuwait	1.20
50	Stockholm	Sweden	1.20
50	Santiago	Chile	1.20
50	Santa Fé De Bogotá	Colombia	1.20
50	San José	Costa Rica	1.20
50	San Juan	Puerto Rico	1.20
50	Montevideo	Uruguay	1.20
50	Caracas	Venezuela	1.20
50	Kampala	Uganda	1.20
59	Belgrade	Serbia and Montenegro	0.80
60	Cairo	Egypt	0.40

Table 4. Average score by continent and OECD member and non-member countries (2007)

	Oceania	Asia	Europe	Average	North America	South America	Africa
OECD	9.20	16.00	7.05	7.74	6.27	-	-
Privacy Averages	9.20	5.92	5.08	4.49	4.35	2.27	0.20
Non-OECD	-	5.0	1.97	2.84	1.52	2.27	0.20

corded in the continents of Europe (9 percent in 2005 to 30 percent in 2007), North America (0 in 2005 to 14 percent in 2007) and South America (0 in 2005 to 11 percent in 2007). Interestingly, the percentage of Asian cities with such a feature has decreased from 13 percent in 2005 to 8 percent in 2007. Table 5 shows the results of evaluation of key aspects of privacy and security by continent.

Cities belonging to OECD countries are found to place more emphasis on privacy and security policies on their official websites, compared to those cities belonging to non-OECD countries. About 79 percent of cities evaluated in OECD countries have developed a privacy or security statement/ policy compared to 67 percent in 2005, while about 31 percent of cities in non-OECD countries have a privacy statement on their web-

Table 5. Results for privacy and security by continent (2007)

	Oceania	Europe	Asia	Average	North America	South America	Africa
Privacy or Security Policy	100%	56%	52%	**47%**	43%	22%	14%
Use of encryption	100%	25%	36%	**26%**	29%	0%	0%
Use of cookies	100%	31%	28%	**27%**	28%	11%	0%
Digital Signature	100%	30%	8%	**20%**	14%	11%	0%

sites in 2007 compared to only 20 percent in 2005. Comparing the performance with regard to the use of encryption in the transmission of data, about 35 percent of cities evaluated in OECD countries have a privacy statement that address this issue, compared to 21 percent of cities in non-OECD countries in 2007. This gap seems to have decreased compared to 2005, when about 43 percent of the OECD cities provided this feature, compared to only 8% in non-OECD nations. In addition, 48 percent of cities evaluated in OECD countries have a privacy policy addressing the use of "cookies" or "web beacons" to track users in 2007 compared to 43 percent in 2005. In the same category, among the non-OECD nations, only 16 percent of cities utilize this feature compared to 12 percent in 2005. Overall, cities in OECD countries that provide digital signatures online have increased from 17 percent in 2005 to 31 percent in 2007. The cities in the non-OECD nations also exhibited a significant increase from 4 percent in 2005 to 14 percent in 2007. Table 6 lists the results of evaluation of key aspects in the category of Privacy and Security by OECD and non-OECD member countries in 2005 and 2007.

When we closely examine the average privacy and security scores by continent, we notice that North America (4.35) scores lowest in comparison to Oceania (9.20), Asia (5.92) and Europe (5.08). Additionally, the average scores from North America are below the world average (4.49). The scores indicate that there may be other factors, beyond the scope of this research, explaining the differences. For example, perhaps an overall lack of trust in government is more pervasive in North American cities than it is in other cities around the world. Another difference explaining the variation in scores may be how much, or little, people accept the use of technology. If users do not perceive the value of technology as high, they are less inclined to use it and this has an adverse effect on what privacy features public-sector organizations are willing to provide to its constituents.

The first step towards increasing the use of privacy policies on municipal websites is to establish benchmarks and make comparisons between cities around the world. This will demonstrate their overall success and shortcomings, thus making municipal governments aware of what needs to be

Table 6. Results for privacy and security by OECD member and non-member nations

	OECD 2007	OECD 2005	Non-OECD 2007	Non-OECD 2005
Privacy or Security Policy	79%	67%	31%	20%
Use of encryption	35%	43%	21%	8%
Use of cookies	48%	43%	16%	12%
Digital Signature	31%	17%	14%	4%

done to make improvements. The next basic step is for municipal governments to develop privacy policies describing specifically what it does and does not collect, who collects the information and exactly what is done with the information once collected. Next, it is important that privacy policies are easily identifiable and accessible on the government website. Finally, national governments need to demonstrate the significance of this issue and adopt federal policies and legislation that require local governments to change their privacy policies. Countries in the EU have strict guidelines that government organizations must follow that include obtaining permission from users when they seek to use personally identifiable information for purposes other than transactions. Also, countries can adopt broad and stringent legislation similar to that of the Children's Online Privacy Protection Act in the United States.

CONCLUSION

Research on e-government indicates an evolutionary approach to the adoption and implementation of ICT, that views its growth in terms of various stages from developing a webpage to fully integrating services and involving all sections of the society (Schelin 2003). Each stage offers higher levels of technical sophistication and will ultimately lead to a state of "one-stop government" for citizens, where all public agencies are inter-connected, and the citizen is able to access services from any public agency at a single location. Layne and Lee (2001)'s four-stage model of e-government adoption in the United States consists of cataloguing, transaction, vertical integration and horizontal integration. In the first stage of cataloging, governments focus their efforts on establishing web portals with minimum features and contain mostly non-transactional information. Gradually citizens' demands lead to websites providing more information including government forms and documents that can be downloaded. During the next transaction stage, citizens begin to conduct transactional services with the government on the web portal thus saving time and money in commuting to the government office. Following the transaction stage is the stage of integrating the web portal vertically with city, state and federal level while the final stage is the horizontal integration stage in which the web portal is linked to other similar level websites.

To ensure that e-government projects progress from the information and cataloging stage to the higher stages of transaction and integration, it is important that municipal governments adopt comprehensive privacy policies on their official websites. This facilitates the adoption of such e-government projects among the citizen users by gaining their trust and confidence and thereby involving them in the transformation process to a one-stop government.

The study of privacy and security practices among municipal governments throughout the world is a significant area that clearly requires more research. Our studies in 2005 and 2007 have produced findings that contribute to the e-governance literature on the longitudinal assessment of performance of municipalities in terms of providing privacy policies and authenticating citizen-users. The 2007 study highlights the increased attention spent on privacy and security while simultaneously upgrading other features of e-government. However a significant number of cities are yet to provide a privacy and security policy and further research is necessary to assess what is currently being done across the world. We believe this research will be useful, as it will yield current policies and characteristics present on municipal government websites worldwide. Furthermore, it may force governments to re-examine their Internet privacy and security practices thereby adopting new policies or changing existing ones.

REFERENCES

Bannister, F. (2005). The panoptic state: Privacy, surveillance and the balance of risk. *Information Polity*, *10*, 65–78.

Baumer, D., Earp, J., & Poindexter, J. C. (2004). Internet privacy law: A comparison between the United States and the European Union. *Computers & Security*, *23*, 400–412. doi:10.1016/j.cose.2003.11.001

Culnan, M. (2000). Protecting privacy online: Is self-regulation working? *Journal of Public Policy & Marketing*, *19*(1), 20–26. doi:10.1509/jppm.19.1.20.16944

Dizard, W. P., III. (2006b). OMB sees improvement in agencies' IT security. *Government Computer News*. Retrieved March 2, 2006, from http://www.gcn.com/vol1_no1/daily-updates/38349l.html

Dutton, W. (2005). The cyber trust tension in e-government: Balancing identity, privacy, security. *Information Polity*, *10*, 13–23.

Garson, G. D. (2006). Securing the virtual state – Recent developments in privacy and security. *Social Science Computer Review*, *24*(4), 489–496. doi:10.1177/0894439306289100

Haag, S., Cummings, M., & Phillips, A. (2007). *Management Information Systems for the information age* (6th ed.). Boston, MA: McGraw-Hill.

Jensen, C., & Potts, C. (2004). *Privacy policies as decision-making tools: An evaluation of online privacy notices*. Paper presented at the Conference on Human Factors in Computing Systems. Vienna, Austria.

Koh, C. E., Prybutok, V. R., Ryan, S., & Ibragimova, B. (2006). The importance of strategic readiness in an emerging e-government environment. *Business Process Management Journal*, *12*(1), 22–33. doi:10.1108/14637150610643733

Layne, K., & Lee, J. (2001). Developing fully functional e-government: A four stage model. *Government Information Quarterly*, *18*, 122–136. doi:10.1016/S0740-624X(01)00066-1

Milne, G., & Culnan, M. (2002). Using the content of online privacy notices to inform public policy: A longitudinal analysis of the 1998-2001 U.S. Web surveys. *The Information Society*, *18*, 345–359. doi:10.1080/01972240290108168

National Institute of Standards and Technology. (2002). *Computer Security Resource Center*. Retrieved on February 26, 2010 at http://csrc.nist.gov/groups/SMA/fisma/overview.html

Satola, D. (2007). Legal aspects of Internet governance reform. *Information Polity*, *12*, 49–62.

Schelin, S. H. (2003). E-government: An overview . In Garson, G. D. (Ed.), *Public Information Technology: Policy and management issues*. Hershey, PA: Idea Group Publishing.

Schuele, K. (2005). Privacy policy statements on nunicipal websites [Electronic Version]. *The Journal of Government Financial Management*, *52*(2), 20–29.

Snijkers, K. (2004). Digital administration and the role of trust. *Information Polity*, *9*, 205–215.

U.S. Federal Trade Commission. (1999). *Child Online Privacy Protection Act*. Retrieved February 26, 2010, from http://www.coppa.org/comply.htm

Warner, J., & Chun, S. A. (2009). Privacy protection in government mashups. *Information Polity*, *14*, 75–90.

Westin, A. F. (1967). *Privacy and freedom*. New York, NY: Atheneum.

Chapter 7
ICT and eGovernance:
The Citizen's Trust Facet

Christos Manolopoulos
Research Academic Computer Technology Institute, Greece

Dimitris Sofotassios
Research Academic Computer Technology Institute, Greece

Paul Spirakis
Research Academic Computer Technology Institute, Greece

Yiannis C. Stamatiou
Research Academic Computer Technology Institute, Greece

ABSTRACT

One of the cornerstones of Democracy is the participation of citizens in decisions that affect their lives. This participation, traditionally, is exercised: a) through national elections and the body of representatives, and b) through binding procedures such as referendums. However, there are decisions that affect citizens' everyday lives that require more frequent, day to day participation. Information and Communications Technologies (ICT) can create fast and secure communication channels, enabling politicians and citizens to engage in a mutually rewarding interaction leading to the development eDemocracy. However, lack of trust either between politicians and citizens or lack of trust of citizens towards ICT can raise barriers to this opportunity. In this chapter we discuss the issue of trust among government, citizens, and ICT. Our view is that it is nowadays possible to, at least, handle effectively the citizen-ICT facet of trust and provide the drivers for the convergence of eGoverment and eDemocracy realizing the concept of eGovernance. As a case study we present our experiences from the design and implementation of an eVoting system, which has the same strong relationship with eGovernance as traditional elections have with Governance.

DOI: 10.4018/978-1-60960-839-2.ch007

INTRODUCTION

We have entered in a phase where old-fashioned state practices are strongly challenged and citizens demand direct involvement to social collective and political issues. Both governments and citizens could benefit from the use of Information and Communications Technology (ICT). ICT can amplify citizens' empowerment and desire for effective involvement in state policies and decision making, overcoming more traditional practices based on indirect involvement through representatives or direct involvement at, usually long-spanned, regular intervals through traditional voting. However, despite the recent progress in technology, one of the main obstacles for the wide adoption of eParticipation tools, such as eVoting, is the reluctance of citizens to participate in or the reluctance of politicians to enable eParticipation services (see (Ekelin, 2007) and (Albrecht *et al.*, 2008)). This reluctance can be, partially, attributed to the, relatively, low penetration of technology among citizens (especially those of higher ages – see (Millward, 2003)) and, even, politicians.

However, our view is that the main reason behind this reluctance is the *lack of trust*. This lack of trust has three dimensions: lack of trust of politicians to citizen's ability to provide useful feedback to decision making processes, lack of trust of citizens to politicians that they will take their opinion and transform it into public policy reform actions, and lack of trust of both parties (i.e. citizens and politicians) in ICT as a vehicle towards a robust implementation of transparent eGovernment services that, in turn, will lead to a successful realization of eGovernance. Trust of the citizens and politicians among themselves, as well as towards ICT, is a basic precondition that can lead to a reform with an eye towards real citizen's needs, as they are expressed by themselves.

The emergence or non-emergence of trust between people or groups of people (e.g. politicians and citizens) cannot, unfortunately, be easily explained and may ignite endless discussions with arguments based on even controversial views from political and social sciences. However, our point of view, which we will discuss in this chapter, is that trust in ICT as it is employed in eGovernance can be considerably enhanced by designing and building eGovernment systems in a way that demonstrates the respect in the privacy of citizens. This requires the application of tools and system representations that can be understood and checked by the specialist and, to a certain degree, by the layman citizen alike. Apart from the technology and engineering approaches, efforts for advancing eParticipation should be *gradual* and develop solutions hand-in-hand with in-field trials that increase (also gradually) in complexity and people inclusiveness, so as to handle the various forms of social trust inertia successfully.

This smooth process seems to work well: 1) it matches bureaucratic and legislative inertia (i.e. time is given to the government to adjust to the new ICT-based, governance model), and 2) time is given to citizens to increase their IT literacy, to understand, trust and finally accept the system used (both in terms of technology and usefulness) before using more complex services (e.g. elections).

It is apparent that voting is a fundamental process in any democratic system. Any effort to migrate from the conventional and long established voting procedures to an electronic voting system is thus very seriously affected by the lack of trust in ICTs and the Internet. Moreover, the abundance of cases of misconduct in electronic voting has resulted in severe decrease of *trust* among citizens (Antoniou *et al.*, 2007). However, eVoting, despite the critique it has attracted (see, for instance, Mercuri, 2007) because it implements one of the most sensitive processes in our democracy, seems to be, still, a hot discussion issue and, possibly, a worldwide reality in the future. Thus, any successful eVoting system should target at increasing *public trust*. Trust, however, is difficult to establish in the eVoting domain since eVoting is necessarily based on complex distributed information systems, involving complicated interactions between many groups of entities and stakeholders: computing systems, software, system operators, auditors, legislation experts etc.

The purpose of the chapter is to examine the relationship between government reform, ICT and trust. Our view is that an effective reform process cannot be based only on the exploitation of ICT to delivering, in one way fashion, simple day to day services (e.g. issuance of birth certificates) or even more complex ones, such as eVoting without incorporating in the whole picture a trust-founded interaction between the state and the citizen. In order to provide a concrete instance of our views, we proceed to summarize our experiences from working in the eVoting domain, which is one of the most important, and difficult to implement by ICT means, pillars of eDemocracy. We discuss how the trust issue was taken into account from the design to the implementation and testing phases as well as how efforts we taken in order to gradually introduce the final system into decision making procedures.

The chapter is structured as follows. In Section 2 we discuss how citizens' trust level towards Information and Communication Technologies affects their attitude towards the use of e-Governance services in their everyday lives. In Section 3 we focus on the complexities of handling the issue of trust in the eVoting domain and ICT trust with good design, implementation, and engineering practices. In Section 4 we describe our layered trust engineering approach that handles trust at various levels ranging from the employment of proper low level cryptographic techniques in the design of eVoting systems to organizing social awareness campaigns for their public acceptance. In Section 5 we discuss how the emerging eIdentity related technology, based on *Attribute Based Credentials* (or ABCs), can enhance eVoting procedures and lead to an increase in citizens' trust and eParticipation. In Section 6 we discuss the gradual adoption model for introducing eVoting to society, according to which this introduction is performed in a gradual, step wise manner to citizen groups of increasing size and influence. In Section 7 we discuss, separately, the importance issue of Open Source Software and eVoting, since deployment of Open Source Software may lead to a system whose properties and, consequently, robustness and security can be evaluated, in principle, by any interested party. In Section 8 we discuss how the principles described in the previous sections were incorporated into the design and implementation of an eVoting platform, called PNYKA, which is able to support distributed eVoting procedures, from simple polls to national binding elections. Finally in Section 9 we summarize our proposal and discuss directions for further considerations on how eVoting procedures founded on citizens' trust may contribute to an increased penetration of reformed eGovernance procedures and services to the society.

E-GOVERNANCE AND THE SOCIAL ASPECTS OF TRUST

According to D. Broster in (European Commission, 2008, p. 5), the next stage in enhancing the relationship between state and citizen is probably "the need to include a strong governance perspective where citizens and businesses seek empowerment and where both geographic boundaries and the role of administrations, the private and civil sectors, are all blurring". This situation entails profound challenges and opportunities for governance. A new governance model where government is seen as just one form of collectivity alongside other forms which are emerging as ICT is taken up, could meet these new challenges. People are becoming increasingly educated and connected and therefore seek to be involved. On the other hand, they demand this involvement to guarantee transparency, collaboration, accountability in information flow through an increased intelligent use of the technology.

In principle this demand could be based on the relationship between eParticipation and eGovernment dynamics and practices. Each one could provide advantages to such a process. For instance, eParticipation could mobilize citizens in order to provide arenas for deep conversations and opinion exchanges and operate as providers of crucial innovative ideas and concepts concerning governance. But at the same time eParticipation practices are not themselves mature to guarantee misuse of the participation processes as well as threats to sensitive data and then identity protection. Besides eGovernment practices, while they are matured to a more or less degree, they seem to be developed and run with no significant relevance to the citizens' needs. In the case where eGovernment policies and practices are not interlinked with eParticipation field, there is no evidence that they could handle effectively the complexities of the interactions between the state and the citizens because this interaction encompasses institutions, subtle and sensitive processes, decisions with long term implications on the political and social life of a country. In modern societies, the principal driving effort behind the well being of the relationships between the state and the citizen is democracy and the processes that enable citizens to participate in decision making processes and, consequently, to state reform efforts.

Therefore, some social and political scientists suggest that the concept of eGovernment itself should be reoriented towards the following three axes: a) relationship with citizens, b) overcoming of border, racial, and other barriers, and c) incorporation of direct, on-line communication and collaboration among government agencies and citizens.

Seang Tae KIM (Kim, 2008) proposes a theoretical model for development and convergence of eGovernment and eDemocracy. According to Kim, the concept and function of eGovernment has been changed because of advanced technology and social needs. The emergence of citizens as policy decision makers and as the focal point of democracy has brought about the emergence of eDemocracy. Current discussions concerning eGovernment have some limitations in addressing possibility and current change, because they ignore developments of civil society and democracy.

J. Millard (Millard, 2007) has proposed that the three axes above should not be seen as independent and equal pillars, but rather as means and ends with the interrelationships that this implies. Therefore, the *public value* is the ultimate goal while effectiveness and efficiency are only means to this higher end and can be provided by governments. These interlinks leading to a public value concept have to rely on trust. According to Millard, trust seems to be one, if not the, common factor in the successful use of ICT for the purposes, not just of empowerment, but also more widely in the economy, the role of the government and in the social lives of citizens and communities.

However, public trust is a *group*, not an atomic property. The social character of trust should at least been distinguished to the following three dimensions: a) trust of the citizens towards the government (politicians), b) trust of the government towards citizens' opinions and c) trust of both citizens and government towards ICT which affect sensitive democratic processes.

In interpreting such a trust framework, (Castells, 2001) proceeds with an analysis of the relationship that holds between the Internet and democracy and he discovers that for the time being Internet use, rather than reinforcing democracy by enhancing knowledge and citizen participation, tends to worsen the crisis resulting from the dissatisfaction of citizens with their representatives. This is evident from the gradual increase of citizen abstention from elections. Thus, trust in the eGovernance process appears to suffer along all its three axes: trust between citizens and government and trust of both towards ICT.

In the European eParticipation study (Panopoulou *et al.*, 2009) 258 eParticipation cases across Europe were identified and discussed. This relatively low number of cases shows a weak eParticipation culture diffusion and lack of a dense citizen–government interrelationship model. One of the main reasons behind this phenomenon is exactly the lack of trust as discussed above. The majority of the results refer to the local level, confirming the fact that participation is usually higher at the local level and consequently indicating that governments are seldom willing to communicate governmental plans, legislature proposals and other important issues to citizens (see Ekelin (2007) and Albrecht *et al.* (2008)).

Trust could emerge at the level of individuals acting collectively, or emerge through a *social diffusion process* propelled by mimetic or collaborative forces underlying the behavior of the individuals. Therefore, to support government reform for the implementation of eGovernance, the governments have to set in motion practices to improve confidence to public policies and enhance mediation. This can only be founded on the *continuous* participation of citizens in decision making procedures overcoming the weak interlinks based on the old fashioned and challenged models of pure citizen's participation only through national elections, every four or five years. ICT could contribute towards increasing the participation through a variety of channels such as open fora, referendums, discussion groups etc. And one of the major ICT pillars of eParticipation is eVoting.

Our view is that eVoting can be designed and implemented in a way that demonstrates the final system's trust properties to citizens, thus increasing their willingness to use it in their everyday, bilateral interaction with the state. Of course, eVoting inherits the dangers of the communication means employed, such as the Internet, as well as the involved technologies. A series of reports worldwide converge to depict the weaknesses of internet-based voting especially due to security reasons. As pointed out in (Alvarez & Hall, 2004) concerning the application of internet voting to US electoral system, eVoting can be implemented and studied in meaningful, although limited and controlled, efforts before it is used in major statewide or national elections. Only through using real voters and real election administrators in carefully controlled settings can researchers learn how internet voting affects the electoral process, in both positive and negative ways. We believe that with increased funding and attention by the politicians and decision makers, research can advance significantly the state of the art and lead to an eVoting technology that can support eParticipation with safety and trustworthiness. This is our main argument in the sections that follows.

TRUST TOWARDS ICT

Despite the impressive recent advancements of technology and ICT devices, the aspect of *trust* continues to play a major role in how people accept and use new technologies in their everyday lives. Lack of trust essentially diminishes the usefulness of technological advancements from the user's perspective. Moreover, when it comes to services delivered through ICT channels, there is another trust level, raising the complexity of decisions with regard to what and/or whom to trust: lack of trust towards the service providers and their own ICT infrastructure.

On the other hand, trust is a hard to formalize concept that also raises philosophical and social (i.e. non-engineering) concerns. Although various formalisms (e.g. mathematical logic, algorithmic theory etc.) can be exploited in order to define and study trust, there are nevertheless some inherent weaknesses in them that prevent them from modeling and handling trust in a completely satisfactory way that allows a systematic derivation of trust-related conclusions. Thus, it appears that reliance on formalism alone is not the answer to the problem of defining and manipulating trust. Rather, entities should better focus on including fast heuristics as well as approximations to reality (even accepting trust in some cases axiomatically, e.g. to avoid the incompleteness pitfalls of powerful formal deductive systems). Moreover, it seems that trust will rely, for some time (until we manage to define it alternatively) on what it relied traditionally for the past few centuries: personal experience, public guidance from organizations and governments, creation of awareness groups, and avoiding trusting a WWW entity whenever one is not totally sure about trusting it (educated decisions). Otherwise, formal trust may either be unattainable (e.g. incompleteness results about formalisms) or hard to verify (NP-completeness results from computational complexity). On another front, Luhmann's research (Luhmann, 1988) considers trust as a mechanism which causes the reduction of complexity. In his work (Coleman, 1990) Coleman distinguishes certain elements that define a trust situation between a trustor and a trustee. By definition a voting procedure is a trust situation, and in this case trust properties have to be reflected both on individual and system level, independently of the voluntary, custom/norm based, institutional or obtruded nature of the procedure. Trust is an emergent social property based on interactions between actors and for this reason, an eVoting procedure could, in principle, be established, if and only if, actors should certainly believe that it complies with certain properties of trust.

There is much ongoing research in the development and analysis of new trust management models for complex and dependable computer systems. In (Blaze *et al.*, 1996) it is proposed the application of automated trust mechanisms in distributed systems. In (Josang, 1996) the focus is on the strong relationship between the notions of trust and security. Moreover, a number of schemes for the design of secure information systems have been proposed (see, for example, (Eschenauer *et al.*, 2002; Hubaux *et al.*, 2001) which are based on automated trust management protocols. The composition and propagation of trust information between elements of information systems is also of pivotal concern and a number of research works are devoted to them, see for example (Richardson *et al.*, 2003; Kamvar *et al.*, 2003; Theodorakopoulos & Baras, 2004; Guha *et al.*, 2004). With regard to trust in the eGovernment domain, specifically, there are specialized research efforts in building trust models based on distributed trust agents, much like as in Public Key Infrastructures (PKI) (Tassabehji & Elliman, 2006). There are many open issues both conceptual and practical, however, that pertain to eGovernment trust, many of which are discussed in (Riedl, 2004) and (Kim *et al.*, 2005). There are even less efforts for trust management in the eVoting domain. Due to the complexity of an eVoting system, most of the efforts are focused on the study of specific security requirements of the system itself such as, for instance, establishing uncoercibility of the voters (Van Acker, 2004). Also, as a common practice for strengthening trust, many approaches focus on the existence of a voter verifiable paper copy of the ballot or the design of strong cryptographic protocols, e.g. (Smith, 2005; Gritzalis, 2003). Finally, the work done by the OASIS consortium (OASIS, 2007) is a first step towards the standardization of secure eVoting architectures based on formal modeling and risk assessment methodologies (e.g. use of the EML language and threat evaluation techniques).

Given the multifaceted nature of trust as well as the difficulties that are inherent in various formalizations proposed in the past, we adopt a *pragmatic* point of view, in the sense that we rely on a *plausible* working definition and proceed in order to satisfy the definition's prerequisites for trust. One possible definition of trust is the following:

Trust of a party A in a party B for a service X is the measurable belief of A in that B will behave dependably for a specified period within a specified context.

In the eVoting domain in particular, A is the voter, B is the eVoting system and X is the eVoting service. Most importantly, by *dependably* we will imply ensuring the following basic voting requirements (which apply to both eVoting and conventional voting): *democracy* (only voters who have the right to vote can vote and one vote per voter is included in the election outcome), accuracy (the election outcome is correct and includes all valid votes), *secrecy* (a voter's vote cannot be seen by any other voter), *receipt-freeness* (no evidence is given to the voter that can be used in order to disclose the contents of his/her vote to another party), *uncoercibility* (protection from outside enforcement of opinion), *fairness* (the outcome of the election will be made public only after all votes have been received and tallied), *verifiability* (all critical stages of the election process are logged for later auditing and the election outcome can be verified by the voters), *verifiable participation* (the participation of a voter can be checked by the election authority, in cases where voting is compulsory), and *robustness* (the election process cannot be hindered either accidentally or on purpose by outside intervention).

Given the above definitions, we can define the means by which the trust prerequisites, i.e. the word "dependably" above, can be satisfied:

Trust management/engineering is a unified approach to interpreting, specifying and incorporating security requirements in a transparent way that allows direct authorization of security-critical actions on behalf of the user.

Thus, this applied view of trust, as pertaining to the eVoting domain, is a property of an eVoting system that emerges in citizens' minds as a result of a systematic process and manifests itself in their will to use the system in order to participate in an election. This emergence is made possible through the proper trust engineering approach. This approach has been applied to the design and development of the eVoting system described below.

HANDLING THE COMPLEXITY OF TRUST IN ICT

The layers of the trust view of the eVoting system are complementary to the other formal views and models of ordinary IT systems (e.g. business view, technical view etc.) and is employed in order to handle the complexity of the security issues pertaining to eVoting, as defined by its security requirements. This complexity can be as high as the complexities that arise in other architectural views of such systems and the layers of trust approach can be used as a tool for managing these issues successfully.

Below we will provide a brief account of these three elements of the approach, which is also depicted in Figure 1 below (Antoniou *et al.*, 2007):

The layers of trust view of the eVoting system is a view complementary to the other formal views and models of ordinary ICT systems (e.g. business view, technical view etc.) and is employed in order to handle the complexity of the security issues pertaining to eVoting, as defined by its security requirements. This complexity can be as high as the complexities that arise in other architectural views of such systems and the layers of trust approach can be used as a tool for managing these issues successfully.

The role of the layers and the correspondence to the eVoting system, is as follows:

Scientific soundness: All the components of the system should possess some type of security justification and be widely accepted within the scientific community. This layer corresponds to the selection of a cryptographically strong eVoting protocol, based on provably secure cryptographic primitives, such as the El Gamal encryption scheme and zero knowledge proofs.

Implementation soundness: A methodology should be adopted that will lead to the verification of the implementation of the separate system components as well as the system as a whole. In addition, such a verification methodology should be applied periodically to the system. This layer corresponds to the adoption of the CORAS methodology (see below) for designing and building the eVoting system.

Internal operation soundness: The design and implementation should offer high availability

Figure 1. The trust-centered approach

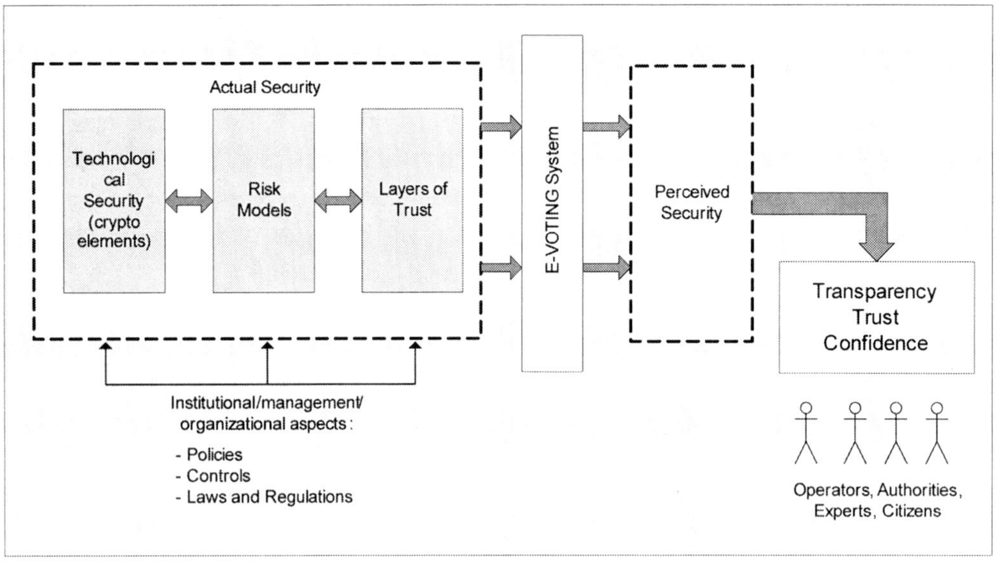

and fault tolerance and should support system self-auditing, self-checking, and self-recovery from malfunction. Interference from the inside with the normal operation of the system should be, ideally, impossible to accomplish and, if ever accomplished, it should be readily detectable. The employment of the cryptographically secure eVoting protocol involves the use of proofs of correctness for all the executed steps.

Externally visible operational soundness: It should be possible for everyone to check log and audit information at some level. The employed cryptographic protocol employs a number of publicly accessible bulleting boards where information is appended concerning the votes cast as well as the proof that the votes where taken into consideration for the computation of the vote outcome.

Convincing the public (social side of trust): It is crucial for the wide acceptance of the eVoting system that the public will trust it when it is in operation. This trust can be, in general, amplified if the eVoting authority publicises the details of the design and operation of the eVoting system to the public. There is provision for publicizing all the details of the system architecture and implementation as well as provide the software source code for scrutiny. In addition, in order to facilitate the system's wide acceptance, the first trials will be conducted on a voluntary basis with closed groups or local associations, whose opinions can be easily gathered and analyzed.

Observe that such a methodological approach for trust management is not apparent between the state and the citizens, since it involves interactions between humans. These interactions have been under a long lasting scrutiny by political and social scientists and, despite copious efforts, no pattern seems to emerge that can be exploited in order t to build a trust handling framework such as the one described above.

ATTRIBUTE-BASED CREDENTIALS AND E-PARTICIPATION

The amount of daily transactions that we perform electronically is rising very fast. Many individuals use the Internet on a daily basis for a number of purposes ranging from accessing information to electronic commerce and e-banking to interactions with government bodies and eVoting. Securing these transactions requires the use of strong authentication. Electronic authentication tokens and mechanisms that provide this become common not only for the use with the Internet but elsewhere. Indeed, electronic identity cards, authentication by mobile phone, RFID tokens are spreading fast. These authentication mechanisms unfortunately have the shortcoming that they use unique identifiers that present the risk that transactions by the same user can be linked, thus seriously threatening the user's privacy. In addition, the carrier of the token can be easily identified by the token issuing authority (e.g. the Certification Authority in a traditional PKI).

In particular, in eVoting applications, unique identification is inappropriate and privacy-preserving attribute-based authentication is therefore desirable. Indeed, a position paper issued in February 2009 by ENISA on "Privacy Features of European eID Card Specifications" (ENISA, 2009) underlines the need for "privacy-respecting use of unique identifiers" (personal number that uniquely identify a user) in emerging European eID cards, and explicitly refers to the emerging *attribute-based credentials (ABC)* technologies ("privacy-enhanced PKI tokens" in their terminology), as having significant potential in this arena.

eVoting procedures can readily gather and summarize the citizens' opinions on various important Governance related processes that range from national elections to simple opinion casting on an open discussion forum. eVoting procedures, in general, rely on two complementary and equally important anchor points: a) preserving citizen anonymity (especially in open forums that discuss candidate Governmental policies), and b) separation of the citizen's opinion from any kind of information that would lead to revelation of his/her identity. Although these two anchor points, if properly supported with strong cryptographic and security techniques, are sufficient for the purpose of gathering citizen's opinions and producing numeric outcomes (e.g. vote tallies or opinion tallies within various categories – e.g. "yes", "no", "do not know", "do not want to answer" etc.) they nevertheless fail in the following important two aspects: a) they do not allow a refinement and further analysis of the opinion gathering results in relation to the *profiles* of the citizens that cast their opinions and/or votes, and b) they do not allow the development of procedures in which only groups of citizens with *specific* profiles can participate. In the following we argue that eVoting procedures that address these two aspects can be more effective for Government policy makers in reforming their tools and practices towards society and its citizens. We further discuss how enhancement of eVoting techniques can be performed so as to address these issues, based on attribute-based credentials. These credentials and protocols, which are used for proving elements of the profiles of citizens, can suitably address these two aspects and may lead to a bilaterally rewarding interaction between Government and citizens.

eVoting and open discussions on the Internet on various proposals for changes or enhancements in governmental practices are commonly used means in order to sense citizens' attitudes and opinions. Of course, anonymity (compulsory in strict eVoting procedures but voluntary on open discussion forums) is the common denominator of all of these processes as one of the major anchor points for protecting the individual's identity.

However, there are situations where knowledge of certain characteristics (or attributes) of individuals' profiles may enhance the conclusions drawn from studying only the responses of the individuals. For instance, the ministry of education may open a discussion as to whether general entrance examinations at the Universities should be abolished and all students enter at the University schools of their choice, depending on their grades only. Then, a discussion result indicating that 90% of the participants support the abolition of general examinations may provide some clue as to what the feelings of society are towards the examinations but a closer examination, according to individuals' profiles, may indicate that only 10% of individuals who are university professors support the abolition and, thus, governmental authorities should be careful in implementing such a radical change without further discussion and elaborations. Moreover, there are also situations where knowledge of characteristics of individuals' profiles may be mandatory. For instance, the ministry of education may want to start a discussion about whether University infrastructures in a country are sufficient for a normal operation of Universities. In order to take as substantiated opinions as possible, the ministry decides to open the discussion only to professors and students who are at least at the 3rd year of their studies. This establishes that those who have had sufficiently many years of university life will participate so as to be in position to judge more accurately the University infrastructures and curricula.

Although all the examples discussed above indicate that having partial information about the profiles of individuals participating in a eVoting process is helpful, there is one major issue that should be taken care of: How can one prove, beyond doubt, something about a certain attribute of his/her credentials/profile without revealing the true identity even to the credentials service provider?

We believe that a debate should be initiated to address the integration of technologies that support attributes based credentials with technologies that are employed for eGovernance, with an emphasis on eVoting. Anonymous credentials technologies allow an Identity Service Provider (IdSP) to issue a credential (or certificate) to a user, in a way analogous to a Public Key Infrastructure issuing a classical certificate such as (X.509, 2005). This credential contains attributes of the user such as address or date of birth but also the user's rights or roles as attributes. Using the credential, the user can prove to a third party that he possesses a credential containing a given attribute or role without revealing any other information stored in the credential. For instance, the user could use a government-issued anonymous ID credential to prove that he is of proper age, i.e., that he possesses a credential that contains a date of birth which is further in the past than 21 years. Thus, anonymous credentials promise to be an important cornerstone in protecting users' privacy in an eVoting environment while, at the same time, providing important enhancement in eVoting processes towards a more effective government policies reform. In the rest of this section we discuss how anonymous credentials may enhance eVoting procedures.

The Attribute-Based Credentials, or ABCs for short, can be viewed as a set of cryptographic protocols which specify a user-controllable framework for defining and managing credential sets. These credential sets may be required for interactions with service providers (either private or governmental) in order to access personalized services that require access only to a subset of the users' credentials. Such services include simple preferences management for e-commerce (e.g. book reading preferences), convincing of one's eligibility (e.g. age or occupation) in order to access public information, and allowing government agencies access personal information that may reside in several other government agencies (e.g. health information). The proposed credential sets may include, except from assertions about a user, hyperlinks to personal information residing elsewhere (e.g. government agencies), that the user desires to disclose to an eVoting service provider (or prove something about this information, not the information itself).

Over the past 10-15 years, a number of technologies have been developed to build ABC systems in a way that they can be trusted, like normal cryptographic certificates, while at the same time protecting the privacy of their holder (e.g. hiding the real holder's identity). Such attribute-based credentials are issued just like ordinary cryptographic credentials (e.g., X.509 credentials) using a digital (secret) signature key. However, ABCs

Figure 2. Attribute-based credentials

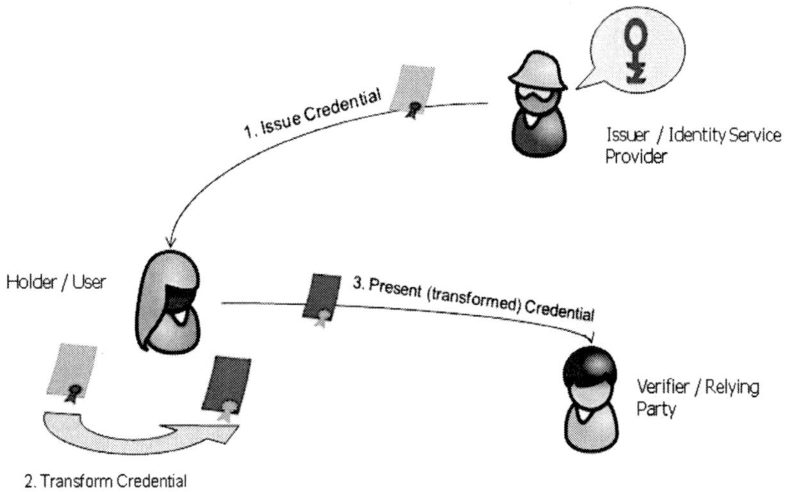

allow their holder to uncover only a subset of the attributes contained in the original credential. Still, these transformed credentials verification procedure just like ordinary cryptographic credentials (using the public verification key of the issuer) and offer the same strong security. See Figure 2 for a high-level view of the ABC concept, as given in Camenisch & Lysyanskaya, 2001 (picture in slides prepared by Camenisch).

A credentials holder/user applies for issuance of a digital credential to the Identity Service Provider or ISP for short. The ISP issues a signed digital credential to the user who, then, can present the credential to the verifier (most often a service provider to whom the user needs to prove something about himself/herself. Note that, in contrast with a classical PKI authentication service, the verifier (service provider) does not contact the ISP (the analogous of the Certification Authority in a PKI). In addition, the user can transform the credential and, thus, present to each verifier a different credential form so that it is not possible for a party to link the different credentials of the user together and, thus, uncover information (e.g. preferences when browsing on the Internet) about the user.

Research has put forth a number of different proposals how to realise anonymous credentials (Brands, 2000; Camenisch & Lysyanskaya, 2001; Camenisch & Lysyanskaya, 2004) which are based on different number-theoretic problems and also differ somewhat in the functionality that they offer. There are two leading anonymous credentials systems: *idemix* of IBM and *U-prove* of Microsoft. These two systems provide functionality for supporting user credentials with the following requirements:

1. Unforgeability (issuing)
2. Selective disclosure with the user controlling the disclosed information set
3. Soundness (no false claims about the validity of a credential)
4. No framing (showing transcript unforgeability)
5. Untraceability (showings, with respect to issuing)
6. Unlinkability (between different showings)
7. Limited-show unlinkability and untraceability.

These two systems provide nearly the same functionality, using different cryptographic primitives. With regard to idemix, it relies, mostly, on the hardness of the strong RSA problem while U-prove relies, mostly, on the difficulty of discrete logarithms. Also, credentials are represented in different formats. In what follows, we will sketch the use of credentials in eVoting using the description given by (Brands *et al.*, 2007). We will only use the basic credentials form in order to demonstrate our idea. The discussion can be extended to work also with the more complex format given in (Brands, 2000) and (Brands *et al.*, 2007) which have been incorporated in Microsoft's U-prove system as well as the other credentials format described in (Camenisch, 2006; Camenisch & Groβ, 2008) which have been implemented into IBM's idemix attribute-based credentials system, see (Camenisch & Van Herreweghen, 2002). We refer the reader to the literature with regard to proofs that the properties listed above in bullets hold for both systems.

TOWARDS A GENERIC TRUST-ORIENTED ICT DEPLOYMENT FRAMEWORK

The application of IT security primitives and protocols as well as technologies lies at the heart of a reasonable eVoting implementation and deployment approach. While strong IT security is a necessary condition for successful eVoting systems, as described in the previous sections, it is by no means (unfortunately) sufficient. In what follows we present the components of a step-wise, trust-driven approach towards the adoption of eVoting by people. The approach involves all stakeholders at the same time and is targeted at convincing them of the usefulness and security of using the eVoting system (see Figure 3).

The principal axes of the approach are the following:

(i) *Proven technological excellence for the system components*: The system should use strong technological tools and computer science primitives, preferably scientifically proven and standard-based. This ensures the sound operation of the system and its robustness against potential attacks. This aspect, though not easy to address, may be approached using the latest technological advances, especially in the field of security.

(ii) *Use of open source software technologies and publicly available information:* System development and operation should be based on open source technologies to allow independence from existing vendors and increase transparency (Neumann, 2004). The system should be open to scrutiny by experts and auditors. An open call for attacks before productive operation is also useful, with an aim to prove system's robustness and attract citizens' trust.

(iii) *In field user assessment:* After the end of the voting process, users/voters should be motivated to assess the system and the whole procedure, in terms of various aspects: user-friendliness, efficiency, perceived trust, etc. This feedback should be taken seriously into account for improving the system and the organization of the voting procedure, for further applications. Apart from the in-field assessment process, users should receive later another assessment form that the system stakeholders should design so as to take into consideration the in-field assessment process as well as the fact that the users have had some time at their disposal to think about the whole election process (off-line user assessment).

(iv) *Organize pre- and post- application information campaigns*: Information campaign before an eVoting event improves stakeholders' understanding of the system's capabilities and operation as well as use, while information days after the eVoting event help stakeholder understand each other's views and propose improvements on the operation

Figure 3. Gradual application model

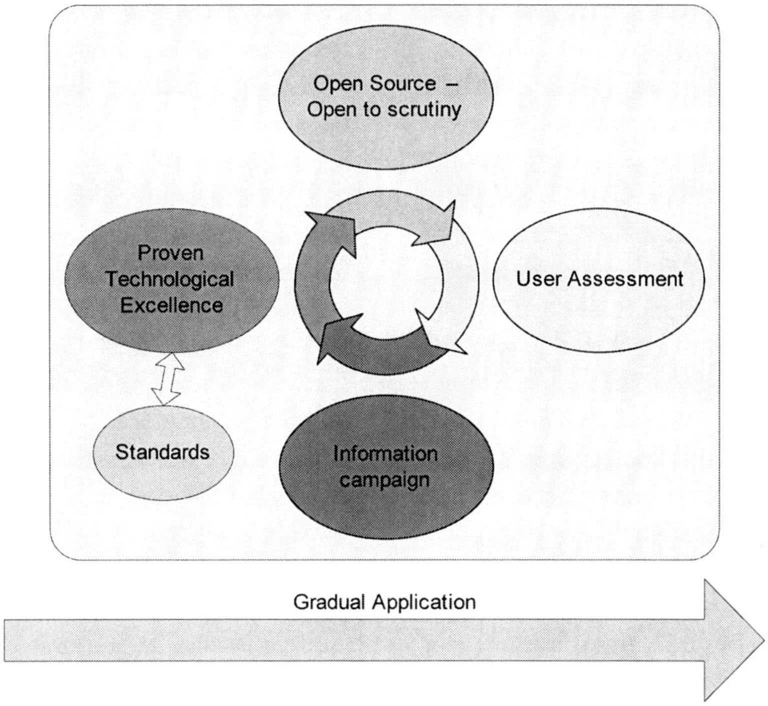

and usability of the system. These information days should include technical people, voters, legislation officials, social scientists etc.

The aforementioned aspects should be accompanied by a step-wise, *gradual application* of the system, as described in the introduction. For instance, the eVoting system should be applied, first, in simple eVoting scenarios (e.g. expression of opinion, polling etc.) and then applied to scenarios of increasing criticality and complexity (e.g. election process in scientific interest groups, elections in societies and organizations, local elections for representatives, and finally to national elections). This gradual adoption effort has multiple benefits: first of all, it allows for thorough, in-field evaluation of the system, using increasingly more complex eVoting scenarios. In addition, time is given to stakeholders to develop opinions and views about the system that will contribute to its improvements in order to face a more demanding eVoting procedure. In this way, eVoting will be gradually established and trusted by citizens as well as the involved stakeholders, something which could not be achieved (and has not been achieved, as witness by documented cases of eVoting failures) if one attempted to penetrate eVoting technology to the whole population of a country and for a critical eVoting process.

This approach was used for the first, real-life application of an eVoting prototype/system that was developed by our team, as described in the following section.

THE ROLE OF OPEN SOURCE SOFTWARE

Any eVoting system should be a democratic system. This implies that it should be open to scrutiny by everyone. Of course, the majority of people lack the e-skills required to validate the design soundness or to assess test results. However, they may be motivated by others who are experts.

The most natural way to achieve this is to use open source software in the development process of an eVoting system, using a model/procedure similar to the one described hereafter: A group of developers implements the system and subsequently distributes it for free use by all, e.g. through the web. In addition, if the development process is combined with typical design methods and risk analysis techniques, as opposed to ad-hoc system design, the result will be an extended documentation of all design and development details. The software is open and extendable and allows the easy incorporation of new protocols.

Expert programmers from around the world may download the software, execute it and identify and fix potential security flaws. Various user communities (e.g. blogs) may test the software and provide feedback to the open source community for possible modifications, refinements and improvements that might ensure ease of use and thus greater user acceptance.

Scientists and security professionals may check the documentation thoroughly and provide mathematical evidence for the security and the scientific soundness of the system (e.g. quality and length of cryptographic keys). The State or other authorities may organize open calls for attackers who will in turn help the system mature and become more robust.

This mobilization of an international community actually creates added value for the system. This approach may require fairly long time but is an open and democratic procedure, fully compatible with the character of voting. What is more, the adoption of an open source model ensures independence from specific vendors and offers lower costs in relation to commercial software.

But, how safe is the open source software? The usual critique against using open source software in eVoting is that the provision of an open system to malicious users may make it an easy target for attacks. However, after the maturity stage, one expects that the system will be secure and robust against such attempts. Just to set an example, Linux kernel, Apache server and openVPN, are among the most secure open source systems. The AES algorithm that substituted DES was the result of an open contest, its source code was published and analyzed for a long time, it was approved by the National Institute of Standards and Technology (NIST) (see, for instance, (Richards, 2003) for the details on the NIST contest) and was the first to be openly released for use by everyone. Many cryptographic libraries have been developed based on the open source model and are freely distributed over the web.

Similar examples also exist in the eVoting domain, the example of Australia being the most characteristic. In Australia, the eVoting system used in Australian Capital Territory elections on October of 2001 was developed by a private company but subsequently, the source code was opened to public, which led to the identification of some problems that needed to be fixed.

PNYKA: TOWARDS THE REALIZATION OF TRUST ORIENTED E-PARTICIPATION

In this section, we will discuss a general trust-oriented framework for building systems capable of supporting eGovernance. This framework was applied for the design and implementation of an Internet-based eVoting platform based on a system-oriented trust and privacy management approach that handles eVoting at a system engineering level.

Our approach, originally appearing in (Antoniou *et al.*, 2007) and (Manolopoulos *et al.*, 2008a), relies on two general methodologies and one cryptographic eVoting specific protocol. The two methodologies are the *layers of trust decomposition* of a system (Konstantinou *et al.*, 2004, Konstantinnou *et al.*, 2005) and the *CORAS*

Figure 4. (a) The distributed architecture of the eVoting system, (b) The EA block

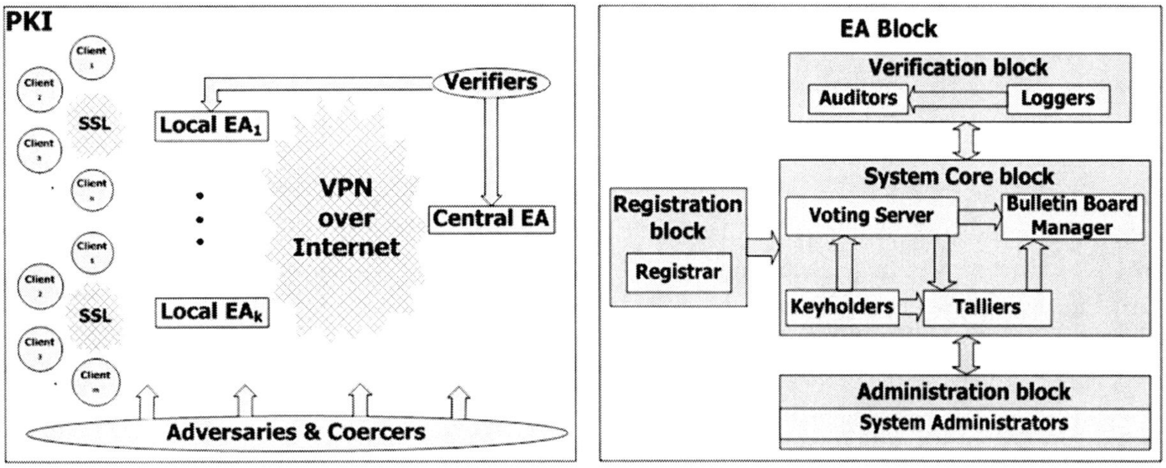

risk assessment framework for security-critical systems (see Stølen at al., 2003). The eVoting protocol is the protocol described by Warren Smith in (Smith, 2005) which is based on the homomorphic properties of the ElGamal encryption function and the hardness of computing the discrete logarithm (see (Lenstra & Lenstra, 1990) for complexity theoretic issues pertaining to the discrete logarithm problem).

The focus is on designing and building the application in a transparent way that produces a sufficient and verifiable security level at each layer, able to establish and maintain trust in all involved agents: technical people, government and the people who will use the system. The goal of the CORAS methodology is to assure that all threats to the system are discovered in time, before the deployment of the system, and to provide sufficient documentation of the system that can be made publicly available. Finally, the cryptographic protocol (any other protocol could be used in its position) assures that all the basic requirements of eVoting are secured, at least in principle. This approach was successfully applied for the design, implementation, and testing of an Internet-based eVoting system that was initially deployed in an actual voting process by engineers-members of the Technical Chamber of Greece (see below for more on this process).

In Figure 4a we see the overall system's architecture. It consists of a number of *local Election Authorities* (local EAs), which control the election process at a local (e.g. municipality) level, a *central Election Authority*, which controls all the local EAs and verifies their operation, a *VPN over the Internet* that handles the communication among the EAs and *SSL* connections of local EAs with *clients*, which are the computers accepting the votes. In the same figure, there also appear the entities that may attempt interference with the system. By taking the worst case scenario we assume their existence and their will to attempt disruption of normal operation.

In Figure 4.b the components of an EA are shown. Each EA implements, at its core, the eVoting protocol described in (Smith, 2005), which has guaranteed strong cryptographic properties. The components of an EA are the following (most of which directly dictated by the protocol): the *registrar*, which is responsible for checking the voter's eligibility through a connection to a database server containing the id's of eligible voters, the *voting server*, which accumulates and verifies the votes sent by the clients over the VPN, the *key holders*, which cooperatively provide the critical vote encryption key, the *tallier*, which sums the votes and provides the election total, the *bulletin board manager*, which makes publicly available proofs that all votes are taken into account unchanged, the *loggers*, which store critical information about the election process, and the *auditors* which use the information stored by the loggers in order to provide publicly verifiable proof of correctness of the election process. Finally, there is the system administration block that is responsible for the configuration, initialization and coordination of all the other blocks.

With regard to the implementation choices, we have adopted the use of as many free and open source libraries as possible. Our choices include the Java programming language, the use of the Bouncy Castle Java crypto library (http://www.bouncycastle.org/), Open VPN (http://openvpn.net/), OpenCA tool for building PKIs (htt://www.openca.org/), pand the use of the PostgreSQL (http://www.postgresql.org/) data base. This ensures that the system's software can be independently audited and verified by any interested third party (government agencies, expert groups, researchers, industry etc.).

In what follows, we will briefly describe the in-field trial of the system in a realistic eVoting scenario (see (Manolopoulos *et al.* 2008b)). The idea was to perform a poll among 200 of the members of a local professional organization (local Sector of the Technical Chamber of Greece). This group was selected mainly due to the fact that it is a well defined group, with easy access to its members (email, address, etc.). What is more, its members, being engineers, are familiar with ICTs and are a good testbed for the first application of such systems. Finally, the Technical Chamber is anyway interested in modernizing its voting processes (e.g. attempts had already been made to automatically scan and tally votes in their last elections for representatives).

The total trial procedure lasted from Monday 3 December 2008, when began the submission of applications for certificate acquisition, until Friday 7 December 2008, when expired the deadline of vote submission.

1. Registration and receipt of an electronic certificate, as means of authentication.

The voters could submit certificate application from Monday 3 to Wednesday 5 December, by accessing the website of Certification Authority. Voters completed a form with their personal data and sent this form to Certification Authority. During the time remaining up to the beginning of vote submission, the administrator of Certification Authority checked the data of submitted applications and created the digital certificates for all the legal voters.

At 6 December before submitting their vote, the voters installed their certificate on the browser of their computer, accessing again the website of Certification Authority.

2. Vote Submission

From 10:00 up to 22:00 of December 6 the voters submitted their votes. In the initial page of system they gave their credentials (username and password). These credentials were automatically produced before the beginning of voting by the system and sent to voters via e-mail.

Voters could vote as many times as they want, but only their most recent vote was counted at tallying phase. They could see their most recent encrypted vote on the Bulletin Board, a web page actually where were published the public data of voting.After voting period expired, the administrator of the system performed the tallying of the votes and published the results.

The trial was considered successful as a whole, both regarding system operation as well as user acceptance.

Participation: Participation percentages were satisfactory and varied for the two phases of the procedure. 37% of the voting population tried to register electronically, and 31% voted. 20% took part in the assessment phase and completed the questionnaire.

System operation: System operation during pilot was satisfactory regarding the proposed distributed architecture, the interconnection of the tools (OpenVPN, OpenCA, and other implementation tools) and the implementation of system components.

During voting procedure some minor problems were reported, which were immediately solved by the help desk. These problems were mainly associated with the certificate application submission and more specifically with user browser settings (Active X controls activation). Another problem during this phase was the incompatibility of the certification tool (OpenCA) with Windows Vista (only 1 problematic case). During vote submission no problems were reported.

System assessment results: The system was assessed by 40 users, 32 of whom used the system up to the end of the procedure.

From the answers it resulted that the participation of the majority (78,1%) of the voters was motivated by personal interest for the electronic voting, while only a small percentage (9,4%) participated because of the subject of voting.

With regard to the system, the majority of voters found the system functional enough or very functional (40,6% and 25% respectively). The instructions provided also contributed greatly to this. There was a no negligible percentage that found the system little or by no means functional (percentage 18,8% and 15,6% respectively). This is probably due to the process of application and acquisition of certificate, which the 49,6% considered complicated and the 9,3% excessively complicated. Nevertheless, 43,8% found the process of certification simple.

This assessment showed that a large percentage of voters found the registration procedure fairly complicated, although they were well familiar with ICT. This is due to the fact that certification was realized with the use of an open source tool simulating a PKI (OpenCA) and not with an existing PKI where the process would be automated. Nevertheless, this remark raises important issues with regard to the target system's user-friendliness, in particular for non-expert users.

Finally, the majority of the voters, taking into consideration the overall experience from the use of the particular system, answered that the electronic voting is easier than the traditional way.

Users were also asked to respond to some questions concerning eVoting in general. It came up that users consider electronic voting easier compared to the traditional way and believe that it will increase the participation in voting procedures. It appears however that there are serious reservations against such systems, since a percentage of 52,5% considers the electronic voting by no means or little secure. This is also confirmed by the answer to the question "Would you vote electronically in national elections?", where the 52,5% answers NO.

With regard to legal/institutional aspects of eVoting, the answers to the question "Which institutional intervention you consider more important for the application of electronic voting?" indicate as more important the specification of new roles, as well as the application of measures of protection against phenomena of mass coercion and vote selling.

Also, the sample considers more important practice for the gradual maturation of systems of eVoting the possibility of electronic submission of vote only from fixed points (i.e. kiosks) and not remotely over Internet.

Although there are examples of countries that have enacted the use of Internet-based voting additionally with the traditional voting, the adoption of kiosk-based voting is considered as a milestone for the smooth migration to systems of remote eVoting.

DISCUSSION AND FURTHER CONSIDERATIONS

eGovernance is a new concept coined to refer to governance procedures which are strongly founded on Information and Communications Technology (ICT). The major goal of eGovernance is to introduce wide sections of society into the governance sphere, paying particular importance to those who are most likely to remain excluded. In other words, eGovernance is a vehicle for bringing, in a convenient and easily accessible manner, good governance practices to the citizens and society as a whole. In this respect, eGovernance is something more than simple automation of governance procedures (e.g. issuing electronically a birth certificate or signing electronically a document). It is all about *bringing* people closer to these procedures using ICT as the main tool.

Following this viewpoint with regard to eGovernance, in this chapter we presented a discussion on our research into *eVoting*. We believe that voting is at the cornerstone of Democracy and possesses a distinguished place among all conceivable governance concepts and processes. Our belief is that, in analogy, eVoting is also at the cornerstone of eGovernance and can lead to considerable enhancement of citizen participation in important, day to day or long term, decisions about their own lives and well being in society.

However, eVoting, being an automated version of the classical voting procedures, must inevitably be founded upon ICT. And these technologies are, inherently, beset with a number of obstacles that hinder wide acceptance from people: lack of education for using ICT, lack of motivation for employing ICT in day to day activities, and, finally, lack of trust towards ICT. In this chapter we focused on the trust component.

Trust in the context of eVoting, in turn, has three major axes: the trust of citizens towards government, the trust of government towards citizens and the trust of government and citizens toward ICT that can enhance eParticipation in the context of eGovernance. Our view is that the difficulty of handling, in a directly applicable fashion, these three components is decreasing, in the given order.

With regard to trust towards the government, there are many difficulties to be overcome that go beyond the realm of engineering sciences and ICT and, thus, we have not touched this issue in the chapter.

In the context of increasing trust towards the citizens from the politicians' side, we have outlined how the emerging ABC technology can be integrated into eParticipation applications, the major one being eVoting, so as to convince politicians about properties of the participating citizen body. Our viewpoint is that ABC technologies will ultimately replace traditional PKI ones in a unified way and into a single *eID token* (see also (Rannenberg *et al.*, 2009) for a general discussion of eIdentity) that all citizens of a country will carry with them. Therefore, we believe that the time is now ripe for efforts that integrate ABC technologies with protocols that are employed for implementing all kinds of e-services in all sectors of citizens' daily lives.

As far as the trust to the ICT component is concerned, there are ways of handling it successfully. In this chapter we discussed our experiences from researching into the eVoting domain as well as from the implementation of an Internet-based eVoting system. Our conclusion is that trust towards ICT is a *multifaceted* concept (i.e. a combination of, at least, engineering, political, and social aspects) that emerges through the harmonic interaction of all main stakeholders: politicians, engineers, and citizens. Politicians can contribute through their support of legislation and policies that encourage the use of ICT in the utmost expression of democracy, i.e. voting procedures, citizens can play a major role by being educated in new technologies and using them through their interaction with the Government and, finally, engineers can produce eVoting systems that are and, at the same time, also appear to the citizens, trustworthy. In our view, all these three stakeholders are inextricably intertwined in the eGovernment fabric. For instance, politicians can educate citizens (e.g. schools, public discussions, organization of open seminars etc.) but citizens, on the other hand, can be more demanding to the politicians and care about being given a more solid education as well as the technological means to interact with the Government. Moreover, citizens can demand from ICT product developers (especially computing and communication devices) to provide details about the security and trust aspects of their products in, both, layman's terms as well as more advanced descriptions. These three groups of stakeholders, as we discussed in this chapter, can contribute to a mutual positive feedback and effort reinforcement in order to reach the maturity level of transforming ICT into a reliable vehicle for enabling eParticipation and inaugurating the eGovernment era. Our findings during the in-field evaluation of the PNYKA eVoting platform demonstrate that there is a long way to go in order to reach this goal (only about half of the participants would vote electronically in a binding election process). An even in countries which attempted to introduce eVoting in their governance procedures, several security breaches and attack incidents demonstrated that the time is not yet ripe to discard good old-fashioned voting procedures.

As a final remark, we would like to point out that despite the difficulties that beset the trust domain concerning the interactions among the state, the citizens, and ICT we believe (drawing, also, on our experiences in the eVoting domain) that the establishment of trust between citizens and ICT can boost trust also along the other two components, that is between from state to citizens and from citizens to the state. Today's technological advances in ICT and ICT security provide the means for establishing this trust. And engineers can act as the link that can help the emergence of trust of all stakeholders towards ICT. Then social and political science can do the more difficult job for trust among the stakeholders themselves!

REFERENCES

Albrecht, S., Kohlrausch, N., Kubicek, H., Lippa, B., Märker, O., Trénel, M., ... Wiedwald, C. (2008). *E-participation – Electronic participation of citizens and the business community in e-government*. Institut für Informationsmanagement Bremen, Study on Behalf of the Federal Ministry of the Interior, Division IT 1 Bremen, January 2008.

Alvarez, R., & Hall, T. E. (2004). *Point click and vote - The future of Internet voting*. Washington, DC: Brookings Institution Press.

Antoniou, A., Korakas, C., Manolopoulos, C., Panagiotaki, A., Sofotassios, D., Spirakis, P., & Stamatiou, Y. C. (2007). A trust-centered approach for building e-voting systems. In M. Wimmer, J. Scholl, & A. Gronlund (Eds.), *6th International Conference on eGovernment (EGOV 2007)* (pp. 366-377). Berlin/Heidelberg, Germany: Springer-Verlag.

Blaze, M., Feigenbaum, J., & Lacy, J. (1996). *Decentralized trust management*. In IEEE Symposium on Security and Privacy (pp. 164-173). Oakland, CA, USA.

Brands, S. (2000). *Rethinking public key infrastructures and digital certificates: Building in privacy*. MIT Press.

Brands, S., Demuynck, L., & De Decker, B. (2007). A practical system for globally revoking the unlinkable pseudonyms of unknown users . In Pieprzyk, J., Ghodosi, H., & Dawson, E. (Eds.), *ACISP 2007* (pp. 400–415). Berlin/Heidelberg, Germany: Springer-Verlag.

Camenisch, J. (2006). Protecting (anonymous) credentials with the trusted computing group's TPM. In S. Fischer-Hübner, K. Rannenberg, L. Yngström & S. Lindskog (Eds.), *International Information Security Conference (SEC 2006)* (pp. 135-147). Springer-Verlag.

Camenisch, J., & Groß, T. (2008). Efficient attributes for anonymous credentials. In P. Syverson, S. Jha & X. Zhang (Eds.), *15th ACM Conference on Computer and Communications Security* (pp. 345-356). New York, NY: ACM.

Camenisch, J., & Lysyanskaya, A. (2001). Efficient non-transferable anonymous multi-show credential system with optional anonymity revocation. In B. Pfitzmann (Ed.), *International Conference on the Theory and Application of Cryptographic Techniques (EUROCRYPT 2001)*, (vol. 2045, pp. 93-118). Springer-Verlag.

Camenisch, J., & Lysyanskaya, A. (2004). Signature schemes and anonymous credentials from bilinear maps. In G. Goos, J. Hartmanis, & J. van Leeuwen (Eds.), *24rd Annual International Cryptology Conference (CRYPTO 2004)* (pp. 56-72). Berlin/Heidelberg, Germany: Springer-Verlag.

Camenisch, J., & Van Herreweghen, E. (2002). Design and implementation of the Idemix anonymous credential system. Research Report RZ 3419, IBM Research Division, June 2002. In V. Atluri (Ed.), *9th ACM Conference on Computer and Communication Security,* (pp. 21-30). New York, NY: ACM Press.

Castells, M. (2001). *The Internet galaxy: Reflections on the Internet, business and society*. New York, NY: Oxford University Press.

Coleman, J. S. (1990). *Foundations of social theory*. Cambridge, MA: The Belknap Press of Harvard University Press.

Ekelin, A. (2007). *The work to make e-participation work*. Blekinge Institute of Technology Doctoral Dissertation Series No. 2007:1. Retrieved from http:// www.bth.se/ fou/ forskinfo.nsf/ 6753b78eb2944e0ac1256608004f0535/ 06c223cbd4e0037dc12572dd004a9ca1/ $file/ Ekelin_diss.pdf

ENISA (European Network and Information Security Agency). (2009). *Privacy features of European e-ID card specifications*. Position paper. Retrieved from www.enisa.europa.eu/ act/ it/ eid/ eid-cards-en

Eschenauer, L., Gligor, V. D., & Baras, J. S. (2002). On trust establishment in mobile ad-hoc networks. In B. Christianson, B. Crispo, J. A. Malcolm & M. Roe (Eds.), *Security Protocols, 10th International Workshop* (pp. 47-66). Springer.

European Commission. (2008). ICT for Governance and Policy Modelling Consultation Workshop. *FP7 Work Programme 2009-2010.* Workshop Report.

Gritzalis, D. A. (Ed.). (2003). *Secure electronic voting* (*Vol. 7*). London, UK: Kluwer Academic Publishers Advances in Information Security Series.

Guha, R., Kumar, R., Raghavan, P., & Tomkins, A. (2004). Propagation of trust and distrust. In *Proc. of 13th ACM International Conference on World Wide Web* (pp. 403-412). New York, NY: ACM Press.

Hubaux, J.-P., Buttyan, L., & Capkun, S. (2001). The quest for security in mobile ad hoc networks. In *Proc. of ACM International Symposium on Mobile ad-hoc networking and computing* (pp. 146-155). New York, NY: ACM Press.

Josang, A. (1996). The right type of trust for distributed systems. In *Proc. of New Security Paradigms Workshop*, (pp. 119-131). New York, NY: ACM Press.

Kamvar, S. D., Schlosser, M. T., & Garcia-Molina, H. (2003). The Eigentrust algorithm for reputation management in p2p networks. In *Proc. 12th International Conference on World Wide Web* (pp. 640-651). New York, NY: ACM Press.

Kim, D. J., Song, Y. I., Braynov, S. B., & Rao, H. R. (2005). A multidimensional trust formation model in B-to-C e-commerce: A conceptual framework and content analyses of academia/ practitioner perspectives. *Decision Support Systems, 40*, 143–165. doi:10.1016/j.dss.2004.01.006

Kim, S. T. (2008). *Converging e-democracy and e-government model toward an evolutionary model of e-governance: The case of South Korea.* Retrieved from http:// www.apdip.net/ projects/ e-government/ capblg/ casestudies/ Korea-Kim.pdf

Konstantinou, E., Liagkou, V., Spirakis, P., Stamatiou, Y., & Yung, M. (2004). Electronic national lotteries. In A. Juels (Ed.), *8th International Conference on Financial Cryptography* (pp.147-163). Berlin/Heidelberg, Germany: Springer.

Konstantinou, E., Liagkou, V., Spirakis, P., Stamatiou, Y., & Yung, M. (2005). Trust engineering: From requirements to system design and maintenance – A working national lottery system experience. In J. Zhou, J. Lopez, R. H. Deng, & F. Bao, (Eds.), *8th International Conference on Information Security* (pp.44-58). Berlin/Heidelberg, Germany: Springer.

Lenstra, A. K., & Lenstra, H. W. J. R. (1990). Algorithms in number theory . In van Leeuwen, J. (Ed.), *Handbook of theoretical computer science* (*Vol. A*, pp. 673–715). Amsterdam, The Netherlands: North-Holland.

Luhmann, N. (1988). Familiarity, confidence, trust: Problems and alternatives . In Gambetta, D. (Ed.), *Trust: Making and breaking cooperative relations* (pp. 94–107). Oxford, UK: Basil Blackwell.

Manolopoulos, C., Nakou, P., Panagiotaki, A., Sofotassios, D., Spirakis, P., & Stamatiou, Y. C. (2008b). A step-wise refinement approach for enhancing e-voting acceptance. In T. Janowski, & T. Pardo (Eds.), *2nd International Conference on Theory and Practice of Electronic Governance (ICEGOV 2008),* (pp. 275-280). ACM Press.

Manolopoulos, C., Panagiotaki, A., Sofotassios, D., Spirakis, P., &. Stamatiou, Y. C. (2008a). Experiences and benefits from the application of a formal risk assessment framework in the e-voting domain. In E. Ferro, H. J. Scholl, & M. Wimmer (Eds.), *7th International Conference on Electronic Government (EGOV 2008)* (pp. 205-212). Trauner Verlag.

Mercuri, R. (2007). *Rebecca Mercuri's statement on electronic voting*. Retrieved from http:// www. notablesoftware.com/ RMstatement.html

Millard, J. (2007). *E-governance and e-participation: Lessons from Europe in promoting inclusion and empowerment.* Report of the Ad Hoc Expert Group Meeting, E-Participation and E-Government: Understanding the Present and Creating the Future (pp. 91-113). Retrieved from http:// unpan1.un.org/ intradoc/ groups/ public/ documents/ un/ unpan026527.pdf

Millward, P. (2003). The grey digital divide: Perception, exclusion and barriers of access to the Internet for older people. *First Monday, 8*(7).

Neumann, P. G. (2004). The problems and potentials of voting systems. *Communications of the ACM, Special Issue on eVoting, 47*(10).

Panopoulou, E., Tambouris, E., & Tarabanis, K. (2009). *European e-participation: Study and supply of services on the development of e-participation in the EU.* E-Participation good practice cases, Deliverable D4.2b Ver. 2. Retrieved from www.european-eparticipation.eu

Rannenberg, K., Royer, D., & Deuker, A. (2009). *The future of identity in the information society – Challenges and opportunities*. Heidelberg, Germany: Springer. doi:10.1007/978-3-642-01820-6

Richards, M. C. (2003). *AES: The making of a new encryption standard.* SANS (SysAdmin, Audit, Network, Security) Institute. Retrieved from http:// www.sans.org/ reading_room/ whitepapers/ vpns/ aes-making-encryption-standard_740

Richardson, M., Agrawal, R., & Domingos, P. (2003). Trust management for the Semantic Web. In *Proc. of 2nd International Semantic Web Conference* (pp. 351-368).

Riedl, R. (2004). *Rethinking trust and confidence in European e-government.* Retrieved from http:// www.ifi.uzh.ch/ egov/ Trust_v1.0.pdf

Smith, W. D. (2005). *Cryptography meets voting.* Retrieved from http:// www.math.temple.edu/ ~wds/ homepage/ cryptovot.pdf

OASIS Standard. (2007). *EML process and data requirements*, ver. 5.0.

Stølen, K., den Braber, F., Dimitrakos, T., Fredriksen, R., Gran, B. A., & Houmb, S.-H. … Aagedal, J. Ø. (2003). Model-based risk assessment in a component-based software engineering process: The CORAS approach to identify security risks. In F. Barbier (Ed.), *Business component-based software engineering* (pp.189-207). Kluwer Academic Publishers.

Tassabehji, R., & Elliman, T. (2006). Generating citizen trust in e-government using a trust verification agent: a research note. In Z. Irani, O. D. Sarikas, J. Llopis, R. Gonzalez, & J. Gasco (Eds.), *European and Mediterranean Conference on Information Systems (EMCIS 2006).*

Theodorakopoulos, G., & Baras, J. S. (2004). Trust evaluation in ad-hoc networks. In M. Jakobsson, & A. Perrig (Eds.), *ACM Workshop on Wireless Security* (pp. 1-10). Philadelphia, PA: ACM Press.

Van Acker, B. (2004). Remote e-voting and coersion: A risk assessment model and solutions . In Prosser, A., & Krimmer, R. (Eds.), *Electronic voting in Europe - Technology, law, politics and society* (pp. 53–62). Bregenz, Austria: GI-Editions.

X.509. (2005). *Information Technology - Open systems interconnection – The directory: Public-key and attribute certificate frameworks*. Retrieved from http:// www.itu.int/ rec/ T-REC-X.509/ en

KEY TERMS AND DEFINITIONS

Attribute-Based Credentials: A cryptographic technology for authenticating individuals based on attributes that prove certain characteristics about them in a secure way.

eGovernment: ICT infrastructure and services for the support of a convenient and secure interaction between government and citizens (G2C – government to citizens), government and businesses (G2B –government to business enterprises) and between governments (G2G – inter-agency relationship).

eParticipation: ICT-supported participation in procedures employed in government and governance.

eVoting: ICT infrastructure and a set of rules for the support of voting procedures ranging from polling to national binding elections.

Open Source Software: Software for which the source code is made publicly available at no cost under a "no profit" license scheme. In this way, other users obtain the opportunity to exploit, modify and improve the software.

Privacy: The state of affairs where individuals can interact in seclusion, without interference from other unwanted individuals.

Trust: Trust of a party A in a party B for a service X is the measurable belief of A in that B will behave dependably for a specified period within a specified context.

Chapter 8
Social Media-Based Communities of Practice for Education in Citizenship and Sustainability

Dimitra Florou
University of Athens, Greece

Dimitris Gouscos
University of Athens, Greece

ABSTRACT

In this chapter we support the view that communities of practice (CoPs) with the support of social media can serve the education for citizenship and sustainability, with a clear benefit on citizens' culture towards future public reforms. This has led to the development and implementation of the policy for sustainability, which is a European and national strategic objective.

The chapter begins with a small analysis of public sector reform towards sustainability and the presentation of the basic principles of education for sustainability and citizenship (ESDC) and the model of CoPs and the social media that facilitate their use. It focuses on the analysis of the three models of belonging -engagement, imagination, alignment- in the application of CoPs for ESDC. In combination with this analysis we demonstrate that CoPs can be supported by social media.

Finally the chapter reinforces the view that the development of such communities in education offers on the long run the ability to remodel the public sphere, strengthen public consultation, promote proposals from the citizens, promote the policy of sustainability, and finally, the efficient use of new technologies, both in society and education.

DOI: 10.4018/978-1-60960-839-2.ch008

INTRODUCTION

Going through the first decade of the new millennium more and more problems appear in social, economic and environmental terms. The extended and multifaceted crisis that takes place in modern societies is a result of social inequality and conflict, increasing scarcity of natural resources and generally in situations that lead to loss of social, economic and ecological stability.

Addressing these issues is the great challenge of the new millennium and demonstrates the need to encourage active citizenship and greater social cohesion (European Commission 2000) to address social and economic change in the perspective of a democratic and sustainable world. At the same time highlight the need for public sector reform of the state. As it is phrased in the 1st Conference of European Ministers responsible for social cohesion (26-27 February 2009, Moscow, Russia) "*Social cohesion is an essential condition for democratic security and sustainable development because divided and unequal societies are not only unjust, but also unstable in the long term*". (Davis, 2009)

An important factor in achieving these goals is the education because *"Education, including formal education, public awareness and training should be recognized as a process by which human beings and societies can reach their fullest potential." (Agenda 21, 36.3.)*

It also emphasizes on the fact that education (formal) is important when it's turned towards education for sustainability and should be a priority for many countries in the world and combined with the overall efforts to combat poverty and promote social and economic development.

In this context two interlocking and interactive fields of educational emerge: education for citizenship and education for sustainability.

At the same time questions rise, such as: what is the content of such education, what are the critical characteristics of people that will activate them and lead them to involvement and action for sustainability, what knowledge, skills and values must be cultivated, what strategies and what tools would help in this direction?

In any case, the introduction of these fields in formal education requires more flexible curricula and adapting to new realities in terms of content and methodology because *"... sustainable development calls for additional and different processes than those traditionally thought of in education... The quest for sustainability demands new approaches to involve people, rather than convey just a body of knowledge" (Fien & Tilbury &., 2002, p.1 -12).*

Modern democratic societies need active, informed and responsible citizens who are willing and able to take responsibility for their communities and contribute to social and political - economic processes for sustainability.

PUBLIC SECTOR REFORM TOWARDS SUSTAINABILITY

During the last decade of the 20th century, due to the focus of public management reform programs and research on New Public Management (NPM) the public sector reforms have been neglected. (Elke Löffler & Colin Talbot, 2004,). As Talbot argues that there are "four paradoxical models that underpin the NPM: let politicians decide, let managers manage, let customers choose, let stakeholders participate" and since "tensions" between them "will not go away" he believes that "the only real issue is how best manage these contradictions " (Talbot, 2004p. 17).

Public sector has been driven to a different direction to the managerial reforms of the 1980s and 1990s, by new challenges (Bovaird and Löffler, 2002, Bovaird, Tony and Löffler, Elke 2002):

- Political pressure from issues, such as crime and vandalism, terrorism, asylum, economic deprivation, the problem of pensions and quality of life for an ageing population, etc.

- The use of ICT not only in relation to service delivery but also in dealing with public policy issues in general
- Pressure from the media as there is a rapid proliferation of private press, radio and television channels and people have access to much greater information from the Internet
- The great increase of globalization which makes governments an important economic player but which also exposes them to a volatile global economy
- The development of a differentiated civil society, in which many (very vocal, and usually well educated) people are using the new media to engage in debates on 'quality of life' issues and national public policy issues, while others are increasingly isolated by the digital divide.

The lack of balance between the power of the market on the one hand and the institutions of governance on the other has as a result a "global governance gap". A substantial, democratic, public sector reform is not just administrative measures, but is terms and conditions for quality development, sustainability and social consistency, democratic deepening and civil participation as well. So far, the answer to every governance challenge, has been proved to be inadequate in all levels –national, European or international, private or public (European Commission, 2002). A reform towards sustainability requires the development of human potential, which is the new generation, which will be the incubator of new, innovative and pioneering ideas and proposals. In addition, it must promote a positive model of proper social behavior, individual and social action and civic responsibility by participating in the endless process of civilizing and cultivating individual and collective values and moral attitudes and behaviors. With the use of ICT mechanisms for individual improvement, education and training can be created; new skills can be promoted, addicting people to the methods and the value of teamwork and joint formulation of ideas, programs and implementation projects.

EDUCATION FOR CITIZENSHIP AND SUSTAINABILITY

Citizenship is a concept that has many meanings. It indicates a political and legal position: each person belongs to a state with rights and obligations that depend on the laws of this state (Karakatsanis, D., 2004). In this dimension it relates to the nationality and the exercise of political rights.

It also states a psychological state that refers to the conduct and attitude of the individual against social and political phenomena at local, regional and international levels (Audrey Osler & Hugh Starkey, 2005). The term is also used to include participation in public life and affairs – meaning the behavior and actions of a citizen, what is called an active citizen. As a result citizenship covers a wide range of participatory activities - from voting in elections and standing for political office, interest in politics and current affairs to a voluntary action and philanthropy. Citizenship in modern society is directly linked to democracy where the people enjoy the personal, social and political freedom or autonomy.

In the text of the European Commission "Towards a European dimension of education and active citizenship" as well as in the text "Democratic citizenship" there is a more holistic approach to citizenship while it is pointed out the enlargement of elements that constitute the citizenship with the rights referring to different values, identities and traditions (cultural rights). The enlargement of the concept is linked to the overcoming of the limitations of the nation-state and the association of citizenship with society (European Commission, 2000 Karen OShea, 2003) and the global community now talking about a cosmopolitan citizenship (Audrey Osler & Hugh Starkey, 2005).

We are now *"members of a society that goes beyond the borders of the nation... so the term citizenship seems to create a frame of life excessively wide and simultaneously very limited" (Canivez, P., 2000:17).*

Citizenship is directly related to the multiple roles and positions of people in society as workers, consumers, etc. as well as with the views of each individual. These roles are learned through the process of political socialization. An important political institution of socialization is the school through the school curriculum, teachers and school life itself. In the Final Declaration of the Conference of European Ministers of Education (Istanbul, May 2007), citizenship is referred as one of the five basic competencies needed to promote democracy and social cohesion.

Several models have been developed for the education for citizenship. As reported by Scott and Lawson (2002,p1) in these models key elements are: *"knowledge (cf. Usher 1996); action (cf. Habermas 1994); community (cf. Etzioni 1995); rights and responsibilities (cf. Giddens 1994); public and private morality (cf. Beck 1998); inclusivity (cf. Arnot 1997; Lister 1997); and locality (cf. Gellner 1983; Wringe 1999; Cogan and Derricott 2000)».*

The concept of education for citizenship consists of several components, because democratic societies need citizens who are:

- aware of their rights and responsibilities as citizens;
- informed about the social and political world;
- concerned about the welfare of others;
- articulate in their opinions and arguments;
- capable of having an influence on the world;
- active in their communities;
- responsible in how they act as citizens. (Bîrzea, C. et al., 2005,., p. 25)

Its features with Cogan and Derriccott (1998,p 2) are:

- *"A sense of identity*
- *The enjoyment of certain rights*
- *The fulfilment of corresponding obligations*
- *A degree of interest and involvement in public affairs*
- *An acceptance of societal values".*

The education for citizenship *« [..]also involves the dimensions of knowledge and understanding, skills, attitudes and values. These dimensions are brought together through teaching and learning approaches, which have the primary goal of shaping and changing the attitudes and behaviour of young people through their adult lives." (D Kerr, 2003, p.7-8)*

In these directions, as reflected in the curricula for citizenship and through literature (Peter Brett & al, 2009) the education for citizenship concerns:

- *Knowledge and understanding*: of issues such as laws and rules of the democratic process, media, human rights, diversity, money and economy, sustainable development, the world as a global community, and concepts such as democracy, justice, equality, freedom, authority of the state of justice.
- *Skills and competencies*: critical thinking, information analysis, expression of views, participation in discussions and debates, negotiating conflict resolution and participation in community activities
- *Attitudes and values*: respect for justice, democracy and the state of justice, openness, tolerance, courage to defend a viewpoint and a willingness to listen and solidarity.

An important element for the citizenship education is the active participation in and for a democratic society. According to CRELL research on "Active Citizenship for Democracy" active citizenship is defined as *"participation in civil society, community and or political life, characterised by mutual respect and non-violence and in accordance with human rights and democracy" (CRELL, Maria HelenaSalema, 2006, p4)*

Encouragement of social participation aims to develop active citizens who not only participate in the decisions but do so consciously, with full knowledge of the process and parameters that will help them make decisions based on social criticism aiming at nothing less than to create democratic, inclusive and sustainable communities. In the survey mentioned above, education and training for active citizenship is defined as:

"Appropriate and effective formal, non-formal and informal learning opportunities at any stage of the life cycle that facilitate or encourage active citizenship." (CRELL, Maria Helena Salema, 2006, p5)

Through this educational process, young people will become more aware, learn, understand and realize (Denis Lewton, & al., 2000)

- The contemporary local and global issues,
- The rights and responsibilities of individuals and groups in democratic societies,
- The ability of individuals and groups to intervene and change for the better social and environmental conditions,
- The fights they should fight to promote issues such as social justice and sustainable development,
- The reasons, which are mainly due to economic factors and lead to social conflict,
- The barriers created by stereotypes and prejudices for the right of citizenship, self-concept and self-determination of people
- The interdependence of one another and the effects of globalization in modern societies.

It should be noted that an important goal in education for citizenship is sustainability in the sense that there must be a balance between social, environmental and economic development, and this can be achieved *"through increased understanding of the concept of development and the skills needed to work with others in order to build a sustainable future"*(Karen OShea, 2003, p 28).

Sustainability is a multidimensional concept without a commonly accepted definition. The term was first used in the late 80's and explains the harmonious coexistence with our environment. In the 1987 edition of the Our Common Future by the World Commission on Environment and Development the first mention the term in official documents takes place. The Brundtland Commission defines sustainable development as *"development that meets the needs of the present without compromising the ability of future generations to meet their own needs."(World Commission on Environment and Development,, 1987, p 43.).*

In the publication Caring for the Earth: A Strategy for Sustainable Living, sustainable development is defined as a process that aims at "improving the quality of human life while living within the carrying capacity of supporting ecosystems." (IUCN / UNEP / WWF, 1991, p 10.)

Education is an important factor in achieving the goals of sustainability and is present in all the areas it covers. As noted in (Agenda 21, chapter 36.3).

"Education is critical for achieving environmental and ethical awareness, values and attitudes, skills and behavior consistent with sustainable development and for effective public participation in decision-making. Both formal and non-formal education is indispensable to changing people's attitudes so that they have the capacity to assess and address their sustainable development concerns."

At the World Summit in Johannesburg the integration of ESD in all levels of the educational systems was supported.

Given that sustainable development involves three interdependent systems: society, economy, environment, the education for sustainability goes beyond the limits of awareness and environmental protection. Issues emerge concerning social justice, human rights, democracy (Fien & Tilbury, 2002, p 9), which are issues of strong social and political nature. ESD is an innovation in education which reverses its traditional role. Students acquire an active role in the learning content, they research and are introduced to another way of thinking and acting and of course participate in shaping decisions (Tilbury, D. and Wortman, D. 2004).

Sustainability and therefore the education for it concern the perceptions of the world and the forms of social and personal practices that lead to:

- Ethical, strengthened and integrated individuals
- Communities which are based on cooperation, tolerance and justice
- Social systems and institutions that are inclusive, transparent and equitable
- Environmental practices that develop and support biodiversity and life through ecological processesethical, empowered and personally fulfilled individuals

In order for the process of social and economic change to be successful people need to acquire communication and cooperation skills that will help their social life and practice of sustainability. It also seeks the development and cultivation of values such as solidarity, which can ensure fundamental rights such as freedom, equality and environmental sustainability. It coexists with values such as autonomy and responsibility, tolerance and democracy (The Earth Charter, 2002, UNESCO, 2006).

In the cognitive level it aims at acquiring the knowledge and understanding of social institutions and their role in change and development, knowledge of natural resources and their weakening, the effects of human activity on it and the social and political decisions, the limits and possibilities of economic development and impact on society and the environment (UNESCO, 2009). It deals with issues such as International cooperation, combating poverty, conservation and management of resources, problems of specific groups and promotes the opening of the school community and developing partnerships with NGOs and organizations.

Through this process citizens become forces of social change and acquire the ability to ensure sustainable and equitable use of natural resources in democratic societies.

From all of the above we notice that both areas have common themes of education. Therefore we can talk about «Education for Sustainability and Ecological Citizenship» (Huckle, J. 2001) A review of UNESCO and the literature reveal that ESD / EC (Fien 1993) is:

- Interdisciplinary, systematic and holistic
- Oriented towards the development:
    - critical thinking and problem solving
    - participation in decision-making
    - cooperation
- Uses multiple methods
- Seeks to move from local to global

In this type of education it is necessary to adopt modern methods of experimental learning through which students act (learning by doing), interact, approach each issue with critical thinking, collaborate and participate. Education for citizenship and sustainability requires a review of teaching approaches in order to encourage skills such as (UNESCO, 2006):

- creative and critical thinking,
- oral and written communication,
- cooperation,
- dealing with conflicts,
- decision making
- problem solving and planning.

COMMUNITIES OF PRACTICE AND SOCIAL MEDIA

According to J. Lave & Et. Wenger, (1991), learning is based on the interaction of social and physical environment in which people act, meaning that it is a function of the business, social and physical environment and cultural data. Because the education is based on social structure it becomes a process and a product of participating in communities.

The significance of the term community "depends upon the period and circumstances its used" (Herbrecther et al, 2006, p. 10)

Explained by Delanty (2003 p. 44-46) "*According to Turner community is best understood as communitas to distinguish a particular kind of social relationship that exists in all kinds of society and which is not reducible to community in the sense of a fixed and spatially specific grouping [...] But has a symbolic character in the sense of creating powerful links between members of a society or social group*".

The concept of community in its evolution is determined by "locality" or surpassing local definitions it concerns the relationships between people, it concerns building elements or has imaginary, symbolic dimensions. In any case, "*the term community is a strong everyday sense in relation to which people understand their lives and understand the place and environment in which they live*" (Jenkins, 2007, p 171). Throughout our life we participate in various communities that create boundaries and are segregated from other communities. The members of a community are bound together by a sense of identity, after becoming members of the community it's not easy to leave, they share common values, accept and follow the same behavior towards other members and towards non-members, they develop a common language (Tsaousis, D., 1997, p. 18-31).

Communities of practice are *"groups of people who share a concern, a set of problems, or a passion about a topic, and who deepen their knowledge and expertise in this area by interacting on an ongoing basis"* (Wenger E, McDermott RA, Snyder W, 2002, p 4).

A brief definition is given by Kimble which is based on the environment of development of communities, because communities of practice *"provide an environment for people to develop knowledge through interaction with others within an atmosphere where knowledge is created, maintained and enhanced"* (Laister & Koubek 2001)

Wenger identifies the key elements of communities of practice (Wenger, 2000,)

1. The domain: commitment to the thematic field
2. The community: The members participate in joint activities and discussions, help each other and exchange information.
3. The practice: The members develop a shared repertoire of resources: experiences, stories, tools, and ways of solving problems.

The components needed to describe the social participation as a learning process, as the states Wegner, are: meaning, practice, community and identity (see Figure 1).

Three interrelated dimensions are the key features of the practice "*as a source of community coherence*" (Wenger, E, 1998,p 73)

- *Mutual engagement*: which refers to relations among individuals, interactive relationship that is developed between individuals and leads to the creation of common meanings or resolution of problems
- *A joint enterprise*: is the process of achieving the objectives, to "become an integral part of the practice" (Wenger, E,1998, p78)
- *A shared repertoire*: refers to the common resources produced or used in the community to negotiate meanings and to facilitate learning, combines reificative and participating aspects (Wenger, E,1998,p83)

Figure 1. Components needed to describe social participation as a learning process, as proposed by Wegner (1998, p.5)

The elements that distinguish a community from other communities of practice are the purpose, the attributes of the members, the bond and the duration.

A community of practice doesn't include only the technical knowledge or skill associated with the realization of a project, but also the number of relationships developed over time within the community and with other communities (Lave & Wenger, 1991). *"A community implies an experience of togetherness that extends through time and space. The continuity of togetherness is what creates the community but it is experienced by members in a rhythm of specific activities located in time and space."*(Wenger et al, 2005, p 2)

The members involved in joint activities and discussions, help each other, exchange information and build relationships that allow them to learn from each other (Wenger, 1998). The organization around a specific theme area and its practice provides a sense of common action and identity to the members.

Community interaction and negotiation of information in daily practice is shaped by the discussions and exchange of experiences. The new members arrive in the group and have access to existing members and information and learn by

Table 1. Elements distinguishing communities of practices from other social structures (Wenger, & Snyder, 2000)

	What's the purpose?	Who belongs?	What holds it together?	How long does it last?
Community of practice	To develop members' capabilities; to build and exchange knowledge	Members who select themselves	Passion, commitment, and identification with the group's expertise	As long as there is an interest in maintaining the group
Formal work group	To deliver a product or service	Everyone who reports to the group's manager	Job requirements and common goals	Until the next reorganization
Project team	To accomplish a task	Employees assigned by senior management	The project's milestones and goals	Until the project has been completed
Informal network	To collect and pass on business information	Friends and business acquaintances	Mutual needs	As long as people have a reason to connect

observing them work, so they acquire knowledge through the acquisition of experience from their participation in the community. As the student moves from the periphery of the community of practice to its core, he becomes more active through the "legitimate peripheral participation" (Lave & Wenger, 1991) which is a social process during which people learn by approaching full participation in a socio-cultural practice.

The circle of life of a community of practice is determined by the value that the members consider the community to have, and not by an organized schedule. Such a community isn't created with the beginning of a scheduled task or disappears with the end of it. Its creation requires some time and it can continue existing after the end of work.

The development and survival of CoPs is based on common visions and principles, on planning with the involvement of interested people, on collaborative work on the development of identity.

Communities of practice can be applied in:

- Organizations
- Education
- Government
- Companies

In education tentative steps have been made as highlighted by Wenger:

"Schools have been a bit slower at adopting the concept of communities of practice because sharing knowledge is already their main activity and adopting communities of practice as a basic organizing principle implies a deeper rethinking of their structure. (Wenger, 2001, p 4)

Important characteristic of Communities of practice is that they may arise from or be supported by social media because of interactivity of the community in these because we use them in order to work together, share experiences, opinions or to solve problems.

The social media have become an essential element of the culture of the new generation. Very often through these it forms a social and political consciousness and behaviour because they function as a latent and a body of shared political socialization.

The new tools were developed with Web 2.0 and many of them are free and accessible by everyone. Shirky, defines social software as *"software that supports group interaction"* (Shirky 2003).

He suggests three defining characteristics of social software:

- Support for conversational interaction, between individual or groups, real-time or asynchronous (commenting on posts).
- Support for social feedback, leading to digital reputation.
- Support for social networks in order to digitally express the human relationships and create new ones.

In Wenger's (2005, p 1) opinion the issue for the communities of practice is the use of tools for the support of the community because the tools change, evolve, but *"The close, voluntary collaboration in communities enables their members to invent and share new uses for all of the technologies at their disposal—they are a vector for the dissemination of technology. [..] As communities of practice around the globe appropriate technology in new ways to serve their purposes, the technologies becoming available to them are also evolving. So is our understanding of the affordances and community uses of those technologies."*

As seen in Figure 2 the tools used to support the communities support social interaction, facilitate the production and sharing of equipment and tools that have been created or collected and strengthen community ties.

The structure and operation of communities of practice is facilitated by the basic characteristics of social media as they allow the rapid creation

Figure 2. Tools used to support communities (Wenger et al, 2005)

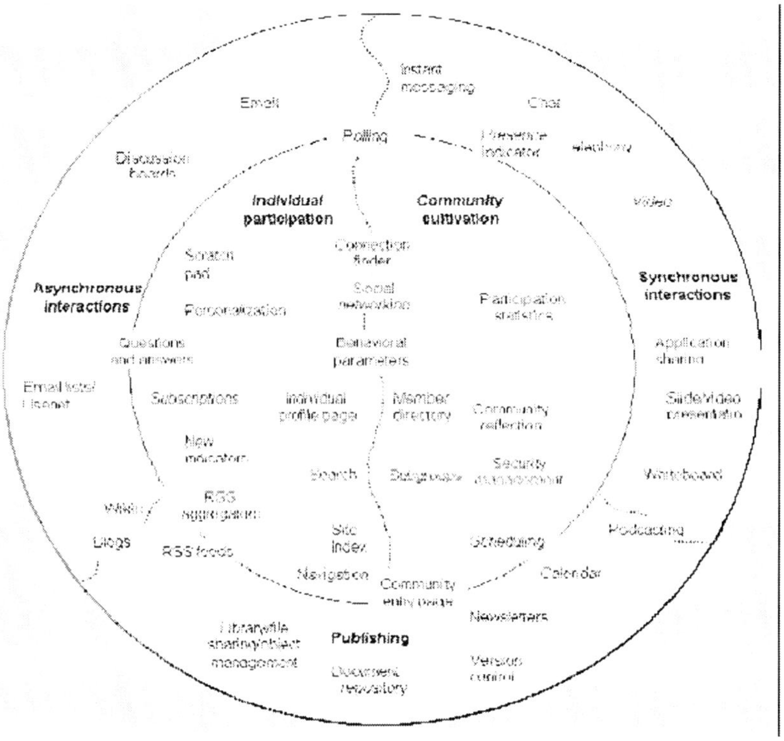

of communities whose members communicate effectively on specific issues, encourage participation and contribution from anyone that is interested, ensure openness by voting, sending relevant content (Feedback), making comments and generally the flow of information, promote conversation and create consistency, gathering and sharing resources, collecting and indexing of information.

Good Practices

The *UN Development Group* (UNDG, http://www.undg.org/index.cfm?P=2) unites the 32 UN funds, programmes, agencies, departments, and offices that play a role in development. It was first established in 1997 in order to co-ordinate the UN development activities and connect the field with the headquarters. Knowledge networks subsequently became institutionalised in order to support countries seeking to attain internationally agreed development goals, people from different regions have become part of flexible communities based on common professional interests, in order to learn from each other, share experiences, bond and acquire a common identity. Besides the electronic network they are supported by face to face meetings.

eTwinning (www.etwinning.net) is a European action of the Life Learning Program, through which schools in different European countries, using tools of Information and Communication Technologies (ICT) cooperate in order to obtain educational, social and cultural benefits. eTwinning is part of Comenius, the EU program for schools. Its goal is to teach students to accept different social and cultural elements while imparting skills in ICT. eTwinning is supported by the Central Support Service (CSS), and a network of National Support Services (NSS). The fraternization is designed in order to provide a very flexible approach to the collaboration between schools and presents a special structure on the level of support offered to teachers. The communication is in English. Students collaborate with schools abroad, on a project and the outcome of their work is brought to the electronic platform of the program. This platform is closed and access is granted only to those registered in eTwinning.

COMMUNITIES OF PRACTICE FOR EDUCATION IN CITIZENSHIP AND SUSTAINABILITY

The main conclusion of the research is the need to develop active citizenship and the important role of education has in this process. Nevertheless, the international analysis of research conducted by the International Association for the evaluation of Educational Achievement for «Civic Education Study» showed that *"education does not produce politically active citizens as it is a need expressed by their respective societies" (Kontogianopoulou-Polidoridi , 2005,p 35).*

An important challenge is the development of methods and teaching techniques - both in formal and informal education-which will lead to achieving the goals of ES/EC. Important feature in such an education is the need to introduce innovative and varied methods.

A critical issue is the effective use of ICT in education. The study of the IEA SITES 2006 of pedagogy and ICT use in schools (IEA 2006) during which it was investigated whether pedagogical practices using ICT promote development skills that are required in the 21st century has shown that:

- The impact of ICT use for students depend greatly on the teaching approaches adopted
- The greatest increase in skills for the 21st Century reported cases used student-centered approaches which provided feedback to students

An innovation - in our opinion-for ESD / C is the creation of CoP's with the support of ICT-social media.

The ESD / C through communities of practice with the support of social media could be a realistic program which would balance reform and maintenance, central and local direction, teacher and student empowerment. Thus, we believe that the development of autonomous and collective skills is promoted; "civil society" is strengthened in order to develop the meshes of the self-regulatory social institutions.

These communities starting from the natural school environment can be developed with the use of social media (blogs, wikis). In this way, ICT are not just tools but aquire a sociocultural dimension, they are used as "mediators" for the development of a social practice that is meaningful to the lives of students.

Moreover, the boundary of this community can be a classroom, a school or evolve to a distribute CoP (*Wenger* &al, 2002, p 25) from the moment it's developed at national level it is not easy to ensure face to face meetings and interactions as its primary vehicle for connecting members.

In order to legitimize the community as a place for sharing and creating knowledge, teachers must involve. The role, however, of the teacher is changing to that of a partner, assistant participant in the process. He is the person who originally organized, who collects and organizes information in order to document practices, encourages, keeps the pace, is a mediator or facilitator and transfers responsibilities to the students.

Although the knowledge which is acquired within communities can't be planned in advance, it can be facilitated. In this context, a design must support three models of belonging (*Wenger,* 1998,p 237) through which we participate in social learning system, which in the field of communities of practice in education are:

- Educational engagement
- Educational imagination
- Educational alignment

Educational Engagement

Finn suggests (1989) two main components of engagement—a behavioural component, "participation" and a psychological component, "identification." (Finn, 1989, p,117-142)

Engagement does not mean uniformity, it is more a result of differences that create the conditions for negotiation of meanings and through this relationships between people are developed. This means active participation, development of relationships and mutuality. Through their participation stereotypes and prejudices are lifted. When, for example, children of different ethnicities or gender work together to develop a project (for example a game for the Environment) they work towards a common goal and do not care about other differences, in contrast they can exploit the creative diversity. Young people create and recognize identities. The lack of identity may provide fertile ground for resentment and anger and create favourable conditions for the exploitation and growth of ethnic and religious issues. To achieve mutuality in education we need activities that require mutual engagement, challenges and responsibilities» based on students' knowledge but also the encouragement for expansion and continuity to develop shared practices. " The motivation of members of society to acknowledge mutuality, to deliberate with others and to search for shared understanding is more likely to succeed if they regard each other as citizens with shared responsibility for making the communities in which they are to live. (Ranson, 2000, p 4)

Educational Imagination

Wegner considers imagination to be a procedure which launches from our personal experiences and during which we create images of the world and see connections through time and space.

This process is very important for EDSC «We must imaginatively develop and apply the vision of a sustainable way of life locally, nationally, regionally and globally» (Earth Charter Commission 2000, *p.4*). It is prerequisite to move on to the development of a sustainable society, to create for ourselves a realistic, compelling and engaging vision of the future that can simply be told and this constitutes motivation for the adoption of practical ways to participate in creating that future in our daily lives» (Elgin, 1991, p. 77)

Concepts such as "sustainability" or "political participation", "equality" and "tolerance", are elements of a future, visionary society. This visualization "encourages us to take responsibility for actions and decisions, to think ahead and to participate in processes of social innovation, recovery and renewal». (Steven Slaughter cited in Tilbury & Wortman 2004,p 26)

Wegner (Wegner,1998, p272) defines three aspects of imagination:

- *Oriented:* it places us in time and space. «it is about identity formation as an expanding image of the world"
- *Reflection:* "is about looking at ourselves and our situations with new eyes"
- *Exploration:* "not accepting things the way they are"

These features constitute critical elements in Dewey's definition of reflective thinking which is specified as an active, persistent, and careful consideration of any belief or supposed form of knowledge in the light of the grounds that support it and the further conclusions to which it tends' (Dewey, 1933, p 118). With this type of thinking, a person, after specifying his/her personal beliefs, information and lived experience in general, he/she distances himself/herself from them and examines the real and logical data that support and interpret concepts, information, reasoning, phenomena, and searches for strong ways of looking into things from a different angle, reviews the experimental knowledge and arranges future energies.

Education for sustainable development must explore the economic, political and social implications of sustainability by encouraging learners to reflect critically on their own areas of the world, to identify non-viable elements in their own lives and to explore the tensions among conflicting aims. (UNESCO, 2002, p.12 4)

This procedure of thinking, during which cases will be examined and critically evaluated, is part of a decision process. One of the fundamental prerequisites for the achievement of sustainable development is broad public participation in decision-making.(*'Agenda 21' Section 23.2)*

In ESD/C, through critical thinking previous conceptions are reconsidered and hidden social structures, established authorities (government, media), the power of companies or non-governmental organisations involved in these issues, are clarified, discovered and recognised. Students discover, individually or collectively their power in shaping their lives.

Educational Alignment

In communities, according to Wegner, opportunities for interaction with other communities, for multi-membership and institutional participation must be offered and the styles and discourses of broader constellations in which they belong should be detected. In ESD/C students-members of the community, in their effort for definition and finding alternative ways of approaching things, turn to those who they believe to be better informed, less prejudiced and more logical in their critical evaluation of facts. Furthermore, in their effort to gain new experiences, to evaluate new information and not to accept things as they seem to be but to understand them as they truly are contacted with members outside of the school environment, they get involved in social practices so that they can see the real process and acquire the new living experience. This way, school opens up and connects with the wider community and students develop actions with the "peripheral participation" in other communities. As John Annette points out, "community-based learning or active learning in the community [...] encourages civic participation as well as the development of civic virtues and political knowledge" (John Annette, 2000, p 78). The experiences of other communities are transferred inside the community, are evaluated and some of them altered or adopted. An education of this kind is a process of introduction in some social practices, in which people, words, beliefs, actions, tools, values, foretypes, objectives and aims take part and from which we realize the abilities required to adopt a particular role and to play this role as satisfactorily as possible. «People are not unaware of the social and environmental problems they face, and more often than not, they have learned quite a lot about them from the media, scientists, governments and daily experience. Consequently, there is a need to move beyond awareness to engage people critically and creatively in their own communities, planning and engaging for action. » (UNESCO, 2002, *p. 38)*

Weblogs

Students' familiarity with blogs in addition to the easy learning of them as well as wikis, make them efficient social software for supporting communities of practice in education. Their use can assure elements such as:

- *Interacting:* To discuss issues, agree and disagree, brainstorm, work on tasks, ask and answer, questions, etc., in order for the members need to connect
- *Publishing:* To produce, share, and collect documents that are relevant to their practice, members need to organize communal

repositories as well as individual access to them.

- *Tending:* To strengthen their common identity, members need to find ways to participate personally as well as cultivate their community

Recent developments of the Web enable people to interact in numerous new ways such as to write together, to post their thoughts, information and links. Tools as Blogger, founded in 1999 by Pyra Labs, made online publishing extremely easy, thereby allowing every web user to publish their thoughts on the Internet. The introduction of commenting, the ability to write a response to postings, took this online discussion platform even further. Weblogs are a type of web page that is simple to create and disseminate and are used as a form of online diaries where people can post their thoughts, information, links or interests. A blog's main characteristic is that it combines text, images, videos and links to blogs, webpages and other media related to the topic being discussed. This is, of course a more technical oriented description of weblogs. What is really interesting is the possibility for visitors to add comments to posts, likely resulting to discussions. Thus, blogs can function as a platform for conversations. Due to their simplicity of use and their flexibility blogs have become a fast-growing feature of educational establishments, corporate businesses and the public sector. The network of more or less interconnected weblogs is called the 'blogosphere'

Blogging is an easy tool for structuring thoughts, communication with others and reflection of interesting things. It can encourage the skills of writing and self-expression. New resources and ideas can be easily added to the discussion for sharing and further feedback, so blogs make it easy to access new resources very quickly. More specifically an important characteristic of blogs is the dialogue through which they learn to take a wider, more differentiated view, and thus acquire sensitivity, subtlety and capacity for judgement. Through blogs there is the possibility of recording personal in narrative format; it's a medium through which the student can share his opinions, emotions and dreams. The student (author) can be subjected to criticism but he can also challenge other opinions and ideas. Through blogging they are trained for public debate. Through the exchange of opinions and personal experiences they realize that other teenagers have the same concerns and face the same problems. Everyone can participate as it is not based on an unbent detailed schedule that sometimes leads some students to «self-exclusion". An additional tool is *feeds* which inform the blogger for any new information (for example reduce of water funds). *Links* give him direct access to the source of the information (at the particular article or web site the information was spotted), he has also ability to connect with web pages of public services (at the public service that is responsible for the management and supply of water) and he is granted access to public information without the intervention of third parties.

As Gilmor (2003) states it can become a genre of «participating journalism" or "journalism of civilians"(Witt, 2004). Students can research local problems (for instance the use of water, energy, garbage disposal in their school, neighborhood or municipality). The use of photographs and videos allows them to record and present the subjects in question and to compare different regions. Using maps (for example Google maps) they can spot the region where increased problems of sustainability management exist (decrease of biodiversity etc) In this way they are encouraged to take action locally. They can also contact scientists or other people with credibility in a specific subject. Finally the blogger-student can come to a conclusion based on all the information and material provided. Through tools like *permalinks* (each post has its own permanent address) new field of interaction are created and new members can enter. Students become accustomed to the democratic proceedings, participating in the dialogue, the final decision and the resolution of conflicts.

And finally another advantage is that blogging creates a readable and searchable report of discussion. A blog in a community favours the "private" dimension, through free speech and personal responsibility and through development of autonomy moves forward to the "social" dimension based on the collaboration for creation, the gathering of knowledge, tolerant behavior, respect, managing of everyday problems and "public" participation.

Wikis

Over the last few years, services have been developed that enable collaborative writing on the Internet. A wiki is a flexible and editable website where anyone has the ability to intervene and modify its pages. Its content can be accessed like any other web page; the important characteristic is that it can be edited by every user or user group requiring a single tool, a Web Browser. Wikis also support hyperlinks and has simple text syntax. A wiki can be defined as "a freely expandable collection of interlinked Web 'pages,' a hypertext system for storing and modifying information–a database, where each page is easily editable by any user with a forms-capable Web browser client" (Leuf and Cunningham, 2001, p.14). The first wiki engine, WikiWikiWeb, was developed in 1995 by Ward Cunningham. Wikis are often used as a tool for personal information management, knowledge management, team collaboration, and as a more flexible kind of weblog. This, together with the low barriers and costs of starting a wiki and its efficiency explains the wide adoption of wikis worldwide, and makes it interesting to study this phenomenon more closely. The most famous example of a wiki in action is Wikipedia, the online encyclopaedia.

Wikis are often used to organize and cross-link knowledge, by making it extremely easy to add or edit links and texts. Another important aspect of a wiki is that it is inherently democratic, which means that every user has the exact same rights and capabilities of every other user. These characteristics make it very easy for a group of people to write collaboratively on a specific topic of interest. Advantages of collaborative writing are an increase in the number of ideas and viewpoints, assurance that various subsections are written by experts, increased motivation among participants, possibilities for less experienced writers to improve their skills, and higher levels of acceptance of the final product. During the process of writing, students negotiate meanings and the result is a full project and not individual sums. This collaborative learning is based on socially structured information exchange and on the sense of responsibility that each member of the team has for the progress of other members and promotes the mutual engagement of community members.

In order to have a large value in common, all of the members of group must have an equable opportunity to receive and take from others. There must be a large variety of shared undertakings and experiences." (Dewey 2007 p.87) Group and social issues also play an important role during the writing process. For instance, the group has to deal with different abilities of participants and conflicts among them. In addition, large wikis sometimes deal with vandalism. People sometimes deliberately destroy the content of the wiki to affect the quality and reliability. Vandalism is considered a problem, but not an insuperable one, since previous versions of a wiki page can be easily restored. As Kolbitsch and Maurer (2006) argue, the fundamental idea of a wiki is that errors will be found and corrected because a vast number of users read and edit the content and over time, the document will become more and more complete.

Wegner (2004) defines blogs as knowledge repositories, where every post functions as an individual repository and wikis as knowledge repositories but are also a form of expressing collective lived memory of the community.

COMMUNITIES OF PRACTICE, EDUCATIONAL EFFECTIVENESS AND SOCIAL EFFICIENCY

Promoting a Culture Favorable to Public Sector Reforms

The integration of innovative strategies in education, which is part of the public sector, creates a mechanism for the achievement of public sector reform in the context of sustainability and citizenship. With the creation of practical communities and through learning a strategy for citizen empowerment through participation is developed, reducing social disadvantages at personal, local and state level, addressing diversity through community, and promoting the ability of citizens' community (without reducing the term to elective ability) to participate in local-national political discussions and decision making. Develop a consensus not only around reforms goals but also the common values that underlie those goals and participation in a public sector reform, as these concern every citizen.

An education with such a content and practice constitutes a subversive educational process, in which people:

- participate in a new way of thinking, learning and working
- acquire the ability to investigate the relationships between them, the environment, social systems and institutions, but also to become active participants in the process of change
- develop social partnership and acquire the intellectual tools in order to think in accordance with the principles of democracy, solidarity, tolerance and freedom

In this communication network that is created an exchange of views takes place, conflicts arise and acceptable solutions that lead to free submission to collective rules are found.

It promotes social cooperation and communication through social networks that highlight common interests and objectives, whereas students are motivated to take collective action. This promotes the "peripheral participation" of students in larger communities outside the natural boundaries of the classroom. Through this process the notion of belonging is cultivated and of participation that can be constant. The conditions for the development of social capital are created, meaning that the ability of people to join forces, cooperate for common purposes in groups and organizations, is cultivated. The development of such communities in education has prospectively the ability of re-modelling of the public sphere, strengthening public consultation, promoting proposals from the citizens, promoting the policy of sustainability. As Dewey (1916,p 87) wrote, 'democracy is more than a form of government: it is primarily a mode of associated living, a conjoint communicated experience'.

Moreover, new technologies are exploited both in education and in the society since they are used as a tool to empower social participation and cooperation. Through social media in community practices, youngsters learn about institutions, democracy problems and objectives, and how civilians can contribute effectively in social life in local, regional and national level. The plural character of today's democracy requires public dialog to achieve social consensus. Participation in public dialog requires informed citizens and is a procedure with rules in which someone to participate; he needs to have the relative education that emerges from experiences gathered through participation in communities of practice. Attachments of cooperation and mutual help that are developed in school through practical communities, in the neighbourhood through volunteer associations created by civilians for public interest, are at the same time source and aim for any kind of public reform and its success.

FUTURE RESEARCH DIRECTIONS

Two major research directions stem out of the discussion presented in this chapter.

Firstly, communities of practice can be employed at multiple levels of education, with varying degrees of control and sophistication, according to criteria and guidelines that need to be further investigated. The same holds true for the application of social media as enabling technology for CoPs, according to norms and interaction netiquettes that need be further elaborated.

Secondly, the actual participation of young people in communities of practice (and so much so in communities of social practice), the identities that are eventually created, the influences on participants' point of view and attitude shifts regarding critical issues, as well as the extent to which participation of CoP members in other communities, the local society for example, is promoted, all call for further research.

CONCLUSION

The main goal of this chapter was to develop a proposition for a public reform which would be based on the citizens' participation and would have sustainability as a goal. Such a public reform has to deal with and manage problems of citizenship, cultural difference and in the same time promote different ways of citizen participation in political and social life.

In this chapter an alternative proposal towards this direction was illustrated, which works for a reform through education, a part of the public sector with special social interest.

During the application of CoPs in education for citizenship and sustainability it was noted that there are basic common elements, both in methodology and in goals. Additionally the significance of the use of social media for the support of these communities was underlined, as they facilitate the formation of identity, make proper use of diversity and promote the management of conflicts in their birth, issues that concern the modern multi-cultural societies.

This proposal is plausible as it does not require structural changes in the educational system but re-orientation based on existent data. A very important aspect is that it concerns both trainers and trainees and it creates bonds in the educational community at a local, national and international level. The issues that emerge from the members themselves encourage the participation in local society but create the conditions for the growth of social activity as well.

The circumstances are created for the proper use of ICTs in education in order to become a tool for the spillover of reform proposals and the development of public discourse in order to achieve public acceptance.

REFERENCES

Annette, J. (2000). Service learning in the community. In Lewton, D., Cairns, J., & Gardner, R. (Eds.), *Education for citizenship*. London, UK: Continuum.

Birzea, C. (2005). *Tools for quality assurance of education for democratic citizenship in schools*. Strasbourg, France: Council of Europe.

Canivez, P. (2000). *Ποια Αγωγή για τον Πολίτη*. Αθήνα: SCRIPTA (in greek)

Cogan, J. J., & Derricott, R. (1998). *Citizenship for the 21st Century: An international perspective on education*. New York, NY: Routlege.

Davis, T. (2009). *Speech by the Secretary General of the Council of Europe*. 1st Conference of Ministers responsible for Social Cohesion of Council of Europe Member States. Moscow, 26 February 2009.

Deans, P. C. (2008). *Social software and Web 2.0 technology trends*. New York, NY: Information Science Reference.

Delanty, G. (2003). *Community key ideas*. London, UK: Routlege.

Dewey, J. (1916) *Democracy and education: An introduction to the philosophy of education* (1966 ed.). New York, NY: Free Press.

Dewey, J. (1933). *How we think*. Boston, MA: D. C. Heath.

Dewey, J. (2007). *Democracy and education: An introduction to the philosophy of education*. NuVision Publications, LLC, (digital book). Retrieved from http:// books.google.gr/books?id=dSmhXutgD4oC&printsec=frontcover&dq=Democracy+and+Education:+An+introduction+to+the+Philosophy+of+Education.&source=bl&ots=kgUy1rn_A5&sig=S_H25Cc-QYRSIefwCWQXzfZayFk&hl=el&ei=maOaS8WVOMz64AaU-oF_&sa=X&oi=book_result&ct=result&resnum=2&ved=0CBEQ6AEwAQ#v=onepage&q=&f=false

Earth Charter Commission. (2000). *The Earth charter.* Earth Charter Commission. Retrieved from http:// www.earthcharter.org/ files/ charter/ charter.pdf

Elgin, D. (1991). Creating a sustainable future. *Re-vision*, *14*(2), 77.

Fien, J. (1993). *Education for the environment: Critical curriculum theorising and environmental education*. Australia: Deakin University.

Fien, J., & Tilbury, D. (2002). *The global challenge of sustainability*. In D. Tilbury, R. B. Stevenson, J. Fien & S. Danie (Eds.), *Education and sustainability responding to the global challenge* (pp. 1-12). IUCN, Switzerland: IUCN Commission on Education and Communication CEC.

Finn, J. D. (1989). Withdrawing from school. *Review of Educational Research*, *59*(2), 117–142. doi:.doi:10.3102/00346543059002117

Herbrecther, S., & Higgins, M. (Eds.). (2006). *Returning (to) communities: Theory, culture and political practice of the communal*. Amsterdam, The Netherlands/New York, NY: Rodopi.

IEA. (2006). *Second Information Technology in education study 2006*. Retrieved from http:// www.iea.nl/ sites20060.html

IUCN/UNEP/WWF. (1991). *Caring for the Earth: A strategy for sustainable living*. Gland, Switzerland: IUCN-The World Conservation Union.

Jenkins, R. (2007). *K*. Athens, Greece: Savalas. (in Greek)

Kerr, D. (2003). Citizenship: Local, national and international. In Gearon, L. (Ed.), *Learning to teach ctizenship in the secondary school* (pp. 7–8). London, UK: Routledge.

Kidd, T. T., & Chen, I. L. (Eds.). (2009). *Wired for learning: An educator's guide to Web 2.0*. USA: Information Age Publishing.

Kolbitsch, J., & Maurer, H. (2006). The transformation of the Web: How emerging communities shape the information we consume. *Journal of Universal Computer Science*, *12*(2). doi:.doi:10.3217/jucs-012-02-0187

Kontogiannopoulou-Polydoridi, G. (2005). *Η δημοκρατία, ο πολίτης και οι "άλλοι": πολιτισμική οικείωση της κοινωνικής και πολιτικής εκπαίδευσης /επιμέλεια*. Athens, Greece: Gutenberg. (in greek)

Laister, J., & Koubek, A. (2001). 3rd generation learning platforms. Requirements and motivation for collaborative learning. *EURODL – European Journal of Open and Distance Learning*. Retrieved from http:// www.eurodl.org/ ?p=archives&year=2001&article=54

Lave, J., & Wenger, E. (2005). *Κοινωνικές όψεις της μάθησης, N*. Athens, Greece: Savalas. (in Greek)

Leuf, B., & Cunningham, W. (2001). *The wiki way*. USA: Addison-Wesley.

Mason, R., & Reenie, F. (2008). *E-learning and social networking handbook: Resources for higher education*. USA: Routledge.

O'Shea, K. (2003). *Council of Europe* (pp. 2001–2004). Greece: Strasburg. (in Greek)

Ranson, S. (2000). *The new learning for inclusion and capability: Towards community governance in the education action zones*. Retrieved from http:// www.oecd.org/ dataoecd/19/22/1855975.pdf

Salema, M. H. (2006, September). *Education and training for active citizenship in formal education*. Paper presented in Working towards indicators on active citizenship of CRELL, Center for Research on Lifelong Learning. Retrieved from http:// crell.jrc.ec.europa.eu/ActiveCitizenship/ Conference/ 04_Salema_final.pdf

Scott, D., & Lawson, H. (2002). *Citizenship education and the curriculum*. Westport, CT: Ablex Publishing.

Shirky, C. (2003). A group is its own worst enemy. *Clay Shirky's writing about the Internet*. Retrieved from www.shirky.com

Shirky, C. (2005). Ontology is overrated: Categories, links and tags. *Clay Shirky's writing about the Internet*. Retrieved from www.shirky.com

Talbot, C. (2004). Paradoxes of human nature and public management reforms. In J. Jabes (Ed.), *The role of public administration in alleviating poverty and improving governance*. Malaysia: ABD, NAPSIPAG, INTAN.

Tilbury, D., Stevenson, R. B., Fien, J., & Schreuder, D. (Eds.). (2002). *Education and sustainability, responding to the global challenge. IUCN Commission on Education and communication (CEC)*. Gland, Switzerland: IUCN – The World Conservation Union.

Tsaousis, D. (1997). *H K*. Athens, Greece: Gutenberg.

UNCED (United Nations Commission on Environment and Development). (1992). [*Programme of action for sustainable development: Rio declaration on environment and development*. Rio de Janeiro, Brazil: UNCED.]. *Agenda (Durban, South Africa)*, 21.

UNESCO. (2002). *Education for sustainability, from Rio to Johannesburg: Lessons learnt from a decade of commitment*. Report from World Summit on Sustainable Development Johannesburg, 26 August – 4 September 2002

Wenger, E. (1998). *Communities of practice: Learning, meaning, and identity*. Cambridge, UK / New York, NY: Cambridge University Press.

Wenger, E. (2000). Communities of practice and social learning systems. *Organization*, *7*(2), 225–246. doi:10.1177/135050840072002

Wenger, E. (2001). *Supporting communities of practice a survey of community-oriented technologies*. Retrieved from http:// www.ewenger.com/ tech

Wenger, E., McDermott, R. A., & Snyder, W. (2002). *Cultivating communities of practice*. USA: Harvard Business School Press.

Wenger, E., White, N., Smith, J. D., & Rowe, K. (2005). *Technology for communities*. In CEFRIO. Retrieved from http:// technologyforcommunities.com/ CEFRIO_Book_Chapter_v_5.2.pdf

Wenger, E. C., & Snyder, W. M. (2000). Communities of practice: The organizational frontier. *Harvard Business Review*, *78*(1), 139–145. Retrieved from http:// search.epnet.com/login.aspx ?direct=true&db=buh&an=2628915./ 2/22/2000 and http:/ /hbswk.hbs.edu/ archive/ 1317.html.

World Commission on Environment and Development (WCED). (1987). *Our common future*. Oxford, UK: Oxford University Press.

ADDITIONAL READING

Bovaird, T., & Löffler, E. (2002). Moving from Excellence Models of Local Service Delivery to Benchmarking of "Good Local Governance". *International Review of Administrative Sciences*, *67*(1), 9–24. doi:10.1177/0020852302681001

Brett, P., Mompoint-Gaillard, P., & Salema, M. H. Contributions by Virgílio Meira Soares, Vedrana Spajic-Vrkasˇ,Sulev Valdmaa & Ulrike Wolff-Jontofsohn. Keating-Chetwynd S. (Ed.) (2009) *How all teachers can support citizenship and human rights education: a framework for the development of competences*. Council of Europe Communication from the Commission to the European Parliament, the Council, the Economic and Social Committee and the Committee of the Regions, (2002,February) *Towards a global partnership for sustainable development* [COM(2002) 82 final - Not published in Official Journal].

Council of the European Union. (2006) Renewed EU Sustainable Development Strategy. Retrieved from: http:// register.consilium.europa.eu/ pdf/ en/ 06/ st10/ st10117.en06.pdf

European Active Citizenship: Introductory Guidelines for Adult Educators (2007), Grundtvig G2 Learning Partnership, EUROPEAN PUZZLE

European Commission. Hoskins B., CRELL, Joint Research Centre. *Working towards indicators for Active Citizenship*, Report from the Active Citizenship for Democracy conference, September 20-21, 2006. JRC Ispra

Fien, J. (1993) *Education for the Environment: Critical curriculum theorising and environmental education*. Australia: Deakin University Press, Huckle, J. (2001). *Education for Sustainability and Ecological Citizenship in Europe: A Challenge for Teacher Education in the 21st Century.* Paper presented at a University of Thrace Conference, Aexandroupolis, Greece

Karakatsani, D. (2004), *Εκπαίδευση και Πολιτική Διαπαιδαγώγηση*. Athens: Metaixmio (in greek)

Osler, A., & Starkey, H. (2005). *Changing citizenship: democracy and inclusion in education*. Maidenhead: Open University Press.

Peters, B. G., & Pierre, J. (2007) *Handbook of Public Administration*. University of Pittsburgh, USA, University of Gothenburg, Sweden, SAGE Publications Ltd The Earth Charter (2002) www.earthcharter.org

Tilbury, D., & Wortman, D. (2004) *Engaging People in Sustainability*. Gland, Switzerland & Cambridge, UK.: Commission on Education and Communication, IUCN

UN. (2005). *Decade of Education for Sustainable Development 2005-2014*. International Implementation Scheme DRAFT.

UNESCO. (2005). *UN Decade of Education for Sustainable Development 2005 – 2014, International Implementation Scheme*. Paris: UNESCO.

UNESCO. (2006). Education for Sustainable Development Toolkit, *Education for Sustainable Development in Action Learning & Training Tools N°1*

UNESCO. Björneloo I. & Nyberg E. (Eds.) (2007) Education for Sustainable Development in Action, Drivers and Barriers for Implementing Learning for Sustainable Development in Pre-School through Upper Secondary and Teacher Education Göteborg Workshop, 27-29 March 2006t

UNESCO. (2009). *Education for Sustainable Development, Second Collection of Good Practices*. UNESCO Associated Schools.

Section 2
Applied E-Government

Chapter 9
An Integrated Information System to Support the Management of World-Widely Spread Educational Resources for the Greek Ministry of Education

John Garofalakis
Research Academic Computer Technology Institute, Greece

Andreas Koskeris
Research Academic Computer Technology Institute, Greece

Theofanis-Aristofanis Michail
Research Academic Computer Technology Institute, Greece

Flora Oikonomou
Research Academic Computer Technology Institute, Greece

ABSTRACT

In this chapter, a Government Resource Management System for the efficient organization of wide-spread manpower resources is presented. It concerns the case of the Greek Ministry of Education which manages several educational resources (educational units and teachers) spread around the globe to provide education opportunities for students with Greek origin. After reviewing the problems which have arisen from previous situation concerning the administration of this wide-spread man-power and the primitive tools used to collect information for effective operational activities (e.g. appointment of teachers to several educational units, selection of teachers to be transferred in educational units abroad, payment procedures), an integrated Web-based solution has been designed, developed, and applied. This case study is presented in detail in the following pages along with the benefits of this implementation and the concepts for its further exploitation.

DOI: 10.4018/978-1-60960-839-2.ch009

INTRODUCTION

The purpose of this chapter is to present a specific case of a web based tool aiming to assist the Greek Ministry of Education for the management of widely distributed educational resources (teachers and schools) around the World (for the provision of Greek education for students with Greek origin World Wide). The presented work is based on a complete initial research concerning Governmental Resource Management Systems (GRM) and Governmental Enterprise Resource Planning Systems (GERP).

Based on one of the Greek government's "Digital Strategy 2006-2013" (http://www.infosoc.gr/infosoc/el-GR/sthnellada/committee/default1/top.htm) objectives to "let the Greek Public Administration improve its internal procedure by effectively using new Information and Communication Technologies ", and in combination with the above mentioned initial research, an "umbrella" of applications have been developed and integrated to one Information System. This information system is used in order to help the Greek Ministry of Education for the daily activities related with the management of the educational units offering Greek education around the Globe.

The functional requirements of the system were based on the detailed study of the way the whole operation management worked until now. This includes the way that teachers were selected to be transferred outside Greece, how they were appointed to specific educational units, how the daily education operation was assessed, as well as issues concerning payment procedures administration. The functional requirements were also based on the conclusions obtained from the problems of the non-ICT based approach which was followed in the past. This analysis led the research team to design several applications to focus on each procedure, dealing with all of its specific problems and difficulties. However, in order to be able to establish a "new way of administration" it was important to integrate all these applications in one Environment adapted to the user level.

Through an evaluation of System's operation until now, this paper also attempts to suggest a set of methodological guidelines that could be used in the future by organizations with similar widely spread resources, in their effort to follow an ICT-based resource planning and management approach.

The methodological approach for contents of the forthcoming sections includes the following:

- Firstly, we present a Framework of Analysis including an overview of the situation world widely, in relation with Governmental Resource Management and Resource Planning systems.
- In the Sections to follow, the specific case study of the Greek Ministry of Education, is presented in detail, along with an evaluation (in qualitative and quantitative basis) and suggestions for further work

THE USE OF GOVERNMENT RESOURCE MANAGEMENT SYSTEMS

Resource management is the efficient and effective deployment for an organization's resources (human capital, infrastructures etc) when they are needed (Project Management Institute, 2004). Current Research and Practice in Resource Management, and especially in Human Resource Management, are targeting to the identification of practices and tools adapted to context specific nature of different organizations (Budhwar, P., Debrah, Y., 2008), resulting to optimal Organization performance (Boon, C., Boselie, J.P., Dietz, G.,2005).

Information and Communications Techologies (ICT's) can play a very important role towards the achievement of this goal and there are several *resource management software tools* available which automate and assist the process of resources allocation and resources visibility (ICTC, 2010) (www.assembla.com; www.egroupware.org). Such systems allow complex organizations to automate many aspects of their resources management (Ljubica, K., et al, 2008), leading to:

- reducing the workload related with management
- effective planning of operations
- improvement of quality and productivity
- delivery of services/products in faster rate with lower costs
- effective Business Processes Reengineering when needed (Willmott, H., 1994)

A step forward towards effective resource management is the so-called *Enterprise Resource Planning (ERP)* which concerns systems and procedures used to manage and coordinate all the resources, information, and functions within Organization/Company etc. (Esteves, J., Pastor, J.,2001). ERP purpose is to facilitate the flow of information between all business functions inside the boundaries of an organization (Bidgoli, Hossein, 2004).

ERP Systems centralize the data in one place. *Benefits* of this include:

- Implementing solutions using sophisticated Software tools (www.openerp.com; www.fedena.com) provides a means by which multiple, heterogeneous procedures within an Organization can be integrated for maximum performance and efficiency (Mutt, N., 2009).
- Another area where ERP can be an indispensable tool is the area of security. It can protect an Organization against crimes such as embezzlement or industrial espionage (Exforsys, 2010).
- Organization/corporations who introduce the ERP system are generally better in economic performance than non-ERP users (Nanjing, J.,2009).

Within the last years Governments have turned to ICT as a lever for better public sector performance to meet increasing internal and external demands, and looking at e-government applications development as a tool for public sector transformation (Organization for Economic Co-operation and Development, 2007). This is mainly achieved by providing new opportunities to improve the government agencies` efficiency and coordination. Examples of such applications include:

- public financial management (Los, 2010),
- human resources management, (Centre of Expertise for local government reform, 2010),
- land and asset management (http://www.accela.com/),
- government purchases through e-procurement (PublicTendering.com, 2009) etc

Resource Management Systems and ERPs at the *Governmental level* are very important tools towards the achievement of such a more effective government. They are part of the category of e-government applications called "Government to government" –G2G. G2G applications improve the amount, quality, and speed of information exchange between various levels of government and departments within governments. They help governments to use resources more wisely and allow departments to tackle large-scale problems (Thomas, C., 2009).

The *adoption* of Resource Management and Enterprise Resources Planning (ERP) tools, is therefore appreciated more and more (Allen, D., Kern,T., Havenhand, M., 2002) for Governments. Motivations behind this trend (Bergeron, F., Raymond, L., Uwizeyemungu, S., 2005) mainly include: operational motivations concerning the need for improvement of processes; performance motivations which are contingent on the will to improve results, both quantitative and qualitative (e.g. reduction of operative costs); motivations of a strategic order which are linked to the need for a change in orientation in the design and delivery of governmental services to personnel and general public. This is important especially for the case of managing Human Resources to allow their effective management, especially in cases where the personnel is increasing above a specific level and it is located on several locations (Thompson, J.R., Seidner, R., 2009).

In the following paragraphs we present briefly selected showcases of Governmental resource management systems/experiences.

ESKADENIA Jordan CRP System (Eskadenia CRP System, 2004) has been designed to meet the largest set of requirements in the Governmental sector. The system automates the governmental departments' work cycles, reduces operational cost, simplifies operations, speeds up work, decreases the routine procedures to the minimum, maintains historical data, and ensures a high level of security. It provides any governmental department with the proper tools to efficiently plan and manage government resources. The experience derived from the application of this system shows that any Governmental Resource planning project for any public sector is a very difficult challenge and requires the involvement and active involvement of specialized Information Technologies experts in all evolution stages.

AMS Advantage ERP (AMS Advantage ERP, 2010) has helped 190 U.S. state and local organizations better serve their more than 90 million citizens and more effectively manage over $500 billion in public funds; it addresses all major administrative requirements in areas such as finance, procurement, budgeting, reporting, payroll and human resources. AMS Advantage is built specifically for state and local government, addressing their requirements out-of-the-box, by streamlining business processes, eliminating redundant data entry, and enhancing access to information.

Agência de Tecnologia da Informação de Pernambuco (ATI), the organization responsible for planning, coordinating and executing IT programs for the government in the *state of Pernambuco in Brazil,* implemented a government resource planning (GRP) system to assure ease of use and application and data integration with the taxes administration system, the services administration integrated system, the financial administration integrated system, and the human resources and payroll administration system; and the processing of the payroll records for 190,000 employees (Intersystems, 2010). The first priority was to create an electronic bidding system, with the goal of making the relationships between the government and its thousands of suppliers more transparent and purchasing processes more agile, and to improve control of expenses. An important issue on the evolution of this system was to assure proof-of-concept project, which required the merging with existing previous relevant systems of the state.

The *City of San Buenaventura (Ventura), California* in 2007 proceed to a replacement of its back-office software systems with a city-wide implementation of a software to help the city in its efforts to upgrade and modernize internal and customer-centric government processes and transform the pace and quality of services to the citizens of Ventura. The motivation behind this decision was the understanding that it was important to proceed and implement a system which will assure improvement of response time for users (Government Technology, 2007).

In *European level* all relevant initiatives (and policies adapted) are leading mainly to national level improvement of governance activities which is a different approach than the one mainly found in US (extended efforts on municipal level). (ePractice, 2010).

The experiences from these applications in real cases shows that ERP and Resources Management systems' adoption from governments/

administrations is *difficult to achieve due to the following factors*:

- Governments in most cases are characterized by strong diversity (Bergeron, F., Raymond, L., Uwizeyemungu, S., 2005) and therefore their organization culture is difficult to model.
- The success stories presenting a basis of successful application are mainly fragmented and not integrated approaches solving specific problems and not getting the "whole" picture. (Washington State Digital Government Plan., 2001) (Bergeron, F., Raymond, L., Uwizeyemungu, S., 2005).
- In some cases some of the internal systems developed may not be welcomed by users (Kevin K.W. HO., 2007) due to low level of Computer Literacy and unsuccessful previous experiences and lack of technical, procedural, and/or functional maturity (ERP Headlines, 2010).

To overcome the beforehand obstacles it is evident that two main goals must be achieved:

- There is a need for integrated (Bergeron, F., Raymond, L., Uwizeyemungu, S., 2005) but yet customized approaches based on each specific situation (especially for heavily diversified administrations). In European political level, this need leaded to concrete plans to achieve government reform through new ICTs strategic utilization (Centre of Expertise for local government reform, 2010), (European Commission, 2010).
- Solutions must be easily expandable (for further adaptation/customization) and user friendly (ERP Headlines, 2010). To achieve this, it is important to base the development and delivery on open source web environments.

Following the conclusions of this Section the authors present next a success story of an integrated information system to support the world widely spreaded, educational resources management of the Greek Ministry of Education. This system has the potential to support the effective day to day management of a very complex and distributed organizational environment (teachers, students and educational units all around the world, managed centrally from Athens) assuring expandability and user friendliness.

IN GENERAL

We live in times of ubiquitous presence of computers. Information and communication technology (ICT) have been present in our environment for quite some time. Therefore, the opportunity of making profits from ICT was first perceived by manufacturing enterprises. These opportunities were later perceived by the state and institutions and ERP systems were introduced in order to improve their operations and make them manageable and more transparent.

Some of these ERP systems have been used to assist the academic world not only from the point of education and research activities but also from business aspect, which uses ICT to support other business functions (administrative, organizational, accounting, etc). One representative example is the case of Slovenian higher educational institutions which made use of ERP systems in order to assist their educational and research activities (Zornada, L., Velkavrh, T., 2005). Another example of an ERP system's use in education is the case of the Student Management System (Paulsen, M., 2002) which is mainly used in Nordic countries. Denmark has the STADS system, Sweden the LADOK, Norway the MSTAS. All of these are national systems which are used for management of students, entities, faculty, courses, applications, admissions, payment, exams and grades.

According to the aforementioned systems, the application presented here is merely a governmental project that involves the Greek government and its employees at the disposal of Greek education provided abroad. It is an e-government project that implements G2G (Government to Government) and G2E (Government to employees) processes. The government and especially the Ministry of National Education decided the implementation of an information system that would support all the processes starting from the selection of the teachers, up to the overview of their distribution into school units along with the cost supervision and finally the forecast and planning of future transfer needs. The success of this information system requires the involvement and participation of every level of the educational system.

More specifically, the system facilitates the process of collection and evaluation of teachers' applications who wish to teach abroad, which is performed by the Ministry's central services. The next step involves the coordinator offices, which are distributed world wide, and each one is responsible for school units and teachers at specific countries. The coordinator, records in details all the information about the school units and the corresponding number of students under his responsibility as well as the detailed employment of each teacher including additional salary information.

The collected information is available through statistical reports to all users involved. As far as the teachers are concerned, they can retrieve useful reports about their employment and salary. The coordinator can extract information useful in managerial decisions, while the Greek Ministry can utilize the system as a decision support for planning future transfer needs.

System's Functionalities

The integrated information system which was implemented for the Greek Ministry of National Education has two distinct user's roles. As depicted in Figure 1, on the one hand there are the governmental users who supervise the whole process and have total access to all data and from now on will be referred as administrators, and on

Figure 1. System's architecture

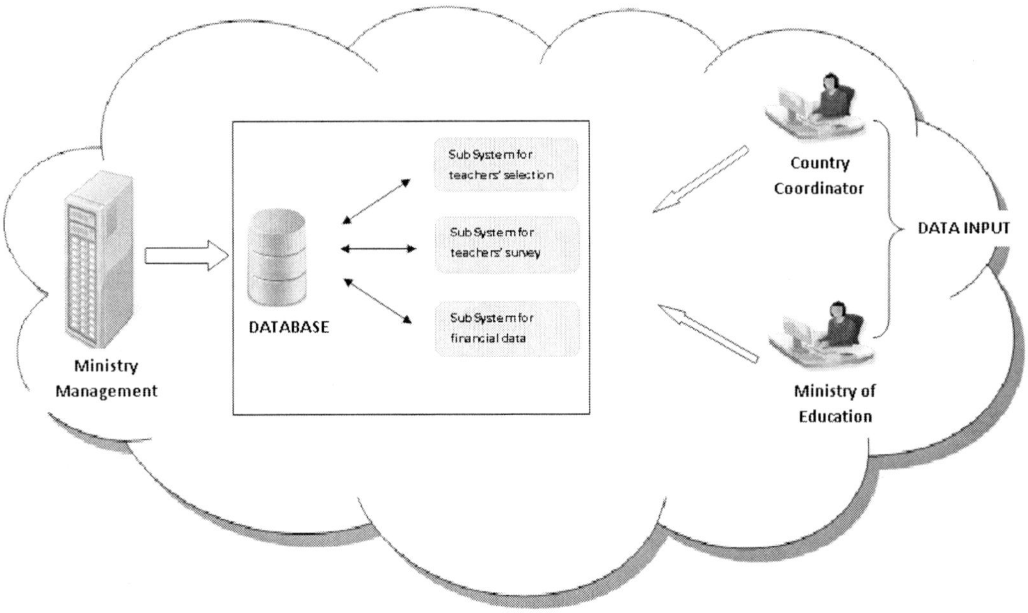

the other hand there are the coordinators, Greek educational directors around the globe who have access only on their area of interest. A central database stores the data from the three subsystems which are integrated to the whole application and the whole process is under the Ministry's Management supervision.

The whole system is a web application resembling a portal. The application is accessed after authentication through a browser and the system is personalized based on the user logged into the system, and different menus and functionalities are provided to each one of them. Three concrete functionalities are included to the system, which are analyzed in the following paragraphs.

Support the Process for the Selection of Teachers to be Transferred Around the World

Every year, the Greek Ministry of National Education announces a call for applications for teachers in order to staff the Greek schools around the world. Every teacher will be examined at a foreign language (or languages) which are defined by his country of interest. For example if someone wants to go to United Kingdom, he will be examined in English. The system's administrators register the teachers' application forms to the integrated information system as seen in Figure 2.

A lot of automated operations have been implemented in order to facilitate the data input process. If a teacher has been registered to the system in the past, then by entering his /hers unique registration number most of his already entered data will be filled in to his registration form automatically. Moreover when the administrators fill in the teachers' countries of interest, the system automatically shows only the languages which correspond to the selected country. For example, if Spain is selected then the administrator has to select Spanish as an examined language. Furthermore, if a teacher has been examined in a specific language in the previous contest and wants to use the acquired grade for the running contest, the system can recover this grade and auto-complete all the necessary fields in the registration form.

Now, for every teacher who is interested in teaching abroad there is a record at the system with his personal data and his countries and languages of interest. The system automatically provides a list with the examination centers and the teachers who will be examined there to their language (or languages) of interest. When the exams are over, the administrators access the system and fill in the teachers' examination results to the appropriate fields of their forms. A lot of statistical results are provided in order to facilitate the systems' administrators for the better supervision of the whole process.

Based on the data entered in the previous year for the number of the school units in every country around the world and the number of the needed teachers, the administrators calculate how many teachers will be needed the current year and what specialty these teachers must have. For example, the previous year 10 mathematicians and 20 nursery school teachers were needed in Sydney and the half of them will return in Greece the current year. As a consequence, at least 5 mathematicians and 10 nursery school teachers would be needed in Sydney. The number of the needed teachers' specialties for every country around the world is filled in to the system in order to acquire the selection lists.

In a final stage the system automatically calculates the selections lists of successful candidates per country. These selection lists contain the successful candidates ordered by their exam grade at each country's corresponding language and the values on more that 10 criteria. These lists comprise the basis for the operation of the second concrete functionality, described below.

Figure 2. Form for inserting teachers' data who are applying for transfer

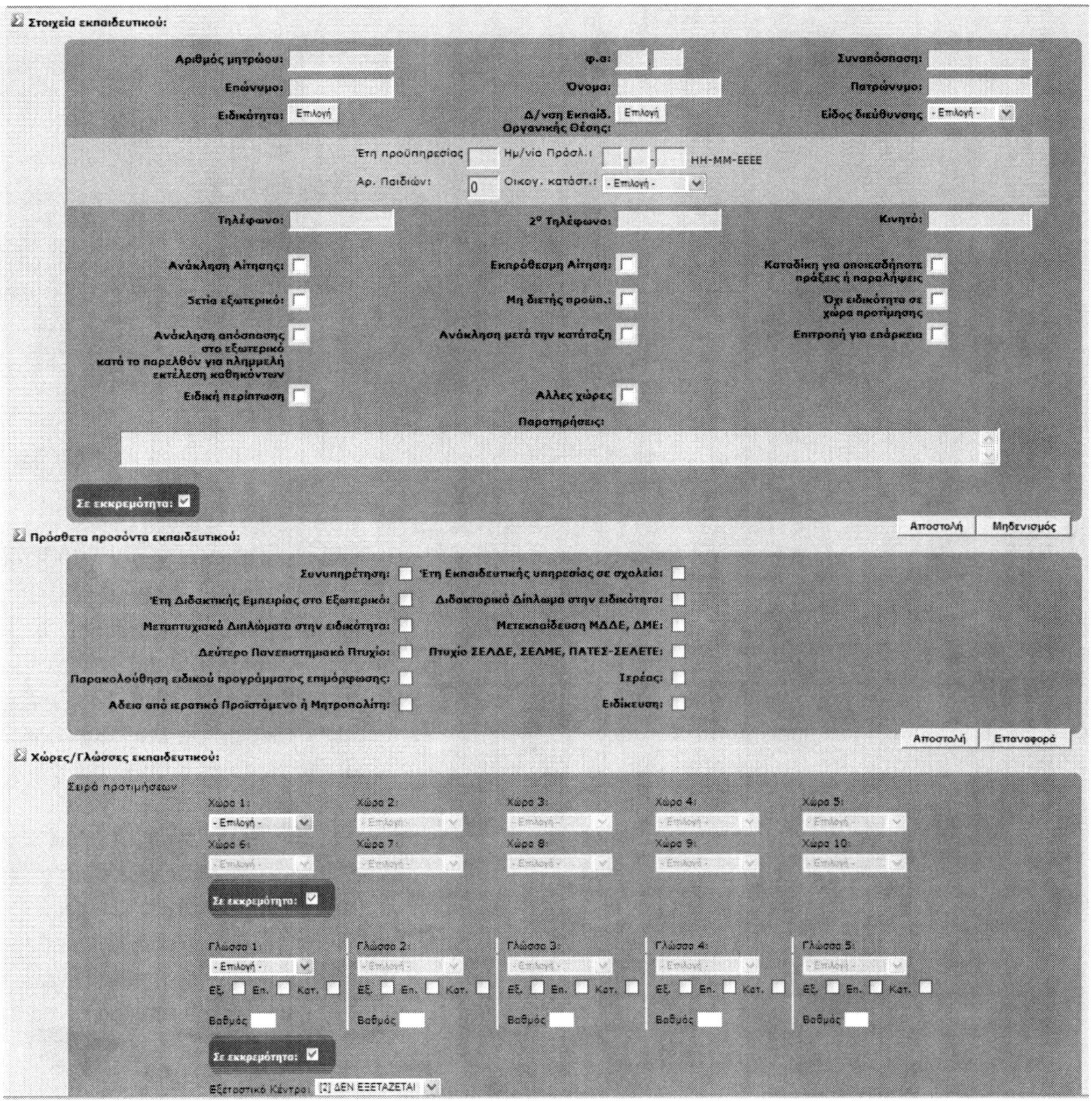

Survey Module

In each country the Ministry appoints a local coordinator to act as supervisor of the local educational units. Every coordinator surveys the educational and scholastic power for the educational units of his area of interest, providing information concerning which school each teacher is appointed to and how many students are attending the courses of this school. This provides important statistical information to the Ministry of National Education on how many teachers will be needed for the following year for every country based on the total number of students and educational units operating per country as previously mentioned. A more detailed description of the survey module is analyzed in the following paragraphs.

Figure 3. Example statistics report: "Primary education school units in Berlin"

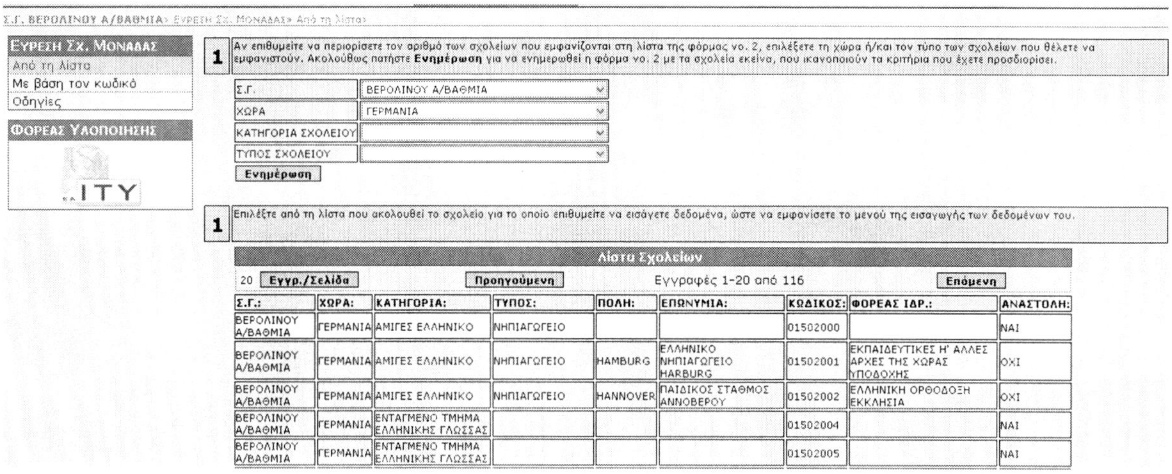

At first a coordinator must provide some general information about the location and the people who work at the coordination office. Additionally, the educational units of his area of interest are entered to the system. For every educational unit the coordinator enters basic information such as the schools location, its contact information (such as telephone, email), the supervisor of that school, the town in which this school is located and many more. Moreover, the coordinator enters data about the teachers who teach at the aforementioned school unit, the courses this school unit has and the number of students who attend these courses.

When the data entering procedure is finished, the coordinator can see a list of all the school units he has entered to the system and of all the teachers who work at these school units. A lot of statistic results are provided in order to facilitate the coordinators for the supervision of the whole process. For example, statistics about the number of students per class, the number of teachers per school unit, the list of all the school units for a specific coordinator's office and many more have been implemented.

A coordinator can have a limited access to the application and only to the data concerning his area of interest. On the other hand system's administrators (i.e. ministry of education employees) can access all the inserted data. Due to the system's personalization, administrators see a different context with more menu options and more statistic results. An administrator can check the data which the coordinators have entered to the system and make proper suggestions if needed. Moreover, he can extract data concerning the educational power of the Greek teachers around the globe as a whole (for example, the current year 2299 teachers are registered to the system) or he can extract data concerning a specific area of interest (for example, in Germany there are 116 primary education school units). The aforementioned results are depicted in the following figures (Figures 3 and 4) and the obtained results can be saved in .pdf of .xls format for further editing.

The statistics provided in the survey module have been implemented in such a way allowing a dynamic execution of database queries. Specifically, a lot of filters are used in every statistic allowing the execution of a different query based on the user's needs. For example, if an administrator wants to see the number of Greek teachers around the globe he does not have to select something at the query's filters. If he wants to see the number of Greek teachers in a specific hemisphere, continent, country all he has to do is to select the appropriate choice from the dropdown menus

Figure 4. A statistic showing the educational Greek power around the globe

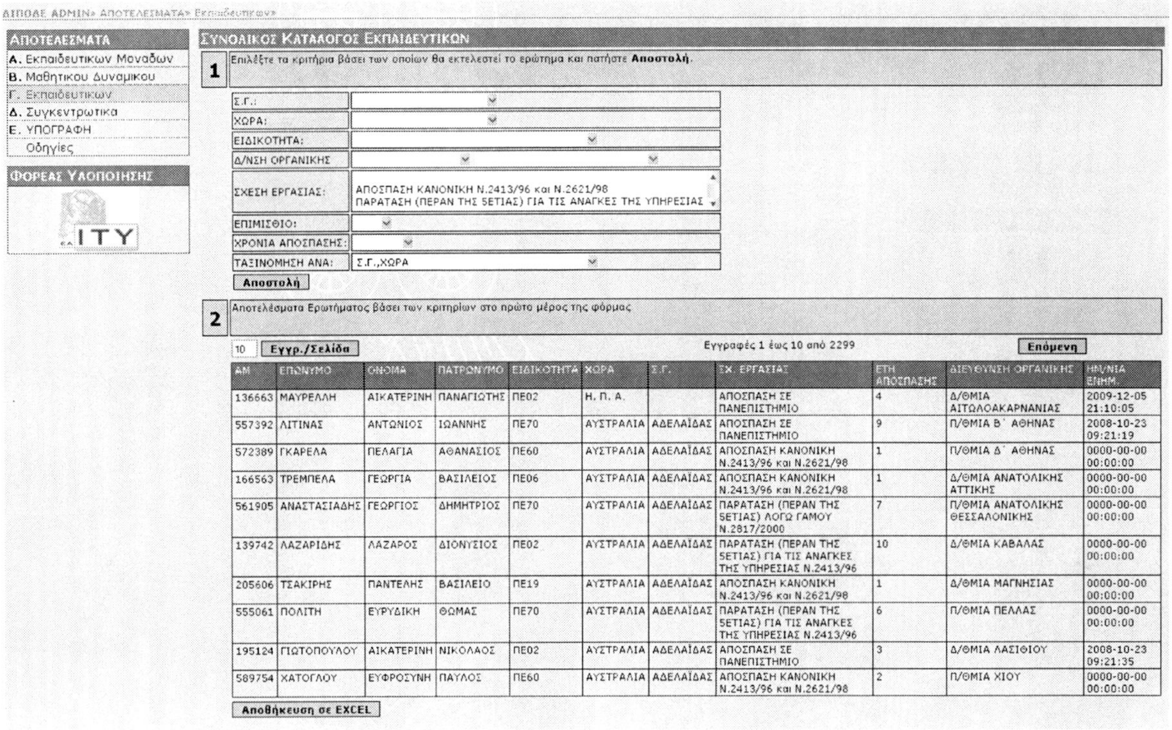

which are provided at the system. The dynamic way, in which the queries are implemented and executed at the system, allowed the administrators to have a plethora of options for the information they want to obtain.

Support of the Payment Process

Apart from the aforementioned functionalities the integrated information system records every month the needed information in order to automatically calculate teachers' salaries (which are calculated differently comparing with their salary costs when they were working in Greece), as seen in figure 4 below. The local coordinators are responsible for this job. All the additional necessary information is retrieved from data already been inserted to the survey module allowing the central management and the transparency of the whole process. It must be mentioned that only system's administrators have access to the salaries calculation.

System's Interconnection

The whole interconnection of the three subsystems described above, is depicted in the following, Figure 6.

The data entered at the teacher's selection subsystem are used for the teacher's survey system and vice versa. When the lists of the teacher's selection system have been created an authorized employee of the Ministry of Education can appoint these teachers to their country of interest with the press of one button. Thus, the records in the database which are associated with the selected teachers are stored to proper tables based on the country in which every teacher was appointed to. With this functionality, a coordinator has a minimum amount of data to enter ensuring a more prone free system. Furthermore, all the results

Figure 5. Monthly salary data inserted

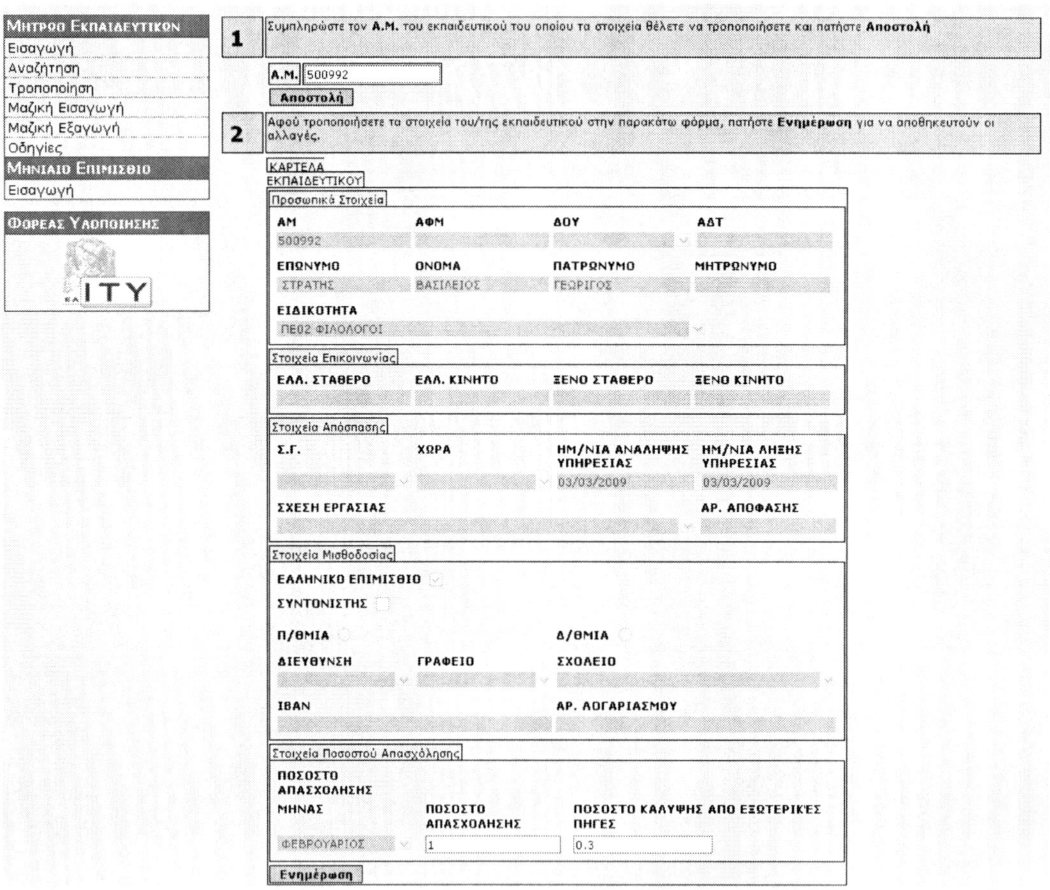

Figure 6. Subsystems' interconnection

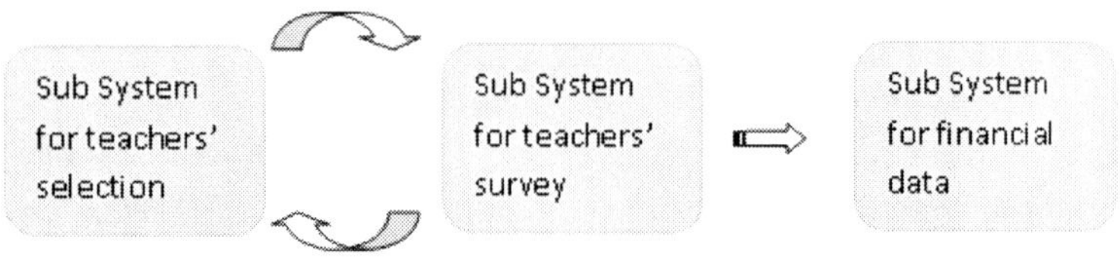

which are collected from the teacher's survey system are substantial in order to extract information for the following year teachers' selection process as already mentioned.

The financial data subsystem uses all these information in order to automatically calculate teachers' salaries allowing the central management, the transparency and the elimination of mistakes of the whole process.

Technologies Used

The whole technical approach used for the system's development and operation is based on open source technologies allowing easy expandability and adaptability with other existing applications of the Greek Ministry of Education (Garofalakis J., Koskeris A., Vopi A., 2007). The application stores the data in MySQL database. MySQL is the most popular, free, open-source database management system. The scripting language that has been used for the developing of the web applications is the PHP, an open source and free software. XML is used to export information from statistical reports, where they are needed.

RESULTS OBTAINED

Prior to the development of this system, the previously described processes where supported by the services of the Greek Ministry of Education with the least technological support. The selection lists where evaluated through the manual processing of the applications and the examination results. Moreover, only few summary statistical data where collected from coordinator offices through excel files leading to only a small number of reports available for the administrators and insufficient management and teacher transfer planning capabilities.

The whole system presented in previous sections started its operation 4 years ago. Since then it has never stopped working. Each year data collected concern approximately 2300 teachers, 90000 students, and 2500 educational units from over 80 countries around the world. Moreover an average number of 2000 teachers' petitions for transfers are handled through the relevant module and about 900 transfers result from them. From the reporting module more than 50 statistical analysis reports are available to the users.

It is evident that, from a *quantitative point of view,* the system is highly successful since it manages all the resources concerning Greek education outside Greece, providing constant online presentation of the actual situation per country. The more important aspect is that the integration of the three subsystems enabled the recording of a wide variety of detailed information with the least effort of all users involved.

From a *qualitative point of view,* the feedback provided by the System through the statistics and the ability to monitor the school entries and the information about the teachers, resulted in the speed up of the procedures related with transfers and redistributions of the educational power for coverage specific needs. As far as the selection process is concerned, the first subsystem supports ideally the operating procedures, providing useful statistics and creating the selection lists on the click of a button. The second subsystem provides very useful reports (especially the comparatively reports on the number of students each year and the detailed teacher employment) that support the planning process of needed teacher transfers abroad. This results in the elimination of the lost teaching hours for the students and the improvement of the whole educational process outside Greece in general with the minimal and absolutely necessary teacher transfers. Finally, the third subsystem provides a detailed view of the cost of the provided educational services to all Greek students international, which is very important especially with the current economy crisis.

In overall, the unlimited provision of statistics and the complete and integrated view of the resources in the distributed environment of the educational units established the System as a very useful Resources Management tool.

FURTHER WORK

The planned further work includes several additional functionalities and integration with additional Governmental ERPs of the Greek Ministry of Education. In mode detail, the development team is willing to:

- Integrate the whole information Environment to the existing Information System which carries out the Multi-level Management of Large Scale resources of the Greek Primary and Secondary Education (Garofalakis J., Koskeris A., Vopi A., 2007). This system manages all educational resources (manpower, students, and schools) in Greece. A first level of integration has been already developed assuring that all teachers' data who apply for transferring around the world are easily found and multiple data entries are unnecessary. Further integration will give the opportunity to the Greek Ministry to have an even more comprehended approach on managing effectively the education system.

- Provide additional functionalities to periodically collect data about educational excursions planned from the Greek Schools around the world, allowing the improvement of their security and educational impact. Such a system already exists for the educational excursions within Greece (Garofalakis J., Koskeris A., Michail A.T., Vopi A., 2008) and its impact was very important allowing local authorities / targets of educational excursions to be prepared and provide better educational and security services.
- Provide additional functionalities to collect daily statistics on students' absences from schools around the world, produce important statistics for the effectiveness of education around the world and provide useful feedback to monitor the situation in cases of increased absences' rates (e.g. in periods of epidemies).
- Search for similarities with other educational systems in Europe and world widely and use the presented system for the effective management of each country's educational resources.

CONCLUSION

As already mentioned in this Chapter, Resource Management Systems at Governmental level are very important tools towards the achievement of a more effective government. This is important especially for the case of managing Human Resources to allow their effective organization (especially in cases where the personnel is increasing above a specific level and it is located on several locations).

Adoption of such tools from governments/ administrations is difficult to achieve due to their strong diversity. Successful applications are mainly fragmented and not integrated approaches, solving specific problems and not getting the "whole" picture. To overcome the beforehand obstacles there is a need for integrated but yet customized approaches based on each specific situation (especially for heavily diversified administrations).

In this chapter, the authors presented a successful story of such an integrated information system to support the world widely spreaded, educational resources management of the Greek Ministry of Education. This system has the potential to support the effective daily management of a very complex and distributed organizational environment (teachers, students and educational units all around the world, managed centrally from Athens).

This system provided an effective way to monitor the school entries and the information about the teachers, resulted in the speed up of the procedures related with transfers and redistributions of the teaching power for the coverage of the Ministry's needs around the Globe. Moreover, this resulted in the elimination of the lost teaching hours for the students and the improvement of the whole educational process outside Greece in general. The unlimited provision of statistics and the complete and integrated view of the resources in the distributed environment of the educational units established the System as a very useful Resources Management tool, which can set the basis for relevant future exploitation in similar governmental environments.

REFERENCES

Allen, D., Kern, T., & Havenhand, M. 2002. ERP critical success factors: An exploration of the contextual factors in public sector institutions. In: *35th Hawaii International Conference on System Sciences (HICSS 2002)*, January 7-10, 2002, Waikoloa, Hawaii

AMS Advantage ERP. 2010, *CGI*, Retrieved February 10, 2010 from: http:// www.cgi.com/ web/ en/ library/ solutions/ governments/ 74072.htm

Bergeron, F., Raymond, L., & Uwizeyemungu, S. 2005, ERP adoption for e-government: An analysis of motivations.In: E-*Government Workshop '05 (eGOV05)*, September 13, 2005, Brunel University, West London, UK.

Bidgoli, H. (2004). *The Internet encyclopedia* (*Vol. 1*, p. 707). John Wiley & Sons. doi:10.1002/047148296X

Boon, C., Boselie, J. P., & Dietz, G. (2005). Commonalities and contradictions in research on human resource management and performance. *Human Resource Management Journal*, *15*(3), 67–94. doi:10.1111/j.1748-8583.2005.tb00154.x

Budhwar, P., & Debrah, Y. 2008, Future research on human resource management systems in Asia, *Asia Pacific Journal of Management*, 26(2), 197-218 Springer Netherlands, Retrieved from: http:// www.springerlink.com/ content/ k7427514p1022838/

Centre of Expertise for Local Government Reform. 2010, *Tools for capacity building*, Retrieved from: http:// www.coe.int/ t/ dgap/ localdemocracy/ Centre_Expertise/ Tools/ default_en.asp.

E-practice. 2010, E-practice editorial team, *eGovernment Factsheets, European Commission*, Retrieved July 2, 2010, from http:// www. epractice.eu/ factsheets.

Eskadenia, C. R. P. System, 2004, *ESKADENIA launches a government resource planning software (GRP)*, Retrieved on February 10, 2010, from http:// www.1stjordan.net/ actuuk/ archivesuk/ resultat.php?id=725&debut=0

Esteves, J., & Pastor, J. (2001). Enterprise resource planning systems research: An annotated bibliography. *Communications of AIS*, *7*(8), 2–54.

European Commission. 2010, *e-government on the fast track* Retrieved July 2, 2010, from http:// ec.europa.eu/ information_society/ activities/ egovernment/ policy/ index_en.htm

Exforsys Inc. 2010, *The advantages and disadvantages of ERP*, Retrieved February 11, 2010, from http:// www.exforsys.com/ tutorials/ erp/ the-advantages-and-disadvantages-of-erp.html

Garofalakis, J., Koskeris, A., Michail, A. T., & Vopi, A. (2008). A Web based tool to assist management, control and security in schools' educational excursions. In: *8th European Conference on e-Government (ECEG2008)*, July 10-11, 2008, Ecole Polytechnique, Lausanne, Switzerland, Retrieved from http:// www.academic-conferences. org/ eceg/ eceg2008/ eceg08-home.htm

Garofalakis, J., Koskeris, A., & Vopi, A. (2007). An e-Government application for integrated, multi-level management of large scale resources of the Greek primary and secondary education, In: *7th European Conference on E-Government (ECEG 2007)*, June 21-22, 2007, Hague, Netherlands.

Government Technology. (2007), *City of Vendura to modernize govenrment ERP system* Retrieved February 14, 2010, from http:// www.govtech. com/ gt/ 219833

Headlines, E. R. P. 2010, *High profile government ERP software failures continue*, Retrieved on February 10, 2010, from http:// www.erpheadlines. com/ government_erp_software.htm

Ho, K. K. W. (2007). The e-government development, IT strategies, and portals of the Hong Kong Sar government. Hershey, PA: Idea Group Publishing. Retrieved from http:// www.infosci-journals.com/ downloadPDF/ pdf/ ITJ3596_RA-F9OKgFC6.pdf

ICTC. (2010), *Human resource tools, Information and Communication Technology Council*, Retrieved on February 11, 2010, from http:// www.ictc-ctic.ca/ en

Intersystems, (2010), *Brazilian government agency completes an integrated resource planning system*, Retrieved February 11, 2010, from http:// www.intersystems.com/ casestudies/ ensemble/ ati.html

Kevin, K. W. H. O. 2007. The E-Government Development, it Strategies, and portals of the hong Kong Sar Government. *IDEA GROUP PUBLISHING*, Available at: http:// www.infosci-journals.com/ downloadPDF/ pdf/ ITJ3596_RA-F9OKgFC6.pdf

Ljubica, K., Radulovic, B., Dragic, R., & Zvonko, S. (2008). Web based human resource management system. *Journal of International Research Publication: Materials, Methods & Technologies*, Vol 3, ISSN 1313-8014.

LoS. (2010), *The management Information System of the Austrian tax and customs administration*, Retrieved on Jyly 3, 2010, from: http:// english.bmf.gv.at/ EGov/ WhatisLoS/ _start.htm

Mutt, N. (2009), Benefits of enterprise resource planning software (ERP), *EzineArticles*, Retrieved February 12, 2010, from http:// ezinearticles.com/ ?Benefits-of-Enterprise-Resource-Planning-Software-(ERP)&id=2823574

Nanjing, J. (2009), Research on economic benefit from ERP-Evidence from Y Software Company's users, In: *First IEEE International Conference on Information Science and Engineering*, December 26- 28, 2009, Nanjing, Jiangsu China.

Organization for Economic Co-operation and Development. (2007), *E-government as a tool for transformation*, Retrieved July 3, 2010, from http:// www.olis.oecd.org/ olis/ 2007doc.nsf/ 4582bc8915d31134c12573a70050a430/ c5bfb886ebcafe06c12572ac0057513c/ $FILE/ JT03224646.PDF [Accessed 03 July 2010]

Paulsen, M. (2002), *Online education systems: Discussion and definition of terms*, Retrieved June 22, 2010, from http:// nettskolen.nki.no/ forskning/ Definition%20of%20Terms.pdf

Project Management Institute (PMI). (2004). *A guide to the project management body of knowledge* (3rd ed.). Newtown Square, Pennsylvania: PMBOK Guides.

PublicTendering.com. (2009), *Analysis: PEPPOL - Pan-European Public eProcurement On-Line* Retrieved July 3, 2010, from http:// www.publictendering.com/ analysis-peppol-pan-european-public-eprocurement-on-line/

Thomas, C. (2009), *Are you ready for g-government?* Retrieved February 10, 2010, from http:// www.esri.com/ news/ arcuser /0101/ umbrella13.html

Thompson, J. R., & Seidner, R. (2009), *Federated human resource management in the federal government: The intelligence community model*, IBM Center for the Business of Government, Retrieved February 10, 2010, from http:// www.businessofgovernment.org/ pdfs/ thompsonseidner_magazine.pdf

Washington State Digital Government Plan. (2001), *National Association of State Information Resource Executives. Nomination for 2001 recognition awards for outstanding achievement in the field of Information Technology*, Retrieved February 10, 2010, from http:// www.nascio.org/ awards/ nominations/ 2001Washington9.doc

Willmott, H. (1994). Business process re-engineering and human resource management, *Emerald publishing, Journal for Personnel Review*, *23*(3). doi:10.1108/00483489410064559

Zornada, L., & Velkavrh, T. (2005). Implementing ERP systems in higher education institutions. In: *27th Int. Conf. Information Technology Interfaces (ITI 2005)*, June 20-25, 2005, Cavtat, Croatia

KEY TERMS AND DEFINITIONS

e-Government: Refers to the maximization of ICT as a transformational agent for improving effectiveness and service delivery by State and Local government agencies.

Government-to-Employees (G2E): Are the online interactions through instantaneous communication tools between government units and their employees.

Government-to-Government (G2G): Is the online non-commercial interaction between Government organizations, departments, and authorities and other Government organizations, departments, and authorities.

Government Resources Planning (GRP): Government Resources Planning facilitates effective and efficient management of government resources and human capital, and provides Government Departments with an integrated suite of services for all resource management (human, financial and material). GRP is based on the accrual accounting system, and reinforces decentralization and self-service within management.

Integrated Information System: An expansion of a basic information system achieved through system design of an improved or broader capability by functionally or technically relating two or more information systems, or by incorporating a portion of the functional or technical elements of one information system into another.

Resources Management: In organizational studies, resource management is the efficient and effective deployment for an organization's resources when they are needed. Such resources may include financial resources, inventory, human skills, production resources, or information technology (IT).

Resources Planning: Is an integrated computer-based system used to manage internal and external resources including tangible assets, financial resources, materials, and human resources. It is an application and software architecture whose purpose is to facilitate the flow of information between all business functions inside the boundaries of the organization and manage the connections to outside stakeholders.

Chapter 10
Evaluating the Use of Structured E-Forum Tools in Consultations on Public Policies

Euripidis Loukis
University of the Aegean, Greece

Alexander Xenakis
Panteion University, Greece

Pedro Soto-Acosta
University of Murcia, Spain

ABSTRACT

The governments of many countries all over the world attempt to reform and improve their communication and interaction with citizens in important public policies issues through electronic channels mainly based on the Internet. It is therefore highly important to develop and systematically evaluate ICT tools that can facilitate and support high quality interaction and consultation among citizens and government agencies on public policies. This chapter investigates and evaluates the use of a structured e-forum tool, which has been designed and developed for this purpose, based on the Issue Based Information Systems (IBIS) framework. Using this tool an e-consultation pilot has been conducted on new legislation, which usually constitutes the most important, complex, and extensively debated component of every public policy. It has been evaluated using multiple methods: analysis of the discussion tree, quantitative evaluation through a structured questionnaire, and qualitative evaluation through an in-depth discussion in a small focus group. The conclusions of them were consolidated revealing the advantages offered by the structured e-forum, and also its limitations.

DOI: 10.4018/978-1-60960-839-2.ch010

INTRODUCTION

The governments of many countries all over the world attempt to reform and improve their communication and interaction with citizens on public policies issues through electronic channels, mainly based on the Internet. The rapid development and diffusion of information and communication technologies (ICT), and especially the Internet, which offer new cheap, inclusive and interactive channels and environments for public political communication and interaction, and at the same time the observed 'democratic deficits' and the trend to overcome them through more participation and involvement of citizens, have been the main drivers of the rapid development of e-participation in the last decade (Macintosh, Malina, & Whyte, 2002; OECD, 2003a, 2003b and 2004; Saebo, Rose, & Flak, 2008; Davis, 2009). According to the relevant reports of OECD (2003b and 2004) electronic participation (or e-participation) is defined as the extension and transformation of participation in societal democratic and consultative processes mediated by ICT. Its main objective is to exploit the continuously increasing capabilities and penetration of ICT in order to inform citizens on government activities and policies, and to broaden and deepen political participation, increasing both its quantity and quality. The potential of ICT and especially the Internet in this direction has been strongly emphasized by the relevant literature. OECD (2004) argues that 'The unprecedented degree of interactivity offered by new ICTs has the potential to expand the scope, breadth and depth of government consultations with citizens and other key stakeholders during policy-making'. In the same direction recently Todd Davis (2009) states that 'Imagine technology and democracy uniting to overcome distance and time, bringing participation, deliberation, and choice to citizens at the time and place of their choosing'. These new technologies can drive significant transformations in the quantity and quality of communication and interaction of government agencies with citizens. This will enable government agencies to gain a better and deeper understanding of the problems, needs, concerns and values of the groups of citizens and in general the societies they are serving, and therefore make in-time the required adaptations and reforms in their public policies, programs, operations and legislations whenever conditions change. Therefore e-participation has the potential to be a strong driver of innovation and reform in government.

It should be emphasized that these e-participation ideas have been based on the ideas of 'strong' or 'participatory' democracy that had emerged about 20 years ago and keep evolving. Their basic proposition is that the role of citizens in modern democracy cannot be limited to voting in the elections taking place every three or five years, but should also include their deliberative engagement in public decision-making; they argue that the informed opinion of citizens should be taken seriously into account in all the decisions of government organizations. Barber (1984) highlights the concept of 'strong democracy', which is based on active citizen participation and discussion among opposing views, which however 'entails listening no less than speaking, it is affective as well as cognitive...'. Held (1987 and 1996) distinguishes nine different models of democracy, one of them being the 'participatory' model, which reflects the need to engage both citizens and civil society organisations (CSOs) in the policy process, which however necessitates informed and active citizens. Fishkin (1991 and 1995) calls for "mass" deliberation by citizens instead of "elite" deliberation by their elected representatives, and argues that 'A major part of the problem of democratic reform is how to promote mass deliberation – how to bring people into the process under conditions where they can be engaged to think seriously and fully about public issues'. The development, reduction of prices and rapid penetration of ICT, and especially the Internet, provided effective means for the wide application of these ideas.

In this direction government agencies of various layers (e.g. national, regional, local) organize e-consultations about important public policies in all the stages of their lifecycle, both in the design stages (agenda-setting, analysis, policy creation) and in the execution ones (implementation, monitoring/evaluation). However, the high expectations have not been fully realized so far (e.g. McNeal, Hale, & Dotterweich, 2008; Macintosh, Gordon, Renton, 2009); this indicates that further research and improvement is required in many areas (both technical and non-technical), so that higher maturity can be achieved in e-participation. One of these areas is definitely the improvement of the ICT tools used for e-participation. Several types of tools have been researched, deployed and tested for this purpose, such as e-form (e.g. for complaints or suggestions), e-forum and e-petition tools, which however are in general characterised by low levels of structure (OECD, 2003b and 2004; Macintosh, 2004; Schlosberg, Zavestoski, & Shulman, 2007; Cartwright, & Atkinson, 2009). For instance the e-forum tools used for most e-consultations are unstructured or minimally structured, since they allow participants to enter just 'opinions' (without any discrimination between different types of opinions), or in some cases opinions on other previously entered opinions. It is therefore highly important to develop and systematically investigate and evaluate more structured ICT tools, which can facilitate and support higher quality interaction and consultation among citizens and government agencies on public policies, based on arguments and contra arguments. Furthermore, such structured ICT tools would make the analysis of participants' contributions easier, so that they can be more efficiently summarized and used in the following stages of the decision-making process. However, limited research and even less systematic evaluation has been made concerning more structured ICT tools for this purpose, such as the 'structured e-forum' (Karacapilidis, Loukis, & Dimopoulos, 2005). It can be defined as an electronic discussion space, which allows participants to enter semantically annotated postings (e.g. problems, proposed solutions, advantages and disadvantages), and also associate them to previous postings, according to some rules based on a predefined discussion ontology.

This chapter investigates and evaluates systematically the use of a structured e-forum tool, which has been designed based on the Issue Based Information Systems (IBIS) framework (Kunz, & Rittel, 1979; Conklin, & Begeman, 1989; Conklin, 2003), for e-consultations on public policies in order to improve their quality. Using this structured e-forum tool an e-consultation pilot on legislation under formation has been conducted in cooperation with the Greek Parliament. Legislation usually constitutes the most important, widely debated and at the same time the most complex component of every public policy, so it is worth focusing on it. This pilot has been evaluated using multiple methods: analysis of the discussion tree, quantitative evaluation though a structured questionnaire and qualitative evaluation through an in-depth discussion in a focus-group. The quantitative and qualitative evaluation have been based on the 'Technology Acceptance Model' (TAM) (Davis, Bagozzi, & Warshaw, 1989; Davis, 1989), which constitutes a well established and mature foundation from the information systems domain. From this evaluation interesting conclusions have been drawn concerning the advantages offered by the structured e-forum, and also its limitations. The research presented in this chapter has been part of the LEX-IS project ('Enabling Participation of the Youth in the Public Debate of Legislation among Parliaments, Citizens and Businesses in the European Union') (www.lex-is.eu) of the 'eParticipation' Preparatory Action of the European Commission (Loukis et al., 2007).

This chapter consists of eight sections. This introduction is followed by a section briefly describing the theoretical background of our research. Then the research methodology is presented, followed by a description of the abovementioned pilot. In the following three sections the results of the multi-method evaluation of the pilot are presented (from the analysis of the discussion tree, the quantitative evaluation and the qualitative evaluation respectively). In the final sections a discussion of findings is provided followed by the conclusions.

THEORETICAL BACKGROUND

Rittel and Weber (1973), as part of a contribution to planning theory, proposed a division of the problems that societies and organizations face into 'tame' and 'wicked' ones. The main characteristics of the tame problems are that, though they are not necessarily simple, they have been sufficiently understood, so they can be analysed using established 'first generation' methods through algorithms, which consist of sequences of predefined steps, and it is clear when a solution has been reached (i.e. there are clear stopping rules). On the contrary the wicked problems are the most difficult to address, since they are characterised by many stakeholders with different and heterogeneous problem views, values and concerns, so there is not agreement among them on the exact definition of the problem; such problems lack mathematically 'optimal' solutions and pre-defined algorithms for calculating them, and have only 'better' and 'worse' solutions, the former having more positive arguments in favour of them than the latter (i.e. there are not clear stopping rules). In order to solve them several iterations are required, each of them usually resulting in a redefinition or elaboration of the problem to be solved.

Kunz and Rittel (1979) suggest that wicked problems cannot be addressed by the usual first generation methods, and require second generation methods, which are based on high quality consultation and argumentation among stakeholders, aiming to build a common understanding of the problem, its possible solutions and the advantages and disadvantages of each of them. Based on this, a 'balanced' solution, which has the highest possible acceptance of the various stakeholders' groups, can be hopefully formulated, having considerable advantages and fewer disadvantages. Furthermore, they suggest that this can be facilitated and enhanced by using an 'Issue Based Information System' (IBIS), which aims to 'stimulate a more scrutinized style of reasoning which more explicitly reveals the arguments. It should help identify the proper questions, to develop the scope of positions in response to them, and assist in generating dispute'. The IBIS framework is based on a simple but powerful discussion ontology, whose main elements are 'questions' (issues-problems to be addressed), 'ideas' (possible answers-solutions to questions-problems) and 'arguments' (evidence or viewpoints that support or object to ideas).

In the same direction Forester (1985) views complex planning in both the public and the private sector as a process of 'Making Sense Together in Practical Conversations', in which stakeholders (i.e. individuals or groups affected by the outcome of this planning) make together sense of the problematic context and discover other participants' values and concerns. This requires a high quality deliberation, resulting in a shared understanding concerning problem definition, alternative actions and also arguments and counterarguments for each of them, which lays the foundation for finding a good and acceptable solution.

The development of public policies for addressing the highly complex and multidimensional problems that modern societies face is usually a complex and wicked planning problem. Most public policies have many stakeholders affected by them, with quite different problem views, values and interests, and very often in conflict with one another. It is very usual that one stakeholder group proposes strongly some policy directions, but other stakeholders' groups have strong objections to them. For these reasons the development of public policies necessitates well-organized participation of stakeholders and efficient consultation and argumentation among them. The relevant literature (Barber, 1984; OECD, 2004;

Macintosh, Gordon, Renton, 2009; Davis, 2009; Fishkin, 2009) emphasizes that this requires not just simple political discussion, but a high quality 'deliberation' based on arguments and contra arguments, in which participants: i) are sufficiently informed, ii) thoughtfully formulate and express their arguments, iii) are willing to listen to, think over and understand the arguments of the other participants, iv) are prepared to change their opinions if they are persuaded by the arguments of others, and v) prefer collaboration and synthesis to competition. However, very often this is not achieved in real life, for various reasons including political culture and also distance, time and budget limitations. Therefore it is of critical importance to use appropriate ICT tools for facilitating and supporting not just discussion among stakeholders, but high quality deliberation among them with the above properties. In this direction OECD (2004) states that a major challenge 'is how to build capacity and active citizenship by harnessing ICTs to constructively encourage deliberation by citizens on public issues – listening to, and engaging in, argument and counter arguments'. Taking into account the above characteristics of public policy development, it is would be interesting to investigate the use of structured e-forum tools based on the IBIS framework for this purpose.

Such a tool requires from the participants to make semantic annotation (i.e. define the type) of each new posting in an electronic discussion, which reflects its content. The allowed semantic annotations will be predefined, based on the discussion ontology of the IBIS framework: each participant will be allowed to enter a new 'question', or 'idea', or 'argument' ('pro' or 'contra'). This will guide the participants to think in a more structured way about the public policy under discussion and make more thoughtful and focused contributions, so it is expected to increase the quality and effectiveness of the discussion. Also, the participants have to associate their postings with previous ones according to the rules defined in the discussion ontology of the IBIS framework, e.g. an 'idea' should be associated with an 'question', while a 'pro' or a 'contra' argument should be associated with an 'idea', etc. This will guide the participants to examine more carefully and understand better the postings of others, so it is expected to improve the communication and interaction among the participants, and in this way to increase further the quality and effectiveness of the discussion. From a knowledge management perspective, such structured electronic discussions allow a more efficient transformation of the valuable 'tacit knowledge' possessed by the stakeholders into 'explicit (codified) knowledge' (knowledge externalization) (Nonaka, 1994; Cohendet, & Steinmueller, 2000), which can be processed, combined with other relevant knowledge and disseminated. Moreover, such a sequence of semantically annotated and associated postings creates threads of in-depth discussions which are more convenient to be tracked, analysed and summarized, so that useful conclusions can be drawn and used in the following stages of the decision-making process.

However, in the area of e-participation have been traditionally used and researched mainly ICT tools characterised by low structure, such as e-forum, e-petition and e-community tools (OECD, 2003b and 2004; Macintosh, 2004; Schlosberg, Zavestoski, & Shulman, 2007; Cartwright, & Atkinson, 2009). For instance, most of the political e-consultations on various public policies are conducted in e-forum environments, which allow participants to enter postings, or postings on other participants' postings, without any semantic annotation or structure. There are a few previous publications describing structured electronic discussion and argumentation tools for public policy consultations (Gordon, & Karacapilidis, 1997; Karacapilidis, & Papadias, 2001; Pingree, 2009), however quite limited research has been conducted concerning the systematic evaluation of such tools (Karacapilidis, Loukis, & Dimopoulos, 2005). Therefore further research is required in order to investigate and evaluate systematically, based on 'real life' evidence, the suitability, advantages and disadvantages of using structured ICT tools for e-consultations on public policy.

RESEARCH METHODOLOGY

In order to contribute to filling this research gap we investigated and evaluated systematically the use of a structured e-forum tool based on the IBIS framework for consultations on legislation under formation, which is usually the most important, widely debated and at the same time complex component of every public policy. It requires high quality deliberation and argumentation among many heterogeneous stakeholders, with thoughtful and focused opinions and arguments, which take into account seriously other stakeholders' opinions (e.g. Coglianese, 1997; Schlosberg, Zavestoski, & Shulman, 2007).

In particular, for meeting the above research objective we adopted the following methodology.

Initially the process of legislation formation in the Greek Parliament was analyzed.

Then, based on this analysis, a pilot e-consultation on a law under formation in the Greek Parliament was designed. This included definition of the bill to be discussed, the participants, the discussion ontology, the timing of the discussion and also the informative material to be provided to the participants. Concerning the discussion ontology, it was decided to use the one of the IBIS framework, since previous literature supports its suitability for discussing wicked problems (e.g. Kunz, & Rittel, 1979; Conklin, & Begeman, 1989; Conklin, 2003). An adaptation of the naming of the basic types of postings provided by IBIS was adopted (as 'issues', 'alternatives', 'pro-arguments', 'contra-arguments', adding also the type of 'comments' allowing more neutral postings), which was used in our previous research (Karacapilidis, Loukis, & Dimopoulos, 2005), being more appropriate for discussions on public policy.

Next this pilot e-consultation was conducted in cooperation with the Greek Parliament, being monitored and moderated by the first two authors (since their native language is Greek).

Finally this pilot was evaluated using multiple methods:

1. Analysis of the discussion tree which was formed by the postings of the participants. We calculated the number of postings entered by the participants in total (as an overall measure of the extent of this e-consultation), per type (for each of the allowed types: key issues, comments, alternatives, pro-arguments, contra-arguments, for assessing the composition of the e-consultation) and per level of the discussion tree (for assessing the depth of the discussion and the interaction among the participants). Also, we calculated the percentages of the simplistic postings (= postings that just agree or disagree with previous postings, without adding any new information/value) and the postings assigned a mistaken type (as indicators of the ease of use of the structured e-forum).
2. Quantitative Evaluation based on the statistical processing of participants' responses to a number of relevant questions of an evaluation questionnaire which was distributed electronically to them. This questionnaire included many questions asking the participants to assess various aspects of this e-consultation. Among them there were five questions focusing on the structured e-forum tool (they are shown in the Appendix), based on the 'Technology Acceptance Model' (TAM) (Davis, Bagozzi, & Warshaw, 1989; Davis, 1989), which constitutes a well established and mature foundation from the information systems domain. These questions were asking participants to assess two basic aspects of the structured e-forum tool, its perceived ease of use (Q1 and Q2) and its perceived usefulness (Q3, Q4 and Q5), which according to the TAM are the main determinants of its adoption.

3. Qualitative Evaluation based on a semi-structured in-depth discussion in a focus-group, consisting of some of the participants in the e-consultation and also Officials of the Greek Parliament. It aimed to provide a deeper understanding of the main strengths and weaknesses of the structured e-forum with respect to the above two basic aspects, its ease of use and usefulness. The discussion was tape-recorded and transcribed. Then coding of the transcript was performed manually, in which each of the two first authors (since their native language is Greek) processed separately the above document, in order to identify the main issues, strengths and weaknesses expressed by the participants in the discussion concerning its ease of use and usefulness, using an open coding approach (Maylor & Blackmon, 2005). The results of these two authors were compared and differences were resolved.

PILOT DESCRIPTION

Our e-consultation pilot, which was implemented as part of the LEX-IS project (Loukis et al., 2007), involved an electronic discussion on a highly controversial law under formation regulating the 'Contract of Voluntary Cohabitation' in a structured e-forum tool. This law formalized an existing social situation in Greece for long time: many couples, especially among the younger age groups, are reluctant to proceed directly to marriage, and instead choose to live together under the same roof, sharing their lives for long periods of time, and during that time have children, share living expenses and buy property, just to mention some of their most important common actions. However these couples are not legally bonded, leaving the weaker partner unprotected in case that such an informal co-habitation ends. In order to cover this legal gap this law was proposed to regulate the formalization of the voluntary co-habitation of couples, and along with that to settle the issues arising when such unions are dissolved. There were two groups who expressed strong objections to the settlements of this law: the young couples and the homosexual couples. The young couples were not satisfied with some of the settlements regulating mainly inheritance and child support issues. The homosexual couples complained that they were excluded from the right to form a union under the scheme that this law regulated; this gave rise to a big debate in the Greek society about whether homosexual couples were justly excluded or not.

The e-consultation on this law was held between 79 participants, aged between 18 to 35 years old, coming mainly from the University and the Parliament environment, and were characterized by levels of education and computer skills. Initially a workshop was held to in order to give them general information about this e-consultation and demonstrate the capabilities of the ICT platform used, including the structured e-forum tool. Next the Parliament provided to them the complete documentation of this law: i) the justification report of the law, ii) the main content of the law (articles), iii) the minutes of the discussion on this law in the Parliament. Then the electronic discussion started, and lasted for a period of 5 weeks. Each participant, once logged in, could either join the discussion on an existing issue or introduce a new issue. In the former case, a participant could either comment on an existing issue, or suggest an alternative addressing it; also, he/she could enter a pro argument in favor, or on the contrary a con argument against an alternative. For each new posting the participant had first to define its type (i.e. semantically annotate it), then enter a short title summarizing it which was shown in the discussion tree), and finally enter a longer text describing and explaining the posting in detail. The discussion was moderated, which meant a delay of several hours between the time a new posting was entered and the time it was approved by the moderator and became visible

Figure 1. Partial view of the discussion tree formed in the structured e-forum

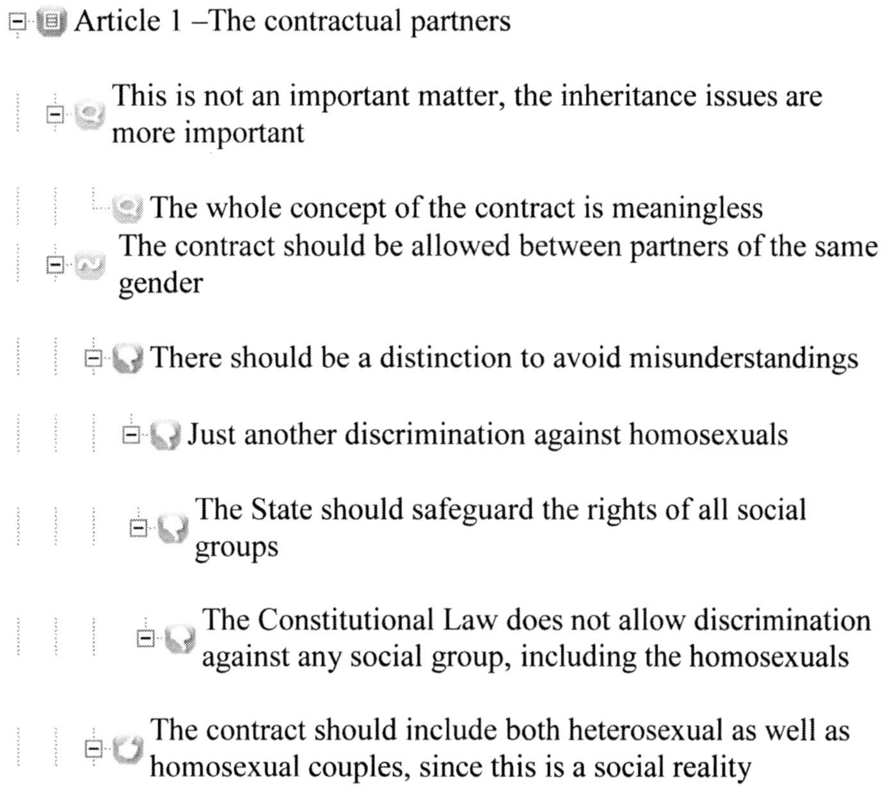

on the e-forum for the other participants to comment on. The conclusions of this e-consultation were given to the competent Parliamentary Committee.

ANALYSIS OF THE DISCUSSION TREE

The first step of the evaluation of this e-consultation was the analysis of the discussion tree that was formed in the structured e-forum tool; we can see a partial view of it in Figure 1 (translated from Greek into English), showing some of the postings entered by the participants.

In total the participants made 4192 visits in the structured e-forum tool and entered 131 postings on this highly debated topic. Initially we calculated the number of postings per type and found that we had:

- 8 'issues',
- 13 'comments',
- 15 suggested 'alternatives',
- 35 'pro-arguments',
- 60 'con-arguments'.

The above indicate that a good and balanced discussion tree was formed, with the expected composition and structure from a well-developed electronic discussion: with several new issues (8) entered by the participants on the root topic (=the law on the 'Contract of Voluntary Co-habitation'), a higher number of alternatives (suggestions for changes) (15), and also a similar number of comments (13) on these issues, and a much higher number of pro-arguments (35) and con-arguments (60). It was encouraging that we did not have a problem of too many comments that we initially feared, which would indicate that participants had difficulty in semantically annotating their postings, and preferred to use the more broad and neutral comment type (since an issue, alternative, pro- or contra-argument, question or answer can be broadly characterised as a comment, however a more detailed mental processing of it reveals that it requires a more 'specific' characterization). Therefore we can conclude that a structurally well-developed electronic discussion took place. This provides a first evidence that these highly educated and computer skilled participants managed to use efficiently the rich 'discussion language' provided by the IBIS framework (consisting of the above six types of postings and the allowed associations among them); however, in order to draw more sound conclusions on this we have to calculate some additional metrics.

So next we calculated the percentage of the simplistic postings (= postings not adding value/ new information), and found only 8, which make a 6% of the total number of postings. Additionally, we calculated the percentage of postings assigned a mistaken type (e.g. some postings were characterized as issues, while from their content we could see that they were alternatives), and found 13 such postings, which makes a 10% of the total number of postings. These results indicate that this structured e-forum tool and the discussion language it provides were not difficult to be used by our highly educated and computer skilled participants, but at the same time they were not very easy and intuitive (as the above non-negligible percentages of postings with mistaken type and simplistic postings, even by these sophisticated users, shows). This can be understood taking into account that in our everyday discussions we are not accustomed to having such structured discussions, which require much mental effort for structuring and semantically annotating our opinions (i.e. selecting the correct type for them).

Finally, in order to assess the level of depth of this electronic discussion, we calculated the number of postings per level, and found:

- 8 first level postings,
- 24 second level postings,
- 38 third level postings,
- 27 fourth level postings,
- 20 postings of fifth level,
- 13 sixth level postings,
- 1 seventh level posting.

Therefore it can be concluded that the electronic discussion of the pilot was characterized by considerable depth and interaction among the participants. This indicates that the stimulation and guidance provided to the participants by a structured e-forum tool, through the predefined types of postings and associations among them (guiding the participants to think which are the main issues, what are the main alternatives for addressing each of them, which are the main advantages and disadvantages of each alternative, etc.), results in discussions of considerable depth and interaction among the participants.

QUANTITATIVE EVALUATION

The second step of the evaluation was quantitative. The evaluation questionnaire was returned by 27 out of the 79 registered participants in this e-participation pilot (34% response rate). The relative frequencies of the responses to the five questions concerning the structured e-forum are presented in Table 1.

With respect to ease of use we can see that most of the respondents found as medium to easy using the structured e-forum (68%), and also accessing, reading and understanding the postings of other participants (56%). It should also be noted that in both these questions the response with the second highest relative frequency was 'medium to difficult' (20% and 28% respectively).

Table 1. Partial view of the discussion tree formed in the structured e-forum

	difficult	medium to difficult	medium to easy	easy
Q1. How easy it was to use the structured forum, i.e. to correctly characterize your idea as an issue, an alternative, a pro-argument, a contra-argument, or a comment, and then correctly enter it in the structured forum??	0%	20%	68%	12%
Q2. How easy it was to access, read and under-stand the postings of other participants and the connections among them in the structured forum?	4%	28%	56%	12%
	much worse	slightly worse	slightly better	much better
Q3. What is your general assessment of the structured forum as a tool for important e-consul-tations in comparison to the normal forum tools?	0%	8%	28%	64%
	low	medium to low	medium to high	high
Q4. How do you assess the quality of the contributions (postings) entered by the participants in this e-consultation?	0%	8%	76%	16%
	to a poor extent	to medium extent	to a good extent	to a very good extent
Q5. To what extent did you learn new things and ideas from the contributions (postings) entered by the other participants in this e-consultation?	4%	40%	44%	12%

Therefore the respondents on one hand do not find the structured e-forum difficult, but on the other do not find it easy either, and believe that it requires considerable mental effort (e.g. in order to correctly characterize an idea as issue, alternative, pro-argument, contra-argument, or comment, to correctly enter it in the structured forum, to access, read and understand the postings of the other participants, etc.), despite their high educational level and computer skills. This conclusion is in agreement with the non-negligible percentage of entries assigned a mistaken type (10%) identified from the analysis of the discussion tree.

With respect to usefulness, the structured e-forum tool is perceived by most of the respondents as much better than the normal forum tools (64%), or slightly better (28%). Also, a big majority of the respondents assess the quality of contributions (postings) of other participants as medium to high (76%), or high (16%). Finally, most of the respondents believe that they learnt new things and ideas from the contributions (postings) entered by the other participants in this e-consultation to a good extent (44%), or to a medium extent (40%). Therefore the respondents find the structured e-forum as useful, and superior to the normal (unstructured) forum, due to the mechanisms of structuring and focusing the discussion it provides, which improve its quality and effectiveness.

QUALITATIVE ANALYSIS

In the semi-structured focus-group discussion we conducted with some of the participants in this e-consultation and also Officials of the Greek Parliament one of the topics was whether it was easy to use the structured e-forum, and also its main advantages and disadvantages in this respect. One of the main difficulties mentioned was the correct assignment of type to the postings; this is confirmed by the findings of the quantitative evaluation (from questions Q1 and Q2) and the non-negligible percentage of mistakes (about

10%) identified in the analysis of the discussion tree. As another difficulty in using the structured e-forum was mentioned the appropriate wording of the title of each posting, which is directly shown in the discussion tree of the structured forum box, so that it reflects the content of the posting in a few words and other participants can easily understand it. By examining the discussion tree we identified several postings in which the title was not representative of the more detailed description and explanation presented in corresponding box, so it was difficult for the other participants from the title to understand the content of the posting. This can reduce the communication and interaction among the participants.

Also, some additional weaknesses were mentioned during this discussion, which had more to do with the design and implementation of the particular platform and the structured e-forum tool used in this pilot, rather than the concept of the structured forum itself. For instance, some participants said that the platform provides a very small space (box) for the structured e-forum, so the users have to use much scrolling up and down when trying to access previous participants' postings. With respect to the moderation of the postings all participants agreed that it caused a big problem: from the time one posting was entered by a participant it usually took several hours until the moderator approved it and the posting became visible; so it was not possible for the same participant and the other ones to see it immediately, and possibly enter more postings associated with it.

Another topic in the semi-structured focus-group discussion was the usefulness of the structured e-forum. It was generally accepted that overall the use of the structured e-forum was considered a strength of the pilot, since it enables a more focused and effective e-discussion. Also, the semantic capability it offers allows users to quickly form an opinion as to the progress of the discussion on a particular key issue of interest. The postings were judged by the focus group to be well informed and of relatively good quality. It was mentioned that the adopted moderation processes had a positive impact on the quality of the postings was; that was known to all participants beforehand, so they were careful anyway when making a posting. The above findings are in agreement with the assessments of most of the respondents in the quantitative evaluation that the structured forum is a superior tool than the normal (unstructured) forum, providing proper structuring mechanisms, which result in better quality of participants' postings and discussion.

The Parliament Officials mentioned that such tools can be useful in order to get a better feeling of public opinion on the issues discussed in the Parliament and better quality of contributions and arguments from the citizens. The focus-group was generally positive towards the idea that such e-participation tools could prospectively offer a stand to the less powerful, excluded and non-participating in politics citizens; however, the higher mental effort that the structured e-forum tool requires, in comparison with the formal (unstructured) forum tool, might prevent citizens with lower education from using it. Another point raised by the Parliament Officials was the anonymity of postings (opinions) entered in this tool, which has some advantages (freedom of expression), but at the same time does not allow them to be seriously considered by the Parliament, which traditionally takes more seriously into account opinions from persons representing important stakeholder groups (e.g. chairpersons of affected trade unions, or sectoral/professional associations).

DISCUSSION

From the above multi-method evaluation of this pilot, which included analysis of discussion tree, quantitative evaluation and qualitative evaluation, some encouraging conclusions have been drawn concerning the potential of using structured e-forum in the e-participation domain for improving the quality of e-consultations on public policies.

In particular, with respect to its usefulness, the highly sophisticated participants in our pilot find that the structured e-forum is better than the simple (unstructured) forum, enabling a more focused and effective electronic discussion. Furthermore, the big majority of the participants find the contributions of their co-participants to be of high or medium quality. However, with respect to the ease of use, these highly sophisticated participants in our pilot do not regard the structured e-forum platform as easy to use and intuitive (which is a critical requirement for e-participation systems); they rather find it medium to easy to use, and believe that it requires considerable mental effort, and mention some difficulties they had in using it (e.g. for the correct characterization of their postings as issues, alternatives, comments, pro- or contra-arguments, for the appropriate wording of the title of each posting so that it reflects the content of it in a few words and other participants can easily understand it).

These conclusions are in general in agreement with the ones drawn from the abovementioned study of Karacapilidis, Loukis & Dimopoulos (2005), who evaluated the use of a similar structured e-forum tool for supporting G2G collaboration in public policy making, based on smaller pilot e-consultation concerning the potential establishment or not of non-state universities in Greece among fourteen public servants from several involved public authorities. From this evaluation it was concluded that participants found the system useful for supporting efficient and effective electronic discussions on difficult and complex public policies; however, at the same time they report some difficulties they had in participating in such a highly structured e-consultation, which is perceived by them as much more demanding than the usual face-to-face ones they often participate in as part of their jobs. Also, our positive conclusions as to the usefulness of structured e-forum are in agreement with the ones of previous studies of other mechanisms of structuring electronic discussion and cooperation in group decision support systems, such moderation, different leadership styles, scripts providing guidance to participants (e.g. Mark et al, 1999; Farnham et al., 2000; Munkvold, 2003; Kahai et al., 2007); their overall conclusions is that these mechanisms of structuring electronic discussion and cooperation have a positive impact on their efficiency and effectiveness.

Our investigation provides evidence that structured e-forum tools can be efficient means of high quality e-consultations on public policies among more sophisticated and knowledgeable discussion groups. They provide significant advantages, associated with the guidance and facilitation they provide to the participants: i) for thinking in a more structured way about the public policy under discussion, ii) for making more thoughtful and focused contributions, and iii) for examining more carefully and understanding better the postings of others. The above properties are expected to improve the communication and interaction among the participants, and the quality of their postings, contributing to a better realization of the 'deliberation models' proposed by the public participation literature.

Furthermore, the use of such advanced structured e-forum tools can drive significant transformations in the quantity and quality of communication and interaction of government agencies with citizens. This will provide government agencies more and higher quality information about the problems, needs, concerns and values of the groups of citizens and in general the societies they are serving, and thus stimulate and enable them to make in-time the required transformations and reforms in their public policies, programs, operations and legislations whenever conditions change. Such a high quality e-participation can be a strong driver of innovation government. Also, the use of structured ICT tools makes the analysis of participants' contributions easier, as it allows a more efficient summarization of them, and then a better exploitation in the following stages of the policy and decision making process.

However, we do not expect these benefits and the resulting transformations/reforms to be realized automatically. On the contrary there are three basic preconditions:

a. Government agencies should develop appropriate mechanisms (e.g. specialized units with highly skilled and motivated personnel) for studying and processing these citizens' contributions, and then forwarding the main conclusions to the highest political management, in order to be integrated in the policy and decision making process at the highest level (avoiding possible filtering and attenuation by middle management layers).
b. Also, a strong political will is necessary to 'hear' these valuable citizens' contributions, and take them seriously into account in policy and decision making, to a similar extent to the various organized groups ('lobbies'), which usually have too much influence on government decisions and policies.
c. Overcome the 'inertia' that very often characterises government agencies, mainly due to their complexity (in terms of processes, rules and legislation), culture and lower exposure to competition (despite the growing trend for benchmarking and comparisons among similar government agencies and also with analogous private companies).

Also, it should be emphasized that on the contrary less sophisticated, knowledgeable and coherent groups might find the structured e-forum a less good and suitable solution, having difficulties in structuring their thoughts according to the requirements of this tool, and semantically annotating their opinions; this means that the mechanistic substitution of the unstructured ICT tools currently in use for e-participation by such structured ones might result in further exclusion of less sophisticated and knowledgeable groups from the political debates increasing 'digital divide'. Therefore a good solution would be the adoption by Parliaments of an appropriate mix of approaches, i.e. for each law under discussion to organize:

- *one closed* electronic discussion in a structured e-forum tool, in which will participate only invited representatives of stakeholder groups, who will be normally more sophisticated and knowledgeable on the law under discussion, and also experts; this will give to more representatives of stakeholder groups the opportunity to express their opinions on laws under discussion (today due to time limitations are invited only a few of them – the most important ones - to come to the Parliament and express their opinions),
- *and also one open* and anonymous electronic discussion for the general public, using a normal (unstructured) forum tool.

This mixed approach could also include the exploitation at the same time of the emerging web 2.0 social media (enabling communication, collaboration, news sharing, social networking, multimedia publishing, broadcasting, etc.) as well, which have managed to attract high numbers of users; this will enable an even wider and more inclusive citizens' e-participation in the formulation of significant public policies, involving various different groups who do not usually visit the official e-participation stages of government organizations (Charalabidis et al., 2010).

CONCLUSION

In the previous sections of this chapter has been presented an investigation and systematic evaluation of the use of a structured e-forum tool, which is based on the IBIS framework, for e-consultations on public policy, focusing on its the most important, widely debated and at the same time most complex component, the formation of legislation. For this purpose we designed and implemented an e-consultation pilot in cooperation with the Greek Parliament on a highly controversial law regulating the 'Contracts of Voluntary Co-habitation'. It was evaluated using multiple methods: analysis of discussion tree, quantitative evaluation and qualitative evaluation. The conclusions were consolidated revealing advantages that the structured e-forum can offer, and at the same time its limitations.

It was concluded that the structured e-forum is better than the simple (unstructured) one, since it can enable a more focused and effective electronic discussion. However, it cannot be characterized as easy to use and intuitive (which is a critical requirement for e-participation systems); on the contrary it requires considerable mental effort, and poses significant difficulties and challenges to its users (e.g. correct characterization of their postings as issues, alternatives, comments, pro- or contra-arguments, or appropriate wording of the title of each posting so that it reflects the content of it in a few words and other participants can easily understand it).

The management implication of this study is that public organizations should adopt an appropriate mix of approaches in this domain: they can organize e-consultations on important public policies both with the wider public using simple unstructured e-forum tools, and also with the more sophisticated and knowledgeable representatives of stakeholders and with domain experts using more structured e-forum tools.

More empirical research is required for investigating the suitability of the structured e-forum for e-consultations on public policies among various citizens groups, covering both more and less educated/knowledgeable groups, and also various kinds of public policies, and different cultural and political contexts. Further research is also required for the development of advanced structured e-participation tools, which can drive efficient electronic discussions and at the same time are usable by wider citizens' groups (e.g. with less discussion structure, or other models of discussion structure). Finally it is necessary to conduct research on the exploitation of the emerging web 2.0 social media by government agencies for e-participation purposes, in combination with their 'traditional' e-participation channels (based on their own government e-participation websites).

REFERENCES

Barber, B. (1984). *Strong democracy*. Berkeley, CA: University of California Press.

Cartwright, D., & Atkinson, K. (2009). Using computational argumentation to support e-participation. *IEEE Intelligent Systems*, *24*(5), 42–52. doi:10.1109/MIS.2009.104

Charalabidis, Y., Gionis, G., Ferro, E., & Loukis, E. (2010). Towards a systematic exploitation of Web 2.0 and simulation modeling tools in public policy process. In *Proceedings of the IFIP Second International Conference on e-Participation - ePart 2010* (August 29 - September 2, 2010, Lausanne, Switzerland). London, UK: Springer Verlag.

Coglianese, C. (1997). Assessing consensus: The promise and performance of negotiated rulemaking. *Duke Law Journal*, *46*(6), 1255–1349. doi:10.2307/1372989

Cohendet, P., & Steinmueller, W. E. (2000). The codification of knowledge: A conceptual and empirical exploration. *Industrial and Corporate Change*, *9*(2), 195–209. doi:10.1093/icc/9.2.195

Coleman, S., & Gotze, J. (2002). *Bowling together: Online public engagement in policy deliberation*. Retrieved from http:// bowlingtogether.net

Conklin, J. (2003). Dialog mapping: Reflections on an industrial strength case study . In Kirschner, P., Buckingham Shum, S., & Carr, C. (Eds.), *Visualizing argumentation: Software tools for collaborative and educational sense-making*. London, UK: Springer Verlag.

Conklin, J., & Begeman, M. (1989). gIBIS: A tool for all reasons. *Journal of the American Society for Information Science American Society for Information Science*, *40*(3), 200–213. doi:10.1002/(SICI)1097-4571(198905)40:3<200::AID-ASI11>3.0.CO;2-U

Davis, F. D. (1989). Perceived usefulness, perceived ease of use and user acceptance of Information Technology. *Management Information Systems Quarterly*, *13*(3), 319–340. doi:10.2307/249008

Davis, F. D., Bagozzi, R. P., & Warshaw, P. R. (1989). User acceptance of computer technology: A comparison of two theoretical models. *Management Science*, *35*(8), 982–1003. doi:10.1287/mnsc.35.8.982

Davis, T. (2009). The blossoming field of online deliberation . In Davis, T., & Gangadharan, S. P. (Eds.), *Online deliberation – Design, research and practice*. Stanford, CA: CSLI Publications.

Farnham, S., Chesley, H. R., McGhee, D. E., & Kawal, R. (2000). Structured online interactions: Improving the decision-making of small discussion groups. In *Proceedings of ACM 2000 Conference on Computer-Supported Cooperative Work (CSCW 2000)* (299-308). New York, NY: ACM Press.

Fishkin, J. S. (1991). *Democracy and deliberation*. New Haven, CT: Yale University Press.

Fishkin, J. S. (1995). *The voice of the people - Public opinion and democracy*. New Haven, CT: Yale University Press.

Fishkin, J. S. (2009). Virtual public consultation: Prospects for Internet deliberative democracy . In Davis, T., & Gangadharan, S. P. (Eds.), *Online deliberation – Design, research and practice*. Stanford, CA: CSLI Publications.

Forester, J. (1985). Designing: Making sense together in practical conversations. *Journal of Architectural Education*, *38*(3), 14–20.

Gordon, T. F., & Karacapilidis, N. (1997). *The Zeno argumentation framework*. Paper presented at the Sixth International Conference on Artificial Intelligence and Law (ICAIL '97).

Held, D. (1987). *Models of participation*. Cambridge, UK: Polity Press.

Held, D. (1996). *Models of Democracy*. Cambridge, UK: Blackwell Publishers.

Kahai, S., Fjermestad, J., Zhang, S., & Avolio, B. J. (2007). Leadership in virtual teams: Past, present, and future. *International Journal of e-Collaboration*, *3*(1), 1–8.

Karacapilidis, N., Loukis, E., & Dimopoulos, S. (2005). Computer-supported G2G collaboration for public policy and decision making. *Journal of Enterprise Information Management*, *18*(5), 602–624. doi:10.1108/17410390510624034

Karacapilidis, N., & Papadias, D. (2001). Computer supported argumentation and collaborative decision making: The HERMES system. *Information Systems*, *26*(4), 259–277. doi:10.1016/S0306-4379(01)00020-5

Kunz, W., & Rittel, H. (1979). *Issues as elements of Information Systems*. Working Paper No. 131. California, USA: Berkley. Retrieved from http://www-iurd.ced.berkeley.edu/pub/WP-131.pdf

Loukis, E., Wimmer, M., Triantafillou, A., Gatautis, R., & Charalabidis, Y. (2007). *Electronic support of participation in the development of legislation: The LEX-IS project*. Paper presented at the 5th Eastern European eGov Days 2007, 11-13 April, Prague, Czech Republic.

Macintosh, A. (2004). *Characterizing e-participation in policy making*. Paper presented at the 37th Hawaii International Conference on System Sciences.

Macintosh, A., Gordon, T. F., & Renton, A. (2009). Providing argument support for e-participation. *Journal of Information Technology & Politics*, *6*, 43–59. doi:10.1080/19331680802662113

Macintosh, A., Malina, A., & Whyte, A. (2002). Designing e-participation in Scotland. *Communications: The European Journal of Communications*, *27*, 261–278.

Mark, G., Grudin, J., & Poltrock, S. (1999). Meeting at the desktop: An empirical study of virtually collocated teams. In the *Proceedings of the Sixth European Conference on Computer-Supported Cooperative Work*. Norwell, MA: Kluwer Academic Publishers.

Maylor, H., & Blackmon, K. (2005). *Researching business and management*. New York, NY: Palgrave-Macmillan.

McNeal, R., Hale, K., & Dotterweich, L. (2008). Citizen-government interaction and the Internet: Expectations and accomplishments in contact, quality and trust. *Journal of Information Technology & Politics*, *5*(2), 213–229. doi:10.1080/19331680802298298

Munkvold, B. E. (2003). *Implementing collaboration technologies in industry: Case examples and lessons learned*. London, UK: Springer-Verlag.

Nonaka, I. (1994). A dynamic theory of organizational knowledge creation. *Organization Science*, *5*(1), 14–37. doi:10.1287/orsc.5.1.14

Organisation for Economic Cooperation and Development (OECD). (2004). *Promise and problems of e-democracy: Challenges of online citizen engagement*. Paris, France: OECD.

Organization for Economic Co-operation and Development (OECD). (2003a). *Engaging citizens online for better policy-making - Policy brief*. Paris, France: OECD.

Organization for Economic Co-operation and Development (OECD). (2003b). *The e-government imperative*. Paris, France: OECD.

Pingree, R. J. (2009). Decision structure: A new structure to three problems in deliberation . In Davis, T., & Gangadharan, S. P. (Eds.), *Online deliberation – Design, research and practice*. Stanford, CA: CSLI Publications.

Rittel, H. W. J., & Weber, M. M. (1973). Dilemmas in a general theory of planning. *Policy Sciences*, *4*, 155–169. doi:10.1007/BF01405730

Saebo, O., Rose, J., & Flak, L. S. (2008). The shape of e-participation: Characterizing an emerging research area. *Government Information Quarterly*, *25*, 400–428. doi:10.1016/j.giq.2007.04.007

Schlosberg, D., Zavestoski, S., & Shulman, S. W. (2007). Democracy and e-rulemaking: Web-based technologies, participation, and the potential for deliberation. *Journal of Information Technology & Politics*, *4*(1), 37–55. doi:10.1300/J516v04n01_04

Whyte, A., & Macintosh, A. (2002). Analysis and evaluation of e-consultations. *e-Service Journal*, *2*(1), 9-34.

APPENDIX

Questions about the Structured E-Forum Tool

Q1. How easy it was to use the structured forum, i.e. to correctly characterize your idea as an issue, an alternative, a pro-argument, a contra-argument, or a comment, and then correctly enter it in the structured forum?
□ difficult □ medium to difficult □ medium to easy □ easy
Q2. How easy it was to access, read and understand the postings of the other participants (issues, alternatives, pro-arguments, contra-arguments, comments) and the connections among them in the structured forum?
□ difficult □ medium to difficult □ medium to easy □ easy
Q3. What is your general assessment of the structured forum as a tool for important e-consultations in comparison to the normal forum tools (where you do not have to characterize your posting as an issue, an alternative, a pro-argument, a contra-argument, or a comment, and then enter it correctly)?
□ much worse □ a little worse □ a little better □ much better
Q4. How do you assess the quality of the contributions (postings) entered by the participants in this e-consultation?
□ low □ medium to low □ medium to high □ low
Q5. To what extent did you learn new things and ideas from the contributions (postings) entered by the other participants in this e-consultation?
□ to a very good extent □ to a good extent □ to a medium extent □ to a poor extent

Chapter 11
A New Model for Transparency and E-Participation:
Who Transforms What Policy into Whose Practice?

Ronit Purian
Tel-Aviv University, Israel

Niv Ahituv
Tel-Aviv University, Israel

Phillip Ein-Dor
Tel-Aviv University, Israel

ABSTRACT

The analysis of transparency depends on the objectives and the research discipline in which the evaluation is undertaken. This study follows two main lines: to provide a framework for transparency evaluation, and to develop guidelines for the design and management of citizen-orientated Internet websites and e-participation initiatives. This is done in three stages: defining the research discipline, defining the concepts and terms, and defining measures for evaluation. Finally, the suggested framework is examined in the context of real estate planning in Israel, where the use of online systems – designed and implemented independently by a few local authorities – seems to bypass a controversial national planning reform. A close acquaintance with governance processes has raised the inevitable question, perhaps typical to many systems in the public sector: who transforms what policy into whose practice?

DOI: 10.4018/978-1-60960-839-2.ch011

Scales for measuring and evaluating the progress of Internet websites are usually based on their evolution, from brochure-like pages to interactive services (Ein-Dor and Segev, 1993). The number of contact channels may reflect openness levels in relatively simple Internet websites; while Web 2.0 applications, which express a higher level of Internet evolution, are more complicated for evaluation. Moreover, the spectrum of e-participation initiatives requires also a user-view framework of analysis.

The knowledge hierarchy, which is widely used in Information Systems (IS) research, may provide the desired user-view framework. The knowledge hierarchy can support the selection of targeted stakeholders in accordance with their skills and abilities. This can be done by matching each type of e-participatory activity to the appropriate level in the knowledge hierarchy. For example: matching processed inputs on a conceptual level, termed knowledge, with the wide community; matching specific information with engaged citizens that possess local knowledge in their areas of interest; and matching data with semi-professional local representatives that produce value out of data much as experts do. This model should help understand conflicts such as the ban of mosque minarets in a country with Muslim minority, or the often heard accusation of "too much democracy," the disfavor of open debates and other expressions of imbalance in the new era of e-participation. Governments and communities may benefit from the proposed user-view framework while designing and implementing new e-participation initiatives.

INTRODUCTION

The evaluation of Internet websites success depends on the objectives and the research discipline in which the evaluation is undertaken. So is the analysis of transparency which is the main topic of this study. Transparency may encompass additional concepts such as accountability and collaborativeness that are crucial for the effective use of information technology (IT) and systems (IS).

Value of information is a concept that was evolved in the IS literature and is supposed to fit to the point more than common success indicators such as return on investment (ROI) or user satisfaction. These objectives do not capture various externalities, whereas measurements of the value of information might be linked to services that are public goods and to values and norms that are embedded in the IT (Walsham, 2009).

Different IT architectures may provide different levels of access, communication, flexibility and collaborativeness, and accountability. For example: to what extent does the owner of the system – the governor or regulator – hold a direct and exclusive control of the system; initiate open discussions; encourage public debate; publish information; and mainly increase "organizational effectiveness through flattening hierarchies and enhancing public sector creativity" (Chadwick 2006, p.194). This optimistic vision expresses the nature of IT: "the introduction of new technologies not only fostered more rapid communication, it also caused fundamental long-term shifts in internal power structure. Vertically integrated hierarchies of command and control were being displaced by looser, more flexible, horizontally integrated networks. [...] Access to centralized databases allows rapid retrieval of information necessary for good decision making. In this perspective, e-government goes beyond simple task automation" (p.194). Moreover, the concepts of information and power are going through a radical change following the creation of the new Web 2.0 practice of sharing (Ahituv, 2001).

Indexing and theorizing the growing variety of e-participation initiatives, which clearly go "beyond simple task automation", is a new challenge in e-government research. In an attempt to capture the "Value for Citizens", Nordfors et al. (2009) proposed the value to "be of personal or private nature to individuals, be they citizens, communities, groups, localities companies etc. It can also be a participative value, created collaboratively and interactively between two or more individuals, or a public value created by the governance structure and proactively promoting collective benefits" (p.72). However, this descriptive division does not provide tools for explaining e-government initiatives, for predicting their success, or for planning and implementing them.

A dichotomy proposed by Paivarinta and Saebo (2006) is more attractive in this sense. The seemingly objective and professional decisions, that actually shape the public sphere, can be divided into two types, according to the question "who sets the agenda, governors or citizens?" (Paivarinta and Saebo, 2006). Different models of democracy are implemented in each category and its resulting IT structure. Defining such criteria contributes much to indexing e-participation initiatives. The power shift from governors to citizens is fundamental especially for a user-view framework. E-government is no longer only in the hands of governments.

The Internet has evolved to a point where its applications offer higher flexibility and collaborativeness. Does it imply a higher evolution of government? Not necessarily. Mature and successful government should incorporate with local constrains and characteristics, which is the objective of this paper to map and model

E-GOVERNMENT

ICT are powerful tools, which need to be managed and used properly in order to alter "the principal agent-client relationship in the public sector-citizen interface, most notably through e-governance" (Rumel 2004, p.247-373). To this end, ICT enables and supports three main concepts: "Accountability, meaning that it is possible to identify and hold public officials to account for their actions; Transparency, meaning that reliable, relevant and timely information about the activities of government is available to the public; Openness, meaning governments that listen to citizens and businesses, and take their suggestions into account when designing and implementing public policies" (Kondo 2001, p.7).

The next section presents e-government as a unique technological service that is supposed to be adopted by all groups of society.

DEFINITIONS FOR E-GOVERNMENT

E-government is defined as the use of Information and Communications Technology (ICT) and its application by the government for the provision of information and public services to the people (OECD, 2001). "Government" comprises the executive, legislative and judiciary organs of the government while the "consumer" or "citizen" includes any member of the civil society (individuals as well as organizations). E-government includes electronic interactions of three types: government-to-government (G2G); government-to-business (G2B) and its reverse (B2G); and government-to-consumer/citizen (G2C), and its reverse (C2G) (OECD, 2001).

The ELOST Consortium (E-government for LOw Socio-economic sTatus groups) defined e-government as "the application of information and communications technology (ICT) to enhance and improve the relationship and interaction between citizens and the government at large, including municipalities and other public authorities" (ELOST 2006, p.59).

The words "to enhance and improve the relationship and interaction between citizens and the government" may imply intentions to implement e-democracy processes. The same is true for the definition proposed by the Center for Democracy and Technology (CDT) and The Information for Development Program (InfoDev): "e-government is the use of ICT to transform government by making it more accessible, effective and accountable" (CDT and InfoDev 2002, p.1).

Indeed there are different definitions of e-government, which expose the variety of attitudes towards the concept: from managerial, technological, operational and social points of view; from a focus on procedure enhancement and better information and service delivery, to equal access to ICT and citizen empowerment. For example, an operational definition for e-government refers to: "a situation in which administrative, legislative and judicial agencies (including both central and local governments) digitize their internal and external operations and utilize networked systems efficiently to realize better quality in the provision of public services", according to the Global Business Dialogue on Electronic Commerce (GBDe 2001, p.42).

A broad technical definition for e-government, which refers mainly to technology and applications, was proposed by the United Nations and the American Society for Public Administration: "E-government can include virtually all information and communication technology (ICT) platforms and applications in use by the public sector" (United Nations 2002, p.1). The following definition widens the technological scope and emphasizes: "everything from 'electronic government services over the Internet' to 'exchange information and services with citizens, businesses, and other arms of government'", according to the United Nations Knowledge Base (United Nations, 2005).

The aim of e-government therefore is not only to efficiently provide information and services to the citizen, but also to encourage their participation in public policy design and decision making. This is a cultural challenge, not a technological one. Reforms in the public service, such as national programs to eliminate corruption, are possible when capable and committed leadership supports the idea (Cho and Choi, 2004; Rumel 2004, p.368). The question that arises here is whether e-government changes the role of government merely by the adoption of more productive technologies for services delivery.

E-GOVERNMENT EVALUATION METHODS

E-government can be implemented on various levels, from the lowest level of online static informative pages to the highest level of interactive services, with not only transaction facility but also participating in democratic processes, open discussions with the public and making decisions together (Layne and Lee, 2001; United Nations, 2005).

The wide scope of e-government research was emphasized by various scholars. E-government should efficiently provide information and services to the citizen, as well as promote participation in public policy design and decision making. The multiple goals were identified in the various definitions for e-government, as were presented in the previous section.

In economic or strategic terms, the success of IS and Internet website applications should be defined and measured in certain functions of organizational performance, including customers, workers or citizens satisfaction (e.g., inward migration to a city). Nevertheless, e-government literature proposed certain measurements that are presented here.

Basically, e-government can be implemented on various levels, from the lowest level of online static informative pages to the highest level of interactive services. A four stage model for e-government, suggested by Layne and Lee (2001), includes: cataloging, transaction, vertical integration, and horizontal integration. These four stages are explained in details in terms of the complexity involved and the different levels of integration (Lee, Tan and Trimi, 2005). Figure 1 presents the model (Layne and Lee 2001, p.124).

Other works describe different stages of e-government development. For example, the UN Department of Economic and Social Affairs proposed the classification of E-Information, E-Consultation and E-Decision (United Nations

Figure 1. E-government development stages (Source: Layne and Lee (2001, p.124))

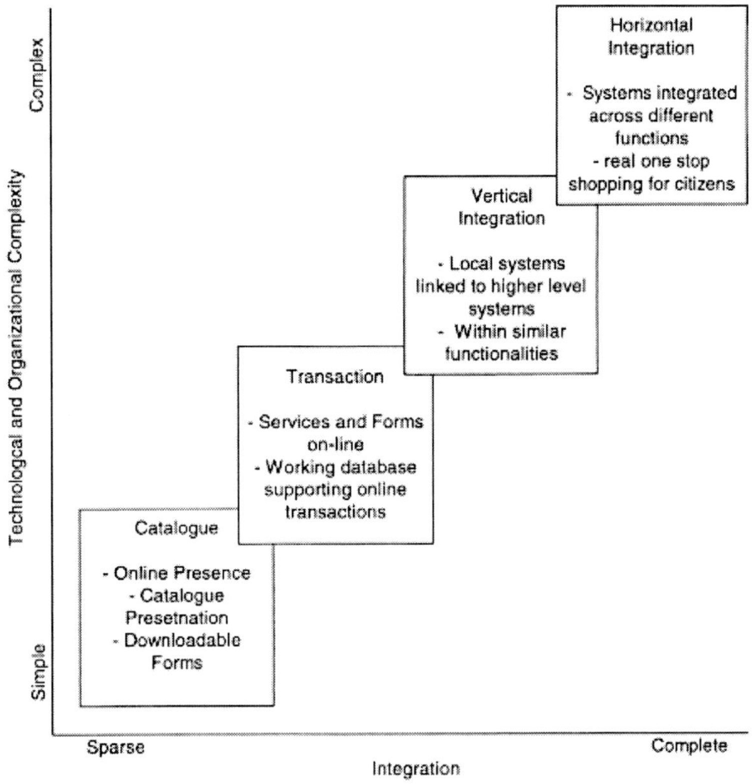

2005, p.20). The UN Global e-Government Readiness Index (2005, p.16) proposed:

- Stage I: Emerging: Online presence; links to ministries may/may not exist. Much of the information is static.
- Stage II: Enhanced: Governments provide more information. They have created links to archived information, and newsletters.
- Stage III: Interactive: Governments deliver online services such as downloadable forms for tax payments.
- Stage IV: Transactional: Governments introduce two-way interactions between 'citizen and government'.
- Stage V: Connected: Governments transform themselves into connected entities that respond to the needs of their citizens by developing an integrated back-office infrastructure.

A critical analysis of the main existing methods of monitoring, evaluating and benchmarking e-government development was proposed by Kunstelj and Vintar (2004), presenting a holistic model. The model integrated measurements of the back-office and the front-office with measurements of the environment, maturity of the government and the customers (citizens and businesses), and the impacts on them. Warkentin et al. (2002) have also recognized the political nature of government agencies as a feature distinguishing e-government from e-commerce. They noted that mandatory relationships exist only in e-government. Jorgensen and Cable (2002) identified three major differences between e-government and e-commerce: Access, Structure and Accountability. Decision-making authority is less centralized in government agencies than in businesses, according to Jorgensen and Cable (2002), and this structural dispersion of authority usually tends to impede the development and implementation of new government services. The third difference they identify is accountability. In a democratic government, public sector agencies are constrained by the requirement to allocate resources and provide services "in the best interest of the public" (Jorgensen and Cable, 2002).

A comprehensive review of recommended measurements, proposed by Scott (2005), includes five categories (pp.152-153):

1. Transparency – The site makes it easy for users to monitor official public records and to communicate with city officials.
2. Transactions – The site allows users to complete a wide range of online transactions.
3. Connectivity – The site connects users with other individuals or organizations that contribute to the local civic interest.
4. Personalization – The site personalizes Web content based on analysis of user preferences and behavior.
5. Usability – The site is reliable and easy to use" (Scott 2005, pp.152-153).

The recent years have brought the next stage of social media that was not included in the methods reviewed here. The change that the new era of Web 2.0 created is not yet incorporated in new evaluation models, neither in the public sector nor in private firms that strive to evaluate ROI for social media and realize that this revolution can not be measured quantitatively. However, the question repeats: what variables should be measured in order to produce a reliable and valid e-government index?

E-GOVERNMENT IN SOCIAL MEDIA

The evaluation of e-government depends on the objectives and the research discipline, whether measuring return on investment, economic efficiency, value of information, users' satisfaction, democratic ideals and more. This study considers the Internet as "a diverse collection of infrastructures delivering an even more diverse collection of technologies" (Saebo et al. 2008, p.411). As with e-participation, the same with e-government, there is "little agreement or discussion of what constitutes a valid evaluation criterion, the different roles of qualitative and quantitative evaluation, which indicators should be measured, and how results can be interpreted as successful or not" (Saebo et al. 2008, p.420).

Additional features that were not widely used a few years ago and should be examined are:

- The municipalities' presence in social media such as Facebook and Twitter, comments in forums and responses ("talk-backs");
- The existence of local wiki and e-petitions sets, in addition to other communication channels.
- Applications of mobile services (m-government).
- Special ICT initiatives that are aimed at policy execution, for example: educational or environmental activities, affordable housing, urban planning and revitalization, natural environment (open\common areas), transportation and energy (smart cities) and more.

Termed "collaborative democracy", Beth Noveck (2009) has developed mechanisms for increasing transparency, collaboration and participation, targeting specific objectives for each category. Examples for such innovative initiatives are quite diversified. Baumgarten and Chui (2009) present the United States District of Columbia's "Apps for Democracy":

"... a contest to encourage developers to create applications that would give residents access to data such as crime reports and pothole repair schedules. Forty-seven applications were created in 30 days. Hiring contract developers would have cost approximately $2.6 million, whereas the cost of running the contest was a mere $50,000" (p.30).

Other examples:

"[The US government] adopted software code developed by a nonprofit organization for USAspending.gov, a database of government grants and contracts. The government had initially estimated that it would cost $10 million to create the database and $2 million a year to maintain it, but it adopted the code developed by OMB Watch to run FedSpending.org, which had been funded through a $334,272 grant [...] roughly $200,000 from the grant was used to pay for the initial launch of the Web site" (p.30).

"[In Europe, a health authority has developed] an information architecture that allows health care providers to access aggregated data and build tailored applications to improve clinical care" (p. 30).

"[The South Korean government's ePeople] site invites civil petitions online (for example, policy suggestions or corruption complaints), moderates online discussion of submitted petitions, and reports back on its decisions. Moreover, governments can use Web 2.0 technologies to break down barriers between and within organizations. For example, the US intelligence community has created Intellipedia to share information among previously unconnected organizations, while the US Food and Drug Administration employed Web 2.0 tools to better engage and capture the knowledge of its internal experts" (p.31).

Goldman (2006) provided a selection of Gov 2.0 cases:

- Estonia's "Today I Decide" allows citizens to comment on draft laws and submit ideas for new ones. If a majority of online voters support a draft bill, it is forwarded to the relevant government department for review.
- A wiki serves for new national Policing Act in New Zealand.
- The Parliament Law Commission in France simplifies laws to make them more readable and understandable in run an online forum.
- The Sunlight Foundation operates PublicMarkup.org around a draft bill on government transparency in the US.
- In England, e-petition on the 10 Downing Street website directly connects with each other around particular issues.
- Twitter brought police departments on the Internet, sometimes instead of press releases.

Up to now we have presented the evolution of e-government, towards an increased voluntary activity of sharing and collaborating. What about those who cannot afford it, or can but still avoid new technologies?

After presenting basic definitions and frameworks for e-government, the following chapter presents prominent theories that are used in IS research, regarding technology adoption.

TECHNOLOGY ADOPTION

Theories used in IS research integrate, among other things, models from social and cognitive literature. The user is central in these theories, whether the level of analysis centers on either the individual or the organization. In this chapter,

Figure 2. Theory of reasoned action (Source: Fishbein and Ajzen, 1975)

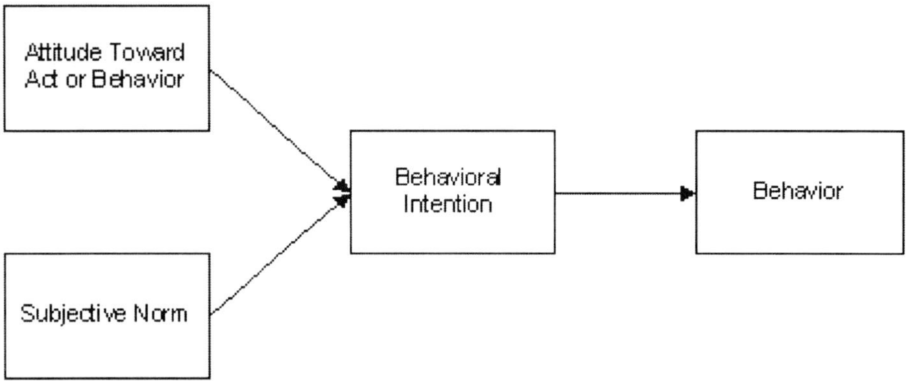

theories based on the individual level of analysis will be presented first.

The first part of this section introduces prominent theories that are used in IS research, regarding technology adoption.

INDIVIDUAL-LEVEL MODELS

Attitude toward behavior is defined, according to the Theory of Reasoned Action, as "an individual's positive or negative feelings (evaluative affect) about performing the target behavior" (Fishbein and Ajzen 1975, p.216). The attitude is determined by assessing one's beliefs regarding the consequences of a behavior and by evaluating the desirability of these consequences. The overall attitude can be expressed as the sum of the desirability assessments times the individual consequence for all expected consequences of the behavior.

In addition to the individual's attitude toward the behavior, behavioral intentions can be influenced also by subjective norms surrounding the performance of the behavior. Subjective norm is defined as "the person's perception that most people who are important to him think he should or should not perform the behavior in question" (Fishbein and Ajzen 1975, p.302). The overall subjective norm can be assessed as the sum of the motivation assessments times the individual perception for all relevant referents.

Figure 2 presents the Theory of Reasoned Action.

According to the Theory of Reasoned Action (Fishbein and Ajzen, 1975) individual behavior is driven by behavioral intentions which are a function of an individual's attitudes and environmental norms. However, the risk of confounding attitudes and norms is one limitation of the model. A second limitation of the model is the potential constraints on the freedom to act. In practice, even if someone forms an intention to act, there may be various constraints.

The Theory of Planned Behavior (Ajzen, 1991) attempts to resolve this limitation by adding a third factor, perceived behavioral control, that is defined as "the perceived ease or difficulty of performing the behavior" (Ajzen 1991, p.188). The Theory of Planned Behavior views the control that people have over their behavior as lying on a continuum from behaviors that are easily performed to those requiring effort, skills, resources and more. Although Ajzen (1991) suggested that the link between behavior and behavioral control should be between behavior and actual behavioral control, the difficulty to assess actual control has led to the use of perceived control instead of actual behavioral control.

Figure 3. Theory of planned behavior (Source: Ajzen, 1991)

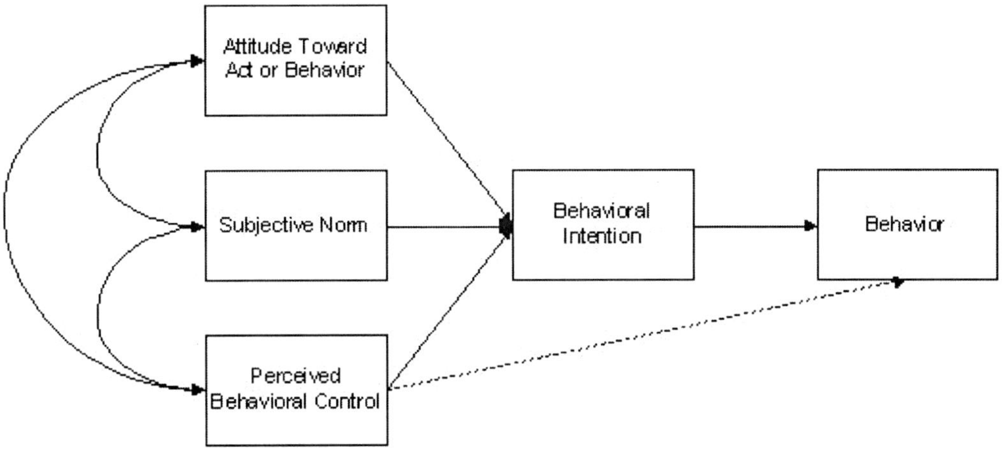

Figure 3 presents the Theory of Planned Behavior.

The Technology Acceptance Model (TAM) (Davis 1989; Venkatesh et al. 2003) integrates constructs from the Theory of Reasoned Action into the field of IS (Mathieson, 1991). According to TAM, an individual's intention to use a new product or technology is determined by the Perceived Ease of Use (PEU) and the Perceived Usefulness (PU) of the new product or technology, and mediates the actual use. The perceived ease of use directly impacts perceived usefulness (Davis, 1989). Figure 4 presents the Technology Acceptance Model (TAM).

A large number of articles have been published about TAM, followed by meta-analysis studies on technology acceptance (King and He 2006; Lee et al. 2003; Legris et al. 2003; Ma and Liu 2004; Schepers and Wetzels 2007; Sun and Zhang 2006; Yousafzai et al. 2007). Schepers and Wetzels (2007) reframe the concepts of Subjective Norm (SN) and Perceived Usefulness (PU) as "compliance effect" and "internalization effect", respectively. They propose: "…people often choose to perform an action when one or more important referents say they should, though they do not like or believe in it" (p. 91). This is the compliance effect. The internalization effect "represents the human tendency to interpret information from

Figure 4. Technology acceptance model (TAM) (Source: Davis, 1989)

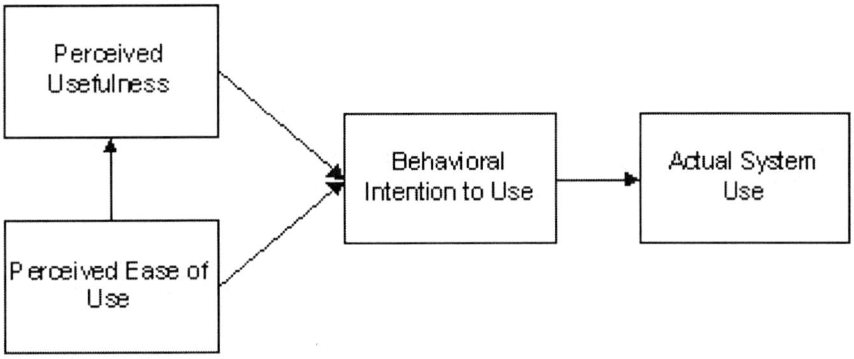

Figure 5. Unified theory of acceptance and use of technology (UTAUT) (Source: Venkatesh et al. 2003)

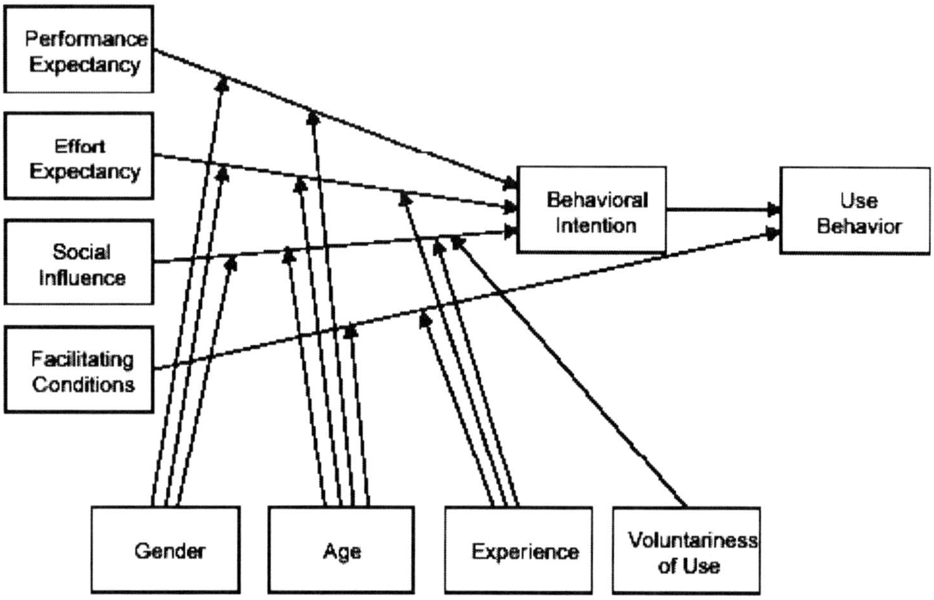

important others as evidence about reality" (p. 91).

Both the Theory of Reasoned Action and TAM have strong behavioral elements, assuming that when someone forms an intention to act, he or she will be free to act without limitation. In practice constraints such as limited ability, limited skills or organizational limits may possibly constrain the freedom to act. The Unified Theory of Acceptance and Use of Technology (UTAUT) aims to explain user intentions to use an IS and usage behavior under various limitations (Venkatesh et al. 2003).

The UTAUT was formulated with four core determinants of usage intention and behavior, and up to four moderators (Venkatesh et al. 2003). The four core determinants are: Performance Expectancy, Effort Expectancy, Social Influence and Facilitating Conditions. The four moderators are: Gender, Age, Experience and Voluntariness of Use, mediating the impact of the four core determinants on Usage Intention and Behavior (Venkatesh et al. 2003). The unified model was formulated through a review of user acceptance literature and the empirical comparison of eight prominent models.

Figure 5 presents the Unified Theory of Acceptance and Use of Technology (UTAUT).

Most of the key relationships in the model are moderated: The strength of the performance expectancy as a determinant of behavioral intention varies with gender and age (more significant for men and younger workers). The effect of effort expectancy on behavioral intention is also moderated by gender and age (more significant for women and older workers). Those effects decrease with experience. The effect of social influence on behavioral intention is contingent on all four moderators and is not significant without them. The effect of facilitating conditions on use behavior was significant only when examined in conjunction with the moderating effects of age and experience; meaning, they only matter for older workers in later stages of experience (Venkatesh et al. 2003).

According to Venkatesh et al. (2003, p.469):

"The complex nature of the interactions observed, particularly for gender and age, raises several interesting issues to investigate in future research, especially given the interest in today's societal and workplace environments to create equitable settings for women and men of all ages [...] While gender and age are the variables that reveal an interesting pattern of results, future research should identify the underlying influential mechanisms – potential candidates here include computer literacy and social or cultural background, among others".

In order to provide an even richer understanding of technology adoption and usage behavior, Venkatesh et al. (2003) suggested that possible questions might take the form of additional theoretically motivated moderating influences, different technologies (e.g., collaborative systems, e-commerce applications), different user groups (e.g., individuals in different functional areas), and other organizational contexts (e.g., public or government institutions).

For the purpose of this research, we will further examine the importance of not only the adoption of new information technologies but also the emotional motivation that constitutes the positive attitudes towards them in the first place. Hence, extrinsic motivation for using technology "because it is perceived to be instrumental in achieving valued outcomes" (Davis et al. 1992, p.1,112) is not enough as an explanation for behavior.

The attitude construct in the TAM is based on the Theory of Self Efficacy. Self Efficacy (Bandura, 1977) is people's perception of their ability to plan and take action to reach a particular goal. Computer Self-Efficacy (CSE) refers to individuals' assessment of their capabilities to perform a behavior (e.g., use a computer) that evokes emotional reactions such as anxiety. Emotional core constructs are affect, defined as an individual's liking for a particular behavior (e.g., computer use), and anxiety (Compeau and Higgins, 1995).

Davis (Davis et al., 1992) also applied motivational theory to understanding new technology adoption and usage, presenting intrinsic motivation versus extrinsic motivation. The perception that users want to perform an activity "for no apparent reinforcement other than the process of performing the activity per se" is opposed to considerations such as "improved job performance, pay or promotions" (Davis et al. 1992, p.1,112).

However, in order to simplify TAM, researchers removed the attitude construct, and so the theory of Self Efficacy was excluded. In their paper "Quo vadis TAM?", Benbasat and Barki (2007) have criticized "the restricted context in which TAM was tested (p.214) and stated that "going back to TPB is not a complete solution, since TPB has its own problems, such as its exclusion of emotions (e.g., enjoyment) and habits" (p.215).

Indeed, the theory of Self Efficacy, the attitudes, or the "intrinsic motivation" – are all crucial for predicting technology adoption. Following this line of thought, the implications of motivation gaps on digital divide measures and indices should be evaluated. Moreover, how would the contribution of innovative individuals be evaluated, assuming their accumulated influence?

After presenting prominent theories that are used in IS research regarding technology adoption, the next section presents definitions and frameworks for digital divide and digital literacy.

DIGITAL DIVIDE AND DIGITAL LITERACY

Digital divide covers a wide spectrum of phenomena (OECD, 2001). In fact, there are many digital divides of different types, e.g. age, gender, location (Ein-Dor, 2006).

OII and LSE (2010) refer to three groups suffering high levels of digital exclusion: those who are economically disadvantaged, being unemployed and low income; those who are elderly, retired and disabled; and those who are educationally disadvantaged and employed. Elaborating these categories beyond economic, educational and age levels is evidently specific to the user-segments that are situated in different conditions. Population groups that are more prone to exclusion in most of the countries include, according to a generic list by ELOST (2008, p.59), the following populations: ethnic minorities; new immigrants whose command of the local language and the governance structure is weak; people with low income; unemployed people; homeless citizens; people with low education; elderly people; young people at risk.

However, although end user segmentations are required for specific policy initiatives, the study of digital divide and digital literacy in developed countries should not be limited to physical barriers. What are the motivational factors that initiate any technological activity or are likely to inhibit digital literacy? In an attempt to address this challenge, barriers to technology adoption were classified by ELOST into four categories: awareness, access, skills and attitudes; or a combination of barrier categories (ELOST 2008, p.44). Positive attitude and especially high motivation may play a key role in technology adoption and innovation. But first, what are the variable that characterize the successful adopter? Digital literacy provides a suitable definition. Digital literacy is the ability to operate within four types of skills: communicate with others on the Internet; obtaining software on a computer; questioning the source of information found on the Internet; and search for required information on the Internet (SIBIS 2003, p.205). This definition is based on the definition of the minimum list of digital literacy skills from the European Commission Digital Literacy Workshop, which also includes a life-long learning perspective (European Commission, 2001).

Digital literacy, as well as digital divide, may be referred to as social or cultural expressions of the individual "intrinsic motivation" (Davis et al., 1992). The desire to use technology, the enthusiasm with no preconditions – are presumed to empower and be empowered by cultural forces. The following section integrates the theories into a new model of participation, where motivational aspects may sharpen the gaps of digital literacy.

THE NEW DIGITAL GAP

ICT are, among other things, social systems. Their impact on government and governance depends on the specific audience that interacts with them. Gregor and Jones (2007) admit that ICT, like traditional crafts, is based "on the knowledge implicit within the object itself of how best to shape, make and use it" (p.314).

In an overview of current practices in leading e-government countries, Lee et al. conclude: "It appears evident that e-government practices mirror each country's ICT diffusion and government efforts toward political reform" (Lee et al. 2005, p.104). The levels of ICT adoption and technology-sophistication of e-government practices vary greatly among governments, even among the leading ones. There are crucial differences in factors such as ICT infrastructure and organizational culture, and other resources required for the transformation: integration of appropriate ICT, information quality, engaged public employees, good administrative processes, and government leadership (Lee et al., 2005).

In the context of e-government, public considerations are injected in highly professional IS decisions. For this reason, ICT should be investigated as the phenomenon that emerges when technology and society interact. The next section sets the framework for possible interactions according to the types of content and users.

Figure 6. The knowledge hierarchy (Source: Tuomi 2000, p.106)

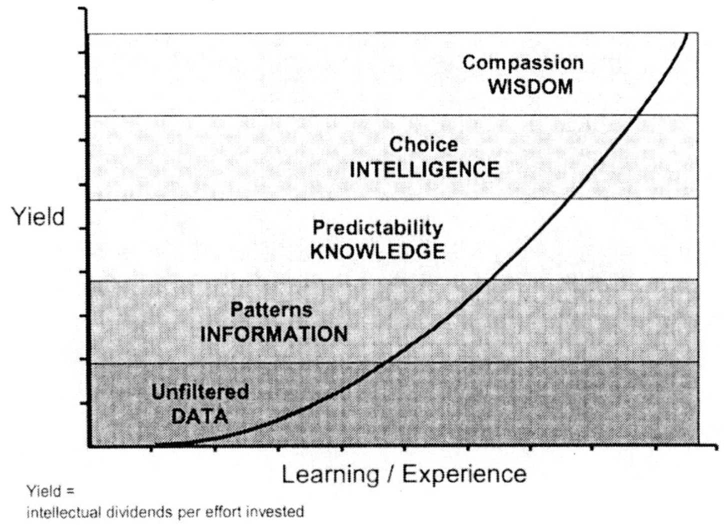

PERCEIVED VALUE OF INFORMATION

The value of information, or the knowledge hierarchy, is in question in this section. Different users may perceive similar inputs differently, depends on their attitudes, skills, and many other variables. Civic mindedness and technological sophistication are the factors to be examined here. Civic mindedness characterizes citizens who are "more engaged in civic affairs. In general, those citizens are likely to have more social contacts in their communities, be politically more active, and pay closer attention to the news media. […] Although many definitions of civic mindedness exist, they encompass the following three aspects: social contact, prior interest in government, and media use for public affairs" (Dimitrova and Chen 2006, p.177).

The knowledge hierarchy, which is widely used in IS research (Tuomi, 2000), matches the heterogeneity of users in the public sphere. Based on the knowledge hierarchy (Figure 6), the citizen-view model is best explained as the ability to retrieve knowledge out of data; or, the ability to produce value out of data (high ability), from information, and from knowledge. A rough division to three groups would be:

- **High-level abilities:** user is expected to produce value out of data, thus turn raw data into knowledge and action according to their needs and purpose.
- **Medium-level abilities:** user may need the assistance of a mediator to process the data into the structured level of information. Information-brokers such as NGOs are expected to turn data into information according to certain stakeholders' demands and purposes.
- **Low-level abilities:** user should consume the proposed alternatives in the shape of knowledge, ready for action; make the appropriate decision and behave based on processed data, or just react to an adverse situation (register complaints). Typical for the most disadvantaged and vulnerable groups in society.

This framework can be developed further in a comparison of participatory regimes, with points of comparison in time (along with the evolution of technology; in relation to differences between regulatory regimes). This interdisciplinary field of research provides an opportunity to understand information dynamics in the public sphere from the citizens' perspective.

Referring to any type of user and decision, the creation of value along the knowledge hierarchy raises additional research questions. For example, two phenomena that should be investigated are:

- **Transparency-efficiency trade-off:** A related research question deals with the trade-off transparency-efficiency; or the costs of e-participation. Is it possible to eliminate the downside? There are centralized local authorities that demonstrate low disclosure and high efficiency. From the opposite direction, the publicity given to long-term plans over short periods of time may reduce efficiency.

Other implications might be a disfavor of open debate, accompanied by the accusation of "too much democracy"; or conflicts such as veil criticism or the ban of mosque minarets in countries with Muslim minority. The design of e-participation mechanisms should consider the complex conditions and implications.

- **Standards-uniqueness trade-off:** A related research question deals with the trade-off between a standardized approach to transparency evaluation, which may reduce the value of reporting into technical data provision (or data flooding), and the fair value approach which reflects relevant activity but its creation and monitoring is more demanding.

A possible solution is a distinction between data that should be the fundamental objective of reporting (data that standards can accomplish), and flexible reporting and e-participation that may be subject to a knowledge standard and provide information value. Increased trust should be one possible output of such a system. Instruments for trust creation are required not only for the citizens but also to satisfy the authorities' need to provide information and obtain successful e-participation.

With these trade-offs in mind, in the design of any level of decision making, the creation of value along the knowledge hierarchy should be a guiding principle.

A NEW FRAMEWORK FOR E-PARTICIPATION

The knowledge hierarchy can support the selection of targeted stakeholder in accordance with their skills and abilities. The new citizen-view model proposed here incorporates the heterogeneity of users in the public sphere according to three knowledge categories of participation. Or, to be more precise, the knowledge level should not characterize the inputs but should refer to the knowledge level of the user in a specific context. In other words, since similar inputs may be perceived differently by different users in different contexts, the categories might be set according to the value that each user produces from the input. One way or the other, the categories may be as follows:

- **Knowledge (high value of information):** The approach to the wide community should be made on a conceptual level of processed inputs.
- **Information (medium value of information):** Informed citizens that possess local knowledge and are involved in the community should be engaged in the intermediary level. Information can be provided to

Table 1. E-participation framework based on the knowledge hierarchy

Target audience	Types activities' inputs
Communities	Knowledge level: e.g., consolidated statements, ready to consume by citizens; may lead to a defined action.
Participants	Information level: e.g., discussions with public representatives.
Decision makers	Data level: e.g., for analysis by experts, professional use.

the skilled stakeholders according to their areas of interest and participation.

- **Data (low value of information):** The local representation semi-professional users are expected to create value of data much as experts are able to.

Table 1 presents the framework that the knowledge hierarchy provides for the spectrum of e-participation initiatives. Governments and communities may benefit from this citizen-view model while designing and implementing new e-participation initiatives in a much more accurate way.

The contribution of the citizen-view model for understanding Gov 2.0 may be illustrated by user satisfaction monitoring. According to Capgemini (2009): "Clear policy shifts towards more user-centric, user-driven government are causing a marked change in user satisfaction monitoring practice" (p.54), therefore some "metrics link to policy goals such as transparency and accountability, inclusion, and accessibility" (p.56). Table 2 was adopted from Capgemini (2009) to illustrate the link between the knowledge hierarchy and the new system of Gov 2.0.

These measurement tools and metrics are of great importance since the engagement of users

Table 2. Framework for user satisfaction monitoring

Tools	Metrics
Knowledge level (monitoring of user needs before a service is put online)	
User co-design Ethnographic work User charter Living labs	EASE OF USE Error rates Time savings Cost savings Convenience Accuracy
Information level (tracking of user satisfaction during usage)	
Online for specific service Online general Online Feedback forms Pop-up survey Mystery user	FULFILMENT Satisfaction score Completeness Return? Recommend?
Data level (satisfaction surveys after the service has been used)	
SERVICE IMPROVEMENT Channel mix POLICY GOALS Inclusion Transparency EMOTIONS and PERCEPTIONS Privacy and Security/Trust	Face-to-face/phone interviews Portal and Websites data Household/Business surveys Focus Groups/Panels

Source: Capgemini 2009, p.55, Figure 32

in e-government systems implementation contributes to their acceptance (Chan and Pan, 2008). The evidence so far "indicates that e-government development is currently characterized by a technocentric approach with minimal engagement of citizens. [...] The crucial enabling role of capacity building is highlighted. Providing citizens with the necessary skills and capabilities to engage effectively offers the key to the successful development of systems such as e-government" (Olphert and Damodaran 2007, p.491). Moreover: "There is overwhelming evidence from many studies worldwide to suggest that e-government systems, like many previous public sector information systems, are falling short of their targets for performance, effectiveness, and adoption by citizens – their intended users. The evidence shows that achieving the goals of enhanced democracy, increased social inclusion, and faster adoption of technology continue to be elusive (p.504).

Aware of the obstacles, a systematic review of community-empowerment initiatives was carried out in the UK in the attempt to find how can governments maximize the benefits of openness towards the community. Pratchett et al. (2009) analyzed the design and the implementation of a wide selection of interventions, their context and their impact. A series of workshops with expert practitioners were convened to reflect on three issues: who benefits and engages with empowerment; the cost-effectiveness of empowerment; and the potential risks of empowerment (p.8).

Six mechanisms were investigated (quoting pp.22-23):

1. Asset transfer and other facilitative mechanisms for community management and/or ownership of assets and social enterprise.
2. Citizen governance, covering the role of citizen or community representatives on partnerships, boards and forums charged with decision making about public services and public policy.
3. Electronic participation, for example, e-forums and e-petitions, as a means of offering substantively different forms of engagement, and alternative or complementary channels for participation.
4. Participatory budgeting as a form of deliberative participation in communities facilitating decision making on devolved budgets.
5. Petitions as a mechanism for citizens and groups to raise issues of concern.
6. Redress as a mechanism for citizens to register complaints, have them investigated and receive feedback and response.

For each mechanism, around twenty cases were selected out of over 3,500 articles and reports on community empowerment. The selected articles referred to "at least one of the criteria to be used for evaluating 'empowerment success'" (p.25).

The methodology applied by Pratchett et al. (2009) relies on a Boolean approach that "allows qualitative researchers to go beyond the usual claims of 'suggest', 'indicate' and 'appear' to identify the conditions for 'empowerment success'. Much of the evidence base on community empowerment is qualitative and case based. The Boolean approach is viewed as a key method in developing systematic findings in comparative case study research" (p.11). This approach made it possible to produce a report on the six specific mechanisms, focusing on practical delivery implications of local initiatives. Table 3 presents the variables and factors for examining empowerment success.

The suggested knowledge-hierarchy framework for e-participation can be applied in the body of evidence presented here. Each target audience requires different inputs and is capable of creating different outcomes. Thus, the effect of the intervention depends on the specific stakeholders' skills and abilities. Indeed, Pratchett et al. (2009) recognize four types of citizen governance. "Looking at the clustering of factors across cases, it is possible to develop a typology of different forms

Table 3. Empowerment success

Outcome factors Three categories	Influencing factors Two categories
Effect on communities: improvements in a community's level of political efficacy, social capital and social cohesiveness.	Design of mechanism/intervention: Open to all; Support mechanisms; Links to formal political decision making.
Effect on participants: the extent to which participants have developed skills such as confidence, social networks, specialist policy knowledge, and the perception that they can influence their local government.	Context of mechanism/intervention: Low resource base; Ethnic diversity; Political 'buy-in'; Bureaucratic 'buy-in'; Highly salient issue (p.26).
Effect on decision making: ability to exercise more influence on decision making, particularly in previously excluded groups (p.25).	

Source: Pratchett et al. 2009, pp.25-26

of citizen governance. These we call: local representation; local knowledge; semi-professional; and organisational proxy" (p.58). For example, "To have a major impact on a community appears to be harder to achieve than advancing the skills of those citizens that do engage" (p.107).

These observations provide an indication about where the suggested framework can be implemented. There is a lack of "both strategic thinking and skills" in how to engage "'hard to reach' groups and new communities" (Pratchett et al., p.9). The suggested framework aims to direct this process. As opposed to the research design applied by Pratchett et al. (2009) where only "outcome factors" were divided according to the knowledge hierarchy – the suggested framework should be applied also to "initiatives" and "research design" which currently do not follow this line.

Chadwick (2006) studied the influence of IS on governments and concluded that there is "mixed evidence" that the introduction of IS in the public sector has increased organizational effectiveness. Why is that?

The existing information and services in Internet websites may tell us much on their strategic management. With no obligation on authorities and ministries to distribute data and information in a transparent manner – for example, certain periodical reports that can be accessible to the public by an Internet website – the differences in transparency and collaborativeness reflect local desires and perceptions. The local initiatives, as revealed in previous study (Purian, 2010), are expressions of personal initiatives, made by devoted individuals. The suggested framework should identify differences in the effective use of particular technologies under different levels of transparency and collaborativeness.

DISCUSSION

Understanding and designing e-participation mechanisms in the knowledge age are of great interest, theoretically and practically. This chapter provides a framework for planning and evaluating transparent system that engages citizens, integrates data and supports actionable public decisions.

Value of information is a concept that was evolved in the IS literature and is presented here versus common economic concepts such as return on investment (ROI), economic efficiency, or users' satisfaction. These operational objectives do not capture the democratic ideals that may be embedded in IT. Moreover, the evolution of IT in the public sector requires new evaluation concepts. The lack of solid theories is of special concern in the emerging stage of "e-government 2.0". What are the moderating principles for development, design, implementation and management? How should the effective use and application be evaluated? Transparency may encompass additional concepts such as accountability and collaborativeness, which is crucial for the effective use and application of IT.

The maturity of e-government systems is in question. The number of contact channels in an Internet website may reflect openness levels in relatively simple e-government websites. E-government 2.0 expresses a higher level of evolution. Within this system, measurements should be applied mainly to the flexibility of communication channels between the stakeholders. Does the governor or regulator hold a direct and exclusive control on the system? To what extent is he or she aware of the possibility to initiate an open discussion and encourage public debate? Different IT may provide different architectures, with different levels of access, communication, flexibility and collaborativeness.

An analysis of discussion forums provides support to the suggested framework. Paivarinta & Saebo (2006) concluded that the conflict is not between satisfying hard-line bureaucratic stakeholders versus increasing the level of service offered to millions of citizens. The conflict is between different models of democracy that may be reflected in each implemented IT structure. Paivarinta & Saebo (2006) mapped models of democracy by following the guiding question: Who sets the agenda, governors or citizens? This way or the other, e-government is no longer only in the hands of governments. E-government should efficiently provide information and services to the citizen, as well as promote participation in public policy design and decision making.

CONCLUSION

This study presents an overarching model for e-participation, based on the integration of new and recently-studied mechanisms. The contribution of the proposed model might be misperceived as a structured disadvantage, stressing that certain participatory activities should be directed to those who posses the suitable level of skills and abilities. However, democracy and equal rights do not necessarily impose absolute distribution of power. On the contrary, the real democratic challenge in the realm of information technology is to shape the appropriate mechanisms of open information and control. The challenge is to protect fair access, avoid biases, and yet balance the flow of information and decision making. Responsible leadership will resolve the trade-off between free access to effectiveness by careful design of initiatives, and by defining the target audience. Perhaps not always identifying it in advance, but drawing the line of participation's goals and the citizens that will contribute to the process for the benefit of all.

The suggested framework does not imply that a selection of specific population segments should be carried out in the design of participatory initiatives; it address the need to observe differences in demands, qualifications and aspirations. Highlighting the differences is aimed at providing suitable solutions for the heterogenic society, and at the same time enhance collaboration with the individuals that can produce more value from data. The questions that should be asked are who is transforming what policy into whose practice.

REFERENCES

Ahituv, N. (2001). *A world without secrets: On the open information society*. Tel Aviv, Israel: Am Oved Publishers. (in Hebrew)

Ajzen, I. (1991). The theory of planned behaviour. *Organizational Behavior and Human Decision Processes*, *50*(2), 179–211. doi:10.1016/0749-5978(91)90020-T

Bandura, A. (1977). Self-efficacy: Toward a unifying theory of behavioral change. *Psychological Review*, *84*, 191–215. doi:10.1037/0033-295X.84.2.191

Baumgarten, J., & Chui, M. (2009). E-government 2.0. *The McKinsey Quarterly*, *4*, 26–32. Retrieved from www.mckinseyquarterly.com/Public_Sector/E-government_20_2408.

Benbasat, I., & Barki, H. (2007). Quo vadis TAM? *Journal of AIS*, *8*(4). Retrieved from http://jais.aisnet.org/articles/8-16/default.asp?view=html.

Capgemini. (2009). *Smarter, faster, better e-government: 8th benchmark measurement of European e-government services*. Prepared for the European Commission Directorate General for Information Society and Media by Capgemini, Rand Europe, IDC, Sogeti and DTI. CDT and InfoDev. (2002). *The e-government handbook for developing countries*. The Center for Democracy and Technology (CDT) and the Information for Development Program (InfoDev). Retrieved from www.cdt.org/egov/handbook

Chadwick, A. (2006). *Internet politics: States, citizens, and new communication technologies*. Oxford, UK: Oxford University Press.

Chan, C., & Pan, S. (2008). User engagement in e-government systems implementation: A comparative case study of two Singaporean e-government initiatives. *The Journal of Strategic Information Systems*, 17.

Cho, Y. H., & Choi, B. D. (2004). E-government to combat corruption: The case of Seoul metropolitan government. *International Journal of Public Administration*, *27*(10), 719–735. doi:10.1081/PAD-200029114

Compeau, D. R., & Higgins, C. A. (1995). Computer self-efficacy: Development of a measure and initial test. *Management Information Systems Quarterly*, *19*(2), 189–211. doi:10.2307/249688

Davis, F. D. (1989). Perceived usefulness, perceived ease of use, and user acceptance of Information Technology. *Management Information Systems Quarterly*, *13*(3), 319–339. doi:10.2307/249008

Davis, F. D., Bagozzi, R. P., & Warshaw, P. R. (1992). Extrinsic and intrinsic motivation to use computers in the workplace. *Journal of Applied Social Psychology*, *22*, 1111–1132. doi:10.1111/j.1559-1816.1992.tb00945.x

De, G. B. *(2001)*. E-government. Section I – Private sector recommendations to government on realization of e-government. Global business dialogue on electronic commerce, *(p. 42)*.

Dimitrova, D. V., & Chen, Y. (2006). Profiling the adopters of e-government information and services: The influence of psychological characteristics, civic mindedness, and information channels. [Thousand Oaks, CA: Summer.]. *Social Science Computer Review*, *24*(2), 172. doi:10.1177/0894439305281517

Ein-Dor, P. (2006). *Digital divides: Definitional and research issues. Department Seminar (December 5)*. Faculty of Management, Tel-Aviv University.

Ein-Dor, P., & Segev, E. (1993). A classification of Information Systems: Analysis and interpretation. *Information Systems Research*, *4*(2), 166–204. doi:10.1287/isre.4.2.166

ELOST. (2006). *Work package 4: Foresight study. D4.1: Review of foresight studies and emerging technologies, D4.2: Technology-related questions for ELOST surveys*. Retrieved from www.elost.org

ELOST. (2008). Work package 6: Recommendations for future policy and research priorities for the EU. Retrieved from www.elost.org/D6-2.pdf

European Commission. (2001). *Digital literacy workshop*. A discussion paper from the eLearning Summit on Digital Literacy, Brussels 10-11 May.

Fishbein, M., & Ajzen, I. (1975). *Belief, attitude, intention, and behavior: An introduction to theory and research*. Reading, MA/ Don Mills, Ontario: Addison-Wesley Pub. Co.

Goldman, J. (2008, April 4). Online deliberation: Expecting more from your e-government. *Politico (Pavia, Italy)*, *4*, 59.

Gregor, S., & Jones, D. (2007). The anatomy of a design theory. *Journal of the Association for Information Systems*, *8*(5), 312–335.

King, W. R., & He, J. (2006). A meta-analysis of the technology acceptance model. *Information & Management*, *43*(6), 740–755. doi:10.1016/j.im.2006.05.003

Kondo, S. (2001). *Fostering dialogue to good government: Public sector transparency and accountability – Making it happen* (pp. 7–11). OECD.

Kunstelj, M., & Vintar, M. (2004). Evaluating the progress of e-government development: A critical analysis. *Information Polity*, *9*, 131–148.

Layne, K., & Lee, J. (2001). Developing fully functional e-government: A four stage model. *Government Information Quarterly*, *18*, 122–136. doi:10.1016/S0740-624X(01)00066-1

Lee, M., Tan, X., & Trimi, S. (2005). Current practices of leading e-government countries. *Communications of the ACM*, *48*(10), 99. doi:10.1145/1089107.1089112

Lee, Y., Kozar, K. A., & Larsen, K. R. T. (2003). The technology acceptance model: Past, present, and future. *Communications of the Association for Information Systems*, *12*(50), 752–780.

Legris, P., Ingham, J., & Collerette, P. (2003). Why do people use Information Technology? A critical review of the technology acceptance model. *Information & Management*, *40*(3), 191–204. doi:10.1016/S0378-7206(01)00143-4

Ma, Q., & Liu, L. (2004). The technology acceptance model: A meta-analysis of empirical findings. *Journal of Organizational and End User Computing*, *16*(1), 59–72. doi:10.4018/joeuc.2004010104

Mathieson, K. (1991). Predicting user intentions: comparing the TAM with the theory of planned behaviour. *Information Systems Research*, *2*(3), 173–191. doi:10.1287/isre.2.3.173

Nordfors, L., Ericson, B., Lindell, H., & Lapidus, J. (2009). *E-government of tomorrow - Future scenarios for 2020*. Gullers Grupp. Vinn ova Report VR 2009:28. VINNOVA – Verket för Innovationssystem/Swedish Governmental Agency for Innovation System. November. Case No: 2009-02921.

Noveck, B. S. (2009). *Wiki government: How technology can make government better, democracy stronger, and citizens more powerful*. Brookings Institution Press.

OECD. (2001). *Understanding the digital divide*. OECD papers, DSTI, Paris. Retrieved from www.oecd.org/dataoecd/38/57/1888451.pdf

OII and LSE. (2010). *Methodology for costing the impact of digital exclusion*. Research project. Retrieved from http://microsites.oii.ox.ac.uk/digital-exclusion/

Olphert, W., & Damodaran, L. (2007). Citizen participation and engagement in the design of e-government services: The missing link in effective ICT design and delivery. *Journal of the Association for Information Systems*, *8*(9), 491–507.

Paivarinta, T., & Saebo, O. (2006). Models of e-democracy. *Communications of the Association for Information Systems*, *17*, 818–840.

Pratchett, L., Durose, C., Lowndes, V., Smith, G., Stoker, G., & Wales, C. (2009). *Empowering communities to influence local decision making – A systematic review of the evidence*. Retrieved from http://fastlink.headstar.com/clg1

Purian, R. (2010). *Technophilia: From entertainment to digital literacy and e-government – A new multilevel concept for technology adoption*. Unpublished Doctoral Dissertation. Tel Aviv University, Tel Aviv, Israel.

Mahmood, M. (2004). Can Information and Communication Technology help reduce corruption? How so and why not: Two case studies from South Asia. [Koninklijke Brill NV, Leiden P.]. *Perspectives on Global Development and Technology*, *3*(3), 347–373. doi:10.1163/1569150042442539

Sabo, O., Rose, J., & Flak, L. S. (2008). The shape of e-participation: Characterizing an emerging research area. *Government Information Quarterly*, *25*(3), 400–428. doi:10.1016/j.giq.2007.04.007

Schepers, J., & Wetzels, M. (2007). A meta-analysis of the technology acceptance model: Investigating subjective norm and moderation effects. *Information & Management*, *44*(1), 90. doi:10.1016/j.im.2006.10.007

Scott, K. J. (2005). Assessing the quality of municipal government websites. *State and Local Government Review*, *37*(2), 151–165. doi:10.1177/0160323X0503700206

SIBIS. (2003). *SIBIS indicator handbook*. (WP6) in Statistical Indicators Benchmarking the Information Society. Information Society Programme of the European Commission. Retrieved October 27, 2008, from www.sibis-eu.org/files/Sibis_Indicator_Handbook.pdf

Sun, H., & Zhang, P. (2006). The role of moderating factors in user technology acceptance. *International Journal of Human-Computer Studies*, *64*(2), 53–78. doi:10.1016/j.ijhcs.2005.04.013

Tuomi, I. (1999-2000). Data is more than knowledge: Implications of the reversed knowledge hierarchy for knowledge management and organizational memory. *Journal of Management Information Systems*, *16*(3), 103–117.

United Nations. (2002). *Benchmarking e-government: A global perspective*. New York, NY: American Society for Public Administration.

United Nations. (2005). *UN global e-government readiness report 2005: From e-government to e-inclusion*. United Nations Knowledge Base (UNKB). United Nations Publication, Publication No.: UNPAN/2005/14. UNKB Framework. Retrieved from http://unpan1.un.org/intradoc/groups/public/documents/un/unpan021888.pdf

Venkatesh, V., Morris, M. G., Davis, G. B., & Davis, F. D. (2003). User acceptance of Information Technology: Toward a unified view. *Management Information Systems Quarterly*, *27*(3), 425–478.

Walsham, G. (2009). *Interpreting Information Systems in organizations*. Global Text.

Warkentin, M., Gefen, D., Pavlou, P., & Rose, G. (2002). Encouraging citizen adoption of e-government by building trust. *Electronic Markets*, *12*(3), 157–162. doi:10.1080/101967802320245929

Yousafzai, S, Y., Foxall, G. R., & Pallister, J. G. (2007). Technology acceptance: a meta-analysis of the TAM: Part 2. *Journal of Modeling in Management*, *2*(3), 281. doi:10.1108/17465660710834462

Chapter 12
Improving Performance and Customer Satisfaction via the Use of Information Technologies in Public Transportation and Logistics Systems

Dicle Yurdakul Şahin
Izmir University of Economics, Turkey

Deniz Türsel Eliiyi
Izmir University of Economics, Turkey

ABSTRACT

During the last two decades, the enhancements in Information Technologies (IT) and the extension of their usage have transformed completely the ways of doing business. In addition to providing a competitive advantage, the utilization of information technologies help businesses to organize all information related with their customers, increasing their level of satisfaction from the good or service provided, support decision making processes and increase the collaboration between supply chain members. Due to the increase in overseas trade and the globalization trends, the usage and importance of Information Technologies in transportation have risen up extremely. This chapter aims to emphasize the growing need for and role of IT in Turkish public logistics systems, present examples of these systems' implementation around the world, and specific benefits to be gained in terms of efficient operations and improved performance, profitability, customer satisfaction, and social welfare. In this respect, the authors aim to draw attention to the significance of the management Information Systems in different areas of public service.

DOI: 10.4018/978-1-60960-839-2.ch012

INTRODUCTION

Information technologies can be used in all operations and logistics systems in order to improve the decision making activities and increase utilization and efficiency in a competitive environment. The increasing demand regarding the improvement of logistics infrastructure and systems in countries that are in hub positions for global transportation networks makes the use and implementation of information technologies a necessity for ensuring effective and efficient transportation of goods across the world. In consideration of the importance of Turkey as a gateway between Europe and Asia, the use of management information systems and IT is vital in the successful management of logistics systems connecting these two continents. Turkey has a strategic position as a bridge between Europe and Asia, which makes the country a hub and a logistics center operating between three continents. In addition to its geographically advantageous position, Turkey's trade with European Union, Middle East, Asia and Africa could be considered as another important reason of the potential of the country to be a regional logistics center.

The Turkish government is aware of the importance of IT systems and adopting them in various areas of implementation. In public sector, projects of e-treasury and e-government are implemented and started to be used effectively with the core aim of public welfare. In spite of the expansive use of these systems, many governmental institutions such as Turkish State Railways and public ports have not yet adopted any sophisticated information technology systems. There are various reasons for this situation, including the high initial investment cost for such systems, insufficient traffic intensity to justify the need for such a system, or simply inattentive management. However, there are many successful implementations of information technologies in logistics systems that should be taken into consideration for improving the efficiency and effectiveness of these governmental institutions. The employment of information technologies alone can be the source of growth through the improvement of main performance measures. The public reform in the logistics systems of the country can be realized by the adoption of information technologies.

Turkish State Railways and public ports are facing an aggressive competition, as global transportation companies operating in Turkey have highly effective operations. Therefore, improvements in the service quality and the satisfaction levels of customers are crucial for public railways and ports to have a competitive edge in this market.

In consideration of the opportunities that can be obtained via the effective use of IT systems, this chapter aims to emphasize the growing need for such systems, and the role they can have in public logistics. For this purpose, we first illustrate the lack of IT systems in public logistics in Turkey, and then examine some exemplary implementations around the world, and the specific benefits to be gained in terms of efficient operations and improved performance, profitability, customer satisfaction and social welfare.

HISTORY AND CURRENT SITUATION: TRANSPORTATION IN TURKEY

Turkish State Railways (TCDD) was established in 1927 as a governmental institution to take over the existing railways in Anatolia which were held by private companies during the Ottoman Empire. Most of the country had no railways during 1930's and 1940's, and the main expenditure of the government was the extension of the existing railway network. Although some major lines were added to the network connecting the main cities of the country in the beginning, this extension came to a halt after the Second World War.[1] After 1990's, the need for urban mass transportation has given a rise to the investments for light rail and heavy metro systems (see Figure 1).

Figure 1. Total length of railways by years(Source:http://www.mmo.org.tr/genel/bizden_detay.php?kod=6197&tipi=4&sube=0)

Years	Total Length of Railways (Km)
Before 1923	4559
1923-1931	6011
1940	8637
1950	9204
2001	10940
2003	10984
2005	10984
2007	10991
2008	11005

In addition to improving the railway network, Turkey focused on the extension of highway systems which reached to approximately 427,000 km during the 1990s. According to the General Directorate of Highways, currently 91.7% of freight transportations are by highways, which is a very high percentage compared to 5.3% share of railways in freight transportations.[2] Since 1927, TCDD holds a monopoly as the only railway operator in the country controlling all passenger, freight and suburban traffic in addition to the operation of the major ports in Turkey (Figure 2). After 2004, the new governmental policy started the privatization process of all ports excluding Haydarpaşa Port in Istanbul.

In contrast with its monopoly position, TCDD has losses in railway transportation, mostly due to the highly unprofitable freight transportation. Profits gained from the operations in major ports of the country (Haydarpaşa, Derince, İzmir, Bandırma, Mersin, Iskenderun, and Samsun), which were operated by TCDD before the privatization process, were used to support railways and prevented new investments to improve the port operations. In addition to the losses faced, globalization and the increase in international trade put pressures on transportation held by the governmental institutions. The operational inefficiencies have effects on the national economy, as most of the cargo between Europe and Asia are being routed beyond the borders of Turkey due to the insufficient transportation infrastructure.

In consideration of this situation, the government started the railway and port reforms in order to ensure that the elimination of unprofitable operations. Currently, six major ports formerly operated by TCDD are either in the process of privatization or already contracted and now is operated by private firms (Thompson, 2009). In addition, some private firms started to buy their own wagons in order to operate them with the railway engines and the infrastructure provided by the government. In consideration of the privatization policy of the government, it can be easily argued that TCDD should re-organize and adapt to the state-of-the-art technology in order to improve its performance, profitability and share in the transportations.

As a hub country between three continents, Turkey holds a very important position. Railways and ports are very important modes of transportation which can be the focal points of economic

Figure 2. Container traffic in Turkey's ports through 2001-2009 (operated by TCDD)(Source:http:// www.tcdd.gov.tr/Upload/Files/ContentFiles/2010/liman-bilgi/konteyner.htm)

	Haydarpaşa	Mersin	İskenderun	Samsun	Derince	Bandırma	Izmir	Total (TEU)
2001	224.544	290.354	30	1.403	687	1.110	491.377	1.009.505
2002	224.642	363.920	32	374	687	4	573.211	1.162.870
2003	244.467	467.111	1.745	0	1.936	0	700.795	1.416.054
2004	316.982	532.999	607	0	1.509	36	804.563	1.656.696
2005	340.629	596.289	0	0	550	0	784.377	1.721.845
2006	400.067	643.749	52	0	609	0	847.926	1.892.403
2007	396.637	232.181	603	0	488	9	898.217	1.528.135
2008	356.272	0	0	0	402	69	884.906	1.241.649
2009	187.365	0	0	254	251	34	826.645	1.014.549

activity in the case of effective and profitable operations. Therefore, in order to implement planned reforms successfully, the focus points of improvement should be identified carefully and benchmarking of successful operators should be taken into consideration. In the next sections, we investigate the implementation of information technologies in transportation operations as a vital competitive force in the highly competitive transportation sector. We discuss the need for and implementation of these technologies in Turkey in order to ensure effective, efficient and profitable operations in the public sector.

USE OF INFORMATION TECHNOLOGIES IN LOGISTICS AND TRANSPORTATION

The implementation and development of IT plays a key role in the transportation and logistics fields. Recent studies have suggested that IT improves the performance of supply chains by passing the information to different parties in the system (Disney et al., 2004). In addition to increased competence capabilities due to the quality of service provided, costs of the overall system are also decreasing (Stock and Lambert, 2001). According to the study of Lai et al. (2005), information technologies have significant effects on creating a competitive advantage to firms. In a similar pattern to other sectors, IT affect the firms in logistics sector to be more competitive in dynamic transportation, which enables them to enhance logistics capabilities, decreasing costs and improving the satisfaction level of customers (Bowersox and Daugherty 1995; Daugherty et al., 1995). Investments in computer based applications and databases are growing rapidly among the firms in the sector, while the reach of information is revolutionized by the wide use of internet communication tools (Sutton and Gillingwater, 1997). With the implementation of IT in logistics operations, firms ensure providing faster and reliable service, increasing revenues, reducing the costs of personnel, loading and delivery time and empty miles of travel and communication (Feng and Yuan, 2006).

There are mainly two systems which are used widely in logistics: geographic information systems (GIS) and Global Positioning by Satellite (GPS). GIS enables its users to configure transportation data with geographic features and factors which causes its rapid diffusion in logistics sector. In order to support logistics and distribution activities, GIS provides database operations using statistics and queries and the results are shown in geographical maps (Samah et al., 2000). GPS is basically a satellite navigation system operated by US Department of Defense. Using 24 navigational satellites, the system coverts satellite signals to position, velocity and time estimates (Wang et al., 2004).

In addition to these systems, the usage of information systems in port operations has risen up tremendously in the recent decades. The information systems applications are accepted to be the main indicators to place a port according to world standards. Information systems are used in various operations in container ports to improve the decision making process, and to increase utilization and efficiency. Complex nature of inter-related resource allocation decisions for the optimization of port performance measures requires information systems to be used. Information systems are used in berthing the ships optimally using the models developed, optimizing the truck routes within the terminal and the positioning of containers in the yard automatically based on user-defined constraints, preventing congestion and promoting throughput.

According to Western and Ran (2009), the applications of IT that can be used in transportation are mainly in the areas of developing intelligent vehicles, vehicle and highway automation, collision warning and avoidance systems and information dissemination. Customers of today are highly demanding in terms of the availability of high degree of timely information and in order to survive in the highly-competitive logistics sector, hence the service providers should focus on this demand of their customers by adopting the related technologies.

How IT Contributes to Customer Satisfaction, Service Quality and Profitability in Transportation

Customer satisfaction is one of the major predictors of a company's future profits. According to the service management literature, customer loyalty is affected by customer satisfaction which will lead in high profitability (Zeithaml et al., 1990; Anderson and Fornell, 1994). The study of Reichheld and Sasser (1990) stated that higher levels of customer satisfaction have the potential to double the firm profits.

In addition, product and service performance is mostly evaluated by customer satisfaction metrics (Anderson and Sullivan, 1993). According to the previous studies in the service sector, customer service is the result of customer's value perceptions in regard of the service provided by the companies (Zeithaml et al., 1990). In order to increase the perceived value of the service provided, many firms in the service industry are adopting IT in creating better and customized services.

Major impacts of IT on customer satisfaction in logistics operations is achieved by providing faster and reliable service as well as timely information to key customers. Many firms in the service industry enjoy the benefits of IT by improving reliability, ensuring consistent levels of performance, minimizing errors and enabling users (customers) to reach up-to-date and reliable information. Due to the information-intensive nature of service industry, IT-enabled processes may have a significant effect on the value perceptions of the customers leading in a higher degree of satisfaction. Providing related easy-to-use IT tools for customers will increase customers' perceptions of logistics process quality (Bienstock et al., 2008) Therefore, it is vital for firms operating in logistics industry to realize the opportunities provided by the use of IT in satisfying customer needs and providing a high quality logistics service.

Successful Use of Information Technologies in Logistics Systems

In spite of the lack of IT expertise, difficulties in changing the ongoing organizational cultures and justification of the implementation costs (Saatcioglu et al., 2008), there are many exemplary implementations of IT systems in the logistics infrastructure.

Giving a considerable importance on IT investments, the information management process of China in Qinghai-Tibet Railway needs special attention as an exemplary case. Information management planning in Qinghai-Tibet Railway to provide accurate location-tracking systems is developed in three stages: geographic information system (GIS), global positioning system (GPS), and global system for mobile communication (GSM). GIS system is used as a tool for storing information in thematic layers which also provides an opportunity to run queries and statistics and providing the results by geographic maps. GPS system includes 24 navigational satellites which receive positioning signals from user-owned receivers. GPS receivers can convert these signals to position, velocity and time estimates. Finally, GSM system is a cellular communication system which enable voice communication between all users, data message exchange, and most importantly, train communication systems which are used for data exchange between trains and traffic control systems (Wang et al., 2004).

The railway system consists of many user tools which are described by Lu et al. (2003):

1. Communication network systems: Used in data, voice and image transmission.
2. Operation Management Information System: Designed to assist managers to acquire, deliver and use timely information.
3. Process Control and Safety Assurance Systems: Designed to ensure the safety of on-line vehicles by monitoring work status of equipments and timely alerting in irregular cases.
4. Office Information Systems: Designed for more affective office management.
5. Decision Support and Composite Application System: Designed to provide managers decision support systems.
6. E-business System: Designed for intra-organizational flow of services, information and communication. It also provides customer service as information resources, seat reservations and selling over internet.

Information technologies are used more widely in world ports compared to railways and there are many examples of successful implementation of information systems all over the world. One of these exemplary implementations is Port of Hamburg which is considered to be one of the most modern ports in Europe. Container Terminal Altenwerder operates 24 hours and nearly all activities are automated. There are driverless equipments and cranes in the port, which are coordinated by the software called Container Terminal Information System (CTIS). The system also supports EDI which enables intra-organizational information sharing. CTIS enables the minimization of manual data entry in the system which provides the users with accurate and timely information. By the help of user-friendly interfaces, the system provides managers with an easy tool for effective decision making. CTIS consists of modules of gate and truck monitoring, vessel call and berth planning, yard planning, ship stowage planning, container freight station, custom access, EDI, report generator, internet and invoicing/tariffs (Keceli and Choi, 2008).

Another example of successful implementation of IT is in Busan Port, the biggest port in Korea. In Busan Port, all communications and EDI is provided by KL-Net, a private company. The IT provide many opportunities to companies by enabling online applications and service requests such as booking and customs clearance, railroad transportation, payments of operational services and taxes. The system connects all parties in the logistics system; it provides them accurate and timely information and many opportunities to ease their operations, which will eventually lead to higher levels of customer satisfaction and effective management.

CONCLUSION

Considering the successful implementations of IT in various transportation systems presented in the previous sections, the importance of these systems in achieving high levels of service quality, performance, customer satisfaction and profitability is clearly predictable. Still, Turkish railways and ports are not using IT effectively, and most of the operations do not even involve the basic uses of information or communication technologies. Although the importance of the country as a gateway between three continents and its potential as a logistics center is obvious, the implementation levels of IT is still very low, causing the loss of the competitive advantage brought by the geographical location.

The current state in the technology usage of the Turkish Railways is lacking modern techniques and programs. IT tools are used in areas such as signalization; however, most operations are planned manually including wagon tracking; responsible personnel keep the records of the entering and leaving wagons in each station manually, and this sometimes leads to various mistakes and hinders transportation. Dissatisfactory operations and unsolved complaints alienate customers, which is one of the main reasons of the small percentage of freight transportation among all transportations. Moreover, the increasing competition and the entrance of global logistics giants into the logistics sector brings lowering tons of freight and passenger transportations per year.

There have been various attempts to implement some decision support systems in Turkish ports. However, evidence suggests that almost none of these attempts could turn into realized implementation of effective systems. TCDD prepared TCDD Port Services Telecommunication Project (DELIMTEL) in 1990, which aimed to analyze container terminal activities. The authorities planned to develop a management information system and apply this system in the pilot ports of Mersin, Haydarpaşa and İzmir (3 major ports of the country operated by TCDD). TCDD also participated in MEDITEL project of European Union, which aimed to develop computer-based applications to increase the effectiveness of the services provided by ports in the Mediterranean Sea. Haydarpaşa port was selected as the pilot implementation arena; however, the implementation could not take place as the software package developed for the project did not fit the existing infrastructure. The project was cancelled in 1999. Such positive efforts could not reach their ultimate goal due to major mistakes in the planning of the IT systems. Hence, in spite of all efforts on implementing IT in port operations, the effective management of ports could not be realized. As a result, as of 2005, the High Council of Privatization Administration started the privatization process of all ports excluding Haydarpaşa Port in Istanbul.

At the moment, the main problems of information systems focusing on public logistics are classified by Keceli and Choi (2008) as:

- Tracking and planning the operations of the port manually. Data is input to the system manually after manual reporting, which is one of the main sources of error. In addition, port operations cannot be monitored on a real-time basis in such an environment.
- The current system does not include yard management modules, which causes the waste of limited resources such as space, time and labor.
- Customers can not reach up-to-date information such as the specific location of their containers, the whereabouts of the wagons or vehicles, approximate arrival dates, etc.

Marport is the only container port in Turkey which uses information systems. This indicates that the attention given to the use of information systems by port authorities is not sufficient. The reasons behind may include the high initial investment costs, lack of management support and insufficient traffic in small ports to justify these investments. However, as observed in many successful implementations of information systems in various world ports, these systems can contribute directly to the improvement of port performance measures, customer satisfaction, and profitability. In realization of this fact, the private operators have a recent tendency in adapting the necessary IT tools.

Turkey has not been able to reap the benefits of its strategic position due to the unsuccessful and late attempts in implementing IT in logistics systems. There is a strong need for public reform in the field of logistics in order to compete with the strong rivals in the industry. This reform is crucial for taking the position of being a hub and a logistics center in the global transportation network. The first step in this reform is to immediately start several simultaneous projects of IT implementation especially in railways, in order to gain a competitive edge by providing quality logistics service and profitability. In order to develop effective transportation systems, current situation of exemplary systems should be reviewed and factors that contribute most to the effectiveness and efficiency of these systems should be identified. With the careful planning of these efforts and possible successful outcomes, the country may be an exemplary logistics hub for many developing countries sharing the same situation.

REFERENCES

Anderson, E. W., & Fornell, C. (1994). A customer satisfaction research prospectus. In Rust, R. T., & Oliver, R. (Eds.), *Service quality: New directions in theory and practice* (pp. 241–268). Thousand Oaks, CA: Sage Publications.

Anderson, E. W., & Sullivan, M. W. (1993). The antecedents and consequences of customer satisfaction for firms. *Marketing Science*, *12*(2), 125–143. doi:10.1287/mksc.12.2.125

Bienstock, C. C., Royne, M. B., Sherrell, D., & Stafford, T. F. (2008). An expanded model of logistics service quality: Incorporating logistics Information Technology. *International Journal of Production Economics*, *113*, 205–222. doi:10.1016/j.ijpe.2007.03.023

Bowersox, D. J., & Daugherty, P. J. (1995). Logistics paradigms: The impact of Information Technology. *Journal ofBusiness Logistics*, *16*(1), 65–80.

Daugherty, P. J., Ellinger, A. E., & Rogers, D. S. (1995). Information accessibility: Customer responsiveness and enhanced performance. *International Journal of Physical Distribution & Logistics Management*, *25*(1), 4–17. doi:10.1108/09600039510080117

Disney, S. M., Naim, M. M., & Polter, A. (2004). Assessing the impact of e-business on supply chain dynamics. *International Journal of Production Economics*, *89*, 109–118. doi:10.1016/S0925-5273(02)00464-4

Feng, C. M., & Yuan, C. Y. (2006). The impact of information and communication technologies on logistics management. *International Journal of Management*, *23*(4), 909–924.

Keceli, Y., & Choi, H. R. (2008). Level of Information Systems in Turkish public ports and direction of improvement. *International Journal of. Logistics Systems and Management*, *4*(6), 673–691. doi:10.1504/IJLSM.2008.019185

Lai, K. H., Ngai, E. W. T., & Cheng, T. C. E. (2005). Information Technology adoption in Hong Kong's logistics industry. *Transportation Journal*, *44*(4), 1–9.

Lu, X. R., Wang, Q. R., & Gao, P. P. (2003). Operation and maintenance modes of Qinghai-Tibet railway. *Journal of Southwest Jiaotong University*, *38*(1), 60.

Reichheld, F. F., & Sasser, W. E. Jr. (1990). Zero defections: Quality comes to services. *Harvard Business Review*, *68*(5), 105–111.

Saatcioglu, O. Y., Deveci, A. D., & Cerit, A. G. (2008, May 25-26). *Logistics and transportation Information Systems in Turkey: E-government perspectives*. Paper presented at European and Mediterranean Conference on Information Systems,Al Bostan Rotana, Dubai.

Samaha, J., Kayssi, A., Achkar, R., & Azar, M. (2000). G3 integrated three system technologies. *Computer*, *33*(10), 107–110.

Stock, J. R., & Lambert, D. M. (2001). *Strategic logistics management*. New York, NY: McGraw-Hill.

Sutton, J., & Gillingwater, D. (1997). Geographic Information Systems and transportation — Overview. *Transportation Planning and Technology*, *21*(1), 1–4. doi:10.1080/03081069708717598

Thompson, L. S. (2009, February). *Railway and ports organization in the republic of South Africa and Turkey: The integrator's paradise?* Paper presented at International Transport Forum, Discussion Paper No. 2009-5, Prepared for the Round Table of 5-6 on Integration and Competition Between Transport and Logistics Businesses.

Wang, B. Wei, Q., Tan, Q., Yang, S., & Cai, B. (2004). *Integration of GIS, GPS and GSM for the Qinghai-Tibet railway information management planning*. Retrieved February 27, 2010, from http:// citeseerx.ist.psu.edu.tr

Western, J. L., & Ran, B. (2009). *Information Technology in transportation, key issues and a look forward*. Committee on Information Systems and Technology. Retrieved February 21, 2010, from www.trb.org/ publications/ millennium/00054.pdf

Zeithaml, V., Parasuraman, A., & Berry, L. L. (1990). *Delivering quality service*. New York, NY: The Free Press.

ADDITIONAL READING

Barua, A., Kriebel, C. H., & Mukhopadhyay, T. (1995). Information technologies and business value – an analytic and empirical investigation. *Information Systems Research*, *6*(1), 3–23. doi:10.1287/isre.6.1.3

Bitner, M. J., Brown, S. W., & Meuter, M. L. (2000). Technology infusion in service encounters. *Academy of Marketing Science Journal.*, *28*(1), 138–149. doi:10.1177/0092070300281013

Brynjolfsson, E. (1996). The contribution of information technology to consumer welfare. *Information Systems Research*, *7*(3), 281–300. doi:10.1287/isre.7.3.281

Choi, H. R., Kim, H. S., Park, B. J., Park, N. K., & Lee, S. W. (2003). An ERP approach for container terminal operating systems. *Maritime Policy & Management*, *30*, 197–210. doi:10.1080/0308883032000089549

Cooper, M. C., Lambert, D. M., & Pagh, J. D. (1997). Supply chain management: More than a name for logistics. *International Journal of Logistics Management.*, *8*(1), 1–14. doi:10.1108/09574099710805556

Cubukcu, F. (1998). Liman yonetiminde etkinligin artirilmasi bakimindan yonetim bilgi sistemlerinin rolu. Master Thesis, Department of Maritime Business Administration, Dokuz Eylul University, Turkey.

Dedrick, J., Gurbaxani, V., & Kraemer, K. L. (2003). Information technology and economic performance: A critical review of empirical evidence. *ACM Computing Surveys*, *35*(1), 1–28. doi:10.1145/641865.641866

Eugene, W. A., & Mary, W. S. (1993). The antecedents and consequences of customer satisfaction for firms. *Marketing Science*, *12*(2), 125–143. doi:10.1287/mksc.12.2.125

Fay, A., & Schnieder, E. (1997). Knowledge-based decision support system for real-time train trac control (pp. 109-125). *7th International Workshop on Computer-Aided Scheduling of Public Transport*. Boston, MA.

Glazer, R. (1991). Marketing in and information intensive environment: Strategic implications of knowledge as an asset. *Journal of Marketing*, *55*(4), 1–19. doi:10.2307/1251953

Goodchild, M. F. (1998). Geographic information systems and disaggregate transportation planning. *Geographical Systems.*, *5*, 19–44.

Grönroos, C. (1991). Scandinavian management and the Nordic School of Services – contributions to service management and quality. *International Journal of Service Industry Management*, *2*(3), 17–25.

Hallowell, R. (1996). The relationships of customer satisfaction, customer loyalty, and profitability: an empirical study. *International Journal of Service Industry Management*, *7*(4), 27–42. doi:10.1108/09564239610129931

Hooghiemstra, J. S., Kroon, L. G., Odijk, M. A., Salomon, M., & Zwaneveld, P. J. (1999). Decision support systems support the search for win-win solutions in railway network design. *Interfaces*, *29*(2), 15–32. doi:10.1287/inte.29.2.15

Keceli, Y., Choi, H. R., Kim, H., Kwon, H. K., & Choi, P. J. (2006). Improvement of port information systems for TCDD ports (pp. 343-352). *4th Logistics and Supply Chain Congress*. Izmir, Turkey.

Kia, M., Shayan, E. & Ghotb, F. (2000). The importance of information technology in port terminals operations. *International Journal of Physical Distribution & Logistics*

Lee-Partridge, J. E., Teo, T. S. H., & Lim, V. K. G. (2000). Information technology management: the case of the Port of Singapore authority. *The Journal of Strategic Information Systems*, *9*, 85–99. doi:10.1016/S0963-8687(00)00035-4

Ma, J.H., Zhang, Z.Y., Ren, Y. & Sun, M.C. (2002). Safety application on radio frequency identification and communication based train control system in Qinghai-Tibet railway. *Progress in Safety Science and Technology, Management*, 30(3),331-344. Part A(3),772-777.

Menon, N. M., Lee, B., & Eldenburg, L. (2000). Productivity of information systems in the healthcare industry. *Information Systems Research*, *11*(1), 83–92. doi:10.1287/isre.11.1.83.11784

Mukhopadhyay, T., Rajiv, S., & Srinivasan, K. (1997). Information technology impact on process output and quality. *Management Science*, *43*(12), 1645–1659. doi:10.1287/mnsc.43.12.1645

Parasuraman, A., & Grewal, D. (2000). The impact of technology on the quality-value-loyalty chain: A research agenda. *Journal of the Academy of Marketing Science*, *28*(1), 168–174. doi:10.1177/0092070300281015

Petzold, R. G., & Freund, D. M. (1990). Potential for geographic information systems in transportation planning and highway infrastructure management. *Transportation Research Record*, *1261*, 1–9.

Roth, A. (1993). Performance dimensions in services: an empirical investigation of strategic performance. In Swartz, T. A., Bowen, D. E., & Brown, S. W. (Eds.), *Advances in Services Marketing and Management: Research and Practice* (*Vol. 2*, pp. 1–47). Greenwich, CT: JAI Press.

Sunil, M., Krishnan, M. S., & Fornell, C. Effect of information technology investments on customer satisfaction: An empirical analysis. Working Paper. Retrieved January 10, 2010 from http:// ssrn.com/ abstract=901643

Thill, J.-C. (2000). Geographic information systems for transportation in perspective. *Transportation Research*, (Part 8): 3–12.

Tuna, O. (2002). *The impact of hub ports on the logistics strategies of Turkey. 2nd International Gwangyang Port Forum* (pp. 211–228). Gwangyang City. The Korean Association of Shipping Studies.

Yeni, K., & Tuna, O. (2003). Logistics oriented developments in container ports: a review on Turkish ports (pp.736–743). Proceedings of the *IAME 2003 Annual Conference International Association of Maritime Economists*. Busan, South Korea.

Yilmaz, A. B., & Cerit, A. G. (2005). Exploring strategies to increase the potential of Turkish domestic cargo shipping. Proceedings of *IAME 2005 Annual Conference, International Association of Maritime Economists*, Limassol, Cyprus.

Yurt, O., Yumurtaci, I. O., & Yercan, F. (2006). Maritime related logistics services and developments in the port industry: Port of Izmir case. *4th International Logistics and Supply Chain Conference* (pp.464-472). Izmir University of Economics, Izmir, Turkey.

Zahorik, A. J., & Rust, R. T. (1992). Modeling the impact of service quality on profitability: a review. In Swartz, T. A., Bowen, D. E., & Brown, S. W. (Eds.), *Advances in Services Marketing and Management* (*Vol. 1*, pp. 247–276). Greenwich, CT: JAI Press.

Zeithaml, V., Parasuraman, A., & Berry, L. L. (1990). *Delivering quality service*. New York, NY: The Free Press.

Zwaneveld, P. J., Kroon, L. G., & Ambergen, H. W. (1996). *A decisionsupport system for routing trains through railway stations* (pp. 219–226). Southampton: Berlin Computational Mechanics Publication.

KEY TERMS AND DEFINITIONS

Customer Satisfaction: A measure of how products and services supplied by a company meet or exceed customer expectation.

Effectiveness: Measure of whether and to what extent set goals have been achieved.

Efficiency: The ratio of the output to the input of any system.

Information Technology: The study, design, development, implementation, support or management of computerized information systems which basicly consists of computer software and hardware.

Logistics Systems: Logistics systems are systems that are made up of a set of facilities linked by transportation services.

Profitability: The amount of profit received relative to the amount invested, often measured by a rate of profit or rate of return on investment.

Rail Transport: Conveyance of passengers and cargo by means of wheeled vehicles running on steel rails.

Transportation: The movement of people and goods from one location to another.

ENDNOTES

1 http://internationaltransportforum.org/jtrc/DiscussionPapers/DP200905.pdf -- accessed on 12.01.2010

2 http://www.kgm.gov.tr/ - accessed on 12.01.2010

Chapter 13
E-Government Developments in Turkey for Supporting Public Sector Transformation

Asim Balci
Selçuk University, Turkey

Tunc Medeni
Turksat, Turkey

ABSTRACT

This work presents the specific case of Turkey for public sector transformation by e-Government services development. The Turkish case will be presented with an aim to provide interesting and useful information for practitioners as well as academicians in the field of e-government and public transformation, and a focus on central government examples and policy orientations affecting daily lives of citizens. The rationale and perspective of the paper reflects practitioners' viewpoint, and assumes that the experiences of Turkey case will have echoes on other places, as the experienced and discussed issues have common characteristics with other cases. This practitioner analysis chapter is then based on the co-authors' personal involvement in and reflections on the various aspects of the Turkish case, while the chapter is written mostly as a result on secondary research. These reflective analyses are embedded within background information about e-government development in Turkey, presented together with academic perspective of transformational government. E-Government Gateway, MERNIS, UYAP, e-tax projects in Turkey are specifically highlighted. A discussion of policy orientations that affect daily lives of citizens follows, and suggestions for future work and directions are also provided. The discussion especially underlines the shared service and citizen-oriented approach to e-government service development with implications for process integration and improvement, if not yet for thorough transformation. It is hoped that the reflections and directions with respect to Turkish case presented in this work provides useful guidelines for new e-government initiatives in Turkey and all around the world.

DOI: 10.4018/978-1-60960-839-2.ch013

INTRODUCTION

This work aims to provide a country specific case, that is, the Turkish case, for public sector transformation by e-Government services development and maturation (transformational government, or T-Government). The Turkish case will be presented, benefiting from central government examples, and policy orientations affecting daily lives of citizens. Examples of customer-centric and shared services will be underlined as important aspects of the public sector transformation in general and in Turkey.

The paper presents the practitioners' viewpoint that is based on the authors' personal involvement in and reflections on the various aspects of the Turkey case. This practitioner analysis chapter is then prepared, mainly based on secondary research on publicly available information on the Internet.

As the outline of the chapter, these reflective analyses will be embedded within background information about e-Government development in Turkey presented together with academic perspective of transformational government. E-Government Gateway, MERNIS, UYAP projects in Turkey will be specifically emphasized. A discussion of policy orientations that affect daily lives of citizens will follow, and suggestions for future work and directions will also be provided.

As hoped by the co-authors, the resulting work provides a good, reflective documentation of the recent e-government developments towards public transformation in Turkey. It is also hoped that the reflections and directions with respect to Turkish case presented in this work will provide useful guidelines for new e-Government initiatives all around the world.

TRANSFORMATIONAL GOVERNMENT

Evolving from basic information provisioning towards more integrated, joined up and citizen-centric service offerings, e-Government services are now working towards realising T-Government – as the highest level of maturity for e-Government development. T-government redefines the delivery of government services by providing a single point of contact to citizens', making the government transparent to citizens, businesses (and state). From a demand perspective, extensive efforts are also needed to increase citizens' awareness about the transformation of the delivery of government services. This awareness could result in increased e-participation, as well.[1] Development of new services and improvement of existing services may then be an area where citizen demand and government provision meet.

Research, yet, has shown that the e-government initiatives are mostly away from reaching the state of t-Government. For instance, West (2004) acknowledges that while e-government transformation and revolution has the possibility to enhance democratic responsiveness and boosts beliefs of effective government, it falls short of its potential to transform service delivery and public trust in government. Torres, Pina and Royo (2005) also discuss that e-government initiatives (at regional and local levels in EU) still reflect present service delivery patterns, not transform them.

The recent OECD report (2009) encourages rethinking e-Government services, considering user-centered approaches. Within these approaches improving, monitoring and evaluating user take-up are especially highlighted, representing the paradigm shift from government centricity to citizen centricity. Meanwhile UN (2008) underlines increased integration in service delivery based on commonality of infrastructures, data, and business processes, and service innovation achieved by multi-channel service delivery and *smaller and smarter* use of back-end processes and systems to support *bigger and better* front-end operations encourage more collaborative models of service delivery. These models of "connected or networked government" request government agencies again rethink their operations, to move towards a chain-oriented paradigm with respect to structure, culture, knowledge and management, and to look towards technology as a strategic tool and an enabler for public service innovation and productivity growth. (UN, 2008)

In response to the various highlighted need of rethinking the services of e-Government and realising the state of t-Government, for instance, Sahraoui *et al.*. (2008) suggest a research agenda of t-Government for benefit realization. Accordingly, "the main threads of t-Government encompass:

- A citizen-centric delivery of public services or e-inclusion
- A shared service culture to maximise value added to clients
- The effective delivery and management of resources and skills within government – or professionalism.

The research agenda needs to include the management of change dimension of these phenomena." (p. 323). These authors suggest a strategic governance model for transformation and benefit realization.

In accordance with this research agenda, for instance, Melin and Axelsson (2009) elaborate upon the management of e-service development through the life cycle of the e-government system; or, Kanat and Özkan (2009) explore perceptions of citizens regarding e-government services, basing their analysis on the theory of planned behaviour, among other examples. Besides, Janssen, *et al.*. (2007) explore the relationships of shared service arrangements (in local government), investigating the case of Municipality of Amsterdam. These authors find that strategic and organizational, financial, political and technical antecedent conditions determine the basis for for designing and operationalizing the shared service center, which in return leads to increase in trust, cooperation and satisfaction among the collaborating parties, as well.

As Janssen (2009) adds, integrated service delivery and orchestration then requires transformations at the strategic, organization and technical level. While traditionally citizen performs the role of orchestrator, as they select, invoke and monitor the services, for integrated service delivery the orchestration role needs be performed by the government, necessitating a shift of activities from the citizen or businesses to the government. Centralized and hierarchical orchestration and coordination represents the most efficient and least expensive coordination mechanism for mostly standardized services with well-defined pathways that are selected to create a service delivery chain, which are not likely to change. Decentralized or network orchestration and coordination provides greater responsive and flexibility to adapt to changing circumstances, enabling different business processes that run in parallel throughout the network while interacting with the client and other processes. (Figure 1) (ibid)

To understand the e-Government phenomenon and development from an evolutionary point of view, there are commonly accepted and applied maturity models that apply a staged approach by dividing the e-Government development process of progressive steps in a continuous process (for a summary of these models, see, for instance, Coursey & Norris, 2008). Here the development starts from the 'immature' and moves to the 'mature' (Irani, *et al.*., 2006; Anderson & Henriksen, 2006 cited in C.E.E.S., 2009). As Flak *et al.* (2009) suggest, these widely used stage models alone can form the prescriptive basis for changing the way governments utilize ICT.

Meanwhile, theories such as the magic bullet theory in ICT-enabled transformation (Markus & Benjamin, 1997) warns of the dangers of technology determinism i.e. that technology in itself will guaranty the resolve of a particular challenge or problem. These magic bullets are to be complemented with entrepreneurial efforts to be assumed by governments. (Flak *et al.*, 2009)

Figure 1. Hierarchical orchestration based on central control (above) versus network orchestration based on mutual agreements (bottom) (Adapted from Jansen, 2009, Fig 2, pp 43, 45)

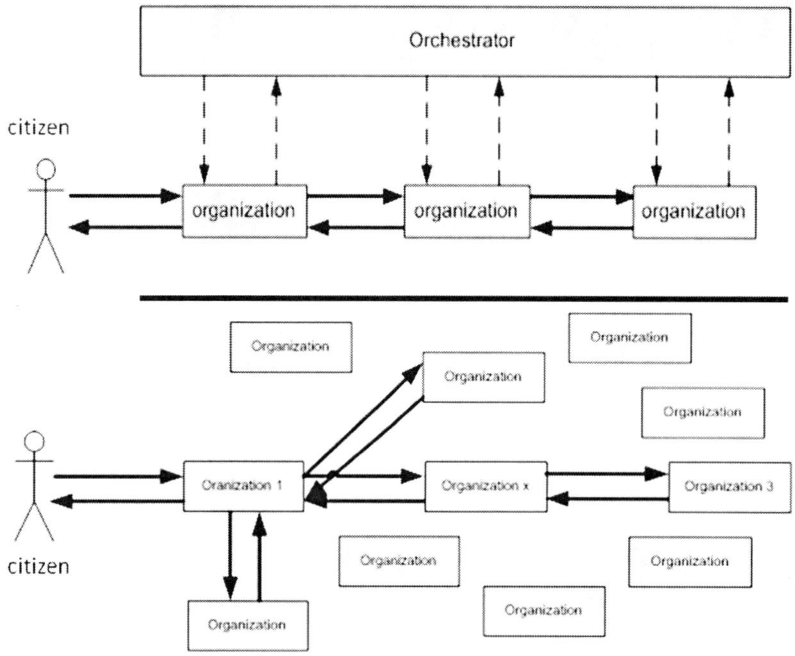

Besides, Norris (2010) discusses that many of the early predictions about e-government especially of claims for e-democracy and e-transformation were, at best, pure, optimistic speculation without basis whatsoever in the prior relevant literature. These large, unsubstantiated claims about the power of the technology to reform and change are complemented by this erroneous technologically-deterministic thinking: 'If we build e-government, really good things (and only good things) will result.' (Norris, 2010, p. 11) Technology is, however, not independent of the people, institutions and societies that adopt it, and it is implemented to serve the interests of those who control organizations.

As Norris (2010) argues, there is actually not enough evidence to surface that ICT produced any fundamental, revolutionary changes in public organizations. In fact, ICT has not reformed or transformed governmental administration. Also, predicted results about e-transformation and e-democracy have largely not materialized from e-government. Surely over time the relationships between citizens of nations and their governments will change nevertheless, technology will not cause the transformations in the relations between citizens and their governments.

All these arguments support the importance of considering technology, people and organization all together at different epistemological, ontological, (and societal) levels for development of e-government services and assessment of t-government. Accordingly, for instance, Afacan and Arifoğlu (2010) then introduces a new metric system model, as objective evaluation of e-transformation is crucial to shift governments' e-performance to an advanced level. The suggested model takes into account core e-transformation measurement factors to be used for assessing nations' performance in their adoption of e-transformation. Commonly utilized set of metrics under six measurement categories that have impact on e-transformation are; "Technology Infrastructure", "e-Society", "Human Capital", "Political and Regulatory Environment", "Economy Environment", "Online Services and Applications", as included in the modelling.

E-GOVERNMENT IN TURKEY AND TURKISH CASE OF GOVERNMENT TRANSFORMATION

Within such a strategic governance model and research agenda discussed above (as the literature review section), issues of change management, process integration, citizen-centric integrated delivery, and shared service culture as a part of benefit realizing transformation are also among the hot topics in the Turkish case. This above section is now followed by background information on the Turkish case and specific projects of E-Government Gateway, MERNIS, UYAP that provide a perspective on these hot topics.

Although previous initiatives (such as building up a central civil registration system) can also be traced back to the 1970s, in Turkey, e-Government initiatives could be said to start in 1998 with the "Kamunet" project that was aimed at establishing a national information system. Soon after this in the framework or the "e-Europe plus" project Turkey prepared its own action plan named the e-Türkiye initiative in 2001. In 2006 the Information Society Strategy document published by the State Planning Organization (Devlet Planlanma Teşkilatı, DPT) continued the development of e-Government services for transforming Turkey into an information society. (DPT, 2006)

The Strategy document provides a perspective for the process which is called an "e-transformation" and includes subtitles such as "social transformation", "citizen-focused services transformation", "ICT adaptation by business", "modernization in the public administration", "competitive, widespread and affordable communication infrastructure and services", and "improvement of R&D and innovation" Uçkan, 2009b). The document, however, receives substantial criticism (Gökmen, 2009; Uçkan, 2009b; among others). For instance Uçkan (2009b, pp.405-406) argues that

"apart from the question that these subtitles can ever sufficiently cover a large spectrum concept such as "information society", the suggestion that a mobilization effort that would transform the society with all its parts and institutions is limited to public sector modernization already gives a concrete idea about the "success" of this strategy! The "information society" becomes an abstract and hollow concept unless handled with its socioeconomic aspects. "Information society", which should accompany the concept of "knowledge economy", is a concept that qualifies societies which create value in producing, sharing, disseminating and using information, and shares this in a fair and equalitarian way."

Uçkan (2009b) adds, for instance, that "social transformation" requests more than just being "ready" to the information society. Thus, relating social transformation just to "e-readiness" standards, such as improving infrastructure and penetration for computer and Internet usage, providing public access opportunities, Internet security and content development, which is the case in the strategy document, is not enough. Uçkan concludes that to use a dynamic such as "knowledge" to enable a country's social, economic and cultural development, a more complex targeting system is required, as well. A "policy convergence" that counters technological convergence, as suggested by EU's "i2010" strategy, can also be considered within such system.

Nevertheless strategy document has become the base for various initiatives in Turkey for "citizen-focused services transformation", and "modernization in the public administration", among others, within such e-transformation perspective. For instance, feasibility studies have been conducted for broadening and disseminating

Figure 2. Feasibility studies (Acar & Kumas, 2009, Adapted from Figure 1, p. 263)

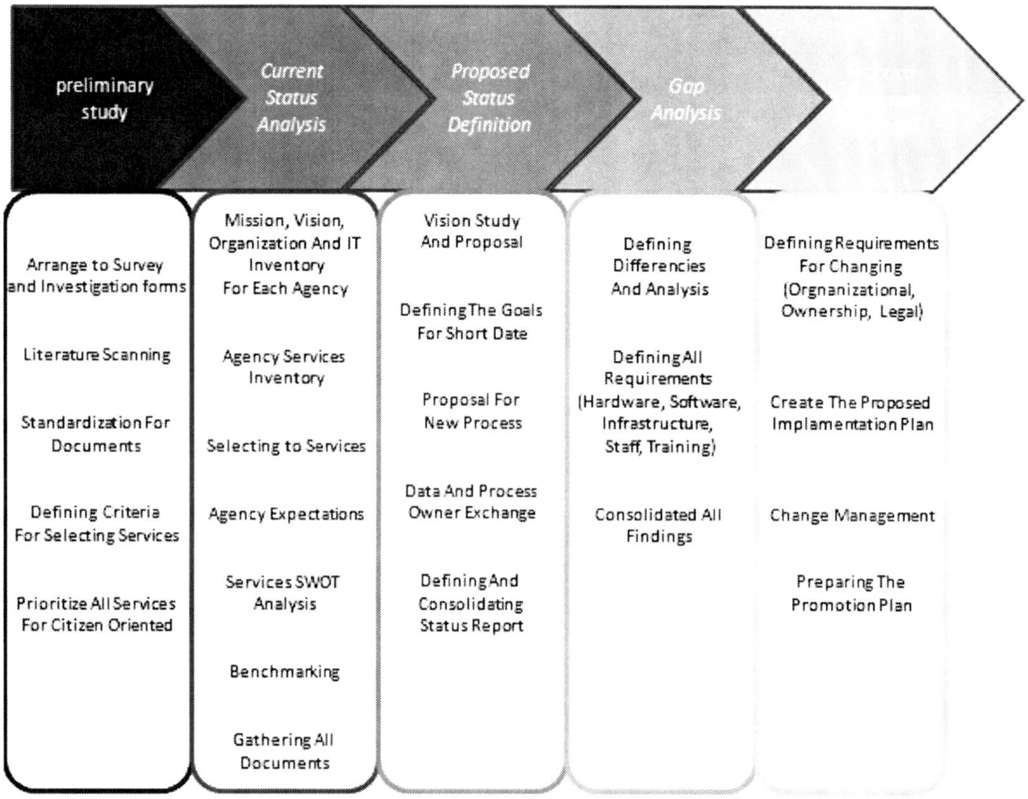

e-services. Following a model-based approach methodology that aimed at prioritizing services that maximize benefits to citizens and conducted "gap analysis" between 'as-is' and 'to-be' situations, these feasibility studies identified more than 100 feasible public services, carried over by 40 governmental organs, that can be served electronically. (Acar & Kumas, 2009) (Figure 2). These feasibility studies are accompanied by various presentations and meetings for awareness, information and updating among the related public institutions. (Balcı, et.al., 2009)

Based on these feasibility studies and intensive interactions among various government agencies and public institutions, a government gateway & portal has been developed. Officially launched in December 2008, the E-Government Gateway (EGG) is a major milestone for transforming into the Information Society for and achieving the related Strategic Goals set by Turkey. It aims to provide Turkey's 70 million citizens and business entities with a single point of access, one-stop-shop, to e-Government services. The implementation process of EGG is based on service transformation. The main principle will be the consideration of user satisfaction issues when re-designing the business processes of public institutions and services delivered to citizens and enterprises. The priority in services transformation will not be merely to transfer available business processes to electronic channels without making any improvements; on the contrary, the aim will be to deliver these electronic government services, as processes which are redesigned according to user needs for integration or simplification when necessary, in an effective, uninterrupted, fast, transparent, reliable way.

There are currently more than 160 e-services integrated into EGG and new services are under development. Selected e-services are presented in Figure 3. Besides these services, EGG provides links to hundreds of electronic services provided by individual agencies from their own websites. Currently EGG services do not "take over" agency web site services, however it provides a trustworthy, user-friendly choice with a single sign-up mechanism to securely access all services in one place. Identity management using personal password and e-signature are integrated into the system, and limited financial transactions and higher levels of personalization are planned for the near future.

Figure 3. Selected e-services provided via EGG (Adapted from Balcı and Medeni 2010)

Organization and Name of Service	*Explanation*
BİMER- Prime Ministry Communication Center New Application	With this service, citizens can send their requests, complaints, opinions, suggestions and information.
Ministry of Justice Court Case File Inquiry	Through this service, citizens may list any lawsuits filed about them in national courts and may monitor their details.
Ministry of National Defense- Logistics Mobilization Data for Work Machinery	This is a service by which you can inquire whether or not work machinery has Mobilization Duty Order.
Ministry of Finance e-Payroll Service	This is a service whereby the citizens can list their payrolls and inquire about the details of their payrolls.
Ministry of Internal Affairs e-Internal Affairs Project Document Follow up	With this service, the user may inquire about the progress of documents at the Ministry of Internal Affairs.
General Directorate of Police- Driver's License Penalty Points Inquiry	With this service, you can access to general information registered in the system about the driver.
Ministry of National Education- MEB Examination Results Inquiry	You can inquire about the examinations organized by the Ministry you have taken
Ministry of Industry and Trade- Operation Manual Inquiry	With this service, you can have access to the Turkish User's Manual and Operation Manual of the purchased product
Undersecretariat of Shipping - International Oil Pollution Prevention Certificate	This is a service used to calculate and pay the fee required for the related certificate.
Social Security Agency- SGK Registry Inquiry	Utilizing this service, you can learn your registry number from the Turkish Social Security Agency
İŞKUR- Unemployment Compensation Application	This is a service allowing you to apply for the Unemployment Benefits provided by İŞKUR.
PTT- Registered Mail Follow up	This is a service whereby the citizens can follow the mails they have sent, entering the barcode number on the mail.
General Directorate of Civil Aviation- Flight Crew Licensing/Rating Application	This service is used by student pilots wishing to apply for flight crew license/rating.
TCDD- e-Ticket Reservation and Sales	e-ticket sales and reservation services of Railways.
DMİGM- Daily Weather Forecast	Using this service, you can display daily Weather Forecast.
Inland Revenue Service - e-Tax Sign Inquiry	With this service, you can display the tax sign of a person or organization, and learn the accrued tax and taxable amount
TCMB- Exchange Rates	Using this service, you can display the daily foreign exchange rates broadcast by the Turkish Central Bank.
KOSGEB- Business Status Inquiry	You can have information as to whether the business is registered, can benefit from and apply for supports.

Recognizing that not all the actions and projects aimed by the Information Society Strategy will be realized, lately, specific e-Government projects have been prioritized for managing e-government innovation and leading a large-scale transformation in Turkey (Yildiz *et al.*, 2008, Table 1). A critical analysis of the process, outcome and outlook of the general Strategy and prioritised projects, as well as the related developments in the political arena are out of the scope of this work; nevertheless, it should be noted that interlink between public sector reform and e-Government development has not been able to be fully established in Turkey (Balci & Kirilmaz 2009).

The approach to prioritize specific projects that would lead to a large-scale transformation could also be considered to reflect that in Turkey e-Government is led by a specific community of e-Government technicians (Uçkan, 2009a). This community of technicians knows the standards of this business and has fought for development based on these standards for the last 15 to 20 years (Uçkan, 2009a). During this period there seems to have been no strong citizen demand for e-Government. Moreover, Alican (2007), and Gökmen (2009) criticize the Information Society Strategy of Turkey for having a weak social content. Specifically these authors argue that the development of Turkey's e-Government capabilities ignores underdeveloped regions and that it does not consider that more than 10% of the population is illiterate, or lack the necessary ICT capabilities. Thus, low citizen demand and a persistent digital divide remain issues that hinder e-Government development in Turkey[2]. As recently identified by research conducted by Saruç (2009), a lack of trust is another important handicap to the development of e-Government services. Fifty two percent of 650 research respondents indicate that they do not trust making payments to government offices over the Internet.

EXAMPLES OF RECENT DEVELOPMENTS AS NATIONAL FRAMEWORKS, CENTRAL GOVERNMENT PROJECTS

E-Government Gateway (EGG) and Shared Service Approach

Turkey was considered to have an ad-hoc approach for e-Government applications using electronic signatures (IDABC, 2007), considering, for in-

Table 1. High-Priority e-Government Projects and their Selection Criteria in Turkey (Adapted from: Yildiz, et.al., 2008)

Project Title Responsible Agency
1. Online Vehicle Registration Ministry of Internal Affairs **2. e-Criminal Record** Ministry of Justice **3. Online Establishment of Firms** Ministry of Industry & Trade **4. e-Appointment in Healthcare** Ministry of Health **5. e-Contracting** Public Contracting Agency **6. e-Taxation in Municipalities** Ministry of Internal Affairs **7. Online Trial Procedures** Ministry of Justice **8. Consumer Portal** Ministry of Industry & Trade **9. Culture Portal** Ministry of Culture & Tourism **10. Foreign e-Trade** Undersecretary of Customs & Undersecretary of Foreign Trade **11. e-Environment Permits** Ministry of Environment & Forestry
Based on the following criteria-weight % (Total-100): Impact-20, Supporting/Pledged Senior Management-15, Time-15, Extra Cost-10, Supporting/Pledged Project Team-10, External Support for the Project (Private Sector, NGOs, etc.)-10, Does it Appear on the Information Society Action Plan Document?-5, Number of Affected Government Agencies-5, Is it One of the 20 EU Basic Public Services?-5, Is it on the 2008 Turkish Government Program?-5

stance, the implementation of Inward Processing Regime. Nevertheless, with the recent launch of EGG in December 2008 that implements unified access and centralized authentication module, a shared service approach should be considered to represent the national framework (Figure 4). Thanks to this approach, issues of security, the management of sign-up mechanisms, back office management, handling of user problems, addressing back-up could be solved more easily and adequately in a unified way by the EGG. As the Figure 1 illustrates, Turkey moves from the ad-hoc approach towards shared service approach, benefiting from the national initiatives such as EGG.

The EGG provides a centralized, shared service approach, enabling the orchestration of different service applications from various government agencies, i.e. "helps them to communicate". However as a specific characteristic of the Turkish case, the situation with data and information ownership is different: the ownership of the cross-communicated data and information is not centralized, but distributed among the government agencies that are responsible from the respective services.

Central Civil Registration System (MERNIS) as a Process and Product of Transformation

The Identity Information Sharing System (abbreviated KPS in Turkish) went into operation in 2005 as an extension of Central Civil Registration System (abbreviated MERNIS in Turkish) introduced in 2000 (although the initiation of the project could be traced back to 1970s). Public agencies can access citizens' identity information stored in "MERNIS database via the KPS under strictly specified conditions in the respective access protocols." The system keeps logs of every user and conducted enquiries over the Virtual

Figure 4. Turkish national e-government applications (using e-signatures) framework towards shared service approach (CSP: Certificate Service Provider) adapted from IDABC, 2007[3])

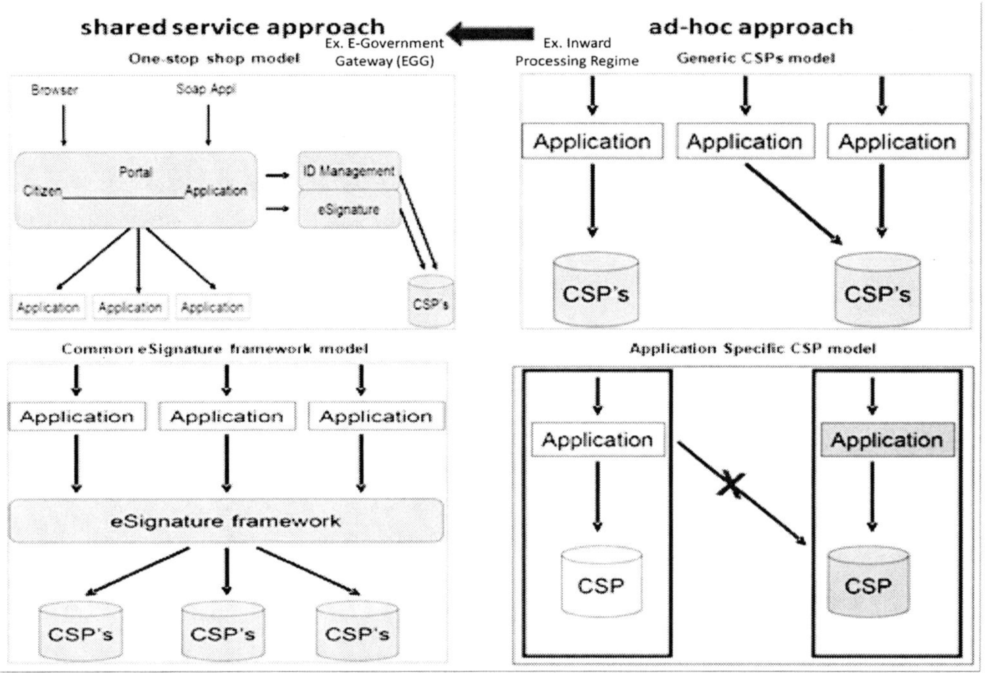

Private Network.[4] The system is complemented with the centrally administered Address Registration System (abbreviated AKS in Turkish).[5] KPS offers the following enquiry services [6]:

Web Sites:

- Enquiry of personal information using the TR Identity Number
- Enquiry of TR Identity Number using personal information
- Enquiry of identity information based on information of the place of registration
- Enquiry of copy of civil status records using various criteria.

Web services (XML Infrastructure): Users of the system are able to conduct inquiries by accessing KPS web services using add-ons to their existing applications or by developing new applications. They are also able to view the enquired data directly from their own applications and automatically update their own databases with the enquired information.

The unified access and centralized authentication module implemented by EGG also benefits from the enquiry services provided by KPS built upon MERNIS, which is:

a centrally administered system where any changes in civil status are registered electronically in real time over a secure network by the 966 civil registration offices spread throughout the country. The information kept in the central database is shared with the public and private agencies for administrative purposes... Currently, the MERNIS database houses more than 130 million personal data files and (as of January 2009) more than 2000 public bodies are using the up-to-date data from the MERNIS database.[7]

MERNIS are expected to contribute to public transformation via these Civil Registration Offices. Transactions related to civil status can be carried out at the civil registration office at the place of domicile instead of the office at the place of registration. Population and vital statistics are also produced and shared instantly. Legislative, operational, informational controls can be effectively made, as well. For other public agencies, aspects of expected public transformation are the following[8]:

- **Economic and Financial:** Tax collections and controls would be carried out more easily and informal economy would be brought under control, fraudulent acts in notary, title deeds and banking operations would be prevented. Banks and notaries would be able to validate the accuracy of persons' records by accessing the KPS database. In this way, fraudulent and counterfeiting incidents would be prevented.
- **Planning and Investment:**· Investing agencies would be able to use data in MERNİS classified according to information such as age groups and number of population, and therefore make accurate future planning and investments based on real data.
- **Security:** Assistance would be provided in monitoring entries and exits from the country, monitoring and arresting convicted persons, outlaws and drivers who committed traffic offences endangering the life and property of others. Security forces would be able to validate identity information of wanted persons by accessing records in MERNIS database using parameters such as the TR Identity Number or Name and Surname. Counterfeit identities would be determined.
- **Military Service:**· Assistance would be available in drafting conscription lists by ASAL (Department of Military Conscription), since the lists of persons reaching the conscription age could be obtained from

MERNIS on time. In addition, since data on male population classified by age groups can be obtained from MERNIS, military personnel needs for the next years can be determined and planned accordingly.

- **Health Services:** Since patient files would be opened based on the identity number, health records of a person would be possible to maintain as a whole. Health policies such as the hospital and health centre needs by region would be planned based on real data from MERNIS.
- **Education:** Since all kinds of nationwide or regional education statistics would be available instantly, planning and policies related to education would be better determined.
- **Social Security:** Since social security agencies will be also accessing the MERNIS database, copies of civil and family status previously requested form the civil registration offices will be provided in electronic form, thereby abolishing the intra-agency correspondence. In addition, memberships with multiple social security agencies by the same person or attempts to register with fake identities would be prevented to a great extend.
- **Electoral Registers:** Assistance would be provided in the establishment of electoral registers, since the details of persons reaching the age of voting would be instantly available.
- **Justice:** Identifications during court trials could be made by accessing MERNIS database from the court's computer terminal. In addition, copies of civil and family status requested during inheritance trials would be accessed in the same way.

These different aspects of social transformation can be summarized as better planning, implementation, control and assessment in all services related with public affairs. The efficiency and speed of public services should also be specifically noted.

MERNIS records related to the identity of the persons are stored and accessed using the Turkish Republic Identity Number[9]. The TR Identity Number used via KPS and MERNIS actually plays a key role for enabling the exchange of data and information among public agencies, thus making possible to achieve such public transformation. (Figure 5)

With its journey of quarter century, MERNIS reflects the purposes, challenges and prospects associated with public transformation via information and communication technologies, although a related thorough analysis is out of the scope of this work. The services integrated into EGG, nevertheless, could also be expected to enhance the achievement of such long-anticipated public transformation. Lately, many of the high-priority e-Government projects will have become operational via EGG. (It is also expected that, integrated with AKS, address change will have also be possible via EGG in a couple of months.) As a part of these new operations, for instance the unified access and centralized authentication module will lead users to specific service websites, providing a new option beside the services provided via EGG or service-providing institution website.

This approach of shared and centralized service but distributed and decentralized data and information could transform the relations among government agencies and citizens. For instance, such approach could address citizen concerns about trustworthiness regarding the risks that could accompany the central ownership of private data. Furthermore, the service processes would be reorganized to establish the necessary communication and interoperation among different agencies and organizations, as well as different internal units within organizations.

Figure 5. Illustration of public agencies: KPS - MERNIS relationship[10]

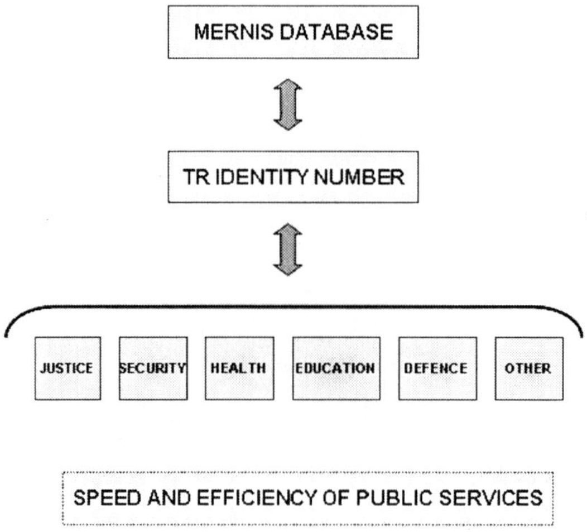

National e-Justice Project (UYAP), Examples of Process Integrations and Improvements

There are also specific success stories of central e-government initiatives that are worth-noting. In this work, Turkish e-justice project UYAP will be discussed as one particular example of success in public transformation[11].

UYAP is an e-justice system as a part of e-government project, which has been developed in order to ensure fast, reliable, and accurate judicial system. UYAP is developed by IT Department of the Ministry of Justice of Turkey by using the most updated technology and methodologies. As a central information system it covers all of the judicial institutions and other governmental departments. All judicial units were fully equipped with computers, case and document management software and other updated hardware. Each judicial unit connected to others by a secure network and given access to legal sources such as legislation, case law, bulletins and circulars. UYAP has been designed in order to improve the functioning and efficiency of the judiciary and to create an effective and less bureaucratic judicial system for the concerned institutions and individuals. All of the judicial units and agencies currently make use of ICT in their daily lives as all processes and transactions were transmitted into electronic environment.

Accordingly, UYAP consists of these sub-systems: Penal and Civil Law System, Administrative Law System, Public Prosecutors Services System, Court of Cassation System, Probation System, Verdict Support System, Lawyer Information System, Enforcement-Bankruptcy System, Convict-Arrest Management System, Citizen Information System, Personal Management System, Financial Management System, Supply and Procurement Management System, Training Management System, Document Management System, Forensic Medicine System, General Support System, Inspection Management System.

Within UYAP, also, establishment of e-learning, a central control system for distance training; citizen and lawyer portal; decision support system, document management system, electronic signature, intelligent warning, SMS (messaging service via mobile phones) information system should be underlined. With these advanced characteristics, the importance and merits of UYAP have been nationally and internationally recognized. Among various benefits of the project, the improvements in processes comparing the times before and after the UYAP are provided in Table 2.

These process time improvement statistics are especially striking for the Justice system in Turkey that is long-known for its slow- proceeding. Furthermore, saving from UYAP are counted to be 243.521.207€ in total. (15.884.989€ of this total amount, for instance, credited to the integration with MERNIS.)[13] Moreover, as for another statistics, for instance, 7,837 pine trees are also saved in a year thanks to the paperless environment provided by UYAP (Hamurcu, 2009).

Even, UYAP itself keeps evolving. With respect to this evolution, Aydın and Polat (2008, p. 4) provides an example of steps and time spent for lawyers in file a suit process:

In minimum 15, maximum 60 minutes, a typical process lawyer

- physically goes to court desk in the court house,
- declares the necessary information about the case, such as the sides of the case, content etc.
- requests the court staff to enter this information into the UYAP electronically,
- receives the document showing the amount of the case fee that needs to be deposited.

It again takes 15-30 minutes for a lawyer to deposit the case fee to the cash desk, and receive the receipt from the cash desk. Then again in 15-30 minutes, Lawyer

- goes back to the court desk,
- presents the receipt to the court desk,
- submits the statement of claim in paper to the court desk,
- finishes the process after the desk staff distributes the case through UYAP electronically.

Thus, with the initial service delivery since 2000 with UYAP (, in spite of all the benefits and improvement), for lawyers still process of filing a suit typically takes 45 minutes to 2 hours for the last 5-6 years (, excluding the time for travel to the court house). As Aydın and Polat (2008, p. 8) discuss, however, as the most developed e-government service over the portal for lawyers, a service for "Filing a Suit and Paying Court Fees Online" has also become available since 2005. Using this service, lawyers can complete the whole filing a suit process within 5 minutes without an obligation of physical presence and time-consuming processes. As opposed to steps

Table 2. Process improvements with respect to UYAP (Source[12]:, Aydın & Polat, 2008, p. 6)

Processes	Before	After
Writing a writ	3-5 min.	3 min.
Writing a postal distribution list	10-20 min.	1 min.
Year-end turnover and preparing statistics	15-20 days	15-20 min.
Requesting a criminal record	1-15 days	1 min.
Requesting a birth certificate	1-15 days	1 min.
Sending a writ, order or file to another court	7-15 days	1 min.
Preparing statistics tables used for judge promotions every two years	1 day	0-1 min.
Creating annual statistics of a court	7 days	0-5 min.

discussed above, lawyers complete the following steps online:

- Select the relevant court,
- Select the type of suit from the pull-down menu,
- Submit information about concerned parties (MERNIS integration allows automatic filling of identity information by submitting only the citizen number),
- Pay court fees online (After submitting the type of suit and information about concerned parties, the portal calculates the court fee and transfers the lawyer to online banking screens. Lawyer logs into his or her account and transfers the certain amount to the relevant court's account.
- Submit electronically signed petition.
- Receive online confirmation, including information about case file, such as file number.

Thus UYAP Lawyer Portal improves the transformative benefits of UYAP that is already a significant development towards provision of better public services via electronic means in the Justice domain in comparison to physical provision of the same services in the old-fashioned way. While, similar process improvements and service evolutions could also be accounted for other public institutions and e-Government services, in conclusion, UYAP can be considered to be a significant means for transforming and revolutionizing the Turkish Judiciary. [14]

UYAP has enhanced the quality of services provided to citizens and the effectiveness of justice. As a result public confidence has been achieved in justice services thanks to transparent and rapid justice, aiding stability and peace in society and growth in the economy. These developments mentioned, in terms of their consequences represents progress that augments the confidence of citizens in the judiciary and shows ongoing improvements.

Still, the portal itself has yet to be fully utilized among lawyers by the time Aydın and Polat (2008) has presented their research. Aydın and Polat (2009) discuss that while the majority of transactions on the Lawyer Portal are for viewing and querying case information, only a small portion is for completing the filing of a law suit process, confirming that 'lawyers have not been prepared or willing to go through the whole process online' (p. 423). In practice, there are still impediments in front of successful penetration of the lawyer portal. Improvement of legislation and payment mechanisms can facilitate further online transactions.

In this work, then, while specific success stories of central e-government initiatives are highlighted, it should be also reminded that these success stories result from learning-by-doing and lessons-learned from mistakes. One other example of this learning-by-doing can be given about e-Tax services as below.

E-Tax Services and Learning from Experiences

While a recent good example of e-tax services can be given as the provision of municipality tax payment via EGG, until this time a (steep) learning curve for e-tax services can also be traced back. For instance, during the diffusion into 30 tax offices after the pilot implementation, a system mistake was discovered by internal auditors during e-auditing. According to this system mistake, people who have tax debts could get official proof that state they do not have tax debt. While the reason of this situation seemed to be the result of simple coding error, actually the whole system needed a close scrutiny due to the black hole(s) among the ongoing processes. Just to illustrate: one person comes to the tax office and says "I owe 100 TL tax debts" and goes to the payment collection unit to get a payment collection slip. As soon as the slip is given by the system, the system also deduces 100 TL from the tax debt. The person then goes to the unit that provides the official proof of having no tax debt and gets it. Next, with this proof of no debt, the person again goes to the payment collection unit, and tells "there was a last minute change, today I cannot pay any money, or I can only pay 10 TL", getting another payment slip respectfully. Finally the person leaves the office with the official proof of no debt but without paying the debt, using this official proof to do business. Meanwhile, another human error was that there was no fee charged due to repetition. Having no repetition fee and thus repetition was impossible in reality, as there had to be various repeated mistakes. The e-auditing identified such machine or human errors in the system, and the system was revised accordingly. [15]

Similar errors and mistakes could be made anytime and anywhere, some of which are properly identified, fixed, and publicized as in this case of e-Tax service. However, what these examples also show, which could be more important, is that still the internal processes of the institution and organized system could need to be reengineered and integrated. In UYAP, still court staffs have roles for processes which lawyers can fulfill more efficaciously, if they do themselves; or in e-Tax services, the careless involvement of different units for various physical, virtual, and bridging-in-between processes could cause system to produce errors, as discussed above. Another example is the processes within and among institutions for ordinary passport application to the General Directorate of Police. Ordinary passport applications can be initiated online, but the applicant still has to apply personally to finalize the application. Also while the application is processed, the applicant may have to go to other government agencies to provide supporting documents in certain cases. (Even, the application could then be finalized without internal control of whether these documents from other agencies are actually presented or not, as personally experienced by one co-author).

Without development and maturation of interoperable, integrated internal and external processes of "information and communication", it would not be possible to fulfill a thorough public transformation with technologies of information and communication. This concludes the discussion regarding national frameworks and central government projects (while local municipality level analyses have been excluded from this discussion, it should be reminded that these entire national, central government projects are within institutions with a diverse network spread within the country.)

DISCUSSION: POLICY ORIENTATIONS THAT AFFECT DAILY LIVES OF CITIZENS

These issues discussed from the perspective of government provision can also be complemented with a discussion from a perspective of citizen demand. For instance, as a part of social transformation, for Citizens MERNIS aims the following[16]:

- *Since all civil registration operations are carried out electronically, waste of time is minimised and documents are issued without any informational errors.*
- *Copies of civil status and identity cards can be obtained from the civil registration offices at the place of domicile, using computer technology thus preventing material errors.*
- *With the introduction of the Identity Information Sharing System (KPS), public agencies would be able to carry out their operations without requesting further documents from the citizen.*

In most of the applications to government agencies, citizen identity and address confirmation is needed. This confirmation used to be received from local neighbourhood authorities named Mukhtars. While currently, for various e-government services KPS and AKS integrated into MERNIS provides the necessary information and documentation, for the other public services civil registration offices facilitate the electronic and physical documentation whenever needed.

As another example, the SMS information system within UYAP provides the following benefits to citizens (Çam, 2009, pp 2-3):

UYAP ... provides a perfect legal protection and alarm system for citizens enabling them learning proceedings first hand. Citizens are given the possibility to check their cases without time and location restrictions ensuring full transparency in legal proceedings... After the system was put into practice which brings easiness to lawyers and citizens, it is not necessary to go to courthouses to get information about the phase of the case or to learn the date of the hearing and also they no longer have to pay travel costs to go to remote courts... use of this system makes the justice system more efficient and transparent, engendering greater public trust and confidence in the judiciary and respect for the rule of law... It also facilitates better access to justice for the disabled people, allowing them to learn about their cases without need to go to courts. In addition SMS information system has increased the awareness and the knowledge of the citizens making them strong in relations with their advocates and confident before courts. This may contribute to the quality of the judiciary. In addition, SMS information system works as a perfect alarming service, enabling citizen to take precautions without delay in case their ID is stolen, used and as a result they became a culprit.

With respect to addressing the citizen perspective, there is also significant work-in-progress in Turkey with respect to measuring citizen satisfaction with the "Citizen Satisfaction Index." A collaboration between Türksat and Kahramanmaraş Sütçü İmam Üniversitesi has been initiated in order to develop a methodology for measuring citizen satisfaction from e-Government services (T-VOHSU Project for measuring satisfaction from provision of citizen-oriented e-Government services). Based upon the existing literature, a draft model using variables such as trust, website quality and citizen services will be proposed. A multi-equation cause-and-effect model and Structural Equation Modeling will be used for data analysis of the relationships among the variables. Regarding the Structural Equation Modeling, "Path Analysis with Observed/Latent Variables", and "Confirmatory Factor Analysis" will be applied to the specific Turkish case, for developing indices at three different levels (e-service, e-institution, e-Government) as suggested by Bakan, Aydın, Kar, and Öz (2008, 2009). While certain initial qualitative results are available (Kutluoglu 2010 [17]), the comprehensive quantitative analyses will be available at the end of 2010.

In addition to this national project, an international project for citizen-oriented evaluation of e-Government services has been developed in collaboration with Brunel University, UK and American University of Beirut, Lebanon in 2008. The project, called CEES (citizen-oriented evaluation of e-Government services), will use the Data Envelope Analysis (DEA) framework, a reference process model that will allow the application of findings to Turkey as well as to other EU countries. (Lee *et al.*, 2009)

Moreover, development of a Ubiquitous Participation Platform for Policy Making (UbiPOL) project, into which Turkish partners are also involved, is also going to start soon. UbiPOL project aims to develop a ubiquitous platform that allows citizens be involved in policy making processes (PMPs) regardless of their current locations and time.

It is suggested that the more citizens find connections between their as-usual life activities and relevant policies, the more they become pro-active or motivated to be involved in the PMPs. For this reason, UbiPOL aims to provide context aware knowledge provision with regard to policy mak-

ing. That is citizens using UbiPOL will be able to identify any relevant policies and other citizen's opinion whenever they want wherever they are according to their as-usual life pattern. (UbiPOL project document 2009[18])

As for the digital divide issue, the Ministry of Transport and Communication has been establishing public internet access points throughout the country. Also, ICT classrooms have been equipped in almost all primary and secondary schools in Turkey, financed by the universal service fund. As an affiliated organization of the Ministry of Transport and Communication, Türksat has devised satellite-based internet connection to more than 5,000 schools in geographically remote areas in the country where other means of communication are unavailable.

In conclusion, "social transformation", "ICT adoption by business", "citizen focused service transformation", and "modernization in public administration" are among the top priorities of the Information Society Strategy and Action Plan (DPT, 2006) that aims to transform Turkey into a developed information/knowledge society. While the Strategy incorporates initiatives to direct the e-Government development, in Turkey, it should be reminded that e-Government development has not been able to be fully interlinked with the public sector reform (Balci & Kirilmaz 2009), some more basic problems need to be solved beforehand. Going back to the basics, for instance, according to Rehan and Koyuncu (2009, p. 385), in short, the main problem of Turkey towards e-Government developments is the weakness of ICT usage and ICT infrastructure. Therefore, by all means certain necessary actions to improve ICT usage and further develop the current infrastructure should be realized within a short period of time.

In order to take action for and realize the improvement of ICT infrastructure and usage, interoperability is then a significant issue to underline, as well. The European Interoperability Framework identifies three aspects of interoperability: Organizational, Semantic and Technical (European Commission, 2004). Accordingly, as generally accepted, in order to make inter-operation and collaboration possible, not only identifying common norms and standards and develop information systems and integrated e-Government services with respect to them, but also enabling coordination and collaboration within and among public institutions are important requirements. In Turkey, also, the necessity of inter-institutional interaction among various societal entities for the integration and interoperability of e-Government services in Turkey is widely recognized (DPT 2006, DPT 2008, DPT 2010). However, specifically in the progress reports of the Strategy, DPT (2008, 2010) highlights the idea that the priorities and objectives of the Strategy still need to be appreciated and owned by all stakeholders, and other responsible and interested entities in the society. Issues of intra-institutional and inter-institutional coordination problems with respect to not only managerial but also technical aspects are among the most significant issues experienced in the implementation of the strategy. Finally, the strategy provides a framework until 2010, and what will come next is currently uncertain.

SUGGESTIONS FOR FUTURE WORK

Following the above discussion, discussion continue that in addition to access to basic Internet services, access to broad-band Internet could also be considered to be a part of the universal service.[19] Moreover, empirical data collection and documentation as well as contributing academic perspectives from different fields are needed to further the reflections and directions discussed in this work.

When process re-organizations for e-Government services are also reflected in physical Government services, this paves the way for the transformation of government agencies and public institutions. While in most cases, still the old processes and continue side by side with the new, transformed processes, evidence of such process and service transformation are also needed to be provided on a case by case basis. The cases can be selected among services integrated within EGG, while other, un-integrated services can be also provided as complementary examples – presented as practices of success stories and lessons-learned, providing empirical data collection, analysis and assessments, as well.

As for contributing academic perspectives from different fields, knowledge management with its technological and technical as well as social and organizational aspects, for instance, can be used to facilitate establishment of interlink between public sector transformation and e-Government development. To diffuse particular good practices into the government system as a whole, knowledge management can also provide certain guidelines. Public organizations have certainly their own structure such as high centralization, bureaucratization and formalization that are considerably differ from the private organizations, and need to apply specific knowledge management strategies for which technology is an important determinant (Bengshir and Sagsan 2009). These knowledge management strategies that are interlinked with overall organizational strategies can lead the institutional transformations. A perspective of knowledge technologies could also contribute to convergence and advancement of information and communication technologies.

Development of various public-oriented social computing applications also opens up new (e-) governance channels for political participation and public engagement (JRC EC, 2009, pp. 121-127) that enhances adoption and diffusion of institutional transformations and t-Government:

- Collaborative sites to build and share knowledge for learning (Connexions)
- Self organizing communities of professionals (such as Doctors.net.uk)
- Websites that facilitate citizen participation in policy decision-making (such as Theyworkforyou)
- Websites that allow citizens to report offences (such as Mybikelane)
- Websites that publish anonymous reports of corruption or other wrongdoings of public institutions (such as Wikileaks) (p. 16)

Such developments enable to connect, share, collaborate, and co-produce content for social or public goals, and should be expected to have more weight on future practical and academic work.

CONCLUSION

To sum up, this chapter aimed to provide a country specific case for public sector transformation by e-Government service development and maturation, i.e. transformational government. The Turkish case has been presented, benefiting from analyses at general national, and citizen levels. These reflective analyses have been embedded within background information about e-government development in Turkey and grounded upon academic perspective of transformational government, as well as public reform, knowledge management. E-Government Gateway, MERNIS, UYAP, e-tax projects in Turkey have been specifically highlighted. A discussion of policy orientations that affect daily lives of citizens has followed, as well as suggestions for future work and directions have also been provided. While customer-centric and shared services have been underlined, ICT professionalism as important aspects of public sector transformation has been left for future work.

The above discussion that gives examples from ongoing work, best practices and lessons-learned especially underlines the shared service and citizen-oriented approach to e-Government service development with implications for process integration and improvements, if not yet for thorough transformation. It is hoped that the reflections and directions with respect to Turkish case presented in this work will provide useful guidelines for new e-Government initiatives in Turkey and all around the world.

ACKNOWLEDGMENT

This work is partially supported by the Ubiquitous Participation Platform for POLicy Makings (UbiPOL), EU FP7-ICT-2009-4 STREP project and by CEES (Citizen-oriented Evaluation of E-Government Services: A Reference Process Model), EU FP7 IAPP PEOPLE (Industry Academia Partnerships and Pathways) project. We also would like to thank Türksat, Turkey for supporting this work. As not only our part of fulfilling the responsibility to contribute to future work, but as part of our affiliations with these above-mentioned projects and institutions, as well, we also try to disseminate the findings of this academic work by presenting certain parts of this paper in various platforms including the transformative government workshop in Brunel University, UK, and new technologies seminar in Science and Technology Policies Centre, METU, Turkey (2010).

REFERENCES

Acar, M., & Kumaş, E. (2009). *A model proposal for the e-transformation infrastructure: The case of Turkey*. ICEGOV 2009, Ankara, Turkey

Afacan, G., & Arifoğlu, A. (2010). *A new metric system for assessment of e-transformation*. ICEGEG 2010. Antalya, Turkey

Alican, F. (2007). Experts without expertise: E-society projects in developing countries – The case of Turkey. *Information Polity*, *12*, 255–263.

Andersen, K. V., & Henriksen, H. Z. (2006). E-government maturity models: Extension of the Layne and Lee model. *Government Information Quarterly*, *23*, 236–248. doi:10.1016/j.giq.2005.11.008

Aydın, E. S., & Polat, M. (2009). *How Information Systems helped Turkish justice system speed up? An analysis on UYAP's lawyer portal and its benefits*. ICEGEG 2009. Ankara, Turkey.

Bakan, İ. A., Aydın, H., Kar, M., & Öz, B. (2008). (submitted to). T-VOHSA project phase 1. [Türksat.]. *Report*.

Bakan, İ. A., Aydın, H., Kar, M., & Öz, B. (2009). (submitted to). T-VOHSA project phase 2. [Türksat.]. *Report*.

Balcı, A., & Kirilmaz, H. (2009). Kamu Yönetiminde Yeniden Yapilanma Kapsaminda E-Devlet Uygulamalari. (Reorganization of Public Administration and e-Government Applications. *Türk İdare Dergisi*, *81*(463-464), 45–71.

Balci, A., Kumaş, E., Medeni, T., & Medeni, İ. T. (2009). Development and implementation of e-government services in Turkey . In Cunha, M. M., Oliveira, E. F., & Antonio, J. T. (Eds.), *Handbook of research on social dimensions of semantic technologies and Web services*. New York, NY: Information Science Reference.

Balcı, A., & Medeni, T. (2010). E-government gateway development in Turkey: Some challenges and future directions for citizen focus . In Downey, E., Ekstrom, C. D., & Jones, M. A. (Eds.), *E-government website development: Future trends and strategic models*. Hershey, PA: IGI Publishing.

Bengshir, T. K., & Sagsan, M. (2009). *Knowledge orchestration: The compatibility with organization, people, technology, and process in public organization*. eGovShare 2009, Antalya, Turkey.

Çam, A. R. (2009). *SMS Information System* (in Turkish e-justice project "UYAP"). Retrieved March 4, 2010, from http:// www.uyap.gov.tr/ english/ makale/ SMS_information_system-TURKEY.pdf

C.E.E.S. (2009). *Citizen-oriented evaluation of e-government services*. EU Marie Curie IAPP funded Project. Unpublished literature review as project deliverable document.

Coursey, D., & Norris, D. F. (2008). Models of e-government: Are they correct? An empirical assessment. *Public Administration Review*, (May-June): 523–535. doi:10.1111/j.1540-6210.2008.00888.x

DPT. (2006). *Bilgi Toplumu Stratejisi ve Eylem Planı (Information/Knowledge Society Strategy Document). Devlet Planlanma Teşkilatı (State Planning Organization)*. Both in Turkish and English.

DPT. (2008). *Information/knowledge society strategy progress report*. Devlet Planlanma Teşkilatı. (in Turkish)

DPT. (2010). *Information/knowledge society strategy progress report*. Devlet Planlanma Teşkilatı. (in Turkish)

European Commission. (2004). *European interoperability framework for pan-European e-government services*. Retrieved June 4, 2010, from http:// ec.europa.eu/ idabc/ servlets/ Doc?id=19528

Flak, L. S., Furuli, K., Kongsrud, S., & Sæbø, Ø. (2009). *Magic bullets or entepreneurial efforts? Two ways to develop national citizen portals?* ICEGOV 2009. Ankara, Turkey

Gökmen, A. (2009). *Developments and prospects in e–government implementations in Turkey*. ICEGOV2009, Ankara, Turkey.

Hamurcu, E. (2009). *Paperless environment and saving the trees with UYAP*. Retrieved March 4, 2010, from http:// www.uyap.gov.tr/ english/ makale/ rolhamurcu.pdf

IDABC. (2007). *Preliminary study on mutual recognition of e-signatures for e-government applications*. Retrieved March 4, 2010, from http:// ec.europa.eu/ idabc/ servlets/ Doc?id=29484

Irani, Z., Al-Sebie, M., & Elliman, T. (2006). Transaction stage of e-government systems: Identification of its location & importance. *Proceedings of the 39th Hawaii International Conference on System Sciences (HICSS-39)*, Hawaii.

Janssen, M. (2009). *Orchestrating networks for integrated service delivery*. ICEGEG 2009. Ankara, Turkey.

Janssen, M., Joha, A., & Weerakkody, V. (2007). Shared service arrangements in the public sector: An exploratory study. *Transforming Government: People . Process and Policy*, *1*(3), 271–284.

JRC EC. (2009). The impact of social computing on the EU information society and economy.

Kanat, İ. K., & Ozkan, S. (2009). Exploring citizens' perception of government to citizen services: A model based on theory of planned behaviour (TBP). *Transforming Government: People . Process and Policy*, *3*(4), 406–419.

Lee, H., Irani, Z., Osman, I., Balcı, A., Ozkan, S., & Medeni, T. (2008). Research note: Toward a reference process model for citizen-oriented evaluation of e-government services. *Transforming Government: People, Process and Policy*, *2*(4), 297-310.

Markus, M. L., & Robert, I. B. (1997). The magic bullet theory in IT-enabled transformation. *Sloan Management Review*, *38*(2), 55–68.

Melin, U., & Axelsson, K. (2009). Managing e-service development – A comparative e-government case study. *Transforming Government: People . Process and Policy*, *3*(3), 248–270.

Norris, D. F. (2010). *E-government, e-democracy, e-transformation? Now? Soon? Ever?* ICEGEG 2010. Antalya, Turkey

OECD. (2009). Re-thinking e-government services: User-centred approaches.

Rehan, M., & Koyuncu, M. (2009). *Towards e-government: A survey of Turkey's progress*. ICEGOV2009. Ankara, Turkey.

Sahraoui, S., Ghoneim, A., Irani, Z., & Özkan, S. (2008). T-government for benefit realization: A research agenda . In Irani, Z., & Love, P. (Eds.), *Evaluating Information Systems*. London, UK: Elsevier. doi:10.1016/B978-0-7506-8587-0.50019-6

Saruç, N. T. (2009). *The factors effecting use of e-government services and perceived quality of public services: An empirical study*. ICEGOV2009, Ankara, Turkey.

Torres, L., Pina, V., & Royo, S. (2005). E-government and the transformation of public administrations in EU countries: Beyond NPM or just a second wave of reforms? [Emerald Group Publishing Limited]. *Online Information Review*, *29*(5), 531–553. doi:10.1108/14684520510628918

Uçkan, Ö. (2009a). *Everyone is governed as they deserve*. Retrieved March 4, 2010, from http://arsiv.sabah.com.tr/ 2009/ 01/ 04/ pz/ haber,0499516A4921456CA2DA627988C1E222.html

Uçkan, Ö. (2009b). *Weakness of ICT policy-making process in Turkey: The governance phobia*. ICEGOV 2009. Ankara, Turkey.

United Nations. (2008). *E-government survey 2008 - From e-government to connected governance*. United Nations.

West, D. M. (2004). E-government and the transformation of service delivery and citizen attitudes. *Public Administration Review*, *64*(1). doi:10.1111/j.1540-6210.2004.00343.x

Yildiz, M., Sadioglu, U., & Altinok, R. (2008). *Managing e-government innovation In Turkey: The case of e-government advisory group in the office of the Prime Minister*. Rotterdam European Group of Public Administration e-Government Study Group. September 3, 2008.

KEY TERMS AND DEFINITIONS

CEES: EU-funded international project for "citizen-oriented evaluation of e-Government services". Initiated in 2009 in collaboration with Brunel University, UK and American University of Beirut, Lebanon, the project will use the Data Envelope Analysis (DEA) framework, a reference process model that will allow the application of findings to Turkey as well as to other EU countries.

E-Government Gateway (EGG): A major milestone for transforming into the Information Society for and achieving the related Strategic Goals set by Turkey, aiming to provide Turkey's 70 million citizens and business entities with a single point of access, one-stop-shop, to e-Government services. The implementation process of EGG is also based on service transformation

MERNIS: Central Civil Registration System (Abbreviated in Turkish). Public agencies can access citizens' identity information stored in MERNIS database via the Identity Information Sharing System. The system is also complemented with the centrally administered Address Registration System

T-Government (Transformational Government): Public sector transformation by e-Government services development and maturation. Citizen-centric delivery shared service culture, professionalism of service provision are significant aspects of t-government.

T-VOHSU: A collaborative project between Türksat and Kahramanmaraş Sütçü İmam Üniversitesi with respect to measuring citizen satisfaction from e-Government services with the "Citizen Satisfaction Index." A multi-equation cause-and-effect model and Structural Equation Modeling is used for data analysis of the relationships among the variables.

Ubiquitous Participation Platform for Policy Making (UbiPOL): International project that aims to develop a ubiquitous platform, allowing citizens be involved in policy making processes regardless of their current locations and time. (EU FP7-ICT-2009-4 STREP project)

UYAP: National e-Justice Project (Abbreviated in Turkish), developed by IT Department of the Ministry of Justice of Turkey as a central information system that covers all of the judicial institutions and other governmental departments with continuously improved benefits to not only these institutions but also individual users as lawyers and citizens.

ENDNOTES

1 (http://www.iseing.org/tgovwebsite/CFP.pdf)

2 Please visit http://epractice.eu/files/download/i2010_eInclusion_Reports.pdf for an e-Inclusion report done by an e-practice.eu sub-group to have a good basis of comparison for digital divide issues.

3 http://ec.europa.eu/idabc/servlets/Doc?id=29484

4 (http://www.nvi.gov.tr/English/KPS_EN,KPS_EN.html)

5 (For further information on AKS: http://www.nvi.gov.tr/English/Address_EN,Address_Registration_System.html)

6 (http://www.nvi.gov.tr/English/KPS_EN,KPS_EN.html)

7 (source: http://www.nvi.gov.tr/English/Mernis_EN,Mernis_En.html)

8 (source: http://www.nvi.gov.tr/English/Mernis_EN,Mernis_En.html?pageindex=2)

9 (For further information on TR Identity Number: http://www.nvi.gov.tr/English/Mernis_EN,Mernis_En.html?pageindex=1)

10 (Source: http://www.nvi.gov.tr/English/Mernis_EN,Mernis_En.html?pageindex=3)

11 (http://www.uyap.gov.tr/english/makale/UYAP_article.pdf)

12 (http://www.uyap.gov.tr/english/makale/UYAP_article.pdf)

13 (http://www.uyap.gov.tr/english/savings/savings.html)

14 (http://www.uyap.gov.tr/english/makale/UYAP_article.pdf)

15 (http://www.milliyet.com.tr/Ekonomi/SonDakika.aspx?aType=SonDakika&KategoriID=11&ArticleID=1026088&PAGE=1)

16 (http://www.nvi.gov.tr/English/Mernis_EN,Mernis_En.html?pageindex=2)

17 1.113 sorted responses from 1.500 qualitative feedbacks within 3-month pilot survey for 28 (including general service provision) within total 160 services. https://prezi.com/secure/?lock=e632c51a2cf54331d0e4e25e86744529d7a070ca

18 http://www.ideal-ist.net/Countries/UK/PS-UK-3051, for further information: http://www.ubipol.eu/

19 (For Ex. @ European broadband Portal, www.broadband-europe.eu http://www.broadband-europe.eu/ Lists/ Universal%20Service%20Obligation%20%20Discussion%20Forum/ Flat.aspx?RootFolder=%2FLists% 2FUniversal%20Service%20Obligation%20%20Discussion%20Forum%2FDo%20you%20think%20the%20USO%20should%20be%20extended%20to%20include%20broadband&FolderCTID=0x01200200B78740AC04679846981F-FA7B0B9F5BB2)s

Chapter 14
Addressing Contextual Influences During ICT Innovation for Public Sector Reform:
The Case of TAXIS

Elpida Prasopoulou
Athens University of Economics and Business, Greece

ABSTRACT

In recent years, ICT innovation is explicitly linked to deep structural reforms in public administrations. In this chapter, I examine the role of context, during the establishment of a minimal and accountable government apparatus, using the concept of negotiation space as my theoretical lens. The process of imbricating ICT innovation within the local context is viewed as a clash between local institutions and the ones carried by new Information Technologies. This clash is empirically examined in the case of TAXIS, the flagship Information Technology project of the Greek government in the mid 1990s. TAXIS's implementation has been strongly supported by both the political system and Greek society. Nevertheless, ICT innovation did not trigger radical changes in taxation. Instead, it was infused by strongly engrained political practices which resulted in the implementation of an Information System functional yet unable to support radical tax reform.

DOI: 10.4018/978-1-60960-839-2.ch014

INTRODUCTION

ICT innovation[1] has been heralded, by both politicians and citizens, as the principal means to trigger changes in the institutional fabric of public administrations (Dunleavy, 2007). Nevertheless, results have been rather limited. The idiosyncrasies of the local hosting contexts cause various deviations from predicted outcomes (Noir & Walsham, 2007), despite the diligent implementation of standard methodologies, acceptable techniques and state-of-the-art technological solutions.

Most research accounts (e.g. Layne & Lee, 2001; Wyld, 2004), adopting a deterministic point of view, trace such failures to the inability of the government apparatus, in the hosting countries, to properly implement and sustain ICT innovation (Bekkers & Homburg, 2007). By identifying the phenomenon as a problem of implementation such research efforts view existing failed attempts as temporary setbacks attributed to the lack of a comprehensive digital environment (Cordella, 2007). Therefore the suggested solution to problematic implementations is further automation of administrative processes in order to oblige public administrations to redesign and simplify their operational activities (Ciborra, 2005).

In this chapter, ICT innovation is addressed as a socio-technical phenomenon unravelling in tandem with its context (Pettigrew, 1985). Such an approach is in line with a growing literature (e.g. Avgerou, 2002; Noir & Walsham, 2007) challenging mechanistic and a-contextual understandings of ICT innovation in public administration. It is the interplay of new information and communication technologies (ICT) with long-standing material practices and imageries on proper administration (Unger, 2004), inherent in the hosting public sector, which shapes the potential of ICT innovation as a vehicle for state reform.

For such a contextualized reading of ICT innovation, research is situated in the Greek public sector during the period of implementation (1996-1999) of the Greek taxation information system (TAXIS). TAXIS is the first electronic government project in Greece aiming at reforming one of the most critical operations of the public sector, the tax system. TAXIS' implementation is analyzed in tandem with core practices of the Greek public sector and the political circumstances of the period (i.e. the rise of modernization as a political ideology).

In the following section (2), the importance of context in the study of ICT innovation in public administration is discussed. Moreover, negotiation space as the core concept guiding analysis is presented. Section 3 presents the methods followed during empirical work and subsequent analysis. Then, an overview of the Taxation Information System (TAXIS) in tandem with some core issues is presented in section 4. The way ICT innovation has been imbricated to existing practices on the Greek political system and its repercussions are analysed in section 5. The following section (6) associates these themes with theory in order to further analyze how these two phenomena co-evolved. The chapter concludes with observations on this interaction and areas for further research.

CONTEXTUALISING ICT INNOVATION: OVERVIEW OF THE LITERATURE

Context constitutes an inseparable component in the study of ICT innovation. As Avgerou (2001) observes, the very nature of the object of study, information technology as a changing entity within its environment, essentially turns every study into a contextual one. The imbroglio of institutional arrangements and cognitive imageries on the desirable forms of human association (Unger, 2004), which constitutes context as an analytical entity, lifts focus from technology as such in order to incorporate societal factors which adequately explain what seems paradoxical in the interaction of the new technology with its environment.

In the following sections, the way context has been examined in the information systems literature is presented. Then, the concept of negotiation space and the theoretical angles it provides in the study of ICT innovation are discussed.

Context in Information Systems

ICT innovation is a composite phenomenon intertwining socio-material practices (Orlikowski, 2007) and symbolic systems within specific institutional contexts. The objective of most contextualist accounts (e.g. Davidson & Chiasson, 2005; Madon et al., 2007) is to increase awareness to the existence of context as a parameter that must be taken into consideration during ICT innovation. Thus, such an approach pays special attention to "action that is political, unintended, and inexplicable by the techno-economic logic" (Avgerou et al., 2004: 2). Implementation projects overflowing with controversy are not perceived as external nuisances (Avgerou & Madon, 2004). They become part of the analysis and provide a more informed account which situates ICT innovation in its proper institutional environment giving more fine-grained explanations for the observed phenomena.

There are several in depth accounts of technology-induced changes, within public organizations in late-development countries (e.g. Avgerou, 2002; Walsham, 1993), incorporating rich descriptions of the broader socio-economic and political environment. Noir & Walsham (2007) acknowledge the importance of long-standing institutional practices and mentalities in the adoption of ICTs. In the same vein, Avgerou and McGrath (2007) attribute failed attempts of IKA (e.g. the largest pension agency in Greece) to host ICT innovation to resistance on behalf of local actors (both end users and political personnel necessary for its success) to novel practices challenging long standing administrative operations. The new way of doing things was perceived as a potential threat to institutionalized relationships between public servants and the state as employer. Finally, Ciborra (2005) challenges deterministic understandings of ICT innovation by displaying the richness and complexity of the institutional complex in the case of the Kingdom of Jordan. A fast track information technology project, the Drivers & Vehicles Licensing (DVDL), chosen for implementation precisely because of its perceived simplicity and the potential of immediate results, presented significant problems even from the analysis stage (Ciborra, 2005). Different underlying assumptions on the importance of a driver's license in the context of the Middle East significantly stalled process re-engineering which has been elevated from a standard procedure, during system development, to an issue of national security.

Yet, none of these research endeavours explicitly addresses the interplay between the meanings and imageries conveyed by ICT innovation and local habitualised practices. They remain at the level of simple observations on how context influences the adoption of successfully implemented information systems. Interest does not rest on the dialogue between ICT innovation and the institutional arrangements shaping its environment. Nor there is an adequate examination of the origins, nature and role of the local institutions. The idiosyncrasies of local contexts are never viewed as parameters which shape and are potentially shaped by the new information technologies. As a result, empirical research produced detailed enumerations of the particularities of local hosting contexts, which have restrained research at the level of empiricism (Mouzelis, 2008).

As a result, the link between the "technical/rational" and the political remains vague (Avgerou & McGrath, 2007). As Kallinikos (2004b: 141) observes, "situated accounts of technology must be supplemented by wider reflection that captures the complex web of dependencies, interoperabilities, and institutional relations that sustain the embeddedness of technology in local contexts". This observation suggests the need for a theoretically informed examination on the role of contextual influences on ICT innovation. The notion of 'negotiation space' (Law & Callon, 1994) is introduced in the following section as a theoretical angle for the study of context during ICT innovation.

Opening the Negotiation Space: The Clash Between ICT Innovation and Local Institutional Arrangements

ICT innovation as enabler of institutional change takes place in contexts embodying specific institutional structures and understandings (Avgerou & Madon, 2004). Yet, despite strong commitment of the hosting countries, the local institutional contexts are not always conducive to ICT innovation and subsequent government reform. The reason for such results lays on the complex mechanisms through which CIT innovation is imbricated to local institutional arrangements and understandings about social reality.

More specifically, firmly engrained institutional and historical arrangements when in contact with the socio-material practices conveyed by new information technologies produce a 'negotiation space' (Law & Callon, 1994); that is a space, a period of time and a set of resources in which innovation may take place. This negotiation space contains institutional elements and ideas different, to varying degrees, than the ones for which information technologies were originally designed. Thus, ICT innovation must be imbricated with local practices in order to become a fixture of the hosting society (Avgerou, 2002). The outcome of this negotiation is highly contingent and depends on the strength and coherence of local institutional arrangements. As Mouzelis explains (1978: 138):

In all societies where institutions did not develop endogenously but, together with advanced technologies, were introduced or rather imposed by Western imperialism, the organic links between native and imported institutions are often lacking. The latter either play a purely decorative role [...] or, when they take strong roots in the host country, do not merge effectively with the older institutional structures. Their co-existence is such that neither of the two works properly.

It follows that contextual recalcitrance (Sørensen et al. 2001) should not be perceived as a phenomenon observed during the initial stages of ICT innovation, as suggested by technical/rational accounts. Nor, it is the outcome of IT implementations that do not take into account contextual parameters, as suggested by contextualist IS research (e.g. Madon et al., 2007; Noir & Walsham, 2007). It is the manifestation of the negotiation space formed during ICT innovation in the hosting countries. The imbrication[2] (Sassen, 2004) of technologically-induced material practices and symbolic systems into local social practices is a conflictual process. The final positioning of ICT innovation within the new institutional context is shaped by a clash between local institutions and the ones carried by new information technologies. Once this clash subsides, new concoctions combining elements of imported and local institutions are incorporated in the socio-material practices and assumptions of the hosting contexts. Thus, research becomes able to trace the multiple mediations taking place between ICT innovation and institutionalised practices in the political and administrative system of the hosting country (Lanzara, 2009).

In this chapter, these mediations are examined in the case of the Greek taxation information system (TAXIS). Before, however, delving into the particularities of the case, the research method adopted is presented in the following section.

RESEARCH METHODS

The aim of this research is to "*produce an understanding of the context of the information system, and the processes whereby the information system influences and is influenced by the con-*

text" (Walsham, 1993: 4-5). The need to present the implementation of an information system in tandem with the Greek institutional context guided me to present my research in the form of a historical account. The value of this approach has been discussed by Mason and colleagues (1997) while it has already been deployed by Avgerou and McGrath (2007) in their study of IKA, a Greek public organization struggling with ICT innovation.

Historical research invites the association of rich case descriptions with contextual elements and theoretical underpinnings. It is therefore quite appropriate for capturing "*the contingencies of organizational context and the situatedness of action in IS innovation [...] when the innovation being studied overflows with controversy, unexplainable actor behaviour, obstinacy in failing to "learn" and perform the expected technical roles, and an inability to improvise successfully*" (Avgerou & Madon, 2004: 168).

Evidence on TAXIS and the way the Greek political system negotiated with ICT innovation is based primarily on the collection of texts (i.e. press articles and opinion articles) as well as interviewing in order to supplement and verify the events. Empirical research drew mainly on Parliamentary minutes, in order to give voice to political parties, as collective actors, through first hand qualitative data. These are verbatim transcripts of any activity – programmed speeches, reactions, events - occurring during sessions of the Greek Parliament. Therefore, they constitute an invaluable source of discussions among representatives of collective actors but they also provide additional cues since they also described the reactions of the deputies (i.e. applause, disapproval). Their direct link to actorial activity allowed a first-hand appreciation of how actors through 'statements' constitute objects and subjects (Peräkylä, 2005). Their collection is in line with the guidelines of Peräkylä (2005) for naturally occurring empirical material that serve as direct testimonies of the way collective actors structure the world.

Documentary material has been supplemented by interviews on key actors during TAXIS' implementation, mainly members of the developing team and supervising authority. These people, traced during the initial reading of the collected material, were contacted and interviewed in order to verify the course of events as presented in the press.

Finally, to capture the values, structures and institutional aspects of Greek state's public administration, I collected an extensive range of academic studies on the matter. The idiosyncrasies of Greek public administration, the patterns of administrative reform as well as the problems experienced during each reform effort are extensively discussed by prominent Greek intellectuals (e.g. Mouzelis, 1995; Sotiropoulos, 2004; Spanou, 1996; Tsoukalas, 1995). Thus, I was able to establish significant insights on the nature of Greek public administration and further elaborate on its interaction with ICT innovation.

The outcome is an historical account of TAXIS during its implementation (1993-2000). For the presentation of the findings I have followed the approach adopted by Avgerou and McGrath (2007) in the case of IKAnet (the second bigger IS project in Greece at the time of TAXIS's implementation). The case narrative presents a "time line of events distilled from a wide range of empirical material" (Avgerou & McGrath, 2007: 300). Events are selected based on my understanding of empirical material through the lens of the adopted theoretical perspective. Then, analysis associates these themes of the case narrative with the theory in order to develop a more concrete account of the interplay of ICT innovation with the local context. Evidence from the case is incorporated in all subsequent sections of the chapter since theory and evidence unravel together to produce an understanding of the case. In the next section, I present a brief overview of the Greek Taxation Information System.

THE GREEK TAXATION INFORMATION SYSTEM (TAXIS)

The establishment of an equitable and efficient tax system is a persistent theme in Greek society. The influence of various social groups over a clientelistic political system has led, over the years, to the creation of a "complex, non-transparent system with generous individual allowances and a web of preferential incentives for the business sector" (Bronchi, 2001: 4). As a result, the tax system never managed to attract a high degree of social and political acceptance hampering compliance while promoting tax evasion (Mavraganis, 1994).

Tax policy was done in a way incompatible to the practices of a modern state in command of its finances. Complicated legislation coupled with lack of an appropriate administrative mechanism supporting the collection and processing of information forced the Ministry of Economics and Finance to base its tax policy on estimates. It follows that the re-organization of the Greek tax system was a recurring theme, during every state reform, without ever producing any tangible results.

In the mid 1990s, however, the circumstances were particularly pressing in view of the eminent European Monetary Union. The country would not successfully follow its counterparties in the European Union without having its finances under control. The government ought to control its tax income and have a more organized view of state's finances. Otherwise, it was impossible to formulate, implement and monitor an efficient financial policy.

TAXIS, at the time, was at the stage of implementation, facing however significant problems. The core visions of modernisation for battling administrative inefficiency and corruption fitted the visions of order and control conveyed by ICT innovation. As a result, TAXIS became the flagship IT project of modernization. The system underlined the commitment of the new government to achieve the Maastricht criteria. Moreover, it instantiated the decisiveness of the new government to battle corruption at the street level since it was implemented in one of the most corrupted public agencies of the country. Its successful roll-out would signal the government's decisiveness to contain clientelism and corrupted practices which hampered state finances and the country's image to the world.

TAXIS' operation would give the opportunity to group dispersed information and perform various controls that would first reveal the volume of tax evasion and then allow its containment[3]. Thus, fiscal policy making would be more realistic while monitoring and control would also be easier to implement. More specifically, the system would collect and organize available financial information, dispersed at local tax authorities, in order to improve the collection process of assessed debts and taxation, reduce tax evasion and increase taxation revenues. Moreover, TAXIS was envisaged to improve decision-making and gradually lead to a more fair financial policy, a persistent demand of Greek society. In a nutshell, TAXIS ought to ensure the following:

- Improvement of the collection process of assessed debts
- Increase in the total collections from all kinds of taxation
- Reduction of tax evasion and subsequent increase of taxation revenues
- Improvement of the decision-making procedure regarding short-term measures about taxation
- Improvement of the capability for evaluation of the measures and for long-term taxation policy planning
- Evaluation of the consequences of such policies within the general macroeconomic policy.

TAXIS was launched in 2000, after seven years of systematic design and implementation efforts. It provided IT support to the central tax authorities, located in Athens, as well as to the local tax agencies in the rest of the country, for carrying out tax filing, calculation and payment transactions with citizens and businesses.

Yet, even to this date, the contribution of TAXIS on tax evasion remains a contested terrain. TAXIS is an operational public information system which did not however lead to a reform of the fiscal system. Tax evasion is still a problem of the Greek state. Changes were contained at the level of its direct users with the establishment of new, more efficient work practices. Most importantly, ICT innovation is still treated as a purely technological issue, despite claims on a more visionary approach. At the same time, the highly bureaucratic and legalistic treatment of IT projects is the dominant practice in the context of the Greek public sector.

Such observations, despite TAXIS's unique success as a large-scale ICT implementation of in Greece, beg for a deeper examination of the negotiation space that opened during the implementation of TAXIS (an innovative ICT project) with public administration. This is done in the following section.

THE NEGOTIATION SPACE DURING TAXIS' IMPLEMENTATION

The Greek political environment, in the mid 1990s, as discussed in the previous section, was conducive to ICT innovation. The new government was determined to follow the path of ICT innovation in order to address the long-standing under-performance problems of tax administration which were hindering the country's developmental potential. Nevertheless, during TAXIS implementation, the negotiation space (Law & Callon, 1994) that emerged hosted a clash between long-standing material practices and symbolic systems in the Greek public sector and those carried by ICT innovation.

The enframing of ICT innovation to old political practices is showcased, in the following sections, by the way political parties monitored the system's progress and understood the first application to be delivered, the tax payers registry.

Monitoring System Progress: Legalistic Practices and Political Debates

The legalistic tradition of the Greek public administration stresses the importance of thorough examination of contractual agreements which constitute essentially the basis for inspecting a public project's progress and attributing responsibility in case of disputes. In the case of TAXIS, this rigid approach to the monitoring of ICT innovation has been further aggravated by the socio-political conditions in Greece during the previous years. Political unrest, scandals implicating the two major political parties and instances of corruption in the public sector have irreversibly influenced the way political control was conducted. Political parties were less tolerant than before towards delays due to contractual renegotiations since they increased costs and triggered suspicions on illegal transactions.

Towards the end of 1996, TAXIS's development is just resuming after a long-lasting lock-out caused by differences between the state and the contractor responsible for the software. The system ought to have been completed the previous year. Yet, none of the software applications had been delivered, since the Ministry disagreed with Sogei-Intrasoft S.A. (i.e. the software subcontracting consortium) on the development tool to be used. After laborious negotiations, Ministry officials were expecting the following year (i.e. 1997) the delivery of the first software applications. According, however, to spokespersons from opposition parties, TAXIS, regardless of announcements for its progress is nowhere near completion. As observed by an opposition deputy:

The original control anticipated full system roll-out by November 1995. You [i.e., the government] avoided committing on the actual delivery date of the system. Thus far you have made three amendments to the contract, the third one being that of the forthcoming December, while you have also delayed delivery three times. In the meantime, nobody is certain whether the system will actually be operational. There is a great delay which is your responsibility. [Parliamentary Minutes[4], 1996 pg. 1916]

Such observations shifted discussions to administrative issues. Political parties were not discussing TAXIS' progress in relation to the eminent tax reform. Discussions evolved around contracts, delays, technical choices and political decisions. Essentially, the core issue was which of the two parties alternating in power during TAXIS design and implementation was responsible for the delays. Thus, political parties entered the familiar terrain of seeking evidence to appoint responsibility to their political rivals for their deeds. In parallel, they also attempted to defer their part of responsibility by justifying their own choices or attributing some of their actions to past commitments of their rivals that had to be fulfilled or at least amended. However, this focus on administrative aspects of TAXIS shows that political parties may have understood the importance of ICT innovation without however grasping the need for more flexible controls and emphasis on results.

Debates on the root cause for TAXIS delays and attempts from both parties to defer this responsibility to their rivals continued until the system roll-out in 1998. Once the various sub-systems started to be delivered, political parties abandoned discussions on system progress and redirected their debates to more technical issues. The case of the tax payers' register analyzed below is quite indicative of this practice.

The Tax Payers Registry: Imbricating Technical and Political Issues

TAXIS is based on a register which ensures single identification of each tax payer. The main purpose of the tax payers register is to manage tax payers' personal details and their relationships with other tax payers. It also stores details on legal persons, background information, information on representatives, branches, holdings, main and secondary activities and various other administrative information. The register of tax payers is the core of the Greek taxation information system since it is essentially the system's pool of single identifiers for all citizens and businesses registered in it. It was the first software application to be implemented and one of the most critical ones since it would provide an initial picture on the actual number of citizens and businesses liable to taxation. It would also reveal an initial estimate of tax evaders.

The necessary legal amendment for making obligatory the existence of a single tax registration number has been refuted in many points during the relevant parliamentary discussion[5]. First some parties refused to vote on its favour suggesting that such close monitoring of citizen's transactions was quite similar to the information kept by the military junta[6]. During the same period, the ratification, by the Greek Parliament, of the Shenghen treaty for the free movement of citizens and goods across the European Union had caused substantial societal unrest. The Greek society, the Greek Orthodox Church and several political parties saw it as a direct attempt of extra-state powers to monitor citizen activity. During the discussion on the single tax registration number there were political parties (i.e. DHKKI[7]) which tried to link the two issues. The imposition for a single tax registration number was perceived as yet another effort of the government apparatus to take control of citizens' lives. This attempt was, however, fiercely declined by the government. As the Under Secretary of the Ministry of Economics and Finances stated in the Parliament:

The parties voting against a single tax registration number harness tax evasion and allow those practicing to continue their doings. I cannot explain differently why they are blocking the exploitation of a possibility provided by a modern information system. [...] What more should the government do in order to convince political parties that it is critical to modernize, at last, the Ministry of Economics and Finances? Unless they believe that it should remain at the computerization levels of 1988, 1989, 1990, 1991. Because it cannot. [Parliamentary Minutes[8], 1997, pg. 28]

The efforts of opposition parties to establish a link between regulations on the single tax registration number and citizens' constitutional rights is also evidenced by the detailed discussion in Greek Parliament regarding authority issues on voting for the regulation. Most opposition parties were arguing that the issue was quite important since it touched upon civil rights. The greatest concern was that maintaining a central archive with all available data would violate citizens' right to privacy. According to opposition parties, the issue ought to be discussed by the entire legislation body and not a section of it. The response of the government was first to stress that the issue was purely technical. It was the way novel information systems were built that required a single identifier. It was not the government trying to invade the citizen's personal life.

The treatment of the single tax registration number by political parties raises many questions on the way ICT innovation was understood. The issue was a sign of progress of system's implementation. It should therefore be welcomed instead of criticized. Yet, discussions on the Greek Parliament showed that it revived all the negative reflexes of Greek political parties. The alignment of a technical and administrative issue with fears for potential breaches of citizen's constitutional rights accentuated citizens' natural distrust towards the government and compromised the system's further implementation and eventual roll-out.

This stance, paradoxical from the outset, when situated in the context of the Greek administrative tradition provides more informed insights. Political parties feared that ICT innovation would destroy the web of preferential allowances solidifying clientelistic relationships. The obsolete practices of the Ministry of Economics and Finances and the complex tax legislation have created a bureaucratic maze inviting continuous legal regulations. Thus, the involvement of political parties was sought instead of repelled in favour of administrative autonomy. The revealing of the Ministry's internal processes would, gradually, lead to the containment of clientelism. Subsequently, political parties would see their domination over public administration to gradually fade. This was an instinctive reflex on behalf of political parties and not an organized attack to ICT innovation. Nevertheless, it should be perceived as an expression of the clash of institutions during ICT innovation hidden under concerns on citizen's rights.

The stance of Greek political parties towards ICT innovation, apart from the immediate outcomes on the design and implementation of TAXIS, had also long-term effects. The instrumental understanding of ICT innovation focused subsequent control on the system's progress to technical issues. The fact that TAXIS was not supplemented by a structured reform of the tax system has been silenced amidst the various heated debates on its technical properties. It follows that the opportunity for the Ministry of Economics to reconsider, in the event of TAXIS' implementation, its practices and the entire rationale of tax legislation was missed. TAXIS continues to operate as a purely technical infrastructure supporting the majority of the Ministry's financial activities. However, a holistic operational model for the Ministry of Economics, comprising a simple and more equitable legislation, controlling procedures for the enforcement of law and more efficient revenue procedures, is still missing debilitating the Greek state.

In the following section, these issues are further analysed and discussed in tandem with the theoretical angle adopted in this chapter.

DISCUSSION

E-government is adopted, by countries like Greece, with a double objective; exploit what is presented in a teleological fashion as the only pathway to progress and preserve their position in the global system; and induce their institutional arrangements into further alignment with more economically advanced countries. Nonetheless, the inevitable interaction between old and new institutionalized practices is a ground favouring conflictual situations. The ambivalence between new institutions, believed to reinforce the country's economic development, and old ones does not allow ICT innovation to be smoothly introduced as an acceptable way for reforming the government apparatus.

In this chapter, the erratic results observed during ICT innovation have been examined as instances of the process through which novel technologies are imbricated in local institutional settings. The imbrication (Sassen, 2004) of material practices and symbolic systems carried by ICT innovation into local social practices is a conflictual process. This means that the final positioning of ICT innovation within the new institutional context is shaped by a clash between local institutions and the ones carried by new information technologies. Such negotiation process between novel institutional arrangements and imageries (Unger 2004) and context-specific practices has been examined in the case of the Greek taxation information system (TAXIS).

TAXIS is the first successfully implemented large-scale information system in the Greek public administration. As a technological infrastructure, it has introduced substantial changes to the daily administrative practices and tax operations of the Ministry of Economics and Finance. Yet, it did not trigger the long-awaited modernization of the tax system which was among the core objectives of the 1990s modernisation political project. The paradox with TAXIS' implementation allows a deeper examination of the interplay of ICT innovation, as carrier of specific socio-material practices and symbolic systems, with local contexts, contributing to the growing problematic on the matter in the field of information systems.

From the evidence presented thus far, it follows that during TAXIS implementation visions of state reform where combined with an instrumental understanding of ICTs, inherited from previous computerization attempts, leading to an awkward arrangement. ICT innovation, in the context of the Greek public administration was considered to entail only changes in organizational operations. These new, efficient operations were to become the basis for a simplified, parsimonious legal framework regulating economic activity.

Modernist elites, to successfully introduce ICT innovation in the highly institutionalised environment of the Greek public sector, brought forward its purely instrumental properties. Information technology was considered an infrastructure facilitating administrative work. Long-standing practices and power alliances within hosting public organizations were not to be affected; otherwise computerization projects were resisted by both upper and low level civil servants. As Avgerou (2002: 169) also observes in the case of IKA, "resistance was oriented to the reforms that attempted to shake the established organizational structures and processes, and within which the technical innovation was to be deployed. The holding on to posts attained through investment in a regime of political favouritism made the efforts to instil the logic of management meaningless and ultimately dangerous". Yet, this non-invasive, at the macro-level, process through which ICT innovation was incorporated within Greek public administration stripped it from the upper-level imageries accompanying it (i.e. reform and modernization) reducing it into a low-level technical issue.

Thus, ICT innovation was institutionalized, in the context of the Greek public administration, as a vehicle for state modernization (qua changes in administrative operations) while state reform remained a purely legalistic exercise. This internally inconsistent role of ICT innovation has been the outcome of the clash between the material practices and symbolic systems carried through new information technologies and firmly engrained practices and understandings in Greek public administration. The effort to fit ICT innovation into long-established practices, typical to the Greek public sector, neutralized its potential to trigger deep structural reforms. Most importantly, this ambivalent translation of state modernization to ICT innovation, during TAXIS implementation, was institutionalised in the context of the Greek public sector, influencing all subsequent IT projects. ICT innovation, despite rhetoric on the contrary, remained a micro-level (i.e. organizational) phenomenon that did not trigger any changes at the macro-level (i.e. government apparatus).

At a more general level, this research has shown that the negotiation of ICT innovation with local institutional arrangements is an ambivalent process where local institutionalised practices and imageries play a significant role. This is an important observation for the implementation of e-government projects in late-development countries. A context-aware implementation, taking into account specific habitualized routines and assumptions, may lead to successful implementations. These, however, still may not trigger large scale reforms at the government apparatus, as in the case of Greece. Put it simply, the systematic use of information technology for reforming the government apparatus may produce operating IT infrastructures without, as strange as it may seem, triggering deeper reforms. The reason lays on the reflexive nature of ICT innovation.

The development and implementation of information and communication technologies is a reflexive practice revealing the inner workings of any system of material practices and adjoining imageries. This view is also supported by Ciborra (2005) who considers ICT innovation as an interplay between ordering and revealing. The automation of work practices and the extensive re-engineering, accompanying such activity, leads to the ordering of "resources, processes, people and relationships" (Ciborra, 2005: 261). This way, information technology reveals the mechanism and interrelationships between the various constituent parts of societal activity. This revealing highlights aspects of everyday activities, which remained unquestioned because of their frequent use. Thus, ICT innovation is eroding institutional practices by bringing them to the spotlight (Zuboff, 1988).

The process of reflexive appreciation of existing practices during ICT innovation generates a negotiation space containing the possibility for both success and failure. Local contexts may endorse the imageries related to state modernisation. Nevertheless, technology-induced changes in material practices are not always welcomed despite rhetorical endorsement. Contestations of long-established rational accounts regarding the existence and appropriateness of strongly engrained relationships may result in actions neutralizing ICT innovation. The process of deinstitutionalization of routinised practices is a difficult one since it triggers resistance aiming at the preservations of the status quo. This resistance is not a straight-forward phenomenon. ICT innovation may be infused by elements of the hosting institutional context which inhibit its reformatory potential without openly questioning its necessity. More specifically, during this process, ICT innovation is engulfed by long-established practices while new imageries are instilled with old understandings.

These findings provide an alternative view on the limited results characterizing e-government projects in late-development countries. They also challenge deterministic accounts of ICT innovation. The reason for failed or poorly functioning IT projects lays on their misalignment with firmly engrained institutionalised practices on the local contexts. Such local practices and institutionalized understandings on the operations of the government apparatus are rarely taken into account during the design of technological interventions. This is not an accidental omission or ignorance of behalf of developers as Ciborra (2005) suggests. It is rather the outcome of the firm belief that the introduction of information technology will force local actors to re-align their practices and assumption regarding their work around the new IT system. Yet, this is not always the case. Local actors, especially dominant ones, have the power to impose understandings of ICT innovation that allow IT systems to operate without touching upon firmly established practices.

CONCLUSION

Existing accounts of ICT innovation for state reform focus primarily on technical aspects of information technology implementations. Nevertheless, there are behavioural, historical and institutional elements which ought to be incorporated in the analysis in order to enrich our understanding of the phenomenon and provide more complete explanations of implementation outcomes. The contextualist account, presented in this chapter, on the role of ICT innovation in public administration, has unravelled the efforts of countries like Greece to diligently pursue the path of technological innovation. Focus has been shifted away from the idiosyncrasies of local contexts as the source of unexpected outcomes to the interplay between local and imported institutionalised practices.

The paradoxical outcomes of the TAXation Information System (TAXIS), implemented by the Greek state in the mid 1990s, have been examined as instantiations of such interplay. From the case analysis, it became evident that the imbrication of material practices and symbolic systems into local social practices is a conflictual process. The final positioning of ICT innovation within the new institutional context is shaped by a clash between local institutions and the ones carried by new information technologies. The legalistic character of Greek public administration, in tandem with the highly symbolic nature of policy implementation allowed only for the automation of paper-based processes. The re-design of organizational processes, a core element of ICT innovation, was contained in a superficial level which did not disturb the operational logic of the tax system. Administrative reform was considered the next stage of automation, following the traditionally legalistic path.

These findings provide a richer understanding of poor reform results from ICT innovation in the public sector. They shift attention from implementation issues to contextual parameters. Thus, they address issues of concern not only restricted to the Greek public sector. Therefore, insights from this chapter are also of relevance to other public organizations all over the world, which find themselves in similar circumstances. Nevertheless, the chapter attempts a general overview of the interplay of ICT innovation with local contexts. To this end, it tackles a number of important issues without delving into the specifics of each one. Subsequent research will need to address any one of these issues separately in order to bring to the surface details which better explain the interaction of ICT innovation with each element of a country's institutional context.

REFERENCES

Agapitos, G. J. (1986). *Income tax in Greece*. Athens, Greece: KEPE. (in Greek)

Avgerou, C. (2001). The significance of context in Information Systems and organizational change. *Information Systems Journal*, *11*(1), 43–63. doi:10.1046/j.1365-2575.2001.00095.x

Avgerou, C. (2002). *Information Systems and global diversity*. New York, NY: Oxford University Press.

Avgerou, C., Ciborra, C., & Land, F. (Eds.). (2004). *The social study of information and communication technology: Innovation, actors, and contexts*. Oxford, UK: Oxford University Press.

Avgerou, C., & Madon, S. (2004). Framing IS studies: Understanding the social context of IS innovation. In Avgerou, C., Ciborra, C., & Land, F. (Eds.), *The social study of information and communication technology: Innovation, actors and contexts* (pp. 162–182). New York, NY: Oxford University Press.

Avgerou, C., & McGrath, K. (2007). Power, rationality, and the art of living through socio-technical change. *Management Information Systems Quarterly*, *31*(2), 295–315.

Bekkers, V., & Homburg, V. (2007). The myths of e-government: Looking beyond the assumptions of a new and better government. *The Information Society*, *23*, 373–382. doi:10.1080/01972240701572913

Bronchi, C. (2001). *Options for reforming the tax system in Greece (No. 291)*. Paris, France: OECD.

Ciborra, C. (2005). Interpreting e-government and development: Efficiency, transparency or governance at a distance? *Information Technology & People*, *18*(3), 260–279. doi:10.1108/09593840510615879

Cordella, A. (2007). E-government: Towards the e-bureaucratic form? *Journal of Information Technology*, *22*(3), 265–274. doi:10.1057/palgrave.jit.2000105

Davidson, E., & Chiasson, M. (2005). Contextual influences on technology use mediation: A comparative analysis of electronic medical record systems. *European Journal of Information Systems*, *14*(1), 6–18. doi:10.1057/palgrave.ejis.3000518

Dunleavy, P. (2007). Governance and state organization in the digital era. In Mansell, R., Avgerou, C., Quah, D., & Silverstone, R. (Eds.), *The Oxford handbook of Information and Communication Technologies* (pp. 404–426). Oxford, UK: Oxford University Press.

Kallinikos, J. (2004). Farewell to constructivism: Technology and context-embedded action. In Avgerou, C., Ciborra, C., & Land, F. (Eds.), *The social study of information and communication technology: Innovation, actors, and contexts* (pp. 140–161). Oxford, UK: Oxford University Press.

Lanzara, G. F. (2009). Building digital institutions: ICT and the rise of assemblages in government. In Contini, F., & Lanzara, G. F. (Eds.), *ICT and innovation in the public sector: European studies in the making of e-government* (pp. 9–48). Houndmills, UK: Palgrave Macmillan.

Law, J., & Callon, M. (1994). The life and death of an aircraft: A network analysis of technical change. In Bijker, W. E., & Law, J. (Eds.), *Shaping technology / building society: Studies in sociotechnical change* (pp. 21–52). Cambridge, MA: The MIT Press.

Layne, K., & Lee, J. (2001). Developing a fully functional e-government: A four stage model. *Government Information Quarterly*, *18*(2), 122–136. doi:10.1016/S0740-624X(01)00066-1

Madon, S., Sahay, S., & Sudan, R. (2007). E-government policy and health Information Systems implementation in Andhra Pradesh, India: Need for articulation of linkages between the macro and the micro. *The Information Society*, *23*(5), 327–344. doi:10.1080/01972240701572764

Mason, R. O., Mckenney, J. L., & Copeland, D. G. (1997). Developing an historical tradition in MIS research. *Management Information Systems Quarterly*, *21*(3), 257–278. doi:10.2307/249497

Mavraganis, G. (1994). Greece: The 1994 tax reform. *European Taxation*, *34*(7), 219–220.

Mouzelis, N. P. (1978). *Modern Greece: Facets of underdevelopment*. London, UK: Macmillan Press.

Mouzelis, N. P. (1995). Greece in the twenty-first century: Institutions and political culture. In Constas, D., & Stavrou, T. G. (Eds.), *Greece prepares for the twenty-first century* (pp. 17–34). Washington, DC: The Woodrow Wilson Center Press.

Mouzelis, N. P. (2008). *Modern and postmodern social theorizing: Bridging the divide*. Cambridge, UK: Cambridge University Press.

Noir, C., & Walsham, G. (2007). The great legitimizer: ICT as myth and ceremony in the Indian healthcare sector. *Information Technology & People*, *20*(4), 313–333. doi:10.1108/09593840710839770

Orlikowski, W. J. (2007). Sociomaterial practices: Exploring technology at work. *Organization Studies*, *28*(9), 1435–1448. doi:10.1177/0170840607081138

Peräkylä, A. (2005). Analyzing talk and text. In Denzin, N. K., & Lincoln, Y. S. (Eds.), *The Sage handbook of qualitative research* (3rd ed., pp. 869–886). Thousand Oaks, CA: Sage Publications.

Pettigrew, A. M. (1985). Contextualist research and the study of organizational change processes. In E. Mumford, R. Hirschheim, G. Fitzgerald & T. A. Wood-Harper (Eds.), *Research methods in Information Systems* (pp. 53-72). Amsterdam, The Netherlands: Elsevier Science Publishers B.V. (North-Holland).

Sassen, S. (2004). Towards a sociology of Information Technology. In Avgerou, C., Ciborra, C., & Land, F. (Eds.), *The social study of information and communication technology* (pp. 76–99). Oxford, UK: Oxford University Press.

Sørensen, C., Whitley, E., Madon, S., Klyachko, D., Hosein, G., & Johnstone, J. (2001). Cultivating recalcitrance in Information Systems research. In Fitzgerald, B., & Russon, N. (Eds.), *Realigning research and practice in IS development: The social and organisational perspective*. Boise, ID: Kluwer Academic Publishers.

Sotiropoulos, D. A. (2004). Southern European public bureaucracies in comparative perspective. *West European Politics*, *27*(3), 405–422. doi:10.1080/0140238042000228077

Spanou, C. (1996). Penelope's suitors: Administrative modernisation and party competition in Greece. *West European Politics*, *19*(1), 97–124. doi:10.1080/01402389608425123

Tsoukalas, C. (1995). Free riders in wonderland; Or, of Greeks in Greece. In Constas, D., & Stavrou, T. G. (Eds.), *Greece prepares for the twenty-first century* (pp. 191–219). Washington, DC: The Woodrow Wilson Center Press.

Unger, R. M. (2004). *False necessity: Anti-necessitarian social theory in the service of radical democracy* (Paperback ed. Vol. 1 of Politics). London, UK: Verso.

Walsham, G. (1993). *Interpreting Information Systems in organizations*. Chichester, UK: John Wiley.

Wyld, D. C. (2004). The 3 Ps: The essential elements of a definition of e-government. *Journal of E-Government*, *1*(1), 17–22. doi:10.1300/J399v01n01_03

Zuboff, S. (1988). *In the age of the smart machine: The future of work and power*. New York, NY: Basic Books.

ENDNOTES

1 ICT innovation, as defined by Avgerou and Madon (2004: 162), "is concerned with design and implementation of a new technology but also addresses issues of information and knowledge, and it has an interest in IS-related changes of the organization and content of work tasks".

2 The term imbrication has been coined by Sassen (2004) in order to describe the overlapping of information and communication technologies into pre-existing social practices. It was also used to stress the dynamic nature of such overlapping which may not simply change institutionalised social practices, as advocates of new ICTs suggest, but also fortify them and solidify their use.

3 During the period of TAXIS' implementation (i.e. 1993-1996), Agapitos (1995) has calculated that, tax evasion accounted for 7% per cent of GDP in 1995 while informal economy was estimated to generate output equivalent to 40% of GDP.

4 Parliamentary Minutes. Θ' Presidential Democracy Term, Plenary Session A', Session ΜΣΤ', Monday, December 16th 1996, pg. 1916.

5 Parliamentary Minutes. Θ' Presidential Democracy Term, Plenary Session A', Summer Session, 1997, Tuesday, July 1st, 1997.

6 During the years of military junta, the then military government kept detailed folders with information for each citizen considered suspect of illegal actions against the state. The Greek term for it is «fakeloma» which derives from the Greek word for folder (i.e. fakelos). Ever since the junta period, every attempt of the state to collect and maintain information on citizens is treated with mistrust since it alludes to that troubled period of Greek history.

7 DHKKI stands for Democratic Social Movement (DemoKratiko Kinoniko Kinima). It is a political party established in 1995 by a former prominent minister of the major socialist Greek party PASOK (Panhellenic Movement). The party was represented in the Greek Parliament during TAXIS' implementation years. Its leader, being a former Minister of Economics, was particularly interested in the taxation information system since he considered himself one of its founders during its term in the Ministry of Finance. Currently, the party is part of a coalition of socialist political parties.

8 Parliamentary Minutes. Θ' Presidential Democracy Term, Plenary Session A', Summer Session, 1997, Tuesday, July 1st, 1997, pg.28.

Chapter 15
Administrative Flexibility and Knowledge in Policy Delivery

Nick Letch
The University of Western Australia, Australia

ABSTRACT

Information and communications technologies are emerging as important drivers of reform in the public sector. This chapter explores both enabling and constraining aspects of the role that ICTs can play in transforming the development and delivery of public policy. Two issues are explored: the reduction in flexibility of decision making that frequently accompanies ICT-based initiatives, and the critical role of knowledge embedded in networks of stakeholders in policy development and delivery. A case study, which traces the knowledge embedded in networks of relationships of actors involved in developing and implementing operational policy in an Australian public sector agency, is presented to illustrate the unintended constraints on knowledge activities. A framework for analyzing socio-technical networks involved in integrating ICTs into the cycle of public policy is presented.

INTRODUCTION

Knowledge is central to the activities involved in developing and implementing public policy and information and communication technologies (ICTs) undoubtedly have the capacity to transform how knowledge is managed and applied. This potential for leveraging of knowledge occurs within the context of an evolving administrative infrastructure which is being shaped by e-Government initiatives. While the capacity for ICTs to transform public policy delivery are continually expounded, large-scale IT implementations can also have unintended – and potentially negative consequences.

"Knowledge Management" (KM) and "e-Government" are two related trends to emerge over the past twenty years which have significant

DOI: 10.4018/978-1-60960-839-2.ch015

implications for the activities and performance of public administration. ICTs are at the heart of e-Government initiatives which promise to transform the operation of public sector agencies and in a similar vein, the effective leveraging of knowledge within public administration through KM initiatives can also be facilitated through the application of ICTs. The benefits of applying ICTs in the public policy development and delivery are generally seen in terms such as improved service delivery, better administrative decision making, efficiency of processing and improved communication. Outcomes such as these will in time undoubtedly be achieved on an ongoing basis as governments become more and more experienced and sophisticated in the approaches they take when applying ICTs. However, research and experience in the implementation of ICT systems over many years has consistently shown that the disruptive nature of change driven by large-scale ICTs can have unintended impacts. Therefore, in addition to investigating the potential benefits of ICT transformations in public policy, these consequences and the potentially constraining nature of the technologies themselves need be considered.

The objective of this chapter is to highlight and explore two issues in relation to the application of ICTs in policy development: the reduction in flexibility of decision making that frequently accompanies ICT-based initiatives; and the critical role of knowledge embedded in networks of stakeholders in policy development and delivery. It is argued that the (re-)structuring of activities, roles and procedures which are brought about by the implementation of large ICT-based systems can lead to disconnects between the knowledge embedded in the activities of policy development and the knowledge embedded in the implementation of policy through the delivery of services.

A case study of organizational units within an Australian public sector agency is used to illustrate how different forms of knowledge are embedded across variety of activities from policy development through to service delivery. This analysis is set against the background of the implementation of a large-scale e-Government system which acts as the primary technological infrastructure for the agency's activities. The analysis examines the relationship between the knowledge activities and the system implementation to suggest that when integrating ICTs into activities which develop and deliver policy, specific attention should be given to the networks of relationships and associations between various stakeholders and actors.

BACKGROUND

E-Government Transformation and Impacts

The use of ICT in public administration and e-Government initiatives in particular, will provide many long-term benefits for the community and over time, will transform relationships between citizens and government. Many e-Government initiatives focus on streamlining the delivery of services to the community and the role of ICTs is usually seen in terms of providing efficiencies in information transfer and the removal of layers of bureaucratic "red tape" (Landsbergen & Wolken, 2001). These initiatives often have the underlying assumption that public service is all about taking a customer (or citizen) focus and providing efficient and effective service delivery. The benefits of service–oriented initiatives are self-evident but only represent the more publicly visible outcomes of ICT-based public administration transformation. The transformative capacity of ICTs goes beyond service delivery and includes the back-office activities which are at the heart of public administration. For public sector organizations, the "service" delivered to the community is the tangible outcome of public policy processes. Activities involved in public policy process include community and stakeholder consultation, policy analysis, policy instrument development, policy implementation, policy co-ordination, and evaluation (Althaus et al., 1998). Many of the activities involved in these "back-office" functions of public sector agencies can be facilitated and improved through the ICTs. For example, several governments are investigating the use of Web 2.0 technologies to facilitate community consultation.

Countering the frequently claimed benefits of e-Government are a small but significant number of studies which examine the impacts of ICT applications in public administration. Bekkers and Homburg (2007) argue that the realistic outcome of many e-government initiatives is less than the rhetoric that surrounds them. Several reports note that many e-Government initiatives have not delivered expected cost savings and have not generally improved social inclusion, innovation or participation (Taylor, 2004). Danziger and Andersen's (2002) analysis of the impacts of ICTs in public administration shows that of nineteen studies of ICT impacts in public administration, in half the impacts have been positive while one-third report negative impacts. Positive impacts largely relate to improved service delivery while negative impacts tend to be associated with a reduction in the level of flexibility available to "street-level" bureaucrats when dealing with citizens. These findings reflect the inherent tension in service delivery initiatives where the efficiency benefits that accrue from the standardization of processes across agencies must be balanced against local knowledge and expertise when dealing with constituent citizen clients (Ellingsen et al., 2007).

Understanding both the positive and negative consequences of ICTs in public administration is necessary in order to gain a full appreciation of their transformative capacity. Furthermore, impacts are not isolated to service delivery but can occur across a range of activities in the wider public policy cycle.

Embedded within the broad activities of policy development and implementation is the knowledge and expertise of politicians, experts, bureaucrats and other interested stakeholders, as well as vast repositories of information that are the product of administrative activity. ICT can be used to leverage this knowledge but in order to do so, it is critical that the interactions and relationships between the ICT infrastructure and the knowledge-related activities of stakeholders is well understood.

Knowledge Management in Public Administration

Public administration is knowledge-intensive work and so when examining the role of ICTs in transforming public services, questions about the impacts that ICTs have on knowledge activities are relevant. ICTs can support knowledge management through a capacity to develop an infrastructure and environment that supports a variety of forms of knowledge (from tacit to explicit), and across various knowledge processes (creation, storage/retrieval, transfer, and application) (Alavi and Leidner, 2001). Knowledge management (KM) initiatives have been identified as a way of improving public administration effectiveness and subsequently improving the services to the clients that that public administration serves (Wiig, 2002).

Although KM projects and systems continue to develop within public administration, specific research in the area is scarce (Taylor & Wright, 2004; Manavvarian and Kesai, 2007). Of the research that has been published, familiar dictums for knowledge management such as "having a project champion", "fostering human networks", and "creating a vision" (Osborne, 2004) are common. For example, in translating the objectives of private sector KM into the requirements for public administration, Wiig's (2002) approach identifies elements of public administration KM practice such as, "assure competent and effective public service", "develop capable knowledge workers", "build and leverage public and private IC", and "prepare effective policy partners". While useful in guiding KM strategy in public administration in general, such suggestions do not provide a depth of understanding how knowledge management systems can be deployed.

To address the potential difficulties in implementing KM in public administration, many analyses take an overarching perspective and identify factors and issues that affect the overall performance of KM. For instance, Omar et al. (2004) developed a factor model of influences on the effective transfer of knowledge within public administration and tested their model within a Malaysian public sector organization. Factors that were hypothesized and found to have a significant influence on knowledge transfer performance were related to organizational culture and structure, IT infrastructure, human resources and political directives. Similarly, Liebowitz & Chen's (2003) investigation of knowledge cultures in public organizations identified the bureaucratic structure typical of public sector organizations as a barrier to the effective sharing of knowledge. Barriers to KM are also the focus of Taylor and Wright's (2004) factor model of effective knowledge sharing in the UK health sector. The six factors they identified in their analysis are associated more with the culture and information infrastructure of the organization than the interactions between senders and receivers of knowledge. Their model identifies issues that need to be addressed in order to alleviate resistance and inertia among knowledge workers which would otherwise ultimately condemn knowledge management initiatives to failure (Gold et al., 2001). Manavvarian and Kesai's (2007) analysis focuses on identifying variables which impact on knowledge management processes (eg knowledge creation, sharing, storage and use).

Identifying cultural and structural enablers and barriers to KM and knowledge sharing in the public sector are important background to the implementation of general knowledge management programs. However the effective leveraging of knowledge through ICTs is also dependent on how knowledge is embedded in the processes of developing policies and delivering services.

Knowledge and Knowledge Management Systems in Public Policy

Knowledge is – and always has been - inextricably linked into the activities of the public sector. Politicians and public sector workers use knowledge to shape their environment and perform their duties in the public service (Riege and Lindsay 2006) and different forms of knowledge are applied throughout the public policy cycle (Adams 2004). The participants in public policy range from the general public who are the source of populist values and attitudes, through interest groups who lobby and advocate with respect to specific policy areas, political functional departmental experts who bring managerial and bureaucratic perspectives to the policy domain, as well as the situational, local knowledge of those who deliver and receive the outputs of the policy. Policy development and implementation involves a range of explicit and tacit knowledge types and it is how this knowledge is bound within policy activities that needs to be understood so that it can be effectively leveraged.

Within the bureaucratic context of public administration it is not uncommon to take a rationalist and linear perspective of how knowledge exists in public sector activities. For example, both Peristeras & Tarabanis (2000) and Misra et al. (2003) develop models which identify a linear set of activities from needs identification through policy development and service delivery in order to understand the role knowledge. Such approaches are useful for descriptive purposes but don't address the view that knowledge is socially constructed (Berger and Luckman, 1966) and furthermore are limited in how they conceive of the ongoing social and political interactions of various stakeholders.

An alternative to the rational perspective of knowledge within public policy activities is that provided by a network view (Adams, 2004; Mischen and Jackson, 2008; Weber and Khademian, 2008). Under this perspective, knowledge is viewed as being constructed within the various social networks of stakeholders who interact in the course of developing and delivering public policy. It is among the various stakeholders and actors in policy networks that knowledge is created, shared and applied in delivering public services. Knowledge management systems can play a fundamental role in facilitating interactions in these networks through enhancing collaboration between stakeholders in communities of practice as well as developing stronger relationships with the general community in policy development activities.

The network view of knowledge in public policy takes better account of the social nature of knowledge than a linear approach but any leveraging of knowledge occurs within the administrative infrastructure which supports the wider policy development and delivery cycle. Given the potential for e-Government initiatives to transform how public services are delivered, the ICT infrastructure will potentially impact on how knowledge is created, stored, shared and used in delivering public policy. The case study in the following section examines this relationship between ICT infrastructure and knowledge networks.

CASE STUDY: LICENSING SERVICES

The organizational units responsible for formulating and implementing operational policy associated with motor vehicle and driver licensing in a large Australian state government agency is now presented. The case study identifies and traces the creation, sharing and use of knowledge among the various actors involved. The data informing this case study were gathered as part of an information requirements analysis project which aimed to identify the potential for KM systems to enhance communication and collaboration between policy personnel and the personnel involved in delivering services.

The study examines organizational units that belong to a large state government that is responsible for several legislative areas and crosses two Ministerial portfolios. Among its legislated responsibilities, this agency (named the Department of Infrastructure (DoI)), develops and implements all vehicle and driver-related policies for the state jurisdiction. The largest and most visible aspect of these responsibilities relate to licensing. This is one of the most common transaction services provided by government and is heavily reliant on a large database infrastructure. The transaction services of driver and vehicle licensing bring a large proportion of the population into direct contact with government bureaucracy, but licensing activities represent only one aspect of the overall policy cycle. The formulation of policy governing the training and testing of drivers, the application of various license classes and associated conditions, and recording of infringements add complexity to a process which appears on the surface to be relatively straightforward.

The focus of the analysis is on three organizational sub-units within the Licensing Services section of the department. Two of the units Policy and Projects (P&P) and Standards and Information (S&I) are each staffed by 10 policy officers and are located at Head Office. The other logical unit under analysis includes the Licensing Centre Branches of which there are 37 throughout the state, as well as the centrally located Call Centre which handles telephone enquiries. Figure 1 illustrates a process view of the key activities involved in the formulation and application of licensing and registration policies.

Organisational Information and Knowledge Culture

Motor vehicle and driver licensing were historically performed and regulated by the Police Department until a public sector restructure heralded by a change of government in the mid 1990's transferred vehicle and driver licensing to

Figure 1. Key activities of licensing services

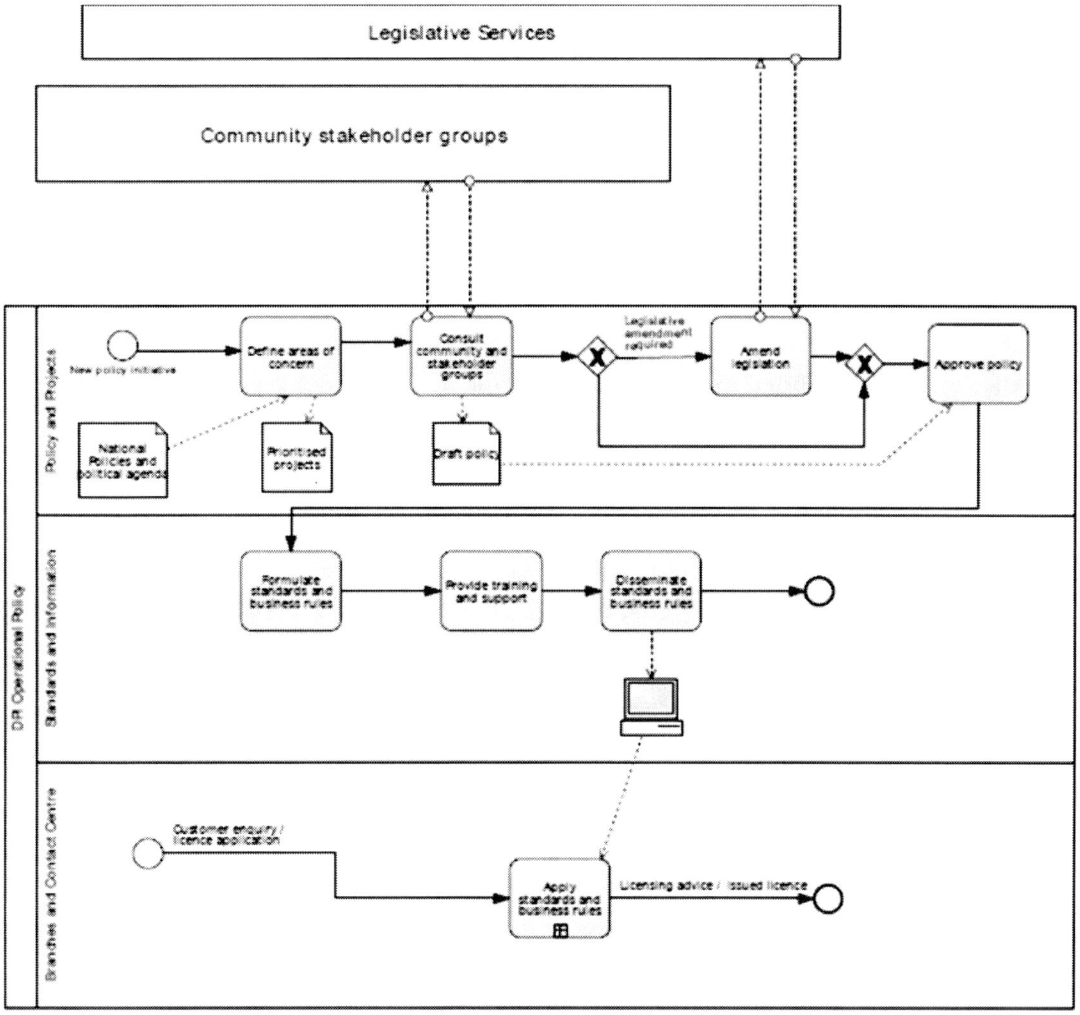

the DoI. The transferral of responsibilities meant that and a significant number of personnel who commenced their public service employment in an administrative arm of the Police Department became employees of a new department with a different organizational mission and ethos. However, Police Department values such as a tendency to "look out for one another" a strong sense of "family" have persisted through to the current organisation. Knowledge work in the DoI benefited from these values because the organizational environment nurtures learning, tolerates mistakes and readily makes advice available. However, this strong communal sense also has the tendency to be highly resistant to any changes that may disturb communal practices (for example, structural changes and new information systems developments).

IT Infrastructure

At the heart of the licensing services provided by the DoI is the LIS system (Licensing Information System). Central to LIS is an integrated database of drivers and vehicles, various licensing data and complex business rules which govern transactions.

Auxiliary functions such as cashier functionality, payment handling and revenue collection management are also incorporated in LIS.

Prior to the development of LIS, motor vehicle licenses and driver licenses were maintained in separate databases and transactions were processed at licensing centres through dumb terminals connected to centrally located AS-400 boxes. The development of the new LIS was a multi-million dollar undertaking that took over ten years to develop and implement. The business case for LIS envisaged a single client view of vehicle and driver data enabling enhanced executive reporting, improved service for clients, closer integration with internal financial and external agents' systems. In the early stages of its development the LIS was championed as the State's leading investment in ICT under the emerging banner of e-Government. Unfortunately, the grand promises of the LIS belied the problems that plagued its development and implementation. When LIS did eventually come on line (two years late), it caused major disruption to operational services and became the subject of front page headlines in the major state newspaper. For example "Motorists Stung by Licensing Delays"; "One Licence, Two Emails, and Eight Busy Bureaucrats"; and "Licensed to Complain"; were just three of the headlines that appeared around the time of going live.

Given the poor publicity surrounding the implementation of LIS, the government threw significant additional resources into alleviating the growing backlog of transactions. After about six months of continuous adjustments and workarounds, the processing of licenses returned to what would be considered a normal level. A subsequent investigation into the LIS project by the Auditor General revealed a range of underlying project management shortcomings as well as issues related to political "turf wars". Given the significant investment in LIS, the DoI continues to promote the potential benefits of the system and integrate the system into strategic and operational activities.

In addition to LIS, other information technologies support day-to-day activities of providing licensing services. An internal intranet and email system supports the flow of information while web-based system support the publication and dissemination of organizational information. These systems have an in-built organizational logic that reinforces the roles, positions and programs of the bureaucracy.

The problems associated with the LIS implementation is not the focus of this analysis but as the major ICT infrastructure of the DoI, the LIS has significant impacts on how knowledge is used and shared among each of the different sections in this study.

Knowledge and Policy Development (Policy and Projects)

The Policy and Projects (P&P) section has the key role of formulating policies. Policy formulation (be it an entirely new policy or the reform of an existing policy) is normally a response to new national initiatives or through Ministerial direction in response to changing community needs. As the overall impact of policies can affect very large sections of the community, policy formulation involves significant research and consultation with the wider community in order to ensure that policies fit within existing legislation and that address local as well as national needs.

In terms of knowledge activities, policy development is primarily concerned with knowledge creation. Within P&P, the process of developing administrative policy involves activities that include internal and external stakeholder consultation, researching best practices, evaluating alternatives and the formal approval and writing of the policy. Typically, this involves an iterative process in which the policy officers develop position papers or discussion notes which are then distributed to stakeholders for comments and feedback. Feedback is evaluated and incorporated into the policy where it is appropriate. As commented by the manager of Policy and Projects section:

"It is all about consultation with internal and external stakeholders. So we get all the advice internally and externally, and we work on that."

External consultation usually involves discussions and meetings with relevant industry representatives (eg motor vehicle dealers), interest groups (eg National Farmers Federation) and other government agencies that might be affected by the policy. External knowledge is thus integrated into policy through public consultation activities.

The skills and capabilities required for policy development go beyond knowledge of the policy development process because much of the input to policy development relies on the expertise of the policy officers themselves. An over-reliance on the tacit knowledge of a few experienced officers has developed in part due to poor record keeping practices that have meant that past decisions have not been documented or at least cannot easily be located.

"We have a departmental filing system but we have been very bad at keeping things in files. So there will be decisions that have been made but you won't be able to find it in files."

While the importance of the knowledge of a handful of experienced staff who work in policy development is recognised by fellow policy officers, there is a perception that senior management does not fully recognise the value these staff. As noted by the manager of P&P:

"...what they have is 30 years of experience which is about as good if not better than a degree. But there is not any acknowledgement of that...the degree is everything...that [experience] doesn't seem to be a skill that senior management values."

This has created tension in the relationship between policy staff and senior management.

"They might have very good management skills but they come from a different area... They think they have an understanding of licensing and how they can fix it. But it is very, very complicated. They sometimes don't make very good decisions."

Policy development also relies on consultation with internal stakeholders so that organisation-wide perspectives can be integrated into the policy. The current practice is to designate managers of different areas as "gateways" between Policy and Projects Section and the operational staff. Draft policies are distributed to these gatekeepers who are then expected to pass them on to whoever they see as relevant. However, this practice opens up the possibility for information hoarding and for bottlenecks to occur – which does happen from time-to time. As commented by the Manager of P&P:

"If the information is about their work area, they will be more than happy to read it. If it is about something else, they are not interested. I suppose you've got to expect that from people, they do a job and that is their key focus."

Policy work is seen here to be heavily reliant on the tacit expertise of individuals in different areas both internal and external to the department. Interaction with stakeholder groups is largely through formal, static channels of communication.

Knowledge and Policy Implementation (Standards and Information)

Once administrative policy has been developed it needs to be translated into business rules and integrated within operational documentation. This translation is essentially a codification of the knowledge embedded in the new or revised policy and involves knowledge storage for subsequent retrieval by operational staff. This is the responsibility of the Standards and Information (S&I) section which sits in a unique position between policy development and operations. On one hand, S&I has to cater for the strategic needs of management in that business rules must follow the general principles of the policy. On the other hand however, business rules must be clear and address operational issues and needs. This activity of translation involves a delicate balance in creating business rules that satisfy these different audiences.

"And that's one of our biggest problems too, ... trying to put something that is reasonably complex and varied into simple language that people can understand. What happens is you lose that background knowledge, and the person would say... "it says down here so we have to do it." That fine line between giving them too much information and too little."

The importance for providing context to the published business rules was noted by one of the operational staff members we interviewed:

"...it is useful to know why- because if you have to explain it to somebody, particularly members of the community want to know why they have to do a certain thing, then I can say "look, there was an enquiry and as a result, we have to ask you this." And it is helpful for staff too because they can put it into context and understanding..."

The process of codifying policies aims to address both management and operational perspectives. All information that represents new policies (be it printed or online) passes through a committee made up of executive managers who comment and provide feedback. Efforts are also made to get feedback from operational staff but their responses are usually limited at best. Any subsequent changes that are incorporated usually involve altering the wording of the rules which can lead to a lack of clarity. As noted by one Licensing Centre staff member:

"You've got policy for management or legal jargon, that's what we like to call it...Why don't you write it in English for the rest of us? It is ridiculous...you don't want to spend half-a-day thinking about what that means..."

A potentially more damaging outcome of the review of published information is that simple wording changes can alter the meaning of policy or business rule.

" it may be phrased perfectly... but it gets changed, and the total content ... is wrong."

The process of codifying business rules is a critical activity in policy implementation as it is through the interpretation of these rules by operational staff that the wider community directly interacts with government policy. Bridging this gap between policy and the community however, remains problematic.

"Those people have no idea on the impact it will have on the community... they didn't deal with it, they don't have to deal with it... the community doesn't care much about paperwork, they just think it is a Government imposition... I don't think they see the impact"

"Policy people are very black and white in their thinking ... they are writing policies for an environment that they really don't understand."

Knowledge and Service Delivery (Licensing Centres)

The core function of licensing centres is to handle licensing queries and needs of customers over the counter. It is here that policies are applied in the form of business rules. Customers of licensing centres come from all walks of life with and a diversity of linguistic, cultural, and socio-economic backgrounds. It is within this dynamic environment that the frontline customer service officers develop specialised experience in dealing with a wide range of problems from routine transactions to specialised queries.

Even though most interactions with customers are standard, there are often times when staff need to diverge from standard operational policy to allow for exceptions, bypass rules, or to adapt the rules to fit the specific needs of the situation.

"I would not override the intent (of the policy), but the method to achieve the objective is what I reserve the right to be flexible on."

"The law is the law and you can't change it ... but how you comply depends on circumstances."

"... it is a case of evolution... We are not breaching the policy but we do it different from what we received- we modify it or update it to meet the circumstance. So we are doing things differently but we don't have it in writing."

This level of flexibility in the application of knowledge however, is a double-edged sword. On one hand, if done within the legislation, it is an invaluable mechanism for the localisation of licensing policies. On the other hand, it can lead to the inconsistent application of policies.

When staff encounter situations that are beyond the scope of their experiential knowledge, they seek help or get a second opinion from their co-workers. The formal internal support structure that staff can draw on begins with immediate supervisors, who then refer the more difficult problems to the centre manager. If necessary, the centre manager will call up relevant sections within the Agency for advice or directions. In some circumstances, staff will also call other licensing branches for their expertise and input.

"we'll talk to or call anyone we think we can get an answer from."

The formal help procedure requires counter staff to go through a chain of authority, starting with their supervisors and managers. However, customer problems usually require immediate resolution. So instead of going through the chain of authority, staff often by-pass the formalised process and go straight to people who they believe can provide them with an answer. The resolution of customer problems in such cases relies on the staff member's social knowledge of "who knows what".

Licensing centre managers, have responsibility for making decisions regarding the application of licensing policy and they are be held accountable. Because there are often 'grey' areas that the policies do not specifically cover, or are politically sensitive, licensing centre managers are sometimes hesitant to because they are unwilling to be solely accountable for the consequences of those decisions.

"...because they are mindful about some organisational perspective especially some of the things that are politically sensitive - or outside of the law. ... they don't want to make the decisions because of the ramifications. So they move elsewhere to get their advice."

Those with the expertise to clarify the "grey areas" are usually those experienced members of staff who now work as policy officers at Head Office. Given their substantial experience in licensing centres, these experts are generally sympathetic toward the pressures faced by counter staff. As a result, licensing centre managers continue the practice of calling on them, even though in most cases, it is just to get a confirmation of answers.

However, it is not uncommon for unique problems to arise and policy staff need to make up policies on the spot to satisfy the situation. These "policies-on-the-run" are not formally documented and are developed without proper research and consultation. As a result, inconsistencies arise when a similar problem resurfaces.

"It is policy on the run. It really is. The person has a problem at the counter. The difficulty is that it needs to be resolved very quickly....but I am sure the next time you will scratch your head and someone might give another answer that is totally different from the one you have given."

While this informal practice of going straight to the recognised experts can quickly deal with an individual customer's issue, there are also consequences in terms of overall efficiency and productivity. Firstly, dealing with operational queries distracts policy staff from their normal work as some of the queries require staff to follow up with other people.

"It's distracting. Some of them are not straightforward and you need to make a few phone calls yourself and clarify in your own mind whether that is the right way to go...You really need to ring [someone else] or liaise with legal services or... yes, it can be time consuming."

Secondly, the advice given remains with the operational staff member who asked the question in the first place. That knowledge is not shared and reinforces the reliance on informal knowledge to carry out the actual work practices. It also means that policy officers continue to receive questions on the same issues from different people.

DISCUSSION

LIS and Knowledge Activities

The implementation of LIS was a major e-Government investment which was a technical necessity but also built on a business case that envisaged a transformation in the capabilities and delivery of licensing services to the public. This major infrastructure initiative was plagued with problems throughout its development and its initial implementation was catastrophic. The LIS design was driven primarily as a database for transaction processing and data integration and although it is a major repository of licensing knowledge (in the form of business rules and operating procedures inscribed within it), the LIS implementation did not fit with the way that knowledge is created, managed and applied within Licensing Services.

The complexity of LIS and the difficulties associated with its development appear to have marginalised attention to finding out how the wealth of information the LIS contains can be best integrated into existing operational workflows. Rather than being viewed as an integral part of operational activities, it is perceived as being overly complex and disruptive. For example, common comments from interviewees were related to both performance and effectiveness: *"Information is not up to date"*, and *"LIS is too slow"*. Although a learning curve is expected for uptake of any new system, the LIS imposed an immense strain on both the resources and morale of the staff. While it was expected that some long-term and experienced staff would resist to the system, newer staff also experienced difficulties in using the system. As one respondent commented, *"we don't really know what we are looking at"*.

With its implementation now stabilised, the LIS acts as the centralised registry for all licenses issued within the State and formally embodies a wealth of institutionalised licensing information that has been developed over the years. However, the LIS implementation has overridden the traditional repository of licensing knowledge. The provision of licensing services produces large amounts of information in terms of licensee information, operating procedures, licensing instructions and business rules. The complex nature of licensing consequently requires an established protocol for managing information. Much of this information developed over the years both under the jurisdiction of Police and DoI is maintained manually. Notably, most operating procedures are kept in an instructional book affectionately known as the "blue book" by staff members. When new procedures are introduced, the associated information is filed as an addendum in a folder known as the licensing notice folder. Together, these manual filing systems are the main non-automated sources of licensing information available to staff involved in licensing. The Blue Book was the source for most of the procedural rules built into the LIS.

In addition to formal channels of information distribution, staff members have established a complex web of informal information channels. These "corridor chats" and "smokers' gossip sessions" play a crucial role in disseminating information. In one account a policy officer recalled how an informal conversation led to the rectification of a major legislative violation. In licensing branches, informal communications are vital ways in which information is disseminated. Often when faced with over the counter service enquiries, branch personnel do not have the time to systematically go through information formally provided (eg in LIS) and it is often easier and faster to call someone from P&P for information.

It has only been in recent years that any significant attention has been paid to the technical maintenance and development of knowledge and information (beyond the actual licensing database). Knowledge and information to a large extent have been maintained in a social sense and woven into the fabric of interrelated actions, experiences and relations which bind the social activities of Licensing Services. The strong social dimension of Policy and Standards also carries over to knowledge activities where the validity of certain information is determined by social trust rather than by reference to published "facts".

Policy development is reliant on the expertise of policy officers as well as their networks with key stakeholders internal and external to the agency. The knowledge work of policy development is not directly affected by the LIS as it largely involves research and consultation. However, because several of the policy officers have years of expertise and licensing knowledge, they are frequently called upon by branch staff to provide advice in resolving difficult counter enquiries. This creates tension with management who do not see providing advice to branches in the job description of policy officers. The informal flexibility of the existing social network that has emerged over the years has been removed as policy officers are directed to ignore requests for advice from branch managers.

The translation of new or revised policy into business rules which can be implemented within LIS has proven to be a major bottleneck for Licensing Services. For example, when the Government introduced a new administrative policy that suspended driver licenses for unpaid fines, the Department's policy officers proposed some exemption categories to take account of individuals who would face undesirable and unnecessary hardship as a consequence of the new policy. The S&I section devised the necessary business rules and sent the necessary change requests to the LIS Development team. However, given the backlog of LIS change requests, six to twelve months was the estimated timeline for the necessary changes to be made in LIS. The previous licensing systems while unwieldly, were much more flexible in accommodating changes to policy and legislation at short notice.

The staff in licensing branches encounter the public on a daily basis. Traditionally the source of knowledge for making street level decisions on how policies should be applied has been through the "blue book" and licensing notices. While the blue book rules and policy interpretations were a significant source of the LIS business requirements and programming, for the counter staff, LIS became a disruptive element in their daily activities. The intention of LIS was to enhance existing processes but on implementation, LIS operation became a separate, additional process that counter staff had to deal with. Management directives to make use of the help system within

LIS rather than resorting to their existing social networks imposed restrictions on the capacity of counter and call centre staff to make timely decisions regarding the application of administrative policy.

Solutions and Recommendations

It is apparent that in a process which spans different organisational sub-units and includes both internal and external stakeholders, that the organisational knowledge management processes of creation, storage, transfer and application (Alavi & Leidner 2001) all require support. These KM processes however are not discretely confined to any single subunit or set of activities. The implication of this that any KM initiative should examine the policy cycle as a whole rather than identify solutions based on functional areas in isolation to one another.

What is even more apparent from the preceding analysis is the inherently social nature of the organisational culture and reliance on a few key individuals with significant domain expertise. The way that operational personnel continue to rely on selected colleagues rather than make use of the "help" embedded within the Licensing Information System is an indicator that the existing platform for operational knowledge is not trusted and informal systems have developed to circumvent formal procedures. This situation can be potentially leveraged through the development and nurturing of online communities (Wenger et al. 2002; Seufert et al. 1999).

Online communities could be used to leverage knowledge within the policy process and provide benefit across several dimensions including:

- The one-to-many mode of knowledge sharing enables advice to be verified by participants of the community, addressing inconsistent understanding and practices and strengthening the validity and consistency of information.
- Rather than one-to-one knowledge transfers, knowledge shared with the community will develop a common body of knowledge that all participants can benefit from.
- Instead of directing queries to a single person who may not have the appropriate depth and range of knowledge, staff can seek advice from a group – reducing the burden on individuals and opening up the query to the wider community for consideration.
- By engaging the participation of staff across different levels, a community-based knowledge strategy provides a means of integrating strategic and operational knowledge, keeping operational staff informed of strategic directions and enabling higher level staff to stay in touch with operational activities.

Summary

The newly introduced LIS has been poorly received by operational staff. The prospect of incorporating online communities into the LIS presents an opportunity to better integrate LIS into the existing work practices. Where the LIS represents the formalised system for managing information content, its introduction has imposed new ways of working that are incompatible with the informal system that staff rely on to carry out their daily work. The integration of LIS and the informal system through online community development can potentially reduce user resistance toward LIS and enhance the ability for LIS to reach its full potential.

Both enabling and constraining aspects of ICT application and their (potential) impact on policy delivery have been explored in the Licensing Services case study. Firstly, from an enabling perspective, an examination of knowledge activities embedded in policy development and delivery broadly suggests how ICTs may be applied in leveraging the knowledge in the communities of practice and the networks of social knowledge that have developed over time. Secondly, the LIS system is fundamental to the services delivered as an outcome of operational licensing policy and its development was premised on a transformation of client service delivery. However, the case has shown that the design and implementation of this system was not integrated with existing practices and no specific change management programs were put in place during the rollout of the LIS. The existing knowledge practices were consequently constrained by the initial LIS implementation.

FUTURE RESEARCH DIRECTIONS

As illustrated by the foregoing case, investments in ICT-based infrastructure to improve the delivery of services to the community do not necessarily have entirely positive impacts in terms of public sector reform. In part, this was due to a failure to recognise and design for the wider policy cycle. As noted earlier, a perspective that views knowledge as being socially constructed through the interactions of networks of actors in policy activities is more conducive to capturing the social and political dimensions of knowledge in public policy. Similarly, one approach to examine the role of ICTs in public policy transformation is to conceptualise the integration of ICTs in public policy from a socio-technical network perspective whereby ICTs are embedded within an ensemble of relationships between people and technological artifacts in organisational contexts (Orlikowski and Iacono, 2001).

From this perspective, three generic networks can be identified to guide analysis of the integration of ICTs in public policy activities (Figure 2). Firstly, service delivery networks represent the operational outcome of policy development and design. These operational service delivery mechanisms are viewed as socio-technical systems that interact with the community and are delivered by line agencies within institutional and social contexts. They are an ensemble of relationships, processes, procedures and technologies that represent the administrative interface with citizens. The construction and activities of this socio-technical ensemble draws on and is influenced by the activities and interactions of actors in networks of policy design and technical systems design. In the policy design network, government departments respond to the changing needs of the community through the policy directions driven by set by Ministers and other lobbyists within the political framework. As new policies are formulated, the infrastructure necessary to deliver the services and administer the policy is set in place. ICTs also play a central role in the delivery of services and contribute to the infrastructure of service delivery. Large-scale e-government initiatives are developed through interactions of a network of actors including consultants and IT contractors, vendors and IT steering committee members whose interests are oriented toward technical systems design. These networks are linked by associations and co-membership of key stakeholders. Knowledge is embedded in the relationships between various actors across these networks. This embedded knowledge can both leveraged and constrained by the ICT infrastructure that is ultimately set in place.

Understanding how the linkages and associations between the policy design networks, the technical system design networks, and the service delivery networks are established, developed and maintained is an area for further research. It is proposed that these associations will influence ultimate quality of systems that are implemented for interaction and benefit of the community at large. In the Licensing Services case presented in this paper, it is suggested that the technical systems design network developed the LIS in relative isolation from the policy development and service delivery networks. Consequently, the fit between the implemented ICT infrastructure and the socially embedded knowledge networks was poor and in part counterproductive. Further research into understanding the interactions and knowledge

Figure 2. Socio-technical networks of administrative policy delivery

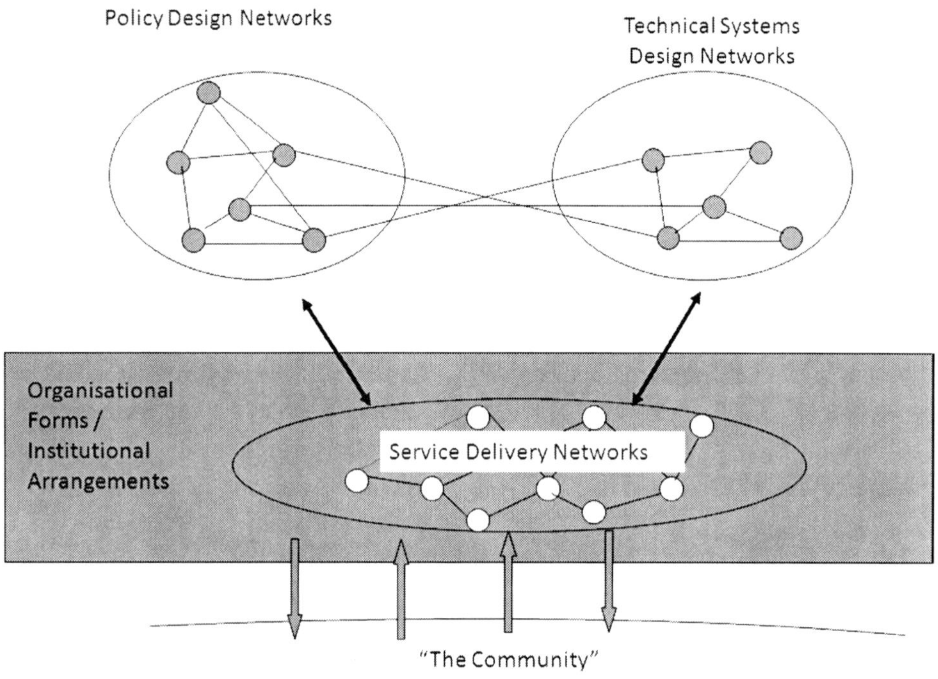

flows among and between actors in these networks can enhance understanding of appropriate ways in which ICT-based infrastructure can be used to transform the operational outcomes of policy delivery.

CONCLUSION

This chapter has examined the relationship between two aspects of public policy transformation using information and communications technology. Rather than focusing on the potential benefits of e-Government initiatives, the potential constraints on administrative flexibility that large-scale ICT systems can impose are examined in terms of the knowledge embedded in the delivery of public policy. It is suggested that the approach taken to understanding and managing knowledge within public administration is usually in terms of a rational and linear management of knowledge as a resource. While this approach fits well with models of public management, it does not address the social and political dimensions of knowledge within public policy development. Furthermore, when implemented with a similar mindset, the ICT-based systems which provide the infrastructure for the delivery of public policy can constrain the effective use and application of the socially embedded knowledge.

The case study of Licensing Services policy development and delivery activities illustrates how different forms of knowledge are embedded across sections responsible for a variety of activities from policy development through to service delivery. The case study showed that policy activities are highly dependent on the expertise developed over many years and located across the different sections. The large LIS system was supposed to transform many of the service delivery and business intelligence aspects of Licensing Services but its implementation did not fit with the existing culture and processes. The LIS was from the outset treated as an ICT project and subsequently largely focused on technical aspects of system design. Only cursory and limited attention was paid to process redesign and training with a resultant mis-match with the organizational culture of Licensing Services. The lack of fit has meant that the LIS has become a separate process of Licensing Services which reduces the flexibility and approaches to staff administering policy.

The transformation of administrative policy through the use of ICTs is a double edged sword. e-Government initiatives can be used to re-design government service delivery and improve efficiencies and policy outcomes. Knowledge management systems also have the potential to in leverage knowledge which is embedded within the social relationships across public administration. However, any ICT-based initiative and transformation has potentially negative or disruptive consequences on implementation. It is suggested that research from a perspective that views the activities of public policy development and delivery as socio-technical networks of associations between a variety of actors can enhance our understanding of the potential impacts that ICT implementations can have on policy activities.

REFERENCES

Adams, D. (2004). Usable knowledge in public policy. *Australian Journal of Public Administration*, *63*(1), 29–42. doi:10.1111/j.1467-8500.2004.00357.x

Alavi, M., & Leidner, D. E. (2001). Review: Knowledge management and knowledge management systems: Conceptual foundations and research issues. *Management Information Systems Quarterly*, *25*(1), 107–136. doi:10.2307/3250961

Bekkers, V., & Homburg, V. (2007). The myths of e-government: Looking beyond the assumptions of a new and better government. *The Information Society*, *23*, 373–382. doi:10.1080/01972240701572913

Berger, P., & Luckman, T. (1966). *The social construction of reality: A sociology of knowledge*. London, UK: Penguin Books.

Ellingsen, G., Monteiro, E., & Munkvold, G. (2007). Standardization of work: Co-constructed practice. *The Information Society*, *23*, 309–326. doi:10.1080/01972240701572723

Gold, A. H., Malhotra, A., & Segars, A. H. (2001). Knowledge management: An organizational capabilities perspective. *Journal of Management Information Systems*, *18*(1), 185–214.

Liebowitz, J., & Chen, Y. (2003). Knowledge sharing proficiencies: The key to knowledge management. In Holsapple, C. W. (Ed.), *Handbook on knowledge management 1: Knowledge matters* (pp. 409–424). Berlin, Germany: Springer-Verlag.

Mischen, P., & Jackson, S. (2008). Connecting the dots: Applying complexity theory, knowledge management and social network analysis to policy implementation. *Public Administration Quarterly*, *32*(3), 314–339.

Misra, D. C., Hariharan, R., & Khaneja, M. (2003). E-knowledge management framework for government organizations. *Information Systems Management*, *20*(2), 38–48. doi:10.1201/1078/43204.20.2.20030301/41469.7

Omar, S., Syed-Ikhsan, S., & Rowland, F. (2004). Knowledge management in a public organisation: A study on the relationship between organizational elements and the performance of knowledge transfer. *Journal of Knowledge Management*, *8*(2), 95–111. doi:10.1108/13673270410529145

Orlikowski, W. J., & Iacono, C. S. (2001). Research commentary: Desperately seeking the "IT" in IT research – A call for theorizing the IT artifact. *Information Systems Research*, *12*(2), 121–134. doi:10.1287/isre.12.2.121.9700

Osborne, M. (2004). Making the most of the best: Formulating a knowledge management strategy for a government advisory body. *Australian Journal of Public Administration*, *63*(3), 43–52. doi:10.1111/j.1467-8500.2004.00389.x

Papavassiliou, G., Ntioudis, S., Abecker, A., & Mentzas, G. (2003). Supporting knowledge-intensive work in public administration processes. *Knowledge and Process Management*, *10*(3), 164–174. doi:10.1002/kpm.176

Periseras, V., & Tarabanis, K. (2000). Towards an enterprise architecture for public administration using a top-down approach. *European Journal of Public Administration*, *9*, 252–260.

Riege, A., & Lindsay, N. (2006). Knowledge management in the public sector: Stakeholder partnerships in the public policy development. *Journal of Knowledge Management*, *10*(3), 24–39. doi:10.1108/13673270610670830

Seufert, A., von Krogh, G., & Bach, A. (1999). Towards knowledge networking. *Journal of Knowledge Management*, *3*(3), 180–190. doi:10.1108/13673279910288608

Shields, R., Taborsky, E., Jones, K. E., & O'Hara, C. (2000). A critical analysis of knowledge management initiatives in the Canadian federal public service. Retrieved from www.carleton.ca/innovation/km-fed.pdf

Syed-Ikhsan, S., Sharifuddin, O., & Rowland, F. (2004). Knowledge management in a public organization: A study on the relationship between organizational elements and the performance of knowledge transfer. *Journal of Knowledge Management*, *8*(2), 95–111. doi:10.1108/13673270410529145

Taylor, W. A., & Wright, G. H. (2004). Organizational readiness for successful knowledge sharing: Challenges for public sector managers. *Information Resources Management Journal*, *17*(2), 22–37. doi:10.4018/irmj.2004040102

Weber, E., & Khademian, A. (2008). Wicked problems, knowledge challenges and collaborative capacity builders in network settings. *Public Administration Review*, *68*(2), 334–349. doi:10.1111/j.1540-6210.2007.00866.x

Wenger, E., McDermott, R., & Snyder, W. (2002). *Cultivating communities of practice: A guide to managing knowledge*. Boston, MA: Harvard Business School Press.

Wiig, K. M. (2002). Knowledge management in public administration. *Journal of Knowledge Management*, *6*(3), 224–239. doi:10.1108/13673270210434331

KEY TERMS AND DEFINITIONS

Administrative Policy Delivery: The service provided to clients which represents the implementation of an instrument of policy.

Administrative Flexibility: The ability of public servants to interpret administrative procedure to meet the needs of the individual case.

e-Government: The application of information and communication technology in public sector organizations in ways that transform operations and service delivery.

Knowledge Network: A social network of stakeholders who construct knowledge through their interactions.

Knowledge Management System: Applications of information and communication technology that facilitate and / or enhance knowledge processes.

Knowledge Management: An initiative or managed set of practices that aims to facilitate and enhance knowledge processes in an organization.

Socio-Technical Network: An ensemble of people, technology, process and procedures which interact in of a range of formal and informal organizational activities.

Section 3
Infrastructure for E-Government

Chapter 16
IT Progress Stage and Management Level Growth in Local Governments:
The Modeling of the Japanese Government Using Empirical Surveys

Sadaya Kubo
Setsunan University, Japan

Tomohide Akebe
Setsunan University, Japan

Keiko Nakagawa
Setsunan University, Japan

ABSTRACT

This chapter considers the management of local governments in a growing information society. We highlight two proposed models for the management of local governments. The first model is the IT progress stage. This stage considered the previously published literature. The second model is the management level model. This model indexed the appearance of management activities learned from an original empirical survey completed in 2009. We analyzed the relationship between the IT progress stage and the management level model. Thereafter, we proposed a common progress stage model for local governments.

INTRODUCTION

Since 2001, local governments in Japan have been showing strong progress in e-transformation, in accordance to the e-Japan strategy (Prime Minister of Japan and his cabinet, 2001). As a result, the infrastructure of Information Technology (IT) has spread and citizens have become frequent users of Information and Communication Technology (ICT). Although the use of ICT has spread, there

DOI: 10.4018/978-1-60960-839-2.ch016

is little system satisfaction among the citizens of Japan. Therefore, improvements and initiatives are required for the future of ICT. Citizens also require an approach that promotes the use of local resources and provides security within a changing society.

With an increasing number of tasks, local governments are faced with significant management problems. Local governments are managed from the optimization of one part of an activity as well as all local government activities. However, it is difficult to define the management of local government in a changing society. Therefore, a management level model for real local activities is required (Anttiroiko, 2003; Kubo & Shimada, 2007; Shimada & Ushida, 2003; Kubo & Shimada, 2008a; Kubo & Shimada, 2008b).

Previous studies have proposed several IT progress stages for local governments. These studies consisted of empirical surveys or case studies. Since e-transformation is a current topic in management issues, the above research methods are effective. Thus, the use of these previous studies will be appropriate in our research.

In this study, we focus on newer issues in management activities based on the IT progress stage. We discuss this premise by using empirical surveys as follows: First, the background of this study is described, showing the framework of the analysis. We denote the IT progress stage from our previous empirical surveys. Next, we verify the validity of the stage model. The other model for management level is discussed, using our empirical survey under the following categories: organization reform, personnel training, life safety, and regional brands. For these four categories, we create a level model by the index of difficulty of the questions in our empirical survey. We show progress directions for these four categories and compare them to the IT progress stage. We indicate the relationship between the IT progress stage and management level model to improve the service in an advanced information society. Furthermore, we discuss the common characteristics of progress models, which we hope will assist in the management of local governments. Finally, we show the impact that our research could have on local governments.

BACKGROUND

IT effects major changes to many activities and many situations. It has especially altered the management of most corporations and organizations, recently including the management of local governments.

The Ministry of Economy, Trade and Industry in Japan has defined the e-transformation stage of corporations. This is composed of four stages. The first stage is "the introduction of electronic computers". The second stage is "e-transformation of business". The third stage is "optimization of corporate process". The fourth stage is "cooperation, integration, and standardization outside the corporation" and "optimization of communications". The first and second stages are called the stages of the sub-optimization (implementation rate is 65.8%). The third and fourth stages are called the entire optimization stage (implementation rate is 34.2%).

In corporations, e-transformation occurs in the individual business to the complete organization. Furthermore, it has changed to e-transformation of the business between organizations. The local government also has been subject to change from sub-optimization, like individual administrative services such as ledger management and call center installation, etc., to complete optimization such as BPR. These changes include web technology, ICT, and new activities involving citizens and government officers.

ICT has had a significant impact on advanced IT societies. In Japan, most citizens have mobile phones and can access the Internet at home and in their offices and schools. People are able to exchange a great deal of information, resulting in a more interactive society. ICT growth provides business opportunities and raises the importance of good management. Because the use of ICT in general, is increasing, it is important to manage information and activities in local governments effectively.

Thus, IT has not only advanced management power; management consists of choice information, design information, and must fit the organization and the ability of its members. Carr (2004) denoted that information technology has become a social infrastructure similar to electronic power. Furthermore, improvements in the management of local governments are enhanced by IT and ICT. Brynjolfsson (2002) described the intangible assets affected by a corporation's improvement by IT. It seems that the intangible assets depend on management policy, organization type, collaboration with people both outside and within the organization, and the organization's resources. It is difficult to clarify these intangible asset factors. However, if several scales (e-transformation level, output level of services, and personnel training level, etc.) exist, we would be able to determine an outline for these assets, as in Brynjolfsson's work (Brynjolfsson, 2002).

Research involves the e-transformation of the local government. These studies showed the scale of e-transformation based on these empirical surveys and many case studies. Local governments in Japan are focusing on promoting regional brands. Regional brands consist of local resources (sightseeing spots, regional foods, regional events, etc.). For instance, in Kyoto, there are many historical buildings such as temples, and shrines. Moreover, we can eat local Kyoto cuisine. These regional brands lead to not only revenue growth through sightseeing but also increased migration to the region. Any combination of these resources would be attractive to promote on a web site or in a book. Local governments are also interested in safety and security in local areas, minimizing the threat of any danger, such as muggings, abductions, or burglaries. Therefore, community policing requires improvement. However, most people dislike security cameras using network technology because they feel that they are an invasion of privacy.

Systematic correspondence and human resources are necessary for promoting regional brands and maintaining safety and security. However, the local government requires budget and staff reductions. Therefore, local governments focus on organizational reform and personnel training.

Proper management is of the utmost importance. However, management is often not clear in how to advance. Moreover, if neither the example nor the situation of other local governments is understood, then the local government will not implement the measures.

Therefore, it is necessary to show the current state of these approaches. In addition, it is shown whether the result of the studies about e-transformation of the local government can be applied to other issues (ex. regional brands, safety and security, and organization reform and the personnel training to support these). If this is shown, then this method of creating scales will prove useful in analyzing the management levels in local governments. There are also many comparable points among local governments worldwide. These points provide the link between local government management to common management.

Framework

The purpose of this study is to clarify the relationship between the IT progress stage and the management level model in local government. In this study, we indicate the management level by our empirical survey and use the e-transformation level from former works.

The empirical survey contains the following research categories:

1. Organization reform
2. Personnel training
3. Life safety
4. Regional brands

We assume that these categories are important factors for local government in Japan and that they denote the surface of management level effects.

The research contents of the organization reform category are collaboration activities with citizens and Non Profit Organizations (NPOs), special departments, measurement of reform profit, etc.

The contents of personnel training include training policy, goal setting, and training style.

The research contents of life safety include special departments, effects of security cameras and information services for older citizens, crimes, and disaster.

The regional brands contents include special departments, collaboration with other organizations, and estimation of resources.

These four categories are not only significant indicators in the management of local Japanese governments but are also important indicators in the local governments of many foreign countries.

In the e-transformation of local governments, several studies have designated level or stage models. Shimada and Ushida (2003) researched the condition of local government e-transformation by a questionnaire survey in 2003. Kubo and Shimada (2007) researched continuous situations of e-transformation in Japanese local governments and analyzed e-transformation levels from 2004 to 2008. They proposed the IT progress stage of local governments in Japan in their studies. Their proposed stages are based on e-transformation levels. Their study showed that a government having advanced e-transformation has excellent management activities, development style, and organizational methods (Kubo & Shimada, 2008a). Other stages or e-transformation levels are exemplified by case studies.

In the present study, we consider the IT progress stage, which was formed from these studies. Using the above assumptions, we discuss the management levels of local governments in Japan with the IT progress stage as the basis of consideration.

IT PROGRESS STAGE IN LOCAL GOVERNMENT

In this study, we used the following IT progress stages (Kubo & Shimada, 2008b):

Stage 5 is Value Generation
Stage 4 is Evaluation
Stage 3 is Ingenuity in Practice
Stage 2 is Organizing
Stage 1 is Preparation
Stage 0 is Nonexistent

We indicated each assumption in stages from 1 to 5.

Preparation (stage 1) includes the development of the information infrastructure and basic information disclosure; that is, the start of digitalization. Organizing (stage 2) is gaining an understanding of the citizens' needs and their participation by web site or Social Network Services (SNS). Ingenuity in practice (stage 3) is the development of cooperative relationships with other organizations, utilizing the resources of other organizations, and improving the citizen's ability to use government services effectively. Evaluation (stage 4) refers to surveys conducted to determine citizens' satisfaction and the satisfactory achievement of public management quality through public-private partnerships. Value Generation is the highest stage in the stage model. It indicates the collaboration between various stakeholders for mutual purposes and the demarcation of the responsibilities of the government, the citizens, and other organizations.

Additional benefits of these collaboration activities are citizen satisfaction, regional brands, original education style, etc. Our progress stage model is based on the following five key factors.

1. Development of information infrastructure.
2. Development of cooperative relationships with other stakeholders(citizens, corporations, NPOs).

Figure 1. The concept of the relationship among the five key factors

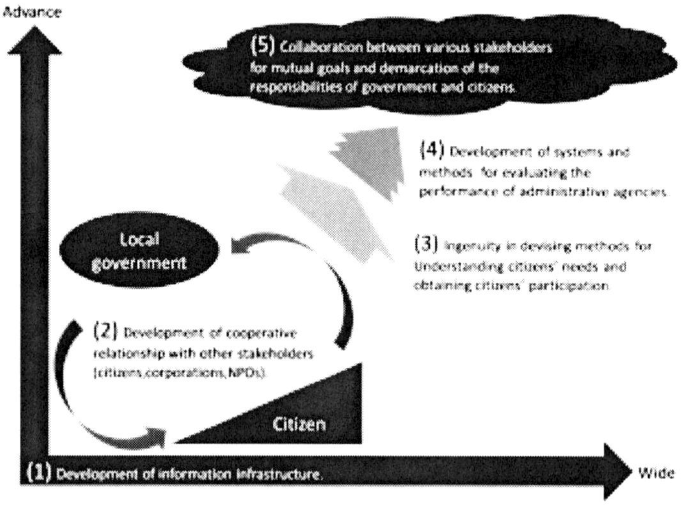

3. Ingenuity in devising methods for understanding citizens' needs and obtaining citizens' participation.
4. Development of systems and methods for evaluating the performance of administrative agencies.
5. Collaboration between various stakeholders for mutual goals and demarcation of the responsibilities of the government and citizens.

These factors are produced by our interview surveys and case studies (Kubo & Shimada, 2008a; Kubo & Shimada, 2008b). The target cases of advanced IT local government services are as follows: collaboration with citizens and administrative agencies by using the electronic conference room (Fujisawa city), collaboration with disclosure of all relevant information by ICT (Saga prefecture), one stop service convenience stores that are present all over the area (Adachi city), multi-purpose citizen service (book reservation, public facilities reservation, health management information) by using integrated circuit (IC) cards (Oushu city), questionnaire survey among all the citizens to determine their needs and evaluate the government (Shiwa town). These local governments carry out advanced utilization of IT or ICT and are worthy of note in Japan. Figure 1 shows the concept of the relationship among the five key factors.

We verified our proposed model by empirical surveys of e-transformation in local governments. We showed the yearly ranking list of e-transformation of local governments. Based on the ranking list, we classified the more difficult questions, which were achieved by highly ranked governments, and the easier questions, which were achieved by most governments. In other words, we analyzed the difficulty of these questions, and verified our model with the difficulty scale.

The following activities in the Preparation stage are undertaken by most local governments:

1. Enactment of the information disclosure ordinance.
2. Publication of the main government policies, such as a master plan for the city.

The following activities in the Organization stage and the Ingenuity in Practice stage are undertaken by middle ranking local governments:

Table 1. Comparison of our IT progress stage and those proposed by previous studies

<table>
<tr><th>Stages</th><th>Our IT progress stage</th><th>Shimada</th><th colspan="2">Arnstein</th><th>Yoshida et.al.</th><th>Anttiroiko</th><th>Mirvis and Googins</th></tr>
<tr><td>5</td><td>Value Generation</td><td rowspan="2">Outcome</td><td colspan="4"></td><td rowspan="2">Transforming</td></tr>
<tr><td rowspan="2">4</td><td rowspan="2">Evaluation</td><td>Citizen Control</td><td rowspan="3">Citizen Power</td><td>Autonomy originated at the citizen-level</td><td>Interaction</td></tr>
<tr><td rowspan="2">Output</td><td>Delegated Power</td><td rowspan="2">Public-private partnership</td><td>Integration</td><td>Integrated</td></tr>
<tr><td>3</td><td>Ingenuity in Practice</td><td>Partnership</td><td>Influence</td><td>Innovative</td></tr>
<tr><td>2</td><td>Organizing</td><td rowspan="3">Input</td><td>Placation</td><td rowspan="3">Tokenism</td><td rowspan="3">Exchange of opinions between citizens and officers</td><td rowspan="3">Institutions</td><td rowspan="2">Engaged</td></tr>
<tr><td rowspan="2">1</td><td rowspan="2">Preparation</td><td>Consultation</td></tr>
<tr><td>Informing</td><td>Elementary</td></tr>
<tr><td rowspan="2">0</td><td rowspan="2">Nonexistent</td><td rowspan="2"></td><td>Therapy</td><td rowspan="2">Nonparticipation</td><td rowspan="2">Exchange of opinions among citizens</td><td rowspan="2" colspan="2"></td></tr>
<tr><td>Manipulation</td></tr>
</table>

1. Community facility reservation system.
2. Citizen PC training.
3. Hearing public options.

The following activities in the Evaluation stage are undertaken by highly ranked the local governments:

1. Research to determine citizens' satisfaction.
2. Evaluation of the effectiveness of the services provided.

The following activities in the Value Generation stage are rarely undertaken by the local governments:

1. A database of frequently asked questions for citizens.
2. A call center to resolve citizens' queries.
3. Allowing citizens to create content.
4. Customized services through the citizen card.

The difficulty of the questions/activities indicated in our survey, as above, is similar to the proposed IT stage model. Therefore, it seems that a series of proposed models for the IT progress stage has validity in actual situations and management concepts.

Table1 shows our stage model and other previous studies.

Shimada (2003) denoted his stage model with Input - Output - Outcome in view of administrative evaluation. Arnstein (1969) showed eight rungs on the ladder of citizen participation. Yoshida et al. (2003) expanded her ladder model to adjust to the information society in Japan. Anttiroiko (2003) denoted the Four Is model consisting of (1) Institutions, (2) Influence, (3) Integration, and (4) Interaction. Mirvis and Googins (2006) presented the corporate citizenship model with (1) Elementary, (2) Engaged, (3) Innovative, (4) Integrated, and (5) Transforming. Any model has a relationship on the horizontal level and a common direction on the vertical level. Therefore, it seems that our proposed model involves an integrated view from all of these studies.

Figure 2. The analysis result of a combination by integral type and modular type

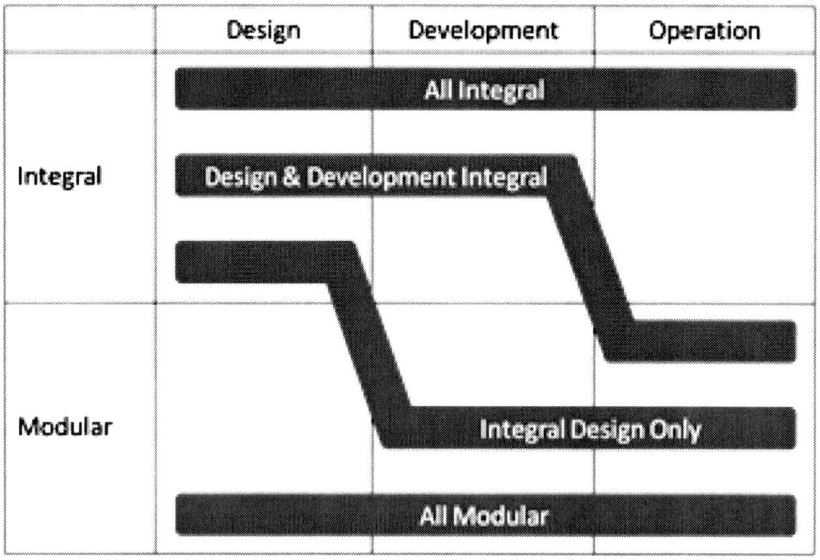

We also analyzed the situations of the construction and operation of advanced information services (Kubo & Shimada, 2008a). In the analysis, we classified e-transformation processes by design, development, and operation. We analyzed these processes by Manufacturing Architecture (Fujimoto, 2006).

Manufacturing architecture has an integral type and a modular type. The integral type is used to produce Japanese car and video game software, which are popular industries. The modular type is used to produce DOS/V PC and web technologies, which are de facto standard products. We focused on a combination of the two types for the advanced e-transformation of local governments. Figure 2 depicts the analysis result.

There are differences in the various e-transformation styles; however, it is important to use the integral type for the design phase. Collaboration and integration are important topics on a management level.

Administrative service is a very important category in which to determine the level of e-transformation. However, for the achievement of effective administrative service, a local government has to consider the other categories in e-transformation. Therefore, our previous empirical surveys took into account computerization in the office and information security.

Computerization in local government offices is the foundation for the implementation of e-transformation. Information security is essential for the smooth operation of government activities. We analyzed these categories in the same manner as administrative services.

The IT progress stage has five levels that are determined by the difficulty of the questions/activities. It appears there are common classifications between the proposed IT progress stage model and these two models. Our proposed model seems to be appropriate for the improvement of e-transformation activities.

Empirical Survey (2009) Result

Overview

This study is based on several empirical surveys done for local Japanese governments. It was the outcome of an original survey, which had four

Table 2. Rates of response to the survey

	Prefectures	Cities and Special Wards	Towns and Villages	Total
Targets	47	806	992	1845
Respondents	36	288	189	513
Percentage of respondents	77%	36%	19%	28%

questionnaire ranges. These ranges are organization reform, personnel training, life security, and regional brands. These ranges are an expansion of the survey on e-transformation of local governments (2004-2008).

This survey was conducted using a questionnaire creation system that uses PHP and MySQL on Linux. This study is uncommon, as is the Japanese e-transformation survey from 2004. The period of this survey was from July to September 2009. It targeted 1,845 local governments in Japan (47 prefectures, 806 cities and special wards, and 992 towns and villages). Table 2 indicates the rates of response to the survey.

The percentage of respondents was lower as compared to the past survey, but the results provided useful information.

Composition of Questions

Questions regarding organization reform examine the flexibility and activity power of management in local governments. This category contains questions:

1. About special departments or organizations promoting organization reform in the office
2. About the existence of cross-departmental activities in the office
3. About collaboration with citizens
4. About measuring the effects of organizational reform

This category is composed of 21 questions.

Questions regarding personnel training examine setting goals, personnel training activity, and the relationship between personnel evaluation and personnel training. This category contains questions:

1. About setting goals for personnel training and creating documentation for personnel training
2. About measuring the effects of personnel training
3. About collaborating with other organizations in the region
4. About the relationship between a system for personnel evaluation and personnel training

This category is composed of 23 questions.

Questions regarding life safety examine collaboration with citizens and the effect of each policy, service, and information. This category contains questions:

1. About the methods of sharing and sending information
2. About collaboration with citizens
3. About the subjective effects of each policy and service
4. About the measurement effects of each policy and service

This category is composed of 30 questions.

Questions regarding regional brands examine the present state of regional brands and the local government's role in the regional brands construction process. This category contains questions:

1. About the presence of regional brands
2. About the types of regional brands

3. About the organization structure of work on the regional brands
4. About the regional brands construction process

This category is composed of 26 questions.

Organization Reform

Organization reform and citizen participation in local governments are promoted based on a document by the Ministry of Public Management "the New Guidelines for the Promotion of Administrative Reform in Local Governments", issued in 2005.

Most organizations and local governments are based on bureaucratic sectionalism. Local governments sometimes need to change their organizational structure to have flexibility for meeting the needs of a diverse population. Collaboration with citizens and other organizations in the region is important to get a grasp on the nature of the citizens' demands. Therefore, an important factor in organization reform is to measure the effects of the reform and provide feedback for future policies.

In our research survey, the category of organization reform questions how to provide training flexibility and diversity in an organization. We pay particular attention to the presence of people and activities that cross organizations. We also pay attention to places where there is collaboration with citizens and other organizations.

There are three aspects of organization reform:

1. The relationship between the progress of the vertical structure and the scale of the local governments
2. The relationship between good collaboration activity and the scale of the local governments
3. How to measure the effects of organization reform

1. Relationship between the Progress of the Vertical Structure and the Scale of the Local Governments

Our questions regarding the relationship between progress of the vertical structure and the scale of the local government deal with the following: the presence of special departments for organization reform, the presence crossing activities, and a project team working under a chief clerk.

Special departments for organization reform were established by 57% of local governments (88% of prefectures, 71% of cities and special wards, and 31% of towns and villages). Over 70% of prefectures and cities and special wards have special departments for organization reform. However, it is difficult for towns and villages to have special departments for organization reform, indicated by the low rate.

Departments with citizen participation are operated by 46% of local governments (59% of prefectures, 61% of cities and special wards, and 20% of towns and villages). Prefectures and cities and special wards are at almost the same rate, and towns and villages are a bit lower. It appears that towns and villages are short of hands to provide citizen participation.

Activities that cross departments run by a staff working under a chief clerk occur in 27% of local governments (47% of prefectures, 33% of cities and special wards, and 16% of towns and villages). Large-scale local governments are at a higher rate in this category than small-scale local governments.

Project teams that cross departments run by a staff working under a chief clerk are established by 42% of local governments (prefectures 56%, cities and special wards 47%, and towns and villages 32%). Large-scale local governments indicate a higher rate in this category than small-scale local governments. More local governments answered that they have cross-departmental project teams than cross-departmental activities.

2. Relationship between Good Collaboration Activity and the Scale of Local Government

Our question referred to collaboration with citizens and other sections (collaboration with citizens, NPOs, universities, enterprises).

Collaboration with citizens was reported by 69% of local governments (71% of prefectures, 75% of cities and special wards, and 59% of towns and villages). Prefectures and cities and special wards are at almost the same rate. Towns and villages are a bit lower.

Collaboration with NPOs was reported by 46% of local governments (91% of prefectures, 59% of cities and special wards, and 19% of towns and villages). Large-scale local governments indicated a higher rate than small-scale local governments.

Collaboration with educational institutions, e.g., universities, was reported by 38% of local governments (76% of prefectures, 44% of cities and special wards, and 23% of towns and villages). Large-scale local governments indicated a higher rate than small-scale local governments.

Collaboration with private enterprises was reported by 20% of local governments (62% of prefectures, 25% of cities and special wards, and 6% of towns and villages). Large-scale local governments indicated a higher rate than small-scale local governments. However, collaboration with private enterprises is at a lower rate than collaboration with other organizations. Large-scale local governments show stronger collaboration with private organizations than small-scale local governments. Collaboration with citizens shows a lower difference than collaboration with other organizations. We also think that collaboration with private enterprises is at a lower rate than collaboration with the private organization because it is still in the developmental stages.

3. How to Measure the Effects of Organization Reform

The effects of organization reform were measured by 14% of local governments (52% of prefectures, 16% of cities and special wards, and 5% of towns and villages). Half of the prefectures reported measured effects. However, few cities, special wards, towns, and villages reported these measurements.

Most local governments measure these effects using a numerical target. For example, local governments use cut down strength, control of personnel costs, amount of overtime work, and the effects of personnel costs. Some local governments do not have measuring indexes. Many local governments use questionnaires and simply listen to citizens and staff in their office. The other methods used are exchanges of opinion, investigations, and comparisons with similar cities.

4. Consideration

The results of our survey indicate the following: First, the most organized bureaucratic sections are prefectures. Towns and villages are the least organized in cross-section activities. Second, the strongest organizations in collaboration with other organizations are prefectures. Collaboration with citizens is similar across the board. Third, the effects of organizational reform are measured using numerical targets; for example, personnel costs could be used as measurement targets.

Personnel Training

The most important factor in effective management is human resources. This factor is also true in the management of local government. In 1997, the Ministry of Home Affairs announced to prefectural governors and mayors in specific cities to "formulate guidelines for a basic policy of personnel training in a new era of local autonomy" (This is the guideline for personnel training in local governments).

We included questions regarding the characteristics and problems of personnel training in our survey. Local governments set goals for personnel training and perform training in their office and in collaboration with other organizations in their region. Questions regarding personnel training activities were answered by 494 local governments (34 prefectures, 280 cities and special wards, and 184 towns and villages).

1. Setting Definite Goals for Personnel Training

An effective personnel training allows an organization to develop a personnel image. The survey shows that local governments set goals for personnel training and have clearly documented their goals. The most popular goal is "aim for government office". The next most popular goal is "aim for an official position".

Local governments have documents for personnel training: over 90% of prefectures and cities and special wards, and 65% of towns and villages. This rate in towns and villages is very low. Small-scale local governments do not have a high enough budget, human resources, or know-how. Therefore, there are not clear guidelines for personnel training. However, they are required to set definite goals.

2. Performing Personnel Training and Measuring its Effects

Local governments perform personnel training to enhance their personnel image. The average number of local governments engaged in personnel training is not much different between prefectures and cities and special wards. However, fewer towns and villages have established a system for personnel training.

Local governments measure the effects of personnel training. Positive effects are reported by 67% of prefectures, 43% of cities and special wards, and 3% of towns and villages. The effects of personnel training are clearly different across the scale.

Local governments measure the effects of personnel training by various indexes and methods. The indexes of effective training are reported by the students themselves (satisfaction, useful for the job, useful to the business, evaluation by instructors and superiors). Local governments rarely use Objective Indexes. Their main method of evaluation is student questionnaire. Other methods used are reports, tests, and evaluation by superiors or instructors. Some local governments measure the effects of personnel training using citizen questionnaires.

Local governments should research methods of evaluation using Objective Indexes and initiate a Plan-Do-Check-Action cycle.

3. Collaboration with Other Organizations in the Region

Local governments utilize collaboration with other organizations in their region for personnel training. Prefectures and cities collaborate with educational institutions, companies, NPOs, and citizens. Towns and villages mostly collaborate with citizens.

Local governments hope for positive effects with regional collaboration; for example, cultivating the perspectives of citizens, enhancing personal skills, providing a sense of business, understanding of local issues, and promoting regional cooperation. It is expected that this collaboration will result in improved staff management skills in private enterprises and the development of close business relationships within the region.

4. The Relationship between Personnel Training and a System of Personnel Evaluation

A system for personnel evaluation is a good tool for measuring the effectiveness of personnel training. Over 60% of local governments do not have a system in place for personnel evaluation. Some local governments still do not have a system for personnel training, so do not yet use a system for personnel evaluation.

5. Consideration

Our survey indicated that prefectures and cities and specific wards are at almost the same rate of personnel training. On the other hand, towns and villages are several points lower on the personnel training scale because of insufficient budgets, manpower, or know-how. Therefore, it appears that it is difficult for small-scale local governments to advance personnel training; however, it is essential that these organizations support the development of effective systems for personnel training.

Life Safety

A common problem in Japanese regions is decreasing population as a result of the lower birth rate, the aging of present citizens, and depopulation. Moreover, national administrative policies have brought about restructuring of grant and of tax systems in local areas. Therefore, local governments need to improve resources for decentralization.

The settlement of citizens and migration outside the region is necessary to solve these problems. In other words, it is important that local governments offer regional environment safety. The category of life safety, then, investigates the following matters:

1. Information sharing and sending
2. Collaboration with citizens
3. The subjective effects of each policy and service
4. Measurement of the effects of each policy and service

1. Information Sharing and Sending

The average rate of sharing and sending information about citizen safety is 87% (prefectures 100%, cities and special wards 90%, and towns and village 80%). Almost all local governments share and send information on safety. "Public relations magazines" is one of the most common methods of sending information. There are also "web sites for each department in local government", "courses and meetings", and "mail service".

2. Collaboration with Citizens

The rate of collaboration with citizens about safety is 64%. The rate of collaboration with citizens is 71% in prefectures, in cities and special wards it is 69%, and in towns and villages it is 57%. Citizen collaboration activities provide the following:

- Creation of a regional safety map
- Training of leaders and staff to promote safety
- Independent activities by communities in small areas

3. Subjective Effects of Each Policy and Service

The questionnaire investigated the subjective effects of the following policies and services.

[Policy and service]

Q1: Security camera
Q2: Emergency alert system for persons of advanced age at home
Q3: Crime prevention information notice by mail
Q4: Sending disaster information by website
Q5: System of information sharing by regional SNS
Q6: Training person to promote safety
Q7: Citizen patrol group
Q8: A personal information network

Subjective effects are classified as "very effective", "rather effective", "so-so", "rather not effective", and "not effective".

All approaches were "very effective" or "rather effective". Q6, Q7, and Q8 are assumed to be very effective. These are the approaches on which the citizen actually acts. It is assumed that very little effect exists for Q3 and Q4. These are the approaches that involve information sending. The policy and service for which the effect was not indicated was Q5 because of the following:

- The confirmation of the actual effect of SNS is difficult
- The reliability of the information is low
- Understanding and participation in SNS are difficult

A difference was seen on the local government scale for the approach of Q1. The rate of the approach that promotes the installation of security cameras was 13% on average. The concrete rates were 48% in prefectures, 16% in cities and special wards, and 3% in towns and villages. Moreover, 11% of local governments had adopted a policy for installation of security cameras. The concrete rates were 47% in prefectures, 14% in cities and wards, and 1% in towns and villages. The installation of security cameras is costly. Moreover, there is sometimes an overlap between the local government's efforts and private citizens voluntarily setting up cameras. In other words, the use of security cameras is difficult for small-scale local governments. Therefore, it seems that small-scale local governments have not made policies regarding this approach to life safety.

4. Measurement of the Effects of Each Policy and Service

The effects of policies and services are measured by 15% of local governments. The concrete rates of measurement effects are 66% in prefectures, 19% in cities and special wards, and 1% in towns and villages. Towns and villages do not normally measure the effects of policies and services.

Local governments chiefly measure the effects of "the rate of crime occurrence" and "citizen's satisfaction". The effects of medical treatment, education, and welfare are measured by a section of the local government. The measurement methods are, primarily, questionnaires, listening, and gathering information from data. Small-scale local governments are not able to measure the effects of policies and services because of the costs in money, time, and manpower and because the range of measurement is so wide.

Regional Brands

Recently, many regions in Japan have constructed regional brands. It seems that establishing a regional brand begins from the revision of the registration system of a regional organization's trademark. Promotion of a regional brand is different from an industry's promotion of a product because the construction of a regional brand aims not only to gain income from consumers inside and outside of a region, but also to develop a citizen's pride and attachment to a region. In other words, a similar strategy for the branding of an enterprise can be applied to the branding of a region. Therefore, the aspect of management is also necessary for a region.

However, the concept of regional branding is fairly new. The survey included a field to investigate the following matters pertaining to a regional brand:

1. Presence of regional brands
2. The types of regional brands
3. Organization structure
4. The construction process

1. Presence of Regional Brands

Regional brands exist in 96% of prefectures, 81% of cities and special wards, and 78% of towns and villages. Most local governments have regional brands. It seems that local governments recognize special products in conventional industry promotion as regional brands.

2. The Types of Regional Brands

The types of regional brands were obtained from the question that consists of the following choices:

[Choices]

"Farm products", "Livestock products", "Marine products", "Craft goods", "Person", "Nature", "Historic sites", "Hot springs", "Culture and history", "Sightseeing spots", "Tourist facilities", "Regional gourmets", and "Regional events".

[Results]

The highest regional brand on any local government scale was "Farm products" (the rate in prefectures was 93%, cities and special wards

68%, and towns and villages 73%). The lowest rate was for "Person" (the rate in prefectures was 13%, cities and special wards 9%, and towns and villages 4%). It is difficult to construct "Person". Moreover, the regional resource of "Person" does not exist.

The rate in prefectures is higher than in cities and special wards and in towns and villages in any type of regional brand, excluding "Nature". This is because the role of administrative divisions is to understand and to manage the regional brands of the city, the special wards, and the town and village to which it belongs. The brand type "Nature" works in towns and villages and not in prefectures, cities, and special wards. Nature exists in greater abundance in towns and villages and is therefore capitalized on as a regional brand.

3. Organization Structure

The organization structure of work on regional brands was obtained from the question that consists of the following choices:

[Choices]

"Establishment of special department", "Approaches that crossed departments", and "Cooperation with other organizations".

[Results]

There are few local governments in which special departments are established (prefectures 29%, cities and special wards 17%, and towns and villages 11%). It is thought that a regional brand works in each department.

The rates for approaches that crossed each department are 65% in prefectures, 39% in cities and special wards, and 26% in towns and villages. This process is difficult for small scale local governments. The approach by each department is mainly used in towns and villages.

The construction process on which any local government scale was executed was "cooperation with other organizations" (the rate in prefectures was 90%, cities and special wards 83%, and towns and villages 74%). It seems that cooperation between departments and relating to an organization is the basic system that works for a regional brand.

4. The Construction Process

The construction process was obtained from the question that selected and executed one of the following choices:

[Choices]

"Grasp of resource", "Clarification of target", "Original approach", "Information sharing and dissemination", "Ex post facto evaluation of brand".

[Results]

The construction process on which all local government scales were built was "Information sharing and sending". It is thought that this process provides the basis for local governments to work on a regional brand. In contrast, differences were found in "grasp of resource" and "Ex post facto evaluation of brand". From the results of "grasp of resource", the role of prefectures is to grasp the region to which the resource belongs. In the towns and villages where a regional brand is constructed, the rate in which "grasp of resource" is executed is actually low, probably because the main industry has already been decided. In other words, it is unnecessary to grasp another resource. The rate of "Ex post facto evaluation of brand" is low because there is no evaluated index. It is thought that prior target-setting is difficult, and it is not possible to evaluate it after the fact.

Management Level Model

In this section, we suggest the management level model. We demonstrate the stage model using each category in our survey. At first, Figure 3 and Figure 4 show the result from our survey. Figure 3 shows the results with an answer rate less than 50%. Figure 4 shows results with an answers rate over 50%. The scatter analysis is used for authorization in Figure 3-4 and Table 3. These are shown that results are based on the scale of local government, there is a difference in the execution of the measure from the result of the scatter analysis.

Next, Figure 3 show the results from our survey used for creating the management level model.

In the organizational reform result, we focused on achievements and the executed situation. They are classified as follows. The question with an answer rate of 60% or greater was "existence of collaboration with citizens". The questions with an answer rate of 40% or greater were "existence of special departments for organization reform", "existence of special departments with citizen participation", "existence of project teams that crossed departments with a staff working under a chief clerk", and "existence of collaboration with a NPO". The questions with an answer rate of 20% or greater were "existence of activity that crossed departments with a staff working under a chief clerk" and "existence of collaboration with colleges". The questions with an answer rate of 20% or less were "existence of collaboration with private enterprises" and "existence of measuring

*Figure 3. The result from our survey; Answer rate less than 50% (Note: *p<0.05; **p<0.01; ***p<0.001)*

Category	Question	Prefectures	Cities and Special wards	Towns and Villages	Average
Organization reform	Measurement of the effects ***	52%	16%	5%	14%
	Collaboration with an enterprise ***	62%	25%	6%	20%
	Activity that crosses departments with a staff working under a chief clerk ***	47%	33%	16%	27%
	Collaboration with colleges ***	76%	44%	23%	38%
	Establishment of project teams that cross departments with a staff working under a chief clerk **	56%	47%	32%	42%
	Establishment of special departments with citizen participation ***	59%	61%	20%	46%
	Collaboration with an NPO ***	91%	59%	19%	46%
Personnel rainning	Collaboration with other organizations is used as personnel training ***	42%	21%	15%	20%
	Measurement of the effects ***	67%	43%	3%	29%
	Approaches that refer to other local governments ***	48%	41%	12%	31%
Life safty	Policy decisions concerning security camera installation ***	47%	14%	1%	11%
	Approach that promotes security camera installation ***	48%	16%	3%	13%
	Measurement of the effect ***	66%	19%	1%	15%
	Establishment of special departments ***	42%	39%	11%	29%
	Original approach ***	70%	33%	17%	29%
Regional brands	Ex post facto evaluation of brand ***	38%	7%	4%	8%
	Clarification of target *	30%	13%	10%	13%
	Establishment of special departments *	29%	17%	11%	15%
	Original approach *	77%	34%	20%	31%
	Approach that crosses departments ***	65%	39%	26%	36%
	Grasp of resources ***	87%	47%	25%	41%

*Figure 4. The result from our survey; Answer rate is over 50% (Note: *p<0.05; **p<0.01;***p<0.001)*

Category	Question	Prefectures	Cities and Special wards	Towns and Villages	Average
Organization reform	Establishment of special departments of organization reform ***	88%	71%	31%	57%
	Collaboration with citizens **	71%	75%	59%	69%
Personnel trainning	Training policy ***	97%	90%	65%	81%
Life safty	Collaboration with citizens *	71%	69%	57%	64%
	Grasp of problem ***	90%	75%	61%	71%
	Information sharing and sending ***	100%	90%	80%	87%
Regional brands	Grasp of problem ***	87%	70%	55%	65%
	Information sharing and sending ***	97%	71%	59%	68%
	Cooperation with other organizations *	90%	83%	74%	80%

Table 3. Management level model

	Organization reform	Personnel training	Life safety	Regional brands
5	Collaboration with an enterprise *** Measurement of the effects ***	Collaboration with other organizations is used as personnel training ***	Measurement of the effect *** Approach that promotes security camera installation *** Policy decisions concerning security camera installation ***	Establishment of special departments * Ex post facto evaluation of brand *** Clarification of target *
4	Activity that crosses departments with a staff working under a chief clerk *** Collaboration with colleges ***	Measurement of the effects *** Approaches that refer to other local governments ***	Establishment of special departments *** Original approach ***	Approach that crosses departments *** Original approach *
3	Establishment of special departments of organization reform *** Establishment of special departments with citizen participation *** Establishment of project teams that cross departments with a staff working under a chief clerk ** Collaboration with an NPO ***			Grasp of resources ***
2	Collaboration with citizens **	Training policy ***	Collaboration with citizens * Grasp of problem ***	Cooperation with other organizations * Grasp of problem *** Information sharing and sending ***
1			Information sharing and sending ***	

Note: *p<0.05; **p<0.01;***p<0.001

the effects of organization reform". It was difficult to evaluate and distinguish "collaboration with other organizations" from "citizens' participation".

For the personnel training results, we grouped the results that refer to the presence of achievement and action as follows. The question with an answer rate of 60% or greater was "existence of an objective document for personnel training policy". There were no questions with an answer rate of 40% or greater. The questions with an answer rate of 20% or greater were "existence of measuring the effects of personnel training", "refer to other organizations for personnel training". The question with an answer rate of 20% or less was "using personnel training to collaborate with other organizations". It was difficult to evaluate and distinguish "collaboration with other organizations" from "consciousness of personnel training".

In life safety results, we grouped the categories as follows. The questions with an answer rate of 60% or greater were "information sharing and sending", "collaboration with citizens", and "grasp of the problem". There were no questions with an answer rate of 40% or greater. The questions with an answer rate of 20% or greater were "establishment of special departments" and "original approach". The questions with an answer rate of 20% or less were "measurement of the effect", "approach that promotes security camera installation", and "decision of policy concerning security camera installation". It was difficult to evaluate "action of means" and "information sharing".

For the regional brands results, we grouped the categories as follows. The questions with an answer rate of 60% or greater were "region has regional brands", "cooperation with other organizations", "grasp of problem", and "information sharing and sending". The question with an answer rate of 40% or greater was "grasp of resource". The questions with an answer rate of 20% or greater were "approach that crossed departments" and "original approach". The questions with an answer rate of 20% or less were "establishment of special departments", "ex post facto evaluation of brand", and "clarification of target". It was difficult to evaluate from "combinations in organizations".

We think that there is flow from "information sharing and sending" and "collaboration with citizens" to "measurement of the effects" and "collaboration with organizations" in management levels of local government.

THE RELATIONSHIP BETWEEN THE IT PROGRESS STAGE AND THE MANAGEMENT LEVEL MODEL

In this section, we discuss the relationship between the IT progress stage and our management level model within four categories. Figure 5 illustrates these relationships.

All categories denote the difficulty to evaluation, which is achieved at less than 40%. The evaluation is set on the 4th stage of the IT progress stage. Therefore, it seems that there is the same flow in these categories of management and the e-transformation of local government.

At each category, organization reform flows from individuals (citizen collaboration) to evaluation and collaboration with other organizations. Personnel training flows from policy setting to evaluation and collaboration. Life safety flows from information sharing and setting to evaluation and carrying out preventative methods. These three categories are similar to the IT progress stage.

Only regional brands has two flows. The flows start at cooperation with others as Ingenuity in Practice (stage 3 of e-transformation). The one flow goes to evaluation, as stage 4, and the other flow goes to organization. The reverse flow of e-transformation exists on regional brands. The characteristics of the flow occur for the following reasons. The regional brands started from a local product or a local characteristic, which are not a product of the local government. The local government cannot choose a brand because of the strong commercial effect. However, newer

Figure 5. The relation between the IT progress stage and our management level model

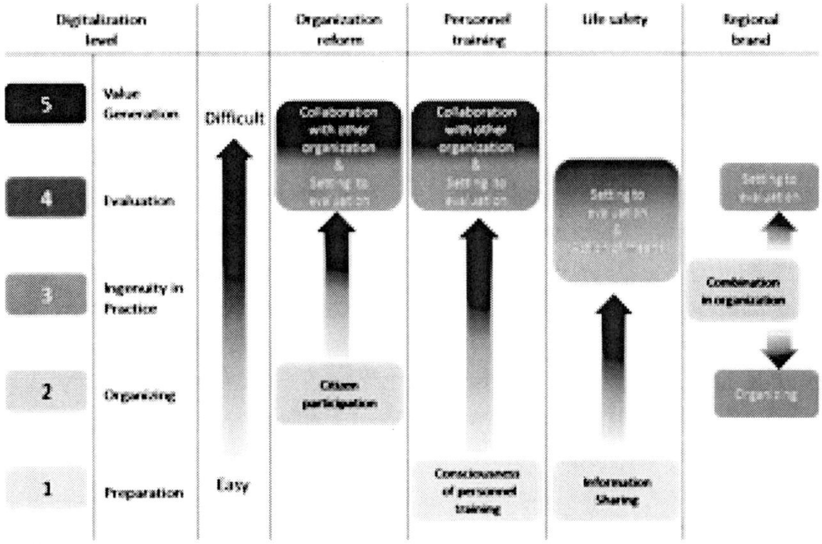

local government issues as regional brands have the collaboration of others, and they are closely positioned at "Value Generation".

Thus, these categories are important for the future management of local governments in that they have the possibility of becoming an essential factor in the future management of local government. Previously, e-transformation did not have such a connection to the management of local government. However, e-transformation has become a vital part of any type of management. There is a real possibility that e-transformation become the entire essence of management. At the least, we can say that the fundamental growth of the management levels of local governments are at least partially related to e-transformation.

The partial factor including these categories has the possibility of changing into essence of the entire management. We assume that we approach the essence of the entire management by creating management level models of these categories, and showing the relation to the model of e-transformation.

FUTURE RESEARCH DIRECTIONS

This study focused on the relationship between the IT progress stage model and the management level model for local government. Our analysis results indicated that management level is related to other progress models of e-transformation. For example, there is the common characteristic of organization reform at the flow from individual to organization. On the other hand, the characteristic of personnel training has a mirror flow. These results give new insight into management that is based on IT and ICT.

Several previous studies focused on profitability, IT equipment, or the number of participants, providing a limited index. These indexes provided validity in a limited range, but their generality was weak. It seems that these approaches, which explore the depths of management, are sufficiently effective to overcome the problem. It is important to find efficient indexes for management.

The categories of life safety and regional brands in this study are new topics in Japanese local government. Other topics indicating the efficiency of management will emerge in the future.

Future research based on this study should expand to include newer management issues, such as:

1. Organization reform should be expanded to estimate the effect and the flexibility against the reform.
2. Personnel training should be expanded to estimate training profit and the contribution of actual activity.
3. Life safety must consider citizen satisfaction for realizing management activity.
4. Regional brands must expand to evaluate the recognition of citizens of other regions and the advantages for other cities.
5. An index to indicate management range will also be required.

In addition, improvements to the wording of the questions in the survey are needed, so that they can be easily understood. With this survey, we should also consider financial situations and the effect of local activation on the management of local governments. Finally, we think that this research method will be appropriate for use in local governments of foreign nations.

CONCLUSION

In this study, we proposed a management level model for local governments. First, we analyzed previous studies on the progress stage by IT and ICT, and we denoted an IT progress stage model. The model had five stages:

Stage 1 is Preparation
Stage 2 is Organizing
Stage 3 is Ingenuity in Practice
Stage 4 is Evaluation
Stage 5 is Value Generation

We compared the stage model to models in previous studies and showed their relationship. Next, we analyzed an empirical survey, which consisted of the four categories "organization reform", "personnel training", "life safety", and "regional brands". We performed an analysis to clarify the management level. We denoted the flows of the management level in each category involved in our empirical questionnaire. The results of these flows involve the direction from individual to organization, and the other direction from office to collaboration. We denoted that multi-direction flows existed on the management level and that there were several common characteristics.

Furthermore, we compared the management level model and the IT progress stage model and discussed their relationship. We considered the following findings in this study:

1. There are the same flows in almost all categories of management level model and IT progress stage in local government.
2. "Organization reform", "personnel training", and "life safety" are similar to the IT progress stage.
3. Concretely, the most common characteristic is seen in the 4th stage (evaluation level).
4. Organization level is different among the management categories, but organization level provides an opportunity for improving management ability.

Using the above considerations, we denoted that this flow might be a factor for future management, promoting the specialization of organizations and expanding the range of stakeholders from citizens to local government. In addition, local government management requires both improvement of their services and IT progress stage. Our management model is an index for local governments to follow when implementing effective and efficient measures. Finally, we described that the future direction of our study is toward the local governments of foreign nations.

REFERENCES

Anttiroiko, A. V. (2003). Building strong e-democracy—The role of technology in developing democracy for the information age. *Communications of the ACM*, *46*(9), 121–128. doi:10.1145/903893.903926

Arnstein, S. R. (1969). A ladder of citizen participation. *JAIP*, *35*(4), 216–224.

Brynjolfsson, E., Hitt, L. M., & Shinkyu, Y. (2002). Intangible assets: Computers and organizational capital. *Brookings Papers on Economic Activity: Macroeconomics*, *1*, 137–198. doi:10.1353/eca.2002.0003

Carr, N. G. (2004). *Does IT matter?*Boston, MA: Harvard Business School Press.

Fujimoto, T. (2006). Architecture-based comparative advantage in Japan and Asia. *MMRC Discussion Paper, 94*, 1-8.

Kubo, S., & Shimada, T. (2007). Local e-governments in Japan: IT utilization status and directions. In Al-Hakim, L. (Ed.), *Global e-government theory, applications and benchmarking* (pp. 300–318). Hershey, PA: Idea Group Publishing.

Kubo, S., & Shimada, T. (2008a). An analysis based on the manufacturing architecture of the computerization of local governments in Japan. *CONF-IRM 2008 Proceedings.*

Kubo, S., & Shimada, T. (2008b). Model presenting the stages of progress of administrative services provided by e-local governments. *ICBI 2008 Proceeding.*

Mirvis, P., & Googins, B. (2006). Stages of corporate citizenship. *California Management Review*, *48*(2), 104–126.

Prime Minister of Japan and his Cabinet. (2001). *E-Japan strategy*. Retrieved February 23, 2010, from http:// www.kantei.go.jp/ foreign/ it/ network/ 0122full_e.html

Shimada, T., & Ushida, K. (2003). Electronic government in Japan: IT utilization status of local governments. In Gingrich, G. (Ed.), *Managing IT in government, business & communities* (pp. 111–126). Hershey, PA: IRM Press.

Yoshida, M., Kubo, S., & Shimada, T. (2003). Information sharing with citizens through the website of the local government. *Proceedings of the 31st Conference on Japan Association for Management Systems (in Japanese)*, (pp. 165-168).

Chapter 17
Broadband Infrastructures as a Common Service and the Role of Local Governments

Christos Bouras
University of Patras, Greece

Petros Ganos
Municipality of Patras, Greece

Vaggelis Kapoulas
Research Academic Computer Technology Institute, Greece

ABSTRACT

Broadband infrastructure is widely viewed as a major development driver. In addition, access to broadband networks is considered by many as a common service to be offered to all. This chapter presents interesting national strategies as well as practices and initiatives of municipalities for to broadband and next generation access networks. It, also, presents five scenarios for business models showing the way in which public agencies and the private sector may work together to offer fibre-to-the-home. Finally, it presents a case study of a Greek inter-municipal company emphasizing to the operating environment, the technical and economic factors, the results of financial analysis, and the assessment of sustainability.

INTRODUCTION

This chapter focuses on the role of the Local Governments/Authorities in the development of open access broadband infrastructures and their involvement in the management, operation, maintenance and expansion of the broadband networks. This role is emphasized through the concise presentation of most important national strategies and practices/initiatives of various municipalities. In addition five selected scenarios for business models on municipal broadband infrastructure exploitation are briefly described. A considerable part of this chapter is dedicated to the presentation of a Greek inter-municipal company which has as main task the holding, management, maintenance and expansion of passive equipment of broadband

DOI: 10.4018/978-1-60960-839-2.ch017

metropolitan networks installed in 24 participating Greek municipalities.

The term "broadband" means an advanced and innovative environment, from a social and technological view, which consists of fast network connections and appropriate network infrastructure for the development of new applications and services. Broadband in simple terms means a constant connection to the Internet without complicated settings, high speed (10-100 times the conventional connection) for new applications and reliable digital connections with guaranteed and consistent high performance. The provision of broadband services is now a key factor for improving the quality of life, education and economy. According to the i2010 (European Information Society 2010) initiative, broadband access is intended to stimulate the development of services, applications and content while providing a safe speed broadband access to Internet, modern online public services, electronic government (e-government), electronic learning services (e-learning), electronic health services (e-health), dynamic environment for electronic business (e-business), secure information infrastructure, mass availability of broadband access at competitive prices, benchmarking progress and dissemination of good practices.

The importance of broadband infrastructure is internationally confirmed by the activation of various advanced countries, which take initiatives to develop appropriate broadband infrastructure, adapt an alternative way to develop their economy and overcome any "technological blockades" of their citizens (Chlamtac, Gumaste, & Szabo, 2005). Next Generation Networks (NGNs) and Broadband infrastructure in general is a key element in the provisioning of e-government services to all citizens, which are both means and targets for the public sector reform. In addition the access to broadband infrastructure is increasingly recognized as a public good (common) and the local and national governments have the task of ensuring its proper and wide deployment.

Apart from providing basic services to citizens and businesses, a lot of local authorities have embraced the provision of broadband services to the list of their strategies as a means to the development of the local economy. There are various reasons and motives for which the local government decided to invest in broadband, whether to develop networks or provide services. The most important are: promotion of economic development, revenue increase of the municipality, services in remote and rural areas, e-government services, public security services, applications that make efficient routine services provided by municipalities (e.g. GIS) and projection of the municipal authority activities.

In general, a large number of Broadband Metropolitan Area Networks (BMAN) has been developed in municipalities along different parts of the globe, using the fibre optic technology as the "communication avenue" for the next decades. But to fully exploit the optic infrastructure and the benefits offered by broadband services, there is an urgent need for the creation of a group of cooperating partners allowing neutral management of broadband infrastructure, so as to ensure maintenance, expansion and most of all sustainability of these networks. Local governments internationally take a series of initiatives to provide broadband infrastructure, mainly optical fibre to each building. These initiatives address the broadband as a common and aim to ensure the connection of all buildings with fibre (FTTx), regardless of geographical distribution. The general term Fibre-to-the-x (FTTx), describes any architecture that uses fiber optics to replace part or all of the copper or other technologies to the local loop, and even to the buildings or homes (as is the case for FTTB and FTTH respectively). There are several variants such as FTTC: Fibre-to-the-Curb or Fibre-to-the-Cabinet where the optical fibre reaches up to the street cabinet that is near the subscribers' premises (typically approx up to 300m from the premises), FTTB: Fibre-to-the-Building, where the fibre reaches the entrance or boundary of a building, and FTTH: Fibre-to-the-Home, where the fibre reaches the individual homes /apartments of the subscribers. FTTP: Fibre-to-the-Premises is used as a blanket for FTTH and FTTB. (FTTH Council, 2009) has definitions for FTTH and FTTB, but no formal definitions for other variants of FTTx.

The chapter is organised as follows: Section 2 presents the broadband infrastructure as a common and the role of the local governments in supporting this common for the public good; Section 3 presents the national strategies of various countries to develop broadband infrastructures and international practices/initiatives undertaken by local authorities; Section 4 briefly presents the business models that can be used for the optimal exploitation of the Broadband Metropolitan Area Networks by local authorities; Section 5 presents the pertinent activities taken by a consortium of municipalities in Southwest Greece as a case study.

BROADBAND AS A COMMON (COMMODITY)

The recent times, a movement is growing for the protection and support the commons of the 21st century. The commons, seen as an economic sector, complements corporations and their commercial economic activity, and come to a balance with them (Tomales Bay Institute). Therefore, it is expected that in the long run economies will be influenced by the proper management, use and evolution of the commons. An active commons sector can help with the reduction of inequalities and contribute to the improvement of the quality of life.

The New Commodities of the 21st Century

When referring to the commodities, most people only think about the traditional commons, usually offered by nature, such as air, water, forests, meadows, beaches, public spaces etc.

However in our era, there are also new goods, made possible by the evolution and use technology, that a growing movement thinks that can and should be considered as commons, see e.g. (Berra, 2006). Examples are the free distribution of the results of creative works, software, digital content, infrastructure to provide access to the Internet etc. The recent years broadband infrastructures, Wi-Fi access, access to fibre-to-the-home/building (FTTH/B) infrastructures, and use of the frequencies reallocated by the transition to digital television for public wireless networking (i.e. unlicensed use of the freed "white space") have been added to the list of the new commons.

True to this new way of thinking, several local and regional administrations, organisation and even groups of individuals have gone on and implemented open access wireless (Wi-Fi) networks in numerous cities around the world.

Broadband Access and Broadband Infrastructures as a Common

Broadband is considered by several nations (especially the developed ones) as the infrastructure of the 21st century. This pertains to the effects that broadband has and the advantages it offers on education, development, economy, public administration, research, innovation, leisure, and in general on all those aspects that constitute the well fare and progress of a community.

Given that almost everybody recognises the opportunities broadband offers and the benefits it brings, it is not unexpected that many formed the opinion that the access to broadband infrastructures should be a common and it should be offered to all citizens.

Broadband has often been seen as the roads, the canals, the railroads and the interstate highways of the Information Age, and its foreseen impact has often been compared to the impact of electricity and the electric grid deployment.

The Role of Local Governments

Although, a large number of local governments wireless deployed municipal networks to offered broadband access to their citizens, wireless networks cannot offer very high capacity in a large scale, cannot support all the forthcoming broadband services (such as high definition IPTV), and are not suitable for a true broadband experience.

Therefore, a need arises to have modern infrastructures that can scale to large numbers while still providing adequate capacity to each home/building not only for today's but also for tomorrow's applications. This infrastructure is fibre-to-the-home/building (FTTH/B).

Deploying an FTTH/B access network is not an easy task, and for some cases it is not economically viable. This is the reason that the private telecommunication companies has not yet undertook such tasks in large scales (and when they did it was only for specific areas where the task was deemed viable).

However, as already mentioned, FTTH/B is increasingly seen by local governments as an infrastructure that must be build for all and as an opportunity that cannot be missed, both because the infrastructure can be considered as common and because it is a means for economic development.

In places where building an FTTx infrastructure with wide coverage is not seen as viable and the private sector is reluctant to invest, there is a clear role for the local government to support and facilitate, and possibly (co-)invest in the deployment of such networks.

That does not mean, of course, that local governments should be elevated to telecom operators. Their role only lies in facilitating the deployment of open access infrastructure and ensuring that all can use them to offer telecommunication services.

There are several ways that local government can be involved in the deployment of FTTH/B networks, ranging from just enabling and facilitating other to do it to building and a totally public network. But in most cases a more balanced approach is used where the public and private sector partner to build the FTTH/B infrastructure.

INTERNATIONAL EXPERIENCE AND PRACTICES/INITIATIVES

National Strategies for Broadband

The importance of Broadband internationally is affirmed from the initiatives and activities of various countries to develop broadband infrastructures. Several countries start to treat broadband infrastructures as a utility (which pertains to the view that broadband infrastructures should be considered a common).

In several developed countries the deployment of high-speed broadband infrastructures is a main strategic target, and there are provisions both for the regulatory frame work and for the co-finance of the various plans and initiatives. An indicative list of summaries of the strategies for various countries follows.

The federal government of the United States of America stimulates the development of broadband infrastructures at a federal level, by loans and grants for broadband infrastructure projects in rural areas, and grants to fund broadband infrastructure, public computer centres and sustainable broadband adoption projects.

In Canada, as part of the Economic Action Plan, there is funding for strategy to deploy broadband coverage to as much un-served or under-served households, as possible (Canada's Economic Action Plan). The scope of the plan is to extend broadband coverage to all underserved communities, and the financing approach is to encourage the private sector to develop rural broadband infrastructure (Qiang 2009).

The Australian Government announced a project of AU$ 43bn to build a FTTP (fibre-to-the-premises) network to 90% of the country's buildings (Australia's broadband plan). To this end Australian Government established NBN Co Limited to design, build and operate the wholesale-only National Broadband Network (NBN). The NBN will provide the infrastructure that will allow wholesale and retail service providers to deliver advanced digital services. NBN will be a wholesale-only, open-access network, and it provide equal, wholesale access, to all retailers. Australia invites the private sector to participate in NBN, but private ownership is apped at 49%. The plan is to connect 90% of all Australian premises with fibre and the rset 10% with next generation wireless and satellite networks (Qiang 2009). In June 20101 NBN and Telstra (the incumbent telecommunication provider) reached an agreement that Telstra would provide NBN access to its facilities, and Telstra's traffic will progressively migrate onto the National Broadband Network (subject to regulatory approval). This agreement can maximise the use of existing infrastructure and accelerate the roll out of the NBN, and means that Telstra is likely to become NBN Co's largest customer providing greater certainty about the future of NBN.

The New Zealand intents to invest NZ$ 1,5bn (apart from the private investments) to build a FFTP network, that would cover 75% of the country (New Zealand Government, 2009).

In South Korea there is a mid- to long-term plan to develop the Broadband Convergence Network (BcN) with 1Gbit/s for wired connections (Korea Communication Commission). The plan aims to help South Korea strengthen its position as one of the world leading countries in IT, by increasing broadband speeds ten-fold by year 2012 (Qiang 2009).

France, with its plan France Numérique 2012 (Digital France 2012), aims at equipping all house holds with Internet connections, while telecommunication suppliers offer FTTH solutions in urban areas (Preparing 'Digital France 2012'). France has a developed regulatory setting for the provision of access to fibre optic cables, and has been the first European country to adopt rules for fibre optic cables in buildings (Bourreau, Cambini & Hoernig, 2010). In ARCEP (2008) duct access is imposed on the incumbent operator, while in ARCEP (2009) the conditions of access to fibre inside buildings in very dense areas is detailed. France has put a strong focus on very dense areas hoping for a development of competition in infrastructure (Bourreau, Cambini & Hoernig, 2010). For the rural and suburban areas there are concerns; either that the areas will not be covered with fibre, or that there will be duplication of networks with viability. Recently the French government launched a consultation on a national program for high-speed broadband (DGCIS 2010) and plans to spend 2 billion Euros to accelerate fibre deployment. Public support is envisioned in two forms: Through public loans for projects in "viable" zones, and through direct state aid for "less viable" zones (Bourreau, Cambini & Hoernig, 2010).

In Germany, Deutsche Telecom rolled out fibre to the street cabinets to offer VDSL service to large German cities. Initially, the relevant regulatory authority (Bundesnetzagentur) did not want to force Deutsche Telecom to allow access to its fibre access network to competitors. However, the European commission, filed an action against Germany which required that Bundesnetzagentur mandate subsidiary access to ducts (and when space in the ducts is not available, to unused dark fibre) so that competitors can roll out their own fibre network. Deutsche Telecom attributes its hesitation to roll out additional fibre network to this mandates subsidiary access (Czernich, et al. 2009). However, the federal government of Germany, with its Breitbandstrategie (Broadband strategy), calls for 50 Mbit/s connections to 75% of the population by the end of 2014 (Breitbandstrategie).

In the United Kingdom, the Digital Britain report set the objective of broadband connections to all house holds, of at least 2 Mbit/s by the end of 2012 (Digital Britain – the report). In mid 2008 British Telecom announced that it will roll out

FTTC for 7-10 million households by 2012 (Ofcom 2008). Ofcom, the relevant regulatory authority, considers British Telecom obliged to provide access to the copper wire at the street cabinet, where it deploys FTTC, and obligates it to allow fibre or wavelength unbundling, or duct access whet it deploys FTTH (Czernich, et al. 2009).

Finland has become the first country in the world to make broadband a legal right for every citizen. From July 1st 2010, every Finn will have the right to access to a 1Mbps broadband connection. The Finnish law means that all telecommunications companies will be obliged to provide all residents with broadband lines that can run at a minimum 1Mbps speed. Finland has plans to connect everyone to a 100Mbps connection by 2016, and it plans to foot one-third of the cost of building a fibre optic network in areas that are underserved (Qiang 2009).

In Greece, the government studies the feasibility of co-funding (in a public-private partnership scheme) an FTTH access network that could cover up 2 million households in the (if not all) major cities (more than 50) of the country (Strategy for electronic communications and new technologies 2008 - 2013).

The Netherlands has a well developed broadband access market. There is strong infrastructure competition between the dominant telephony provider and the cable providers which reach more than 94% of the households (Czernich, et al. 2009, Kirsch & von Hirschhausen 2008). The incumbent operator (KPN) had plans to replace part of its network with fibre rolled out to street cabinets or to homes. The regulatory authority (OPTA) imposed regulatory obligation to KPN so that competitors would not lose interconnection. Also, with interventions in the regulatory framework, it encourages investments for FTTH networks that would cover all country (OPTA 2008).

Portugal took steps to regulate duct (and other infrastructure able to carry fibre) access by imposing it to all telecom operators as well as other public and owned by the state entities. This way it significantly increased the number of ducts available to telecom operators for fibre deployment. In addition Portugal in order to facilitate fibre deployment in the rural interior of the country launched public contest for subsidies for the construction and operation of "open" Next Generation Networks (NGNs) in a number of different regions. The novelty of the competition is that he winners in each region will have to apply for state aid (with a significant part handed out by the EU). This allowed the contest to progress while the guideline for the state aid procedures where still under consultation. However, the rules of the contest conform to the state aid legality as outlined in the EC's guidelines. Furthermore, the Portuguese state committed itself to the creation of a 800 million Euros credit line for NGN construction as part of agreement with telecom operators to invest 1 billion Euros and help combat the economic crisis (Bourreau, Cambini & Hoernig, 2010).

Italy does not seem to have a clear national strategy for the deployment of NGNs, as the Italian government facing problem with the deficit, has suspended its commitment to provide subsidies to spur investment in broadband connections. As a result many Italian telecom operators turned to signing agreements with local governments and municipalities to extend broadband coverage in areas where the return on investment is considered low or non-existent (Bourreau, Cambini & Hoernig, 2010).

It should be noted that, similarly to what Katz (2000) argues, applying different policies strategies to different countries and/or areas may allow policy makers to understand what works and what does not. Bourreau, Cambini & Hoernig (2010) argue that this kind of "experimentation" is called for and it might be efficient to allow different countries to follow different routes in the early phases of the deployment of large scale fibre networks.

Most countries with a high broadband penetration rate focus on the preservation and increase of this rate, but mostly on the increase of the quality and the speed of the broadband connections (e.g. by focusing on fibre optic connections) and the increase of the coverage to up to the whole population of the country.

The European Union is considering making high-speed Internet access compulsory; i.e. obliging member states to provide or ensure nation wide broadband coverage. This line of thinking come from the fact that existing infrastructure in the countryside does not provide as wide coverage as in urban areas.

Both as part of the above considerations, an as part of the Economic Recovery Plan, the EU wants to effectively involve the local and regional authorities in the deployment of new broadband infrastructures as to ensure that no community in rural areas is left behind.

In addition, in several countries, independent of the national strategy for the deployment of NGNs and fibre optic infrastructure there is an involvement of the regional and local authorities in relevant issues; either in developing the policy and strategy to be adopted (especially in rural and suburban areas), or in seeking subsidies, or in forming partnerships with telecom operators, etc.

Therefore, not only there is a role for the local governments in the plans to deploy broadband infrastructures, but the local governments are actually expected to assume this role and pursue their plans to offer access to broadband infrastructure to their citizens.

Broadband Practices and Initiatives of Various Municipalities

This section describes some example practices and initiatives, undertaken by some municipalities (with or without the involvement of private entities), both in European and international level, which are aimed at deploying and exploiting fibre optic network infrastructure.

A lot of municipalities all over the world have already recognised their role in the broadband scene and have already been involved in the successful deployment of high speed optical networks. Their practices now constitute examples that may be followed by other municipalities. Several other municipalities are deploying or expanding their broadband infrastructures and a sufficient number of them are planning to do so. As all the cases are numerous to present here, we mention only a few representative cases that attracted a lot of attention.

Stockholm – Stokab

Stokab is a fibre optic network deployed in the area of the municipality of Stockholm. Stokab was built by the company group Stockholms Stadshus AB, owned by the City of Stockholm (Dobers, 1999; Stokab in english).

The development of the fibre-optic network was started in 1994 in the commercial districts of inner-city Stockholm, and was thereafter extended to the major industrial areas of Stockholm. Now, there are interurban networks to all municipalities in the County of Stockholm, to Uppsala, parts of the archipelago, to some of the municipalities in the Mälar region via Mälarringen and also to Gotland. This network comprises 5,600 kilometres of cable and in total 1,200,000 kilometres of fibre (Stokab in english - The infrastructure).

The company is competition-neutral and provides a network that is open to all players on equal terms (Stokab in english - About Stokab).

Amsterdam

The local authorities in the city of Amsterdam realised, early enough, that the existing communication networks were not enough to satisfy the ever increasing telecommunication demands of the citizens. In 2000, some low-income housing complexes in the city connected to the fiber optic network that was developed by a Swedish company. Then there was the fact that, whereas previously these buildings attracted mainly foreign immigrants, after connecting with FTTH network, they became an attraction for young professionals. Following that observation, the city realised the importance of the fibre optic network infrastructure. When the negotiations with telecommunication providers were fruitless, the city of Amsterdam proceeded to the formation of a public-private partnership, called GNA, to build a fibre optic network (Citynet Amsterdam; Sadowski, Nucciarelli, & Rooij, 2009).

The city of Amsterdam participates in the first phase of the deployment of the network with 20% of the budget. The network has open access architecture and the consortium GNA does not fix the retail prices, because it uses only the passive part of the network. Each provider will determine retail prices and features of the services provided to households and businesses. According to the design, the network will connect the total of 420,000 homes in the city and all businesses. In mid-2009 the second phase of the network began, covering 100,000 optic connections.

LocalRet

LocalRet (or Local Network for Catalonian Municipalities) is a consortium of municipalities, created in 1998, aiming at providing cable TV services to 800 municipalities in Catalonia. Since then its aim changed to include the deployment of broadband infrastructures.

The main aim is to create the necessary network infrastructure by the public sector and maintain this network infrastructure as the property of the public sector. The role of the involved authorities (LocalRet) is to create an organisation to manage this project and to promote broadband in Catalonia.

The government of Catalonia has the necessary resources to build the network even without the help of the central Spanish government. Once completed, the network will provide open access to all at competitive (cost-oriented) prices. The plan is to initially offer only passive network connections (dark fibre); other communication services will be also offered later (Cook Network Consultants 2005).

Wien

According to the plan for the Fiber to the Premises (FTTP) infrastructure in the city of Wien (Broadband Properties; FTTH in Vienna to all households), there will be connections of 1 Gbit/s to 1 million households. The project, which has already started, is implemented by a consortium of the municipality of Wien with Wienstrom (energy provider) and Wienkanal (cable provider). The consortium does not aim at creating a monopoly, but rather an open network where all service providers will have access on equal terms.

Interestingly, where in other cities the fibre-optic network is built as GPON (Gigabit Passive Optical Network), and the capacity of one fibre cable is shared between several households, the network in Wien uses one separate fibre connection per households and implements active Ethernet infrastructure.

Utah: UTOPIA

The Utah Telecommunication Open Infrastructure Agency (UTOPIA) is a consortium of cities in Utah, USA, responsible for the deployment and operation of a FTTP network that connects all enterprises and households in the participating cities. The access provided is 1 Gbit/s for enterprises and 100 Mbit/s for households.

The network, UTOPIA Community MetroNet, is built in three phases, with the first phase concluding and the second phase beginning. The business model used is that of the open wholesale access. Several services providers have already been selected, and UTOPIA seeks to co-operate with other providers for offering retail services. UTOPIA does not dictate the prices for the retail services, as it is just a wholesale provider. Every retail service provider defines the characteristics of the service offered as well as the price. UTO-

Table 1. Characteristics of practices/initiatives for fibre optic infrastructures by some municipalities

Characteristics	Stokab	Amsterdam	LocalRet	Wien	UTOPIA
Local Government	X	X	X	X	
Private Sector		X			
Joint Venture		X	X		X
Dark Fiber Network	X	X	X	X	X
Last Mile Connections		X		X	X
Government Funding		X	X	X	X
Private Support		X			
Collocation Facilities	X		X		
Rental to telecom providers	X		X	X	X
Services Provision	X (municipal services)			X	

PIA financed the network with a loan to be paid back by the income of the network (UTOPIA Feasibility Study).

Review of Practices and Initiatives

The following table (Table 1) presents the characteristics of the cases discussed in this section.

The examples above indicate that there is a variety of approaches that a local government can follow in order to support the deploying of a high speed broadband network within its area. These approaches range from building a neutral infrastructure financed and owned by local government, to co-investing usually through the formation of public-private partnerships, to just mediating and facilitating the private sector to build the broadband infrastructure.

However, in most cases, the local governments form a kind of cooperation with the private sector. This happens because, in most cases, and especially in rural areas, such an investment is not justified for the private sector, and some public funding is needed. Similarly, in most cases the local government or the public sector in general, cannot dispose the whole fund for such a big project. Therefore, in most cases the way forward is to form a public-private partnership that can stand on the fund (both public and private) to build the infrastructure. In this case the partnership leases the infrastructure to network or service providers in order to balance the investment.

Also in most cases, the infrastructure is neutral, which means that it is available to reasonable price to all that request it, including service providers that may offer their services (including Internet access) to the citizens. This is usually a requirement for the building of the broadband infrastructure due to the public co-financing. In order to ensure fair competition, the infrastructure has to remain neutral and be offered at a cost-oriented rate to all.

BROADBAND BUSINESS MODELS

In literature, several business models for the exploitation of broadband infrastructure have been presented. Four representative papers with collected information are (Troulos, Merekoulias, & Maglaris, 2009; Kyriakidou, Chipouras, Katsianis, & Sphicopoulos, 2009; Alexiou, Bouras, Primpas, & Papagiannopoulos, 2008; Bouras, Gkamas, Theofilopoulos, & Tsiatsos, 2008). Figure 1 shows the three main levels of a well known business model (Hughes, 2003):

- The first level determines who (a private or public enterprise, etc.) exploits the net-

Figure 1. The basic levels of a business model

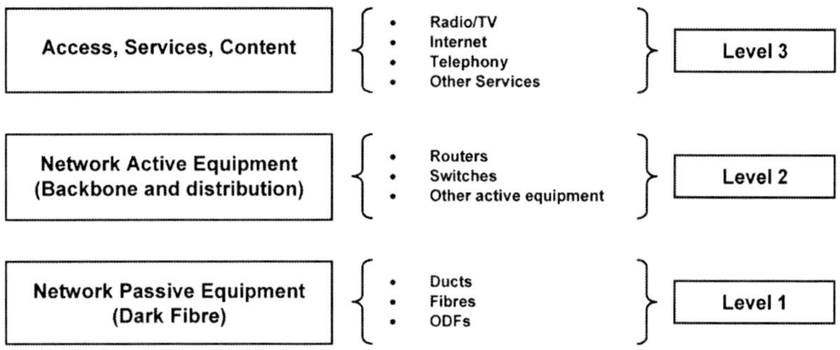

work's passive equipment (channels, optical fibres etc.).

- The second level determines who provides and exploits the active equipment of the network (switches, routers etc.).
- The third level determines who offers access to the network, the services and the content.

A table detailing the characteristics, advantages and disadvantages (with reference to Figure 1) of the main local and regional models for broadband deployment is given in (Bouras, Gkamas, Papagiannopoulos, Theofilopoulos, & Tsiatsos, 2009).

Scenarios for Business Models

Based on Figure 1 five scenarios for business models, that are presented in (Bouras, Gkamas, Theofilopoulos, & Tsiatsos, 2008), are briefly described. These scenarios show how public agencies and private providers of infrastructure, equipment and services may work together to benefit of the end user.

Scenario 1: Equal Access

The objective of this scenario is to ensure equal access to the passive network equipment. Specifically:

- At the first level the operating entity provides the passive network equipment in a cost-oriented manner to the provider of active equipment. Because of that, the entity must be a utility company or a municipal authority (in the form of a public, non-profit company).
- At the second level many providers are involved who offer the active network equipment.
- At the third level there are also many service providers who operate in competitive and offer broadband services to users.

Scenario 2: Full Public Control Through Public – Private Partnerships (PPPs)

This scenario involves the local government in all parts of the broadband network (passive infrastructure, active infrastructure and services). This ensures the State intervention and control at all levels, through State participation in joint ventures of public and private sector.

Scenario 3: Public-Private Partnerships – PPPs orchestrated

In this scenario a public - private consortium is created for the control of the passive network equipment and the provided services. In this consortium, the local government is involved with a small percentage, usually less than 20%, while the other participants are private entities and companies. The active part of the network is owned and managed exclusively by a private company.

Scenario 4: Public Sector Telco

In this scenario the objective is the use of passive and active part of the network by a public utility. Specifically:

- In the first and second level a utility company or a municipal authority (in the form of a public, non-profit enterprise) operates, which provides the passive and active network equipment.
- The third level involves many private companies which operate competitively, offering broadband services to users.

Scenario 5: Sole Private Provider

In this model, the active network equipment, network management and services are provided by a single private provider. A public body (e.g. a municipality) owns the passive network equipment.

Business Model for the Greek Case

In (Bouras *et al.* 2009), the most appropriate business model for the effective exploitation of the broadband metropolitan area networks in Greece is proposed. According to this model, the network's passive equipment is proposed to be public, while competition exists among private companies in the two upper levels (services and active equipment). The main objectives of the proposed business model are the following:

- The passive network infrastructure may be used by a large number of service providers.
- The users have the choice of selecting one of the multiple service providers, according to their needs.
- Management of the infrastructure is performed by a neutral operator.
- Low operational expenditure (OPEX) and capital expenditure (CAPEX) are ensured.
- Financial viability of all parts of the infrastructure is secured.

Also in the same reference, table 3 shows the relevant stakeholders, roles, costs (Capital Expense - CAPEX and Operation Expense - OPEX) and the revenues in each layer (services, active network equipment and passive network equipment).

CASE STUDY OF A GREEK INTER-MUNICIPAL COMPANY

Operating Environment and Main Objectives

The need for broadband access in Greece is as given just as in other countries. The advantages of the spread and use of new technologies will be an essential tool for open and effective governance and the improvement of business competitiveness. Although considerable efforts have been made in recent years, Greece lags significantly in an advanced telecommunications infrastructure and provision of modern and advanced network services to its citizens. In Greece the provision of broadband services is now a key factor in improving the quality of life, education and economy. But to fully exploit the benefits offered by broadband services, it is necessary the installation of optic infrastructure and the construction of metropolitan broadband fibre optic networks.

Large cities of Greece have approved proposals in the Operational Program "Information Society" through the calls 93, 145 and 195, for building metropolitan broadband fibre optic networks with the basic objective of linking the buildings of public interest (Bouras, Papagiannopoulos, Katsikas, & Gritzalis, 2008). The need to establish and operate a new regional form for the proper operation and further development of metropolitan networks in Greek regions main stems from the fact that the developed broadband infrastructure in these areas are diffused and have no interconnection. These networks are essentially independent islets of fibre infrastructure, thereby creating both an unattractive business model and also limited possibilities for future use. The issue that deserves special attention is the way of use and further development of these metropolitan fibre optic networks. The proposal to establish an inter-municipal company faces the broadband as an infrastructure, which means that it should be offered as a public good, without any exclusion. A key to the success of this proposal is the local government (Bouras *et al.*, 2007).

On the initiative of the Municipality of Patras an Inter-municipal Company of Broadband Network of Southwest Greece (summary IBC: Inter-municipal Broadband Company) was created to support broadband infrastructure that was developed throughout the southwest axis of Greece and especially in the regions of Western Greece, Ionian Islands, Epirus and Peloponnesus. Figure 2 shows a map of the 24 participating municipalities.

The task of IBC is the holding, management, maintenance and expansion (in various stages) of passive equipment (physical layer) of broadband metropolitan networks of 24 participating municipalities. The IBC has a dual role:

- The supervision of management and maintenance of the network
- The supervision and planning of network expansion

The company's foundation has obvious advantages that have to do with central planning in relation to the maintenance, operation and expansion of networks in the wider area of Southwest Greece. Therefore, with this approach, competition among telecommunications providers and service providers ensures benefit to the consumer. Telecommunications providers will have available cheap passive infrastructure on equal terms. The provision of passive infrastructure reduces costs in the required initial investment, resulting in greater number of active telecommunications providers. Competition among service providers is ensured by the fact that they have the option to choose between telecommunications providers as a platform for their services. The construction of metropolitan fibre optic networks in conjunction with the disposal of broadband services is expected to promote healthy competition in bodies, companies and businesses. In particular, the expected indirect effects are:

- Improvement of the functionality of public sector and particularly in the areas of health, education and public administration.
- Stimulation of competition and growth of entrepreneurship in the region.
- Reduction of the factors discouraging investment in the region by private companies.

IBC has an organizational scheme which allows centrally monitoring of fibre optic networks and also the provision some of the company activities as a sub-contract (outsourcing) to legal entities of public or private sector. The funding sources of the proposed company could be found among private investment, the NSRF (National Strategic Reference Framework) and the Greek development law. Also another funding source can be Standard Innovative Development Projects which will be exploited through Global Grants (www.ggea.gr/globalgrants).

The long term goal of IBC is the global creation of broadband infrastructure. In particular:

- The interconnection of broadband networks that were created under the calls 93,

Figure 2. Municipalities participating in the IBC

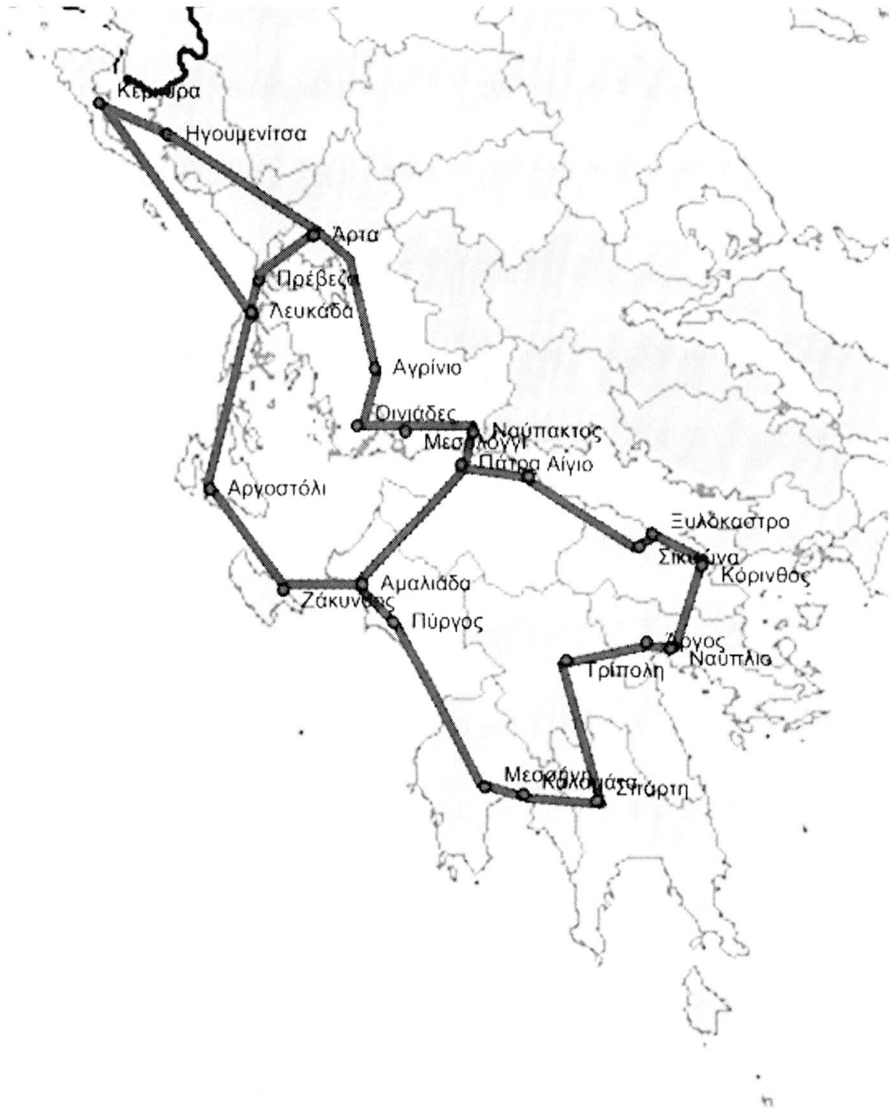

145 and 195 in the region of Southwest Greece.

- The expansion of broadband networks created under the calls 93, 145 and 195 in Southwest Greece with a view to providing fibre to the final user (Fibre To The x - FTTx).
- The provision of broadband access with Wi-Fi, WiMax technologies for remote users.

TECHNO-ECONOMIC STUDY

The Patras Municipality, which is the third largest city of Greece and the owner of the longest fibre optic network (through the above calls), commissioned the University of Patras to prepare a techno-economic study. The ultimate goal of this study is to find the optimal business model to ensure the sustainability of the metropolitan networks and fully exploit the offered possibilities. In the following paragraphs an executive summary and major results of this study are presented.

In the four Greek regions considered in the study, a major infrastructure of metropolitan broadband fibre optic networks has already been developed in 24 municipalities. The total length of routes is 376.157 km. In the regions of these municipalities the indexes of use the Internet and broadband penetration are in general lower than the national averages, while in the considered 24 urban areas these indexes are higher than the ones of the corresponding region. Also in these urban areas optical fibre infrastructures have been developed by various private telecommunication companies (OTE, OTEGlobe, HoL, Tellas etc.).

For the involvement of local authorities in the development of broadband infrastructure, there are many business models (Bouras, Gkamas, Papagiannopoulos, Theofilopoulos, & Tsiatsos, 2009). But in no way the purpose of local authorities should be to become a telecommunications provider. The ultimate objective of the local government regarding its involvement in the provision of broadband services should be the creation of an open competitive environment in which access and services will be offered by many providers. This reduces the cost of provided services for citizens and businesses and promotes the development of advanced and high quality services. The investment in the passive infrastructure of a network is long and, although it requires large capital investment at the beginning, has long life-cycle of the order of twenty years. It can be considered a low risk investment with a payback period of 15 to 20 years.

Regarding the technological side and having regard to long-term planning to cover all citizens, broadband infrastructure that can meet the demands of the future is the one of optical fibre based on architecture FTTH (or temporarily FTTB) and specially the architecture Point – to – Point. This architecture authorizes the activation of many service providers and thus creates competition in service provision. Another advantage of such infrastructure is its relatively easy expandability.

In Greece, there are some initiatives to public sector involvement in Next Generation Access Networks. It is remarkable the Greek State plan to create FTTH network in two million households. Also the proposal of the Central Union of Municipalities and Communities indicates the immediate integration and operation of fibre optic networks of local authorities. In this context, regional forms have been created by municipalities trying to promote the utilization of their optical infrastructure. Four initiatives are these of the Municipalities of Central Greece, the Municipalities of Kriti and Aegean Sea, the Municipalities of East Macedonia and Thraki and the 24 Municipalities of Western Greece, Epirus, Ionian Islands, and Peloponnesus. At the same time throughout the Greek territory, there are two large public networks, SYZEFXIS and Greek School Network. SYZEFXIS (www.syzefxis.gov.gr) is a project of Greek Ministry of the Interior, Public Administration and Decentralization, which aims at the development and updating of Public Sector's telecom infrastructure. It's about a core and access network for the Public Sector's organizations aiming to satisfy all their needs for communication through Telephony (telephone communication between organizations), Data (PC's communication - Internet) and Video (teleconference - training). The Greek School Network (GSN - www.sch.gr) is the educational intranet of the Ministry of Education and Religious Affairs (www.ypepth.gr), which interlinks all schools and provides basic and advanced telematics' services. Thus, it contributes to the creation of a new generation of educational communities, which takes advantage of the new Informatics' and Communication Technologies in the educational procedure. These two networks have many common physical points with the Metropolitan Broadband Networks, while optic infrastructure covers additional points of public interest. Therefore, these two large public networks can be extended and improve their provided services by the use of the municipal optic infrastructure.

SUMMARY AND RESULTS OF FINANCIAL ANALYSIS

For the financial analysis some initial considerations - assumptions were used that are considered necessary for the calculations. These are the following:

- The construction cost of the optical fibre network per kilometre is equal to 50,000 €/km.
- The maintenance cost of the optical fibre network per kilometre is equal to 2% of construction cost per kilometre thus equal to 1,000 €/km.
- The average length of the optical loop (from network distributor to telecommunications centre) is equal to 1.3 km.
- Assuming that at least two providers will undertake action in the local area and request the use of the network, the estimated average number of optical pairs rented per cable is equal to 1.5.
- The period of depreciation is equal to 25 years.
- The fixed charge for the provision of any new connection is equal to 1.500 €.

Also the following data are taken into account:

- The total population of the involved 24 municipalities is equal to 729,770.
- The total of the public sector points for the 24 municipalities is 629, while 598 connections will gradually be activated (relocation of some public points).
- The total of the educational and research points for the 24 municipalities is 418.
- The total length of the optical infrastructure for the 24 municipalities is 376.157 km.

Based on these initial considerations and assumptions the following initial variables can be calculated:

- The construction cost of the optical loop (from network distributor to telecommunications centre) is equal to 50,000 € / km x 1.3 km = 65,000 €.
- The annual construction cost of the optical loop is equal to 65,000 € / 25 years = 2,600 €.
- The total annual cost or equivalently charge (construction and maintenance) of the optical loop is equal to (2,600 € + 1,000 €) / 1.5 = 2,400 €.
- The total monthly cost or equivalently charge of the optical loop is equal to 3,600 € / 1.5 / 12 = 200 €.

The financial analysis was based on the above assumptions leading to the calculation of basic critical operation elements of IBC for five years, which are shown in the following table (Table 2).

Figure 3 shows the cash flow of IBC.

The above analysis results that the IBC shows positive financial flows from the year 2014. The above does not mean that the IBC will be profitable by the year 2014 as there are negative financial flows in previous years which have to be covered. But it means that, IBC with positive financial flows from 2014 onwards may reach the point where the total (cumulative) income will be equal to the total (cumulative) cost (break-even point). Therefore, although the creation of the IBC does not seem attractive in the short term, the analysis shows that there is a basis for its sustainability.

However, the above analysis focused on basic initial assumptions such as the fact that at least two providers operating in the region will be in-

Table 2. Basic financial elements for the operation of IBC

	2010	2011	2012	2013	2014
Revenue	**629.601 €**	**877.988 €**	**1.052.315 €**	**1.162.785 €**	**1.245.331 €**
Marketing costs	12.592 €	17.560 €	21.046 €	23.256 €	24.907 €
Selling, General and Administrative Expenses (SG & A)	614.372 €	624.985 €	675.436 €	723.742 €	731.095 €
Earnings Before Interest, Taxes, Depreciation and Amortization (EBITDA)	**2.637 €**	**235.444 €**	**355.832 €**	**415.787 €**	**489.329 €**
Depreciation	403.584 €	597.127 €	831.324 €	579.500 €	521.832 €
Earnings Before Interest and Taxes (EBIT)	-400.948 €	-361.684 €	-475.492 €	-163.713 €	-32.503 €

terested to purchase pairs of optical fibre. Also, we considered that some of the connections to be requested will require constructions of network expansion. Cases such as these affect the process of the company and its results.

The main objective of the business plan was to keep the company operating costs low. However, the revenue guarantee is a parameter which sets the project in risk. This concerns the demand from private providers and the accounting or actual income from the public bodies. To make the whole project much more attractive, company costs have to be reduced, while revenue has to be increased. One way to achieve this is through scale economy if the range of metropolitan fibre optic networks is not limited to those considered in the present study (Western Greece, Epirus, Ionian Islands and Peloponnesus). The management of many more networks would allow first the distribution of less construction costs per km and second the negotiation in better terms of maintenance cost which could be reduced to 1.5% or even lower (by 2% estimated in this study). Also, the overall discussions and negotiations with providers for the use of broadband metropolitan optical fibre networks would be done in better terms. These negotiations could lead to initial agreements that would allow more precise calculation of the connections, removing the uncertainty that put the initial assumptions and the possible redefinition of the cost of each connection at most attractive price. The last would increase the possible sales to other stakeholders.

ASSESSMENT OF SUSTAINABILITY

The implementation of fibre optic networks results in different risks, which may be economic and/or technological. To study the economic risks, the

Figure 3. The cash flow of IBC

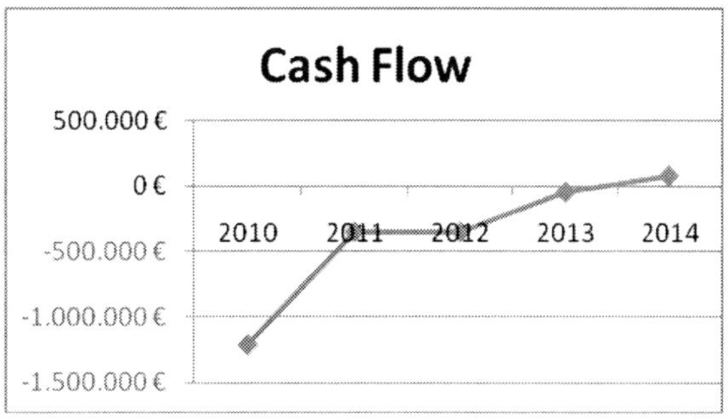

implementation of the network has to be separated into two sections, the implementation of passive optical network infrastructure (the subject of the IBC) and the implementation of active network equipment and services which, according to the business model proposed for the IBC, will provide competition from other private companies.

The implementation of passive infrastructure likes enough to the establishment of public good infrastructure (such as water supply or electricity). It is a long term investment, which requires large capital investment at the beginning of the project and has a long lifecycle. A typical lifecycle of a passive infrastructure is at least 20 years and can be considered an investment, which will be repaid over 15-20 years. The creation of a passive optical network infrastructure is considered as a public good and for that reason it should be supervised to ensure global access and low cost to end-users. To ensure this, the building process of broadband infrastructure usually receives support from the government (as in the calls of Operational Programs) and especially through the financing of infrastructure in areas which are expected to be not profitable or low profit. These infrastructures are considered low-risk financial investments (in terms of investment in active equipment and services) and are attractive to investors who are interested in long-term safe investment.

On the other side, the investment in active broadband equipment and services is a high tech investment with significantly lower life-cycle (around 5-7 years). This investment adds value to citizens and businesses and enables higher profits, but the financial risk is significantly greater than the implementation of passive infrastructure. Therefore, the loans that finance the installation of active equipment and development services are considerably more expensive.

The above reinforce the policy followed by the IBC in which the management of passive infrastructure is separated by the active equipment and development of services. With this practice, lower cost is provided and the financial risk is shared among large (for the active equipment and services) and low (for the passive infrastructure).

The disadvantages and potential risks of the policy of IBC include the fact that substantial investment by network providers and internet service providers for the provision of related services are required. Given that the investment required by the providers is a relatively risky, this may lead to the fact that some metropolitan optical networks may not be considered particularly attractive by the providers. The above fact may lead to a situation where some metropolitan optical networks (especially in small towns) will attract a few providers (so there will be low competition), or, at worst, none provider. To address the above risk, promotion of broadband services should be increased to the citizens, to make clear the advantages and to increase the demand for broadband services. These, in synergy with the fact that the IBC will provide its infrastructure with a cost-oriented manner (resulting in the provision of services to citizens in a low cost), will boost the demand for broadband services and attract a sufficient number of providers in the metropolitan optical networks supported by the IBC.

A significant risk is the further consolidation in the telecommunications sector. Today, several providers are active, but their presence in the remote areas is lower than the big cities. The basic assumption for generating revenue to IBC from customers - service providers is that during the five years period more than two service practitioners in the IBC's area should be active, who will be interested to use fibre pairs of the IBC. Risk also exists on the revenue expected from the connection of government agencies which are estimated to 50% of the total revenue of the IBC. In case that such income is accounting and is not collected at all or collected with delay, the operation of the company is compromised. Another risk is that the IBC should gain experienced and skilful staff in technology and promotion issues of broadband infrastructure. The above risk will be addressed by attracting capable managers in the human resources of the IBC and the use of outsourcing policy in fields where the IBC can not handle alone (for example, the network maintenance).

Having therefore a key objective to reduce the costs of IBC, applying a national business model under the auspices of Central Union of Municipalities and Communities would contribute significantly to sustainability. By applying such a model the conditions for reducing the costs to the levels of management, maintenance and expansion of the network are created and significant economies of scale can be achieved. In addition to this solution better conditions are created for the expansion of existing networks, the links between the MAN and the links between MAN and other broadband networks.

CONCLUSION

The purpose of this chapter was to highlight the broadband infrastructures as a common and focus the important role of local governments in the development and use of municipal fiber optic networks. The ultimate objective of the local government regarding its involvement in the provision of broadband services is the creation of an open competitive environment, in which access and services are offered by many providers, thereby reducing the cost of services for citizens and businesses, while developing advanced, high-quality services. Depending on the prevailing conditions, the local authorities have to engage actively to achieve this goal while ensuring cost-oriented operation of infrastructure.

The installation of broadband infrastructure in a country is considered as a common that can lead to significant changes in both the public and private sectors. It is commonly accepted that the local authorities and government bodies focus on the creation of passive infrastructure to encourage the creation of broadband networks. Understanding the benefits, advantages and potential of the broadband, a summary of international experience is described. Several countries develop and adopt strategies and policies for broadband growth and expansion. Most of these efforts are initiatives of local government or based on public – private partnerships, which have shown successful best practices in developing and maintaining of municipal fibre optic networks, while the efforts of the private sector are a minority.

Also, five scenarios for broadband business models are briefly presented. The business model that draws much attention indicates that there is no relationship between the owners of the infrastructure (public sector) and the services provided to the subscribers by the services providers (private sector).

Finally in this chapter a case study of a Greek inter-municipal broadband company (IBC) is presented. IBC has been created to support broadband infrastructure that was developed throughout the southwest axis of Greece. The techno-economic study shows that IBC has to be active only in the operation, management, maintenance and expansion of passive equipment of broadband metropolitan networks. The results of the financial analysis show that having as a key objective to reduce the costs of the IBC, its sustainability depends on the application of a national business model which can perform significant economies of scale. The application of this model creates the preconditions for cost reduction in the levels of management and maintenance of the network. In addition, this solution creates the conditions for the expansion of existing networks, interlinking MAN and connecting MAN with other broadband networks.

REFERENCES

Alexiou, A., Bouras, C., Primpas, D., & Papagiannopoulos, J. (2008). Metropolitan broadband networks: Design and implementation aspects and business models. In *Global diffusion of broadband data transmission: Factors affecting the adoption, usage and economics of broadband* (pp. 196–210). Hershey, PA: IDEA Group Publishing.

ARCEP–Autorité de Régulation des Communications électroniques et des Postes. (2008). *Décision n° 2008-0835*. République Française. Retrieved July 1, 2010, from http:// www.arcep.fr /uploads/ tx_gsavis/ 08-0835.pdf

ARCEP–Autorité de Régulation des Communications électroniques et des Postes. (2009). *Décision n° 2009-1106*. République Française. Retrieved July 1, 2010, from http:// www.arcep.fr/ uploads/ tx_gsavis/ 09-1106.pdf

Berra, M. (2006, March 23-25). *New commons or IPR extension? The future of innovation*. IASCP Europe Regional Meeting: Building the European Common: from Open Fields to Open Source, Brescia, Italy. Retrieved March 1, 2010, from http:// iascpeurope.eco.unibs.it/ papers/ Berra.pdf

BMWI. (2010). *Breitbandstrategie*. Retrieved March 1, 2010, from http:// www.bmwi.de/ BMWi/ Navigation/ Technologie-und-Innovation/ Telekommunikation-und-Post/ breitbandstrategie,did=257532.html

Bouras, C., Gkamas, A., Papagiannopoulos, J., Theofilopoulos, G., & Tsiatsos, T. (2007). *Business models for broadband municipal optical networks: A proposed model for the Greek case*. The Twelfth IEEE Symposium on Computers and Communications, (pp. 727-732). Aveiro, Portugal.

Bouras, C., Gkamas, A., Papagiannopoulos, J., Theofilopoulos, G., & Tsiatsos, T. (2009). Broadband municipal optical networks in Greece: A suitable business model. *Journal of Telematics and Informatics*, *26*, 391–409. doi:10.1016/j.tele.2009.03.003

Bouras, C., Gkamas, A., Theofilopoulos, G., & Tsiatsos, T. (2008). Business models for municipal broadband networks. In Khosrow-Pour, M. (Ed.), *Encyclopedia of Information Science and Technology* (pp. 457–465). Hershey, PA: IGI Global. doi:10.4018/978-1-60566-026-4.ch076

Bouras, C., Papagiannopoulos, J., Katsikas, S., & Gritzalis, S. (2008). The status of broadband in western Greece: A study on the supply and the demand of broadband services for e-government promotion. [IJEG]. *International Journal of Electronic Governance*, *1*(3), 326–344. doi:10.1504/IJEG.2008.020453

Bourreau, M., Cambini, C., & Hoernig, S. (2010). *National FTTH plans in France Italy, and Portugal. Robert Schuman Centre for Advanced Studies, Florence School of Regulation European University Institute*. Florence, Italy: European University Press.

Broadband Properties. (2006). *Issues*. Retrieved July 2, 2010, from http:// www.broadbandproperties.com/ 2006issues/ mar06issues/ vienna_march.pdf

Chlamtac, I., Gumaste, A., & Szabo, C. (Eds.). (2005). *Broadband services business models and technologies for community networks*. John Wiley & Sons. doi:10.1002/0470022515

Citynet. (2010). *Citynet Amsterdam*. Retrieved June 28, 2010, from http://www.citynet.nl/

Cook Network Consultants. (2005). *Building regional open access fiber infrastructure in Catalonia* (Northeastern Spain). The COOK Report on Internet, September-October 2005. Retrieved March 1, 2010, from http:// www.cookreport.com/ catalonia.pdf

Czernich, N., & Engl, F. Falck, O., Kiessl, T., & Kretschmer, T. (2009). *Regulatory framework for next-generation access networks across Europe*. CESIfo Dice Report 1/2009.

DGCIS - Direction générale de la Compétitivité, de l'Industrie et des Services. (2010). *Consultation publique - Programme national très haut débit*. République Française. Retrieved July 1, 2010, from http:// www.telecom.gouv.fr/ fonds_documentaire/ consultations/ 10/ consthd.pdf

Digital Britain. (2010). *What we do: The report.* Retrieved March 1, 2010, from http:// www.culture.gov.uk/ what_we_do/ broadcasting/ 6216.aspx

Dobers, P. (1999). *Netting the information infrastructure of Stockholm.* Paper presented at the Conference of Managing the Big City, Göteborg University, Sweden.

Epractice. (2008). *Preparing Digital France 2012.* Retrieved March 1, 2010, from http:// www.epractice.eu/ en/ news/ 284991

European Commission. (2010). *European information society 2010.* Retrieved June 28, 2010, from http:// ec.europa.eu/ information_society/ eeurope/ i2010/ index_en.htm

FTTH Council. (2009). Definition of terms. (Revision Date: January 9th 2009). Retrieved August 4, 2010, from http:// www.ftthcouncil.eu/ documents studies/ FTTH-Definitions-Revision_January_2009.pdf

Government of Canada. (2010). *Canada's economic action plan.* Retrieved March 1, 2010, from http:// www.actionplan.gc.ca/ eng/ index.asp

Hughes, G. (2003) Local & regional models for broadband deployment. In *Proceedings of eEurope: Broadband Local & Regional Best Practises Workshop.* Retrieved August 4, 2010, from http:// ec.europa.eu/ information_society/ eeurope/ 2005/ doc/ all_about/ broadband/ bb_regional /g_hughes.ppt

Katz, M. (2000). Regulation: The next 1000 years. In R. M. Entman (Ed.), *Six degrees of competition: Correlating regulation with the telecommunications marketplace.* A Report of the Fourteenth Annual Aspen Institute Conference on Telecommunications Policy. The Aspen Institute, Washington.

Kirsch, F., & von Hirschhausen, C. (2008). Regulation of next generation networks: Structural separation, access regulation, or no regulation at all? *Communications & Strategies, 69,* 63–85.

Korea Communication Commission. (2010). *Important issues.* Retrieved March 1, 2010, from http:// eng.kcc.go.kr/ user.do?page=E02010100&dc=E02010100

Kyriakidou, V., Chipouras, A., Katsianis, D., & Sphicopoulos, T. (2009). Business models for municipal metro networks: Theoretical and financial analysis. In Chochliouros, I. P. (Ed.), *Optical access networks and advanced photonics: Technologies and deployment strategies.* Hershey, PA: IGI Global. doi:10.4018/978-1-60566-707-2.ch010

LocalRet. (2009). *Website.* Retrieved July 1, 2010, from http:// www.apd.cat/ media/ 888.pdf

New Zealand Government. (2009). *Broadband investment initiative.* Retrieved March 1, 2010, from http:// www.med.govt.nz/ upload/ 63958/ Final-broadband-initiative-consultation-document.pdf

Ofcom. (2008). *Delivering super-fast broadband in the UK.* London.

OPTA. (2008) *Policy rules: Tariff regulation for unbundled fibre access.* OPTA/AM/2008/202874. The Hague. Retrieved July 1, 2010 from http:// www.opta.nl/ en/ download/ publicatie/?id=2832

Qiang, C. Z.-W. (2009). *Broadband infrastructure investment in stimulus packages: Relevance for developing countries.* Washington, DC: World Bank.

RadioAustralia News. (2009). *Australia's broadband plan.* Retrieved March 1, 2010, from http:// www.radioaustralianews.net.au/ stories/ 200904/ 2538028.htm

Sadowski, B., Nucciarelli, A., & Rooij, M. (2009). Providing incentives for private investment in municipal broadband networks: Evidence from the Netherlands. [Elsevier B.V.]. *Telecommunications Policy*, *33*(10-11), 582–595. doi:10.1016/j.telpol.2009.08.005

Stokab in English. (2010). *Home*. Retrieved March 1, 2010, from http:// www.stokab.se/ templates/ startpress.aspx?id=1115

Stokab in English. (2010). *About Stokab*. Retrieved March 1, 2010, from http:// www.stokab.se/ templates/ StandardPage.aspx?id=306

Stokab in English. (2010). *The infrastructure*. Retrieved March 1, 2010, from http:// www.stokab.se/ templates/ StandardPage.aspx?id=775

Tomales Bay Institute. (2006). *The commons rising, a report to owners*. Retrieved August 30, 2007, from http:// onthecommons.org/ files/ Commons_Rising_06.pdf

Troulos, C., Merekoulias, V., & Maglaris, V. (2009). A business model for municipal FTTH/B networks: The case of rural Greece. *Info - The Journal of Policy, Regulation and Strategy for Telecommunications* [Emerald Group Publishing Limited.]. *Information and Media*, *12*(3), 73–89.

UTOPIA. (2003). Feasibility study, part II: Financial analysis, dynamic city Metronet advisors.

UTOPIA. (2010). *Utopianet*. Retrieved March 1, 2010, from http:// www.utopianet.org/

VoIP and ENUM. (2006). *FTTH in Vienna to all households*. Retrieved July 2, 2010, from http:// voipandenum.blogspot.com/ 2006/ 01/ ftth-in-vienna-to-all-households.html

YME. (2008). *Strategy for electronic communications and new technologies 2008 – 2013*. Retrieved March 1, 2010, from http:// www.yme.gr/ index.php?tid=21&aid=1532 (in Greek)

ADDITIONAL READING

Bouras, C., Alexiou, A., Kapoulas, V., Paraskevas, M., Scopoulis, I., & Papagiannopoulos, J. (2005, 7-8 October). Deployment of Broadband Infrastructure in the Region of Western Greece. *2nd IEEE/Great e-net International Workshop on Deployment Models and First/Last Mile Networking, 2*, pp. 1510-1515. Boston, MA, USA.

Burney, P., Parsons, S., & Green, J. (2000). Forecasting market demand for new telecommunications services: an introduction. *Telematics and Informatics*, *19*(3), 225–249. doi:10.1016/S0736-5853(01)00004-1

Cava-Ferreruela, I., & Alabau-Munoz, A. (2006). Broadband policy assessment: a cross-national empirical analysis. *Telecommunications Policy*, *30*(8–9), 445–463. doi:10.1016/j.telpol.2005.12.002

Choudrie, J., & Dwivedi, Y. K. (2006). Examining the socio-economic determinants of broadband adopters and non-adopters in the United Kingdom. In *Proceedings of the 39th Annual Hawaii International Conference on System Sciences (HICSS'06), 4*. p. 85a.

Ebusiness Forum. (2005). *Study about the Use of New Information and Telecommunication Technologies in Small and Medium-sized Enterprises*. Retrieved March 1, 2010, from http:// www.ebusinessforum.gr/

European Commission. (2004). *Challenges for Europe's Information Society Beyond 2005: Starting Point for a New EU Strategy*. EC communication, p. 757.

Government of Sweden (2006). *Broadband for Growth, Innovation and Competitiveness*. The Government and the Government Offices of Sweden, December 2006.

Greek Research and Technology Network – GRNET. (2005). *National Survey on New Technologies and the Information Society*. Retrieved March 1, 2010, from: http:// www.grnet.gr/

Henderson, A., Gentle, I., & Ball, E. (2005). WTO principles and telecommunications in developing nations: Challenges and consequences of accession. *Telecommunications Policy*, *29*(2–3), 205–221. doi:10.1016/j.telpol.2004.11.003

Höffler, F. (2007). Cost and benefits from infrastructure competition. Estimating Welfare Effects from Broadband Access Competition. *Telecommunications Policy*, *31*(6–7), 401–418. doi:10.1016/j.telpol.2007.05.004

Jones, R. (2006, 25–26 January). *Business Case Study for Municipal Networks – FTTH Project Funding*. FTTH Council Europe Conference 2006: Europe at the Speed of Light, Vienna.

Weis, G., Pink, F., & Kadrnoska, H. (2006, 25–26 January) *Fibre–Optic Technology in Vienna*, FTTH Council Europe Conference 2006: Europe at the Speed of Light, Vienna.

KEY TERMS AND DEFINITIONS

Broadband: An advanced and innovative environment, from a social and technological view, which consists of fast network connections and appropriate network infrastructure for the development of new applications and services.

Commons: Resources that are shared by a large number of individuals and resists sole ownership, i.e. they collectively owned.

Fibre-to-the-x (FTTx): Any architecture that uses fiber optics to replace part or all of the copper or other technologies to the local loop, and even to the buildings or homes. FTTx is a collective term for FFTC, FFTB, FTTH and/or FTTP.

Fiber-to-the-Building (FFTB): An architecture for fibre optic networks where the optica; fibre reaches the entrance or boundary of a building.

Fiber-to-the-Curb: or **Fiber-to-the-Cabinet (FFTC):** An architecture for fibre optic networks where the optical fibre reaches up to the street cabinet that is near the subscribers' premises (typically approx up to 300m from the premises).

Fiber-to-the-Home (FFTH): An architecture for fibre optic networks where the fibre reaches the individual homes /apartments of the subscribers

Fiber-to-the-Premises (FFTP): A term used as a blanket for FTTH and FTTB (FTTH/B is also used)

Next Generation Networks (NGNs): Next Generation Networks is a term to describe the networks that will be deployed over the next years. Their main characteristic is that one network achives very high transmission rates (using optical fibre technologies) and transports all information and services, including voice, video, TV, data etc.

Optical Fibre: An optical fibre is a flexible, glass or plastic fiber that carries light along its length. Optical fibres can be used as a medium for telecommunication and networking, and can achieve very high transmission rates.

Chapter 18
Service Oriented Architectural Principles for Interoperable and Secure E-Government Frameworks

Teta Stamati
National and Kapodistrian University of Athens, Greece

Athanasios Karantjias
University of Piraeus, Greece

Drakoulis Martakos
National and Kapodistrian University of Athens, Greece

ABSTRACT

The objective of the chapter is to analytically examine the materialization towards the transformational government. It presents the case of implementing an innovative Local Government Access Framework, LGAF, deployed for the Central Union of Municipalities and Communities of Greece. The LGAF integrates almost two hundred and fifty government services in many different domains of the public administration, implementing peak XML technologies, worldwide standards and specifications. The chapter presents an advanced interoperable and secure large scale e-government framework built for Greek LGOs, and provides insights to critical success design factors that should be established in order for the provided services to gain end-users' acceptance and allow the coordination and alignment of business processes and information architectures that span both intra- and inter- public organizational boundaries.

DOI: 10.4018/978-1-60960-839-2.ch018

INTRODUCTION

Local Government Organizations - LGOs hold a respectful share in contributing to economic growth and wealth of societies (Moon, 2002; Irani *et al.*, 2005). Delivering fully executable public, national and cross-border electronic services through LGOs has increasingly become a political priority (Kling, 2000). Beyond the core administrative and democratic activities, health, education and security are among the service branches adding public value and creating the right environment for prosperous economies. The local government structures are believed to be the essence of participatory democracy since it is through local government that citizens come into direct contact with their elected government, as the power flows from national to local government (Stamati and Martakos, 2010; Koussouris *et al.*, 2008). Thus, LGOs desks are in many countries an active point of transactions between the government and the citizens.

Although the term transformational government only emerged the last five years, a number of LGOs have already been involved in web related activities. With the emerging popularity of the Internet, various European regions, prefectures and municipalities began to experiment with it to transform their external dealings with the citizens (Ho, 2002; Tan and Pan, 2003). Similarly, Greek local public authorities, through the implementation of e-government initiatives, attempt to transform their stereotypical image of being bureaucratic and inflexible to a new image of being customer oriented and efficiency conscious (Devadoss *et al.*, 2002; Mecella and Batini, 2001). Such investments are often inspired by the promised benefits of greater customer satisfaction, better efficiency, improved effectiveness and reduced bureaucracy (Devadoss *et al.* 2002; Fountain, 2001).

The motivation by LGOs to reduce administrative costs and enhance the provided services to citizens, businesses and general community, has been a driving force for LGOs to build real interoperable and secure systems, enterprise information architects and to define fundamental principles, strategies and policies in designing, implementing and maintaining large-scale, scalable, extensible and high-administrative government solutions (Irani *et al.*, 2005; Carter and Bélanger, 2005). However, such progress is hindered by difficulties connected to design and implementation. Today's e-Government deployments can resemble a patchwork of incompatible information and communications technology solutions rather than flexible and reusable assets that would provide essential building blocks of services for end-users (citizens and employees of LGOs).

Therefore effective guidelines, principles and policies should be established in order for LGOs to accelerate their entrance in the digital society, strengthening their fundamental structure and enhancing the collaboration of the public sector (Stamati and Martakos, 2010). These will allow the coordination and alignment of business processes and information architectures that span both intra- and inter- organizational boundaries. They will enhance the collaboration of public and private aware organizations in critical issues such as workflows, decision-making and business transactions. The vision behind the integration of new and more advanced governmental frameworks is extremely ambitious and therefore also very attractive to any LGO interested in truly improving the effectiveness of its IT enterprise.

The chapter presents an interoperable, secure, privacy-aware, scalable, and high-administrative framework, called *Local Government Access Framework - LGAF* (LGAF project, 2009), deployed for the *Central Union of Municipalities and Communities in Greece* (www.kedke.gr), and outlines the main insights regarding the critical success design factors that need to be adopted when integrating large-scale, user-centric e-Government solutions. The aim of LGAF is to fulfil common goals and benefits such as, to increase intrinsic interoperability, security, federation, vendor diversification options, business and technology domain alignment, Return Of Investment - ROI, organizational agility, and reduce IT burden. The authors were involved in the whole life cycle development process of the project, including design, implementation and system roll out.

It should be noted that in the rest of the paper when we refer to an e-Government service, we specifically mean an enterprise service operated by a public organization that performs one instance of a business function. The terms "enterprise service" and "e-Government service" are therefore interchangeable in this context.

REVIEW OF PREVIOUS E-GOVERNMENT RESEARCH

Well funded formal research programs began to expand and deepen, especially under the digital government research program of the US *National Science Foundation - NSF* and the corresponding *Information Society Technologies - IST* of the EC. With this infusion of government attention and financial support, researchers began to emphasize the prospects for electronic customer-oriented services (eTen, 2007; IDABC, 2007; Millard et al, 2006). Taking a development view, several researchers proposed 'stage' models of e-Government, which describe a sequence of developmental steps that represent a kind of maturity model associated with services and management. However, very few of them have engaged in general e-Government theory development for predicting why information age government behaves the way it does and how it can be effectively changed (Stamati and Martakos, 2010).

Several attempts to build generic e-Government representations and models have been identified, covering all three categories, depending on their modelling perspective, the 'Object' perspective, the 'Process', and the 'Holistic' one. Among them, the *Gartner Government Performance Framework -GGPF* (Gartner, 2003) provides a top-level conceptual categorization of the overall governance domain. These categories are further elaborated but in lower levels it becomes clear that the model constitutes rather an evaluation and assessment tool than an attempt to analyze and model the domain. It actually focuses on the outputs and outcomes of the governance system and not on the description and the model of the overall system.

The *Government Process Classification Scheme - GPCS* (Peristeras and Tarabanis, 2004) presents a conceptual and generic process model that may lead to proper integrations of added value public services, which is highly relevant to the e-Government domain. It proposes a very detailed organization of all governmental processes. However, it focuses on few supportive functions required for the public sector, while their concrete analysis is missing. Although the scheme was a US governmental initiative in the mid-90s, its adoption seems to be low even within the US.

Similarly, the UK *Government Common Information Model - GCIM* (Benson, 2002) is a pure public administration service modelling attempt and it is clearly focused on the service interaction. Although it provides an interesting view of the business services for the public sector, it rather remains on an abstract level, which leads to insuperable differences when trying to secure interconnect them.

The FIDIS e-Government Domain Model (FIDIS IST project, 2004) presents the results of the FIDIS project which is a generic secure framework for the digital public sector. The focus of this model is clearly on the design and implementation of secure privacy-aware processes. However, the efficient management of the privacy of individuals is just one of the application areas of e-Government, and thus the FIDIS proposed model requires further enhancements in order to be considered complete and coherent, addressing all the needs of the public sector.

It becomes obvious that in most cases current strategies, models and activities are only short- to mid-term oriented and do not fully take into account some of the critical issues that can become key enabling success factors. If overlooked, these issues will remain barriers preventing realisation of the promise of e-government.

On the other hand, specific and extensively used local and national solutions and research initiatives, such as the 'LGOL-Net', 'LGOL-X', 'LGOL-Flow', and 'Aplaws' enterprise systems, deployed under the LAWs national project in UK (LAWs project, 2004), the 'MMBase' relational object mapping tool (MMBase, 2006) developed and used in Netherlands and Germany, the 'Mioga 2 groupware solution' in France (Mioga 2, 2004), the strategies and initiatives on the technology-enabled transformation of government services and administrations in Australia (AGIMO, 2006), and others aimed to develop a set of assets and principles that can be implemented and followed on a modular basis, depending on local governmental technological and information management maturity.

The facts that core requirements such as interoperability, strong security and trust, and scalability at the time that many of these solutions were deployed, were very innovative assets, and the primitive status of common technological, interoperability and security standards, led to ineffective and rather closed enterprise solutions. The lack of proper open source technologies and strategies in building advance content repositories, middleware messaging systems, customizable content management systems, business process management systems, strong security and privacy-aware mechanisms and modules, at the time when these attempts took place, necessitates their replacement and the integration of new and more advanced initiatives.

Even if standards were adopted, there are many obstacles in their practical enforcement. A basic problem identified is the lack of common domain ontologies to be used for modelling the semantic of data, ensuring that the precise meaning of exchanged information is understandable by every application and system. Moreover, most of them are relied on application or system level authentication and authorization for establishing simple trusted user identity features, causing the following obstacles:

- LGOs have to implement multiple, different and separate authentication and authorization mechanisms for their applications and systems. This is rather expensive and difficult for a LGO to manage and administer, while is inefficient for the end-users who have to manage multiple identities;
- Every attempt to interconnect different applications in order to add value and build more advanced e-services, often means to link separate user e-access security processes, which is rather complex and difficult to achieve from the technical point of view. The usual solution followed in these cases is to lower the level of security and privacy to these systems.

In general, the majority of these solutions do not adopt the user perspective, who needs to simplify his entrance in a large scale enterprise e-Government framework and receive high quality of services. On the other hand, even if these *Service Oriented Architectures - SOAs* and Web Services - based solutions are properly designed and implemented in a way to satisfy the needs of the end user, they are unable to interconnect with existing, self sufficient, legacy applications and systems, which do not necessarily conform to the assumptions of SOA's distributed application model. Therefore most of the time LGOs are obliged to change or exclude their legacy systems in order to adopt such unified enterprise systems.

In terms of user-friendliness in current e-Government implementations are far from being satisfactory. Long is the list of complaints such as the general lack in targeting the audience; the inadequate and inconsistent design; the sloppiness in maintenance, etc. Even if lately many improvements have been identified, yet essential progress is necessary.

However, technological complexity and incompatibility, described above, are not the only, nor the most difficult, challenges to overcome. Information integration is a critical component in the design and the implementation of advanced e-government information technologies. In a simple conceptualization, information integration allows end-users to work at the same time, with the same information drawn from multiple disparate sources. In a more complex form it has the potential to support the transformation of organizational structures and communication channels between and among multiple agencies residing in different locations. Therefore, besides technical it requires also organizational process and behaviour changes for the individuals and mostly for LGOs involved.

In fact, despite the many potential benefits of using modern ICT, governments still struggle with the problems of rigid and ineffective internal and inter-institutional processes. Apart from that, a severe lack of understanding of citizens' real needs, attitudes and abilities to use ICT-based services also exists and this consequently leads to low take-up of online offers.

Thus, the goals of this study are twofold: firstly to present the case of a large scale e-Government framework such as the LGAF for the Greek LGOs, and secondly to identify the critical success factors for designing effective, real interoperable and secure advanced local government access frameworks. An investigation of Greek LGOs' perception toward an integrated e-Government system for LGOs will help to build a technological theory of e-Government system acceptance, by further enlightening the process of technology adoption and use specifically in the context of local government administration.

GREEK LOCAL GOVERNMENTAL BACKGROUND

The Greek national public administration system is constituted of a large number of LGOs. Specifically, there are more than one thousand LGOs, mostly municipalities that provide a significant number of governmental services to the citizens, visitors, enterprises based within their geographical limits and other governmental bodies. The exact number of services provided by each LGO varies as they have their own operational framework that depends on parameters related to the distinctiveness of each one. Such parameters can be the financial status, the local population composition, region's cultural characteristics, geopolitical and geographical attributes and other organizational and legal parameters that allow or not the LGO to offer some kinds of services (Koussouris, *et al.* 2008). These services can be split in general categories according to their nature and entity they refer to. Some indicative categories refer to payments, applications, registries, records, certificates and licenses.

LGOs' services were, until recently, provided in a conventional way, which meant that no infrastructure had been developed for electronic services and proved the poor level of *Information and Communications Technologies - ICT* adoption. The conventional way of services provision demanded the physical presence of the person that applied for the service in the LGO. Thus the interested person went in a LGO to submit both the application and get the outcome of the requested service (Koussouris *et al.*, 2008). The poor level of ICT adoption by the LGOs was the main reason behind the aforementioned situation and did not allow the electronic provision of services (Moon, 2002).

Given the importance of services offered by LGOs, it is essential, in the modern technological era, for ICTs to provide solutions in order to transform these traditionally offered services into electronic transactions. These can be initiated over the Internet aiming at the facilitation of the citizen's life, who is the eventual 'customer' of any government. LGOs service branches need to keep pace with innovation and technology developments, thus guaranteeing a lasting quality and provision of public services. The great potential of ICTs to contribute to a competitive and wealthy economy needs to be exploited in LGOs activities. Only through investment in ICT research and effective innovation concepts can the local public administration ensure an innovative, knowledge-enabled, and competitive economy.

In the last decade, LGOs attempt to re-establish their mission critical operations and this has lead to persistent organizational transformations. Given this fact, currently an important number of the European regions, prefectures, and municipalities have constructed their own presence on the web. In Greece, the situation also seems to be changing over the last years, as many LGOs implement projects mainly funded by the 6th Framework Program and the Greek Information Society. These are aiming to achieve the goal of providing better services, creating new conditions for social activation and improving the communication with the citizens. Through their online presence, many Greek LGOs have also started offering various categories of online services as introduced by Moon (2002) regarding information, interaction and transaction. Modern ICTs heavily impact and shape these activities for cooperating and interacting with stakeholders within country and sometimes across borders. ICTs are changing local government structures and organizational processes producing significant business and technical benefits (Heeks, 1999).

Electronic projects are becoming increasingly important for the public administration, and LGOs base their decision to move forward with modern e-platforms expecting benefits such as better services, operational savings and increased program effectiveness (Gil-Garcial *et al.* 2007). The exploitation of e-Government from LGOs is the rationale being used to define *local transformational government* (local t-Gov) (Irani *et al.*, 2007).

Although LGOs have travailed to embrace ICTs, these individual attempts resulted frequently in isolated, ad-hoc systems, offering only a part of the services, mainly dissemination of information or at best communication in two ways. Up to now Greek local government structures have not been able to live up to expectations, as they are generally characterized by indolence of service delivery and failure to attract users' participation. The problem is mainly attributed to lack of capacity and technical know-how. Some analysts argue that the local government 'mayhem' has to do with the lack of strong security and interoperability, which are becoming gradually very urgent matters. The absence of these two important challenges result to each governmental authority to come up with short sighted and inflexible business models and Information Systems, which means that the information and the services provided from LGOs are not easily accessible by, or compatible to, information systems, technologies or business services adopted by other LGOs, or even other departments within the same organization.

THE LGAF FRAMEWORK

Objectives and Analysis Methodology Approach

The *LGAF* is a Greek/European co-funded initiative project, deployed for the Central Union of Municipalities and Communities of Greece (www.kedke.gr), which is constituted of more than one thousand (1.000) local administration organizations. It aims to bring together the central government, the local government and the private sector, providing advanced, secure, privacy-aware, interoperable, and high-administrative national electronic services. The motivation by Greek local administration organizations to reduce administrative costs, as well as enhancing the services they offer to citizens and businesses, has been the driving force for the development and implementation of the LGAF framework as a mission critical broadband e-Government infrastructure within Greece. It integrates almost two hundred and fifty (250) public electronic services in many different domains of the public administration such as in *health*, *social care*, *education*, *public transportation*, *cultural*, and other sectors (LGAF project, 2009).

The LGAF consortium first attempted to identify and stimulate the different perspectives of the Greek Municipalities' operations, in order to better predict and shape the innovation processes required to be designed and implemented. These described a coherent set of visions and archetypal images of scenarios, recording the actual situation in the handling of civil status documents, identifying complementary and/or contrasting alternatives, and problematic areas.

Regional and national interviews and workshops with the participation of experts from the LGOs, the Ministry of Interior in Greece, the ICT industry and consulting, and the academia, worked together in collecting all the business and technical information needed, as depicted in Figure 1. Protocols of procedures were defined beforehand in order to guide the group discussion and to document the scenario elements developed. Based on the workshops and the online consulta-

Figure 1. Gathering of requirements and analysis approach

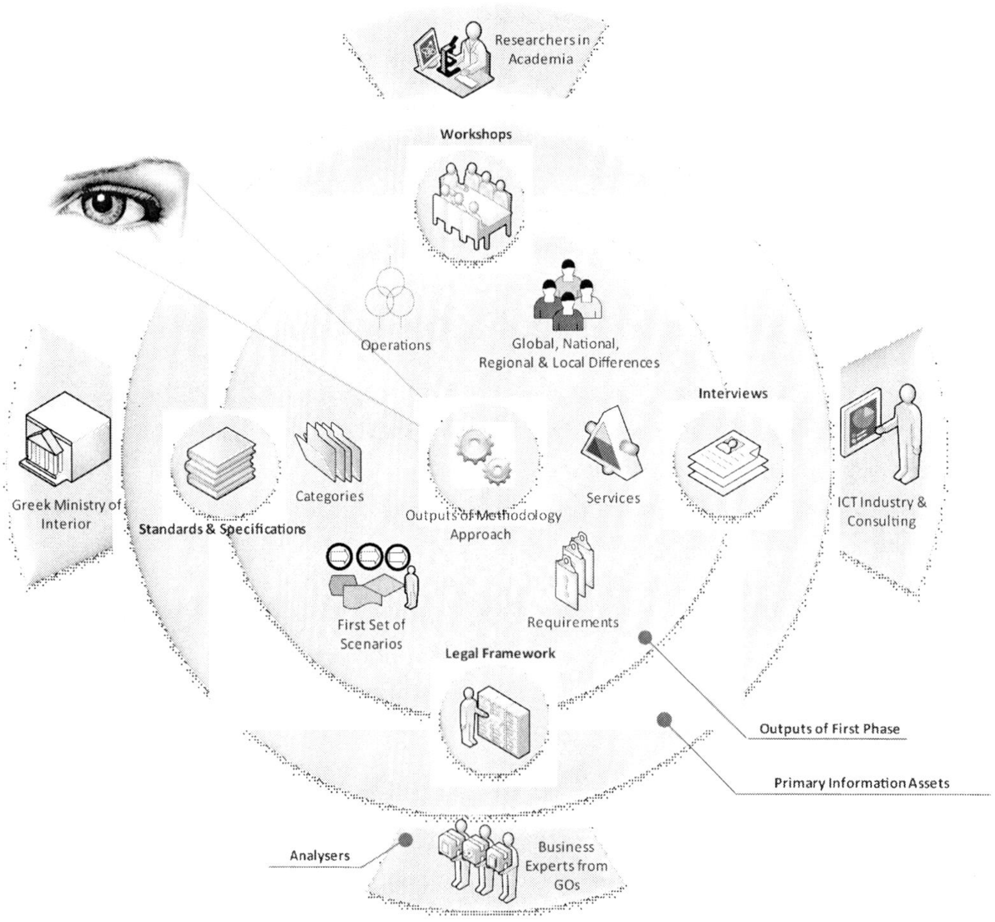

tion inputs the project consortium synthesised and consolidated a first set of scenarios and user requirements. The last mentioned covered the most important issues identified, taking into account existing inventories, policies, initiatives, and the national legal and regulatory framework in Greece. This set was the main input to the next phases (analysis, design, and implementation).

Issues on different levels of government (Global, National, Regional, and Local) were analysed properly and regional differences occurred due to distinct cultures, diverging local constitutions, and organizational structures of LGOs were identified. During this attempt the concept of community of interest was introduced. Organizing e-Government services into communities aimed to reduce the overhead of operating them in small, medium, and bigger Municipalities. Communities are themselves services, created, advertised, discovered, and invoked mostly as Web Services, including three different and concrete parts:

- *Categories*, which contain domain, synonyms, and specialization attributes. Domain provides the area of interest of the community (e.g. public transportation). The synonyms attribute contains a set of alternative domains for the category, while specialization is a set of characteristics of each category.
- *Operations*, which invoke the communities.
- *Services*, which invoke each community operation.

In parallel international standardisation bodies', like the UN/CEFACT, OASIS, W3C and OMG, findings affected many research areas related to LGAF. The fields of research affecting interoperability at organisational and semantic level and security included process modelling (*Business Process Model and Notation – BPMN* (OMG, 2009)), data modelling (Greek eGIF XML Schemas, *Core Components Technical Specification – CCTS* (UN/CEFACT, 2007)), metadata modelling (Dublin Core (http://dublincore.org/)), privacy (WS-Trust (Nadalin et al, 2009)), and Laws and regulations enforced by the national and EU Legal Framework, especially concerning framework enforcement and digital authentication issues (Directives 01/45/EC, 99/93/EC, 97/66/EC).

However, apart from the European and US research efforts, the LGAF consortium performed an in-depth investigation on the way the main framework could interact with national projects, like the National One-Stop Government Portal (http://www.ermis.gov.gr), the National Network of Public Administration (http://www.syzefxis.gov.gr/), and the National e-Procurement System. The whole research was based on the second generation Greek eGIF approach, which interacts on a knowledge exchanged level with the UK and German eGIFs, setting new aims and objectives related to public administration, as well as new areas of interest that were addressed for the first time, especially concerning more than two hundred different electronic documents for the public sector. The Greek eGIF runs over increasing cycles (spiral approach) in LGAF, starting from the definition of the core services for citizens and organisations, continuing with the business modelling and analysis of the processes involved in the provision of these services, and concluding with the designing of the data schemas in order to describe the execution of the processes. Relevant technical specifications for interoperability, security and privacy for systems and users were properly identified and included.

Under this effort the Greek eGIF now includes formal process modelling methodologies and notation that covers the description and management of public electronic services. Our vision is for the full map to include even more public services, towards business and citizens, stemming from the majority of the public administration points in Greece and engaging the aggregation of LGOs' electronic documents.

In the synthesis of the final scenarios and assessment matrices, each issue identified and extracted was tagged with its origin. It actually typed a topic of interest or a dimension, and it was grouped into specific categories. The gap analysis performed on the conducted categories, adopting accepted methodologies such as *Soft Systems Methodology - SSM* (Checkland and Scholes, 1999), SWOT analysis methodology (Harvard Business Press, 2009), and ITPOSMO methodology (Heeks, 1999), allowed us to better identify and validate the differences between the current state of affairs, and a future desired state on LGOs.

Specifically, the identification of commonalities in current research issues and in future needs of governmental e-services was carried out on the basis of dimensions and topics of interest from the scenarios and the current situation. The next step included the identification of lacking dimensions and topics of interest, in order to define emerging issues, which were not addressed in current research. Then the gap assessment according to impact and relevance towards the e-government and the e-Governance model of each region, emerged a policy formulation, which included clear definition of policies, strategic decision-making, issues of constitutions of each region, etc. In parallel the consortium attempted to generate the theoretical base of the LGAF ontology framework and derive the taxonomies required for better organising the various quantities of public information that the LGOs handle.

LGAF DESIGN AND IMPLEMENTATION

In the design and implementation phase the LGAF consortium aimed of addressing the results conducted from the analysis phase in the following core features:

- *Composing advanced, added-value, e-Government services.* A framework for automatically composing e-Government services is proposed based on a set of rules that check composability of governmental services.
- *Developing cross-boundary information sharing.* Significant changes in organizational and technological processes were proposed in order to better support government response capabilities. These changes are influenced by specific types of social interaction, which take the form of group decision-making, learning, understanding, trust building, and conflict resolution, among others.
- *Specifying operational policies.* Rules and constrains were defined in order to govern the behaviour of all services for their successful interaction. These are machine-to-machine specifications that are expressed programmatically as assertions and grouped into various combinations.
- *Integrating SOA Lifecycle Management mechanisms.* LGAF enabled the monitoring and controlling of any change on a service, ensuring that the quality of the service remains consistent. Without it, policies may be violated resulting in noncompliant inefficient services.
- *Preserving privacy.* Privacy credentials with filtering mechanisms were used to ensure that only authorized entities can access sensitive information.
- *Increasing user-friendliness.* LGAF increased system usage by better designed services and knowledge enhancements.

These features are introduced in four district main entities, as depicted in Figure 2:

- A ***Content Management System – CMS***, which undertakes the creation, editing, management and publishing of all the gov-

Figure 2. The LGAF system overview

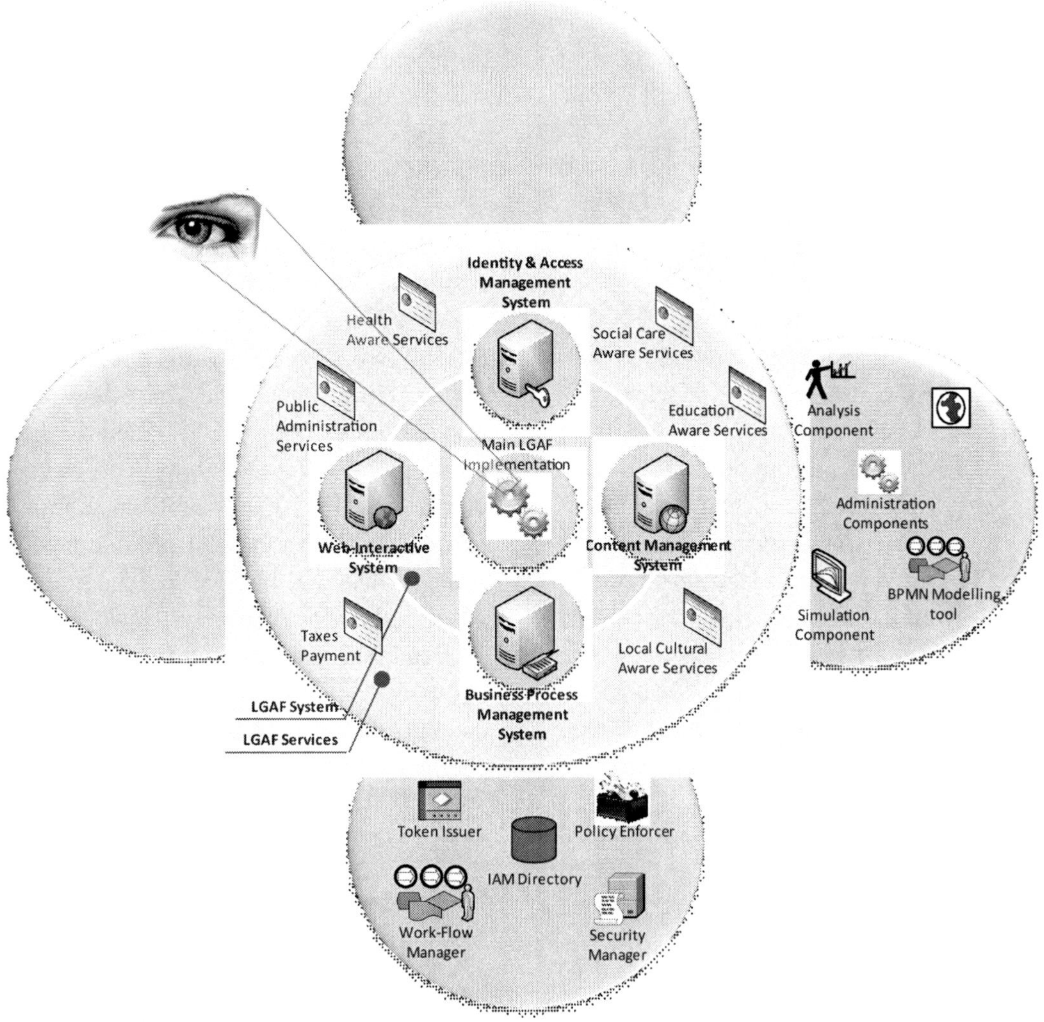

ernmental primary and processed content in a consistently organized fashion.

- A ***Business Process Management System***, which implements powerful new process modelling standards, adding advanced features in managing the business logic of the Governmental enterprise services. It actually defines and mixes human based actions, creating business rules based on workflow data.
- A federated Single-Sign-One user-centric ***Identity and Access Management -IAM*** system, which properly specifies and enforces fine-grained security and privacy policies, used to control access to *LGAF* services.
- A ***Web Interactive System***, which provides electronic secure access to *LGAF* services, information, and content, retrieved and processed from diverse sources, in a unified and user-friendly way.

The aforementioned district systems are integrated in one framework, the LGAF framework, the multitier architecture of which is depicted in the following figure:

The following paragraphs provide an analytical description of the core LGAF technological components and their integration details in one framework.

The LGAF Content Management System

Processing, navigating and dynamically analyzing large amounts of content effectively are known to be difficult problems, especially for the public sector that owns and handles vast amounts of content. The way the information is currently being processed and accessed changes dramatically day by day, and content management system tools already started playing a significant role in it, emerging Web 2.0 technologies, which come with the challenge of efficient web design that gives independence to share information in a user defined way. However, the design phase of web applications based on CMSs is very complex since the integration requires a novel environment in which data is highly coupled and the dependency of different modules on each other is also very increased.

Our open-source, novel solution, called BetaCMS (http://www.betacms.org), in the development of which the LGAF consortium participates, manages both types of content (structure and unstructured) to populate static as well as dynamic dimensions, which allow for roll-up and drill-down operations based on the content and the link-structure of the dynamically selected document subset. It maintains a content model for the metadata, which includes links between the documents, while this metadata can be either simple attributes such as document timestamps, authors, title, purpose, and so on, or more sophisticated attributes extracted from the content itself.

The adoption of the fully conforming implementation of the *Java Content Repository - JCR*, the 'Apache Jackrabbit' (http://jackrabbit.apache.org/), allows the collection of content objects and provides the essential activities for accessibility, use, and reuse, with support for structured and unstructured content, full text search, versioning, transactions, and observations.

The usage of world-wide standards, such as the ISO-2788:1986 and BS-8723:2005 (http://schemas.bs8723.org), for integrating content-aware taxonomies defines the structure of the required LGAF content objects. Among these are the *Integrated Public Sector Vocabulary – IPSV* (http://www.govtalk.gov.uk), published from the *British Government, the Taxonomy of Human Services* (LA Country, 2007), and the *European Communities Glossary* (http://europa.eu) based on e-gif specifications, enable the seamless flow of information assets and provide a long term strategy that will be able to accommodate and adapt in the near future.

BetaCMS also maintains an enriched text index allowing keyword searching functions on both the content and the metadata, and generating several challenges such as:

- *Modelling issues*: Our approach interprets the individual concepts of the BetaCMS (e.g. document, content, metadata, and links) as multidimensional entities (e.g. facts, dimensions, and measures) of each schema.
- *Operational issues*: The BetaCMS system allows any form of querying such as taxonomy search, semantic search, etc. Our query processing consists of a sequence of operations executed each time a query is issued. First the text index on the documents in the CMS is probed with the query keywords to generate a potentially large hit list. Then, the population of the multidimensional schema takes place. The metadata of the documents in the hot list are used for populating the static dimensions in the schema (e.g. dimensions based

on the topics of the documents and the frequent or relevant phrases).

- *Content-based dimension extraction*: The core property of dynamically selected documents comprises of the frequent phrases, which form the foundation for much more elaborate property extraction. Our approach 'enriches' the text index with posting lists for frequent phrases in a preprocessing step in order to generate and discover the phrases.
- *Importance extraction*: Document ranking is extremely important since it helps separate the really important documents from the noise documents. The BetaCMS adopts the *Latent Semantic Indexing - LSI* (Deerwester et al, 1988), which is a technique in natural language processing for analyzing relationships between a set of documents and the terms that they contain by producing a set of topics related to the document and terms. The weighting of the elements of each matrix is integrated using the typical *Term Frequency–Inverse Document Frequency - TF-IDF* (Salton and Burkley, 1988) score.

The LGAF CMS can be considered as the core building block of the overall framework, as it provides content-aware services to all other modules – systems. Furthermore it is the common content repository for all LGAF applications, while all basic operations are provided as SOAP/RESTFUL Web services for easy integration with systems, which adopt SOA design and implementation principles.

The LGAF Business Process Management System

By making information assets available as reusable, independent services that better correspond to the business granularity and needs, each SOA approach renders businesses better prepared for the process improvement methods and techniques, as well as for changes in business operations. Therefore, all governmental services integrated within the LGAF system are designed and implemented by means of a BPM system. This organizes the embedded logic of all LGAF applications into district states in a unified workflow. It actually puts significant emphasis on the integrated processes both in terms of streamlining process logic to improve efficiency and also establishing processes that are adaptable and extensible so that they can be augmented in response to likely the LGAF business changes (Karantjias and Polemi, 2009).

Our primary goal in orientating the integrated advanced electronic services for the public sector was to establish a highly agile automation environment, which will be realized by abstracting the logic of each business process in the public sector into its own tier, covering many different perspectives:

- *Functional*: It actually represents the process elements which are being performed. The basic elements of a business process are activities that can be either atomic or sub-processes, which are recursively refined by activities.
- *Organizational*: It represents where and by whom process elements are performed. In LGAF the metadata-model elements are inspired by the organizational unit, the role, the human, and the actual resource. Thus, if an organizational unit is addressed, its members may perform the selected activity. If a role is addressed, an activity is performed by a role or skill set. A role in this context is a function a human has within an organization, while roles and organizational units represent a human in the overall LGAF meta-model.
- *Behavioural*: It represents when process elements are performed as well as aspects of how they are performed through feedback loops, iteration, complex decision-making

conditions, entry and exit criteria, and so forth. Each data flow connects atomic activities with information resources and every other meta-model element of this perspective is adopted from the workflow control patterns. Moreover, in LGAF we adopt the advanced branching and synchronization patterns in a way that makes sense for the public sector, merging many execution paths.

- *Informational*: It represents the informational entities produced or manipulated by a process, including data, artefacts, and objects. The basic elements of this perspective are resources and events. An event may trigger an activity, while a resource is an entity to be produced or consumed by an atomic activity.
- *Business process Context*: It represents the business processes from a wide angle. It actually provides an overview of the process and describes major characteristics, such as goals and their measures, the deliverables, the process owner, its type and the end-user at a glance. In LGAF all process characteristics are integrated into the meta-model, in order to better represent essential process theory that should be also made transparent in a process model.

The implementation of the processes took place in two phases. During the first phase the LGAF consortium defined the base processes for government content posting, querying and collaboration (which are essentially related to the LGAF CMS), while during the second phase the processes for all applications and services developed in the system were adequate identified. The aforementioned processes were designed and implemented in three different versions:

- For *small-sized LGOs*, which consist of not more than 10.000 citizens
- For *medium-sized LGOs*, in which the number of citizens varies from 10.000 to 30.000
- For *large-sized LGOs*, in which the number of citizens exceeds 30.000

The main reason for designing and implementing these three versions of processes concerns the organizational structure (number of concrete departments, number of civil servants, etc) of these types of LGOs, which presents major differences. For example, in many small-sized LGOs many departments are combined the one with the other, since the number of civil servants is limited. Therefore the whole life-cycle of a process in a specific service contains more workflow steps for a large-sized LGO than in a small one. The LGAF consortium integrated in the final framework all three types of processes enabling the appropriate one in every specific case of LGO.

The LGAF system integrates the Intalio BPM enterprise platform (www.intalio.com), which is built on the Apache ODE BPEL engine (ode.apache.org; www.oasis-open.org), providing all the components required for the design, deployment, and management of the complex governmental business processes.

The LGAF BPM system (Figure 3) enables the design of the all governmental processes in the framework. It consists of four main layers:

- The *Modelling Toolkit*, which models all governmental process in order to organize their embedded logic
- The *Analysis and Simulation Toolkit*, which allows the investigation of impacts and effects of operation and changes in governmental process and organisational structures.
- The *Administration Toolkit*, which manages several configuration settings of the public environment in which the e-Governmental services operate.

Figure 3. The LGAF architecture

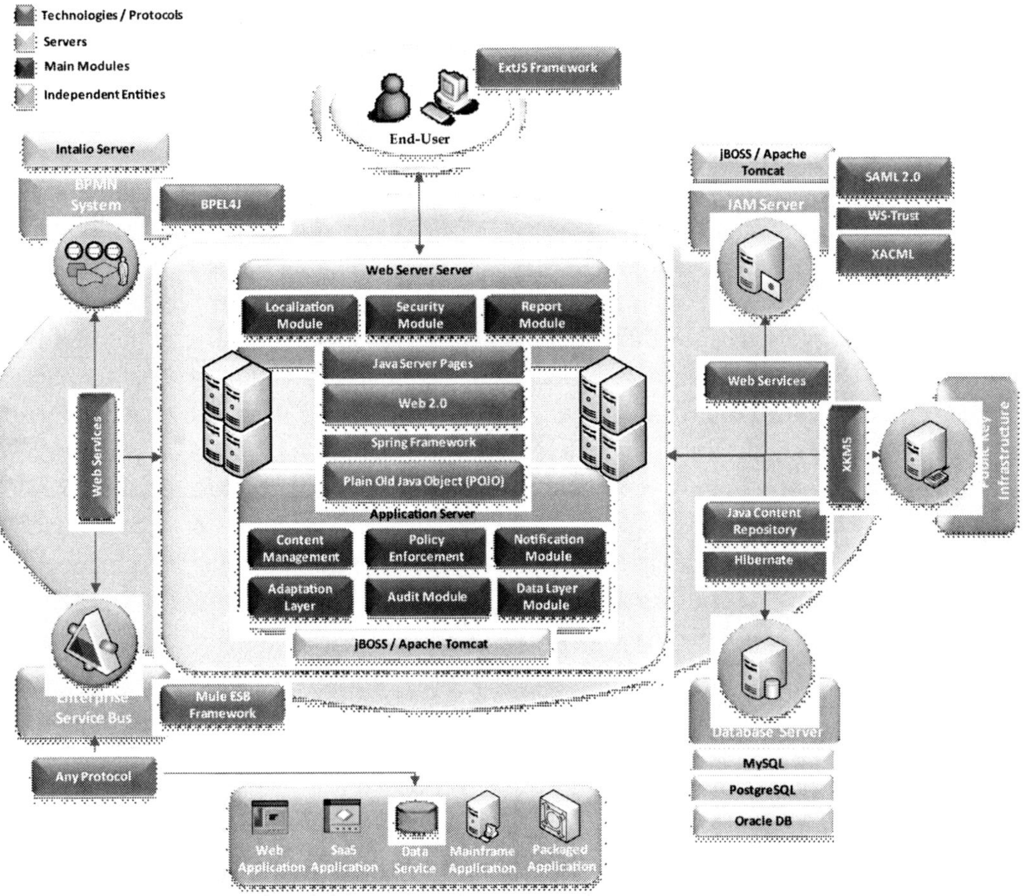

- The *Database*, which stores all the implemented processes and their current status.

The LGAF Identity and Access Management System

Privacy in massively inter-connected public environments and its social acceptance from end-users requires totally novel approaches to identity and privacy management (Karantjias et al, 2009), through trustworthy interfaces, taking into account multiple requirements such as anonymity, pseudonimity, linkability / unlinkability (Haddad, 2008), and data protection regulations (European Commission, 1997; 1999; 2001) in place.

Our approach recognizes the need for broader e-Government solutions, in which the notion of federation is expanded, and the relationship of each user with the overall framework is established, guaranteed and monitored. The LGAF IAM system undertakes the management of users' partial identities and pseudonyms, as well as the provision of proper asserted claims for accessing governmental services deployed in LGOs' SOA oriented enterprise systems.

However, the role of the IAM system is different from traditional federated Single-Sign-On integrations. Even if it provides privacy-aware services, it does not disclose user's *Personal Identification Information – PII* to the other main systems of the LGAF framework. Specifically, every other module of our framework only handles per-session registration (and consequently authentication and authorization) to maintain users' anonymity. At the end of each session the one-time pseudonym of the user is useless. Therefore, a malicious usage of our approach provides only the ability to retain the linked PII of the user for one specific session. It cannot profile user's activities since the next time the user authenticates to the IAM system, a new pseudonym will be assigned to him which means that every other module of the framework will not be able to link the PII revealed from previous sessions with the new pseudonym.

The LGAF IAM, the architecture of which is depicted in Figure 4, system mainly consists of the following main components:

- The OASIS eXtensible Access Control Markup Language (XACML) (Rieger and Neumair, 2007) - based *Policy Enforcement* (Papastergiou, et al, 2007) module specifies and enforces fine-grained, system-readable privacy policies, used to control access to Web Services, digital objects and services, enclosing users' PII preferences and IAM's business requirements. It is actually the component that receives the authorization requests and LGOs' identification information preferences. If these are satisfied it initializes a per-session registration negotiation process for each user, responding with LGOs' identification information list. The same component receives user's PII disclosure preferences and decides whether to accept them or not. Therefore, within this component an initial policy matching of the LGOs' require-

Figure 4. The LGAF IAM system

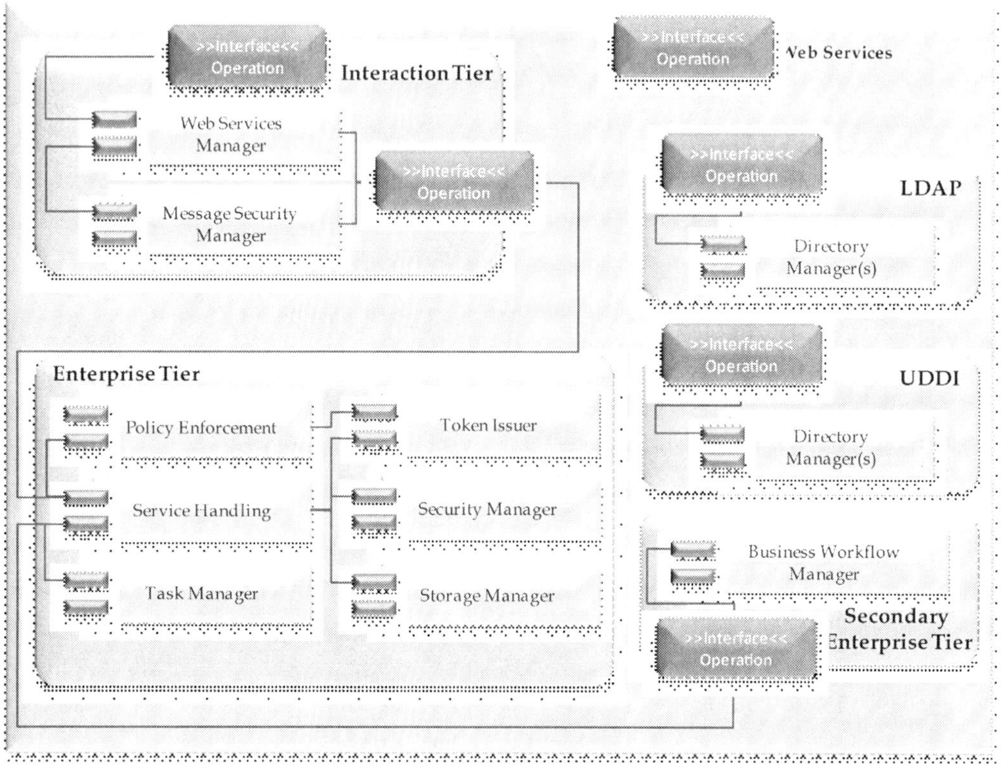

ments with users' preferences and capabilities and vice versa is achieved.

- The *Security Manager* module handles all the security credentials required for authenticating the user or the system in the framework. Our approach integrates two kinds of authentication methods. All citizens use usernames and passwords, while civil servants and main components of the LGAF framework which need to act on behalf of users and interact with other systems on different public organizations use digital certificates provided from a national *Public Key Infrastructure - PKI* (Adams and Lloyd, 1999). Therefore this module implements all the advanced security mechanisms on the IAM system such as the creation/validation of XML digital signatures and XML encryption and decryption. Even if the details of the underlying PKI infrastructure is out of the scope of the LGAF framework we would like to mention that the key-size and the encryption/singing algorithms used are of sufficient length and strength to prevent reasonable adversaries from breaking the cryptographic schemes.
- The *Token Issuer* module issues XML-based security tokens, integrating the WS-Trust standard (Nadalin et al, 2009), and provides strong authorization and advanced auditing mechanisms. To maximize interoperability with e-clients and systems from multiple vendors, the IAM supports the WS-Federation and SAML 2.0 protocols (Lockhart and Campbell, 2007). For higher administrative efficiency, it automates federation trust configuration and management, using the harmonized federation metadata format (Kaler and McIntosh, 2009). This automation enables the IAM system and LGOs to publish their federation metadata in a standard format, which can be exchanged between potential partners. Therefore, the usage of a single specifications that can support both passive web application and active Web Services requestors is a key advantage for effectively operate our IAM system in multiple and heterogeneous environments.
- The *Workflow Manager,* which manages the choreography of the IAM system's services, implementing their business logic, defining and mixing human based actions and creating business rules based on workflow data.
- The *IAM Directory*, in which privacy and security aware data such as the various profiles of the end-users are securely stored.

The LGAF IAM system is built on top of the every tool and application of the overall LGAF framework. It allows for clean separation between the various services that the end-users access and the associated authentication and authorization procedures required, enabling collaboration across the mass LGAF applications and tools, networks, and organizations in different trust realms.

The LGAF Web Interactive System

The LGAF *Web Interactive System* provides electronic based point of secure access to LGAF information and content, retrieved and processed from diverse sources, in a unified and user-friendly way. As every synchronous governmental system, it integrates complex mechanisms and operations, which are transparent to all end users (citizens, organizations and civil servants). Automated processing is linked to the operational costs of the e-services for public organizations, which satisfy a great number of requests with the need of only a handful of personnel under normal operations. In LGAF this is leveraged by integrating innovative technologies, which give to citizens and businesses the opportunity to perform part of processes by themselves, using Web Services for reducing human intervention in *Business-to-Citizen - B2C* and *Business-to-Business - B2B* transactions to the largest possible extent.

The use of strong, open source frameworks and rich User Interface (UI) technologies such as Spring Web Flow - SWF, Java Server Faces – JSF, Ajax4jsf, RichFaces and Facelets, provide a user friendly web component based architecture, improving system performance (Karantjias and Polemi, 2009). Moreover, they offer LGAF the opportunity to easily build interactive interfaces and templates with basic form controls and efficient, reusable operations, while future architecturally developers will be able to separate the presentation logic (the "what") from the UI component's business logic (the "why" and "how").

Overview of the LGAF Architecture

The process map, BPMN models, the document definitions, the XML schemas, and the related technical components of all above-described entities are integrated in one enterprise framework, as depicted in Figure 5.

Figure 5. The LGAF multilayer framework

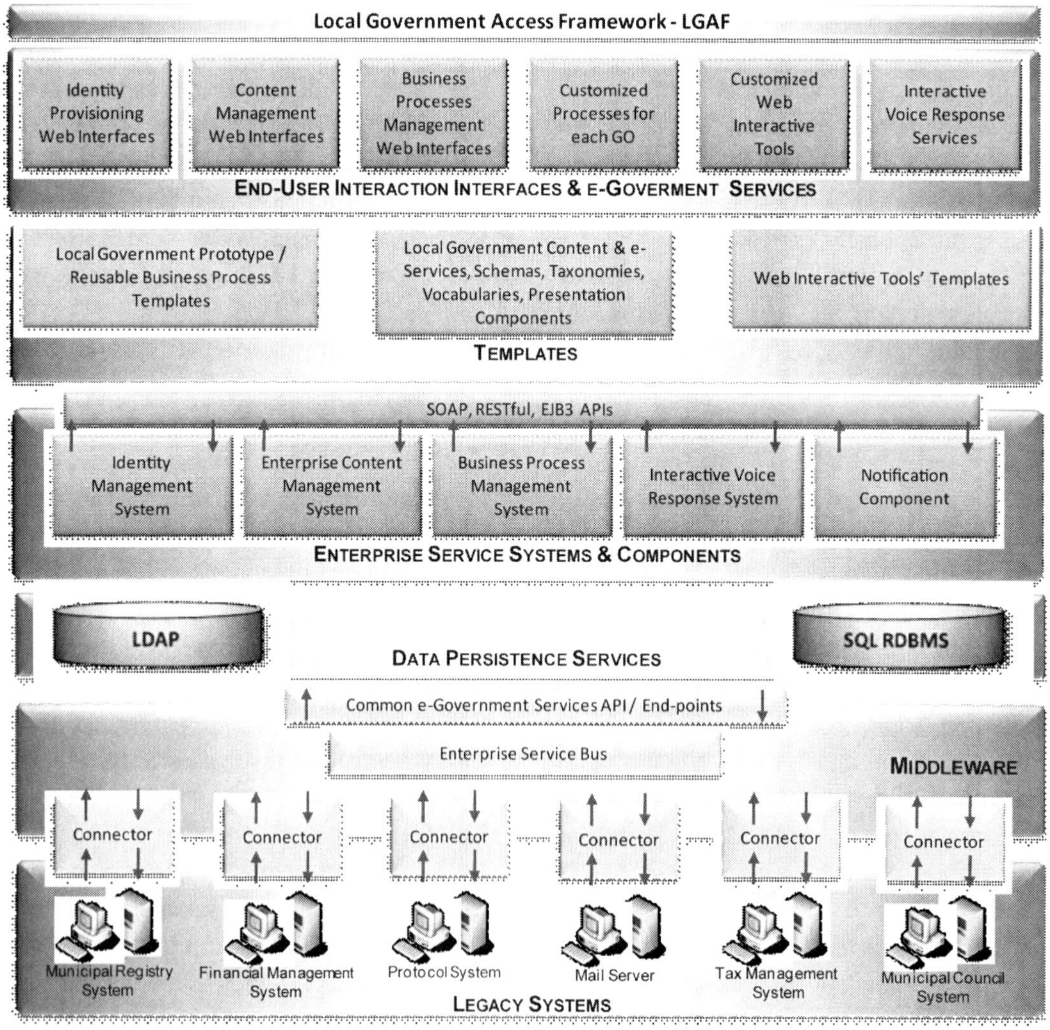

A main difficulty that emerged was to find a universal and standardized way to interoperate with all these different kinds of applications, systems, and tools. In addition to this the interconnection of this core LGAF system component with existing, self-sufficient applications and systems (legacy systems), which do not necessarily conform to the assumptions of SOA's distributed system model, was also an emerging problem that required a solid solution. Specifically, the difficulties faced are summarized as follows:

- *Proprietary Interfaces:* Integration logic in terms of transformation rules, workflow services etc. cannot be ported between the different solutions that most governmental organizations host and operate. In their majority, these solutions are closely linked to different vendors, weakening the durability of integration-related developments.
- *Limited communication protocols:* The end-to-end supervision of business processes, which are executed in more than one system is very difficult. Although the use of SOAP/HTTP protocols provides a bridge between different solutions, it only tackles the rudimentary issue of the session-less RPC, overlooking other fundamental architecture services such as guaranteed delivery and limiting interoperability among them.
- *Lack of scalability:* Deporting all or parts of a central integration logic to Web Services connectors has never been a trivial task and is something very complex to deploy and administer.

A properly integrated and configured middleware tier of LGAF architecture, as depicted in Figure 3 and 5, implementing the Mule *Enterprise Service Bus - ESB,* provides adequately solutions to the aforementioned problems. Specifically this tier is built on top of the LGAF CMS in order to allow further integration with other advanced governmental tools, applications, and services. It manages all interactions between the various components transparently, stipulating that different applications communicate through a common messaging bus, while it orchestrates all the Web Services integrated in the framework

The goal of this middleware tier (Figure 5) is actually that every communication with the main framework is standardised, while the communication with every specific legacy system in LGOs is built appropriately with every possible custom technology and method, without affecting the main architecture of the framework.

THE DIFFERENT ANGLES OF THE LGAF FRAMEWORK

In LGAF there are different diagrammatic representations of the modelled architectures at each level that correspond to different angles from which the main user-roles involved 'understand' the whole system. Among these roles someone could clearly identify the following:

- Software Engineers, who are able to view the technology stack view of the framework and improve its components
- System Engineers, who are able to view the system view undertaking the installation and distribution of the various components of the LGAF servers, and executing the settings of all supporting technologies
- Software Architects, who build new services or modify existing components composing reusable framework's services
- Business Analysts and/or End-Users, who understand the platform as finally delivered operational software components (applicable modules), used to perform their daily operational functions, as depicted in Figure 6, with which each LGO processes and exchanges information, providing advanced electronic services

Once installed in a public agency, the LGAF framework is able to support the whole life-cycle provision of services to citizens and civil-servants, including the following:

- The analytical presentation of services to citizens
- The management of communication and reception of relevant requests from end-users (citizens, organizations)
- The automatic management of workflows required to process and service requests
- The communication between internal and external systems involved in servicing the requests
- The coordination of actions implemented by the executives of local authorities to implement end-users' requests
- Sending messages and notifications to end-users
- The content management of services and related workflows of the executives of local authorities

The goal regarding the provision of default functionality of the LGAF framework is that it enables the direct creation of electronic services in LGOs with a simple installation and high-level configuration. The supplied pre-installed functionality (Figure 6) includes:

- A user-friendly portal with pre-standard web pages and structure, which grants access to a large number of one-stop public electronic services
- A set of XSD Schemas which model:

Figure 6. Out of the box functionality of the LGAF Framework

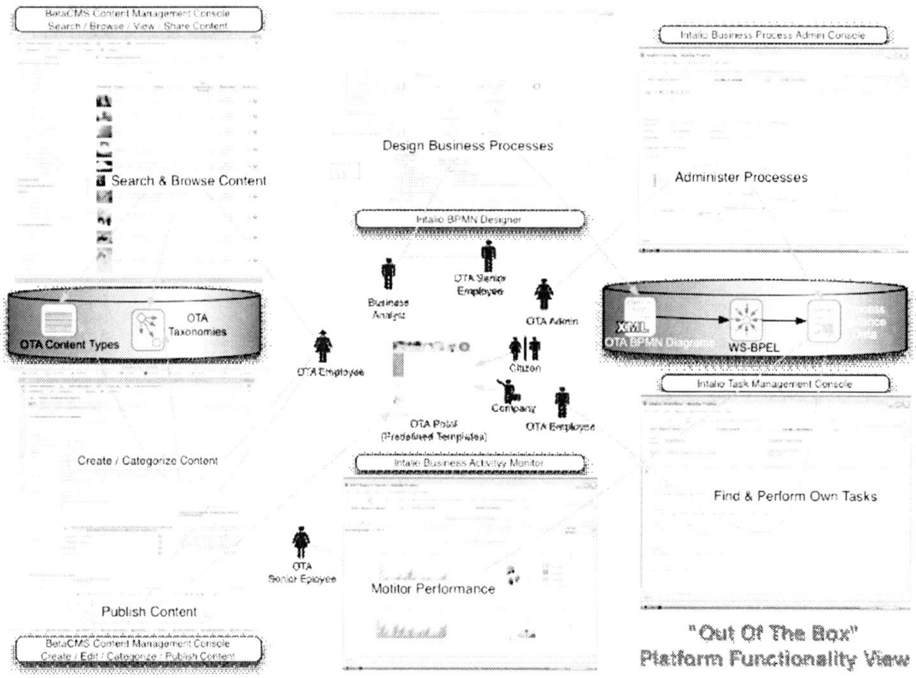

    - The types of information presented on the portal (ex. articles, circulars, newsletters, public documents, requests, public decisions, etc)
    - The information exchanged with end-users and other organizations of the public and the private sector
- A set of taxonomies that describe the types of information provided by local authorities and agencies and the dictionaries used for all advanced services provided (ex. Content classification service levels, descriptions of the Regions / Departments / Prefectures / Municipalities, etc)
- A set of public services' workflows provided in two different forms:
    - BPMN diagrams, which can be furthered be processed and updated from LGOs
    - Executables BPEL workflows, which actually provide the operational flows of services
- A set of Web Services and WSDL descriptions of modelled messages, exchanged between the services that the LGAF framework implements and the legacy systems (Back-Offices) used by local authorities
- A graphical console (WebUI) for managing the content provided by all services and the management of communication forms implemented on the portal

Critical Design Factors

Our involvement in designing and building large, national and international, cross border enterprise frameworks for the public sector (eMayor IST project, 2006; SWEB IST project, 2007, LGAF project, 2009) convince us that effective guidelines, principles and policies should be established in order for the provided services to gain end-users' acceptance and allow the coordination and alignment of business processes and information architectures that span both intra- and inter- public organizational boundaries.

Our proposition is that every governmental implementation should realize the adoption of at least seven fundamental architectural principles, as depicted in Figure 7. The main benefit of these is the consistent usage of standards-based architectures, which provide easily modified and expanded functionality and re-engineered e-Government services, ensuring that end-users perceive the quality of the services provided, and trust of these that being delivered.

The existence of strong relations among the following principles imprints that the satisfaction of one may need to benefit from the satisfaction of another one:

- ***Modularity:*** Every module should be a component of a larger system, and operate within that system independently in its operation, following the LGAF example. Thus, the integrated system will be able to decompose an operating problem into a small number of less complex sub-problems, which are usually connected by a simple structure, and independent enough to allow further work to continue separately on each item (Karantjias et al, 2008). This way the effect of an abnormal condition will remain confined to it, or at worst it will only propagate to a few neighbouring ones.
- ***Open Standards:*** A primary requirement when designing and implementing e-Government prototypes should be the minimization of costs not only for the current integration but also for every future improvement of it, due to the fact that governmental organizations usually lack of financial resources and IT well trained personnel. Besides, private companies are typically compelled by the realities of profit making, while organizations of the public sector do not have such profit-oriented motivations. Essentially, such implementations should

Figure 7. Fundamental non-functional architectural design principles

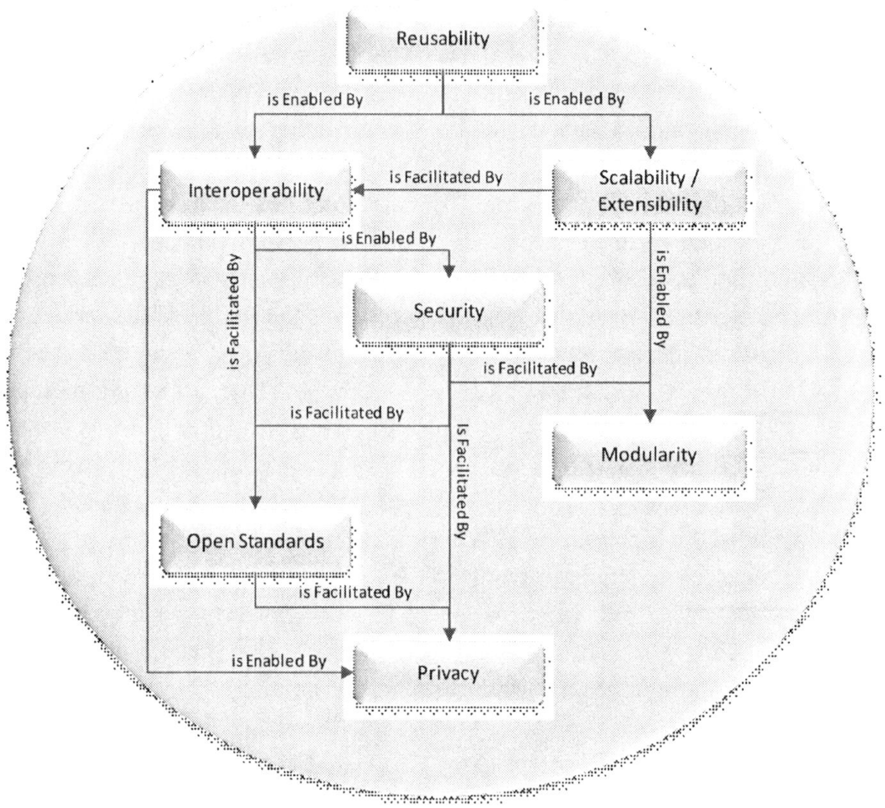

adopt peak technologies and worldwide accepted and mature standards in order to build *Enterprise Application Integration - EAI* and technology frameworks, providing advanced added-value electronic services according to *Software-as-a-Service - SaaS* model (Finch, 2006)

- ***Interoperability:*** Interconnecting many distributed and heterogeneous enterprise systems, is a difficult task, requiring easily identifiable and publishable services, as well as interfaces for the establishment of secure and reliable connection points (Karantjias and Polemi, 2009). Interoperability among the core entities of a large scale enterprise system is achieved by adopting Web Services as the core communication protocol, and advanced XML-based technologies.

The integration of Middleware Layers, which will integrate truly interoperable mechanisms through the use of ESB frameworks (Khoshafian, 2006) is proposed by the authors in such cases. This will undertake to manage all internal and external to the system interactions between the various components transparently, stipulating that different components of applications communicate through a common messaging bus. In this context, semantic interoperability among the different e-Government systems should be handled by using standards-based ontologies following mostly existing European ones (Harris *et al.*, 2008).

- ***Scalability & Extensibility:*** Advanced enterprise solutions demand the creation of a dependency between business and information technologies in order for governmental organizations to be able to maintain scalable and extensible systems that efficiently will support their business activities. An e-Government system should allow the abstraction of proprietary applications through the use of adapters, brokers, and orchestration engines. Thus, the resulting integration architecture will be more robust and extensible, especially with the advent of the open Web Services framework and its ability to fully abstract proprietary technology. The authors believe that the use of BPMN technologies for modelling all business processes in the core enterprise will organize the embedded logic of an application into separate and easily changed 'state machines' (Pasley, 2005), establishing a highly agile automation environment, fully capable of adapting to change, which will be realized by abstracting the business process logic into its own tier. Thereby, the integrators will be able to alleviate other services from the need to repeatedly embed process logic, and support process optimization as a primary source of change for which services can be recomposed.

- ***Security:*** There are five critical security requirements that need to be satisfied (Hartman *et al.*, 2003):
  - *Authentication*, the method with which an entity is uniquely identified and its identity verified.
  - *Integrity*, the method that ensures that every system, resource, file and information in general can be modified only by authorized entities.
  - *Privacy and confidentiality*, the method by which access to the content of information is available only to authorized recipients.
  - *Non-repudiation*, the method that produces cryptographic data that ensure that an entity cannot repudiate its actions.
  - *Availability*, the method that ensures that a system can fulfil its purpose with a given degree of success.

An e-Government service can satisfy the security requirements by making use of set of *security mechanisms* and a set of *security services*. Security mechanisms are stand alone instances of components that are directly embedded within an e-Government enterprise service and that addresses a security requirement based on a policy. Security services on the other hand, are independent services within an e-Government architecture that are available to any enterprise service wishing to perform a security goal as part of a policy. Security services integrate security mechanisms, and may interact with other security services as part of their operation. Security mechanisms may also interact with security services to send and receive information.

Although Web Services and SOAs permit enterprises to create interoperable services and applications, their original definition didn't include a strong, built-in security model. Today, security is one of the primary challenges when implementing e-strategies for the public sector.

Second generation PKIs (Adams and Lloyd, 1999) and advanced XML cryptography mechanisms such as XML digital signature and encryption support a large scale deployment of a number of security services, such as origin authentication, content integrity, confidentiality, and non-repudiation, establishing trust chains at local, national and international level. Electronic signatures and related services that allow data authentication can, therefore, play an important role in this aspect by ensuring security and trust in every e-transactions.

The integration of large-scale e-Government solutions should highly consider existing European Directives such as the 1999/93/EC (EC, 1999) which impose the legal recognition of electronic signatures defining two levels of security that organizations may apply to e-signatures depending on the sensitivity of the transaction:

- Simple e-signatures, for a minimum level of security, integrating the W3C XML Digital Signature - XML-DSIG standard, which defines the appropriate way for rendering digital signatures in XML.
- Advanced electronic signatures, XAdES signatures, for a higher level of security, implementing the ETSI standard (Karantjias et al, 2009).

Privacy: Privacy in massively inter-connected environments and its social acceptance from end-users require totally novel approaches to identity and privacy management (Papastergiou et al, 2007).

These must adopt trustworthy interfaces, taking into account multiple requirements (e.g. anonymity, pseudonimity, linkability / unlinkability) (Hansen et al, 2008) and data protection regulations (EC, 1997; EC, 2001) in place, enabling:

- End-users to administrate and control their identities on their own, and easily e-access advanced business services
- Governmental organizations to harmonise their authentication/authorisation procedures, enhancing the majority of their infrastructures by easily plug-in them to a core IAM system and to effectively secure and manage their enterprises.

The authors believe that a synchronous e-Government approach should recognize the need for broader e-solutions, in which the notion of federation is expanded, and the relationship of each user with the framework is established, guaranteed and monitored by a trusted third entity. A user-centric and federated solution will allow for clean separation between each service and the associated authentication and authorization procedures required. Thus the collaboration across multiple systems, networks, and organizations in different trust realms will be expanded, ensuring that:

- Each user/organization will perceive high quality of the privacy-aware services provided.
- End-users will be able to manage their identities personally, without the involvement of the various Service Providers
- Service Providers will be able to utilize the majority of their systems in an open and scalable privacy-aware IAM framework.

Reusability: The goals behind service reusability are tied directly to some of the most strategic objectives of service-oriented computing, which should be strongly supported by synchronous e-Government integration (Karantjias et al, 2008). These objectives have as follows:

- Allow for service logic to be repeatedly leveraged over time so as to achieve an increasingly high return on the initial investment of delivering the service;
- Increase business agility by enabling the rapid fulfilment of future business automation requirements through wide-scale service composition;
- Enable the realization of agnostic service models;
- Enable the creation of service inventories with a high percentage of these agnostic services.

Rather than embedding functionality that should be deployed across every specific service, an e-Government system should offer advanced and reusable security, storage and Web Services interfaces to application developers in order to easily expand its functionality and build upon it. Integrators' main focus should be to offer an innovative implementation framework, in which all essential public aware functions could be easily reused, configured and customized in every e-service provided.

CONCLUSION

Although, the engineering world appears today more mature than ever in providing stable technology premises in order to build real interoperable and secure systems (Chetty and Coetzee, 2009) for LGOs, enterprise information architects still struggle to define fundamental principles, strategies and policies in designing large-scale, scalable, extensible and high-administrative local government solutions (Karantjias *et al.*, 2009).

Advanced SOAs are considered the most promising way to achieve complex communication among multiple e-government actors across organizational domains. The deployment of an effective e-government policy requires a coherent design and implementation approach that considers fundamental design principles toward the provisioning of customer-centric e-services. Essentially, this paper intends to provide practical and comprehensive coverage of a synchronous, user-centric, federated framework, the LGAF framework, which consists of advanced e-Government enterprise systems that transform the delivery of public services from 'standing in line' to online: anytime, anywhere, by any means, and in interactive mode.

This framework addresses core electronic government requirements of security, interoperability, transparency, scalability and high administration in the communications with their citizens, businesses and other similar organizations. Its "out of the box functionality" facilitates the creation and provision of advanced government business services with a simple installation and customization, thus enabling:

- Developers to easily extend its functionality reusing several architecture modules when implementing new governmental services.
- Business analysts to reengineer the deployed enterprise services, using graphical interfaces of the BPM system on runtime environment, and redeploy the service.

Its adoption enables faster interaction among entities and minimizes effort to obtain public documents from multiple sources, while at the same time providing for privacy, integrity and confidentiality. This solution promotes the modelling procedure of future government services, providing all advanced mechanisms and features to multiple roles of users to participate in this effort, and it achieves the following benefits:

- **Increased productivity:** better output in terms of the quantity and quality of traditional results, or the performance of previously impossible tasks;
- **Cost effectiveness:** due to reduction in time duration, complexity or possible repetition/duplication of tasks;
- **Improved service delivery:** offering equal access to government services, more and better information, choice of level/quality of service and guaranteed standards (including privacy), remedies for failures and, ultimately, value for money.

Application knowledge by government is not only creating more challenges within the public organizations in trying to utilize the knowledge of their employees more productively, but the organizations are also pressured into changing their corporate strategies to encourage this utilization in order to remain competitive. In this process, competitive advantage in today's global and rapidly changing market requires organizations to build and continually replenish capabilities at both individual and organizational levels, to work effectively with uncertainty, especially considering digital gap in developing countries.

Despite the fact that this paper describes many technological solutions for developing cross-boundary information and services sharing to support government response capacities, LGOs must also establish and maintain collaborative relationships in which knowledge sharing will be critical to resolve numerous issues, related to data definitions and structures, diverse database designs, highly variable data quality, and incompatible network infrastructures. These integration processes will often involve new work processes and significant organizational change. Additionally, social processes, which interact with entities such as theoretical frameworks, digital policies, and organizational behaviour, are critical components of integration.

Similarly in order to have successful e-Government policy implementations, it is necessary to establish their legitimacy, secure their efficiency and gain the trust between government and citizens and also provide for the legal aspects to become part of their roadmap. Yet the e-Government legal frameworks are still in infancy. A cohesive legal framework is required for helping the facilitation of a better progress. During LGAF implementation, the main domains of concerns identified, included the 'Back-Office' re-organization, the inclusive access, the trust and confidence, and the better use of public sector information. Therefore, four main sets of legislation are considered relevant: Personal data protection laws; Privacy and security laws; Information (provision) laws; and Administrative laws in National and International level.

ACKNOWLEDGMENT

The authors would like to thank the E.C. and the Greek Ministry of Interior for their support in funding the LGAF project and all the project partners.

REFERENCES

Adams, C., & Lloyd, S. (1999). *Understanding public key infrastructure – Concepts, standards, and deployment considerations* (1st ed.). MacMillan Technical Publishing.

Alcock, R., & Lenihan, D. G. (2001). *Opening the e-government file: Governing in the 21st century-Results of the crossing boundaries cross-country tour* (*Vol. 2*, p. 31). Ontario, Canada: Center for Collaborative Government.

Australian Government Information Management Office (AGIMO). (2006). *E-Government strategy, responsive government: A new service agenda.* Retrieved April 2007 from http:// www.finance.gov.au/ e-government/ strategy-and-governance/ index.html

Benson, T. (2002). *The e-services development framework* (eSDF). UK Cabinet Office, Office of the e-Envoy, Volume 1.0b

BetaCMS. (2008). *An open source JCR-compliant, enterprise content infrastructure & content management platform.* Retrieved from http:// www.betacms.org

Boiko, B. (2004). *Content management bible* (2nd ed.). Wiley Publishing.

BS 8723. (2005). *Structured vocabularies for information retrieval: Exchange formats and protocols for interoperability.* Retrieved from http:// schemas.bs8723.org/

Carter, L., & Bélanger, F. (2005). The utilization of e-government services: Citizen trust, innovation and acceptance factors. *Information Systems Journal*, *15*, 5–25. doi:10.1111/j.1365-2575.2005.00183.x

Checkland, P., & Scholes, J. (1999). *Soft systems methodology in action.* West Sussex, UK: John Wiley & Sons Ltd.

Chetty, J., & Coetzee, M. (2009). *Considering contracts for governance in service-oriented architectures*. Information and Computer Security Architecture (ICSA). Retrieved from http:// icsa. cs.up.ac.za/ issa/ 2008/ Proceedings/ Research/6. pdf

Country, L. A. (2007). *A taxonomy of human services: A conceptual framework with standardized terminology and definitions for the field.* General Social Sciences, Taxonomy Warehouse. Retrieved from http:// www.taxonomywarehouse.com/ vocabdetails_include.asp?vVocID=370

Deerwester, S., Dumais, S., Furnas, G., Harshman, R., Landauer, T., Lochbaum, K., & Streeter, L. (1988). *Latent semantic indexing (LSI).* US Patent 4.839.853.

Devadoss, P. R., Pan, S. L., & Huagng, J. C. (2002). Structurational analysis of e-government initiatives: a case study of SCO. *Decision Support Systems*, *34*(4), 253–269.

Dublin Core Metadata Initiative (DCMI). (n.d.). *Website*. Retrieved from http:// dublincore.org/

eMayor IST project. (2006). *Electronic and secure municipal administration for European citizens.* 6th Framework Programme, IST-2004-507217. Retrieved from www.emayor.org

eTen. (2007).*E-ten programme: Support for trans-European telecommunications networks.* Retrieved from http:// europa.eu/legislation_summaries/ information_society/ l24226e_en.htm

European Commission (EC). (1997). *Directive 97/66/EC of the European Parliament and of the Council concerning the processing of personal data and the protection of privacy in the telecommunications sector*, (pp. 1–8).

European Commission (EC). (1999). *Directive 99/93/EC of the European Parliament and of the Council of 13 December 1999 on a community framework for electronic signatures* (pp. 12 – 20).

European Commission (EC). (2001). *Directive 01/45/EC of the European Parliament and the Council of Ministers on the protection of individuals with regard to the processing of personal data by the community institutions and bodies and on the free movement of such data* (pp. 1–22).

European Commission (EC). (2006). *i2010 e-government action plan: Accelerating e-government in Europe for the benefit of all.* Retrieved from http:// ec.europa.eu/ idabc/ en/ document/ 5763/ 254

European Community. (n.d.). *Europa glossary.* Retrieved from http:// europa.eu/ scadplus/ glossary/ eu_communities_en.htm

FIDIS IST project. (2004). *The future of identity in the information society (FIDIS): Towards a global dependability and security framework.* Sixth Framework Programme, European Commission.

Finch, C. (2006). The benefits of the software-as-a-service model. *ComputerWorld.* Retrieved from http:// www.computerworld.com/ action/ article.do?command=viewArticleBasic&articleId=107276

Finger, M., & Pecoud, G. (2003). From e-government to e-governance? Towards a model of e-governance. *Proceedings of 3rd European Conference on e-Government*, Trinity College Dublin, Ireland. 3-4 July

Fountain, J. (2001). *Building the virtual state: Information Technology and institutional change.* Washington, DC: Brookings Institution Press.

Gartner. (2003). *New performance framework measures public value of IT.* Research Note, Gartner

Hansen, M., Pfitzmann, A., & Steinbrecher, S. (2008). Identity management throughout one's whole life. *Elsevier Advanced Technology Publications. Information Security Technical Report*, *13*(2), 83–94. doi:10.1016/j.istr.2008.06.003

Harris, S., Gibbons, J., & Davies, J. Tsui, A., & Crichton, C. (2008). Semantic technologies in electronic government. *Proceedings of the 2nd International Conference on Theory and Practice of Electronic Governance. ACM International Conference Proceedings*, Cairo, Egypt, 351, (pp. 45-51).

Harvard Business Press. (2009). *SWOT analysis II: Looking inside for strengths and weaknesses*. Cambridge, MA: Harvard Business School Press.

Heeks, R. (1999). Reinventing government in the information age. In Heeks, R. (Ed.), *International practice in IT-enabled public sector reform*. New York, NY: Routledge Publishing. doi:10.4324/9780203204962

Hermes Project. (2009). *Website*. Retrieved from http:// www.ermis.gov.gr

Ho, A. T. (2002). Reinventing local governments and the e-government initiative. *Public Administration Review*, *62*(4), 434–444. doi:10.1111/0033-3352.00197

Intalio Enterprise Cloud Company. (2009). *Intalio BPM open source business process platform*. Intalio Incorporation. Retrieved August 2009 from http:// ww.intalio.com/ products/ bpm/

Intelcities, I. S. T. Project. (2006). *Intelligent cities*. 6th Framework Programme, IST-2004-507860, Retrieved from http:// intelcities.iti.gr/ intelcities

Interoperable Delivery of European eGovernment Services to public Administrations Businesses and Citizens (IDABC). (2007). *The IDABC programme* (2005-2009). Retrieved from http:// europa.eu/ legislation_summaries/ information_society/ l24147b_en.htm

Irani, Z., Elliman, T., & Jackson, P. (2007). Electronic transformation of government in the UK: A research agenda. *European Journal of Information Systems*, *16*, 327–335. doi:10.1057/ palgrave.ejis.3000698

Irani, Z., & Love, P. E. D. (2001). The propagation of technology management taxonomies for evaluating investments in manufacturing resource planning (MRPII). *Journal of Management Information Systems*, *17*(3), 161–177.

Irani, Z., Love, P. E. D., Elliman, T., Jones, S., & Themistocleous, M. (2005). Evaluating e-government: Learning from the experiences of two UK local authorities. *Information Systems Journal*, *15*, 61–82. doi:10.1111/j.1365-2575.2005.00186.x

Jeston, J., & Nelis, J. (2008). *Business process management, 2nd edition: Practical guidelines to successful implementation*. Butterworth-Heinemann Publishing

Kaler, C., & McIntosh, M. (2009). *Web services federation language (WS-Federation) version 1.2: Advancing open standards for the information society*. OASIS Standard.

Karantjias, A., & Polemi, N. (2009). An innovative platform architecture for complex, secure e/m-Governmental services. *International Journal of Electronic Security and Digital Forensics (IJESDF). Special Issue in Mobile Services Technological and Legal Issues*, *2*(4), 338–354.

Karantjias, A., Polemi, N., Stamati, T., & Martakos, D. (2009). A user-centric & federated single-sign-in IAM system for SOA e/m-frameworks. *International Journal of Electronic Government (IJEG), Special Issue on Usability and Privacy Issues in Electronic and Mobile Government, 7*(3).

KEDKE. (n.d.). *Central Union of Municipalities and Communities of Greece*. Retrieved from http:// www.kedke.gr/

Khoshafian, S. (2006). *Service oriented enterprises* (1st ed.). Auerbach Publishing. doi:10.1201/9781420013269

Kling, R. (2000). Learning about Information Technologies and social change: The contribution of social informatics. *The Information Society*, *16*(3), 217–232. doi:10.1080/01972240050133661

Koussouris, S., Tsitsanis, A., Gionis, G., & Psarras, J. (2008). Designing generic municipal services process models towards e-government interoperability infrastructures. *Electronic Journal for E-Commerce Tools and Applications, eJETA Special Issue on Interoperability for Enterprises and Administrations Worldwide.*

Laudon, K. C., & Laudon, J. P. (2002). *Management Information Systems: Managing the digital firm* (7th ed.). New Jersey: Prentice Hall.

LAWs project. (2004). *Local authority websites national project (LAWs).* Retrieved from http:// www.laws-project.org.uk/

LGAF project. (2009). *Local government access framework.* 6th Framework Programme. Retrieved from http:// lgaf.kedke.org/ wiki

Lockhart, H., & Campbell, B. (2007). *SAML V2.0 errata.* Advancing Open Standards for the Information Society. OASIS Standard.

Mecella, M., & Batini, C. (2001). Enabling Italian e-government through a cooperative architecture. *IEEE Computer, 34*(2), 40–45.

Millard, J., Warren, R., Leitner, C., & Shahin, J. (2006).*EU: Towards the e-government vision for the EU in 2010.* Report for the European Commission, Draft Final Report. Retrieved from http:// fiste.jrc.ec.europa.eu/ pages/ documents/ eGovresearchpolicychallenges-DRAFTFINAL-WEBVERSION.pdf

Mioga 2. (2004). *Mioga 2 groupware solution: Collaborative work, shared organizers.* Retrieved from http:// www.mioga2.org

MMBase. (2006). *MMBase relational object mapping tool.* Retrieved from http:// www.mmbase.org/

Moon, M. J. (2002). The evolution of e-government among municipalities: Rhetoric or reality? *Public Administration Review, 62*(4), 424–433. doi:10.1111/0033-3352.00196

Nadalin, A., Goodner, M., Gudgin, M., Barbir, A., & Granqvist, H. (2009). *WS-trust 1.4. Advancing Open Standards for the Information Society.* OASIS Standard.

Ndou, V. (2004). E-government for developing countries: Opportunities and challenges. *Electronic Journal of Information Systems in Developing Countries, 18*(1), 1–24.

Object Management Group (OMG). (2009). *Business process model and notation* (BPMN). OMG standard, version 1.2. Retrieved from http:// www.omg.org/ spec/ BPMN/ 1.2/ PDF/

OECD. (2003). *The e-government imperative: Main finding.* Paris, France: Organisation for Economic Co-operation and Development.

OECD. (2004). The e-government imperative. Cedex 16, Paris, France.

Papastergiou, S., Karantjias, A., & Polemi, D. (2007). A federated privacy-enhancing identity management system (FPE-IMS). *Proceedings of the 18th Annual IEEE International Symposium on Personal, Indoor and Mobile Radio Communications, PIMRC 07*, September, Athens, Greece, (pp. 1-5).

Pardo, T., & Scholl, H. J. (2002). Walking atop the cliffs: Avoiding failure and reducing risk in large scale e-government projects. *Proceedings of the 35th Hawaii International Conference*, Hawaii.

Pasley, J. (2005). How BPEL and SOA are changing Web services development. *IEEE Internet Computing, 9*(3), 60–67. doi:10.1109/ MIC.2005.56

Peristeras, V., & Tarabanis, K. (2004). Governance enterprise architecture (GEA): Domain models for e-government. *Proceedings of the 6th International Conference in Electronic Commerce, ACM International Conferences, 60*, (pp. 471-479).

Rieger, S., & Neumair, B. (2007). Towards usable and reasonable Identity Management in hererogeneous IT infrastructures. *Proceedings of 10th IFIP/IEEE International Symposium on Integrated Network Management – IM'07*, Munich, Germany, (pp. 560-574).

Salton, G., & Burkley, C. (1988). Term-weighting approaches in automatic text retrieval. *Information Processing & Management. Elsevier Science Ltd, 24*(5), 513–523.

Schedler, K., & Scharf, M. C. (2000). *Exploring the interrelations between electronic government and the new public management: A managerial framework for electronic government.* Switzerland: Work report, Institute for Public Services and Tourism, University of St. Gallen. German

Sealy, W. U. (2003). Empowering development through e-governance: Creating smart communities in small island states. *The International Information & Library Review, 35*(2-4), 335–358. doi:10.1016/S1057-2317(03)00020-1

Stamati, T., & Martakos, D. (2011). Electronic transformation of local government: An exploratory study. *International Journal of Electronic Government Research (IJEGR), Special Issue on Scope, Objective, and Achievement of E-government: E-government to E-governance.* IGI Global. In press.

SWEB IST project. (2007). *Secure, interoperable, cross border m-services contributing towards a trustful European cooperation with the non-EU member Western Balkan countries.* 6th Framework Programme, IST-2006-2.6.5. Retrieved from www.sweb-project.org

Syzeyxis Project. (2008). *Website.* Retrieved from http:// www.syzefxis.gov.gr/

Tan, C. W., & Pan, S. L. (2003). Managing e-transformation in the public sector: an e-government study of the Inland Revenue Authority of Singapore (IRAS). *European Journal of Information Systems, 12*(4), 269–281. doi:10.1057/palgrave.ejis.3000479

The Apache Software Foundation. (2007). *Apache Jackrabbit: Content repository for Java technology API (JCR).* Retrieved from http:// jackrabbit.apache.org/

The Apache Software Foundation. (2007). *Apache orchestration director engine (ODE).* Retrieved from http:// ode.apache.org/

UK Government. (2005). *Transformational government: Enabled by technology.*

UK GovTalk. (2005). *Integrated public sector vocabulary (IPSV).* Cabinet Office. Retrieved from http:// www.govtalk.gov.uk

UN/CEFACT. (2007). *Core components technical specification, version 3.0.* Second Public Review.

Waisanen, B. (2002). The future of e-government: Technology-fueled management tools. *Public Management, 84*(5), 6–9.

West, D. M. (2001). *State and federal e-government in the United States.* Providence, RI: Brown University Press.

World Bank Group. (2003). *Definition of e-government.* Retrieved from http:// go.worldbank.org/ M1JHE0Z280

WSBPEL 2.0. (2007). *OASIS Web services business process execution language,* version 2.0. Advancing Open Standards for the Information Society, OASIS Standard.

Chapter 19
Integrating IT Infrastructures in the Public Domain:
A Proposition of Influential Factors for Enterprise Application Integration Adoption

Muhammad M. Kamal
Brunel University, UK

ABSTRACT

Several private and public organisations have realised the significance of integration technologies e.g. database oriented middleware, message based technologies, transaction based technologies, distributed object technologies and interface based technologies (collectively known as Enterprise Application Integration [EAI]) for integrating their heterogeneous Information Technology (IT) infrastructures. Nevertheless, where these integration technologies have supplemented efficacy and strengthened the IT infrastructures in the private domain, public organisations e.g. Local Government Authorities (LGAs) have been slow in adopting cost-effective integration solutions to significantly expand the capabilities of their conventionally inflexible Information Systems (IS). Despite EAI represent an attractive proposition to LGAs and other public organisations and offer the opportunity to leverage the IS into a seamless chain of processes, these integration technologies have not been widely investigated in the public domain and specifically LGAs. Albeit there are several research studies focusing on a number of domain specific factors influencing EAI adoption, nonetheless, the applicability and validity of these research studies in the area of LGAs is arguable and under research. The reason is that these research studies were proposed to support the decision-making process in private or healthcare sectors and not in LGAs.

DOI: 10.4018/978-1-60960-839-2.ch019

There are differences indicating that the factors that influence the decision-making process for EAI adoption differ from one type of organisation to the other depending among others on the nature and size. For instance, literature indicates that one set of factors is used to support EAI adoption in Small and Medium Enterprises (SMEs) and another in large organisations. In addition, there are differences among influential factors that are used in private sector and healthcare organisations. The authors takes into consideration and present Critical Success Factors (CFS) influencing the decision making process for EAI adoption in LGAs. To investigate this less acknowledged phenomenon, the author follows an interpretive, qualitative case study approach to conduct this research.

INTRODUCTION

During the last decades, several LGAs have widely focused on the use of information systems to overcome their organisational problems and automate their business processes and functions (Kamal *et al.*, 2009; Grimsley and Meehan, 2007; Irani *et al.*, 2006). LGAs focused on IS to provide direct support to meet citizens' needs including housing, social services, and the management of a complex service infrastructure that supports communities and businesses (Johnson and King, 2005). However, IS developments within LGAs have resulted in non-integrated IT infrastructures (Lam, 2005; Beaumaster, 2002). The reason is that each LGA autonomously made its own IT operation decisions based on its needs (Janssen and Cresswell, 2005; Di Natale *et al.*, 2003; Aldrich *et al.*, 2002). Additionally, there was rarely a single approach for developing IS, as organisations have developed their applications without a common architectural planning (Markus and Tanis, 1999). Moreover, each LGA displays differences in the way: (a) their business processes are implemented to provide citizen services, and (b) makes its decisions that differs a lot from other private organisations (Johnson and King, 2005; Ward and Mitchell, 2004). Such theorised evidences illustrate that LGAs operate and function independently and do not share information and functionality with other LGAs (Gortmaker and Janssen 2004; Ralphs and Wyatt, 1998).

Such aforesaid concerns have resulted in several problems that have influenced the decision-making process in LGAs. For example, Beynon-Davies and Williams (2003) report that within LGAs there is not enough emphasis on the re-engineering of legacy business processes and applications. The reason is that legacy business processes and applications have been developed over several years to serve their core processing needs and government officials are reluctant to change their operational procedures (Lam, 2005). Furthermore, McIvor *et al.*, (2002) report that the inherent design of many legacy applications was as standalone, typically mainframe-based applications, rather than as network-integrated applications. The reluctance in government officials to bring change in their operational practices and availability of non-integrated legacy applications has resulted in poor citizen service provisioning and making decision-making process more complex (Lam, 2005; McIvor *et al.*, 2002). Thus, the integration of legacy business processes and applications is required to support coordination within LGAs, enhance the decision-making process and provide better services to citizens (Janssen and Cresswell, 2005; McIvor *et al.*, 2002).

While adopting new IT solutions, a major concern for LGAs' management is the investment decision associated with the change in organisation and their IT infrastructure (Signore *et al.*, 2005; Beaumaster, 2002). The reason is that LGAs lack sufficient amount of money for their IT infrastructure (Ward and Mitchell, 2004). Wagnar and Antonucci (2004) support that LGAs' budgets are often reduced and sometimes allocated with appropriations. Lam (2005) and McIvor *et al.*, (2002) also report that government organisations face difficulties in obtaining the level of financial support requested, especially if grant is drawn from a funding pool that is meant to serve multiple initiatives. Therefore, LGAs are seeking for integration solutions that are cost effective and as a result provide better services to their citizens. Virili and Sorrentino (2009) have illustrated that cost-effective and small/pilot IT integration projects based on responsive information system enhancement practices can considerably influence the legacy systems, enhancing the overall degree of IT effectiveness, with positive effects on policy outcomes and policy impacts.

Another problem notable is with the electronic Government (e-Government) policies that are still evolving and are in a state of change (Lam, 2005). In this context, the central government plays a pivotal role in defining policies for citizen privacy and security, which can be interpreted by LGAs in relation to bringing changes to their business processes in e-Government projects (Aileen *et al.*, 2010). Signore *et al.*, (2005) argues that citizens' concerns on privacy and confidentiality of the personal data have been a critical obstacle in implementing e-Government projects. Tillman (2003) also reports that concerns over citizen privacy continue to be a problem in e-Government discipline, whereas Lam (2005) identified citizen privacy as a barrier to integrating e-Government. Lam (2005) also supports that the lack of clarity in the privacy policies among LGAs is a major problem. The reason is that questions regarding: (a) why data is being collected, (b) how it will be used and secured, and (c) with whom it will be shared, require the establishment of clear policies with respect to citizen data privacy and security. In the absence of such policies, decision-making to achieve integrated e-Government may become stagnated (Kamal *et al.*, 2009; Signore *et al.*, 2005; Lam, 2005). Researchers also exemplify and support that e-Government is seen as exemplar of integration of information technology and information policy to influence and facilitate social interaction between government and citizens (Whitmore and Choi, 2010). However, as e-Government begins to mature and disseminate, central government needs to pay increasing attention to the factors that drive e-Government success (Whitmore and Choi, 2010; Aileen *et al.*, 2010).

Moreover, a long-term government sector concern is the need for efficient and effective application integration (Kamal, 2009; Beynon-Davies and Williams, 2003). Janssen and Cresswell (2005) report that service provisioning is likely to fail if the information systems within LGAs that need to work together to provide a service are not integrated. Integration problems are founded in the highly fragmented IS within LGAs (Kamal *et al.*, 2008; Lam, 2005). Such IS were often based on different hardware configurations, functioning under different operating systems, employing distinct database technologies and programming languages (Peristera and Tarabanis, 2000). According to Allen *et al.*, (2001) existing IS are typically built using architectures that do not readily support enterprise-wide integration, thus requiring major efforts to take decision to develop new architectures and systems to implement e-Government.

In addition to aforesaid problems, literature also indicates several differences in the decision-making process within LGAs and other private organisations (Ward and Mitchell, 2004). The rationale is that LGAs are complex organisations and are managed by the consent and rules set by the central government. They are influenced by other government authorities and ministries, and their IS adoption involve distributed decision-making based on a division of control and powers (Worrall, 1994). Additionally, LGAs seek guidance from central government on how to translate their e-Government vision into more explicit specifications for e-Government service provisioning (Lam, 2005). Conversely, private organisations have direct and undivided power over decisions and flexible management style with inter-departmental teams working in central coordination (Ward and

Mitchell, 2004). This distinction illustrates that LGAs have a bureaucratic nature and are committed to outdated cultural values. Such characteristics emphasise risk aversion and insist that structures enhance control rather than connected thinking with silos in LGAs, let alone between them (Janssen and Cresswell, 2005).

Thus, all the aforementioned problems illustrate that there is a need for LGAs to: (a) undergo structural and operational changes to accommodate changing citizen needs, (b) enhance decision-making process, (c) adopt cost-effective integration solutions, (d) integrate their autonomous information systems, and (e) persistent business process transformation. However, in order to understand how the above can be achieved, the author asserts the need to:

1. Comprehend the importance of EAI in accomplishing such transformation in LGAs
2. Explore and understand the critical success factors that influence the decision making process for EAI adoption in LGAs.

Thereafter, the author presents the research methodology employed to explore the adoption and implementation practices of EAI in local government domain. Moreover, test the importance of the CFS influencing the decision making process for EAI adoption in LGAs. Empirical findings are presented along with the limitations and future directions summarised in the conclusion.

ENTERPRISE APPLICATION INTEGRATION

Literature indicates a new generation of integration technologies i.e., EAI technologies that combines a variety of integration technologies such as: (a) message brokers, (b) adapters, and (c) application servers etc, to build a centralised integration infrastructure (Lam, 2005; Themistocleous, 2004; Linthicum, 2000). It incorporates functionality from a diversity of systems and results in the development of flexible and maintainable integrated IT infrastructures (Serian, 2002; Zahavi, 1999). In other words, EAI acts as a software data translator that takes information from, for example, organisational Enterprise Resource Planning (ERP) systems and convert it into formats that other applications can understand (Linthicum, 2000). EAI also allows the organisations to simplify interactions among applications by adopting a standard approach to integration, replacing hundreds or thousands of ad hoc integration designs (Lam, 2005; Ruh *et al.*, 2000; Linthicum, 2000).

Literature indicates that for "***x***" applications a total of "***(x*(x-1)/2)***" interconnections are needed when each application is interconnected with the rest of the applications (Themistocleous, 2004). This can be explained as e.g. when an application is interconnected (through traditional integration) to several other applications that require any change, it affects all other applications because it has equivalent number of interconnections with those applications. On the other hand, when the same application that is integrated through EAI architecture requires some changes; the rest of the system is rarely affected. The reason is that these systems are not directly interconnected with the application that requires those changes. Thus, this way only those applications that require changes are altered, resulting in a reduced maintenance effort and increased flexibility with few interconnections among the applications (Themistocleous, 2004). Figure 1 illustrates the differences in the number of connections when traditional integration approaches and enterprise application integration are adopted.

Organisations that have integrated their IT infrastructures through EAI have reported significant benefits (Bass and Lee, 2002). For example, Themistocleous and Irani (2001) analysed and explained the benefits that derive from the use of EAI technology. They classified the benefits into: (a) organisational (e.g. resulting in organised business processes), (b) managerial

Figure 1. Traditional integration approaches vs. enterprise application integration

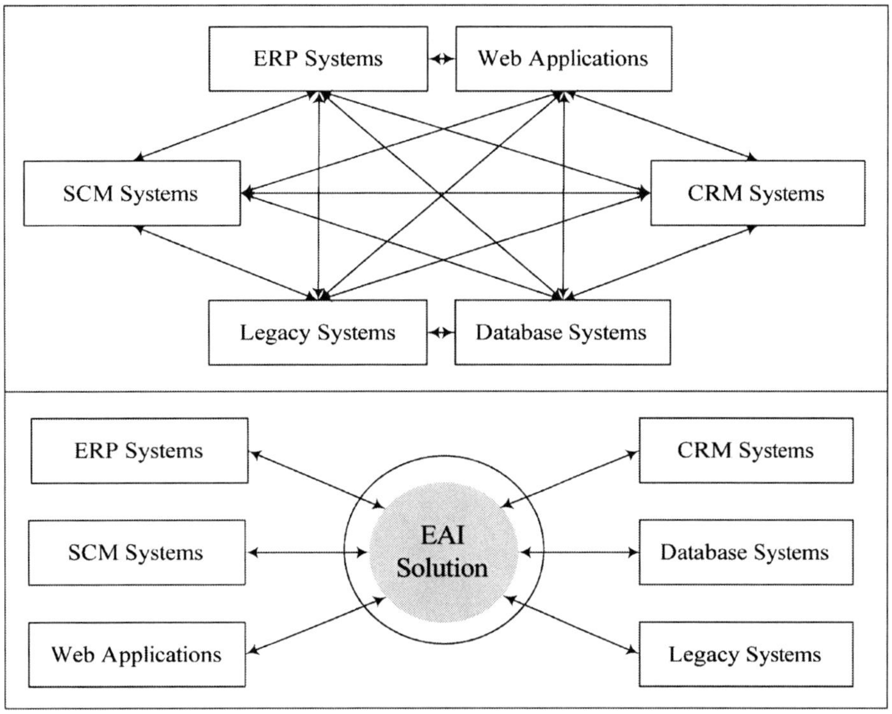

(e.g. achieving significant return on investment), (c) operational (e.g. reducing the operational cost), (d) strategic (e.g. increase in collaboration among different partners and suppliers), and (e) technical (e.g. achieving integration at different levels i.e. data, objects and process). Literature also indicates another significant EAI business benefit i.e. the reduction of overall integration cost and the reason for this is due to the decrease in both integration time and maintenance costs (Linthicum, 2000). In addition, EAI provides a flexible, manageable and maintainable IT infrastructure that supports the changing business and technical requirements (Themistocleous *et al.*, 2005). Based on the EAI integrated organisation-wide architecture, organisations can increase their productivity and provide better services for their customers and improve their relationships with their clients (Ruh *et al.*, 2000).

In this context, by employing EAI effectively, organisations can: (a) leverage their existing assets to provide enhanced services, (b) improve their relationships with customers and other stakeholders, (c) improve their performance, as well as (d) to streamline its operations (Themistocleous, 2002; Ruh *et al.*, 2000). Other benefits include: (a) the provision of a centralised point of control, (b) the reduction of skills level required to integrate applications, and (c) faster time to marketing and increased market share. Moreover, as EAI incorporates organisational and cross-organisational applications (Zahavi, 1999), from this viewpoint, EAI can lead to integrated intra and inter-organisational systems. By enabling all these capabilities, Ruh *et al.*, (2000) claimed that EAI can help an organisation create a competitive advantage. However, the high investment costs associated with EAI have caused much concern for many organisations (Chen, 2005). Sanchez *et al.*, (2002) argued that although the initial cost of investing in EAI may be daunting to several organisations, the cost of integration is in fact more extensive when EAI technological solutions not adopted.

This illustrates that on prolonging the integration problem is likely to be more costly than an initial EAI investment, especially when long-term plans including new technologies and IS into the IT infrastructure. The reason may be that while not taking integration into consideration, each application that is initially developed based on own requirements, may have its own meaning of organisational objects (e.g. citizen data). Therefore, each application that has data (with own meaning) may overlap with data in other applications. This data redundancy and inconsistency generates vital data integrity problems and increases the maintenance and integration cost. As the literature indicates that EAI is based on a set of integration technologies, each EAI package differs from other EAI package (Linthicum, 2000). The reason is that each EAI vendor configures its EAI package using a different subset of integration technologies. Thus, during the selection process organisations need to evaluate their EAI technologies to meet their organisational and integration problems.

CRITICAL SUCCESS FACTORS INFLUENCING EAI ADOPTION IN LGAs

Technological adoption has been an important area for IS research and practice (Fichman, 1992). Several studies on integration technologies e.g. existing EAI adoption models like those proposed by Mantzana *et al.*, (2007); Khoumbati *et al.*, (2006); Chen (2005) and Themistocleous (2004) are domain specific (e.g. healthcare sector, private organisations). These models investigate the adoption of EAI through a set of influential factors. Some of these factors can be considered as common (e.g. benefits, barriers, costs) and therefore can be reused when adopting EAI in LGAs. Other factors like patients' satisfaction or physician and patient relationship are domain specific and thus are of no use by LGAs. In addition to this, there are differences indicating that the factors influencing the decision-making process for EAI adoption differ from one type of organisation to the other depending among others on the nature and size. For instance, one set of factors is used to support EAI adoption in SMEs and another in large organisations or healthcare organisations. However, the applicability and validity of these models is arguable and under research in LGAs, as these were proposed to support the decision-making process in other sectors and not in LGAs. As a result of these distinctions, additional factors may be required particular to a context. Fichman (1992) also supports that such factors merely by themselves are unlikely to be strong predictors for technology adoption and thus, need additional factors according to a particular environment. Taking into consideration this argument, the author presents the factors proposed by Kamal (2008) into this research (these factors are a significant part of PhD research). These factors have supported LGAs in developing an understanding while adopting EAI solutions and helping them transforming their functions. These factors are categorised all according to Pressure Factors (PF), Technological Factors (TF), Support Factors (SF), Financial Factors (FF) and Organisational Factors (OF).

PRESSURE FACTORS

- ***Project Champion (Internal Pressure Factor):*** Championship refers to the existence of a person in the organisation who is committed to introduce IT initiative to the organisation. Project champions are personnel who actively and vigorously promote their personal vision for using IT, pushing the project over or around approval and implementation hurdles (Beath, 1991). Norris (1999) report that within government organisations, the existence of a project champion is one of the most important facilitators in the adoption of technologies.

- ***Project Delivery Time:*** Literature significantly highlights that developing products faster, better and economical than competitors, on the other hand completing IT related projects and delivering on time, has become critical to success in many markets (Ford and Sterman, 1998). Homer *et al.,* (1993) also asserts that the reduction in project delivery times has become a high priority for many companies who are looking for ways to become more competitive and accomplish more within the given resources. However, it can be argued that the reduction in project delivery time is not a simple task and may require sizeable investments and perhaps within uncertain payback tenure (Yardley, 2002).
- ***Data Consistency:*** According to Kamal (2009) and Gamper and Augsten (2003) absence of data consistency and presence of data redundancies and duplication (highlighted as internal pressure) has been identified as the most common problems faced by local government organisations and its related agencies. Empirical evidences illustrate that a fundamental requirement in electronic service delivery and making government information available online is the ability for government applications to be able to exchange consistent and duplication free data in a seamless fashion (Kamal, 2008).
- ***Citizen's Satisfaction (External Pressure Factor):*** Citizen's satisfaction has a significant impact on the performance of LGAs and in the growing push towards accountability between the LGAs (Welch *et al.,* 2005). IT adoption is viewed as a central part of the modernisation of LGAs in improving the quality of LGAs services and achieving citizen satisfaction (Beynon-Davies, 2005). Welch *et al.,* (2005) report that IT appears to offer a useful opportunity to LGAs to enhance citizen satisfaction by improving procedural transparency, cost-efficiency and effectiveness.
- ***Critical Mass (External Pressure Factor):*** Research on critical mass has shown that central government and LGAs are affected by the actions of other governments in IT adoption (Akbulut, 2002). For example, cities adopting innovations were located in close proximity to other innovation-adopting cities. This showed that organisations were affected by the actions of other organisations that were similar in terms of size and budgetary constraints. The benefit of having a critical mass of organisations adopting same technology is one aspect of inter-organisational relationships and IT adoption.
- ***Market Knowledge (External Pressure Factor):*** A majority of successful IT adoption cases are referred to the recognition of demands in the market. Lee and Treacy (1988) report that an unstable organisational environment generates increased potential for IT adoption. This requires an organisation's intent on being up-dated and well informed about the changes in market environment. Contact with environment through development of external information system e.g. can reduce the insecurity for the individual organisation.
- ***Stakeholders Pressure:*** Stakeholders are individuals and groups which can affect the company's performance or who are affected by a firm's actions (Freeman, 1984). Empirical findings indicate that stakeholders represent an influencing factor for EAI adoption e.g. the pressure from: (a) government agencies, (b) peers from other departments (c) peers from other boroughs for the provision of better service delivery to the citizens and (d) partner organisations for improvement in close collaboration,

represent pressure from external stakeholders (Kamal, 2008). In addition, the pressure from citizens for the improvement of facilities such as availability of their records wherever and whenever required to the services providers for better service provision also represent external pressure from the stakeholders (Valor, 2005).

- ***Competition:*** Researchers report that increased competition often pushes organisations to search for new ways to increase their productivity and seek a competitive advantage (Themistocleous, 2004). However, in the context of this research competition does not mean competing for monitory purpose, instead there is competition in terms of being more productive and improving services to community and in turn acquiring more funds from the central government. Empirical evidences suggest that due to the pressure from the central government to achieve the 2005-2008 e-Government targets (in the past) and enhancement in service delivery, LGAs perceive the pressure indirectly as competition among other boroughs to provide integrated services (Kamal, 2008). Literature indicates that increased competition from external business environments has be a source for adopting EAI (Themistocleous, 2004).

Technological Factors

- ***Evaluation Frameworks:*** Themistocleous (2004) proposed two evaluation frameworks such as: (a) framework for evaluating integration technologies and (b) framework for evaluating EAI packages, which can be used by organisations to assess EAI packages and technologies. These frameworks highlight a possible combination of integration technologies and tools and EAI packages that can be used to integrate IT infrastructure. Therefore, these evaluation frameworks facilitate organisations to overcome the confusion regarding the selection of EAI products.
- ***Technological Risks:*** Technological risks can make risk-averse managers require higher, not lower, rates of return before they invest. Studies on risk factor in IT projects have described issues e.g. organisational fit and technology planning. In LGAs, the degree of technological risks is escalating as the use of public networks increases together with databases that hold citizen's profiles and government information (Ebrahim and Irani, 2005).
- ***IT Infrastructure:*** IT infrastructure consists of the computer systems and the supporting software needed to develop, manage and operate IT applications e.g. operating systems, development and management tools (Shaw, 2000). However, the non-integrated nature of IT infrastructure causes integration problems. Thus, raising the need for integration in the organisations. As a result, several researchers have reported IT infrastructure as a factor in their integration technologies adoption models.
- ***Personnel IT Knowledge:*** Personnel IT knowledge refers to the IT capabilities of an organisation (Akbulut, 2002). The available skill set of the personnel is an important factor that constraints the introduction of new technologies. One of the most important factors in the adoption of computer applications by LGAs is staff competence. Norris (1999) reports that employees in LGAs were not very well trained in using information technologies and this inadequate training resulted in resistance to change, resistance to use, and under utilisation of computers.
- ***IT Sophistication:*** IT sophistication is reported as an influential factor in integra-

tion technologies adoption models. The research findings on integration technology adoption represent that organisations with sophisticated IT resources will be likely to be adopters of integration technology. Themistocleous (2004) has reported IT sophistication as a factor for EAI adoption. This is due to the level of understanding in addressing technical problems at an enterprise and cross enterprise level.

- ***Data Security and Privacy:*** Security and privacy of citizens' data has always been important (Signore *et al.,* 2005). Applications that have evolved autonomously rather than as part of an overall architecture inevitably end up having their own security architecture that is incompatible. Key security functions, such as authentication, authorisation, and confidentiality are managed according to the application's own specific set of rules, and thus present a significant challenge to the definition of a single security administration function across an integrated e-Government solution (Lam, 2005). In addition, citizens' concern on privacy and confidentiality of the personal data has been a critical obstacle in implementing e-Government projects.

Support Factors

- ***Top Management Support:*** Top management support has been recognised as one of the most important elements necessary for the successful implementation of integration technologies and integrated packages. Beath, (1991) reports that one of the most successful factors associated with large-scale IT implementation projects is securing the support of top management. In addition, sustained top management support within LGAs in IT projects, is needed throughout the implementation project (Chen and Gant, 2001). The reason is as the project progresses, active involvement of top management remains critical in constantly monitoring the progress of the project and providing direction to the implementation teams.
- ***IT Support:*** EAI requires organisations to invest considerable investment on their IT infrastructure. Therefore, it is essential for organisations to have support from vendors and consultants. For example, consultants support the IT departments to introduce and evaluate EAI in organisations (Themistocleous, 2004). Vendors' support also has a correlation with IT infrastructure since vendors provide services (e.g. maintenance) to the organisations. As reported in several case studies the: (a) close relationships between one organisation and its hardware vendors and, (b) the dependence of the other organisation on the vendor's solution (hardware), influenced the decision for purchasing EAI package from the vendor (Themistocleous, 2004).
- ***Higher Administrative Authority:*** Improving LGA technological facilities depends on whether support from higher administrative authorities elected or appointed top administrators, LGAs and also the central government is available for IT managers who are in charge of implementing technology adoption process and its utilisation. (2004) report that even in the case that IT managers initiate technology adoption; support from higher administrative authorities may play a significant role.
- ***Stakeholders Support:*** The much-quoted Stanford Research Institute's (SRI) definition of stakeholders as "those groups without whose support the organisation would cease to exist" (SRI, 1963; quoted in Freeman, 1984: 31). The growing popularity of stakeholder analysis reflects an increasing recognition of how the char-

acteristics of stakeholders such as their support – influence the decision making processes in organisations (Brugha and Varvasovszky, 2000). According to Themistocleous (2004) and Kamal (2008) stakeholder support e.g. from vendors, management, etc, is considered a significant factor for affects the decision making process for EAI technological solutions.

Financial Factors

- ***Return on Investment:*** In the context of LGAs, ROI is important, as technology budgets of LGAs at times are much lower as compared to other private and public organisations. Within LGAs budgets are often reduced and sometimes allocated with appropriations. Lam (2005) also reports that government organisations face difficulties in obtaining the level of funding requested, especially if funding is drawn from a funding pool that is meant to serve multiple initiatives. As a result, they do not want to invest more in technology, without significant ROI.
- ***Cost:*** Literature indicates cost as a significant factor and many organisations perform a cost benefit analysis before taking any important decision regarding their investment for technology adoption (Themistocleous, 2004). In the context of EAI, Lee *et al.,* (2003) report that the basic concept of EAI is mainly in it externality of enterprise integration with lower cost and less programming using existing applications, whereas a significant benefit of EAI is the reduction of overall integration cost.
- ***Central Government Grant:*** The relationship between different levels of government, and their interactions on the financial side, has been the subject of considerable scrutiny in recent years. Several issues related to monitory funding from the central government have been discussed in the normative literature. For example, empirical evidences proposed by Kamal (2008) suggest that money, resources and the capability of the processes to support them has always been a constraint while adopting integration solutions in the local government domain. This conception is so because EAI is a high risk investment, knowing the fact that LGAs lack knowledge on EAI and their departments are reluctant to spend from their available capital and resources. To overcome this constraint, LGAs seek central government grants to improve their planning and developing processes (Borge and Rattsø 1997).

Organisational Factors

- ***Centralisation:*** Centralisation refers to the degree of power or decision-making authority in organisations and encompasses participation in decision-making and authority hierarchy. In centralised organisations, decision-making is typically concentrated at the top level of hierarchy while in decentralised structures decision-making is distributed across different hierarchical levels. Since the decision-making for technology adoption is typically concentrated at top level of management in public sector organisations (Ebrahim *et al.,* 2004), hence, the degree of centralisation may influence EAI adoption in LGAs.
- ***Managerial Capability:*** Managerial capability refers to the ability of managers to identify problems of the current systems, and to develop and evaluate alternatives to improve the IT infrastructure of the organisation appears to be important. However, Senyucel (2005) argues that some managers are not realistic in their demands regarding IT infrastructure, which can be

traced back to an inward-looking approach in the literature. Several managers were seen as highly suspicious of new initiatives and unsupportive. Such managerial short-sightedness has the potential to jeopardise the success of e-Government facilitation.

- ***Barriers:*** Literature indicates that EAI adoption presents a similar case to ERP systems in terms of its barriers (Themistocleous, 2004). Like ERP systems, EAI: (a) promises to integrate IT infrastructures, (b) introduce changes to the organisational structure and the way of doing business, (c) influences the employees tasks as well as inter-organisational relationships, (d) it costs a lot of money and (e) is more likely adopted by big organisations. Since there are a lot of failures on ERP adoption, organisations tend to estimate the possible impact of EAI adoption before proceeding to its adoption.
- ***Benefits:*** Benefits refer to the level of recognition of the advantages that the integration technologies could provide to the organisation. Iacovou *et al.*, (1995) classified perceived benefits into direct and indirect. Direct benefits were mostly operational saving-related (e.g. reduced transaction cost) and indirect benefits were mostly tactical and competitive advantages that had an impact on business process and relationships (e.g. increased operational efficiency). Bradford and Florin (2003) report benefits as organisational benefits that include the facilities for the integration problems, real-time planning, user satisfaction and support to quick customer response.
- ***Formalisation:*** Formalisation refers to the existence of clear procedures, norms and formal processes for carrying out organisational tasks more effectively and efficiently (Lee *et al.,* 2003). Ebrahim *et al.,* (2004) reports formalisation as an organisational factor that is internal to the public sector, which influences the adoption and design of e-Government applications. IT adoption provides challenges to organisations as it not only addresses changes in technology and systems but also deals with the need for changing the way an organisation runs its business in terms of processes, workflows, policies, procedures, and structure (Ebrahim and Irani, 2005).
- ***Size:*** Akbulut (2002) measures size in terms of the size of the community served and the number of the services provided by the organisation. Norris (1999) reported that larger organisations would adopt more sophisticated and advanced IT compared to smaller as larger organisations: (a) have greater financial resources, (b) are in more need of technologies and, (c) have superior institutional ability such as IT departments, to support the technologies. This is also because larger organisations input sufficient volume to justify the adoption of new technology to accommodate variations in input even when variations occur infrequently. Smaller organisations, however, experience many types of input variations so rarely that they could not reasonably expect to benefit from making similar accommodations.

RESEARCH METHODOLOGY

The author followed an interpretivism, qualitative multiple case study approach to conduct this research and test the factors. Interpretivism assumes that the knowledge of reality is gained only through social constructions such as consciousness, shared meanings, language, documents, tools and other artefacts (Saunders *et al.,* 2000). An interpretivism stance allows the researchers to navigate and better explain this phenomenon. It is also anticipated that as the social world cannot be reduced to isolated variables, such as space and mass, it must be observed in its totality. Therefore, the author asserts that, there is a need for a research approach that may allow LGAs to be viewed in their entirety and permits the author to get close to participants (i.e. the interviewees), penetrate their realities, and interpret their perceptions. Hence, the author considers interpretivism as more appropriate for the research reported herein. Having justified the use interpretive research approach, the author describes the nature of qualitative research approach in order to justify its relevance to the research presented in this paper. Qualitative research is multi-method in focus, involving an interpretive, naturalistic approach to its subject matter (Denzin and Lincoln, 1994). This implies that the qualitative researchers study things in their natural environment, and they comprehend events in terms of meanings that people bring to them. The qualitative paradigm recommends that researchers observe human behaviour and action as it occurs in mundane everyday life (Schutz, 1967). Thus, the author suggests that in the context of this research a qualitative approach is more appropriate as such approach can be used to: (a) investigate less acknowledged phenomena like EAI adoption in the local government authorities, (b) examine the in-depth complexities and processes e.g. analysing the factors influencing the decision making process for EAI adoption, (c) examine the phenomenon in its natural setting, (d) provide considerable flexibility during interviews and observations and (e) learn from practice

A case study examines a phenomenon in its natural setting, employing multiple methods of data collection to gather information from one or a few entities e.g. people, groups, or organisations (Yin, 1994). Case studies can be single or multiple – a single case study may enable the researchers to investigate a phenomenon in depth, getting close to the phenomenon, providing rich primary data and revealing its deep structure within the organisational context (Cavaye, 1996). However, a single case may not provide sufficient insight into the phenomenon of EAI adoption in LGAs. The reason is that most research efforts require multiple cases, as single case studies are only useful in specific instances e.g. useful at the outset of theory generation and late in theory testing (Bonoma, 1985), which is not the case for this research. Instead, the author suggests that multiple case studies might be more appropriate, as multiple case studies may enable the researchers to examine and 'cross-check' findings and may provide the research with a more 'robust' investigation of cause and effect relation of the units of analysis (Herriot and Firestone, 1983). Data was collected via interviews, observation, and archival documentation. Interviews are regarded as the main tool of qualitative research for data collection process (Denzin and Lincoln, 1994). In this research, interviews constituted the main data source in the case organisations. Six participants from each LGA_A and LGA_B were interviewed using structured interviews. Structured interviews were based on the interview agenda. Using the interview agenda, the interviewees replied to specific questions on EAI adoption. Semi-structure interviews also took place but without the use of an interview agenda. Using this type of interviews the authors attempted to clarify some issues that derived from structured interviews. All the structure or semi-structured interviews took place at interviewees' office. Unstructured interviews dealt with discussions that the authors had with interviewees but without using a structured or semi-structured type of interview. The author had unstructured interviews during lunches, coffee breaks, out of office hours. Using unstructured interviews some important data on the case studies were collected (e.g. information about resistance to change). All of the interviews were tape recorded and transcripts prepared as soon as possible after each interview. Tape recording supported the authors in collecting accurate data and interpreting them without time pressures.

Table 1. Importance of factors influencing EAI adoption in LGA_A

		LGA_A					
	Factors	**HBIS**	**PM**	**DSM**	**SD**	**DM**	**SDE**
PF	*Project Champion*	■	■	■	■	■	■
	Citizen's Satisfaction	■	▣	▣	■	■	□
	Critical Mass	▣	▣	□	■	□	■
	Market Knowledge	▣	■	▣	■	■	▣
	Project Delivery Time	■	■	▣	▣	▣	■
	Data Consistency	■	■	■	■	■	■
	Stakeholder Pressure	▣	▣	▣	▣	▣	■
	Competition	■	■	▣	■	■	■
SF	*Top Management Support*	■	■	■	■	■	■
	IT Support	▣	□	▣	□	□	▣
	Higher Administrative Authority	■	■	■	▣	▣	■
	Stakeholder Support	■	■	▣	▣	■	▣
FF	*Return on Investment*	■	▣	▣	■	■	■
	Cost	■	■	■	■	■	■
	Central Government Grants	■	■	■	■	■	▣
TF	*Evaluation Frameworks*	□	□	▣	□	▣	▣
	Technological Risks	▣	▣	■	■	■	■
	IT Infrastructure	■	▣	■	■	■	■
	Personnel IT Knowledge	■	■	■	■	■	▣
	IT Sophistication	■	■	▣	■	▣	▣
	Data Security and Privacy	■	■	■	■	■	■
OF	*Centralisation*	▣	■	▣	▣	■	■
	Managerial Capability	■	■	■	■	■	■
	Barriers	■	■	■	■	■	■
	Benefits	■	■	■	■	■	■
	Formalisation	▣	▣	■	▣	■	■
	Size	■	■	▣	■	▣	■

CASE ORGANISATIONS: LGA_A AND LGA_B

To test the influential factors (as explained earlier), case studies were undertaken conducted within two local government authorities both situated within the region of England. These case organisations are responsible for providing services through various sectors such as: social and environmental services, housing, education and health. For confidentiality reasons the real names of these case organisations cannot be reported. Instead the author uses the coded-names LGA_A and LGA_B to refer to the case organisations. As reported earlier, structure, semi-structured and unstructured interviews were conducted in both case organisations to investigate the decision making process for EAI adoption. In achieving this, those factors considered to influence the decision-making process are identified, when seen from a multiple-stakeholder perspective. These perceptions were seen from those stakeholders that were involved in the EAI adoption, implementation and evaluation process. From LGA_A, the stakeholders that were specifically interviewed included the: Head of Business Information Systems (HBIS), Project Manager (PM), Development Service Manager (DSM), Systems Developer (SD), Development Engineer (DE), and Service Delivery Manager (SDM). At LGA_B stakeholders interviewed included: Head of Information Communication and Technologies (HICT), Senior Systems Developer (SSD), Service Delivery Manager for Applications (SDMA), Web Manager (WM), Project Manager (PM) and Senior Software Engineer (SSE).

EMPIRICAL FINDINGS

During the interview sessions at LGA_A, the interviewees were asked to highlight the importance of factors that influenced the decision making process for EAI technological solution adoption for their respective EAI project. The level of importance as presented in Table 1 follows a scale similar to the one used by Miles and Huberman (1994) i.e. scale of less important (□), medium important (▣) and most important (■).

As highlighted in Table 1, two factors were not validated, i.e. evaluation frameworks and IT support. Regarding the evaluation frameworks, the project manager reported that:

"...we had cheaper in house solution with expertise, knowledge and skills. Basically we just conducted a market survey for cost evaluation, not to procure a solution that may have cost us lots of money. We needed a solution that could assist us in implementing the project quickly, thus we evaluated the solution from the options based how quickly we can implement this project ...".

The interview discussions also illustrate that the project team did not use any support from external consultant. The service delivery manager reported the reason for not selecting IT support from external consultant:

"... we wanted to be able to use our existing staff skills, support the system better and it is better value for money ...".

The remaining factors as highlighted had varied findings as such preference on the importance of factors by the interviewees is simply based on the interviewee's observation, understanding and involvement during their project at LGA_A.

Whereas, during the interview sessions at LGA_B, the interviewees were also asked to highlight the importance of EAI adoption factors in this project. The level of importance as presented in Table 2 follows a similar scale as used for testing the factors used in Table 1.

As illustrated in Table 2, one factor was not tested, i.e. return on investment. According to the EAI project implemented, the project improved data collection with intelligent, dynamic top level e-Forms. Cost fell because quality data reduced the form rejection rates and received e-Forms that did not need to be manually keyed-in, whereas, ROI was not validated. The head of ICT reported that:

"... due to silo mentality in LGA_B we were not able to prove the return on our investment in this project...".

The remaining factors illustrate varied answers from the interviewees, however, comparing the outcome of Tables 1 and 2, it is clear that most of the factors have influenced the decision making process for EAI adoption in LGA_A and LGA_B. Thus, validating the factors influencing EAI adoption in LGAs as reported earlier. These findings

Table 2. Importance of factors influencing EAI adoption in LGA_B

		LGA_B					
	Factors	**HIT**	**PM**	**DSM**	**PSD**	**SDM**	**SDE**
PF	*Project Champion*	■	■	■	■	▣	■
	Citizen's Satisfaction	■	■	▣	▣	■	■
	Critical Mass	▣	▣	■	■	■	▣
	Market Knowledge	▣	▣	■	■	■	▣
	Project Delivery Time	■	■	■	▣	▣	▣
	Data Consistency	▣	■	■	■	■	▣
	Stakeholder Pressure	■	■	■	▣	▣	■
	Competition	■	■	■	■	■	▣
SF	*Top Management Support*	■	■	■	▣	■	■
	IT Support	■	▣	▣	■	▣	▣
	Higher Administrative Authority	■	■	■	▣	▣	■
	Stakeholder Support	■	■	▣	▣	▣	▣
FF	*Return on Investment*	□	▣	□	□	▣	▣
	Cost	■	▣	■	■	▣	■
	Central Government Grants	■	■	■	■	■	▣
TF	*Evaluation Frameworks*	▣	▣	■	■	▣	▣
	Technological Risks	■	▣	■	■	■	■
	IT Infrastructure	■	■	□	▣	■	■
	Personnel IT Knowledge	■	■	▣	■	■	■
	IT Sophistication	▣	■	▣	■	▣	▣
	Data Security and Privacy	▣	▣	■	■	■	▣
OF	*Centralisation*	▣	■	■	▣	▣	▣
	Managerial Capability	■	▣	■	■	■	▣
	Barriers	■	■	■	■	▣	■
	Benefits	■	■	■	■	■	■
	Formalisation	□	■	■	▣	■	▣
	Size	□	■	■	▣	▣	▣

are in accordance with the literature findings (e.g. Kamal, 2006; Khoumbati *et al.,* 2006; Chen, 2005; Themistocleous, 2004) that present these factors for the adoption of different integration technologies in various types of organisations e.g. public sector to private sectors and SMEs to large organisations.

DISCUSSIONS AND SYNTHESIS OF THE RESULTS

This paper empirically studies the importance of factors influencing the decision making process for EAI adoption. As noted from Table 1 and 2, different interviewees (i.e. also termed as internal stakeholders) have diverse views on the importance of factors. If seen individually, for the twenty seven factors all the interviewees provided relatively different importance. This can be attributed to their understanding and involvement in EAI projects within LGA_A and LGA_B respectively. However, some factors such as project champion, data consistency, top management support, cost, benefits, and barriers are primarily denoted with higher importance from almost all interviewees. For example, taking the project champion factor – interviewees recognise the inevitable significant nature of project champions and realise their necessity in effectively supporting and leading EAI projects (Kamal and Alsudairi, 2009). In addition, it can also be debated that project champions play an imperative role in actively and vigorously promoting their personal vision for using IT, pushing the project over or around approval and implementation hurdles. Project champion at LGA_A and _LGA_B played a similar role in actively supporting and endorsing their EAI project. Correspondingly, project champion importance is also highly recognised and reported in normative literature e.g. Garfield (2000) reported that in inter-organisational IS implementation projects the presence of an internal champion in each participating organisation is very important in providing the necessary leadership as the existence of a system-wide sponsor is not always sufficient. Norris (1999) and Beath (1991) also reported that within government organisations, the existence of a champion is one of the most important facilitators in the adoption of technologies. These discussions reported herein, therefore, support the existing published literature evidences on the importance of project champions (e.g. Somers and Nelson, 2004; Garfield, 2000).

Similarly, other factors such as data security and privacy, top management support and benefits respectively, have also been signified with the most importance. Relatively similar higher importance for these factors is also reported in normative literature (e.g. Signore *et al.,* 2005; Janssen and Cresswell, 2005; Pardo and Scholl, 2002; Themistocleous *et al.,* 2005). For example, *security and privacy of citizens'* data has always been important i.e. citizens' concern on security, privacy and confidentiality of the personal data has been a critical obstacle in implementing e-Government projects (Signore *et al.,* 2005; Tillman, 2003); *top management support* has been recognised as one of the most important elements necessary for the successful implementation of integration technologies and integrated packages (Ngai and Gunasekaran, 2004; Colmenares, 2004). Chen and Gant (2001) also report that one of the most successful factors associated with large-scale IT implementation projects is securing the support of top management; *benefits* refer to the level of recognition of the advantages that the integration technologies could provide to the organisation. Themistocleous (2004) reported different types of benefits such as: operational e.g. increase productivity, reduce cost and reduce lost sales, managerial e.g. increase performance, improve data quality, and support decision making, technical e.g. increase flexibility, reduce redundancy, achieves process integration and results in reliable data, strategic e.g. achieve customers' satisfaction and return on investment and organisational e.g. allow organisation to do business effectively.

The author argues that the concept of "*identifying the importance factors influencing EAI adoption*" presented in this paper makes a novel contribution both at the conceptual and empirical level in the context of LGAs for adopting EAI solutions. As highlighted in Tables 1 and 2, it is quite instinctive that each individual presents different views on the importance of the factors (Lam and Chin, 2005). Nevertheless, the views of all individuals should be considered, rather than a single one. Integration is an inescapable dilemma for LGAs and other government agencies for their e-Government projects (Cheng-Yi Wu, 2007; Sarikas and Weerakkody, 2007), which requires the devotion of each stakeholder (i.e. interviewees) involved in EAI projects. Therefore, it is indispensable to take the views of all stakeholders into account in the importance of factors. However, the essence in using this method is that it has the ability of determining the importance of factors as shown in Tables 1 and 2, thus allowing the researchers and practitioners in LGAs in determining which EAI adoption factor must be first given attention. EAI is no longer just an option but a necessity for LGAs aiming for better service delivery. Relevant strategies and organisational-wide policies play the primary role in making EAI projects a success. Therefore, the analysis presented in this paper would be beneficial for evaluating any other LGA enterprise application integration adoption practices while also identifying the importance of its influential factors.

CONCLUSION

While private organisations have continued to take advantage of EAI solutions to develop integrated IT infrastructures and improve their business processes, services offered by government organisations have remained deficient over the years. Implementing EAI is a challenging problem for the local government authorities, as it requires understanding and reengineering of the LGA structure, gaining stakeholder commitment, sharing of knowledge, and negotiating the division of costs and benefits. On the other hand, the concept of e-Government has emerged as a credible solution to improve such services as it allows people to access public services from within their own homes or offices. The importance of electronic service delivery has been widely recognised with 30 European ministers agreed upon a plan to speed up the development of e-Government applications in an attempt to modernise the European public sector.

Recently, many LGAs have attempted to link together their e-Government information systems to gain more advantages and deliver better services. Nonetheless, LGAs have realised that they can gain significant advantages when they integrate their e-Government information systems with their disparate back office solutions. Thus, they are seeking ways to integrate their applications and IT infrastructures. The author suggests that LGAs can focus on integration technologies like EAI to incorporate their systems and processes, and thus, achieving their goals. Yet, the adoption of EAI is still in its infancy within LGAs, researchers need to understand the issues surrounding this technology. This paper analysed and presented the EAI adoption practices by two LGAs, namely LGA_A and LGA_B. Empirical data for the present study were extrapolated through various sources of data like interviews, documentation and observation from these case organisations. The purpose of this data collection was to test and validate the factors influencing the decision making process for EAI adoption. Data was collected until there was enough data to test the proposed EAI adoption model. As highlighted in Tables 1 and 2, most of the factors were validated through the case studies, thus, supporting the author's literature findings on the proposed EAI adoption factors. Although the empirical research tested the factors, the research work presented in this paper is no exception; as a result this research can be further developed.

In the light of the reflections and the limitations it is recommended that further work could usefully be pursed. The theoretical and empirical data collected are confined to the limited context of the LGAs within the region of England. The structure of LGAs varies in different parts of the United Kingdom (UK). There are five different types of authorities in the UK and these are divided into single-tier and two-tier authorities with differences in the organisational structure, nature and size of each authority. In this context, it may be difficult to generalise the results of this research to other parts of the UK and other countries. A recommendation for the future study may be to test all the factors in another LGA across other parts of the UK. The empirical findings on the factors and the observations derived from the case organisation presented in this paper cannot be generalised. Nevertheless, it is not the intention of this paper to offer prescriptive guidelines for EAI adoption in LGAs, but rather to describe case organisation perspectives that allow others to relate their experiences to those reported. Hence, this paper offers a broader understanding of the phenomenon of EAI adoption in LGAs.

REFERENCES

Aileen, K., Joseph, P. C., & Carol, K. (2010). Business process change in e-government projects: The case of the Irish land registry. *International Journal of Electronic Government Research*, *6*(1), 9–22. doi:10.4018/jegr.2010102002

Akbulut, A. Y. (2002). An investigation of the factors that influence e-information sharing between state and local agencies. *Proceedings of the 8th Americas Conference on Information Systems*, USA, (pp. 2454-2460).

Aldrich, D., Berlot, J. C., & McClure, C. R. (2002). E-government: Initiatives, development, and issues. *Government Information Quarterly*, *19*(4), 349–355. doi:10.1016/S0740-624X(02)00130-2

Allen, B. A., Juillet, L., Paquet, P., & Roy, J. (2001). E-governance & government online in Canada: Partnerships, people & prospects. *Government Information Quarterly*, *18*, 93–104. doi:10.1016/S0740-624X(01)00063-6

Bass, C., & Lee, J. M. (2002). Building a business case for EAI. *EAI Journal*, 18-20.

Beath, C. M. (1991). Supporting the information technology champion. *Management Information Systems Quarterly*, *15*(3), 355–372. doi:10.2307/249647

Beaumaster, S. (2002). Local government IT implementation issues: A challenge for public administration. *Proceedings of the 35th Annual Hawaii International Conference on System Sciences*, IEEE Computer Society, (pp. 1725-1734).

Beynon-Davies, P. (2005). Constructing electronic government: The case of the UK inland revenue. *International Journal of Information Management*, *25*(1), 3–20. doi:10.1016/j.ijinfomgt.2004.08.002

Beynon-Davies, P., & Williams, M. D. (2003). Evaluating electronic local government in the UK. *Journal of Information Technology*, *18*, 137–149. doi:10.1080/0268396032000101180

Bonoma, T. (1985). Case research in marketing: Opportunities, problems and a process. *JMR, Journal of Marketing Research*, *22*, 199–208. doi:10.2307/3151365

Borge, L., & Rattsø, J. (1997). Local government grants and income tax revenue: Redistributive politics in Norway 1900–1990. *Public Choice*, *92*, 181–197. doi:10.1023/A:1004955330460

Bradford, M., & Florin, J. (2003). Examining the role of innovation diffusion factors on the implementation success of ERP systems. *International Journal of Accounting Information Systems*, *4*(3), 205–225. doi:10.1016/S1467-0895(03)00026-5

Brugha, R., & Varvasovszky, Z. (2000). Stakeholder analysis: A review. *Health Policy and Planning*, *15*(3), 239–246. doi:10.1093/heapol/15.3.239

Cavaye, A. L. M. (1996). Case study research: A multifacted research approach for IS. *Information Systems Journal*, *6*(3), 227–242. doi:10.1111/j.1365-2575.1996.tb00015.x

Chen, H. (2005). *Adopting emerging integration technologies in organisations*. PhD Thesis, Department of Information Systems and Computing, Brunel University, West London, UK.

Chen, Y. C., & Gant, J. (2001). Transforming local e-government services: The use of application services providers. *Government Information Quarterly*, *18*(4), 343–355. doi:10.1016/S0740-624X(01)00090-9

Cheng-YI Wu, R. (2007). Enterprise integration in e-government. *Transforming Government: People. Process and Policy*, *1*(1), 89–99.

Colmenares, G. L. E. (2004). Critical success factors of enterprise resource planning systems implementation in Venezuela. *Proceedings of the 10th Americas Conference on Information Systems*, New York, USA, (pp. 134-139).

Denzin, N. Y. K., & Lincoln, Y. (1994). *Handbook of qualitative research*. London, UK: SAGE Publications.

Di Natale, M., Cucinotta, T., & Kolachalam, S. (2003). A modular open-source architecture for ICT services in the public administration. *Proceedings of the 2nd International Conference on E-Government Prague,* Czech Republic, (pp. 167-172).

Ebrahim, Z., & Irani, Z. (2005). E-government adoption: Architecture and barriers. *Business Process Management Journal*, *11*(5), 589–611. doi:10.1108/14637150510619902

Ebrahim, Z., Irani, Z., & Sarmad, S. (2004). *Factors influencing the adoption of e-government in public sector*. European & Mediterranean Conference on Information Systems, Tunis, Tunisia.

Fichman, R. (1992). *Information Technology diffusion: A review of empirical research*. 13th International Conference on Information Systems, (pp. 195-206).

Ford, D. N., & Sterman, J. D. (1998). Dynamic modelling of product development processes. *System Dynamics Review*, *14*(1), 31–67. doi:10.1002/(SICI)1099-1727(199821)14:1<31::AID-SDR141>3.0.CO;2-5

Freeman, R. E. (1984). *Strategic management: A stakeholder approach*. Boston, MA: Pitman / Ballinger.

Garfield, M. (2000). Critical success factors for the state telemedicine policy. *Proceedings of the 6th Americas Conference on Information Systems*, Long Beach, California, USA, (pp. 1573-1578).

Gortmaker, J., & Janssen, M. (2004). Business process orchestration in e-government: A gap analysis. *Proceedings of the 15th International Resources Management Association (IRMA) International Conference*, New Orleans, LA, USA, (pp. 1-6).

Grimsley, M., & Meehan, A. (2007). E-government Information Systems: Evaluation-led design for public value and client trust. *European Journal of Information Systems*, *16*, 134–148. doi:10.1057/palgrave.ejis.3000674

Herriot, R. E., & Firestone, W. A. (1983). Multi-site qualitative policy research: Optimising description and generalisability. *Educational Researcher*, *12*, 14–19.

Homer, J., Sterman, J., Greenwood, B., & Perkola, M. (1993). Delivery time reduction in pulp and paper mill construction projects: A dynamic analysis of alternatives. *Proceedings of the 1993 International System Dynamics Conference*, Cancun, Mexico.

Iacovou, C., Benbasat, I., & Dexter, A. (1995). Electronic data interchange and small organisations – Adopting and impact of technology. *Management Information Systems Quarterly*, *19*(4), 465–485. doi:10.2307/249629

Irani, Z., Al-Sebie, M., & Elliman, T. (2006). Transaction stage of e-government systems: Identification of its location & importance. *Proceedings of the 39th Hawaii International Conference on System Sciences, IEEE*, (pp. 1-9).

Janssen, M., & Cresswell, A. (2005). *Enterprise architecture integration in e-government*. 38th Hawaii International Conference on System Sciences, Hawaii, (pp. 1-10).

Johnson, O. A., & King, S. F. (2005). *Best practice in local e-government: A process modelling approach*. e-Government Workshop (Egov05), (pp. 1-14).

Kamal, M. M. (2006). IT innovation adoption in the government sector: Identifying the critical success factors. *Journal of Enterprise Information Management*, *19*(2), 192–222. doi:10.1108/17410390610645085

Kamal, M. M. (2008). *Investigating enterprise application integration adoption in the local government authorities*. PhD Thesis, Department of Information Systems and Computing, Brunel University, London, UK.

Kamal, M. M. (2009). A multiple case study on integrating IT infrastructures in the public sector. *International Journal of Electronic Government Research*, *5*(3), 1–20. doi:10.4018/jegr.2009070101

Kamal, M. M., & Alsudairi, M. (2009). Investigating the importance of factors influencing integration technologies adoption in local government authorities. *Transforming Government: People, Process and Policy*, *3*(3), 302–331.

Kamal, M. M., Themistocleous, M., & Elliman, T. (2008). Extending IT infrastructures in LGAs through EAI. *Proceedings of the 14th Americas Conference on Information Systems*, Toronto, Canada, (pp. 1-12).

Kamal, M. M., Themistocleous, M., & Morabito, V. (2009). Justifying the decisions for EAI adoption in LGAs: A validated proposition of factors, adoption lifecycle phases, mapping and prioritisation of factors. *Proceedings of the 42nd Hawaii International Conference on System Sciences*, Hilton Kaikoloa Village Resort, Hawaii, (pp. 1-10).

Khoumbati, K., Themistocleous, M., & Irani, Z. (2006). Evaluating the adoption of enterprise application integration in healthcare organisations. *Journal of Management Information Systems*, *22*(4), 69–108. doi:10.2753/MIS0742-1222220404

Kim, H. J., & Bretschneider, S. (2004). Local government Information Technology capacity: An exploratory theory. *Proceedings of the 37th Annual Hawaii International Conference on System Sciences*, (pp. 121-130).

Lam, P.-K., & Chin, K.-S. (2005). Identifying and prioritizing critical success factors for conflict management in collaborative new product development. *Industrial Marketing Management*, *34*, 761–772. doi:10.1016/j.indmarman.2004.12.006

Lam, W. (2005). Barriers to e-government integration. *Journal of Enterprise Information Management*, *18*(5), 511–530. doi:10.1108/17410390510623981

Lam, W. (2005). Investigating success factors in enterprise application integration: A case driven analysis. *European Journal of Information Systems*, *14*(2), 175–187. doi:10.1057/palgrave.ejis.3000530

Lee, C. S., Chandrasekaran, R., & Thomas, D. (2003). *Examining IT usage across different hierarchical levels in organisations: A study of organizational, environmental, and IT factors*. 9th Americas Conference on Information Systems, (pp. 1259-1269).

Lee, S., & Treacy, M. E. (1998). Information Technology impacts on innovation. *R & D Management*, *18*(3), 257–271. doi:10.1111/j.1467-9310.1988.tb00592.x

Linthicum, D. (2000). *Enterprise application integration*. Massachusetts, USA: Addison-Wesley.

Mantzana, V., Themistocleous, M., Irani, Z., & Morabito, V. (2007). Identifying healthcare actors involved in the adoption of Information Systems. *European Journal of Information Systems*, *16*(1), 90–102. doi:10.1057/palgrave.ejis.3000660

Markus, L., & Tanis, C. (1999). The enterprise systems experience – From adoption to success. In Zmud, R. (Ed.), *Framing the domain of IT management: Glimpsing the future through the past* (pp. 173–207). Norman, Oklahoma: Pinnaflex Educational Resources, Inc.

McIvor, R., McHugh, M., & Cadden, C. (2002). Internet technologies supporting transparency in the public sector. *International Journal of Public Sector Management*, *15*(3), 170–187. doi:10.1108/09513550210423352

Miles, M., & Huberman, A. (1994). *Qualitative data analysis: An expanded sourcebook*. Newbury Park, CA: Sage.

Ngai, E. W. T., & Gunasekaran, A. (2004). Implementation of EDI in Hong Kong: An empirical analysis. *Industrial Management & Data Systems*, *104*(1), 88–100. doi:10.1108/02635570410514124

Norris, D. F. (1999). *Leading edge Information Technologies and their adoption: Lessons from US cities*. Hershey, PA: Idea Group Publishing.

Pardo, T. A., & Scholl, H. J. J. (2002). Walking atop the cliffs: Avoiding failure and reducing risk in large scale e-government projects. *Proceedings of the 35th Annual Hawaii International Conference on Systems Sciences*, (pp. 1656–1665).

Peristera, V., & Tarabanis, K. (2000). Towards an enterprise architecture for public administration using a top-down approach. *European Journal of Information Systems*, *9*, 252–260. doi:10.1057/palgrave/ejis/3000378

Ralphs, M., & Wyatt, P. (1998). The application of geographic and land Information Systems to the management of local authority property. *Property Management*, *16*, 83–91. doi:10.1108/02637479810214123

Ruh, W., Maginnis, F., & Brown, W. (2000). *Enterprise application integration. A Wiley Tech Brief*. New York, NY: Wiley John Wiley & Sons Inc.

Ruhe, G., & Du, G. (2004). Strategic planning of enterprise application integration. *Proceedings of the Enterprise Application Integration Summit*, (pp. 193-203).

Sanchez, E., Beery, D., & Shehab, J. (2002). *EAI systems bring IT together*. Network Computing.

Sarikas, O. D., & Weerakkody, V. (2007). Realising integrated e-government services: A UK local government perspective. *Transforming Government: People, Process and Policy*, *1*(2), 153–173.

Saunders, M., Lewis, P., & Thornhill, A. (2000). *Research methods for business students*. Essex, UK: Pearson Education Ltd.

Schutz, A. (1967). *The phenomenology of the social world*. Evanston, IL: Northwestern University Press.

Senyucel, Z. (2005). *Towards successful e-government facilitation in UK local authorities*. e-Government Workshop, (pp. 1-16).

Serian, D. (2002). *Middleware and enterprise application integration*. London, UK: Springer Verlag.

Shaw, N. G. (2000). Capturing the technological dimensions of IT infrastructure change. *Journal of the Association for Information Systems*, *2*(8).

Signore, O., Chesi, F., & Pallotti, M. (2005). *E-government: Challenges and opportunities*. CMG Italy – XIX Annual Conference, Florence, Italy.

Somers, M. T., & Nelson, G. K. (2004). A taxonomy of players and activities across the ERP project life cycle. *Journal of International Management, 41*, 257–278.

Themistocleous, M. (2004). Justifying the decisions for EAI implementations: A validated proposition of influential factors. *Journal of Enterprise Information Management, 17*(2), 85–104. doi:10.1108/17410390410518745

Themistocleous, M., & Irani, Z. (2001). Benchmarking the benefits and barriers of application integration. *Benchmarking: An International Journal, 8*(4), 317–331. doi:10.1108/14635770110403828

Themistocleous, M., Irani, Z., & Love, P. E. D. (2005). Developing e-government integrated infrastructures: A case study. *Proceedings of the 38th Annual Hawaii International Conference on System Sciences*, Big Island, Hawaii, IEEE, (pp. 1-10).

Tillman, B. (2003). More information could mean less privacy. *The Information Management Journal, 37*(2), 20–23.

Valor, C. (2005). Corporate social responsibility and corporate citizenship: Towards corporate accountability. *Business and Society Review, 110*(2), 191–212. doi:10.1111/j.0045-3609.2005.00011.x

Virili, F., & Sorrentino, M. (2009). Value generation in e-government from service-based IT integration. *Transforming Government: People, Process and Policy, 3*(3), 227–247.

Wagner, W., & Antonucci, Y. L. (2004). An analysis of the Imagine PA Public Sector ERP Project. *Proceedings of the 37th Hawaii International Conference on Systems Sciences*, Hawaii, (pp. 1-10).

Ward, M. A., & Mitchell, S. (2004). A comparison of the strategic priorities of public and private sector information resource management executives. *Government Information Quarterly, 21*(3), 284–304. doi:10.1016/j.giq.2004.04.003

Welch, E. W., Hinnant, C. C., & Moon, M. J. (2004). Linking citizen satisfaction with e-government and trust in government. *Journal of Public Administration: Research and Theory, 15*(3), 371–391. doi:10.1093/jopart/mui021

Whitmore, A., & Choi, N. (2010). Reducing the perceived risk of e-government implementations: The importance of risk communication. *International Journal of Electronic Government Research, 6*(1), 1–8. doi:10.4018/jegr.2010102001

Worrall, L. (1994). Justifying investment in GIS: A local government perspective. *International Journal of Geographical Information Science, 8*(6), 545–565. doi:10.1080/02693799408902021

Yardley, D. (2002). *Successful IT project delivery: Learning the lessons of project failure*. London, UK: Addison-Wesley.

Yin, R. K. (1994). *Case study research design and methods*. London, UK: Sage.

Zahavi, R. (1999). *Enterprise application integration with CORBA*. New York, NY: John Wiley and Sons Inc.

KEY TERMS AND DEFINITIONS

Enterprise Application Integration (EAI): Unrestricted sharing of information between two or more enterprise applications. A set of technologies that allow the movement and exchange of information between different applications and business processes within and between organisations.

Electronic Government (e-Government): E-Government (from electronic government, also known as e-Gov, digital government, online government or in a certain context transformational government) refers to the use of internet technology as a platform for exchanging information, providing services and transacting with citizens, businesses, and other arms of government. E-

Government may be applied by the legislature, judiciary, or administration, in order to improve internal efficiency, the delivery of public services, or processes of democratic governance.

Information Technology Infrastructure: The term IT infrastructure refers to the part of the infrastructure of an organisation that forms a platform for the IT applications.

Local Government Authorities (LGAs): LGAs are administrative offices that are smaller than a central government and are in direct contact with the community. The term is used to contrast with offices at nation-state level, which are referred to as the central government or national government. The pattern of LGAs is complex, with the distribution of functions varying according to the local arrangements.

Chapter 20
Guidelines for Successful Public Internet Access Points (PIAPs) Implementation

Ali Arifoğlu
METU Informatics Institute, Turkey

Gülgün Afacan
METU Informatics Institute, Turkey

Erkan Er
METU Informatics Institute, Turkey

ABSTRACT

This chapter is prepared to explain important aspects and factors to be considered in PIAPs-related projects, especially implemented in country-level. It is likely a guideline offering step-by-step and systematic approach for successfully implementing PIAP projects. The content of the guideline is divided into following sections: Potential PIAP Types, PIAP Services, Management Structure, Operational Structure, How to Create Public Demand, and Critical Success Factors.

The content of the chapter is as follows: first, related literature is briefly explained to review important PIAP implementations in the world; then, trends in PIAP projects in the world are examined and discussed based on the findings of investigation over 21 PIAPs implementation in the world; after that, the guideline is explained with all details; and finally, the chapter ends with future research directions and the conclusion section.

DOI: 10.4018/978-1-60960-839-2.ch020

INTRODUCTION

Primary objective of Public Internet Access Points (PIAPs) is to provide citizens with access to information and communication technologies. To use PIAPs in full potential, the implementation phase should be managed effectively. For a better implementation, there is a need for planned and systematic approach comprising all related issues (e.g. PIAP types to be established, services to be provided, operational issues, etc) for building PIAPs. The purpose of this study is to propose a guideline for successful PIAP implementation in country-level. This guideline is intended to help executers during the planning of PIAPs-related projects and also during the establishment of PIAPs so that citizens will be able to benefit from them in full-potential.

The chapter begins with the background information part, in which the definition of what PIAP is and the benefits and advantages it provides for citizens are introduced. In addition, some statistical data based on the investigation over 21 PIAP implementations in the world are provided in order to identify the common trends and applications in the world regarding services provided in PIAPs, management structure and operational structure of PIAP projects, financial management etc. After background information is presented, the main part of the chapter comes next. This main part firstly explains the methods of the study and the common problems and difficulties in PIAP implementations leading to need for a comprehensive guideline for better serving PIAPs. Then, the guideline is explained in details under five main titles: (1) Potential PIAP Types, (2) PIAP Services, (3) Management Structure, (4) Operational Structure, (5) Creating Public Demand and (6) Critical Success Factors. Towards the end of the chapter, potential future research studies are discussed in order to improve and extend the scope of the guideline. Finally, the chapter ends with the conclusion section.

BACKGROUND

Definitions

Public Internet Access Points (PIAPs) can be defined as technological tools designed to provide citizens with access to information and communication technologies (ICT). PIAPs are generally established to provide ICT opportunities for poor communities living in rural areas, where the current technology is not available or where affordability of these technologies is not achieved by majority (Kumar and Best, 2003). However, PIAPs can be established in both rural and urban areas depending on the specific purpose of the PIAP. The important point is that intended location should be able to provide the required technological infrastructure so that the PIAP should operate in a way that intended services addressing the needs of local people should be provided effectively.

Having the major purpose as to diminish digital divide and to support socio-economic development, PIAPs serve with variety of content and services. In other words, besides ICT services, PIAPs offer variety of services considering the needs and interests of individuals in order to increase the user demand and consequently source of revenue for PIAPs. These services, for example, can comprise trainings (e.g. basic computer courses or occupational courses), specific e-government services, library services, telecommunication services, multimedia services, etc. Benefits of PIAPs can be explained in three main titles as follows:

Direct Benefits - Financial Profit

a. Contributing to decrease in unemployment rates via employment opportunities for the operation and maintenance of PIAPs,
b. Supporting the e-Transformation of countries with minimal costs (i.e. it could finance itself by charge of users for training and office services, advertisement income, donations)

Table 1. Setup locations

Location	# of PIAP project	Percentage
Rural	21	% 100
Urban	6	% 29

Indirect Benefits – Productivity, Decrease in Cost, Operational Perfection

a. Human resources productivity will be increased because e-government services are offered in PIAPs and citizens are not required to go physically to governmental agencies,
b. Citizen satisfaction interviews/analyses will be performed immediately,
c. Communication and office services will be offered for small enterprises,
d. There will be productivity resulted from internet access availability for e-workers,
e. There will be variety of facilitation for finding local human resources for small enterprises.

Strategic Benefits

a. Decreasing digital divide,
b. Increasing the citizen awareness of e-transformation,
c. New lines for access to e-government services.

Trends in the World

In this part of the chapter, investigation results of successful PIAP implementations in the world are discussed. This investigation was performed over 21 PIAP projects implemented in 17 different countries. The investigation details are explained in details in Methodology section. The results of this investigation were published in 7th Eastern European e-GovDays (Arifoglu, Afacan, Er, 2009). In this part, these results will be summarized under 5 categories to show what other countries did commonly:

- Setup Location
- Services Provided in PIAPs
- Management Structure
- Operational Structure
- Financial Support

Setup Locations

Based on the investigated PIAP cases, setup locations are determined as rural or urban. Investigation results show that all of the PIAP projects are implemented in rural areas, whereas 6 of them are implemented in urban areas as well (See Table 1).

Being established in rural location is actually relevant with the mission of PIAPs, diminishing digital divide between rural and urban people by providing ICT-related services. Hungary case can be given as one major example since it gave significant importance to enable rural people to benefit from ICT with the help of PIAPs. In Hungary, there are totally 3145 PIAPs, of which 2361 PIAPs are operating in villages and towns. That is, most of the Hungary PIAPs were established in rural areas, especially in villages having population less than 5000.

Services Provided in PIAPs

Besides ICT-related services, PIAPs provides various services to address needs of target users. According to investigation results, training & education and telecommunication services are the most popular ones with 17%. Following these two, Office Services and Online information services come next with the percentage of 11 and 9, respectively (See Table 2).

These results show that there is a need for training citizens especially in rural areas so that they can gain basic computer skills and benefit from PIAPs in full potential. One of the useful cases in this regard is Sri Lanka Telecenters Proj-

Table 2. Services provided in PIAPs

Services	Percentage
Training and education	% 17
Telecommunication services	% 17
Office services	% 11
Online information services	% 9
Other services*	% 46

* Library Service, e-commerce services, small enterprise services, Job and Career Planning Services

ect. As instructional and training services, SriLanka Telecenters provide basic ICT training, office programs training, distance education, computer certificate course, computer supported instruction and operator training. Canada's telecenter project (i.e. The Kitimat Community Skills Centre in British Columbia) is another successful implementation that shows how PIAPs can be utilized as a training center that serves for various types of education. In this project, a network that enables access for 10 communities through full interactive, internet based and electronic classes were established.

Management Structure

Bodies responsible for management of PIAPs project can be listed as government, NGOs, private sector corporations and international organizations. In the investigated PIAP projects, there are cases where only one organization manage project alone and cases where more than one organization have the responsibility of managing project.

As it is observed in Table 3, in most of PIAPs projects, governments have responsibility as project manager with 76%. In 16 PIAPs cases of 21, governments have played role in project management in cooperation with other organizations or alone. NGOs are following the governments with 41% as project owner. Private sector organizations and international institutions follow after NGOs with 24%.

Table 3. Management structure

Body	# of PIAP project	Percentage
Government	16	% 76
NGO	8	% 41
Private Sector	5	% 24
International	5	% 24

As an example, AMIC@s project of Paraguay has a well-implemented management approach that merges managerial abilities of government, NGO and private sector. Briefly, in this project, government is responsible for the overall management of the project. NGOs comprising youth club members and local people, are responsible for analysis of society interest and needs, planning towards analysis, support the sustainability of center services and operation, find sponsor and advertising tasks. Finally, private sector companies such as Internet Service Providers, High Education Organizations, Radio TV Stations and US Peace Organizations contribute to technical and technological management of centers.

In addition, Australia Telecenters Project has implemented a different management structure that addresses the needs of PIAPs that are located over larger lands, like West Australia. This type of management has three levels: local level, regional level and government level. Each telecenter is managed by local management committee. To improve regional services and comply with the plans, existing four regions are controlled by regional coordinators. Each telecenter is supported by supporting units whose main offices are located in Ministry of Trade and Industry. Thus, the management structure of Australia Telecenter project seems to be appropriate for countries with large lands.

Operational Structure

After the analysis of PIAP operators in 21 cases from world, potential candidates for PIAP operator

Table 4. Operational structure

Body	# of PIAP project	Percentage
Government	14	% 65
NGO	11	% 53
Private	11	% 53

Table 5. Financial support

Source	# of PIAP project	Percentage
Fee-paying services	8	% 30
Government support	3	% 16
International funding	3	% 16
Private sector	3	% 16
Donations	3	% 16
Municipalities	1	% 4

can be listed as government, NGOs and private sector companies. During this analysis, there are cases where only one organization operates all PIAPs in project alone and cases where operation of PIAPs shared among more than one organization (i.e. hybrid operation model).

As it is observed in Table 4, in most of PIAPs project, governments have responsibility to operate PIAPs with 65%. That is, in 14 PIAPs cases, governments have either full operation responsibility or certain number of PIAPs in hybrid operation model. Following governments, NGOs and private sector corporations separately have responsibility to operate PIAPs with 53% (i.e. 11 PIAPs cases of 21).

One of the useful cases that successfully implements hybrid operational model is UK Online Centers Project. In this project, public organization, private sector and organizations in local, regional and national level operates PIAPs separately.

Financial Support

In the investigated PIAPs cases, various financial resources have been applied in order to overcome the financial difficulties during the PIAP project. Followings are used as financial resources during investigated PIAPs projects: (1) Incomes from services (charged services), (2) governmental support, (3) resources of municipality, (4) international funds, (5) shareholders' support and (6) donations.

As it is observed in Table 5, charged services seems to be mostly applied financial resource with 30% in general. 8 PIAPs cases out of 21 require a reasonable charge for services to maintain its sustainability. It is important to follow an appropriate policy to start service charging. In cases with charged services, it is observed that service charging was not applied at the start of operation and service charges came on later phases. So that citizens can benefit from PIAPs without any negative idea in their minds, and understand the importance of PIAPs for their daily lives. However, in the following years, financial resource planning has been changed so that a reasonable charging for the PIAPs services is started at the beginning and other financial resources (e.g. governmental support) are reduced.

Although financial support was attained by fee-paying services, the other funding opportunities become crucial in rural areas where people could not afford fee of using PIAPs. UNESCO Community Multimedia Centers (CMC) is an important example for such a case. In this project, citizens were able to benefit from all services without any charge.

GUIDELINES FOR SUCCESSFUL PIAP IMPLEMENTATION

Methodology

In order to prepare the guideline for successful PIAP implementation in country-level, 21 successful PIAP projects in the world are examined in order to identify common issues and problems in PIAP implementations and emphasize intended

Table 6. Examined PIAP projects

Case	Country
1. American Community Technology Centers (Stone, 2003)	America
2. Australia Telecentre Network (Latchem, Walker, 2003; McGregor, Latchem, 1991;McGregor, 1992;Oliver, 1996;Short, 2002)	Australia
3. Kitimat Community Skills Centre (Latchem, Walker, 2003)	Canada
4. Remote Community Service Telecentres (Latchem, Walker, 2003)	Canada
5. UK Online Centers [15]	England
6. Hungary Telecottages (UNDP, Europe and the CIS, 2005).	Hungary
7. UNESCO Community Multimedia Centers (Creech, Berthe, Assubuji, Mansingh, Anjelkovic, 2006).	Latin America, Africa and South Asia
8. Distance Learning Support Centre In Maseru (West, Sebatane, Setsabi, Abdo, Howard, 2000).	Lesotho
9. Mexico Digital Community Centers (DTC) (e-Mexico National System, 2008)	Mexico
10. Mozambique Telecenters (Werner, 1996)	Mozambique
11. Paraguay AMIC@s (Latchem, Walker, 2001)	Paraguay
12. Senegal Telecenters (Etta, Parvyn-Wamahiu, 2003)	Senegal
13. e-Sri Lanka Telecenters (Proenza, Hanna, Dewapura, 2004)	Sri Lanka
14. People First Network (PFnet) (PFnet, 2005;Chand, Leeming, Stork, Agassi, Biliki, 2005)	Solomon Islands
15. Gaseleka Telecenters (West, Sebatane, Setsabi, Abdo, Howard, 2000).	South Africa
16. Taiwan Telecentres (Lin, 2005).	Taiwan
17. BBBOP Project	Turkey
18. Belnet Internet Houses in Istanbul	Turkey
19. Internet Cafes in Turkey	Turkey
20. MEB PIAPs	Turkey
21. Uganda Telecenters (Etta, Parvyn-Wamahiu, 2003)	Uganda

solution alternatives applied in those implementations. The examined PIAP projects are listed in Table 6.

During the investigation process, firstly the problems and issues faced in each PIAP project were analyzed. These analyses resulted in a set of problems commonly faced in PIAP implementations, which are categorized into five main problem domains:

- Problems related to usage of PIAPs
- Problems related to management of PIAPs
- Problems related to operations of PIAPs
- Problems related to infrastructure of PIAPs
- Problems related to financial issues

Problems in those domains actually revealed the need for a solution, a guideline for successful PIAP implementation. In the following section issues and problems are discussed and then guideline content is provided.

Issues and Problems: The Need for Guidelines

Potential problems faced in investigated PIAP cases are grouped into five categories which are listed in the following table:

- Problems related to usage of PIAPs
- Problems related to management of PIAPs
- Problems related to infrastructure of PIAPs

- Problems related to operations of PIAPs
- Problems related to financial issues

Problems Related to Usage of PIAPs

Awareness of citizens for PIAPs could not be achieved at expected level because of difficulties faced in presentation of PIAPs to citizens, which leads to lower rates of use below the capacity of PIAPs. Local people living in poor economical conditions could not afford to benefit from PIAPs providing charged services. Consequently, this situation decreases the use of PIAPs. Problems related to use of PIAPs and percentages of each one are illustrated in Figure 1.

Problems Related to Management of PIAPs

Most critical problem related to managerial issues is inadequate support of authorities, which effected financial resources and sustainability of PIAPs deeply in negative way. PIAP cases that have not effective management structure have always faced some difficulties in managerial and operational issues. Problems related to managerial issues and percentages of each one are illustrated in Figure 2.

Problems Related to Operation of PIAPs

Some of the PIAPs cases from world have faced difficulties during employment progress of needed

Figure 1. Problems related to usage of PIAPs

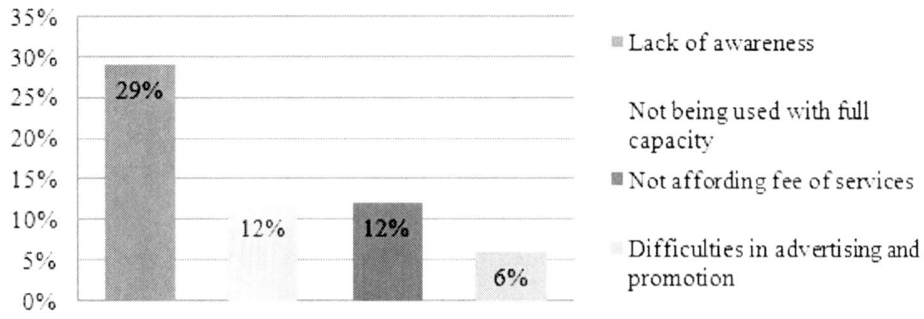

Figure 2. Problems related to management of PIAPs

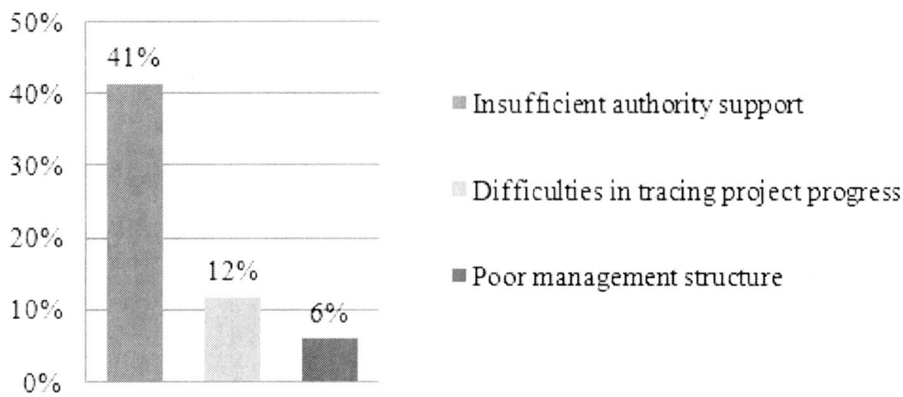

personal. The main reason for that is the lack of qualified technical staff. Furthermore, there are some issues related to sustainability of PIAPs as a result of insufficient support of local administration. In addition, poor communication link among project partners causes operational problems. The other specific problematic issue about operation of PIAPs is that it is hard to educate and enable aged citizens to gain basic computer skills. Problems related to operation of PIAPs and percentages of each one are illustrated in Figure 3:

Problems Related to Infrastructure of PIAPs

There are various problems faced related to infrastructure of PIAPs. Insufficient spaces inside PIAPs and wrong location choice to set up PIAPs decrease the accessibility of PIAPs by citizens. Internet, phone and electricity cut -especially in rural areas distracted the expectation of citizens from PIAPs and consequently decreased the number of PIAPs user. Other problems related to infrastructure are malfunctioning of software hardware, not updating technical infrastructure, difficulties in supplying technical support, limited range of services, unsecure internet connection.

Figure 3. Problems related to operation of PIAPs

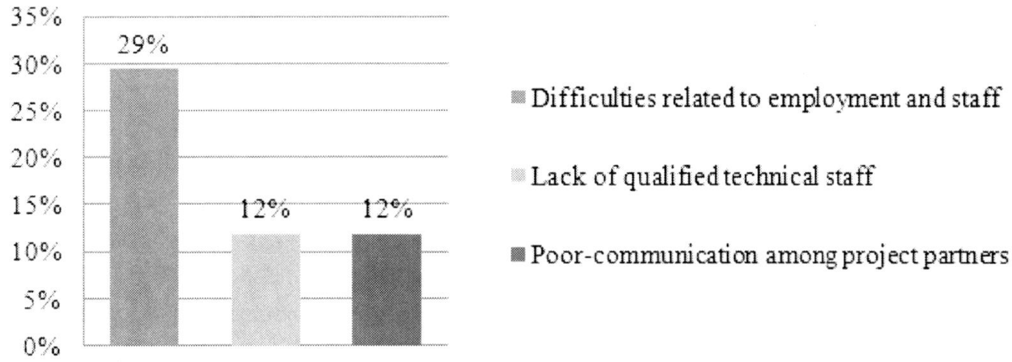

Figure 4. Problems related to infrastructure of PIAPs

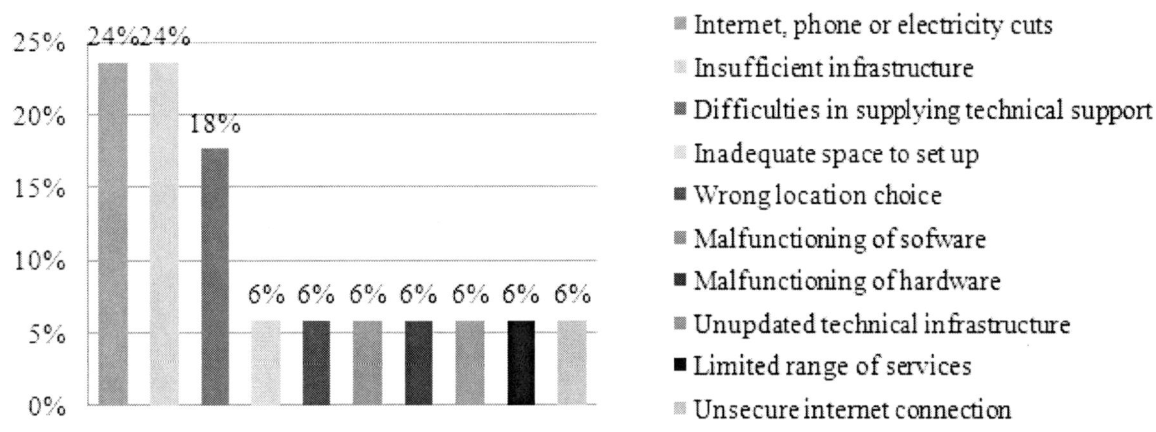

Problems related to infrastructure of PIAPs and percentages of each one are illustrated in Figure 4.

Problems Related to Financing of PIAPs

The typical problem related to financial issues is to get enough financial support. The main cause of that problem is that decision-makers or authorities do not appreciate the value of PIAPs for the citizens. Furthermore, conducting technical maintenance of PIAPs in remote regions is costly, which burdens project budget. Problems related to infrastructure of PIAPs and percentages of each one are illustrated in Figure 5.

Guideline Content

Potential PIAP Types

In this section, specific PIAP types are explained considering their structure, infrastructure and sustainability. These potential PIAP types, which are kiosk, mobile PIAP, multi-purpose PIAPs and mini-PIAPs, are defined by the appropriate classification of PIAP structures of examined world cases.

Kiosk Model

Kiosk model is set up in places that have high number of visitors like railway stations, air ports, terminals, ferry-boats and sea bus, tourism centers, hospitals, shopping centers and its main service is the internet. Kiosks must be situated at busy points where people visit most. Setup locations of kiosks within a building should be chosen carefully so that people can notice and access easily, and use comfortably.

Taiwan Telecenter project can be given as an example for a successful Kiosk implementation. In urban regions of the country kiosks are located in airports, train stations, libraries and cultural centers. Kiosk model consists of only a wall-mounted Internet computer, which was similar to a public phone. Since kiosks are managed within a centralized structure, maintenance costs are low and usage statistics can be obtained.

Mobile PIAPs

Mobile PIAPs are developed to transmit Internet access to rural region with low population density or to the regions with limited access to ICT. With this model, regions in which it is hard to install technology are covered and special vehicles are used to serve citizens through its appropriate technical infrastructure. At the same time, this

Figure 5. Problems related to financing of PIAPs

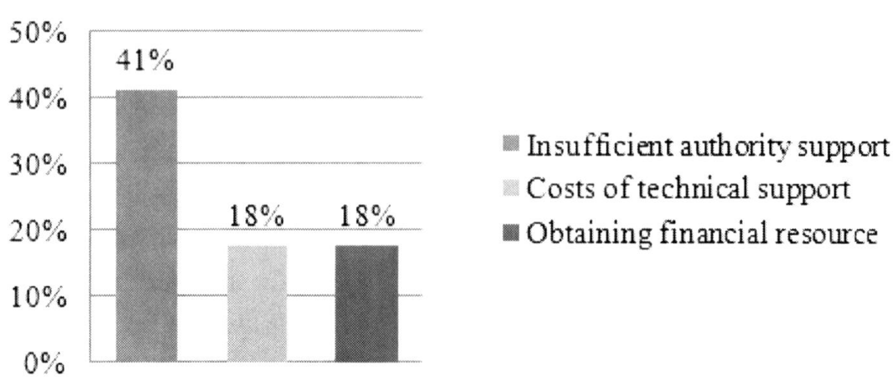

model can also be utilized to increase the awareness of citizens and to introduce new technologies to local people. Instead of permanent structure, special vehicles are equipped with Internet access and other required infrastructure.

There are a few telecenter projects that implement Mobile PIAPs. One of them is Hungarian Telecottages[1]. In this project, mobile PIAPs are not the only PIAP type implemented, but it is implemented in addition to other PIAP types such as Multi-purpose PIAPs. Throughout the project, there have been experiments and solutions in which the telecottage was temporarily installed or being transported on a lorry (or other means of mobility). As far as the community is concerned, these are of a temporary nature, and do not satisfy the requirements of a permanent PIAP building. Nevertheless, they play a positive role in the evaluation and testing of services and opportunities, and in convincing users during the development period.

Multi-Purpose PIAPs

Multi-purpose PIAPs are generally established within governmental organizations, non-governmental organizations, schools, stopping places, small industry complexes, and organized industrial zone. The locations of multi-purpose PIAPs are closed places in which 5-20 computers are installed. This model is mainly preferred to transmit information and communication technologies, and services regarding health, education, women improvement and economical development for regions digitally isolated regions.

One of the most popular PIAP type is the Multi-Purpose PIAP and important example is UK Online Centers for this type. These centers are majorly located in urban areas and intended to increase ICT usage-level. Besides basic services such as internet access and computer games, UK Online Centers provides e-Government services and online content (e.g. child care, special interest areas, etc.). Thus, UK Online Center is an excellent example of multi-purpose PIAP with variety of services it provides for all citizens independent from their socio-economic groups.

Mini-Model

Mini PIAPs are intended to be established in "central village" so that citizens of closer villages will be able to use. Mini PIAPs should be established in public places in the center of settlement. According to usage capacity of mini PIAPs, in buildings of PTT agencies, mini PIAPs can be established. PIAP should be accessible by all citizens (young, olds, children, unemployed, disabled, etc.); design of buildings of PIAPs should be feasible for entrance and exit of users. To contribute to sustainability, content and services should be rich, up-to-date and need-oriented, and should be developed by active participation of project shareholders.

Sri Lanka Telecenters Project is one of those which majorly implemented this type of PIAPs. In this project, telecenters are installed in rural regions having population between 2000 and 5000. Therefore, PIAPs serve majority of population in rural area with variety of services. The main focus of these services is instruction and training. As instructional and training services, Sri Lanka Telecenters provide basic ICT training, office programs training, distance education, computer certificate course, computer supported instruction and operator training. Besides that, telecommunication, e-commerce, office and social services are offered.

Comparison of PIAP Types

In this section, a brief comparison table is provided to let the reader have a general look of unique characteristics of each PIAP type and differences among them.

How to Choose PIAP Type

PIAP types defined in this study have different capabilities that can be utilized depending on the specific needs of citizens and governments. A summary table has been given to indicate which PIAP type should be decided under what circumstances.

PIAP Services

In order to define services to be provided in PIAPs and their priorities, a simple prioritization approach which takes into account expert view and user demand has been applied. In this approach, feasibility of services and user demands for services has been investigated and results were merged to define a reasonable priority-level for each service.

User demand is identified considering the trend in the world and results of a survey which was conducted with 2000 active PIAP users in Turkey. To assess the feasibility of services, IT experts have been consulted to grade feasibility-level of each service over five. The results are illustrated in Figure 6.

Service prioritization graph is divided into three regions to categorize PIAP services. These categories are Initial Services, Intermediate Services and Advanced Services. Initial services could be provided in the first establishment of the PIAPs whereas intermediate services are to be provided in medium-term. Finally, Third region comprises services for long-term. In the following part, these service categories are investigated in details.

Initial Services

Services of orange region should be provided during the initial phase of PIAP formation that is the first year. These services are listed below. They are ordered according to level of user demand and feasibility.

1. Basic Computer Education,
2. Print Services,

Table 7. Comparison of PIAP types

	PIAP Types			
	Multi-purpose PIAPs	**Mini PIAPs**	**Kiosk**	**Mobile PIAPs**
User Capacity	5-20 users	1-5 users	1 user	5-10 users
Region Addressed	Urban	Rural	Urban	Rural
Purpose	Intends to provide wide-range of services in highly populated areas.	It is a minimized version of Multi-purpose PIAPs that provide services applicable for rural areas having low population density.	It provides mainly Internet access in places such as terminals, hospitals, etc.	It mainly supports awareness of public by performing advertorial activities
Management Structure	Three different types of management: central management, local management and branch management	With the cooperation of public sector, universities, private sector and NGOs.	Managed by owner institution/organization in which kiosk is installed.	Managed by private or public organization.
Operational Structure	2 coordinators, conduct training, maintenance, cleaning and security tasks. Controlling unit monitors technical, administrative and financial aspects related to PIAPs.	1 or 2 staff, responsible for daily tasks and technical support of PIAPs. Controlling unit monitors technical, administrative and financial aspects related to PIAPs.	1 staff, responsible for coordination of centers and provision of technical support.	Controlling unit, responsible for control of technical, administrative and financial issues.

Table 8. How to choose PIAP type

PIAP Type	Conditions	Region
Mobile PIAPs	No ICT infrastructure, Hard to access physically to a specific area, No technical staff, Totally technology-illiterate population	Rural
Multi-purpose PIAPs	Technology-literate population, Need for advance and enriched ICT-services, Focus on specific user groups (e.g. elder people)	Urban
Mini PIAPs	Technology-illiterate population, Enough technical infrastructure for the establishment, Need for ICT-related training services to enable citizens gain basic computer skills	Rural
Kiosks	Need for specific purposes at busy public points (e.g. railway stations, hospitals, terminals),	Rural/Urban

Figure 6. Prioritization of PIAP services

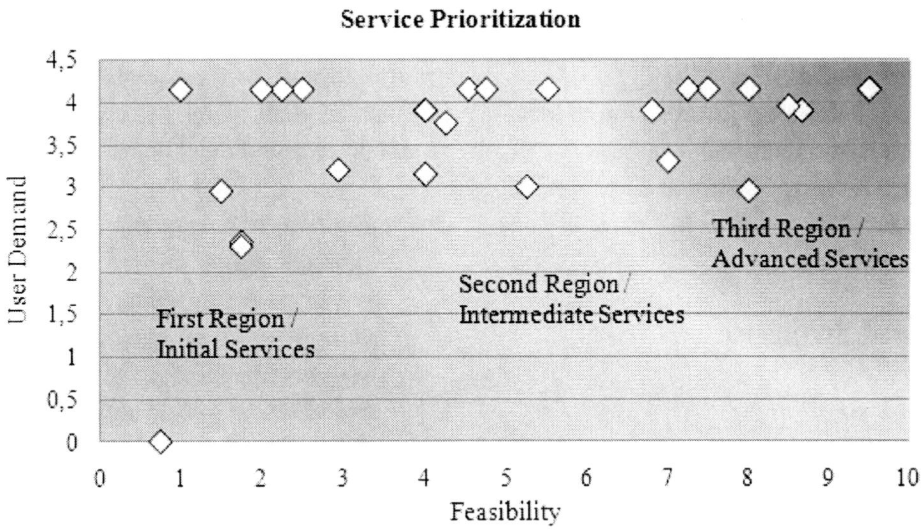

3. Photocopy Services,
4. Scanning Documents,
5. Telecommunication Services,
6. Online Information Services,
7. Vocational Development Trainings,
8. Office Software Trainings,
9. Educational Computer Games,
10. Computer Certification Courses,
11. E-Government Services.

Intermediate Services

Services of yellow region should be provided during the median-term of PIAP formation that is the 2nd and 3rd years. These services are listed below. They are ordered according to level of user demand and feasibility.

1. Web Design Trainings
2. Career Planning Services
3. Language Courses
4. Typing Service

5. Web Design Services
6. Binding Service
7. Lamination Services

Advanced Services

Services of blue region are advanced services that should be provided during the 4th and 5th years of PIAP formation. These services listed below are currently not much demanded and also their feasibility is low. They are ordered according to level of user demand and feasibility.

1. Multimedia Services,
2. Programming Courses,
3. Hardware Trainings,
4. Small Enterprise Services,
5. E-Commerce Services,
6. Electronic Publishing (Preparation of local newspapers and journals)
7. Reading/Writing Courses for Native Language
8. Library Services

Management Structure

Kiosk Model

Control of kiosks can be performed by the management of owner institution/organization in which kiosk is installed. Content providers should cooperate with owner institution/organization while making decisions about installation of kiosks and operational issues of kiosks. Also, a committee can be formed which consists of representatives of organizations owning a kiosk in order to make decisions about kiosks and to define standard service level. For example, representatives of hospitals owning a kiosk, representatives of content providers, and one representatives of Ministry of Health (Computer Center) can meet regularly to discuss the current issues related to kiosks. Related department of Computer Center of Ministry of Health can define the general rules, control and tracking mechanism for kiosks.

Mobile PIAPs

Mobile PIAPs should be coordinated by an organization for which they are running. Separate organizations responsible from management of mobile PIAPs should cooperatively take decisions regarding establishment and operation of mobile PIAPs. Moreover, there should be a top management committee to provide aggregation of owner organizations of mobile PIAPs to take common decisions towards mobile PIAPs. Management of mobile PIAPs in the same status will be accountable to top management of PIAPs regarding general rules, control, and monitoring.

Multi-Purpose PIAPs

Multi-purpose PIAPS requires three different types of management which are central management, local management and branch management.

- *Central management:* a program management office created by government is responsible for several tasks such as development of an agreement defining roles and responsibilities of local authorities, management of this agreement, and evaluation of performances of local authorities, planning of funding value, planning and monitoring quality standards, researching user complaints, and researching for additional financial resources.
- *Local management:* a management committee is formed to perform PIAP related administrative tasks. This committee regularly meets and decides on planning, financial monitoring, funding, and cooperation opportunities with NGOs for volunteer support, personnel employment and training. Management committee should involve representatives from local authorities, citizens, and NGOs. An operational model not considering gain of benefit is applied.
- *Branch management:* Two coordinators are attended for each PIAP by management

committee. These two coordinators work full time and responsible for management, operation, maintenance and advertising of PIAPs. Regular reporting to management committee is also duty of coordinators. Multi-purpose PIAPs are open in hours 10:00 to 20:00 every day. Membership system is applied. Users become members after filling the membership forms. For users aged below 18, parent permission is required. Members can benefit any PIAPs.

Mini-Model

There should be a local coordinator unit which is responsible for determining the villages in which mini PIAPs will be established, planning the near villages that will receive services from these PIAPs, providing cooperation with universities, private sector, and NGOs to develop service and content towards needs and expectations of village citizens, monitoring implementation of services, coordinate the progress regarding the selected model to be utilized. Besides installation of centers and, design, implementation and update of content, this unit will control the operation of PIAPs, learn the complaints and ideas of users and find possible solutions. This unit will be managed by main PIAP administration. Participation of local people should be provided into progress of analyzing needs in order to create demand of users towards use of centers.

Participation of local people should be provided into progress of analyzing needs in order to create demand of users towards use of centers. According to findings, local coordinator unit should be responsible for providing relation between local people and related organizations, and providing content serving to needs of citizens. Local coordination unit can build a consulting committee or management committee from related organizations. Moreover, local coordination unit should cooperate with district/ministry for permit process, and usage limitations regarding public buildings.

Operational Structure

Kiosk Model

Operational costs, which comprises personnel salaries and internet costs, can be accepted by owner institution/organization as running expenses. Project partners are responsible for content development, which is a critical factor for kiosks, design and update of interfaces, and technical support. Donations of shareholders, advertisement incomes, and, incomes obtained from charged services could be considered as important financial resources to meet costs of content development and software used in kiosks.

One personnel should be employed by management. These personnel will be responsible for coordination of centers and provision of technical support for citizens if needed. Personnel should have knowledge and experience about use of information and communication technologies. Cleaning and security related tasks shall be carried out by existing personnel employed by manager organization.

Mobile PIAPs

Since operation of mobile PIAPs will be performed by private organizations, financing will be supported by resources of private sector. Expenses are composed of staff salary, transportation, technical infrastructure and costs of operation. As personnel costs salaries of mobile PIAP coordinators and drivers should be met. A controlling unit, which will be formed by management committee, will be responsible for control of technical, administrative and financial issues of mobile PIAPs and reporting the results to PIAP management structure.

Multi-Purpose PIAPs

Two coordinators are employed to manage PIAPs and provide technical support to the users. These coordinators should have previous knowledge and experience about information and communication technologies. Training, maintenance, cleaning and security tasks are carried out by personnel procured by local authorities, private organizations or NGOs. A controlling unit will be formed and this unit will monitor the technical, administrative and financial aspects of the PIAPs. During monitoring progress, results will be reported by unit to PIAP management.

Mini-Model

Staff responsible for daily tasks of PIAPs should be knowledgeable about use of information and communication technologies. If ICT capabilities of personnel are not good enough, initiative and/ or assistants should be trained in technical area. A controlling unit, which shall be formed by management committee, will be responsible for control of technical, administrative and financial issues of mini PIAPs and reporting the results to PIAP management structure. In order to develop and update content, design interface, provide technical support, public organizations, private organizations, NGOs and local coordinator unit should collaboratively work.

How to Create Demand for PIAP?

Potential ways of creating society demand towards PIAPs are examined under three categories: User Satisfaction, PIAP Advertising, and User Participation.

User Satisfaction: Since PIAPs will be established throughout the whole country, users of PIAPs will be from different socio-economic backgrounds. The socio-economic difference between users will result in distinction according to expectation of users from PIAPs; while some users' expectation are clear, others need personnel support because of their lack of awareness about technology. Because creating user demand is one of the important aims of PIAPs, usage rates should be increased by providing high user satisfaction. In order to provide user satisfaction so that to reach high usage rates, following steps should be considered:

- PIAPs should offer services towards needs of citizens,
- PIAP users should be informed, guided and trained about technology and services,
- The personnel of PIAPs should be competent in operation of PIAPs, be knowledgeable about services and should provide support whenever users need.

PIAP Advertising: Interest of users will be increased if citizens are informed about the opportunities of PIAPs. Primarily, citizens should be informed about operation and services of PIAPs. The use of technical terminology while informing citizens with lack of technology knowledge may cause citizens to hesitate towards technology. Instead, basic terminology should be used to address level of citizens; opportunities of technology, services and aims of PIAPs should be presented; brochure, poster and visual advertising materials should be used while informing citizens.

User Participation: Citizens' opinions should be considered towards the content and services to be offered by PIAPs. For example, citizen expectations towards courses can be analyzed by interview so that prioritization can be conducted among training services. Based on the data obtained, PIAPs will offer training courses relevant to citizens' demand.

Critical Success Factors

Factors effecting success and sustainability of PIAPs are examined under 7 main categories:

- PIAP Infrastructure
- PIAP Services
- PIAP Planning
- PIAP Management
- PIAP Operation
- PIAP Financing
- PIAP Use

Please see Appendix A for a summary table of all success factors under these 7 categories.

PIAP Infrastructure

The primary condition for effective operation of PIAPs is to provide basic infrastructure components in centers. The building of PIAPs shall have relevant features from different perspectives. PIAPs established in secure, clean and well-kept buildings get the attention of users so that usage rates increase and operational sustainability of PIAPs are supported. If PIAPs are located in centre of towns, citizens can easily reach to centers so that any potential transport problem will be omitted. Among the PIAP cases in the world, most common problems encountered are related to interruption of Internet or electricity. Because of these problems, rate of uses tends to decrease. As significant factors, countries shall try to provide continuous Internet and electricity in PIAPs so that usage decrease caused from interruption will be eliminated. Number of PCs to be involved in PIAPs shall be decided according to number of population that PIAPs will address. For instance, while mini model aims to install 1-5 PCs in rural, multipurpose model aims to install 5-20 PCs in urban region. It is not enough to install only PCs for sustainability of PIAPs. Regular controls should be performed for proper functioning of software and hardware, and if necessary maintenance of technical infrastructure should be conducted. At the same time, in case of any technical problem, technical support should be provided to remove the problem.

PIAP Services

To achieve sustainability of PIAPs and high user satisfaction rates, various content and services should be offered in PIAPs. Types of services to be offered in PIAPs can be determined according to users' feedback obtained through interview type assessment methods. The presence of services demanded by users will increase the usage permanency and raise the rate of user satisfaction. In order to make PIAPs appealing to the users, rich content and services shall be offered and regularly updated. At the same time, it shall be considered that services and content should be relevant to language and cultural characteristics of citizens. Opinions and suggestions of users should be attained regularly.

PIAP Planning

Plans related to PIAPs should be decided by top level managers in parallel to general aims and objectives of PIAPs. Initially, a detailed PIAP business plan should be developed. Business plan should involve the plans of budget, workforce and technical infrastructure of PIAPs. Technology needs analysis of people should be conducted to determine the needs and interests of users. For this purpose, PIAP shareholders and end users should be involved into planning process. Gradual approach should be adopted; therefore, scope of program can be enlarged if success is observed or contingency plans should be considered if weaknesses occur.

Management of PIAPs

For the purpose of structuring and sustainability of PIAPs, effective management structure involving government leadership should be adopted. Essential rules, standards and regulations should be developed by management committee of PIAPs. Since, parallel progress between PIAPs is significant, structure of management should enable coordination between shareholders of PIAPs. Moreover, government leaders should support the development of PIAPs.

PIAP Operation

Support of local authorities plays an important role during operation of PIAPs. Local authorities can provide various supports such as human resources, buildings and hardware. Regarding operation, employing qualified personnel will decrease the probability of occurrence of any problem. Qualified personnel imply PIAP coordinators, instructors and volunteer staff supporting PIAPs. As stated in critical success factors of PIAP infrastructure part, employing technical personnel is important factor that ensures operation of PIAPs without any problem. Effective coordination between shareholders responsible for operation of PIAPs is significant for operational sustainability of PIAPs.

PIAP Financing

In order to find financial support, common solution applied by PIAP cases is to benefit from various financial sources. Local authorities and enterprises contribute to budget of PIAPs in different ways. Leadership of local authority and cooperation between local enterprises may meet the costs of rent, water, electricity, furniture and building supplies. Government may support the costs of human resources and maintenance of technical infrastructure. Citizens may charge with small fees for services and membership so that PIAPs will be able to meet their expenses one or two years after the installation. Utilization of international funding will support the costs of installation. Volunteers may support the human resource capacity of PIAPs and donations may meet the costs of operation. Private sector will play an important role to provide essential software and content for services to be offered in PIAPs.

Usage of PIAPs

There are various factors to increase Internet utilization rates of citizens so that to achieve information society. Provision of secure Internet, high awareness towards ICT and high satisfaction of users are important factors to reach intended rates for Internet use. Because of high satisfaction, citizens' motivation will be increased so that a society that can integrate ICT into daily lives will be achieved. Advancing in computer skills will develop the countries according to academic and social fields.

Benefits of PIAPs for Public Sector

There are many potential benefits of PIAPs for public institutions. First of all, analysis of PIAP projects from different countries show that PIAPs have a high capacity of supporting educational activities and one of the common training is ICT and basic computer educations. Especially, developing countries needs to transform public sector including all employers and officials into e-organization. For that reason, besides offering e-government services, people working in public institutes have to be computer-literal and adapt technologies without resistance. Developing countries can use PIAPs as a training center to transform its governmental units into computer literate bodies and therefore enhance the technology adaption by public sector.

Furthermore, governments can easily generalize and disseminate e-government services to citizens who frequently use PIAPs. e-Government services can be integrated effectively in PIAPs and naturally citizens using PIAPs become aware of those services and get familiar with advantageous of e-government easily. The more satisfaction citizens get while using e-government services, the higher demands emerges for this kind of services. Therefore, governments can achieve more effective e-transformation progress, provided that they increase the usage rate of PIAPs.

What is more is that communication among governmental bodies and citizens becomes easier with the help of PIAPs. For example, governmental bodies can ensure that citizens get access to various announcements, advertisements and important notifications through PIAPs. This communication can also be possible at local level.

FUTURE RESEARCH DIRECTIONS

The guideline provided in this chapter could be further enhanced and extended by conducting a study to measure social impact of PIAPs. Roger's Diffusion of Innovation Model or Technology Acceptance Model could be employed to measure the diffusion level of PIAPs among citizens. Such kind of study conducted in different regions may produce clues for why people adapt PIAPs or why they do not accept it, etc. These clues could be benefited for better PIAPs implementation and can provide different dimensions for the proposed guideline.

CONCLUSION

In conclusion, based on the analysis of PIAP cases, this chapter proposes a guideline explaining what to do for better PIAP implementation in country level by addressing the following questions:

- What could be the potential PIAP types?
- What is important for the selection of PIAP services? How could those be categorized?
- How should be the management structure?
- How to operate PIAPs?
- How to create or increase public demand for PIAPs?
- What are the critical success factors?

In the guideline, firstly potential PIAP types (i.e. multi-purpose PIAPs, mini PIAPs, kiosks and mobile PIAPs) are explained by emphasizing infrastructure and sustainability issues. Secondly, PIAP services are categorized according to phases of deployment. In other words, the basic services to be provided at the initial stage, the intermediate services to be provided after PIAPs becomes more popular, and the advanced services to be provided in long term are explained. This categorization is parallel with increasing maturity of PIAPs and citizen awareness.

In the following two parts, management and operational structure related to each PIAP type are introduced. The structures are determined according to the characteristics of PIAP types. Type-specific explanation for management and operation structures worked well in showing what factors should be taken into consideration depending on the type.

At the end of the guideline, critical success factors that are to be considered for achieving intended goals are explained in details. These factors are examined in six PIAP related categories: infrastructure, services, planning, management, operational, financial, and usage. The content of this study includes valuable directions for the researchers and practitioners of PIAPs.

REFERENCES

Arifoglu, A., Afacan, G., & Er, E. (2009). *Public Internet access points (PIAPs): A model to accelerate e-inclusion.* Paper presented at 7th Eastern European e-Gov Days 2009, Prague.

Chand, A., Leeming, D., Stork, E., Agassi, A., & Biliki, R. (2005). *The impact of ICT on rural development in Solomon Islands: The PFnet case.* ICT Capacity Building at USP Project, the University of the South Pacific. ISBN 982-01-0629-X

Creech, H., Berthe, O., Assubuji, A. P., Mansingh, I., & Anjelkovic, M. (2006). *Evaluation of UNESCO's community multimedia centres: Final report.* (Report No. IOS/EVS/PI/54). Paris, France: United Nations Educational, Scientific, and Cultural Organization. e-Mexico National System. (2008). *Digital community centers.* Retrieved October 19, 2008, from http:// www.emexico.gob.mx/ wb2/ eMex/ eMex_Digital_community_centers

Etta, F., & Parvyn-Wamahiu, S. (2003). *Information and communication technologies for development in Africa: Volume 2- The experience with community telecentres.* (pp. 127-148, 72, 113). IDRC, CODESRIA.

Kumar, R., & Best, M. (2006). Social impact and diffusion of telecenter use: A study from the sustainable access in rural India project. *Journal of Community Informatics*, *2*, 3.

Latchem, C., & Walker, D. (2001). *Telecentres: Case studies and key issues*. Vancouver, Canada: The Commonwealth of Learning.

Lin, M. (2005). *Digital divide and telecenter development in Taiwan.* Department of Information Management Research, Development, and Evaluation Commission, Taiwan. Retrieved November 15, 2008, from http:// www.rdec.gov.tw/ public/ Data/ 941716305971.pdf

McGregor, A., & Latchem, C. (1991). *Networks for learning: A review of access and equity in post-compulsory education in rural and remote areas of the State of Western Australia*. Perth, Australia: Western Australian Office of Higher Education.

McGregor, A. L. (1992). *Networks on trial: An evaluation of the WA learning network centres project. Report commissioned by the Western Australian Higher Education Council*. Perth, WA: Western Australian Office of Higher Education.

Oliver, R. (1996). *Networks into the 21st century: An evaluation of the Western Australian telecentre network*. Report commissioned by the Western Australia Department of Training, Perth, WA.

People First Network (PFnet) Rural Development Volunteers Association. (2005). *The Solomon Islands people first Network (PFnet).* Retrieved October 17, 2008, from http:// www.peoplefirst.net.sb/ general/ PFnet.htm

Proenza, J., Hanna, G., & Dewapura, R. (2004). *E-Sri Lanka's tele-center development program: Strategic choices and challenges of a high impact high risk investment.* Retrieved December 13, 2008, from http:// www.e-forall.org/ pdf/ VGKChoicesChallenges_6Sep2004.pdf

Short, G. (2002). *The socio-economic impact of telecentres in rural and remote Western Australia*. Retrieved October 15, 2008, from www.itu.int/ITU-D-UniversalAccess/ seminar/ buda/ final_papers.htm

Stone, A. (2003). *Community technology centers' network: Center startup manual*. Retrieved October 4, 2008, from http:// www.ctcnet.org/ toc.htm

UK Online Centres Team at UFI. (2008). *About UK online centres*. Retrieved October 20, 2008, from http:// www.ukonlinecentres.com

UNDP. Europe and the CIS. (2005). *Telecottage handbook: How to establish and run a successful telecenter*. Bratislava, Slovakia. ISBN 92-95042-48-4

Werner, M. (1996). *Empowering socio-economic development in Africa utilizing Information Technology: Case study of Mozambique.* Retrieved October 11, 2008, from www.bellanet.org/ partners/ aisi/ policy

West, P., Sebatane, L., Setsabi, A. M., Abdo, T., & Howard, L. (2000). *DaimlerChrysler distance learning support centre, Maseru, Lesotho.* The Information Communications Technology (ICT) Centre, The Technology Enhance Learning Initiative of Southern Africa (TELISA Initiative).

ENDNOTE

1 Telecottage Handbook

APPENDIX A: SUMMARY TABLE OF CRITICAL SUCCESS FACTORS

PIAP Infrastructure	*PIAP Services*	*PIAP Planning*	*PIAP Management*
1. Convenient Building 2. Located centre of settlement 3. Continuous Internet and electricity 4. Adequate number of PCs in proportion to population 5. Proper functioning of software and hardware 6. Maintenance of technical infrastructure 7. Technical support	1. Analyzing user demand towards PIAP services 2. Offering services according to demand of users 3. Relevance of service and content to language and cultures of citizens 4. Rich content 5. Updating content in regular intervals 6. Considering users' feedback regarding PIAP services	1. Developing a PIAP business plan 2. Conducting technology needs analysis 3. Involving shareholders and end users into planning process 4. Initiating limited scope program, enhancing the program according to success 5. Creating budget of PIAPs beforehand	1. Government Leadership 2. Rules, standards, regulations 3. Coordination between PIAP shareholders 4. Support for PIAP development
Financial Sustainability of PIAPs	***Usage of PIAPs***	***Operation of PIAPs***	
1. Supports of local authorities and enterprises 2. Government support 3. Paid services and membership 4. International financial sources/ Funding 1. Volunteer works 2. Donations 3. Private sector support	1. User satisfaction 2. Frequency of use 3. Improving computer skills 4. Increasing user motivation 5. Academic and social effects of PIAPs 6. Integration of ICT into daily lives of citizens 7. PIAP advertising 8. Secure Internet Use	1. Support of local authorities 2. Qualified personnel 3. Technical personnel support 4. Coordination between shareholders	

Chapter 21
Data Mining Applications in the Service of E-Government

George Stylios
Patras University, Greece

Dimitris Christodoulakis
Patras University, Greece

Jeries Besharat
Patras University, Greece

Maria-Alexandra Vonitsanou
Patras University, Greece

Ioannis Kotrotsos
Patras University, Greece

Athanasia Koumpouri
Patras University, Greece

Sofia Stamou
Patras University, Greece

ABSTRACT

E-government refers to the use of information and communication technologies for improving government services and interactions with citizens. In today's digital information era the successful delivery of public policy is of paramount importance and significantly dependent upon the effective technology deployment. In this respect, many researches and business organizations have studied the means via which public administrations and citizens can benefit from the availability of e-government applications and services. Despite the plethora of existing studies on how technological means can serve governmental decision-making policies, still there is ample of room for improvement before Information Technology services are fully exploited.

In this chapter we propose the exploration of text and data mining techniques for empowering e-government applications and services for the citizen's benefit. In particular, we start by providing a field overview with respect to the current trends in e-government services and we demonstrate via proofs of concept the limited adaptation existing e-government applications entail. Stimulated by the need to transform e-government services to e-inclusion applications, we suggest the utilization of data mining techniques for processing the governmental data so as to extract and associate information fragments with real citizen needs and thus enable the encapsulation of the latter in future governmental decisions.

DOI: 10.4018/978-1-60960-839-2.ch021

To demonstrate the usability and added value of our proposed approach we have designed an interactive e-government infrastructure, the architecture of which we will present and discuss in our chapter. Moreover, we will elaborate on the system details, its adaptation capacity and we will discuss its usage benefits for both citizens and public sector bodies.

INTRODUCTION

A critical factor of success in today's governments is to effectively communicate their messages to citizens and build strong alliances with them by empowering their participation in the decision-making process. With the advent of the web and the technological advancements, governments around the globe have launched ambitious plans for building electronic government (e-government) applications and services. The quest in establishing e-government applications is on the one hand to facilitate public sector regulations reach society in an instant and cost-effective manner and on the other to get around any obstacles imposed by bureaucracy within the governments' interactions with stakeholders (i.e., citizens, public and private bodies). Despite the resources that have been allocated in realizing e-government, still is deployment is confined to the technological aspects of implementing public services and fails to capitalize on the societal factors involved in the determination of information policies via technological means. In other words, in its current form e-government is mainly perceived as a service system to support the activities of governments and lets aside issues dealing with the socio-political impact of those activities.

In this chapter, we try to fill this void by proposing a novel e-government mechanism that captures the societal impact of public sector regulations in an attempt to decipher the public's stance towards governmental decisions. In particular, we propose the exploitation of data mining techniques towards firstly capturing the public's opinions (communicated online) about governmental decisions and secondly analysing the polarity of the mined opinions so that they are considered in subsequent governmental decisions. Specifically, we introduce a method for decomposing citizens' opinions and comments that are posted in online fora and blogs, in order to evaluate how governmental decisions are perceived by the public and thereafter how the public's implicit feedback should be interpreted by governmental bodies in their subsequent actions. What motivates our study is that up-to-date governmental social web sites are not consistently evaluated in the governmental decision-making process and as such citizens' voices are most of the times heard in a limited audience.

To realize our study objective, we propose a framework that integrates text and data mining methods for modeling the public's opinions and evaluations of the governmental decisions. We then, statistically analyze the mined citizens' feedback in order to derive on the one hand the sentiment orientation of the public opinions and on the other the underlying correlation between mined opinions and the formulation of new governmental decisions on related issues. To demonstrate the functionality of our proposed mechanism, we present as a proof of concept an experiment we carried out in which we mined and automatically organized into polarized clusters citizen opinions published online and discussing governmental regulations. The findings of our experimental study clearly demonstrate that e-government services invoke the citizens' active participation in the decision making process and indicate that by putting together inter-disciplinary methods and tools we can transform e-government from a technological infrastructure to a powerful interactive manifestation of e-inclusion and e-participation.

The remainder of the chapter is organized as follows. We start our discussion with a detailed overview on existing studies addressing the current trends on e-government as well as the encapsulation of data mining applications into available e-government applications. In Section 3, we introduce the utilization of text and data mining techniques for identifying and deciphering the citizen opinions about governmental issues that are communicated online. In particular, we describe how we can exploit the user-generated online content via the use of natural language processing and text mining tools in order to firstly mine user opinions from their posts and then annotate the mined opinions with a suitable polarity label depending on the orientation of the latent user opinions. In Section 4, we present a preliminary experiment we carried out in which we relied on real user comments about governmental decisions and tried to organize the mined user opinions into polarized clusters of citizen comments. We present our experimental results and discuss the implications of our findings. We conclude the chapter in Section 5 where we also sketch our plans for future work.

BACKGROUND

Electronic government, or e-government, is correlated with the use of digital technology in the management and delivery of public services, by enhancing the efficiency of the public sector and developing more personal, customized relationships between citizens and their government. E-government indicates that management services and functions are transferred onto the internet. Thus, it is a way for governments to use the most innovative information and communication technologies to offer citizens, business and employees with efficient access to information and services (Hayat 2009). This way, collaborative web technologies make it possible for the geographically dispersed citizens to participate in the government decision making.

A wide range of services is encompassed by the term Electronic government as dissemination of information commerce with the private sector services to individual citizens and businesses, and participatory democracy (Irani et al, 2005). The motivation by local and central governments to reduce administrative and operational costs, as well as to enhance the services they offer to businesses, citizens and the general community at large, has been a driving force for the development and implementation of an e-government infrastructure.

Despite the benefits of e-government – increased government accountability to citizens, greater public access to information and a more efficient, cost-effective government – the success and acceptance of e-government initiatives, such as online voting and licence renewal, are contingent upon citizens' willingness to adopt this innovation (Carter and Belanger, 2005). Governments around the world are implementing or launching plans for developing electronic government projects. However, the deployment of e-government projects has faced various obstacles and in many cases has failed to satisfy the expectations of both the government and citizens in delivering government services (Haya, 2009). In order to develop 'citizen-centred' services that provide participants with accessible, relevant information and quality services that are more expedient than traditional 'brick and mortar' transactions, government agencies must first understand the factors that influence citizen adoption of this innovation.

Although the internet may be viewed as being a vehicle for government and citizen interaction and a new participatory democracy (Steyaert, 2000), e-government is much more than getting information and services online: It is transforming government administration, information provision and service delivery by the application of new technologies, delivering government services in ways that are most convenient to the citizen, and realizing efficiency gains and streamlining government processes (Rimmer, 2002). E-government applications are very comprehensive; the challenges to e-government are not only technological but also economic, legislative and political (Pilipovic *et al.*, 2002).

Governments began outlining their visions for online service delivery few years ago, and, since that time, have had varying degrees of success in turning those visions into reality. Since the early 1990s Australia (a pioneer in the practices of e-government) began to develop its own e-government strategies. Today, over 1,600 Commonwealth, Public and Stakeholder Opinion, and e-Democracy government services are available online (Macintsoh, and Whyte, 2006). Moreover, a research study on e-government (Accenture, 2004) found Canada for the fourth year in a row as the most e-government-enabled country. The European Commission developed a new strategic framework, "i2010 – A European Information Society for growth and employment", which promotes an open and competitive digital economy and emphasizes ICT as a driver of inclusion and quality of life. The importance of e-Government development in EU forced the elaboration and the adoption of a specific "i2010 e-Government Action Plan" as an integral part of the i2010 initiative. The Action Plan focuses on five major objectives for e-Government: 1) no citizen left behind, 2) making efficiency and effectiveness a reality, 3) implementing high-impact key services for citizens and businesses, 4) putting key enablers in place and 5) strengthening participation and democratic decision-making. E-Government will be accelerated with a view to face major challenges such as ageing, climate change or terrorism, to assure better services, better security and better democracy, to provide seamless public services across borders and to increase citizens' opportunities for mobility and for business in Europe.

Many researchers and business organizations have studied the means via which public administrations and citizens can benefit from the availability of e-government applications and services. In "I 2010" (2005) is mentioned that: There is a list of 20 basic services, development of which is monitored by the European Commission in all its phases. Twelve of them are "citizen" services: Income taxes, Job search services, Social security benefits, Personal Documents, Car registration, Application for a building permission, Declaration to police, Public libraries (catalogues, search tools), Certificates (birth and marriage), Enrolment in higher education, Announcement of moving and Health-related services. Eight of the services are "business" ones: Social contributions for employees, Corporate tax, VAT, Registration of a new company, Submission of data to statistical offices, Customs declaration, Environment-related permits and Public procurement.

It is well known that "What other people think" has always been an important piece of information for most of us during the decision making process. Long before awareness of the World Wide Web became widespread, many of us asked our friends who they were planning to vote for in local elections, requested reference letters regarding job applicants from colleagues, or consulted Consumer Reports to decide what product to buy. But the internet and the Web have now (among other things) made it possible to find out about the opinions and the experiences of those in the vast pool that are neither our personal acquaintances nor well known professional critics – that is, people we have never heard of. And conversely, more and more people are making their opinions available to strangers via the internet (Pang and Lee, 2008). Businesses have used data mining for years to analyze customer demographics and transaction history to better target direct marketing efforts. Recent advances in computer speed and the collecting of data by many businesses have inspired the improvement of software to achieve today's mining abilities. As parallel processing and the use of artificial intelligence have met with improvements in software and growing business awareness of the benefits of database analysis, data mining and related fields, based on both statistical tools and computer science, have emerged.

The Semantic Web plays a crucial role in automatic delivery of customized e-government services. It extends the existing Web by providing a framework for technologies that give meaning to data and applications for automatic processing (Gribble, *et al.*, 2000). Ontologies[1] are integral to the Semantic Web in facilitating knowledge sharing and reuse. Web services constitute a related technology that has recently emerged to deal with the glut of Web applications. Semantic description of Web services is the key to automating customized service delivery (Medjahed et al, 2003). Web 2.0 enhances the creativity, collaboration, information sharing and functionality of the web. Wikis, social networking and folksonomies are often focused on personal life, and many on professional life. In the professional or business environment, both private and public sectors are very interested in offered the best services to the users (Decman, 2009). With the explosion of the Web 2.0 platforms such as blogs, discussion forums, peer to peer networks, and various other types of social media citizens have at their disposal a soapbox of unprecedented reach and power by which to share their experiences and opinions positive or negative, regarding any product or service (Zabin and Jefferies, 2008).

Effective and timely user access to public information is one of the most fundamental requirements for e-government and e-democracy. In this context, the discovery of e-services available to citizens plays a very important role, because it represents one of the most frequent points of contact between public administrations and citizens. Sacco (2006) presented a solution, based on dynamic taxonomies, to end-user discovery of e-services. Differently from mainstream research in semantic web, the solution proposed is intended for the direct use of end-users, rather than for programmatic or agent-mediated access. One of the most overlooked areas in the current debate and research on e-government is e-citizen access to public information. Information available to citizens includes normative material (the official publication of laws and regulations) but also information on the e-services the government offers. Currently, a typical e-government portal provides 100-200 e-services. However, it is already difficult, and becoming more so, to quickly and effectively find the desired e-services from a pool of several hundred.

As is well known, opinions matter a great deal in politics. Some work has focused on understanding what voters are thinking, whereas other projects have as a long term goal the clarification of politicians' positions, such as what public figures support or oppose, to enhance the quality of information that voters have access to. Moreover, Sentiment analysis has specifically been proposed as a key enabling technology in e-Rulemaking, allowing the automatic analysis of the opinions that people submit about pending policy or government-regulation proposals. The field of opinion mining and sentiment analysis is well-suited to various types of intelligence applications e.g. Government intelligent.

Opinion mining has recently become a topic of interest trying to combine statistics, Artificial Intelligence and Data Mining technologies in a unified framework (Pang and Lee, 2008). Negative and positive opinions can be used as guidelines for companies to change their strategies toward specific target groups, customers to decide on the purchase of a product or destination place for their holidays and lately for governments to improve services, launch campaigns etc. (Ku et al, 2007). Traditionally opinion of the people was acquired through Gallup polls and questionnaires. The latest trend however is to extract public opinion expressed in text documents in the web (blogs, forums), information that might be more objective since it is expressed without any "pressure". On the other hand the tendency of a person for or against an argument, a product etc is not as easily extracted as in the case of specific questionnaires.

It is therefore somewhat subjective posing an extra difficulty in the analysis of this information.

Published news articles often contain factual information along with opinions, either as the outcome of analysis or quoted directly from primary sources. Text materials from many other sources (e.g., the web) also mix facts and opinions. Automatically determining which part of these documents is fact and which is opinion would help in selecting the appropriate type of information given an application and in organizing and presenting that information. E-government webs are among the largest webs in existence, based on the size, number of users and number of information providers. Thus, creating a Semantic Web infrastructure to meaningfully organize e-government webs is highly desirable. At the same time, the complexity of the existing e-government implementations also challenges the feasibility of Semantic Web creation (Wagner 2006).

Web opinion mining aims to extract, summarize, and track various aspects of subjective information on the Web. Ku *et al.* (2007) applied web mining techniques to mine positive and negative sentiment words and their weights on the basis of Chinese word structures. Xu and Ramnath (2009) proposed a system for opinion mining using poll results on the web dealing with opinion answering question, opinion mining on a single object and opinion mining on multiple objects. Furuse et al (2007) developed a search engine that can extracts opinion sentences relevant to an open-domain query -based not only on positive or negative measurements but also on neutral opinions, requests, advice, and thoughts- from Japanese blog pages. Miao *et al.* (2009) proposed AMAZING a sentiment mining and retrieval system which mines knowledge from consumer product reviews by utilizing data mining and information retrieval technology based on a ranking mechanism taking temporal opinion quality and relevance into account to meet customers' information needs. Liu *et al.* (2005) developed Opinion Observe to compare consumer opinions of different products based on online reviews, while Sun *et al.* (2006) conducted opinion comparisons among a set of topics via the implementation of BlogHarvest, which is a blog mining and search framework that extracts the interests of the blogger, finds and recommends blogs with similar topics and provides blog oriented search functionality. An opinion utility named Jodange was built in the Leveraging Cornell University. Jodgane identifies opinion holders on issues, organizations, or people of interest. It can track the impact of an issue via publication, region, opinion holder, tonality or any other measurement, uncover important sentiment trends on key issues and correlate opinions against specific outcomes. The VIStology's IBlogs (International Blogs) project, funded by the Air Force Office of Scientific Research's Distributed Intelligence provides blog analysts a tool for monitoring, evaluating, and anticipating the impact of blogs by clustering posts by news event and ranking their significance by relevance, timeliness, specificity and credibility, as measured by novel metrics. This technology allows analysts to discover, from the bottom up, the issues that are important in a local blogosphere, by providing measurements particular to that locale alone. The need for identifying opinions has motivated a number of automated methods for detecting opinions or other subjective text passages (Wiebe, Bruce and O' Hara, 1999; Hatzivassiloglou and Wiebe, 2000; Wiebe, 2000; Wiebe *et al.*, 2002; Riloff, Wiebe and Wilson, 2003; Yu and Hatzivassiloglou, 2003) and assigning them to subcategories such as positive and negative opinions (Pang, Lee and Vaithyanathan, 2002; Turney, 2002; Yu and Hatzivassiloglou, 2003). A variety of machine learning techniques have been employed for this purpose and are generally based on lexical cues associated with opinions. However, a common element of current approaches is their focus on either an entire document (Pang, Lee and Vaithyanathan, 2002; Turney, 2002) or on full sentences (Wiebe, Bruce and O'Hara, 1999; Hatzivassiloglou and Wiebe, 2000; Wiebe, 2000; Wiebe *et al.*, 2002;

Yu and Hatzivassiloglou, 2003) (Bethard, 2004). Choi *et al.*, 2005), focuses on another aspect of opinion analysis: automatically identifying the sources of the opinions. Identifying opinions sources is especially critical for opinion-oriented question-answering systems (e.g., systems that answer question of the form "How does [X] feel about [Y]?") and opinion-oriented summarization systems, both of which need to distinguish the opinions of one source from those of another. The goal of their research is to identify direct and indirect sources of opinions, emotions, sentiments, and other private states that are expressed in text.

The successful delivery of public policy is of paramount importance and significantly dependent upon the effective technology deployment. In this respect, many researchers and business organizations have studied the means via which public administrations and citizens can benefit from the availability of e-government services. Governments are currently struggling with huge information overloads, with new and emerging ICT capabilities, and with a shortage of information management skills and human expertise. Ontologies and knowledge management facilities (such as search, retrieval, visualization, text mining, and intelligent reasoning) seem promising but need to be exploited more effectively to achieve information quality and economy, and to support knowledge management processes in e-Government settings.

Despite the plethora of existing studies on how technological means can serve governmental decision –making policies, still there is ample of room for improvement before information technology services are fully exploited. The utilization of data mining techniques for processing the governmental data so as to extract and associate information fragments with real citizen needs will enable the encapsulation of the latter in future governmental decisions.

MINING USER-GENERATED CONTENT EXPRESSING OPINIONS ABOUT GOVERNMENTAL REGULATIONS

The objective of our work is to design a method that can automatically capture the polarity of the online user-generated content that is published to verbalize citizen opinions about governmental decisions. In this direction, we rely on real web content harvested from e-government social media sites, e.g., blogs, fora, etc., and we analyze the associated user posts in order to firstly identify and extract the citizen opinions from the posts' textual data, then mine the opinions' polarity and eventually train a classifier to automatically organize mined opinions according to their sentiment orientation into positive and negative ones. Unlike traditional approaches that attempt to infer the users' stance against the issues they discuss online by examining their ratings (usually denoted on a numeric/star scale), our approach focuses on the actual text of the user posts and tries to mine the citizens' stance against particular aspects adhering to governmental decisions. This is because we believe that numerical ratings do not convey much information about which decision aspects citizens value positively or negatively and as such they cannot be fruitfully utilized in subsequent governmental regulations. Conversely, the textual content of user posts, if properly processed and analyzed, can be much more revealing about the impact that governmental decisions have on citizens' perception.

To understand how public sector regulations affect the citizens' stance against governmental actions, we conduct a two-level analysis. Firstly, we rely on user online comments, which we process as described below in order to identify the latent user opinions and then be able to extract such opinions, which we call opinion phrases. Then, at the second level of analysis we annotate the sentiment orientation of the identified opinion phrases in order to assign them with a positive or negative polarity label depending on their publishers' underlying stance against the issues they discuss. Based on the output of the above analysis, we may not only capture the citizen's viewpoints on governmental issues but with the proper tools and techniques we may also be able to build predictive models about how citizens value public sector regulations. In the following paragraphs, we describe in detail how we process the user postings to identify and evaluate opinion phrases as well as how to utilize the mined opinions along with their polarity labels in order to train an opinion classifier.

Mining Public Opinions on Governmental Decisions

Given the availability of social networking web sites, our approach aims at collecting online content pertaining to user opinions about governmental decisions and processing it in order to extract both the decision aspects mentioned in the citizens' online postings and the respective citizen evaluations of those decisions. To identify citizen opinions within their postings pertaining to governmental issues, we firstly download the content of the user posts and we process it in order to identify within their textual data the text extracts that contain user opinions. To process the data, we apply tokenization to the posting's body in order to extract the lexical elements of the user generated texts and then we apply Part-of-Speech tagging to the identified elements in order to obtain their grammatical categories. Thereafter, we rely on postings containing adjectives and we further analyze them to derive opinion phrases from their body. The reason for concentrating on postings containing adjectives is because according to the study of Gliozzo *et al.* (2004) people evaluate an item or verbalize an opinion via adjectives. Therefore, user posts containing adjectives are highly probable of indicating implicit user opinions as opposed to posts that contain no adjectives at all. But, relying entirely on the study of adjectives is not sufficient for characterizing the user opinions given that we must firstly identify the topic to which every adjective (i.e., opinion) refers. In other words, we need to detect within a user's post the topic(s) being discussed as well as the user's opinion on those topic(s). Only then we will be able to successfully extract the phrases that communicate user opinions within their online postings. Unlike current approaches that focus on either the entire body of the posting (Pang *et al.*, 2002) or on full sentences (Bethard, 2004), in our work a user opinion is communicated via the use of adjectives, while the topic to which the opinion refers is communicated via the nouns or proper nouns to which the corresponding adjectives refer. To be able to detect such references within the user posts, we employ a syntactic dependency parser, which given as input a piece of text containing adjectives it identifies the noun (or proper noun) to which every adjective refers, i.e., characterizes. Then, we rely on the syntactically dependent adjective-noun pairs[2] to derive the opinion phrases communicated in the user postings.

Extracted adjective-noun pairs constitute the text chunks that contain implicit user opinions about the issues being discussed in the collected postings. To unravel both the topic of the discussion and people's stance toward this topic, we assume that every noun in the dataset represents a specific aspect of a governmental decision, whereas the adjectives that refer to each of the nouns correspond to the user opinions about the respective decision aspect. Based on this assumption, the problem of identifying how people judge governmental decisions translates into deciphering the sentiment of the adjectives that users select in their online government-related postings. To identify how citizens evaluate governmental decisions, we rely on the notion of words' semantic orientation and we try to discriminate between words of positive and negative sentiments as follows.

We examine every adjective extracted from the harvested postings against the FrameNet ontology (FrameNet) in order to obtain the semantic frame

Figure 1. The process of mining user opinions on governmental decisions

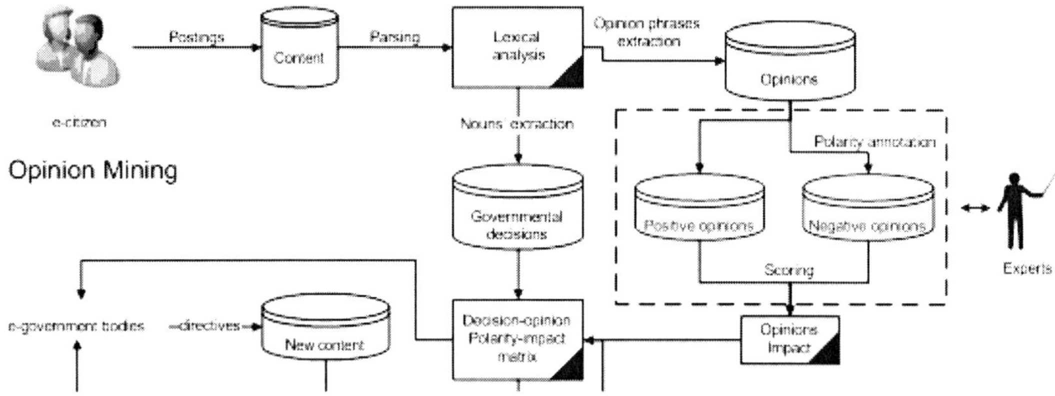

of the adjective. Based on the identified frames, we exclude from our data the adjectives that have been assigned the frames: *Increment*, *Relative Time* or *Similarity*, based on the intuition that these are not indicative of the citizens' opinions about the governmental decisions that they discuss in their online postings. Following on, we manually assign an orientation label, either positive (+) or negative (-), to each of the remaining adjectives in our dataset. The criterion under which labelling takes place is that a positive adjective is one that gives praise to the decision under evaluation, whereas a negative adjective is one that criticizes some or all aspects of the evaluated decision. Note that the manual labelling of the adjectives bears a satisfactory level of objectivity, since several studies (e.g. Hatzivassiloglou and McKeown, 1997) have demonstrated high levels of inter-annotation agreement for the semantic orientation of adjectives. Nevertheless, periodical user studies can always be performed by any interested governmental body before actually putting into action our proposed opinion mining framework. At this point we would like to emphasize that our study objective is not to develop new techniques for text annotation but rather we are interesting in supporting the citizens' participation in e-government issues via the availability of an interactive framework that mines the citizens' opinions about governmental decisions and feeds them back to the decision making process.

The result of the above process is a set of positive and negative adjectives that correspond to the opinions of citizens who discuss a governmental decision in their online postings. We refer to those adjective-noun pairs as opinion phrases and we further explore them in order to deduce their strength and their potential encapsulation in future governmental decisions. The overall opinion mining process we suggest is schematically illustrated in Figure 1. Being able to automatically identify and interpret citizen opinions on governmental issues entails a significant benefit toward transforming public sector administrations from mere government service providers into the public's apprentice for confronting bureaucracy. This is because e-government cannot be reformed into a significant part of our daily lives unless citizen opinions are taken into account and e-inclusion is encouraged.

Having presented our method for mining user opinions as well as annotating mined opinions with a suitable polarity label, our next step is to utilize the mined user data in order to train a classifier for automatically organizing opinion phrases into bimodal clusters of supportive (i.e., positive) and unsupportive (i.e., negative) citizen views on governmental regulations. The details of our opinion classification approach are discussed next.

Classifying Mined User Opinions According to their Polarity Labels

To automatically organize mined user opinions in terms of their sentiment orientations, we employ a decision tree-based classification module and proceed as follows. We rely on the annotated opinion phrases previously extracted from our dataset and we expand them with semantic information harvested from WordNet (Fellbaum, 1998). WordNet is a lexical hierarchy, which organizes concepts into synonym sets and links them together depending on the underlying semantic relations that connect concepts together. In our approach, we explore the adjectives encoded in WordNet and utilize them for expanding our collected opinion phrases. Opinion phrases' expansion follows a two-level expansion: (i) expansion with semantically equivalent adjectives, which we call synonymy expansion and (ii) expansion with antonymous adjectives, which we call antonymy expansion. In the first expansion level, we append to all the adjectives appearing in our collected opinion phrases their synonyms recorded in WordNet, while in the second expansion level we append to all the adjectives appearing in our collected opinion phrases their antonyms recorded in WordNet.

Following opinion phrases' expansion, we proceed with the sentiment annotation of the expanded phrases as follows. Opinion phrases formulated after applying synonymy expansion take the same polarity label with that of their originating opinion phrases, i.e., before expansion, while opinion phrases formulated after applying antonymy expansion take the opposite polarity label from that of their originating phrases. Then, based on the expanded set of polarized opinion phrases, we split them into training and testing examples and use the training set to learn the classifier automatically identify the polarity of opinion phrases. The learning accuracy of the classifier is evaluated against the test set and by running several classification iterations. In the experimental Section, we present the details of a classification evaluation we conducted in which we assessed the classification accuracy of our method when relying on the extracted polarized opinion phrases. Obtained results give useful insights with respect to how citizens comment governmental decisions as well as with respect to the usefulness of opinion phrases into revealing the public's stance against public sector regulations. Before presenting our experimental evaluation we discuss how our opinion mining method can serve as a tool for measuring the influence of citizen opinions on governmental issues and therefore how can governmental bodies account for influential opinions into their subsequent regulations and decisions.

Measuring the Strength of Citizen Opinions for Governmental Issues

As a final step in our opinion mining approach, we statistically analyze the mined user data in order to firstly estimate the overall impact of every opinion mined and then quantify the influence of citizens' opinions on subsequent governmental decisions. By opinion impact, we mean the degree to which an opinion expressed about a governmental directive is commonly shared across citizens, while by opinion influence we denote the probability that an opinion globally shared by the citizens will affect subsequent governmental decisions on similar issues.

To estimate the overall impact of the mined citizen opinions, we work as follows. Firstly, we associate every governmental decision discussed in the citizens' online postings that we have previously extracted with the corresponding opinions that have been mined about this decision. Such decision-opinion associations can be easily performed via the use of a relational database management system for the storage of the harvested web data. Then, for every decision for which there are some user opinions expressed (via the use of adjectives) we formulate two data clusters. In the first cluster, we store the adjectives that refer to that decision and which have been assigned a positive polarity label, i.e. the supportive opinions about the decision. In the second cluster, we store the adjectives that refer to the decision and which have been assigned a negative polarity label, i.e. the unsupportive opinions about the decision. This way, we maintain for every governmental decision that is being discussed online a set of positive and negative user opinions. Thereafter, we estimate the impact of every opinion, denoted as Impact (O), as:

$$\text{Impact}\left(O\right) = \frac{\sum_{i \in O(D)}^{|O\,i(D)|} \left|O_i\left(D\right)\right|}{\left|O\left(D\right)\right|} \qquad (1)$$

Where Oi (D) is the number of times an opinion i appears in the collected e-citizen postings that refer to a decision (D) and O(D) is the number of all opinions contained in the e-citizen postings about D. Impact scores are normalized taking values between 1 and 0; with values close to one indicating that a given opinion is globally shared by the citizens who write a posting about a given decision and values close to zero indicating that the underlying opinion is only representing a few individuals' stance towards the referred governmental decision. Having quantified the impact of every opinion, we associate every mined opinion with its respective polarity label, either positive or negative.

Then, we rely on the above formula and we compute for all the positive opinions about a decision their average impact value in order to quantify the degree to which the decision is generally endorsed by the public. Similarly, we also compute the average impact value of all the negative opinions about a decision in order to deduce the degree to which the latter is rejected by the public. At the end of this process, we annotate every examined governmental decision with the sentiment orientation of the highest average impact in order to indicate how and how much the public values the contribution of the examined governmental decisions.

As a last step, we estimate the probability that the evaluation result of a governmental decision will affect future decisions on relevant issues. This estimation could provide governmental officials with useful insight on the expected outcome of their decisions on a societal level. To deduce whether an opinion will influence subsequent decisions, we rely on the impact values estimated for that opinion and apply the following criterion:

$$\text{Influence}(O) = \begin{cases} \text{significant} & \text{if avg. Impact (D)} > F \\ \text{insignificant} & \text{if otherwise} \end{cases} \qquad (2)$$

Where the value of F can be experimentally set to some threshold based on the statistical analysis of the demographic data collected from the e-citizens whose opinions have been mined. Such data could concern age, popularity, education level, etc. Note though that running experiments to set the value of F goes beyond the objective of our work, which focuses on providing a method for mining the public's opinions about governmental issues in an automated manner.

EVALUATING CLASSIFICATION ACCURACY OF POLARITY-LABELED USER OPINIONS

So far we have presented a novel method for capturing and assessing citizen opinions on governmental issues in an attempt to assist both the public and governments successfully interact with each other. The core of our method is an opinion mining framework, which manages to automatically identify and validate citizen opinions. In

Figure 2. Comparative evaluation of opinion classification accuracy

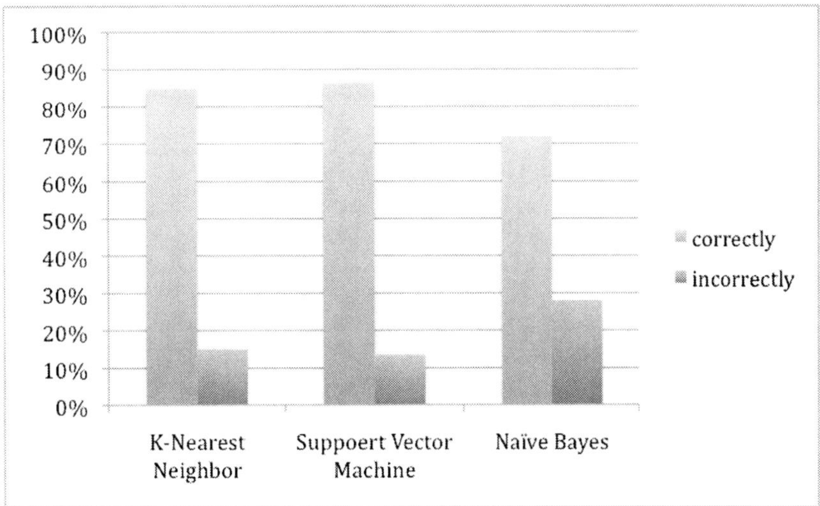

this section, we try to experimentally evaluate the performance of our technique in automatically organizing mined opinions in terms of their polarity, i.e., to group positive and negative user opinions on governmental issues separately so that governments can exploit and account for them in their subsequent regulations. Unless we evaluate the accuracy of our model in capturing the public's stance, we will not be able to estimate its impact into transforming e-government from a technological infrastructure into an e-democracy application.

To assess our study objective, we collected a set of real citizen opinions. This dataset was downloaded from the forum antheorisi[3], which is a Greek forum focusing on policy issues that are being developed by several users, and consists of 124 comments. After processing these comments as previously described we extracted from their body 652 distinct opinion phrases. Then, we trained three different classifiers incorporated into the Weka platform[4]. The three classifiers we use are Support Vector Machine, K-Nearest Neighbor and Naïve Bayes.

Before the training phase, our software prepares the data by randomizing the full dataset and then stratify it because the classification class is nominal. Then, performs a 10-fold cross validation and generates training and test sets. Classification training is vital in order to learn the classifiers discriminate between positive and genitive citizen opinions. After the training, each classifier returns a summary of the results. The following chart shows the average of cases that were correctly and incorrectly predicted for the three classifiers. In particular, Figure 2 depicts the fraction of opinion phrases that were correctly and incorrectly identified by the classifiers as positive or negative.

As the figure shows, the algorithm with the best classification performance is the Support Vector Machine where the average accuracy is about 86% while the worst performing classification algorithm is Naïve Bayes with 72% accuracy. Figure 3 summarizes the performance details of the three classification modules we employed in our study and as results suggest the proposed method is quite effective into automatically organizing opinion phrases in terms of their polarity.

Based on our experimental findings, we may deduce the following. First, that our proposed opinion mining and evaluation technique is quite effective in automatically identifying the public's

Figure 3. Evaluation of opinion classification accuracy

	K-Nearest Neighbor	Support Vector Machine	Naive Bayes
True Positive Rate	67.58%	67.74%	12.07%
True Negative Rate	96.09%	97.71%	99.37%
False Positive Rate	3.905%	2.28%	0.62%
False Negative Rate	32.41%	32.25%	87.92%

stance towards governmental decisions. Moreover, results demonstrate that our method can be easily integrated into existing classification modules in order for the latter to automatically organize mined user opinions according to the positive or negative orientation. Above all, our experimental study shows that with today's technological advancements it is feasible to deploy existing mechanisms into novel applications such ones related to e-government.

CONCLUSION

In this chapter we have presented a method for extracting citizen opinions about governmental decisions from social media sites, as well as a technique for classifying opinion phrases in terms of their sentiment orientation. In addition, we have proposed a metric for quantifying the impact of citizen opinions on governmental decisions so that the former can be fruitfully employed in subsequent governmental regulations. Our method relies on the intuition that there is plentiful data available on social web sites that communicates implicit information about how citizens perceive governmental regulations and directives. Being able to collect, process and mine such data can provide decision-makers with valuable information about how the recipients of their actions evaluate the latter and it can also empower citizens with the ability to actively participate in governmental decision making aspects. Today, all EU Member States have ICT policies and consider them a key contributor to national growth and jobs under the renewed Lisbon agenda. eParticipation is the strongest growing area of eGovernment Action Plan. "eParticipation" is about reconnecting ordinary people with politics and policy-making and making the decision-making processes easier to understand and follow trough the use of new ICT.

As already pointed out by other researchers, one of the most important issues for making e-government effective is to enable citizens participate in the decision-making process. Via our proposed approach we provide both citizens and governments with the means to effectively interact with each other and actively participate into common actions from which both would benefit. Although the work presented in this chapter is still in early stages and only gives a general notion with respect to how opinion mining techniques can be successfully explored in the course of e-government and e-inclusion approaches we believe that it will pave the ground for more initiatives in this respect. As a matter of fact, we are currently working on the incorporation of additional societal aspects in the opinion mining process as well as towards the employment of additional metrics that would evaluate the trustworthiness of the citizen comments and opinions on governmental decisions. Another aspect of future work would be to rely on the mined and polarity-annotated user opinions in order to build and train effective prediction models that would be able to approximate the potential impact of planned governmental decisions on citizens' stance. Finally, it would be interesting to apply our opinion mining technique towards a wide variety of user opinions on governmental decisions and identify the regulations that interest citizens the most and thus offer them the infrastructure to interact with governmental bodies.

REFERENCES

i2010 EUROPA. (2005). *A European information society for growth and employment*. Communication from the Commission to the European Parliament, the Council, the EESC and the Committee of the Regions, Brussels, COM.

Accenture. (2004). E-government leadership: High performance, maximum value. New York, NY: Accenture.

Bethard, S., Yu, H., Thornton, A., Hatzivassiloglou, V., & Jurafsky, D. (2004). Automatic extraction of opinion propositions and their holders. (AAAI 2004), Springer.

Choi, Y., Cardie, C., Riloff, E., & Patwardhan, S. (2005). Identifying sources of opinions with conditional random fields and extraction patterns. In *Proceedings of Human Language Technology Conference on Empirical Methods in Natural Language Processing* (HLT/EMNLP), (pp. 355-362). Vancouver, Canada: Association for Computational Linguistics.

Decman, M. (2009). Web 2.0 in e-government: The challenges and opportunities of Wiki in legal matters. *Proceedings of the 9th European Conference on e-Government*, (pp. 229-236).

Fellbaum, C. (Ed.). (1998). *WordNet: An online electronic lexical database*. The MIT Press.

FrameNet. (n.d.). Retrieved from http:// framenet.icsi.berkeley.edu

Gliozzo, A., Strapparava, C., & Dagan, I. (2004). Unsupervised and supervised exploitation of semantic domains in lexical disambiguation. *Computer Speech & Language, 18*(3), 275–299. doi:10.1016/j.csl.2004.05.006

Gribble, D. S., et al. (2000). Scalable, distributed data structures for Internet service construction. *Proc. 4th Symp. Operating Systems Design and Implementation*, (pp. 319–332). Usenix Association.

Hatzivassiloglou, V., & McKeown, K. R. (1997). Predicting the semantic orientation of adjectives. In *Proceedings of the 35th Annual Meeting of the Association for Computational Linguistics and the 8th Conference on European Chapter of the ACL*, (pp. 174-181).

Hatzivassiloglou, V., & Wiebe, J. (2000). Effects of adjective orientation and gradability on sentence subjectivity. In *Proceedings of the Conference on Computational Linguistics* (COLING-2000).

Hayat, A., Macaulay, L., & Zhao, L. (2009). A collaboration pattern language for e-participation: A strategy for reuse. *Proceedings of the 9th European Conference on e-Government*, (pp. 29-39).

Irani, Z., Love, P. E. D., Elliman, T., Jones, S., & Themistocleous, M. (2005). Evaluating e-government: Learning from the experiences of two UK local authorities. *Information Systems Journal, 15*(1), 61–82. doi:10.1111/j.1365-2575.2005.00186.x

Jian-Tao, S., Xuanhui, W., Dou, S., Hua-Jun, Z., & Zheng, C. (2006). *CWS: A comparative Web search system*. In International Conference on World Wide Web (WWW), 2006.

Ku, L. W., & Chen, H. H. (2007). Mining opinions from the Web: Beyond relevance retrieval source. *Journal of the American Society for Information Science and Technology, 58*(12). doi:10.1002/asi.20630

Macintsoh, A., & Whyte, A. (2006). Evaluating how e-participation changes local democracy. In Z. Inai & A. Ghoneim (Eds.), *Proceedings of the e-Government Workshop 2006*. London, UK: Brunel University.

Medjahed, B. (2003). Business-to-business interactions: Issues and enabling technologies. *The VLDB Journal, 12*(1), 59–85. doi:10.1007/s00778-003-0087-z

Pang, B., & Lee, L. (2008). Opinion mining and sentiment analysis. *Foundations and Trends in Information Retrieval, 2*(1-2), 1–135. doi:10.1561/1500000011

Pang, B., Lee, L., & Vaithyanathan, S. (2002). Thumps up? Sentiment classification using machine learning techniques. In *Proceedings of the 2002 Conference on Empirical Methods in Natural Language Processing* (EMNLP-02).

Qingliang, M., Qiudan, L., & Ruwei, D. (2009). AMAZING: A sentiment mining and retrieval system. *Expert Systems with Applications, 36*(3).

Sacco, M. G. (2006). User-centric access to e-government information: E-citizen discovery of e-services. In *Proceeding of the 8th Annual International Conference on Digital Government Research: Bridging Disciplines & Domains*. American Association Artificial Intelligent. ISBN: 1-59593-599-1

Turney, P. (2002). Thumps up or thumbs down? Semantic orientation applied to unsupervised classification of reviews. In *Proceedings of the 40th Annual Meeting of the Association for Computational Linguistics*.

Wagner, C., Karen, S. K., Cheung, R. K. F., & Ip, S. B. (2006). Building Semantic Webs for e-government with Wiki technology. *Electronic Government, an International Journal, 3*(1), 36-55. Inderscience Publishers.

Wiebe, J. (2000). Learning subjective adjectives from corpora. In Proceedings *of the 17th National Conference on Artificial Intelligence* (AAAI -2000).

Wiebe, J., Bruce, R., & O'Hara, T. (1999). Development and use of a gold standard data set for subjectivity classifications. In *Proceedings of the 37th Annual Meeting of the Association for Computational Linguistics* (ACL-99), (pp. 246-253).

Wiebe, J., Wilson, T., Bruce, R., Bell, M., & Martin, M. (2002). *Learning subjective language. Technical Report TR – 02-100*. Pittsburgh, Pennsylvania: Department of Computer Science, University of Pittsburgh.

Xu, Z., & Ramnath, R. (2009). *Mining opinion from poll results in Web pages*. WWW2009, April 20-24, 2009, Madrid Spain.

Yu, H., & Hatzivassiloglou, V. (2003). Towards answering opinion questions: Separating facts from opinions and identifying the polarity of opinion sentences. In *Proceedings of the Conference on empirical Methods in Natural language Processing* (EMNLP-03).

Zabin, J., & Jefferies, A. (2008). *Social media monitoring and analysis: Generating consumer insights from online conversation*. Aberdeen group Benchmark Report.

KEY TERMS AND DEFINITIONS

E-Government: The availability of a comfortable, transparent, and cheap interaction between government and citizens.

E-Inclusion: It covers the development of appropriate policies, maintenance of a knowledge base, research and technology development and deployment and best pracwtices dissemination.

FrameNet: A lexical database that lists and defines the semantic frames of terms, it offers annotations of selected sentences that contain the above terms and summarizes the semantic and combinational properties discovered for individual lexical units.

Opinion Mining: Opinion mining aims to extract attributes and components of the object that have been commented.

Sentiment Analysis: Aims to determine the attitude of a speaker or a writer with respect to some topic.

ENDNOTES

1. A formal representation of the knowledge by a set of concepts within a domain and the relationships between those concepts.
2. Note that there might apply different patterns to the adjective-noun syntactic structure, e.g. noun-adjective, adjective-noun, determiner-adjective-noun, etc.
3. Anatheorisi.org
4. http://www.cs.waikato.ac.nz/ml/weka/

Compilation of References

Abecker, A., Sheth, A., Mentzas, G., & Stojanovic, L. (2006). *Semantic Web meets e-government. Stanford University*. AAAI Press.

Abie, H., Foyn, B., Bing, J., Blobel, B., Pharow, P., & Delgado, J. (2004). The need for a digital rights nanagement framework for the next generation of e-government services. [Inderscience Publishers]. *International Journal of Electronic Government*, *1*(1), 8–28. doi:10.1504/EG.2004.004134

Acar, M., & Kumaş, E. (2009). *A model proposal for the e-transformation infrastructure: The case of Turkey*. ICEGOV 2009, Ankara, Turkey

Accenture. (2004). E-government leadership: High performance, maximum value. New York, NY: Accenture.

Adam, M. S., & Myers, M. D. (2003). Have you got anything to declare? Neo-colonialism, Information Systems, and the imposition of customs and duties in a third world country. In M. Korpela, R. Montealegre & A. Poulymenakou (Eds.), *Proceedings of the International Federation of Information Processing, IFIP 9.4 and 8.2 Joint Conference on Organizational Information Systems in the Context of Globalization* (pp. 101-116). Dordrecht, The Netherlands: Kluwer.

Adams, D. (2004). Usable knowledge in public policy. *Australian Journal of Public Administration*, *63*(1), 29–42. doi:10.1111/j.1467-8500.2004.00357.x

Adams, C., & Lloyd, S. (1999). *Understanding public key infrastructure – Concepts, standards, and deployment considerations* (1st ed.). MacMillan Technical Publishing.

Adesina, J. O. (2006). When is 'techno-talk' a fatal distraction? ICT in contemporary development discourse on Africa. *Africa Development. Afrique et Developpement*, *31*(3), 118–151.

Afacan, G., & Arifoğlu, A. (2010). *A new metric system for assessment of e-transformation.* ICEGEG 2010. Antalya, Turkey

Affisco, J., & Soliman, K. (2006). E-government: A strategic operations management framework for service delivery. *Business Process Management Journal*, *12*(1), 13–21. doi:10.1108/14637150610643724

Agapitos, G. J. (1986). *Income tax in Greece*. Athens, Greece: KEPE. (in Greek)

Ahituv, N. (2001). *A world without secrets: On the open information society*. Tel Aviv, Israel: Am Oved Publishers. (in Hebrew)

Aichholzer, G., & Schmutzer, R. (2000). *Organisational challenges to the development of electronic government*. IEEE Computer Society, London, paper presented at 11th International Workshop on Database and Expert Systems Applications.

Aileen, K., Joseph, P. C., & Carol, K. (2010). Business process change in e-government projects: The case of the Irish land registry. *International Journal of Electronic Government Research*, *6*(1), 9–22. doi:10.4018/jegr.2010102002

Ajzen, I. (1991). The theory of planned behaviour. *Organizational Behavior and Human Decision Processes*, *50*(2), 179–211. doi:10.1016/0749-5978(91)90020-T

Akbulut, A. Y. (2002). An investigation of the factors that influence e-information sharing between state and local agencies. *Proceedings of the 8th Americas Conference on Information Systems*, USA, (pp. 2454-2460).

Alavi, M., & Leidner, D. E. (2001). Review: Knowledge management and knowledge management systems: Conceptual foundations and research issues. *Management Information Systems Quarterly*, *25*(1), 107–136. doi:10.2307/3250961

Albrecht, S., Kohlrausch, N., Kubicek, H., Lippa, B., Märker, O., Trénel, M., ... Wiedwald, C. (2008). *E-participation – Electronic participation of citizens and the business community in e-government*. Institut für Informationsmanagement Bremen, Study on Behalf of the Federal Ministry of the Interior, Division IT 1 Bremen, January 2008.

Alcock, R., & Lenihan, D. G. (2001). *Opening the e-government file: Governing in the 21st century- Results of the crossing boundaries cross-country tour* (*Vol. 2*, p. 31). Ontario, Canada: Center for Collaborative Government.

Aldrich, J., Bertot, J. C., & McClure, C. R. (2002). E-government: Initiatives, developments, and issues. *Government Information Quarterly*, *19*, 349–355. doi:10.1016/S0740-624X(02)00130-2

Aldrich, D., Berlot, J. C., & McClure, C. R. (2002). E-government: Initiatives, development, and issues. *Government Information Quarterly*, *19*(4), 349–355. doi:10.1016/S0740-624X(02)00130-2

Alexiou, A., Bouras, C., Primpas, D., & Papagiannopoulos, J. (2008). Metropolitan broadband networks: Design and implementation aspects and business models. In *Global diffusion of broadband data transmission: Factors affecting the adoption, usage and economics of broadband* (pp. 196–210). Hershey, PA: IDEA Group Publishing.

Alican, F. (2007). Experts without expertise: E-society projects in developing countries – The case of Turkey. *Information Polity*, *12*, 255–263.

Alkhatib, G., Bataineh, E., Fraihat, H., & Maamar, Z. (2007). An intelligent integrated e-government framework: The case of Jordan. *Proceedings of the 7th European Conference on E-Government*.

Allen, B. A., Juillet, L., Paquet, P., & Roy, J. (2001). E-governance & government online in Canada: Partnerships, people & prospects. *Government Information Quarterly*, *18*, 93–104. doi:10.1016/S0740-624X(01)00063-6

Allen, D., Kern, T., & Havenhand, M. 2002. ERP critical success factors: An exploration of the contextual factors in public sector institutions. In: *35th Hawaii International Conference on System Sciences (HICSS 2002)*, January 7-10, 2002, Waikoloa, Hawaii

Al-Omari, A., & Al-Omari, H. (2004). *A framework model for assessment of e-government readiness*. IMTC 2004 - Information Technology Conference Amman, Jordan.

Al-Qirim, N. (2007). The adoption and diffusion of e-commerce in developing countries: The case of an NGO in Jordan. *Information Technology for Development*, *13*(2), 107–131. doi:10.1002/itdj.20053

Alvarez, R., & Hall, T. E. (2004). *Point click and vote - The future of Internet voting*. Washington, DC: Brookings Institution Press.

AMS Advantage ERP. 2010, *CGI*, Retrieved February 10, 2010 from: http:// www.cgi.com/ web/ en/ library/ solutions/ governments/ 74072.htm

Andersen, D., & Dawes, S. (1991). *Government information management: A primer and casebook*. Englewood Cliffs, NJ: Prentice Hall.

Andersen, K. V., & Henriksen, H. Z. (2006). E-government maturity models: Extension of the Layne and Lee model. *Government Information Quarterly*, *23*, 236–248. doi:10.1016/j.giq.2005.11.008

Anderson, E. W., & Sullivan, M. W. (1993). The antecedents and consequences of customer satisfaction for firms. *Marketing Science*, *12*(2), 125–143. doi:10.1287/mksc.12.2.125

Anderson, E. W., & Fornell, C. (1994). A customer satisfaction research prospectus. In Rust, R. T., & Oliver, R. (Eds.), *Service quality: New directions in theory and practice* (pp. 241–268). Thousand Oaks, CA: Sage Publications.

Angelopoulos, S., Kitsios, F., & Babulak, E. (2008). (in press). From e to u: Towards an innovative digital era. *Heterogeneous Next Generation Networking: Innovations and Platform*. doi:10.4018/978-1-60566-108-7.ch019

Angelopoulos, S., Kitsios, F., & Papadopoulos, T. (2010). New service development in e-government: identifying critical success factors. *Transforming Government: People, Process and Policy*, *4*(1), 95–118.

Angelopoulos, S. (2010). *Ancient Greek values as a paradigm for e-government*. Athens Dialogues. Democracy and Politeia. EUNIC Papers. Available at: http:// athensdialogues.chs.harvard.edu/ cgi-bin/ WebObjects/ athensdialogues.woa/ wa/ dist?dis=86.

Annette, J. (2000). Service learning in the community. In Lewton, D., Cairns, J., & Gardner, R. (Eds.), *Education for citizenship*. London, UK: Continuum.

Antoniou, A., Korakas, C., Manolopoulos, C., Panagiotaki, A., Sofotassios, D., Spirakis, P., & Stamatiou, Y. C. (2007). A trust-centered approach for building e-voting systems. In M. Wimmer, J. Scholl, & A. Gronlund (Eds.), *6th International Conference on eGovernment (EGOV 2007)* (pp. 366-377). Berlin/Heidelberg, Germany: Springer-Verlag.

Antovski, L., & Gusev, M. (2005). *M-government framework*. EURO mGOV 2005, Brighton, UK, (pp. 36-44).

Anttiroiko, A. V. (2003). Building strong e-democracy—The role of technology in developing democracy for the information age. *Communications of the ACM*, *46*(9), 121–128. doi:10.1145/903893.903926

Appiah, K. A. (1991). Is the post- in postmodernism the post- in postcolonial? *Critical Inquiry*, *17*(2), 336–357. doi:10.1086/448586

ARCEP – Autorité de Régulation des Communications électroniques et des Postes. (2009). *Décision n° 2009-1106*. République Française. Retrieved July 1, 2010, from http:// www.arcep.fr/ uploads/ tx_gsavis/ 09-1106.pdf

Archer, M. S., & Tritter, J. Q. (Eds.). (2000). *Rational choice theory: Resisting colonization*. London, UK & New York, NY: Routledge.

Arellano Gault, D. (2004). *Mas allá de la Reinvención del Gobierno: Fundamentos de la Nueva Gestión Pública y Presupuestos por Resultados en América Latina*. Mexico: Centro de Investigación y Docencia Económicas y Miguel Angel Porrúa.

Arifoglu, A., Afacan, G., & Er, E. (2009). *Public Internet access points (PIAPs): A model to accelerate e-inclusion*. Paper presented at 7th Eastern European e-Gov Days 2009, Prague.

Arnstein, S. R. (1969). A ladder of citizen participation. *JAIP*, *35*(4), 216–224.

Auditor General of Ontario. (2009). *Special report: Ontario's electronic health records initiative*. Retrieved February 15, 2010, from http:// www.auditor.on.ca/ en/ reports_en/ ehealth_en.pdf

Australian Government Information Management Office (AGIMO). (2006).*E-Government strategy, responsive government: A new service agenda*. Retrieved April 2007 from http:// www.finance.gov.au/ e-government/ strategy-and-governance/ index.html

Avgerou, C. (2000). Recognising alternative rationalities in the deployment of Information Systems. *The Electronic Journal on Information Systems in Developing Countries*, *7*(3), 1–15.

Avgerou, C. (2000). IT and organizational change: an institutionalist perspective. *Information Technology & People*, *13*(4), 234–262. doi:10.1108/09593840010359464

Avgerou, C. (2001). The significance of context in Information Systems and organizational change. *Information Systems Journal*, *11*(1), 43–63. doi:10.1046/j.1365-2575.2001.00095.x

Avgerou, C. (2002). *Information Systems and global diversity*. New York, NY: Oxford University Press.

Avgerou, C., Ciborra, C., & Land, F. (Eds.). (2004). *The social study of information and communication technology: Innovation, actors, and contexts*. Oxford, UK: Oxford University Press.

Avgerou, C., & McGrath, K. (2007). Power, rationality, and the art of living through socio-technical change. *Management Information Systems Quarterly*, *31*(2), 295–315.

Avgerou, C., & Madon, S. (2004). Framing IS studies: Understanding the social context of IS innovation. In Avgerou, C., Ciborra, C., & Land, F. (Eds.), *The social study of information and communication technology: Innovation, actors and contexts* (pp. 162–182). New York, NY: Oxford University Press.

Avgerou, C. (2003). The link between ICT and economic growth in the discourse of development. In Korpela, M., Momtealegre, R., & Poulymenakou, A. (Eds.), *Organizational Information Systems in the context of globalization* (pp. 373–386). Boston, MA: Kluwer.

Avgerou, C. (2003). New socio-technical perspectives of IS innovation in organisations. In C. Avgerou & R. L. La Rovere (Eds.), *Information Systems and the economics of innovation* (pp. 141-161). Cheltenham, UK & Northhampton, MA: Edward Elgar Pub.

Aydın, E. S., & Polat, M. (2009). *How Information Systems helped Turkish justice system speed up? An analysis on UYAP's lawyer portal and its benefits*. ICEGEG 2009. Ankara, Turkey.

Bai, M. (2010, June 13). Democrat in chief? *The New York Times*.

Bakan, İ. A., Aydın, H., Kar, M., & Öz, B. (2008). (submitted to). T-VOHSA project phase 1. [Türksat.]. *Report*.

Bakan, İ. A., Aydın, H., Kar, M., & Öz, B. (2009). (submitted to). T-VOHSA project phase 2. [Türksat.]. *Report*.

Baker, P. (2009, February 1). New symbol of elite access: Email to the chief. *The New York Times*.

Balcı, A., & Kirilmaz, H. (2009). Kamu Yönetiminde Yeniden Yapilanma Kapsaminda E-Devlet Uygulamalari. (Reorganization of Public Administration and e-Government Applications. *Türk İdare Dergisi*, *81*(463-464), 45–71.

Balci, A., Kumaş, E., Medeni, T., & Medeni, İ. T. (2009). Development and implementation of e-government services in Turkey. In Cunha, M. M., Oliveira, E. F., & Antonio, J. T. (Eds.), *Handbook of research on social dimensions of semantic technologies and Web services*. New York, NY: Information Science Reference.

Balcı, A., & Medeni, T. (2010). E-government gateway development in Turkey: Some challenges and future directions for citizen focus. In Downey, E., Ekstrom, C. D., & Jones, M. A. (Eds.), *E-government website development: Future trends and strategic models*. Hershey, PA: IGI Publishing.

Balutis, A. (2001). E-government 2001a, part I: Understanding the challenge and evolving strategies. *Public Management*, *30*, 33.

Bandura, A. (1977). Self-efficacy: Toward a unifying theory of behavioral change. *Psychological Review*, *84*, 191–215. doi:10.1037/0033-295X.84.2.191

Banerjee, P., & Chau, P. Y. K. (2004). An evaluative framework for analysing e-government convergence capability in developing countries. *Electronic Government*, *1*(1), 29–48. doi:10.1504/EG.2004.004135

Bangura, Y., & Larbi, G. A. (2006). Introduction: Globalisation and Public Sector Reform. In Bangura, Y., & Larbi, G. A. (Eds.), *Public Sector Reform in Developing Countries* (pp. 1–22). New York: Palgrave MacMillan.

Bannister, F. (2001). Dismantling the silos: Extracting value from IT investments in public administration. *Information Systems Journal*, *11*, 65–84. doi:10.1046/j.1365-2575.2001.00094.x

Bannister, F. (2005). The panoptic state: Privacy, surveillance and the balance of risk. *Information Polity*, *10*, 65–78.

Bannister, F., & Lalor, S. (2001). Public service values: Towards an ethical framework for e-government, In *Proc. European Conference on e-Government*, Trinity College Dublin. Reading, UK: MCIL.

Bansal, P. (2005). Evolving sustainably: A longitudinal study of corporate sustainable development. *Strategic Management Journal*, *26*(3), 197–218. doi:10.1002/smj.441

Barber, B. (1984). *Strong democracy*. Berkeley, CA: University of California Press.

Barley, S. R. (1990). The alignment of technology and structure through roles and networks. *Administrative Science Quarterly*, *35*, 61–103. doi:10.2307/2393551

Barley, S. R., & Tolbert, P. S. (1997). Institutionalization and structuration: Studying the links between action and institution. *Organization Studies*, *18*(1), 93–117. doi:10.1177/017084069701800106

Bass, C., & Lee, J. M. (2002). Building a business case for EAI. *EAI Journal*, 18-20.

Baumer, D., Earp, J., & Poindexter, J. C. (2004). Internet privacy law: A comparison between the United States and the European Union. *Computers & Security*, *23*, 400–412. doi:10.1016/j.cose.2003.11.001

Baumgarten, J., & Chui, M. (2009). E-government 2.0. *The McKinsey Quarterly*, *4*, 26–32. Retrieved from www.mckinseyquarterly.com/Public_Sector/E-government_20_2408.

Beath, C. M. (1991). Supporting the information technology champion. *Management Information Systems Quarterly*, *15*(3), 355–372. doi:10.2307/249647

Beaumaster, S. (2002). Local government IT implementation issues: A challenge for public administration. *Proceedings of the 35th Annual Hawaii International Conference on System Sciences*, IEEE Computer Society, (pp. 1725-1734).

Bekkers, V., & Homburg, V. (2007). The myths of e-government: Looking beyond the assumptions of a new and better government. *The Information Society*, *23*, 373–382. doi:10.1080/01972240701572913

Belanger, F., & Hiller, J. (2005). A framework for e-government: Privacy implications. *Business Process Management Journal*, , 11.

Belanger, F., Carter, L. D., & Schaupp, L. C. (2005). U-government: A framework for the evolution of e-government. *Electronic Government, an International Journal, 2*(4), 426-445.

Bellamy, C. A., & Taylor, J. A. (1992). Informatization and new public management: A new agenda for public administration. *Public Policy and Administration*, *7*(3), 29–41. doi:10.1177/095207679200700303

Bellamy, C., & Taylor, J. A. (1994). Reinventing Government in the Information Age. *Public Money and Management, 14*(3).

Benbasat, I., & Barki, H. (2007). Quo vadis TAM? *Journal of AIS*, *8*(4). Retrieved from http://jais.aisnet.org/articles/8-16/default.asp?view=html.

Bengshir, T. K., & Sagsan, M. (2009). *Knowledge orchestration: The compatibility with organization, people, technology, and process in public organization*. eGovShare 2009, Antalya, Turkey.

Bennett, M., Bouma, J. J., & Ciccozzi, E. (2004). An institutional perspective on the transfer of accounting knowledge: a case study. *Accounting Education*, *13*(3), 329–346. doi:10.1080/0963928042000273807

Benson, T. (2002). *The e-services development framework* (eSDF). UK Cabinet Office, Office of the e-Envoy, Volume 1.0b

Berger, P., & Luckman, T. (1966). *The social construction of reality: A sociology of knowledge*. London, UK: Penguin Books.

Bergeron, F., Raymond, L., & Uwizeyemungu, S. 2005, ERP adoption for e-government: An analysis of motivations.In: E-*Government Workshop '05 (eGOV05)*, September 13, 2005, Brunel University, West London, UK.

Bergmann, R. (2002). *Experience management. Lecture Notes in Artificial Intelligence Series, 2432*. Springer.

Berra, M. (2006, March 23-25). *New commons or IPR extension? The future of innovation*. IASCP Europe Regional Meeting: Building the European Common: from Open Fields to Open Source, Brescia, Italy. Retrieved March 1, 2010, from http:// iascpeurope.eco.unibs.it/papers/ Berra.pdf

BetaCMS. (2008). *An open source JCR-compliant, enterprise content infrastructure & content management platform*. Retrieved from http:// www.betacms.org

Bethard, S., Yu, H., Thornton, A., Hatzivassiloglou, V., & Jurafsky, D. (2004). Automatic extraction of opinion propositions and their holders. (AAAI 2004), Springer.

Beynon-Davies, P. (2005). Constructing electronic government: The case of the UK inland revenue. *International Journal of Information Management*, *25*(1), 3–20. doi:10.1016/j.ijinfomgt.2004.08.002

Beynon-Davies, P., & Williams, M. D. (2003). Evaluating electronic local government in the UK. *Journal of Information Technology*, *18*, 137–149. doi:10.1080/0268396032000101180

Bhabha, H. K. (1994). *The location of culture*. London, UK & New York, NY: Routledge.

Bhatnagar, S. (2002). E-government: Lessons from implementation in developing countries. *Regional Development Dialogue*, *24*(Autumn).

Biccum, A. R. (2002). Interrupting the discourse of development: On a collision course with postcolonial theory. *Culture, Theory and Critique*, *43*(1), 33–50. doi:10.1080/14735780210162094

Bidgoli, H. (2004). *The Internet encyclopedia* (*Vol. 1*, p. 707). John Wiley & Sons. doi:10.1002/047148296X

Bienstock, C. C., Royne, M. B., Sherrell, D., & Stafford, T. F. (2008). An expanded model of logistics service quality: Incorporating logistics Information Technology. *International Journal of Production Economics*, *113*, 205–222. doi:10.1016/j.ijpe.2007.03.023

Biesma, R. G., Brugha, R., Harmer, A., Walsh, A., Spicer, N., & Walt, G. (2009). The effects of global health initiatives on country health systems: A review of the evidence from HIV/AIDS control. *Health Policy and Planning*, *24*, 239–252. doi:10.1093/heapol/czp025

Birzea, C. (2005). *Tools for quality assurance of education for democratic citizenship in schools*. Strasbourg, France: Council of Europe.

Blaze, M., Feigenbaum, J., & Lacy, J. (1996). *Decentralized trust management*. In IEEE Symposium on Security and Privacy (pp. 164-173). Oakland, CA, USA.

BMWI. (2010). *Breitbandstrategie*. Retrieved March 1, 2010, from http:// www.bmwi.de/ BMWi/ Navigation/ Technologie-und-Innovation/ Telekommunikation-und-Post/ breitbandstrategie,did=257532.html

Bogdanor, V. (Ed.). (2005). *Joined-up government*. New York, NY: Oxford University Press.

Boiko, B. (2004). *Content management bible* (2nd ed.). Wiley Publishing.

Bonham, G. M., Seifert, J. W., & Thorson, S. J. (2001). *The transformational potential of e-government: The role of political leadership*. European Consortium for Political Research, which was held at the University of Kent at Canterbury, U.K.

Bonoma, T. (1985). Case research in marketing: Opportunities, problems and a process. *JMR, Journal of Marketing Research*, *22*, 199–208. doi:10.2307/3151365

Boon, C., Boselie, J. P., & Dietz, G. (2005). Commonalities and contradictions in research on human resource management and performance. *Human Resource Management Journal*, *15*(3), 67–94. doi:10.1111/j.1748-8583.2005.tb00154.x

Borge, L., & Rattsø, J. (1997). Local government grants and income tax revenue: Redistributive politics in Norway 1900–1990. *Public Choice*, *92*, 181–197. doi:10.1023/A:1004955330460

Borins, S., Kernaghan, K., Brown, D., & Bontis, N. 6, P., Thompson, F. (2007). *Digital state at the leading edge*. Toronto, Canada: University of Toronto Press.

Bouras, C., Gkamas, A., Papagiannopoulos, J., Theofilopoulos, G., & Tsiatsos, T. (2009). Broadband municipal optical networks in Greece: A suitable business model. *Journal of Telematics and Informatics*, *26*, 391–409. doi:10.1016/j.tele.2009.03.003

Bouras, C., Papagiannopoulos, J., Katsikas, S., & Gritzalis, S. (2008). The status of broadband in western Greece: A study on the supply and the demand of broadband services for e-government promotion. [IJEG]. *International Journal of Electronic Governance*, *1*(3), 326–344. doi:10.1504/IJEG.2008.020453

Bouras, C., Gkamas, A., Theofilopoulos, G., & Tsiatsos, T. (2008). Business models for municipal broadband networks. In Khosrow-Pour, M. (Ed.), *Encyclopedia of Information Science and Technology* (pp. 457–465). Hershey, PA: IGI Global. doi:10.4018/978-1-60566-026-4.ch076

Bouras, C., Gkamas, A., Papagiannopoulos, J., Theofilopoulos, G., & Tsiatsos, T. (2007). *Business models for broadband municipal optical networks: A proposed model for the Greek case*. The Twelfth IEEE Symposium on Computers and Communications, (pp. 727-732). Aveiro, Portugal.

Bourn, J. (2002). *Better public services through e-government*. London: The National Audit Office.

Bourreau, M., Cambini, C., & Hoernig, S. (2010). *National FTTH plans in France Italy, and Portugal. Robert Schuman Centre for Advanced Studies, Florence School of Regulation European University Institute*. Florence, Italy: European University Press.

Bovens, M., Zouridis, S., & Tilburg, U. (2002). From street-level to system-level bureaucracies: How information and communication technology is transforming administrative discretion and constitutional control. *Public Administration Review*, *62*(2), 174–184. doi:10.1111/0033-3352.00168

Bowersox, D. J., & Daugherty, P. J. (1995). Logistics paradigms: The impact of Information Technology. *Journal of Business Logistics*, *16*(1), 65–80.

Bozeman, B., & Pandey, S. K. (2004). Public Management Decision Making: Effects of Decision Content. *Public Administration Review*, *64*(5), 553–564. doi:10.1111/j.1540-6210.2004.00403.x

Braa, J., & Hedberg, C. (2002). The struggle for district-based health Information Systems in South Africa. *The Information Society*, *18*, 113–127. doi:10.1080/01972240290075048

Braa, J., & Muquinge, H. (2007). Building collaborative networks in Africa on Health Information Systems and Open Source Software Development - Experiences from the HISP/BEANISH Network. Retrieved August 10, 2010, from http://citeseerx.ist.psu.edu/viewdoc/download?doi=10.1.1.131.8950&rep=rep1&type=pdf

Bradford, M., & Florin, J. (2003). Examining the role of innovation diffusion factors on the implementation success of ERP systems. *International Journal of Accounting Information Systems*, *4*(3), 205–225. doi:10.1016/S1467-0895(03)00026-5

Brands, S. (2000). *Rethinking public key infrastructures and digital certificates: Building in privacy*. MIT Press.

Brands, S., Demuynck, L., & De Decker, B. (2007). A practical system for globally revoking the unlinkable pseudonyms of unknown users. In Pieprzyk, J., Ghodosi, H., & Dawson, E. (Eds.), *ACISP 2007* (pp. 400–415). Berlin/Heidelberg, Germany: Springer-Verlag.

Bretschneider, S. (2003). Information Technology, e-government, and institutional change. *Public Administration Review*, *63*(6), 738–741. doi:10.1111/1540-6210.00337

Brewer, G. A., Hicklin, A. K., & Walker, R. M. (2006, December). *Layers of Red Tape: Using Multilevel Modelling to Study the Effects of Red Tape, Management, and the Environment on Performance*. Paper presented at the Conference on "Determinants of Performance in Public Organizations II", 7-9th December 2006, University of Hong Kong, Hong Kong.

Bridgman, T., & Willmott, H. (2006). Institutions and Technology: Frameworks for Understanding Organisational Change. *The Journal of Applied Behavioral Science*, *42*(1), 110–126. doi:10.1177/0021886305284990

Brinton, M. C., & Nee, V. (1998). *The new institutionalism in sociology*. Stanford, CA: Stanford University Press.

Broad, R. (2006). Research, knowledge, and the art of paradigm maintenance: The World Bank's Development Economics Vice-Presidency (DEC). *Review of International Political Economy*, *13*(3), 387–419. doi:10.1080/09692290600769260

Broadband Properties. (2006). *Issues*. Retrieved July 2, 2010, from http:// www.broadbandproperties.com/ 2006issues/ mar06issues/ vienna_march.pdf

Brodie, M. L. (1992). The promise of distributed computing and the challenges of legacy Information Systems. In P. M. D. Gray & R. J. Lucas, (Eds.), *Advanced database systems: Proceedings of the 10th British National Conference on Databases* (pp. 1-28). New York, NY & Heidelburg, Germany: Springer-Verlag.

Bronchi, C. (2001). *Options for reforming the tax system in Greece (No. 291)*. Paris, France: OECD.

Brown, M. M., & Brudney, J. L. (2001). *Achieving advanced electronic government services: An examination of obstacles and implications from an international perspective*. Paper presented at the National Public Management Research Conference, Bloomington, IN.

Brugha, R., & Varvasovszky, Z. (2000). Stakeholder analysis: A review. *Health Policy and Planning*, *15*(3), 239–246. doi:10.1093/heapol/15.3.239

Brynjolfsson, E., Hitt, L. M., & Shinkyu, Y. (2002). Intangible assets: Computers and organizational capital. *Brookings Papers on Economic Activity: Macroeconomics*, *1*, 137–198. doi:10.1353/eca.2002.0003

BS 8723. (2005). *Structured vocabularies for information retrieval: Exchange formats and protocols for interoperability*. Retrieved from http:// schemas.bs8723.org/

Budhwar, P., & Debrah, Y. 2008, Future research on human resource management systems in Asia, *Asia Pacific Journal of Management*, 26(2), 197-218 Springer Netherlands, Retrieved from: http:// www.springerlink.com/ content/ k7427514p1022838/

Bui, T. X., Sankaran, S., & Sebastian, I. M. (2003). A framework for measuring national e-readiness. *International Journal of Electronic Business*, *1*(1), 3–22. doi:10.1504/IJEB.2003.002162

C.E.E.S. (2009). *Citizen-oriented evaluation of e-government services.* EU Marie Curie IAPP funded Project. Unpublished literature review as project deliverable document.

CAFRAD. NEPAD, & UNDESA. (2003). Plan of action for the implementation of the e-Africa Initiative for Good Governance. *e-Africa 2003: Expert Consultative Meeting on Building e-governance capacity in African Countries*. Tangier, Morocco.

Caituiro-Monge, H., & Rodríguez-Martinez, M. (2004). *Net traveler: A framework for autonomic Web services collaboration, orchestration and choreography in e-government Information Systems. ICWS* (pp. 2–10). San Diego, California: IEEE.

Caloyannides, M. (2003). US e-government authentication framework and programs. *IT Professional*, *5*(3), 16–21. doi:10.1109/MITP.2003.1202230

Çam, A. R. (2009). *SMS Information System* (in Turkish e-justice project "UYAP"). Retrieved March 4, 2010, from http://www.uyap.gov.tr/english/makale/SMS_information_system-TURKEY.pdf

Camenisch, J. (2006). Protecting (anonymous) credentials with the trusted computing group's TPM. In S. Fischer-Hübner, K. Rannenberg, L. Yngström & S. Lindskog (Eds.), *International Information Security Conference (SEC 2006)* (pp. 135-147). Springer-Verlag.

Camenisch, J., & Groß, T. (2008). Efficient attributes for anonymous credentials. In P. Syverson, S. Jha & X. Zhang (Eds.), *15th ACM Conference on Computer and Communications Security* (pp. 345-356). New York, NY: ACM.

Camenisch, J., & Lysyanskaya, A. (2001). Efficient non-transferable anonymous multi-show credential system with optional anonymity revocation. In B. Pfitzmann (Ed.), *International Conference on the Theory and Application of Cryptographic Techniques (EUROCRYPT 2001)*, (vol. 2045, pp. 93-118). Springer-Verlag.

Camenisch, J., & Lysyanskaya, A. (2004). Signature schemes and anonymous credentials from bilinear maps. In G. Goos, J. Hartmanis, & J. van Leeuwen (Eds.), *24rd Annual International Cryptology Conference (CRYPTO 2004)* (pp. 56-72). Berlin/Heidelberg, Germany: Springer-Verlag.

Camenisch, J., & Van Herreweghen, E. (2002). Design and implementation of the Idemix anonymous credential system. Research Report RZ 3419, IBM Research Division, June 2002. In V. Atluri (Ed.), *9th ACM Conference on Computer and Communication Security,* (pp. 21-30). New York, NY: ACM Press.

Cameron, J. D. (2004). The World Bank and the new institutional economics: Contradictions and implications for development policy in Latin America. *Latin American Perspectives*, *31*, 97–103. doi:10.1177/0094582X0403100408

Cammack, P. (2004). What the World Bank means by poverty reduction, and why it matters. *New Political Economy*, *9*(2), 189–211. doi:10.1080/1356346042000218069

Campbell, M. (2008, December 9). Ontario drops plans to limit passengers in teens' cars. *The Globe and Mail.*

Canivez, P. (2000). *Ποια Αγωγή για τον Πολίτη*. Αθήνα: SCRIPTA (in greek)

Capgemini. (2009). *Smarter, faster, better e-government: 8th benchmark measurement of European e-government services.* Prepared for the European Commission Directorate General for Information Society and Media by Capgemini, Rand Europe, IDC, Sogeti and DTI. CDT and InfoDev. (2002). *The e-government handbook for developing countries.* The Center for Democracy and Technology (CDT) and the Information for Development Program (InfoDev). Retrieved from www.cdt.org/egov/handbook

Carden, F. (2009). *Knowledge to policy: Making the most of development research. Los Angeles, CA/ London, UK/ New Delhi, India/ Singapore.* Washinton, DC: Sage.

Carr, N. G. (2004). *Does IT matter?* Boston, MA: Harvard Business School Press.

Carr, D. (2008, November 10). Obama's personal linkedin. *The New York Times.*

Carter, L., & Bélanger, F. (2005). The utilization of e-government services: Citizen trust, innovation and acceptance factors. *Information Systems Journal*, *15*, 5–25. doi:10.1111/j.1365-2575.2005.00183.x

Carter, L., & Bélanger, F. (2005). The utilization of e-government services: Citizen trust, innovation and acceptance factors. *Information Systems Journal*, *15*, 5–25. doi:10.1111/j.1365-2575.2005.00183.x

Cartwright, D., & Atkinson, K. (2009). Using computational argumentation to support e-participation. *IEEE Intelligent Systems*, *24*(5), 42–52. doi:10.1109/MIS.2009.104

Castellano, M., Pastore, N., Arcieri, F., Summo, V., & Bellone de Grecis, G. (2005). An e-government cooperative framework for government agencies. *Proc. of 38th Intern. Conf. on System Sciences, Hawaii, 5*(5), 121c.

Castells, M. (2000a). *End of millennium* (2nd ed.). Malden, MA: Blackwell Publishers.

Castells, M. (2000b). *The rise of the network society* (2nd ed.). Oxford, UK/ Malden, MA: Blackwell.

Castells, M. (2001). *The Internet galaxy: Reflections on the Internet, business and society*. New York, NY: Oxford University Press.

Caufield, C. (1998). *Masters of illusion: The World Bank and the poverty of nations*. London, UK: Pan.

Cavaye, A. L. M. (1996). Case study research: A multifacted research approach for IS. *Information Systems Journal*, *6*(3), 227–242. doi:10.1111/j.1365-2575.1996.tb00015.x

Center for Democracy and Technology (CDT). (2002). E-government handbook for developing countries. *CDT Policy Post, 8*(26).

Central, I. T. Unit. (2000). *E-government: A strategic framework for public services in the Information Age*. UK Cabinet Office, London.

Centre of Expertise for Local Government Reform. 2010, *Tools for capacity building*, Retrieved from: http:// www.coe.int/ t/ dgap/ localdemocracy/ Centre_Expertise/ Tools/ default_en.asp.

Chadwick, A., & May, C. (2003). Interaction between states and citizens in the age of the Internet: E-government in the United States, Britain, and the European Union. *Governance: An International Journal of Policy, Administration, and Institutions*, *16*(2), 271–300.

Chadwick, A. (2006). *Internet politics: States, citizens, and new communication technologies*. Oxford, UK: Oxford University Press.

Chakrabarty, D. (2000). Subaltern studies and postcolonial historiography. *Nepantla: Views From South*, *1*(1), 9–31.

Chan, C., & Pan, S. (2008). User engagement in e-government systems implementation: A comparative case study of two Singaporean e-government initiatives. *The Journal of Strategic Information Systems*, ▪▪▪, 17.

Chand, A., Leeming, D., Stork, E., Agassi, A., & Biliki, R. (2005). *The impact of ICT on rural development in Solomon Islands: The PFnet case.* ICT Capacity Building at USP Project, the University of the South Pacific. ISBN 982-01-0629-X

Chang, A., & Kannan, P. (2008). *Leveraging Web 2.0 in government*. Arlington, VA: IBM Center for the Business of Government.

Charalabidis, Y., Lampathaki, F., & Stassis, A. (2007). *A second-generation e-government interoperability framework. 5th Eastern European e|Gov Days 2007 in Prague.* Austrian Computer Society.

Charalabidis, Y., Gionis, G., Ferro, E., & Loukis, E. (2010). Towards a systematic exploitation of Web 2.0 and simulation modeling tools in public policy process. In *Proceedings of the IFIP Second International Conference on e-Participation - ePart 2010* (August 29 - September 2, 2010, Lausanne, Switzerland). London, UK: Springer Verlag.

Checkland, P., & Holwell, S. (1998). *Information, systems and Information Systems-Making sense of the field.* Chichester, UK: John Wiley & Sons.

Checkland, P., & Scholes, J. (1999). *Soft systems methodology in action.* West Sussex, UK: John Wiley & Sons Ltd.

Chen, W., & Hirschheim, R. (2004). A paradigmatic and methodological examination of Information Systems research from 1991 to 2001. *Information Systems Journal*, *14*, 197–235. doi:10.1111/j.1365-2575.2004.00173.x

Chen, Y. N., Chen, H. M., Huang, W., & Ching, R. K. H. (2006). E-government strategies in developed and developing countries: An implementation framework and case study. *Journal of Global Information Management*, *14*(1), 23–46. doi:10.4018/jgim.2006010102

Chen, Y. C., & Gant, J. (2001). Transforming local e-government services: The use of application services providers. *Government Information Quarterly*, *18*(4), 343–355. doi:10.1016/S0740-624X(01)00090-9

Chen, H. (2005). *Adopting emerging integration technologies in organisations*. PhD Thesis, Department of Information Systems and Computing, Brunel University, West London, UK.

Cheng-YI Wu, R. (2007). Enterprise integration in e-government. *Transforming Government: People, Process and Policy*, *1*(1), 89–99.

Cherns, A. B. (1977). Can behavioral science help design organizations? *Organizational Dynamics*, *5*(4), 44–64. doi:10.1016/0090-2616(77)90039-0

Chetty, J., & Coetzee, M. (2009). *Considering contracts for governance in service-oriented architectures*. Information and Computer Security Architecture (ICSA). Retrieved from http:// icsa.cs.up.ac.za/ issa/ 2008/ Proceedings/ Research/6.pdf

Chilundo, B., & Aanestad, M. (2004). Negotiating multiple rationalities in the process of integrating the Information Systems of disease-specific health programmes. *Electronic Journal on Information Systems in Developing Countries*, *20*(2), 1–28.

Chircu, A. M. (2004). *E-government value assessment: Towards a multidimmensional framework*. Retrieved from http:// www.informatik.umu.se/ ~qron/ Chircu.doc

Chlamtac, I., Gumaste, A., & Szabo, C. (Eds.). (2005). *Broadband services business models and technologies for community networks*. John Wiley & Sons. doi:10.1002/0470022515

Cho, Y. H., & Choi, B. D. (2004). E-government to combat corruption: The case of Seoul metropolitan government. *International Journal of Public Administration*, *27*(10), 719–735. doi:10.1081/PAD-200029114

Cho, D., Irwin, N., & Whoriskey, P. (2008, October 14). U.S. forces nine major banks to accept partial nationalization. *Washington Post*.

Choi, Y., Cardie, C., Riloff, E., & Patwardhan, S. (2005). Identifying sources of opinions with conditional random fields and extraction patterns. In *Proceedings of Human Language Technology Conference on Empirical Methods in Natural Language Processing* (HLT/EMNLP), (pp. 355-362). Vancouver, Canada: Association for Computational Linguistics.

Chun, A. H. W. (2008, Spring). An AI framework for the automatic assessment of e-government forms. *AI Magazine*.

Ciborra, C., & Navarra, D. D. (2005). Good governance, development theory, and aid policy: Risks and challenges of e-government in Jordan. *Information Technology for Development*, *11*(2), 141–159. doi:10.1002/itdj.20008

Ciborra, C. (2005). Interpreting e-government and development: Efficiency, transparency or governance at a distance? *Information Technology & People*, *18*(3), 260–279. doi:10.1108/09593840510615879

Ciborra, C. (1999). A theory of Information Systems based on improvisation. In Currie, W., & Galliers, B. (Eds.), *Rethinking management Information Systems* (pp. 136–155). Oxford, UK: Oxford University Press.

Cilingir, D., & Kushchu, I. (2004). *E-government and m-government: Concurrent leaps by Turkey*. Mobile Government Lab (mGovLab). Retrieved May 9, 2009, from http://www.mgovlab.org

Citynet. (2010). *Citynet Amsterdam*. Retrieved June 28, 2010, from http://www.citynet.nl/

Clark, C. (2000). *Theories of development and the Taiwan experience: Success and challenge from incongruity*. Paper presented at the Annual Meeting of the American Political Science Association, August 31 - September 3, 2000.

Codagnone, C., & Boccardelli, P. (2006). *Measurement framework final version*. E-Government Economics Project. Rome, Italy: eGEP Consortium. Retrieved from http:// 82.187.13.175/ eGEP/ Static/ Contents/ final/ D.2.4_Measurement_Framework_final_version.pdf

Cogan, J. J., & Derricott, R. (1998). *Citizenship for the 21st Century: An international perspective on education.* New York, NY: Routlege.

Coglianese, C. (1997). Assessing consensus: The promise and performance of negotiated rulemaking. *Duke Law Journal, 46*(6), 1255–1349. doi:10.2307/1372989

Cohendet, P., & Steinmueller, W. E. (2000). The codification of knowledge: A conceptual and empirical exploration. *Industrial and Corporate Change, 9*(2), 195–209. doi:10.1093/icc/9.2.195

Coleman, J. S. (1990). *Foundations of social theory.* Cambridge, MA: The Belknap Press of Harvard University Press.

Coleman, S., & Gotze, J. (2002). *Bowling together: Online public engagement in policy deliberation.* Retrieved from http:// bowlingtogether.net

Colmenares, G. L. E. (2004). Critical success factors of enterprise resource planning systems implementation in Venezuela. *Proceedings of the 10th Americas Conference on Information Systems*, New York, USA, (pp. 134-139).

Compeau, D. R., & Higgins, C. A. (1995). Computer self-efficacy: Development of a measure and initial test. *Management Information Systems Quarterly, 19*(2), 189–211. doi:10.2307/249688

Conklin, J., & Begeman, M. (1989). gIBIS: A tool for all reasons. *Journal of the American Society for Information Science American Society for Information Science, 40*(3), 200–213. doi:10.1002/(SICI)1097-4571(198905)40:3<200::AID-ASI11>3.0.CO;2-U

Conklin, J. (2003). Dialog mapping: Reflections on an industrial strength case study. In Kirschner, P., Buckingham Shum, S., & Carr, C. (Eds.), *Visualizing argumentation: Software tools for collaborative and educational sense-making*. London, UK: Springer Verlag.

Cook Network Consultants. (2005). *Building regional open access fiber infrastructure in Catalonia* (Northeastern Spain). The COOK Report on Internet, September-October 2005. Retrieved March 1, 2010, from http:// www.cookreport.com/ catalonia.pdf

Coquery-Vidrovitch, C. (1988). *Africa: Endurance and change south of the Sahara.* University of California Press.

Cordella, A. (2007). E-government: Towards the e-bureaucratic form? *Journal of Information Technology, 22*(3), 265–274. doi:10.1057/palgrave.jit.2000105

Corea, S. (2007). Promoting development through Information Technology innovation: The IT artifact, artfulness, and articulation. *Information Technology for Development, 13*(1), 49–69. doi:10.1002/itdj.20036

Country, L. A. (2007). *A taxonomy of human services: A conceptual framework with standardized terminology and definitions for the field.* General Social Sciences, Taxonomy Warehouse. Retrieved from http:// www.taxonomywarehouse.com/ vocabdetails_include.asp?vVocID=370

Coursey, D., & Norris, D. F. (2008). Models of e-government: Are they correct? An empirical assessment. *Public Administration Review*, (May-June): 523–535. doi:10.1111/j.1540-6210.2008.00888.x

Creech, H., Berthe, O., Assubuji, A. P., Mansingh, I., & Anjelkovic, M. (2006). *Evaluation of UNESCO's community multimedia centres: Final report.* (Report No. IOS/ EVS/PI/54). Paris, France: United Nations Educational, Scientific, and Cultural Organization. e-Mexico National System. (2008). *Digital community centers.* Retrieved October 19, 2008, from http:// www.emexico.gob.mx/ wb2/ eMex/ eMex_Digital_community_centers

Crichton, C., Davies, J., Gibbons, J., Harris, S., & Shukla, A. (2007). Semantic frameworks for e-government. *Proceedings of the 1st International Conference on Theory and Practice of Electronic Governance.* WORKSHOP SESSION: Formal engineering methods for electronic governance, (pp. 30-39). Macao, China.

Crown, U. K. (2000). *E-government interoperability framework* (e-GIF). Office of the e-Envoy. Retrieved from http:// www.uk-online.gov.uk

Culnan, M. (2000). Protecting privacy online: Is self-regulation working? *Journal of Public Policy & Marketing, 19*(1), 20–26. doi:10.1509/jppm.19.1.20.16944

Currie, W., & Guah, M. W. (2007). Conflicting institutional logics: A national programme for IT in the organisational field of healthcare. *Journal of Information Technology, 22*, 235–247. doi:10.1057/palgrave.jit.2000102

Czernich, N., & Engl, F. Falck, O., Kiessl, T., & Kretschmer, T. (2009). *Regulatory framework for next-generation access networks across Europe*. CESIfo Dice Report 1/2009.

Dada, D. (2006). The failure of e-government in developing countries: a literature review. *Electronic Journal of Information Systems in Developing Countries*, *26*(7), 1–10.

Daniels, M. (2002). *E-government strategy: Simplified delivery of services to citizens*. Washington, DC: Office of Management and Budget.

Danish International Development Agency. (2006, November). Health sector programme support to Kenya. [Copenhagen, Denmark: Danish International Development Agency, Ministry of Foreign Affairs.]. *Phase*, *II*, 2006–2011.

Danziger, J. N., & Andersen, K. V. (2002). The impacts of Information Technology on public administration: An analysis of empirical research from the Golden Age of transformation. *International Journal of Public Administration*, *25*(5), 591–627. doi:10.1081/PAD-120003292

Daugherty, P. J., Ellinger, A. E., & Rogers, D. S. (1995). Information accessibility: Customer responsiveness and enhanced performance. *International Journal of Physical Distribution & Logistics Management*, *25*(1), 4–17. doi:10.1108/09600039510080117

Davidson, E., & Chiasson, M. (2005). Contextual influences on technology use mediation: A comparative analysis of electronic medical record systems. *European Journal of Information Systems*, *14*(1), 6–18. doi:10.1057/palgrave.ejis.3000518

Davis, F. D. (1989). Perceived usefulness, perceived ease of use and user acceptance of Information Technology. *Management Information Systems Quarterly*, *13*(3), 319–340. doi:10.2307/249008

Davis, F. D., Bagozzi, R. P., & Warshaw, P. R. (1989). User acceptance of computer technology: A comparison of two theoretical models. *Management Science*, *35*(8), 982–1003. doi:10.1287/mnsc.35.8.982

Davis, F. D., Bagozzi, R. P., & Warshaw, P. R. (1992). Extrinsic and intrinsic motivation to use computers in the workplace. *Journal of Applied Social Psychology*, *22*, 1111–1132. doi:10.1111/j.1559-1816.1992.tb00945.x

Davis, T. (2009). The blossoming field of online deliberation. In Davis, T., & Gangadharan, S. P. (Eds.), *Online deliberation – Design, research and practice*. Stanford, CA: CSLI Publications.

Davis, T. (2009). *Speech by the Secretary General of the Council of Europe*. 1st Conference of Ministers responsible for Social Cohesion of Council of Europe Member States. Moscow, 26 February 2009.

Dawes, S. (2002). Government and technology: User, not regulator. *Journal of Public Administration: Research and Theory*, *12*(4), 627–631.

Dawson, A. (2004). "To remember too much is indeed a form of madness": Caryl Phillips's *The Nature of Blood* and the modalities of European racism. *Postcolonial Studies*, *7*(1), 83–101. doi:10.1080/1368879042000210612

De, G. B. *(2001)*. E-government. Section I – Private sector recommendations to government on realization of e-government. Global business dialogue on electronic commerce, *(p. 42)*.

Deans, P. C. (2008). *Social software and Web 2.0 technology trends*. New York, NY: Information Science Reference.

Decman, M. (2009). Web 2.0 in e-government: The challenges and opportunities of Wiki in legal matters. *Proceedings of the 9th European Conference on e-Government*, (pp. 229-236).

Deerwester, S., Dumais, S., Furnas, G., Harshman, R., Landauer, T., Lochbaum, K., & Streeter, L. (1988). *Latent semantic indexing (LSI)*. US Patent 4.839.853.

Delanty, G. (2003). *Community key ideas*. London, UK: Routlege.

Denzin, N. Y. K., & Lincoln, Y. (1994). *Handbook of qualitative research*. London, UK: SAGE Publications.

Devadoss, P. R., Pan, S. L., & Huagng, J. C. (2002). Structurational analysis of e-government initiatives: a case study of SCO. *Decision Support Systems*, *34*(4), 253–269.

Dewey, J. (1933). *How we think*. Boston, MA: D. C. Heath.

Dewey, J. (1916) *Democracy and education: An introduction to the philosophy of education* (1966 ed.). New York, NY: Free Press.

Dewey, J. (2007). *Democracy and education: An introduction to the philosophy of education.* NuVision Publications, LLC, (digital book). Retrieved from http:// books.google.gr/books?id=dSmhXutgD4oC&printsec=frontcover&dq=Democracy+and+Education:+An+introduction+to+the+Philosophy+of+Education.&source=bl&ots=kgUy1rn_A5&sig=S_H25Cc-QYRSIefwCWQXzfZayFk&hl=el&ei=maOaS8WVOMz64AaU-oF_&sa=X&oi=book_result&ct=result&resnum=2&ved=0CBEQ6AEwAQ#v=onepage&q=&f=false

DGCIS - Direction générale de la Compétitivité, de l'Industrie et des Services. (2010). *Consultation publique - Programme national très haut débit.* République Française. Retrieved July 1, 2010, from http:// www.telecom.gouv.fr/ fonds_documentaire/ consultations/ 10/ consthd.pdf

Dhunpath, R., & Paterson, A. (2004). The interface between research and policy dialogue: Substantive or symbolic? *Journal of Education*, *33*, 125–146.

Di Maio, A., Baum, C., Keller, B., Kreizman, G., Pretali, M., & Seabrook, D. (2002). *Framework for e-government strategy assessment: Strategic analysis report.* 8 March 2002. Stamford, Connecticut: Gartner, pl. 2

Di Natale, M., Cucinotta, T., & Kolachalam, S. (2003). A modular open-source architecture for ICT services in the public administration. *Proceedings of the 2nd International Conference on E-Government Prague,* Czech Republic, (pp. 167-172).

Diedrich, E., Schmidt, D., & Wimmer, M. (2006). A three dimensional framework to realize interoperability in public administrations. *Proceeding of the Workshop on Semantic Web for eGovernment.* Workshop at the 3rd European Semantic Web Conference 12 June 2006, Budva, Serbia & Montenegro.

Digital Britain. (2010). *What we do: The report.* Retrieved March 1, 2010, from http:// www.culture.gov.uk/ what_we_do/ broadcasting/ 6216.aspx

Digital-Opportunity-Initiative. (2001). *Creating a development dynamic: Final report of the Digital Opportunity Initiative: Accenture, Markle Foundation.* UNDP.

Dillon, J., & Pelgrin, W. (2002). *E-government/commerce in New York State.* New York, NY: Office of Technology.

Dimitrova, D. V., & Chen, Y. (2006). Profiling the adopters of e-government information and services: The influence of psychological characteristics, civic mindedness, and information channels. [Thousand Oaks, CA: Summer.]. *Social Science Computer Review*, *24*(2), 172. doi:10.1177/0894439305281517

Dirlik, A. (1994). The postcolonial aura: Third world criticism in the age of globalization. *Critical Inquiry*, *20*(2), 328–356. doi:10.1086/448714

Disney, S. M., Naim, M. M., & Polter, A. (2004). Assessing the impact of e-business on supply chain dynamics. *International Journal of Production Economics*, *89*, 109–118. doi:10.1016/S0925-5273(02)00464-4

Dizard, W. P., III. (2006b). OMB sees improvement in agencies' IT security. *Government Computer News.* Retrieved March 2, 2006, from http://www.gcn.com/vol1_no1/daily-updates/38349l.html

Dobers, P. (1999). *Netting the information infrastructure of Stockholm.* Paper presented at the Conference of Managing the Big City, Göteborg University, Sweden.

Doty, P., & Erdelez, S. (2002). Information micro-practices in Texas rural courts: Methods and issues for e-government. *Government Information Quarterly*, *19*, 369–387. doi:10.1016/S0740-624X(02)00121-1

Dow, A. C., & Dow, S. C. (2005). The application of development economics: General principles and context specificity. *Cambridge Journal of Economics*, *29*, 1129–1143. doi:10.1093/cje/bei072

DPT. (2006). *Bilgi Toplumu Stratejisi ve Eylem Planı (Information/Knowledge Society Strategy Document). Devlet Planlanma Teşkilatı (State Planning Organization).* Both in Turkish and English.

DPT. (2008). *Information/knowledge society strategy progress report.* Devlet Planlanma Teşkilatı. (in Turkish)

DPT. (2010). *Information/knowledge society strategy progress report.* Devlet Planlanma Teşkilatı. (in Turkish)

Dublin Core Metadata Initiative (DCMI). (n.d.). *Website.* Retrieved from http:// dublincore.org/

Duffy, D. (2000). *Q&A: Balancing the role of e-government: Interview with Mike Hernon, vice president of e-government for New York City based Gov Works*. Retrieved from http:// www.cnn.com/ 2000/ TECH/ computing/ 11/ 13/ qna.egov.idg

Dunleavy, P., Margetts, H., Bastow, S., & Tinkler, J. (2005). New public management is dead-Long live digital-era governance. *Journal of Public Administration: Research and Theory*, *16*(3), 467–494. doi:10.1093/jopart/mui057

Dunleavy, P. (2007). Governance and state organization in the digital era. In Mansell, R., Avgerou, C., Quah, D., & Silverstone, R. (Eds.), *The Oxford handbook of Information and Communication Technologies* (pp. 404–426). Oxford, UK: Oxford University Press.

Dussel, E. (2002). World-system and trans-modernity. *Nepantla: Views from South*, *3*(2), 221–244.

Dutton, W. (2005). The cyber trust tension in e-government: Balancing identity, privacy, security. *Information Polity*, *10*, 13–23.

Earth Charter Commission. (2000). *The Earth charter.* Earth Charter Commission. Retrieved from http:// www.earthcharter.org/ files/ charter/ charter.pdf

Ebrahim, Z., & Irani, Z. (2005). E-government adoption: Architecture and barriers. *Business Process Management Journal*, *11*(5), 589–611. doi:10.1108/14637150510619902

Ebrahim, Z., Irani, Z., & Sarmad, S. (2004). *Factors influencing the adoption of e-government in public sector*. European & Mediterranean Conference on Information Systems, Tunis, Tunisia.

Edgren, G. (2003). The unequal dialogue. In Olsson, J., & Wohlgemuth, L. (Eds.), *Dialogue in pursuit of development* (pp. 23–38). Expert Group in Development Studies.

Ein-Dor, P. (2006). *Digital divides: Definitional and research issues. Department Seminar (December 5)*. Faculty of Management, Tel-Aviv University.

Ein-Dor, P., & Segev, E. (1993). A classification of Information Systems: Analysis and interpretation. *Information Systems Research*, *4*(2), 166–204. doi:10.1287/isre.4.2.166

Ekelin, A. (2007). *The work to make e-participation work.* Blekinge Institute of Technology Doctoral Dissertation Series No. 2007:1. Retrieved from http:// www.bth.se/ fou/ forskinfo.nsf/ 6753b78eb2944e0ac1256608004f0535/ 06c223cbd4e0037dc12572dd004a9ca1/ $file/ Ekelin_diss.pdf

Elgin, D. (1991). Creating a sustainable future. *Re-vision*, *14*(2), 77.

Ellingsen, G., Monteiro, E., & Munkvold, G. (2007). Standardization of work: Co-constructed practice. *The Information Society*, *23*, 309–326. doi:10.1080/01972240701572723

ELOST. (2006). *Work package 4: Foresight study. D4.1: Review of foresight studies and emerging technologies, D4.2: Technology-related questions for ELOST surveys*. Retrieved from www.elost.org

ELOST. (2008). Work package 6: Recommendations for future policy and research priorities for the EU. Retrieved from www.elost.org/D6-2.pdf

eMayor IST project. (2006). *Electronic and secure municipal administration for European citizens.* 6th Framework Programme, IST-2004-507217. Retrieved from www.emayor.org

e-México. (2003). *Resumen ejecutivo del sistema nacional e-México.* Retrieved January, 2006, from http://www.emexico.gob.mx/wb2/eMex/eMex_Resumen_ejecutivo_del_Sistema_Nacional_eMexic

Emmerij, L. (2005). *Turning points in development thinking and practice*. Paper presented at the WIDER Jubilee Conference on WIDER Thinking Ahead: The Future of Development Economics.

ENISA (European Network and Information Security Agency). (2009). *Privacy features of European e-ID card specifications*. Position paper. Retrieved from www.enisa.europa.eu/ act/ it/ eid/ eid-cards-en

Epractice. (2008). *Preparing Digital France 2012*. Retrieved March 1, 2010, from http:// www.epractice.eu/ en/ news/ 284991

E-practice. 2010, E-practice editorial team, *eGovernment Factsheets, European Commission*, Retrieved July 2, 2010, from http:// www.epractice.eu/ factsheets.

Eschenauer, L., Gligor, V. D., & Baras, J. S. (2002). On trust establishment in mobile ad-hoc networks. In B. Christianson, B. Crispo, J. A. Malcolm & M. Roe (Eds.), *Security Protocols, 10th International Workshop* (pp. 47-66). Springer.

Escobar, A. (1995). *Encountering development: The making and unmaking of the Third World*. Princeton, NJ: Princeton University Press.

Eskadenia, C. R. P. System, 2004, *ESKADENIA launches a government resource planning software (GRP)*, Retrieved on February 10, 2010, from http:// www.1stjordan.net/ actuuk/ archivesuk/ resultat.php?id=725&debut=0

Esteves, J., & Pastor, J. (2001). Enterprise resource planning systems research: An annotated bibliography. *Communications of AIS*, *7*(8), 2–54.

eTen. (2007).*E-ten programme: Support for trans-European telecommunications networks*. Retrieved from http:// europa.eu/legislation_summaries/ information_society/ l24226e_en.htm

Etta, F., & Parvyn-Wamahiu, S. (2003). *Information and communication technologies for development in Africa: Volume 2- The experience with community telecentres*. (pp. 127-148, 72, 113). IDRC, CODESRIA.

European Commission (EC). (1997). *Directive 97/66/EC of the European Parliament and of the Council concerning the processing of personal data and the protection of privacy in the telecommunications sector*, (pp. 1–8).

European Commission (EC). (1999). *Directive 99/93/ EC of the European Parliament and of the Council of 13 December 1999 on a community framework for electronic signatures* (pp. 12 – 20).

European Commission (EC). (2001). *Directive 01/45/EC of the European Parliament and the Council of Ministers on the protection of individuals with regard to the processing of personal data by the community institutions and bodies and on the free movement of such data* (pp. 1–22).

European Commission (EC). (2006). *i2010 e-government action plan: Accelerating e-government in Europe for the benefit of all*. Retrieved from http:// ec.europa.eu/ idabc/ en/ document/ 5763/ 254

European Commission. (2004). *European interoperability framework for pan-European e-government services*. IDA working document, version 2.4, Brussels.

European Commission. (2008). ICT for Governance and Policy Modelling Consultation Workshop. *FP7 Work Programme 2009-2010*. Workshop Report.

European Commission. 2010, *e-government on the fast track* Retrieved July 2, 2010, from http:// ec.europa.eu/ information_society/ activities/ egovernment/ policy/ index_en.htm

European Commission. (2001). *Digital literacy workshop*. A discussion paper from the eLearning Summit on Digital Literacy, Brussels 10-11 May.

European Commission. (2004). *European interoperability framework for pan-European e-government services*. Retrieved June 4, 2010, from http://ec.europa.eu/idabc/ servlets/Doc?id=19528

European Commission. (2010). *European information society 2010*. Retrieved June 28, 2010, from http:// ec.europa. eu/ information_society/ eeurope/ i2010/ index_en.htm

European Committee for standardization. (2005). *EU e-government metadata framework* (ecs). Retrieved from ftp:// ftp.cenorm.be/ PUBLIC/ CWAs/ e-Europe/ MMI-DC/ cwa15245-00-2005-Apr.pdf

European Community. (n.d.). *Europa glossary*. Retrieved from http:// europa.eu/ scadplus/ glossary/ eu_communities_en.htm

Evans, D., & Yen, D. C. (2005). E-government: An analysis for implementation: Framework for understanding cultural and social impact. *Government Information Quarterly*, *14*, 3–6.

Exforsys Inc. 2010, *The advantages and disadvantages of ERP*, Retrieved February 11, 2010, from http:// www. exforsys.com/ tutorials/ erp/ the-advantages-and-disadvantages-of-erp.html

Farnham, S., Chesley, H. R., McGhee, D. E., & Kawal, R. (2000). Structured online interactions: Improving the decision-making of small discussion groups. In *Proceedings of ACM 2000 Conference on Computer-Supported Cooperative Work (CSCW 2000)* (299-308). New York, NY: ACM Press.

Fellbaum, C. (Ed.). (1998). *WordNet: An online electronic lexical database*. The MIT Press.

Feng, C. M., & Yuan, C. Y. (2006). The impact of information and communication technologies on logistics management. *International Journal of Management*, *23*(4), 909–924.

Fernandes, D., Gorr, W., & Krishnan, R. (2001). *Servicenet: An agent-based framework for one-stop e-government services*. Americas Conference on Information Systems.

Fichman, R. (1992). *Information Technology diffusion: A review of empirical research*. 13th International Conference on Information Systems, (pp. 195-206).

FIDIS IST project. (2004). *The future of identity in the information society (FIDIS): Towards a global dependability and security framework*. Sixth Framework Programme, European Commission.

Fien, J. (1993). *Education for the environment: Critical curriculum theorising and environmental education*. Australia: Deakin University.

Fien, J., & Tilbury, D. (2002). *The global challenge of sustainability*. In D. Tilbury, R. B. Stevenson, J. Fien & S. Danie (Eds.), *Education and sustainability responding to the global challenge* (pp. 1-12). IUCN, Switzerland: IUCN Commission on Education and Communication CEC.

Finch, C. (2006). The benefits of the software-as-a-service model. *ComputerWorld*. Retrieved from http:// www.computerworld.com/ action/ article.do?command=viewArticleBasic&articleId=107276

Fine, B., Lapavitsas, C., & Pincus, J. (Eds.). (2001b). *Development policy in the twenty-first century: Beyond the post-Washington consensus*. London, UK: Routledge.

Fine, B. (2001). The social capital of the World Bank. In Fine, B., Lapavitsas, C., & Pincus, J. (Eds.), *Development policy in the twenty-first century: Beyond the post-Washington consensus* (pp. 136–154). London, UK: Routledge.

Fine, B., Lapavitsas, C., & Pincus, J. (2001a). Preface. In Fine, B., Lapavitsas, C., & Pincus, J. (Eds.), *Development policy in the twenty-first century: Beyond the post-Washington consensus* (pp. x–xvi). London, UK: Routledge.

Finger, M., & Pecoud, G. (2003). From e-government to e-governance? Towards a model of e-governance. *Proceedings of 3rd European Conference on e-Government*, Trinity College Dublin, Ireland. 3-4 July

Finn, J. D. (1989). Withdrawing from school. *Review of Educational Research*, *59*(2), 117–142. doi:. doi:10.3102/00346543059002117

Fishbein, M., & Ajzen, I. (1975). *Belief, attitude, intention, and behavior: An introduction to theory and research*. Reading, MA/ Don Mills, Ontario: Addison-Wesley Pub. Co.

Fishkin, J. S. (1991). *Democracy and deliberation*. New Haven, CT: Yale University Press.

Fishkin, J. S. (1995). *The voice of the people - Public opinion and democracy*. New Haven, CT: Yale University Press.

Fishkin, J. S. (2009). Virtual public consultation: Prospects for Internet deliberative democracy. In Davis, T., & Gangadharan, S. P. (Eds.), *Online deliberation – Design, research and practice*. Stanford, CA: CSLI Publications.

Flak, L. S., Eikebrokk, T. R., & Dertz, W. (2007). An exploratory approach for benefits management in e-government: Insights from 48 Norwegian government funded projects. *Proceedings of the 41st Annual Hawaii International Conference on System Sciences*, (p. 210).

Flak, L. S., Furuli, K., Kongsrud, S., & Sæbø, Ø. (2009). *Magic bullets or entepreneurial efforts? Two ways to develop national citizen portals?* ICEGOV 2009. Ankara, Turkey

Flanagan, T. (2007). *Harper's team: Behind the scenes in the Conservatives' rise to power*. Montreal, Canada: McGill Queen's University Press.

Fletcher, K., & Wright, G. (1995). Organizational, strategic and technical barriers to successful implementation of database marketing. *International Journal of Information Management*, *15*(2), 115–126. doi:10.1016/0268-4012(95)00005-R

Ford, D. N., & Sterman, J. D. (1998). Dynamic modelling of product development processes. *System Dynamics Review*, *14*(1), 31–67. doi:10.1002/(SICI)1099-1727(199821)14:1<31::AID-SDR141>3.0.CO;2-5

Forester, J. (1985). Designing: Making sense together in practical conversations. *Journal of Architectural Education, 38*(3), 14–20.

Fountain, J. E. (1995). *Enacting technology: An institutional perspective*. Cambridge, MA: John F. Kennedy School of Government, Harvard University.

Fountain, J. (2001). *Building the virtual state: Information Technology and institutional change*. Washington, DC: Brookings Institution Press.

Fountain, J. E. (2008). Bureaucratic reform and e-government in the United States: An institutional perspective. In Chadwick, A., & Howard, P. N. (Eds.), *The handbook of Internet politics*. New York, NY: Routledge.

Fountain, J. E. (2004). *Prospects for the virtual state*. Working papers. Retrieved May, 2006, from http:// www.j.u-tokyo.ac.jp/coeps/pdf/040710.pdf

Fountain, J. E., & Gil-Garcia, J. R. (2006). *Comparing integrative models of technology and structure in government*. Paper presented at the 2006 APPAM Fall Conference "Tax and Spend: Designing, Implementing, Managing and Evaluating Effective Redistributional Policies", Madison, WI.

Fountain, J. E., McKinnon, R., & Park, E. (2003). E-government cross-agency and intergovernmental initiatives research project: Web survey results. Boston, MA: Working Papers Series, National Center for Digital Government, John F. Kennedy School of Government, Harvard University.

FrameNet. (n.d.). Retrieved from http:// framenet.icsi.berkeley.edu

Frederic, C., & Michel, L. (2005). *A semantical reasoning framework for e-government of French national retirement system*. Retrieved from http:// www.imu.iccs.gr/ sweg/ papers/ Comte+Leclere.pdf

Freeman, R. E. (1984). *Strategic management: A stakeholder approach*. Boston, MA: Pitman /Ballinger.

Freire, P. (1972). *Pedagogy of the oppressed*. Penguin Books.

Friedman, M. (1966). The methodology of positive economics. In M. Friedman (Ed.), *Essays in positive economics* (pp. 3-16, 30-43). Chicago, IL: Univ. of Chicago Press.

FTTH Council. (2009). Definition of terms. (Revision Date: January 9th 2009). Retrieved August 4, 2010, from http:// www.ftthcouncil.eu/ documents studies/ FTTH-Definitions-Revision_January_2009.pdf

Fujimoto, T. (2006). Architecture-based comparative advantage in Japan and Asia. *MMRC Discussion Paper, 94*, 1-8.

Gallachi, A. (2000). *Project completion report. Ministry of Health, Kenya Health sector support programme, 1995-1998*. Copenhagen, Denmark: Danish International Development Agency, Ministry of Foreign Affairs.

Garfield, M. (2000). Critical success factors for the state telemedicine policy. *Proceedings of the 6th Americas Conference on Information Systems*, Long Beach, California, USA, (pp. 1573-1578).

Garofalakis, J., Koskeris, A., Michail, A. T., & Vopi, A. (2008). A Web based tool to assist management, control and security in schools' educational excursions. In: *8th European Conference on e-Government (ECEG2008)*, July 10-11, 2008, Ecole Polytechnique, Lausanne, Switzerland, Retrieved from http:// www.academic-conferences.org/ eceg/ eceg2008/ eceg08-home.htm

Garofalakis, J., Koskeris, A., & Vopi, A. (2007). An e-Government application for integrated, multi-level management of large scale resources of the Greek primary and secondary education, In: *7th European Conference on E-Government (ECEG 2007)*, June 21-22, 2007, Hague, Netherlands.

Garson, G. D. (2006). Securing the virtual state – Recent developments in privacy and security. *Social Science Computer Review, 24*(4), 489–496. doi:10.1177/0894439306289100

Gartner. (2003). *New performance framework measures public value of IT*. Research Note, Gartner

Gascó, M. (2004). E-Gobierno en Bolivia y Paraguay. In Araya Dujisin, R., & Porrúa Vigon, M. A. (Eds.), *América Latina Puntogob: Casos y tendencias en gobierno electrónico* (pp. 125–150). Santiago, Chile: FLACSO-Chile/ AICD-OEA.

Gefen, D., & Pavlou, P. (2002). *E-government adoption*. Paper presented at Americas Conference on Information Systems.

Giddens, A. (1979). *Central problems in social theory. Action, structure and contradiction in social analysis*. Berkeley/Los Angeles, CA: University of California Press.

Giddens, A. (1984). *The constitution of society*. Berkeley/ Los Angeles, CA: University of California Press.

Gijarro, L. (2004). *Analysis of the interoperability frameworks in e-government initiatives*. EGOV'04

Gil-Garcia, J. R. (2006, January 4-7, 2006). *Enacting state websites: A mixed method study exploring e-government success in multi-organizational settings*. Paper presented at the 39th Hawaii International Conference on System Sciences (HICSS).

Gil-Garcia, J. R., & Luna-Reyes, L. F. (2008). A brief introduction to electronic government: Definition, applications and stages. *Revista de Administración Pública RAP 116, 43*(2), 221-241.

Gillwald, A. (2002). Experimenting with institutional arrangements for communications policy and regulation: The case of telecommunications and broadcasting in South Africa. *The Southern African Journal of Information and Communication, 2*(1).

Giraldo, R. L. (2005). *Public policy and the new regulatory framework on electronic government procurement in Colombia*. AR: Revista de Derecho Informático, ISSN 1681-5726, vol. 88.

Gliozzo, A., Strapparava, C., & Dagan, I. (2004). Unsupervised and supervised exploitation of semantic domains in lexical disambiguation. *Computer Speech & Language, 18*(3), 275–299. doi:10.1016/j.csl.2004.05.006

Gökmen, A. (2009). *Developments and prospects in e–government implementations in Turkey*. ICEGOV2009, Ankara, Turkey.

Gold, A. H., Malhotra, A., & Segars, A. H. (2001). Knowledge management: An organizational capabilities perspective. *Journal of Management Information Systems, 18*(1), 185–214.

Goldman, J. (2008, April 4). Online deliberation: Expecting more from your e-government. *Politico (Pavia, Italy), 4*, 59.

Goldsmith, S., & Eggers, W. D. (2004). *Governing by network: The new shape of the public sector*. Washington, DC: Brookings Institution Press.

Gordon, T. F., & Karacapilidis, N. (1997). *The Zeno argumentation framework*. Paper presented at the Sixth International Conference on Artificial Intelligence and Law (ICAIL '97).

Gortmaker, J., & Janssen, M. (2004). Business process orchestration in e-government: A gap analysis. *Proceedings of the 15th International Resources Management Association (IRMA) International Conference*, New Orleans, LA, USA, (pp. 1-6).

Goudos, S., Loutas, N., Peristeras, V., & Tarabanis, K. (2007). Public administration domain ontology for a Semantic Web services e-government framework. *Proceedings of 2007 IEEE SCC*, (pp. 270-277).

Government of Canada. (2010). *Canada's economic action plan*. Retrieved March 1, 2010, from http:// www.actionplan.gc.ca/ eng/ index.asp

Government of Kenya. (1997). *Sessional paper no. 4 of 1997 on AIDS in Kenya*. Nairobi, Kenya: Government Printer, Republic of Kenya.

Government Technology. (2007), *City of Vendura to modernize govenrment ERP system* Retrieved February 14, 2010, from http:// www.govtech.com/ gt/ 219833

GovTalk. (2003). *Smart cards: Enabling e-government*. Draft Policy Framework. Retrieved from www.govtalk.gov.uk

Grafton, C., & Permaloff, A. (1991). Inexpensive database management software. *Political Science and Politics, 24*(2), 226–231. doi:10.2307/419939

Grant, G., & Chau, D. (2005). Developing a generic framework for e-government. *Journal of Global Information Management, 13*(1), 1–30. doi:10.4018/jgim.2005010101

Gregor, S., & Jones, D. (2007). The anatomy of a design theory. *Journal of the Association for Information Systems, 8*(5), 312–335.

Gribble, D. S., et al. (2000). Scalable, distributed data structures for Internet service construction. *Proc. 4th Symp. Operating Systems Design and Implementation*, (pp. 319–332). Usenix Association.

Grimsley, M., & Meehan, A. (2007). E-government Information Systems: Evaluation-led design for public value and client trust. *European Journal of Information Systems, 16*, 134–148. doi:10.1057/palgrave.ejis.3000674

Grindle, M. S. (2004). Good enough governance: Poverty reduction and reform in developing countries. *Governance, 17*(4), 525–548. doi:10.1111/j.0952-1895.2004.00256.x

Gritzalis, D. A. (Ed.). (2003). *Secure electronic voting* (*Vol. 7*). London, UK: Kluwer Academic Publishers Advances in Information Security Series.

Grönlund, Å., & Horan, T. A. (2005). Introducing e-gov: History, definitions and issues. *Communications of the AIS, 15*(39), 713–729.

Guha, R., Kumar, R., Raghavan, P., & Tomkins, A. (2004). Propagation of trust and distrust. In *Proc. of 13th ACM International Conference on World Wide Web* (pp. 403-412). New York, NY: ACM Press.

Guijarro, L. (2005), Policy and practice in standards selection for e-government interoperability frameworks. In *Proc. of EGOV 2005 Conference*, (pp. 163–173). Copenhaguen (Denmark)

Gunter, B. (2006). Advances in e-democracy: overview. [Emerald Group Publishing Limited. Great Britain.]. *Aslib Proceedings, 58*(5), 361–370. doi:10.1108/00012530610692320

Gupta, M. P., & Jana, D. (2003). E-government evaluation: A framework and case study. *Government Information Quarterly, 20*(4), 365–387. doi:10.1016/j.giq.2003.08.002

Haag, S., Cummings, M., & Phillips, A. (2007). *Management Information Systems for the information age* (6th ed.). Boston, MA: McGraw-Hill.

Halchin, L. E. (2004). Electronic government: Government capability and terrorist resource. *Government Information Quarterly, 21*, 406–419. doi:10.1016/j.giq.2004.08.002

Hamurcu, E. (2009). *Paperless environment and saving the trees with UYAP*. Retrieved March 4, 2010, from http://www.uyap.gov.tr/english/makale/erolhamurcu.pdf

Hancock, G. (2004). *Lords of poverty*. Nairobi, Kenya: Camerapix Publishers International.

Hansen, M., Pfitzmann, A., & Steinbrecher, S. (2008). Identity management throughout one's whole life. *Elsevier Advanced Technology Publications. Information Security Technical Report, 13*(2), 83–94. doi:10.1016/j.istr.2008.06.003

Harbage, B., & Dean, A. G. (1999). Distribution of Epi Info software: An evaluation using the Internet. *American Journal of Preventive Medicine, 16*(4), 314–317. doi:10.1016/S0749-3797(98)00101-9

Harfoush, R. (2009). *Yes we did: An inside look at how social media built the Obama brand*. Berkeley, CA: New Riders.

Harris, S., Gibbons, J., & Davies, J. Tsui, A., & Crichton, C. (2008). Semantic technologies in electronic government. *Proceedings of the 2nd International Conference on Theory and Practice of Electronic Governance. ACM International Conference Proceedings*, Cairo, Egypt, 351, (pp. 45-51).

Harvard Business Press. (2009). *SWOT analysis II: Looking inside for strengths and weaknesses*. Cambridge, MA: Harvard Business School Press.

Hassan, S., & Gil-Garcia, J. R. (2008). Institutional theory and e-government research. In Garson, G. D., & Khosrow-Pour, M. (Eds.), *Handbook of research on public Information Technology* (pp. 349–360). Hershey, PA: IGI Global. doi:10.4018/978-1-59904-857-4.ch034

Hatzivassiloglou, V., & McKeown, K. R. (1997). Predicting the semantic orientation of adjectives. In *Proceedings of the 35th Annual Meeting of the Association for Computational Linguistics and the 8th Conference on European Chapter of the ACL*, (pp. 174-181).

Hatzivassiloglou, V., & Wiebe, J. (2000). Effects of adjective orientation and gradability on sentence subjectivity. In *Proceedings of the Conference on Computational Linguistics* (COLING-2000).

Hayat, A., Macaulay, L., & Zhao, L. (2009). A collaboration pattern language for e-participation: A strategy for reuse. *Proceedings of the 9th European Conference on e-Government*, (pp. 29-39).

Headlines, E. R. P. 2010, *High profile government ERP software failures continue*, Retrieved on February 10, 2010, from http:// www.erpheadlines.com/ government_erp_software.htm

Heeks, R. (2000). The approach of senior public officials to information technology related reform: Lessons from India. *Public Administration and Development*, *20*, 197–205. doi:10.1002/1099-162X(200008)20:3<197::AID-PAD109>3.0.CO;2-6

Heeks, R. (2001). *Reinventing government in the information age: International practice in IT-enabled public sector reform*. London, UK/New York, NY: Routledge.

Heeks, R. (2002a). E-government in Africa: Promise and practice. *Information Polity*, *7*, 97–114.

Heeks, R. (2002b). Information Systems and developing countries: Failure, success, and local improvisations. *The Information Society*, *18*, 101–112. doi:10.1080/01972240290075039

Heeks, R. (2002). Information Systems and Developing Countries: Failure, Success, and Local Improvisations. *The Information Society*, *18*(2), 101–112. doi:10.1080/01972240290075039

Heeks, R. (1999). E-government as a carrier of context. *Journal of Public Policy*, *25*(1), 51–74. doi:10.1017/S0143814X05000206

Heeks, R. (2006). Health Information Systems: Failure, success. *International Journal of Medical Informatics*, *75*, 125–137. doi:10.1016/j.ijmedinf.2005.07.024

Heeks, R., & Stanforth, C. (2007). Understanding e-government project: Trajectories from an actor-network perspective. *European Journal of Information Systems*, *16*, 165–177. doi:10.1057/palgrave.ejis.3000676

Heeks, R. (2003). Most e-government-for-development projects fail: How can risks be reduced? In Heeks, R. (Ed.), *iGovernment working paper series*. Manchester, UK: Institute for Development Policy and Management, University of Manchester.

Heeks, R., & Bhatnagar, S. (2001). Understanding success and failure in information age reform. In Heeks, R. (Ed.), *Re-inventing Government in the information age: International practice in IT-enabled public sector reform* (pp. 49–74). London, New York: Routledge.

Heeks, R. (1999). Reinventing government in the information age. In Heeks, R. (Ed.), *International practice in IT-enabled public sector reform*. New York, NY: Routledge Publishing. doi:10.4324/9780203204962

Heeks, R. (2001). *Understanding e-governance for development*. The University of Manchester, Institute for Development, Policy and Management Information Systems, Technology and Government: Working Papers Series, Number 12/2001. Retrieved from http:// idpm.man.ac.uk/ idpm/ igov11abs.htm

Heeks, R. (2008). *Success and failure in e-government projects*. Retrieved on January 28, 2008, from http:// www.egov4dev.org/ success/ definitions.shtml

Heeks, R., & Bailur, S. (2006). Analysing eGovernment Research: Perspectives, Philosophies, Theories, Methods, and Practice. *iGovernment Working Paper Series*, Paper No. 16.

Heffernan, V. (2008, November 16). Clicking and choosing: The election according to YouTube. *The New York Times Magazine*.

Heijden, H. d. (2003). Making the policy dialogue more effective: What the development co-operation record suggests. In Olsson, J., & Wohlgemuth, L. (Eds.), *Dialogue in pursuit of development* (pp. 78–106). Expert Group in Development Studies.

Held, D. (1987). *Models of participation*. Cambridge, UK: Polity Press.

Held, D. (1996). *Models of Democracy*. Cambridge, UK: Blackwell Publishers.

Herborn, T., & Wimmer, M. A. (2006). Process ontologies facilitating interoperability in e-government: A methodological framework. In K. Hinkelmann, D. Karagiannis, N. Stojanovic, & G. Wagner (Eds.), *Proceeding of the Workshop on Semantics for Business Process Management at the 3rd European Semantic Web Conference 2006*, Budva, Montenegro, June 2006, (pp. 76–89).

Herbrecther, S., & Higgins, M. (Eds.). (2006). *Returning (to) communities: Theory, culture and political practice of the communal*. Amsterdam, The Netherlands/New York, NY: Rodopi.

Hermes Project. (2009). *Website*. Retrieved from http:// www.ermis.gov.gr

Herriot, R. E., & Firestone, W. A. (1983). Multi-site qualitative policy research: Optimising description and generalisability. *Educational Researcher*, *12*, 14–19.

Higgo, H. A. (2003). Implementing an Information System in a large LDC bureaucracy: The case of the Sudanese Ministry of Finance. *Electronic Journal of Information Systems in Developing Countries*, *14*(3), 1–13.

Ho, A. T. (2002). Reinventing local governments and the e-government initiative. *Public Administration Review*, *62*(4), 434–444. doi:10.1111/0033-3352.00197

Ho, K. K. W. (2007). The e-government development, IT strategies, and portals of the Hong Kong Sar government. Hershey, PA: Idea Group Publishing. Retrieved from http:// www.infosci-journals.com/ downloadPDF/ pdf/ ITJ3596_RAF9OKgFC6.pdf

Homburg, V. (2008). *Understanding e-government: Information Systems in public administration*. Abingdon, UK: Routledge.

Homer, J., Sterman, J., Greenwood, B., & Perkola, M. (1993). Delivery time reduction in pulp and paper mill construction projects: A dynamic analysis of alternatives. *Proceedings of the 1993 International System Dynamics Conference*, Cancun, Mexico.

Hood, C. (2000). Paradoxes of public-sector managerialism, old public management and public service bargains. *International Public Management Journal*, *3*(1), 1–22. doi:10.1016/S1096-7494(00)00032-5

Hope, K. R. (2001). The new public management: context and practice in Africa. *International Public Management Journal*, *4*, 119–134. doi:10.1016/S1096-7494(01)00053-8

Hubaux, J.-P., Buttyan, L., & Capkun, S. (2001). The quest for security in mobile ad hoc networks. In *Proc. of ACM International Symposium on Mobile ad-hoc networking and computing* (pp. 146-155). New York, NY: ACM Press.

Hughes, G. (2003) Local & regional models for broadband deployment. In *Proceedings of eEurope: Broadband Local & Regional Best Practises Workshop*. Retrieved August 4, 2010, from http:// ec.europa.eu/ information_society/ eeurope/ 2005/ doc/ all_about/ broadband/ bb_regional /g_hughes.ppt

Hwang, S. D., Choi, Y., & Myeong, S. H. (1999). Electronic government in South Korea: Conceptual problems. *Government Information Quarterly*, *16*(3), 277–285. doi:10.1016/S0740-624X(99)80028-8

i2010 EUROPA. (2005). *A European information society for growth and employment*. Communication from the Commission to the European Parliament, the Council, the EESC and the Committee of the Regions, Brussels, COM.

Iacovou, C., Benbasat, I., & Dexter, A. (1995). Electronic data interchange and small organisations – Adopting and impact of technology. *Management Information Systems Quarterly*, *19*(4), 465–485. doi:10.2307/249629

ICTC. (2010), *Human resource tools, Information and Communication Technology Council*, Retrieved on February 11, 2010, from http:// www.ictc-ctic.ca/ en

IDABC. (2007). *Preliminary study on mutual recognition of e-signatures for e-government applications*. Retrieved March 4, 2010, from http://ec.europa.eu/idabc/servlets/ Doc?id=29484

IEA. (2006). *Second Information Technology in education study 2006*. Retrieved from http:// www.iea.nl/ sites20060.html

Intalio Enterprise Cloud Company. (2009). *Intalio BPM open source business process platform*. Intalio Incorporation. Retrieved August 2009 from http:// ww.intalio.com/ products/ bpm/

Intelcities, I. S. T. Project. (2006). *Intelligent cities*. 6th Framework Programme, IST-2004-507860, Retrieved from http:// intelcities.iti.gr/ intelcities

Interoperable Delivery of European eGovernment Services to public Administrations Businesses and Citizens (IDABC). (2007).*The IDABC programme* (2005-2009). Retrieved from http:// europa.eu/ legislation_summaries/ information_society/ l24147b_en.htm

Intersystems, (2010), *Brazilian government agency completes an integrated resource planning system*, Retrieved February 11, 2010, from http:// www.intersystems.com/ casestudies/ ensemble/ ati.html

Irani, Z., Elliman, T., & Jackson, P. (2007). Electronic transformation of government in the UK: A research agenda. *European Journal of Information Systems*, *16*, 327–335. doi:10.1057/palgrave.ejis.3000698

Irani, Z., & Love, P. E. D. (2001). The propagation of technology management taxonomies for evaluating investments in manufacturing resource planning (MRPII). *Journal of Management Information Systems, 17*(3), 161–177.

Irani, Z., Love, P. E. D., Elliman, T., Jones, S., & Themistocleous, M. (2005). Evaluating e-government: Learning from the experiences of two UK local authorities. *Information Systems Journal, 15*, 61–82. doi:10.1111/j.1365-2575.2005.00186.x

Irani, Z., Al-Sebie, M., & Elliman, T. (2006). Transaction stage of e-government systems: Identification of its location & importance. *Proceedings of the 39th Hawaii International Conference on System Sciences (HICSS-39)*, Hawaii.

IUCN/UNEP/WWF. (1991). *Caring for the Earth: A strategy for sustainable living*. Gland, Switzerland: IUCN-The World Conservation Union.

Jacucci, E., Shaw, V., & Braa, J. (2006). Standardization of health information systems in South Africa: The challenge of local sustainability. *Information Technology for Development, 12*(3), 225–239. doi:10.1002/itdj.20044

Jaeger, P. T. (2003). The endless wire: E-government as a global phenomenon. *Government Information Quarterly, 20*(4), 323–331. doi:10.1016/j.giq.2003.08.003

James, G. (2000). Empowering bureaucrats. *MC Technology Marketing Intelligence, 20*(12), 62–68.

Janssen, M., Joha, A., & Weerakkody, V. (2007). Shared service arrangements in the public sector: An exploratory study. *Transforming Government: People, Process and Policy, 1*(3), 271–284.

Janssen, M. (2009). *Orchestrating networks for integrated service delivery.* ICEGEG 2009. Ankara, Turkey.

Janssen, M., & Cresswell, A. (2005). *Enterprise architecture integration in e-government*. 38th Hawaii International Conference on System Sciences, Hawaii, (pp. 1-10).

Jenkins, R. (2007). *K*. Athens, Greece: Savalas. (in Greek)

Jensen, C., & Potts, C. (2004). *Privacy policies as decision-making tools: An evaluation of online privacy notices.* Paper presented at the Conference on Human Factors in Computing Systems. Vienna, Austria.

Jeston, J., & Nelis, J. (2008). *Business process management, 2nd edition: Practical guidelines to successful implementation*. Butterworth-Heinemann Publishing

Jian-Tao, S., Xuanhui, W., Dou, S., Hua-Jun, Z., & Zheng, C. (2006). *CWS: A comparative Web search system.* In International Conference on World Wide Web (WWW), 2006. [REMOVED HYPERLINK FIELD]

Johne, A., & Storey, C. (1998). New service development: A review of the literature and annotated bibliography. *European Journal of Marketing, 32*(3-4), 184–251. doi:10.1108/03090569810204526

Johnson, O. A., & King, S. F. (2005). *Best practice in local e-government: A process modelling approach*. e-Government Workshop (Egov05), (pp. 1-14).

Josang, A. (1996). The right type of trust for distributed systems. In *Proc. of New Security Paradigms Workshop*, (pp. 119-131). New York, NY: ACM Press.

Joshi, J., & Ghafoor, A. (2001). Digital government security infrastructure design challenges. *IEEE Computer, 34*(1), 66–72.

JRC EC. (2009). The impact of social computing on the EU information society and economy.

Kahai, S., Fjermestad, J., Zhang, S., & Avolio, B. J. (2007). Leadership in virtual teams: Past, present, and future. *International Journal of e-Collaboration, 3*(1), 1–8.

Kaler, C., & McIntosh, M. (2009). *Web services federation language (WS-Federation) version 1.2: Advancing open standards for the information society*. OASIS Standard.

Kallinikos, J. (2004). Farewell to constructivism: Technology and context-embedded action. In Avgerou, C., Ciborra, C., & Land, F. (Eds.), *The social study of information and communication technology: Innovation, actors, and contexts* (pp. 140–161). Oxford, UK: Oxford University Press.

Kalloniatis, C. (2004). Security requirements engineering for e-government applications: Analysis of current frameworks. *Proceedings of the Electronic Government: Third International Conference, EGOV 2004*, Zaragoza, Spain. (LNCS 3183, p. 66). Springer-Verlag.

Kamal, M. M. (2006). IT innovation adoption in the government sector: Identifying the critical success factors. *Journal of Enterprise Information Management, 19*(2), 192–222. doi:10.1108/17410390610645085

Kamal, M. M. (2009). A multiple case study on integrating IT infrastructures in the public sector. *International Journal of Electronic Government Research, 5*(3), 1–20. doi:10.4018/jegr.2009070101

Kamal, M. M., & Alsudairi, M. (2009). Investigating the importance of factors influencing integration technologies adoption in local government authorities. *Transforming Government: People, Process and Policy, 3*(3), 302–331.

Kamal, M. M. (2008). *Investigating enterprise application integration adoption in the local government authorities*. PhD Thesis, Department of Information Systems and Computing, Brunel University, London, UK.

Kamal, M. M., Themistocleous, M., & Elliman, T. (2008). Extending IT infrastructures in LGAs through EAI. *Proceedings of the 14th Americas Conference on Information Systems*, Toronto, Canada, (pp. 1-12).

Kamal, M. M., Themistocleous, M., & Morabito, V. (2009). Justifying the decisions for EAI adoption in LGAs: A validated proposition of factors, adoption lifecycle phases, mapping and prioritisation of factors. *Proceedings of the 42nd Hawaii International Conference on System Sciences*, Hilton Kaikoloa Village Resort, Hawaii, (pp. 1-10).

Kamvar, S. D., Schlosser, M. T., & Garcia-Molina, H. (2003). The Eigentrust algorithm for reputation management in p2p networks. In *Proc. 12th International Conference on World Wide Web* (pp. 640-651). New York, NY: ACM Press.

Kanat, İ. K., & Ozkan, S. (2009). Exploring citizens' perception of government to citizen services: A model based on theory of planned behaviour (TBP). *Transforming Government: People, Process and Policy, 3*(4), 406–419.

Karacapilidis, N., Loukis, E., & Dimopoulos, S. (2005). Computer-supported G2G collaboration for public policy and decision making. *Journal of Enterprise Information Management, 18*(5), 602–624. doi:10.1108/17410390510624034

Karacapilidis, N., & Papadias, D. (2001). Computer supported argumentation and collaborative decision making: The HERMES system. *Information Systems, 26*(4), 259–277. doi:10.1016/S0306-4379(01)00020-5

Karantjias, A., & Polemi, N. (2009). An innovative platform architecture for complex, secure e/m-Governmental services. *International Journal of Electronic Security and Digital Forensics (IJESDF). Special Issue in Mobile Services Technological and Legal Issues, 2*(4), 338–354.

Karantjias, A., Polemi, N., Stamati, T., & Martakos, D. (2009). A user-centric & federated single-sign-in IAM system for SOA e/m-frameworks. *International Journal of Electronic Government (IJEG), Special Issue on Usability and Privacy Issues in Electronic and Mobile Government, 7*(3).

Katz, M. (2000). Regulation: The next 1000 years. In R. M. Entman (Ed.), *Six degrees of competition: Correlating regulation with the telecommunications marketplace*. A Report of the Fourteenth Annual Aspen Institute Conference on Telecommunications Policy. The Aspen Institute, Washington.

Keceli, Y., & Choi, H. R. (2008). Level of Information Systems in Turkish public ports and direction of improvement. *International Journal of. Logistics Systems and Management, 4*(6), 673–691. doi:10.1504/IJLSM.2008.019185

KEDKE. (n.d.). *Central Union of Municipalities and Communities of Greece*. Retrieved from http://www.kedke.gr/

Kernaghan, K. (2008). *Integrating service delivery: Barriers and benchmarks*. Toronto, Canada: Institute for Citizen-Centred Service.

Kerr, D. (2003). Citizenship: Local, national and international. In Gearon, L. (Ed.), *Learning to teach ctizenship in the secondary school* (pp. 7–8). London, UK: Routledge.

Kevin, K. W. H. O. 2007. The E-Government Development, it Strategies, and portals of the hong Kong Sar Government. *IDEA GROUP PUBLISHING*, Available at: http:// www.infosci-journals.com/ downloadPDF/ pdf/ ITJ3596_RAF9OKgFC6.pdf

Khoshafian, S. (2006). *Service oriented enterprises* (1st ed.). Auerbach Publishing. doi:10.1201/9781420013269

Khoumbati, K., Themistocleous, M., & Irani, Z. (2006). Evaluating the adoption of enterprise application integration in healthcare organisations. *Journal of Management Information Systems*, *22*(4), 69–108. doi:10.2753/MIS0742-1222220404

Kidd, T. T., & Chen, I. L. (Eds.). (2009). *Wired for learning: An educator's guide to Web 2.0*. USA: Information Age Publishing.

Kim, D. J., Song, Y. I., Braynov, S. B., & Rao, H. R. (2005). A multidimensional trust formation model in B-to-C e-commerce: A conceptual framework and content analyses of academia/practitioner perspectives. *Decision Support Systems*, *40*, 143–165. doi:10.1016/j.dss.2004.01.006

Kim, H. J., & Bretschneider, S. (2004). Local government Information Technology capacity: An exploratory theory. *Proceedings of the 37th Annual Hawaii International Conference on System Sciences*, (pp. 121-130).

Kim, S. T. (2008). *Converging e-democracy and e-government model toward an evolutionary model of e-governance: The case of South Korea*. Retrieved from http:// www.apdip.net/ projects/ e-government/ capblg/ casestudies/ Korea-Kim.pdf

Kimaro, H. C., & Nhampossa, J. L. (2005). Analyzing the problem of unsustainable health Information Systems in less-developed economies: Case studies from Tanzania and Mozambique. *Information Technology for Development*, *11*(3), 273–298. doi:10.1002/itdj.20016

Kimaro, H. C., & Sahay, S. (2007). An institutional perspective on the process of decentralisation of health Information Systems: A case study from Tanzania. *Information Technology for Development*, *13*(4), 363–390. doi:10.1002/itdj.20066

King, W. R., & He, J. (2006). A meta-analysis of the technology acceptance model. *Information & Management*, *43*(6), 740–755. doi:10.1016/j.im.2006.05.003

Kirkpatrick, G. (2004). *Critical technology: A social theory of personal computing*. Aldershot, UK & Burlington, VT: Ashgate Publishing.

Kirsch, F., & von Hirschhausen, C. (2008). Regulation of next generation networks: Structural separation, access regulation, or no regulation at all? *Communications & Strategies*, *69*, 63–85.

Kling, R. (2000). Learning about Information Technologies and social change: The contribution of social informatics. *The Information Society*, *16*(3), 217–232. doi:10.1080/01972240050133661

Koh, C. E., Prybutok, V. R., Ryan, S., & Ibragimova, B. (2006). The importance of strategic readiness in an emerging e-government environment. *Business Process Management Journal*, *12*(1), 22–33. doi:10.1108/14637150610643733

Kolbitsch, J., & Maurer, H. (2006). The transformation of the Web: How emerging communities shape the information we consume. *Journal of Universal Computer Science*, *12*(2). doi:.doi:10.3217/jucs-012-02-0187

Kondo, S. (2001). *Fostering dialogue to good government: Public sector transparency and accountability – Making it happen* (pp. 7–11). OECD.

Konstantinou, E., Liagkou, V., Spirakis, P., Stamatiou, Y., & Yung, M. (2004). Electronic national lotteries. In A. Juels (Ed.), *8th International Conference on Financial Cryptography* (pp.147-163). Berlin/Heidelberg, Germany: Springer.

Konstantinou, E., Liagkou, V., Spirakis, P., Stamatiou, Y., & Yung, M. (2005). Trust engineering: From requirements to system design and maintenance – A working national lottery system experience. In J. Zhou, J. Lopez, R. H. Deng, & F. Bao, (Eds.), *8th International Conference on Information Security* (pp.44-58). Berlin/Heidelberg, Germany: Springer.

Kontogiannopoulou-Polydoridi, G. (2005). *Η δημοκρατία, ο πολίτης και οι "άλλοι": πολιτισμική οικείωση της κοινωνικής και πολιτικής εκπαίδευσης/επιμέλεια*. Athens, Greece: Gutenberg. (in greek)

Korea Communication Commission. (2010). *Important issues*. Retrieved March 1, 2010, from http:// eng.kcc.go.kr/ user.do?page=E02010100&dc=E02010100

Koussouris, S., Tsitsanis, A., Gionis, G., & Psarras, J. (2008). Designing generic municipal services process models towards e-government interoperability infrastructures. *Electronic Journal for E-Commerce Tools and Applications, eJETA Special Issue on Interoperability for Enterprises and Administrations Worldwide.*

Kraemer, K. L., & Dedrick, J. (1997). Computing and public organizations. *Journal of Public Administration: Research and Theory*, *7*(1), 89–112.

Kraemer, K. L., & King, J. L. (2006). Information Technology and administrative reform: Will the time after e-government be different? *International Journal of Electronic Government Research*, *2*(1), 1–20. doi:10.4018/jegr.2006010101

Krishna, S., & Walsham, G. (2005). Implementing public Information Systems in developing countries: Learning from a success story. *Information Technology for Development*, *11*(2), 123–140. doi:10.1002/itdj.20007

Krueger, A. O. (2003). *Address on globalization at the Seventh St. Petersburg International Economic Forum*. IMF External Relations Dept.

Ku, L. W., & Chen, H. H. (2007). Mining opinions from the Web: Beyond relevance retrieval source. *Journal of the American Society for Information Science and Technology*, *58*(12). doi:10.1002/asi.20630

Kubo, S., & Shimada, T. (2007). Local e-governments in Japan: IT utilization status and directions. In Al-Hakim, L. (Ed.), *Global e-government theory, applications and benchmarking* (pp. 300–318). Hershey, PA: Idea Group Publishing.

Kubo, S., & Shimada, T. (2008a). An analysis based on the manufacturing architecture of the computerization of local governments in Japan. *CONF-IRM 2008 Proceedings*.

Kubo, S., & Shimada, T. (2008b). Model presenting the stages of progress of administrative services provided by e-local governments. *ICBI 2008 Proceeding*.

Kumar, R. (2006). Impact and sustainability of e-government services in developing countries: Lessons learned from Tamil Nadu, India. *The Information Society*, *22*, 1–12. doi:10.1080/01972240500388149

Kumar, (2007). Factors for successful e-government adoption: A conceptual framework. *Electronic Journal of E-Government*, *5*(1), 63–76.

Kumar, R., & Best, M. (2006). Social impact and diffusion of telecenter use: A study from the sustainable access in rural India project. *Journal of Community Informatics*, *2*, 3.

Kunstelj, M., & Vintar, M. (2004). Evaluating the progress of e-government development: A critical analysis. *Information Polity*, *9*, 131–148.

Kunz, W., & Rittel, H. (1979). *Issues as elements of Information Systems*. Working Paper No. 131. California, USA: Berkley. Retrieved from http://www-iurd.ced.berkeley.edu/pub/WP-131.pdf

Kyriakidou, V., Chipouras, A., Katsianis, D., & Sphicopoulos, T. (2009). Business models for municipal metro networks: Theoretical and financial analysis. In Chochliouros, I. P. (Ed.), *Optical access networks and advanced photonics: Technologies and deployment strategies*. Hershey, PA: IGI Global. doi:10.4018/978-1-60566-707-2.ch010

Lai, K. H., Ngai, E. W. T., & Cheng, T. C. E. (2005). Information Technology adoption in Hong Kong's logistics industry. *Transportation Journal*, *44*(4), 1–9.

Laister, J., & Koubek, A. (2001). 3rd generation learning platforms. Requirements and motivation for collaborative learning. *EURODL – European Journal of Open and Distance Learning*. Retrieved from http:// www.eurodl.org/ ?p=archives&year=2001&article=54

Lam, P.-K., & Chin, K.-S. (2005). Identifying and prioritizing critical success factors for conflict management in collaborative new product development. *Industrial Marketing Management*, *34*, 761–772. doi:10.1016/j.indmarman.2004.12.006

Lam, W. (2005). Barriers to e-government integration. *Journal of Enterprise Information Management*, *18*(5), 511–530. doi:10.1108/17410390510623981

Lam, W. (2005). Investigating success factors in enterprise application integration: A case driven analysis. *European Journal of Information Systems*, *14*(2), 175–187. doi:10.1057/palgrave.ejis.3000530

Lambert, S. C., Arenas, A. E., Delaitre, S., Mena Raposo, J., Ferrentino, P., Majewska, M., et al. Procopio, V. (2004). A framework for experience management in e-government: The Pellucid Project. In F. Bannister (Ed.), *Electronic Journal of e-Government, 2*(3), 167-176. Academic Conferences Limited.

Lambo, E., & Sambo, L. G. (2003). Health sector reform in sub-Saharan Africa: A synthesis of country experiences. *East African Medical Journal*, *80*(6), 1–20.

Lambrinoudakis, C., Gritzalis, S., Dridi, F., & Pernul, G. (2003). Security requirements for e-government services: A methodological approach for developing a common PKI-based security policy. *Computer Communications*, *26*(16), 1873–1883. doi:10.1016/S0140-3664(03)00082-3

Landolt, L. K. (2004). (Mis)constructing the third world? Constructivist analysis of norm diffusion. *Third World Quarterly*, *25*(3), 579–591. doi:10.1080/0143659042000191447

Lanzara, G. F. (2009). Building digital institutions: ICT and the rise of assemblages in government. In Contini, F., & Lanzara, G. F. (Eds.), *ICT and innovation in the public sector: European studies in the making of e-government* (pp. 9–48). Houndmills, UK: Palgrave Macmillan.

Latchem, C., & Walker, D. (2001). *Telecentres: Case studies and key issues*. Vancouver, Canada: The Commonwealth of Learning.

Lau, T. Y., Aboulhoson, M., Lin, C., & Atkin, D. J. (2007). Adoption of e-government in three Latin American countries: Argentina, Brazil and Mexico. *Telecommunications Policy*, *32*(2), 88–100. doi:10.1016/j.telpol.2007.07.007

Laudon, K. C., & Laudon, J. P. (2002). *Management Information Systems: Managing the digital firm* (7th ed.). New Jersey: Prentice Hall.

Lave, J., & Wenger, E. (2005). *Κοινωνικές όψεις της μάθησης, N.* Athens, Greece: Savalas. (in Greek)

Law, J., & Callon, M. (1994). The life and death of an aircraft: A network analysis of technical change. In Bijker, W. E., & Law, J. (Eds.), *Shaping technology / building society: Studies in sociotechnical change* (pp. 21–52). Cambridge, MA: The MIT Press.

LAWs project. (2004). *Local authority websites national project (LAWs)*. Retrieved from http://www.laws-project.org.uk/

Layne, K., & Lee, J. (2001). Developing fully functional e-government: A four-stage model. *Government Information Quarterly*, *18*(2), 122–136. doi:10.1016/S0740-624X(01)00066-1

Lee, H., Ko, K., Jang, S., & Heeks, R. (2008). Analysing South Korea's ICT for development and aid programme. *The Electronic Journal on Information Systems in Developing Countries*, *35*(2), 1–15.

Lee, M., Tan, X., & Trimi, S. (2005). Current practices of leading e-government countries. *Communications of the ACM*, *48*(10), 99. doi:10.1145/1089107.1089112

Lee, Y., Kozar, K. A., & Larsen, K. R. T. (2003). The technology acceptance model: Past, present, and future. *Communications of the Association for Information Systems*, *12*(50), 752–780.

Lee, S., & Treacy, M. E. (1998). Information Technology impacts on innovation. *R & D Management*, *18*(3), 257–271. doi:10.1111/j.1467-9310.1988.tb00592.x

Lee, C. S., Chandrasekaran, R., & Thomas, D. (2003). *Examining IT usage across different hierarchical levels in organisations: A study of organizational, environmental, and IT factors*. 9th Americas Conference on Information Systems, (pp. 1259-1269).

Lee, H., Irani, Z., Osman, I., Balcı, A., Ozkan, S., & Medeni, T. (2008). Research note: Toward a reference process model for citizen-oriented evaluation of e-government services. *Transforming Government: People, Process and Policy*, *2*(4), 297-310.

Legris, P., Ingham, J., & Collerette, P. (2003). Why do people use Information Technology? A critical review of the technology acceptance model. *Information & Management*, *40*(3), 191–204. doi:10.1016/S0378-7206(01)00143-4

Lenk, K., & Traunmüller, R. (2000). A framework for electronic government. *Proceedings of the 11th International Workshop on Database and Expert Systems Applications*, (pp. 340-345).

Lenstra, A. K., & Lenstra, H. W. J. R. (1990). Algorithms in number theory. In van Leeuwen, J. (Ed.), *Handbook of theoretical computer science* (*Vol. A*, pp. 673–715). Amsterdam, The Netherlands: North-Holland.

Letch, N., & Carroll, J. (2008). Excluded again: Implications of integrated e-government systems for those at the margins. *Information Technology & People*, *21*(3), 283–299. doi:10.1108/09593840810896037

Leuf, B., & Cunningham, W. (2001). *The wiki way*. USA: Addison-Wesley.

Leys, C. (1975). *Underdevelopment in Kenya: The political economy of neo-colonialism, 1964-1971*. Heinemann.

LGAF project. (2009). *Local government access framework*. 6th Framework Programme. Retrieved from http:// lgaf.kedke.org/ wiki

Liebowitz, J., & Chen, Y. (2003). Knowledge sharing proficiencies: The key to knowledge management. In Holsapple, C. W. (Ed.), *Handbook on knowledge management 1: Knowledge matters* (pp. 409–424). Berlin, Germany: Springer-Verlag.

Lin, M. (2005). *Digital divide and telecenter development in Taiwan*. Department of Information Management Research, Development, and Evaluation Commission, Taiwan. Retrieved November 15, 2008, from http:// www. rdec.gov.tw/ public/ Data/ 941716305971.pdf

Linthicum, D. (2000). *Enterprise application integration*. Massachusetts, USA: Addison-Wesley.

Ljubica, K., Radulovic, B., Dragic, R., & Zvonko, S. (2008). Web based human resource management system. *Journal of International Research Publication: Materials, Methods & Technologies,* Vol 3, ISSN 1313-8014.

LocalRet. (2009). *Website*. Retrieved July 1, 2010, from http:// www.apd.cat/ media/ 888.pdf

Lockhart, H., & Campbell, B. (2007). *SAML V2.0 errata*. Advancing Open Standards for the Information Society. OASIS Standard.

LoS. (2010), *The management Information System of the Austrian tax and customs administration,* Retrieved on Jyly 3, 2010, from: http:// english.bmf.gv.at/ EGov/ WhatisLoS/ _start.htm

Loukis, E., Wimmer, M., Triantafillou, A., Gatautis, R., & Charalabidis, Y. (2007). *Electronic support of participation in the development of legislation: The LEX-IS project*. Paper presented at the 5th Eastern European eGov Days 2007, 11-13 April, Prague, Czech Republic.

Lowry, T. (2008, June 24). Obama's secret digital weapon. *Business Week*.

Lu, X. R., Wang, Q. R., & Gao, P. P. (2003). Operation and maintenance modes of Qinghai-Tibet railway. *Journal of Southwest Jiaotong University, 38*(1), 60.

Luhmann, N. (1988). Familiarity, confidence, trust: Problems and alternatives. In Gambetta, D. (Ed.), *Trust: Making and breaking cooperative relations* (pp. 94–107). Oxford, UK: Basil Blackwell.

Luna-Reyes, L. F., Gil-Garcia, J. R., & Cruz, C. B. (2007). E-Mexico: Collaborative structures in Mexican public administration. *International Journal of Cases on E-Commerce, 3*(2), 57–74.

Luna-Reyes, L. F., Gil-Garcia, J. R., & Estrada-Marroquín, M. (2008). The impact of institutions on interorganizational IT projects in the Mexican federal government. *International Journal of Electronic Government Research, 4*(2), 27–42. doi:10.4018/jegr.2008040103

Luna-Reyes, L. F., Hernández-García, J. M., & Gil-Garcia, J. R. (2009). Hacia un Modelo de los Determinantes de Éxito de los Portales de Gobierno Estatal en México. *Gestión y Política Pública, XVIII*(2), 307–340.

Luna-Reyes, L. F., Gil-García, J. R., & Cruz, C. B. (2006, August 4-6). *Collaborative digital government in Mexico: Some lessons from federal Web-based inter-organizational information integration initiatives*. Paper presented at the 12th Americas Conference on Information Systems, Acapulco, Mexico.

Luo, M. (2008, December 5). Obama hauls in $ 750 million for campaign, with plenty left to spend. *The New York Times*.

Ma, J., Otten, M., Kamadjeu, R., Mir, R., Rosencrans, L., & McLaughlin, S. (2008). New frontiers for health Information Systems using Epi Info in developing countries: Structured application framework for Epi Info (SAFE). *International Journal of Medical Informatics, 77*(4), 219–225. doi:10.1016/j.ijmedinf.2007.02.001

Ma, Q., & Liu, L. (2004). The technology acceptance model: A meta-analysis of empirical findings. *Journal of Organizational and End User Computing, 16*(1), 59–72. doi:10.4018/joeuc.2004010104

Macintosh, A., Gordon, T. F., & Renton, A. (2009). Providing argument support for e-participation. *Journal of Information Technology & Politics*, *6*, 43–59. doi:10.1080/19331680802662113

Macintosh, A., Malina, A., & Whyte, A. (2002). Designing e-participation in Scotland. *Communications: The European Journal of Communications*, *27*, 261–278.

Macintosh, A. (2004). *Characterizing e-participation in policy making*. Paper presented at the 37th Hawaii International Conference on System Sciences.

Macintsoh, A., & Whyte, A. (2006). Evaluating how e-participation changes local democracy. In Z. Inai & A. Ghoneim (Eds.), *Proceedings of the e-Government Workshop 2006*. London, UK: Brunel University.

MacLeod, H. (2008, June 2). Call them CrackBerries: MPs addicted to their little BlackBerries. *The Hill Times*.

Macome, E. (2008). On implementation of an Information System in the Mozambican context: The EDM case viewed through ANT lenses. *Information Technology for Development*, *14*(2), 154–170. doi:10.1002/itdj.20063

Madon, S., Sahay, S., & Sudan, R. (2007). E-hovernment policy and health Information Systems implementation in Andhra Pradesh, India: Need for articulation of linkages between the macro and the micro. *The Information Society*, *23*, 327–344. doi:10.1080/01972240701572764

Mahapatra, R., & Perumal, S. (2006). E-governance in India: A strategic framework. *International Journal for Infonomics: Special issue on measuring e-business for development.*

Mahmood, M. (2004). Can Information and Communication Technology help reduce corruption? How so and why not: Two case studies from South Asia. [Koninklijke Brill NV, Leiden P.]. *Perspectives on Global Development and Technology*, *3*(3), 347–373. doi:10.1163/1569150042442539

Makedon, F., Sudborough, C., Baiter, B., Pantziou, G., & Conalis-Kontos, M. (2003). *A safe information sharing framework for e-government communication*. Retrieved from http:// www.ists.dartmouth.edu/ library/ sis0903.pdf.2003

Manolopoulos, C., Nakou, P., Panagiotaki, A., Sofotassios, D., Spirakis, P., & Stamatiou, Y. C. (2008b). A step-wise refinement approach for enhancing e-voting acceptance. In T. Janowski, & T. Pardo (Eds.), *2nd International Conference on Theory and Practice of Electronic Governance (ICEGOV 2008),* (pp. 275-280). ACM Press.

Manolopoulos, C., Panagiotaki, A., Sofotassios, D., Spirakis, P., &. Stamatiou, Y. C. (2008a). Experiences and benefits from the application of a formal risk assessment framework in the e-voting domain. In E. Ferro, H. J. Scholl, & M. Wimmer (Eds.), *7th International Conference on Electronic Government (EGOV 2008)* (pp. 205-212). Trauner Verlag.

Mansell, R. (2002). Constructing the knowledge base for knowledge-driven development. *Journal of Knowledge Management*, *6*(4), 317–329. doi:10.1108/13673270210440839

Mansell, R., & Wehn, U. (1998). *Information Technology for sustainable development*. SPRU Research and Oxford University Press.

Mansell, R., & Wehn, U. (1998b). *Information Technology for sustainable development: Friend or foe? Developing countries and the international governance system*. SPRU Research and Oxford University Press.

Mantzana, V., Themistocleous, M., Irani, Z., & Morabito, V. (2007). Identifying healthcare actors involved in the adoption of Information Systems. *European Journal of Information Systems*, *16*(1), 90–102. doi:10.1057/palgrave.ejis.3000660

March, J. G. (1981). Footnotes to organizational change. *Administrative Science Quarterly*, *26*(4), 563–577. doi:10.2307/2392340

Mark, G., Grudin, J., & Poltrock, S. (1999). Meeting at the desktop: An empirical study of virtually collocated teams. In the *Proceedings of the Sixth European Conference on Computer-Supported Cooperative Work*. Norwell, MA: Kluwer Academic Publishers.

Markus, L. (2004). Technochange management: Using IT to drive organisational change. *Journal of Information Technology*, *19*, 4–20. doi:10.1057/palgrave.jit.2000002

Markus, M. L., & Robert, I. B. (1997). The magic bullet theory in IT-enabled transformation. *Sloan Management Review*, *38*(2), 55–68.

Markus, L., & Tanis, C. (1999). The enterprise systems experience – From adoption to success. In Zmud, R. (Ed.), *Framing the domain of IT management: Glimpsing the future through the past* (pp. 173–207). Norman, Oklahoma: Pinnaflex Educational Resources, Inc.

Martin, C. R., & Horne, D. A. (1995). Level of success inputs for service innovations in the same firm. *International Journal of Service Industry Management*, *6*(4), 40–56. doi:10.1108/09564239510096894

Mason, R., & Reenie, F. (2008). *E-learning and social networking handbook: Resources for higher education*. USA: Routledge.

Mason, R. O., Mckenney, J. L., & Copeland, D. G. (1997). Developing an historical tradition in MIS research. *Management Information Systems Quarterly*, *21*(3), 257–278. doi:10.2307/249497

Mathieson, K. (1991). Predicting user intentions: comparing the TAM with the theory of planned behaviour. *Information Systems Research*, *2*(3), 173–191. doi:10.1287/isre.2.3.173

Matthews, S. (2004). Post-development theory and the question of alternatives: A view from Africa. *Third World Quarterly*, *25*(2), 373–384. doi:10.1080/0143659042000174860

Mauher, M., & Smokvina, V. (2006). *Digital to intelligent local government transition framework*. Proceedings MIPRO 2006, (vol. 5, p. 47). Opatija-Croatia.

Mavraganis, G. (1994). Greece: The 1994 tax reform. *European Taxation*, *34*(7), 219–220.

Maylor, H., & Blackmon, K. (2005). *Researching business and management*. New York, NY: Palgrave-Macmillan.

Mbembé, J. A. (2001). *On the postcolony*. University of California Press.

McClure, D. L. (2000). *Government online: Strategies and challenges*. Retrieved February 3, 2005, from http:// www.house.gov/ reform/ gmit/ hearings/ 2000hearings/ 000522dm.htm

McGregor, A., & Latchem, C. (1991). *Networks for learning: A review of access and equity in post-compulsory education in rural and remote areas of the State of Western Australia*. Perth, Australia: Western Australian Office of Higher Education.

McGregor, A. L. (1992). *Networks on trial: An evaluation of the WA learning network centres project. Report commissioned by the Western Australian Higher Education Council*. Perth, WA: Western Australian Office of Higher Education.

McIvor, R., McHugh, M., & Cadden, C. (2002). Internet technologies supporting transparency in the public sector. *International Journal of Public Sector Management*, *15*(3), 170–187. doi:10.1108/09513550210423352

McNamara, K. S. (2003). *Information and Communication Technologies, poverty and development: Learning from experience*. Paper presented at the infoDev Annual Symposium, December 9-10, 2003.

McNeal, R., Hale, K., & Dotterweich, L. (2008). Citizen-government interaction and the Internet: Expectations and accomplishments in contact, quality and trust. *Journal of Information Technology & Politics*, *5*(2), 213–229. doi:10.1080/19331680802298298

Means, G., & Schneider, D. (2000). *Meta-capitalism: The e-business revolution and the design of 21st century companies and markets*. New York, NY: John Wiley & Sons Inc.

Mecella, M., & Batini, C. (2001). Enabling Italian e-government through a cooperative architecture. *IEEE Computer*, *34*(2), 40–45.

Medjahed, B. (2003). Business-to-business interactions: Issues and enabling technologies. *The VLDB Journal*, *12*(1), 59–85. doi:10.1007/s00778-003-0087-z

Melin, U., & Axelsson, K. (2009). Managing e-service development – A comparative e-government case study. *Transforming Government: People, Process and Policy*, *3*(3), 248–270.

Mercuri, R. (2007). *Rebecca Mercuri's statement on electronic voting*. Retrieved from http:// www.notable-software.com/ RMstatement.html

Miles, M., & Huberman, A. (1994). *Qualitative data analysis: An expanded sourcebook*. Newbury Park, CA: Sage.

Millard, J. (2007). *E-governance and e-participation: Lessons from Europe in promoting inclusion and empowerment.* Report of the Ad Hoc Expert Group Meeting, E-Participation and E-Government: Understanding the Present and Creating the Future (pp. 91-113). Retrieved from http:// unpan1.un.org/ intradoc/ groups/ public/ documents/ un/ unpan026527.pdf

Millard, J., Warren, R., Leitner, C., & Shahin, J. (2006). *EU: Towards the e-government vision for the EU in 2010.* Report for the European Commission, Draft Final Report. Retrieved from http:// fiste.jrc.ec.europa.eu/ pages/ documents/ eGovresearchpolicychallenges-DRAFTFINALWEBVERSION.pdf

Millward, P. (2003). The grey digital divide: Perception, exclusion and barriers of access to the Internet for older people. *First Monday*, *8*(7).

Milne, G., & Culnan, M. (2002). Using the content of online privacy notices to inform public policy: A longitudinal analysis of the 1998-2001 U.S. Web surveys. *The Information Society*, *18*, 345–359. doi:10.1080/01972240290108168

Mindlin, A. (2009, January 5). Web passes papers as a news source. *The New York Times*.

Ministry of Health. (1994). *National health policy framework.* Nairobi, Kenya: Ministry of Health, Republic of Kenya.

Ministry of Health. (2005). *The second national health sector strategic plan 2005-2010 (NHSS II).* Nairobi, Kenya: Ministry of Health, Republic of Kenya.

Mioga 2. (2004). *Mioga 2 groupware solution: Collaborative work, shared organizers*. Retrieved from http:// www.mioga2.org

Mirvis, P., & Googins, B. (2006). Stages of corporate citizenship. *California Management Review*, *48*(2), 104–126.

Mischen, P., & Jackson, S. (2008). Connecting the dots: Applying complexity theory, knowledge management and social network analysis to policy implementation. *Public Administration Quarterly*, *32*(3), 314–339.

Mises, L. v. (1985). *Liberalism in the classical tradition.* New York, NY /San Francisco, CA: The Foundation for Economic Education, Inc./Cobden Press.

Misra, D. C., Hariharan, R., & Khaneja, M. (2003). E-knowledge management framework for government organizations. *Information Systems Management*, *20*(2), 38–48. doi:10.1201/1078/43204.20.2.20030301/41469.7

Mittal, P. A., Kumar, M., Mohania, M. K., Nair, M., Batra, N., & Roy, P. … Yagnik, L. (2004). A framework for e-governance solutions. IBM Journal of Research and Development, 48(5/6). IBM Research in Asia. Retrieved from www.research.ibm.com/ journal

MMBase. (2006). *MMBase relational object mapping tool*. Retrieved from http:// www.mmbase.org/

Montagna, J. M. (2005). A framework for the assessment and analysis of electronic government proposals. *Electronic Commerce Research and Applications*, *4*(3), 204–219. doi:10.1016/j.elerap.2005.01.003

Moon, M. J. (2002). The evolution of e-government among municipalities: Rhetoric or reality. *Public Administration Review*, *62*(4), 424–433. doi:10.1111/0033-3352.00196

Moon, M. J. (2002). The evolution of e-government among municipalities: Rhetoric or reality? *Public Administration Review*, *62*(4), 424–433. doi:10.1111/0033-3352.00196

Mouzelis, N. P. (1978). *Modern Greece: Facets of underdevelopment*. London, UK: Macmillan Press.

Mouzelis, N. P. (2008). *Modern and postmodern social theorizing: Bridging the divide*. Cambridge, UK: Cambridge University Press.

Mouzelis, N. P. (1995). Greece in the twenty-first century: Institutions and political culture. In Constas, D., & Stavrou, T. G. (Eds.), *Greece prepares for the twenty-first century* (pp. 17–34). Washington, DC: The Woodrow Wilson Center Press.

Mowlana, H. (1997). *Global information and world communication: New frontiers in international relations* (2nd ed.). Sage Publications.

Mudimbe, V. Y. (1988). *The invention of Africa: Gnosis, philosophy, and the order of knowledge*. Bloomington & Indianapolis, IN/London, UK: Indiana University Press/ James Currey.

Mudimbe, V. Y. (2003). Globalization and African identity. *CR (East Lansing, Mich.)*, *3*(2), 205–218.

Mueller, M. L., Kuerbis, B. N., & Pagé, C. (2007). Democratizing global communication? Global civil society and the campaign for communication rights in the information society. *International Journal of Communication*, *1*, 267–296.

Mukherjee, A., & Biswas, A. (2005). Simple implementation framework for m-government services. In *Proceedings of the International Conference on Mobile Business* (ICMG'05). IEEE, (pp. 288-293).

Mullen, H., & Horner, D. S. (2004). Ethical problems for e-government: An evaluative framework. *Electronic Journal of E-Government*, *2*(3), 187–196.

Munck, R. (2000). Deconstructing development discourses: Of impasses, alternatives and politics. In Munck, R., & O'Hearn, D. (Eds.), *Critical development theory: Contributions to a new paradigm*. London, UK: Zed Books.

Munkvold, B. E. (2003). *Implementing collaboration technologies in industry: Case examples and lessons learned*. London, UK: Springer-Verlag.

Muñoz, S. S., Macdonald, A., & Mollenkamp, C. (2009). U.K., U.S. expand bank rescue bids. *The Wall Street Journal*.

Munyua, A. W. (2005). New generation of policy development: The case of multi-stakeholder ICT policy process in Kenya. *Information Technology in Developing Countries*, *15*(1), 2–9.

Mutahaba, G., & Kiragu, K. (2002). Lessons of International and African Perspectives on Public Service Reform: Examples from Five African Countries. *Africa Development. Afrique et Developpement*, *27*(3-4), 48–75.

Mutt, N. (2009), Benefits of enterprise resource planning software (ERP), *Ezine Articles*, Retrieved February 12, 2010, from http:// ezinearticles.com/ ?Benefits-of-Enterprise-Resource-Planning-Software-(ERP)&id=2823574

Mwega, F. M. (2009). *A case study of aid effectiveness in Kenya: Volatility and fragmentation of foreign aid, with a focus on health.* Wolfensohn Center for Development Working Papers no. 8, Washington, DC: The Brookings Institution.

Nadalin, A., Goodner, M., Gudgin, M., Barbir, A., & Granqvist, H. (2009). *WS-trust 1.4. Advancing Open Standards for the Information Society*. OASIS Standard.

Nanjing, J. (2009), Research on economic benefit from ERP-Evidence from Y Software Company's users, In: *First IEEE International Conference on Information Science and Engineering*, December 26- 28, 2009, Nanjing, Jiangsu China.

National AIDS Control Council. (2000). *The Kenya national HIV/AIDS strategic plan 2000-2005*. Nairobi, Kenya: National AIDS Control Council, Republic of Kenya.

National Institute of Standards and Technology. (2002). *Computer Security Resource Center*. Retrieved on February 26, 2010 at http://csrc.nist.gov/groups/SMA/fisma/overview.html

National Research Council. (2002). *Information Technology research, innovation, and e-government*. Washington, DC: National Academy Press.

Navarra, D., & Cornford, T. (2003). *A policy making view of e-government innovations in public governance.* Paper presented at the 9th Americas Conference on Information Systems (AMCIS 2003), Tampa, FL, USA

Ndlovu-Gatsheni, S. J. (2007). *Giving Africa voice within global governance: Oral history, human rights and the United Nations (UN) Human Rights Council*. Leiden, The Netherlands: African Studies Centre.

Ndou, V. (2004). E-government for developing countries: Opportunities and challenges. *Electronic Journal of Information Systems in Developing Countries*, *18*(1), 1–24.

Neumann, L., & Benda, P. (2005). Open ICT e-government architecture as an interoperability framework, *Proceedings, 5th European Conference on E-Government*, University of Antwerp, Belgium, (pp. 585-598).

Neumann, P. G. (2004). The problems and potentials of voting systems. *Communications of the ACM, Special Issue on eVoting, 47*(10).

New Zealand Government. (2009). *Broadband investment initiative.* Retrieved March 1, 2010, from http:// www.med.govt.nz/ upload/ 63958/ Final-broadband-initiative-consultation-document.pdf

Ngai, E. W. T., & Gunasekaran, A. (2004). Implementation of EDI in Hong Kong: An empirical analysis. *Industrial Management & Data Systems*, *104*(1), 88–100. doi:10.1108/02635570410514124

Njihia, J. M. (2008). *ICT for Development reconsidered: A critical realist approach to the strategic context in Kenya's transition to e-governance.* Unpublished PhD thesis University of Warwick, Coventry, UK.

Noir, C., & Walsham, G. (2007). The great legitimizer: ICT as myth and ceremony in the Indian healthcare sector. *Information Technology & People, 20*(4), 313–333. doi:10.1108/09593840710839770

Nonaka, I. (1994). A dynamic theory of organizational knowledge creation. *Organization Science, 5*(1), 14–37. doi:10.1287/orsc.5.1.14

Nordfors, L., Ericson, B., Lindell, H., & Lapidus, J. (2009). *E-government of tomorrow - Future scenarios for 2020.* Gullers Grupp. Vinn ova Report VR 2009:28. VINNOVA – Verket för Innovationssystem/Swedish Governmental Agency for Innovation System. November. Case No: 2009-02921.

Norris, D. F. (1999). *Leading edge Information Technologies and their adoption: Lessons from US cities.* Hershey, PA: Idea Group Publishing.

Norris, D. F. (2010). *E-government, e-democracy, e-transformation? Now? Soon? Ever?* ICEGEG 2010. Antalya, Turkey

North, D. C. (1999). *Institutions, institutional change, and economic performance.* New York, NY: Cambridge University Press.

Noveck, B. S. (2009). *Wiki government: How technology can make government better, democracy stronger, and citizens more powerful.* Brookings Institution Press.

Nustad, K. G. (2001). Development: The devil we know? *Third World Quarterly, 22*(4), 479–489. doi:10.1080/01436590120071731

O'Shea, K. (2003). *Council of Europe* (pp. 2001–2004). Greece: Strasburg. (in Greek)

OASIS Standard. (2007). *EML process and data requirements*, ver. 5.0.

Object Management Group (OMG). (2009). *Business process model and notation* (BPMN). OMG standard, version 1.2. Retrieved from http:// www.omg.org/ spec/ BPMN/ 1.2/ PDF/

Odhiambo-Otieno, G. W. (2005). Evaluation of existing district health management Information Systems. A case study of the district health systems in Kenya. *International Journal of Medical Informatics, 74*, 733–744. doi:10.1016/j.ijmedinf.2005.05.007

OECD. (2000). *Annual report 2000.* Retrieved February 3, 2005, from http:// www.oecd.org/ dataoecd/ 30/ 59/ 1842666.pdf

OECD. (2001). *Understanding the digital divide.* OECD papers, DSTI, Paris. Retrieved from www.oecd.org/ dataoecd/38/57/1888451.pdf

OECD. (2003). *The e-government imperative: Main finding.* Paris, France: Organisation for Economic Co-operation and Development.

OECD. (2004). The e-government imperative. Cedex 16, Paris, France.

OECD. (2009). Re-thinking e-government services: User-centred approaches.

Ofcom. (2008). *Delivering super-fast broadband in the UK.* London.

OII and LSE. (2010). *Methodology for costing the impact of digital exclusion.* Research project. Retrieved from http://microsites.oii.ox.ac.uk/digital-exclusion/

Oliver, R. (1996). *Networks into the 21st century: An evaluation of the Western Australian telecentre network.* Report commissioned by the Western Australia Department of Training, Perth, WA.

Olowu, D. (2006). Decentralisation Policies and Practices under Structural Adjustment and Democratisation in Africa. In Bangura, Y., & Larbi, G. A. (Eds.), *Public Sector Reform in Developing Countries* (pp. 228–254). New York: Palgrave MacMillan.

Olphert, W., & Damodaran, L. (2007). Citizen participation and engagement in the design of e-government services: The missing link in effective ICT design and delivery. *Journal of the Association for Information Systems, 8*(9), 491–507.

Olsen, J. P. (2004). Maybe it is time to rediscover bureaucracy. *Journal of Public Administration: Research and Theory, 16*(1), 1–24. doi:10.1093/jopart/mui027

Olsson, J., & Wohlgemuth, L. (Eds.). (2003). *Dialogue in pursuit of development*. Expert Group in Development Studies.

Omar, S., Syed-Ikhsan, S., & Rowland, F. (2004). Knowledge management in a public organisation: A study on the relationship between organizational elements and the performance of knowledge transfer. *Journal of Knowledge Management*, *8*(2), 95–111. doi:10.1108/13673270410529145

OPTA. (2008) *Policy rules: Tariff regulation for unbundled fibre access*. OPTA/AM/2008/202874. The Hague. Retrieved July 1, 2010 from http:// www.opta.nl/ en/ download/ publicatie/?id=2832

Organisation for Economic Cooperation and Development (OECD). (2004). *Promise and problems of e-democracy: Challenges of online citizen engagement*. Paris, France: OECD.

Organization for Economic Co-operation and Development. (2007), *E-government as a tool for transformation*, Retrieved July 3, 2010, from http:// www.olis.oecd.org/ olis/ 2007doc.nsf/ 4582bc8915d31134c12573a70050a430/ c5bfb886ebcafe06c12572ac0057513c/ $FILE/ JT03224646.PDF [Accessed 03 July 2010]

Organization for Economic Co-operation and Development (OECD). (2003a). *Engaging citizens online for better policy-making - Policy brief*. Paris, France: OECD.

Organization for Economic Co-operation and Development (OECD). (2003b). *The e-government imperative*. Paris, France: OECD.

Orlikowski, W. J., & Barley, S. R. (2001). Technology and institutions: What can research on Information Technology and research on organizations learn from each other? *Management Information Systems Quarterly*, *25*(2), 145–165. doi:10.2307/3250927

Orlikowski, W. J. (1992). The duality of technology: Rethinking the concept of technology in organizations. *Organization Science*, *3*(3), 398–427. doi:10.1287/orsc.3.3.398

Orlikowski, W. J. (1996). Improvising organizational transformation over time: A situated change perspective. *Information Systems Research*, *7*(1), 63–92. doi:10.1287/isre.7.1.63

Orlikowski, W. J. (2000). Using technology and constituting structures: A practice lens for studying technology in organizations. *Organization Science*, *11*(4), 404–428. doi:10.1287/orsc.11.4.404.14600

Orlikowski, W. J., & Iacono, C. S. (2001). Research commentary: Desperately seeking the "IT" in IT research--A call to theorizing the IT artifact. *Information Systems Research*, *12*(2), 121–134. doi:10.1287/isre.12.2.121.9700

Orlikowski, W. J. (2007). Sociomaterial practices: Exploring technology at work. *Organization Studies*, *28*(9), 1435–1448. doi:10.1177/0170840607081138

Osborne, D., & Gaebler, T. (1992). *Reinventing government: How the entrepreneurial spirit is transforming the public sector*. Reading, MA: Addison-Wesley.

Osborne, M. (2004). Making the most of the best: Formulating a knowledge management strategy for a government advisory body. *Australian Journal of Public Administration*, *63*(3), 43–52. doi:10.1111/j.1467-8500.2004.00389.x

Oyomno, G. (2004). Towards a framework for assessing the maturity of government capabilities for e-government. [LINK Centre.]. *The Southern African Journal of Information and Communication*, *4*, 77–97.

Paivarinta, T., & Saebo, O. (2006). Models of e-democracy. *Communications of the Association for Information Systems*, *17*, 818–840.

Pang, B., & Lee, L. (2008). Opinion mining and sentiment analysis. *Foundations and Trends in Information Retrieval*, *2*(1-2), 1–135. doi:10.1561/1500000011

Pang, B., Lee, L., & Vaithyanathan, S. (2002). Thumps up? Sentiment classification using machine learning techniques. In *Proceedings of the 2002 Conference on Empirical Methods in Natural Language Processing* (EMNLP-02).

Panopoulou, E., Tambouris, E., & Tarabanis, K. (2009). *European e-participation: Study and supply of services on the development of e-participation in the EU*. E-Participation good practice cases, Deliverable D4.2b Ver. 2. Retrieved from www.european-eparticipation.eu

Papadomichelaki, X., Magoutas, B., Halaris, C., Apostolou, D., & Mentzas, G. (2006). *Designing government services, A review of quality dimensions in e-government services. Lecture Notes in Computer Science*. Berlin / Heidelberg, Germany: Springer.

Papastergiou, S., Karantjias, A., & Polemi, D. (2007). A federated privacy-enhancing identity management system (FPE-IMS). *Proceedings of the 18th Annual IEEE International Symposium on Personal, Indoor and Mobile Radio Communications, PIMRC 07*, September, Athens, Greece, (pp. 1-5).

Papavassiliou, G., Ntioudis, S., Abecker, A., & Mentzas, G. (2003). Supporting knowledge-intensive work in public administration processes. *Knowledge and Process Management, 10*(3), 164–174. doi:10.1002/kpm.176

Pardo, T. A., & Scholl, H. J. J. (2002). Walking atop the cliffs: Avoiding failure and reducing risk in large scale e-government projects. *Proceedings of the 35th Annual Hawaii International Conference on Systems Sciences*, (pp. 1656–1665).

Paris-HLF. (2005). *Paris Declaration on Aid Effectiveness, Ownership, Harmonization, Alignment, Results and Mutual Accountability*. High-Level Forum on Aid Effectiveness. Retrieved March 6, 2010, from http://www.aidharmonization.org/secondary-pages/Paris2005

Pasley, J. (2005). How BPEL and SOA are changing Web services development. *IEEE Internet Computing, 9*(3), 60–67. doi:10.1109/MIC.2005.56

Patterson, R., & Wilson, E. J. (2000). New IT and social inequality: Resetting the research and policy agenda. *The Information Society, 16*, 77–86. doi:10.1080/019722400128347

Paulsen, M. (2002), *Online education systems: Discussion and definition of terms,* Retrieved June 22, 2010, from http:// nettskolen.nki.no/ forskning/ Definition%20 of%20Terms.pdf

Pender, J. (2001). From structural adjustment to comprehensive development framework: Conditionality transformed? *Third World Quarterly, 22*(3), 397–411. doi:10.1080/01436590120061679

People First Network (PFnet) Rural Development Volunteers Association. (2005). *The Solomon Islands people first Network (PFnet).* Retrieved October 17, 2008, from http:// www.peoplefirst.net.sb/ general/ PFnet.htm

Peräkylä, A. (2005). Analyzing talk and text. In Denzin, N. K., & Lincoln, Y. S. (Eds.), *The Sage handbook of qualitative research* (3rd ed., pp. 869–886). Thousand Oaks, CA: Sage Publications.

Peristera, V., & Tarabanis, K. (2000). Towards an enterprise architecture for public administration using a top-down approach. *European Journal of Information Systems, 9*, 252–260. doi:10.1057/palgrave/ejis/3000378

Peristeras, V., & Tarabanis, K. (2004). Governance enterprise architecture (GEA): Domain models for e-government. *Proceedings of the 6th International Conference in Electronic Commerce, ACM International Conferences, 60*, (pp. 471-479).

Peters, B. G. (2001). *Institutional theory in political science. The new institutionalism.* London, UK: Continuum.

Pettigrew, A. M. (1985). Contextualist research and the study of organizational change processes. In E. Mumford, R. Hirschheim, G. Fitzgerald & T. A. Wood-Harper (Eds.), *Research methods in Information Systems* (pp. 53-72). Amsterdam, The Netherlands: Elsevier Science Publishers B.V. (North-Holland).

Phipps, L. (2000). New communications technologies: A conduit for social inclusion. *Information Communication and Society, 3*(1), 39–68. doi:10.1080/136911800359419

Pieterse, J. N. (1998). My paradigm or yours? Alternative development, post-development, reflexive development. *Development and Change, 29*, 343–373. doi:10.1111/1467-7660.00081

Pieterse, J. N. (1995). Globalization as hybridization. In Featherstone, M., Lash, S., & Robertson, R. (Eds.), *Global modernities* (pp. 45–68). London, UK: Sage Publications.

Pilieci, V. (2008, October 29). Government creates own version of Wikipedia. *The Ottawa Citizen.*

Pingree, R. J. (2009). Decision structure: A new structure to three problems in deliberation. In Davis, T., & Gangadharan, S. P. (Eds.), *Online deliberation – Design, research and practice*. Stanford, CA: CSLI Publications.

Piotti, B., Chilundo, B., & Sahay, S. (2006). An Institutional Perspective on Health Sector Reforms and the Process of Reframing Health Information Systems: Case Study From Mozambique. *The Journal of Applied Behavioral Science*, *42*(1), 91–109. doi:10.1177/0021886305285127

Pithouse, R. (2003). Producing the poor: The World Bank's new discourse of domination. *African Sociological Review*, *7*(2), 118–148.

Polidano, C. (1999). The new public management in developing countries. *IDPM Public Policy and Management Working Papers* (vol. 13). Manchester, UK: University of Manchester.

Powell, W. W., & DiMaggio, P. J. (1991). *The new institutionalism in organizational analysis*. Chicago, IL: University of Chicago Press.

Pratchett, L., Durose, C., Lowndes, V., Smith, G., Stoker, G., & Wales, C. (2009). *Empowering communities to influence local decision making – A systematic review of the evidence*. Retrieved from http://fastlink.headstar.com/clg1

President's Emergency Plan for AIDS Relief. (2004). *Kenya FY 2004. Country Operational Plan (COP). 31 March 2004. Office of U.S. Global AIDS Coordinator and the Bureau of Public Affairs*. Washington, DC: U.S. State Department.

Prime Minister of Japan and his Cabinet. (2001). *E-Japan strategy*. Retrieved February 23, 2010, from http:// www.kantei.go.jp/ foreign/ it/ network/ 0122full_e.html

Proenza, J., Hanna, G., & Dewapura, R. (2004). *E-Sri Lanka's tele-center development program: Strategic choices and challenges of a high impact high risk investment.* Retrieved December 13, 2008, from http:// www.e-forall.org/ pdf/ VGKChoicesChallenges_6Sep2004.pdf

Project Management Institute (PMI). (2004). *A guide to the project management body of knowledge* (3rd ed.). Newtown Square, Pennsylvania: PMBOK Guides.

PublicTendering.com. (2009), *Analysis: PEPPOL - Pan-European Public eProcurement On-Line* Retrieved July 3, 2010, from http:// www.publictendering.com/ analysis-peppol-pan-european-public-eprocurement-on-line/

Purian, R. (2010). *Technophilia: From entertainment to digital literacy and e-government – A new multilevel concept for technology adoption*. Unpublished Doctoral Dissertation. Tel Aviv University, Tel Aviv, Israel.

Puron Cid, G., & Gil-Garcia, J. R. (2004). Enacting e-budgeting in Mexico. *Public Finance and Management*, *4*(2), 182–217.

Qiang, C. Z.-W. (2009). *Broadband infrastructure investment in stimulus packages: Relevance for developing countries*. Washington, DC: World Bank.

Qingliang, M., Qiudan, L., & Ruwei, D. (2009). AMAZING: A sentiment mining and retrieval system. *Expert Systems with Applications*, *36*(3).

RadioAustralia News. (2009). *Australia's broadband plan*. Retrieved March 1, 2010, from http:// www.radioaustralianews.net.au/ stories/ 200904/ 2538028.htm

Ralphs, M., & Wyatt, P. (1998). The application of geographic and land Information Systems to the management of local authority property. *Property Management*, *16*, 83–91. doi:10.1108/02637479810214123

Ramirez, R. (2007). Appreciating the contribution of broadband ICT with rural and remote communities: Stepping stones toward an alternative paradigm. *The Information Society*, *23*, 85–94. doi:10.1080/01972240701224044

Rannenberg, K., Royer, D., & Deuker, A. (2009). *The future of identity in the information society – Challenges and opportunities*. Heidelberg, Germany: Springer. doi:10.1007/978-3-642-01820-6

Ranson, S. (2000). *The new learning for inclusion and capability: Towards community governance in the education action zones.* Retrieved from http:// www.oecd.org/ dataoecd/19/22/1855975.pdf

Rehan, M., & Koyuncu, M. (2009). *Towards e-government: A survey of Turkey's progress*. ICEGOV2009. Ankara, Turkey.

Reichheld, F. F., & Sasser, W. E. Jr. (1990). Zero defections: Quality comes to services. *Harvard Business Review*, *68*(5), 105–111.

Rensburg, J. R. V., Veldsman, A., & Jenkins, M. (2008). From technologists to social enterprise developers: Our journey as ICT for Development practitioners in Southern Africa: View from practice. *Information Technology for Development*, *14*(1), 76–89. doi:10.1002/itdj.20088

Rhodes, R. A. W. (1999). Traditions and public sector reform: Comparing Britain and Denmark. *Scandinavian Political Studies*, *22*(4), 341–370. doi:10.1111/1467-9477.00023

Richards, M. C. (2003). *AES: The making of a new encryption standard.* SANS (SysAdmin, Audit, Network, Security) Institute. Retrieved from http:// www.sans.org/ reading_room/ whitepapers/ vpns/ aes-making-encryption-standard_740

Richardson, M., Agrawal, R., & Domingos, P. (2003). Trust management for the Semantic Web. In *Proc. of 2nd International Semantic Web Conference* (pp. 351-368).

Riedl, R. (2004). *Rethinking trust and confidence in European e-government.* Retrieved from http:// www.ifi.uzh.ch/ egov/ Trust_v1.0.pdf

Riege, A., & Lindsay, N. (2006). Knowledge management in the public sector: Stakeholder partnerships in the public policy development. *Journal of Knowledge Management*, *10*(3), 24–39. doi:10.1108/13673270610670830

Rieger, S., & Neumair, B. (2007). Towards usable and reasonable Identity Management in hererogeneous IT infrastructures. *Proceedings of 10th IFIP/IEEE International Symposium on Integrated Network Management – IM'07*, Munich, Germany, (pp. 560-574).

Rieke, R. (2002). *Projects CASENET and SKe - A framework for secure e-government*. In Telecities 2002 Winter Conference, Siena, Italy, Dec. 2002. Retrieved from http:// www.comune.siena.it/ telecities/ program.html

Rittel, H. W. J., & Weber, M. M. (1973). Dilemmas in a general theory of planning. *Policy Sciences*, *4*, 155–169. doi:10.1007/BF01405730

Rivero, O. d. (2001). *The myth of development: Non-viable economies of the 21st century*. Zed.

Rocheleau, B., & Liangfu, W. (2002). Public Versus Private Information Systems. *American Review of Public Administration*, *32*(4), 379–397. doi:10.1177/027507402237866

Rodney, W. (1972). *How Europe underdeveloped Africa*. London, UK: Bogle-L'Ouverture Publications.

Rostow, W. W. (1960). *The stages of economic growth: A non-Communist Manifesto*. Cambridge, UK: Cambridge University Press.

Ruccio, D. F., & Simon, L. H. (1992). Perspectives on underdevelopment. In C. K. Wiber & K. P. Jameson (Eds.), *The political economy of development and underdevelopment* (5 ed., pp. 119-150). New York, NY: McGraw Hill.

Ruh, W., Maginnis, F., & Brown, W. (2000). *Enterprise application integration. A Wiley Tech Brief.* New York, NY: Wiley John Wiley & Sons Inc.

Ruhe, G., & Du, G. (2004). Strategic planning of enterprise application integration. *Proceedings of the Enterprise Application Integration Summit*, (pp. 193-203).

Rupert, M. (2000). *Ideologies of globalization: Contending visions of a new world order*. London, UK / New York, NY: Routledge.

Rutherford, M. (1999). *Institutions in economics. The old and the new institutionalism*. New York, NY: Cambridge University Press.

Saatcioglu, O. Y., Deveci, A. D., & Cerit, A. G. (2008, May 25-26). *Logistics and transportation Information Systems in Turkey: E-government perspectives*. Paper presented at European and Mediterranean Conference on Information Systems,Al Bostan Rotana, Dubai.

Sabo, O., Rose, J., & Flak, L. S. (2008). The shape of e-participation: Characterizing an emerging research area. *Government Information Quarterly*, *25*(3), 400–428. doi:10.1016/j.giq.2007.04.007

Sacco, M. G. (2006). User-centric access to e-government information: E-citizen discovery of e-services. In *Proceeding of the 8th Annual International Conference on Digital Government Research: Bridging Disciplines & Domains*. American Association Artificial Intelligent. ISBN: 1-59593-599-1

Sadowski, B., Nucciarelli, A., & Rooij, M. (2009). Providing incentives for private investment in municipal broadband networks: Evidence from the Netherlands. [Elsevier B.V.]. *Telecommunications Policy*, *33*(10-11), 582–595. doi:10.1016/j.telpol.2009.08.005

Saebo, O., Rose, J., & Flak, L. S. (2008). The shape of e-participation: Characterizing an emerging research area. *Government Information Quarterly*, *25*, 400–428. doi:10.1016/j.giq.2007.04.007

Sahay, S., & Avgerou, C. (2002). Introducing the special issue on Information and Communication Technologies in developing countries. *The Information Society*, *18*, 73–76. doi:10.1080/01972240290075002

Sahraoui, S., Ghoneim, A., Irani, Z., & Özkan, S. (2008). T-government for benefit realization: A research agenda. In Irani, Z., & Love, P. (Eds.), *Evaluating Information Systems*. London, UK: Elsevier. doi:10.1016/B978-0-7506-8587-0.50019-6

Salema, M. H. (2006, September). *Education and training for active citizenship in formal education.* Paper presented in Working towards indicators on active citizenship of CRELL, Center for Research on Lifelong Learning. Retrieved from http:// crell.jrc.ec.europa.eu/ ActiveCitizenship/ Conference/ 04_Salema_final.pdf

Salton, G., & Burkley, C. (1988). Term-weighting approaches in automatic text retrieval. *Information Processing & Management*. *Elsevier Science Ltd*, *24*(5), 513–523.

Samaha, J., Kayssi, A., Achkar, R., & Azar, M. (2000). G3 integrated three system technologies. *Computer*, *33*(10), 107–110.

Sanchez, E., Beery, D., & Shehab, J. (2002). *EAI systems bring IT together*. Network Computing.

Sander, J. I., Bell, P. J. B., & Rice, S. D. (2005). MIS sustainability in Sub-Saharan Africa: Three case studies from The Gambia. *International Journal of Education and Development using Information and Communication Technology, 1*(3), 135-159.

Sarikas, O. D., & Weerakkody, V. (2007). Realising integrated e-government services: A UK local government perspective. *Transforming Government: People, Process and Policy*, *1*(2), 153–173.

Saruç, N. T. (2009). *The factors effecting use of e-government services and perceived quality of public services: An empirical study*. ICEGOV2009, Ankara, Turkey.

Sassen, S. (2004). Towards a sociology of Information Technology. In Avgerou, C., Ciborra, C., & Land, F. (Eds.), *The social study of information and communication technology* (pp. 76–99). Oxford, UK: Oxford University Press.

Satola, D. (2007). Legal aspects of Internet governance reform. *Information Polity*, *12*, 49–62.

Saunders, M., Lewis, P., & Thornhill, A. (2000). *Research methods for business students*. Essex, UK: Pearson Education Ltd.

Schedler, K., & Scharf, M. C. (2000). *Exploring the interrelations between electronic government and the new public management: A managerial framework for electronic government*. Switzerland: Work report, Institute for Public Services and Tourism, University of St. Gallen. German

Scheela, W., & Van Dinh, N. (2004). Venture capital in a transition economy: The case of Vietnam. *Venture Capital - An International Journal of Entrepreneurial Finance, 6*(4), 333-350.

Schelin, S. H. (2003). E-government: An overview. In Garson, G. D. (Ed.), *Public Information Technology: Policy and management issues*. Hershey, PA: Idea Group Publishing.

Schellong, A. (2007). Extending the technology enactment framework. Boston, MA: Harvard University, Kennedy School of Government, Program on Networked Governance, Working Paper No. PNG07-003.

Schepers, J., & Wetzels, M. (2007). A meta-analysis of the technology acceptance model: Investigating subjective norm and moderation effects. *Information & Management*, *44*(1), 90. doi:10.1016/j.im.2006.10.007

Schlosberg, D., Zavestoski, S., & Shulman, S. W. (2007). Democracy and e-rulemaking: Web-based technologies, participation, and the potential for deliberation. *Journal of Information Technology & Politics*, *4*(1), 37–55. doi:10.1300/J516v04n01_04

Schoepf, B. G. (2004). AIDS. History and struggles over meaning. In Kalipeni, E., Craddock, S., Oppong, J. R., & Ghosh, J. (Eds.), *HIV/AIDS in Africa: Beyond epidemiology* (pp. 15–28). Oxford, UK & Malden, MA: Blackwell Publishing.

Scholl, H. J. (2005). *The mobility paradigm in electronic government theory and practice: A strategic framework.* Paper presented at Euro Mobile Government (Euro mGov), Brighton, UK.

Schuele, K. (2005). Privacy policy statements on nunicipal websites [Electronic Version]. *The Journal of Government Financial Management, 52*(2), 20–29.

Schutz, A. (1967). *The phenomenology of the social world.* Evanston, IL: Northwestern University Press.

Schwartz, N. D. (2003, June 23). Down and out in white-collar America, professionals have never had a tougher time finding a job. It's not just the economy; the rules of the game are changing. *Fortune.*

Scott, W. R. (2001). *Institutions and organizations* (2nd ed.). Thousand Oaks, CA: Sage.

Scott, D., & Lawson, H. (2002). *Citizenship education and the curriculum.* Westport, CT: Ablex Publishing.

Scott, K. J. (2005). Assessing the quality of municipal government websites. *State and Local Government Review, 37*(2), 151–165. doi:10.1177/0160323X0503700206

Sealy, W. U. (2003). Empowering development through e-governance: Creating smart communities in small island states. *The International Information & Library Review, 35*(2-4), 335–358. doi:10.1016/S1057-2317(03)00020-1

Sein, M. K., & Harindramath, G. (2004). Conceptualizing the ICT artifact: Towards understanding the role of ICT in national development. *The Information Society, 20,* 15–24. doi:10.1080/01972240490269942

Senyucel, Z. (2005). *Towards successful e-government facilitation in UK local authorities.* e-Government Workshop, (pp. 1-16).

Serian, D. (2002). *Middleware and enterprise application integration.* London, UK: Springer Verlag.

Seufert, A., von Krogh, G., & Bach, A. (1999). Towards knowledge networking. *Journal of Knowledge Management, 3*(3), 180–190. doi:10.1108/13673279910288608

Sharifia, H., & Zareib, B. (2004). An adaptive approach for implementing e-government in I.R. Iran. *Journal of Government Information, 30,* 600–619. doi:10.1016/j.jgi.2004.10.005

Sharma, S. K., & Gupta, J. N. D. (2003). Building blocks of an e-government – A framework. *Journal of Electronic Commerce in Organizations, 1*(4), 34–48. doi:10.4018/jeco.2003100103

Shaw, N. G. (2000). Capturing the technological dimensions of IT infrastructure change. *Journal of the Association for Information Systems, 2*(8).

Shields, R., Taborsky, E., Jones, K. E., & O'Hara, C. (2000). A critical analysis of knowledge management initiatives in the Canadian federal public service. Retrieved from www.carleton.ca/innovation/km-fed.pdf

Shimada, T., & Ushida, K. (2003). Electronic government in Japan: IT utilization status of local governments. In Gingrich, G. (Ed.), *Managing IT in government, business & communities* (pp. 111–126). Hershey, PA: IRM Press.

Shirky, C. (2003). A group is its own worst enemy. *Clay Shirky's writing about the Internet.* Retrieved from www.shirky.com

Shirky, C. (2005). Ontology is overrated: Categories, links and tags. *Clay Shirky's writing about the Internet.* Retrieved from www.shirky.com

Short, G. (2002). *The socio-economic impact of telecentres in rural and remote Western Australia.* Retrieved October 15, 2008, from www.itu.int/ITU-D-UniversalAccess/seminar/ buda/ final_papers.htm

SIBIS. (2003). *SIBIS indicator handbook.* (WP6) in Statistical Indicators Benchmarking the Information Society. Information Society Programme of the European Commission. Retrieved October 27, 2008, from www.sibis-eu.org/files/Sibis_Indicator_Handbook.pdf

Signore, O., Chesi, F., & Pallotti, M. (2005). *E-government: Challenges and opportunities.* CMG Italy – XIX Annual Conference, Florence, Italy.

Simon, H. A. (1976). *Administrative behavior* (3rd ed.). New York, NY: The Free Press.

Smith, M., Madon, S., Anifalaie, A., Lazarro-Malecela, M., & Michael, E. (2008). Integrated health Information Systems in Tanzania: Experience and challenges. *Electronic Journal on Information Systems in Developing Countries, 33*(1), 1–21.

Smith, W. D. (2005). *Cryptography meets voting*. Retrieved from http:// www.math.temple.edu/ ~wds/ homepage/ cryptovot.pdf

Snijkers, K. (2004). Digital administration and the role of trust. *Information Polity*, *9*, 205–215.

Somers, M. T., & Nelson, G. K. (2004). A taxonomy of players and activities across the ERP project life cycle. *Journal of International Management*, *41*, 257–278.

Sørensen, C., Whitley, E., Madon, S., Klyachko, D., Hosein, G., & Johnstone, J. (2001). Cultivating recalcitrance in Information Systems research. In Fitzgerald, B., & Russon, N. (Eds.), *Realigning research and practice in IS development: The social and organisational perspective*. Boise, ID: Kluwer Academic Publishers.

Sotiropoulos, D. A. (2004). Southern European public bureaucracies in comparative perspective. *West European Politics*, *27*(3), 405–422. doi:10.1080/0140238042000228077

Spanou, C. (1996). Penelope's suitors: Administrative modernisation and party competition in Greece. *West European Politics*, *19*(1), 97–124. doi:10.1080/01402389608425123

Spivak, G. C. (2005). Scattered speculations on the subaltern and the popular. *Postcolonial Studies*, *8*(4), 475–486. doi:10.1080/13688790500375132

Spivak, G. C. (1988). Can the subaltern speak? In Nelson, C., & Grossberg, L. (Eds.), *Marxism and the interpretation of culture* (pp. 271–313). Chicago, IL: University of Illinois Press.

Stamati, T., & Martakos, D. (2011). Electronic transformation of local government: An exploratory study. *International Journal of Electronic Government Research (IJEGR), Special Issue on Scope, Objective, and Achievement of E-government: E-government to E-governance*. IGI Global. In press.

Stiglitz, J. E. (1998). *Towards a new paradigm for development: Strategies, policies, and processes*. Paper presented at the 9th Raul Prebisch Lecture, UNCTAD, Geneva.

Stock, J. R., & Lambert, D. M. (2001). *Strategic logistics management*. New York, NY: McGraw-Hill.

Stojanovic, N., & Stojanovic, L. (2005). A change-aware framework for the knowledge management in e-government. In K. V. Andersen, Å Grönlund, R. Traunmüller, & M. Wimmer (Eds.), *Electronic Government - Workshop and Poster Proceedings of the Fourth International EGOV Conference 2005*, Denmark, (pp. 3-10). ISBN 3-85487-830-3

Stokab in English. (2010). *Home*. Retrieved March 1, 2010, from http:// www.stokab.se/ templates/ startpress.aspx?id=1115

Stokab in English. (2010). *About Stokab*. Retrieved March 1, 2010, from http:// www.stokab.se/ templates/ StandardPage.aspx?id=306

Stokab in English. (2010). *The infrastructure*. Retrieved March 1, 2010, from http:// www.stokab.se/ templates/ StandardPage.aspx?id=775

Stølen, K., den Braber, F., Dimitrakos, T., Fredriksen, R., Gran, B. A., & Houmb, S.-H. … Aagedal, J. Ø. (2003). Model-based risk assessment in a component-based software engineering process: The CORAS approach to identify security risks. In F. Barbier (Ed.), *Business component-based software engineering* (pp.189-207). Kluwer Academic Publishers.

Stoltzfus, K. (2005). Motivations for implementing e-government: An investigation of the global phenomenon. In *Proceedings of the 2005 National Conference on Digital Government Research* (Vol. 89, pp. 333–338). Atlanta, GA: ACM International Conference Proceeding Series.

Stone, A. (2003). *Community technology centers' network: Center startup manual*. Retrieved October 4, 2008, from http:// www.ctcnet.org/ toc.htm

Sumner, A., & Tribe, M. (2004). *The nature of epistemology and methodology in development studies: What do we mean by rigour?* Paper presented at the The nature of Development Studies, DSA Annual Conference, Bridging Research and Policy, Church House, London.

Sun, H., & Zhang, P. (2006). The role of moderating factors in user technology acceptance. *International Journal of Human-Computer Studies*, *64*(2), 53–78. doi:10.1016/j.ijhcs.2005.04.013

Sundar, D. K., & Garg, S. (2005). *M-governance: A framework for Indian urban local bodies*. Paper presented at the Euro mGov 2005: The First European Mobile Government Conference, Brighton, UK.

Sutton, J., & Gillingwater, D. (1997). Geographic Information Systems and transportation — Overview. *Transportation Planning and Technology*, *21*(1), 1–4. doi:10.1080/03081069708717598

SWEB IST project. (2007). *Secure, interoperable, cross border m-services contributing towards a trustful European cooperation with the non-EU member Western Balkan countries*. 6th Framework Programme, IST-2006-2.6.5. Retrieved from www.sweb-project.org

Syed-Ikhsan, S., Sharifuddin, O., & Rowland, F. (2004). Knowledge management in a public organization: A study on the relationship between organizational elements and the performance of knowledge transfer. *Journal of Knowledge Management*, *8*(2), 95–111. doi:10.1108/13673270410529145

Sylvester, C. (1999). Development studies and postcolonial studies: Disparate tales of the third world. *Third World Quarterly*, *20*(4), 703–721. doi:10.1080/01436599913514

Syzeyxis Project. (2008). *Website*. Retrieved from http://www.syzefxis.gov.gr/

Tahinakis, P., Mylonakis, J., & Protogeros, N. (2006). The contribution of e-government to the modernisation of the Hellenic taxation system. *Electronic Government, an International Journal, 3*(2), 139-57.

Talbot, C. (2004). Paradoxes of human nature and public management reforms. In J. Jabes (Ed.), *The role of public administration in alleviating poverty and improving governance.* Malaysia: ABD, NAPSIPAG, INTAN.

Tambouris, E., & Wimmer, M. (2004). Online one-stop government: A single point of access to public services. In Huang, W. (Ed.), *Electronic government strategies and implementation* (pp. 115–139). Hershey, PA: Idea Group Publishing. doi:10.4018/978-1-59140-348-7.ch006

Tan, C. W., & Pan, S. L. (2003). Managing e-transformation in the public sector: an e-government study of the Inland Revenue Authority of Singapore (IRAS). *European Journal of Information Systems*, *12*(4), 269–281. doi:10.1057/palgrave.ejis.3000479

Tapscott, D. (2009). *Grown up digital: how the net generation is changing your world*. New York, NY: McGraw-Hill.

Tassabehji, R., & Elliman, T. (2006). Generating citizen trust in e-government using a trust verification agent: a research note. In Z. Irani, O. D. Sarikas, J. Llopis, R. Gonzalez, & J. Gasco (Eds.), *European and Mediterranean Conference on Information Systems (EMCIS 2006)*.

Taylor, W. A., & Wright, G. H. (2004). Organizational readiness for successful knowledge sharing: Challenges for public sector managers. *Information Resources Management Journal*, *17*(2), 22–37. doi:10.4018/irmj.2004040102

Teswanich, W., Anutariya, C., & Wuwongse, V. (2006). A knowledge management system framework for governmental regulating processes. *Electronic Government, an International Journal, 3*(1), 56-73.

The Apache Software Foundation. (2007). *Apache Jackrabbit: Content repository for Java technology API (JCR)*. Retrieved from http:// jackrabbit.apache.org/

The Apache Software Foundation. (2007). *Apache orchestration director engine (ODE)*. Retrieved from http://ode.apache.org/

Themistocleous, M., & Irani, Z. (2002). (in press). Evaluating enterprise application integration technologies: A novel frame of references. *European Journal of Operational Research*.

Themistocleous, M. (2004). Justifying the decisions for EAI implementations: A validated proposition of influential factors. *Journal of Enterprise Information Management*, *17*(2), 85–104. doi:10.1108/17410390410518745

Themistocleous, M., & Irani, Z. (2001). Benchmarking the benefits and barriers of application integration. *Benchmarking: An International Journal*, *8*(4), 317–331. doi:10.1108/14635770110403828

Themistocleous, M., Irani, Z., & Love, P. E. D. (2005). Developing e-government integrated infrastructures: A case study. *Proceedings of the 38th Annual Hawaii International Conference on System Sciences*, Big Island, Hawaii, IEEE, (pp. 1-10).

Theodorakopoulos, G., & Baras, J. S. (2004). Trust evaluation in ad-hoc networks. In M. Jakobsson, & A. Perrig (Eds.), *ACM Workshop on Wireless Security* (pp. 1-10). Philadelphia, PA: ACM Press.

Therkildsen, O. (2006). Elusive public sector reforms in East and Southern Africa. In Bangura, Y., & Larbi, G. A. (Eds.), *Public sector reform in developing countries* (pp. 19–26). New York, NY: Palgrave MacMillan.

Thiongo, N. W. (1996). *Decolonizing the mind: The politics of language in African literature*. Nairobi, Kenya: East African Educational Publishers.

Thomas, C. (2009), *Are you ready for g-government?* Retrieved February 10, 2010, from http:// www.esri.com/ news/ arcuser /0101/ umbrella13.html

Thompson, M. (2004). Discourse, development & the digital divide: ICT & the World Bank. *Review of African Political Economy*, *31*, 103–123. doi:10.1080/0305624042000258441

Thompson, M. P. A. (2002). Cultivating meaning: Interpretive fine-tuning of a South African health Information System. *Information and Organization*, *12*(3), 183–211. doi:10.1016/S1471-7727(01)00016-1

Thompson, J. R., & Seidner, R. (2009), *Federated human resource management in the federal government: The intelligence community model,* IBM Center for the Business of Government, Retrieved February 10, 2010, from http:// www.businessofgovernment.org/ pdfs/ thompsonseidner_magazine.pdf

Thompson, L. S. (2009, February). *Railway and ports organization in the republic of South Africa and Turkey: The integrator's paradise?* Paper presented at International Transport Forum, Discussion Paper No. 2009-5, Prepared for the Round Table of 5-6 on Integration and Competition Between Transport and Logistics Businesses.

Tilbury, D., Stevenson, R. B., Fien, J., & Schreuder, D. (Eds.). (2002). *Education and sustainability, responding to the global challenge. IUCN Commission on Education and communication (CEC)*. Gland, Switzerland: IUCN – The World Conservation Union.

Tillman, B. (2003). More information could mean less privacy. *The Information Management Journal*, *37*(2), 20–23.

Tomales Bay Institute. (2006). *The commons rising, a report to owners*. Retrieved August 30, 2007, from http:// onthecommons.org/ files/ Commons_Rising_06.pdf

Tondeur, J., Braak, J. v., & Valcke, M. (2007). Curricula and the use of ICT in education: Two worlds apart? *British Journal of Educational Technology*, *38*(6), 962–976. doi:10.1111/j.1467-8535.2006.00680.x

Torres, L., Pina, V., & Acerete, B. (2005). E-government developments on delivering public services among EU cities. *Government Information Quarterly*, *22*, 217–238. doi:10.1016/j.giq.2005.02.004

Torres, L., Pina, V., & Royo, S. (2005). E-government and the transformation of public administrations in EU countries: Beyond NPM or just a second wave of reforms? [Emerald Group Publishing Limited]. *Online Information Review*, *29*(5), 531–553. doi:10.1108/14684520510628918

Toussaint, É. (2004). *Anne Krueger, the white knight of globalisation*. Committee for the Abolition of Third World Debt. Retrieved March 7, 2010, from http:// www.cadtm.org/ Anne-Krueger-the-White-Knight-of

Traunmuller, R., & Wimmer, M. (2004). E-government - A roadmap for progress. *Digital Communities in a Networked Society: E-Commerce, E-Business and E-Govemment: The Third IFIP Conference on E-Commerce*. Hingham, MA: Kluwer Academic Publishers.

Troulos, C., Merekoulias, V., & Maglaris, V. (2009). A business model for municipal FTTH/B networks: The case of rural Greece. *Info - The Journal of Policy, Regulation and Strategy for Telecommunications* [Emerald Group Publishing Limited.]. *Information and Media*, *12*(3), 73–89.

Tsaousis, D. (1997). *H K*. Athens, Greece: Gutenberg.

Tsoukalas, C. (1995). Free riders in wonderland; Or, of Greeks in Greece. In Constas, D., & Stavrou, T. G. (Eds.), *Greece prepares for the twenty-first century* (pp. 191–219). Washington, DC: The Woodrow Wilson Center Press.

Tufts University Center for Information and Research on Civic Learning and Engagement. (2008). Young voters in the 2008 presidential election. Retrieved February 12, 2010, from www.civicyouth.org

Tuomi, I. (1999-2000). Data is more than knowledge: Implications of the reversed knowledge hierarchy for knowledge management and organizational memory. *Journal of Management Information Systems*, *16*(3), 103–117.

Turney, P. (2002). Thumps up or thumbs down? Semantic orientation applied to unsupervised classification of reviews. In *Proceedings of the 40th Annual Meeting of the Association for Computational Linguistics*.

U.S. Federal Trade Commission. (1999). *Child Online Privacy Protection Act*. Retrieved February 26, 2010, from http://www.coppa.org/comply.htm

Uçkan, Ö. (2009a). *Everyone is governed as they deserve*. Retrieved March 4, 2010, from http://arsiv.sabah.com.tr/2009/01/04/pz/haber,0499516A4921456CA2DA627988C1E222.html

Uçkan, Ö. (2009b). *Weakness of ICT policy-making process in Turkey: The governance phobia*. ICEGOV 2009. Ankara, Turkey.

UK Government. (2005). *Transformational government: Enabled by technology*.

UK GovTalk. (2005). *Integrated public sector vocabulary (IPSV)*. Cabinet Office. Retrieved from http:// www.govtalk.gov.uk

UK Online Centres Team at UFI. (2008). *About UK online centres*. Retrieved October 20, 2008, from http:// www.ukonlinecentres.com

UN/CEFACT. (2007). *Core components technical specification, version 3.0*. Second Public Review.

UNCED (United Nations Commission on Environment and Development). (1992). [*Programme of action for sustainable development: Rio declaration on environment and development*. Rio de Janeiro, Brazil: UNCED.]. *Agenda (Durban, South Africa)*, •••, 21.

UNDP. Europe and the CIS. (2005). *Telecottage handbook: How to establish and run a successful telecenter*. Bratislava, Slovakia. ISBN 92-95042-48-4

UNESCO. (2002). *Education for sustainability, from Rio to Johannesburg: Lessons learnt from a decade of commitment*. Report from World Summit on Sustainable Development Johannesburg, 26 August – 4 September 2002

Unger, R. M. (2004). *False necessity: Anti-necessitarian social theory in the service of radical democracy* (Paperback ed. Vol. 1 of Politics). London, UK: Verso.

United Nations & American Society for Public Administration (ASPA). (2002). *Benchmarking e-government: A global perspective*. New York, NY: U.N. Publications.

United Nations. (2002). *Benchmarking e-government: A global perspective*. New York, NY: American Society for Public Administration.

United Nations. (2008). *E-government survey 2008 - From e-government to connected governance*. United Nations.

United Nations. (2005). *UN global e-government readiness report 2005: From e-government to e-inclusion*. United Nations Knowledge Base (UNKB). United Nations Publication, Publication No.: UNPAN/2005/14. UNKB Framework. Retrieved from http://unpan1.un.org/intradoc/groups/public/documents/un/unpan021888.pdf

UTOPIA. (2003). Feasibility study, part II: Financial analysis, dynamic city Metronet advisors.

UTOPIA. (2010). *Utopianet*. Retrieved March 1, 2010, from http:// www.utopianet.org/

Valor, C. (2005). Corporate social responsibility and corporate citizenship: Towards corporate accountability. *Business and Society Review*, *110*(2), 191–212. doi:10.1111/j.0045-3609.2005.00011.x

Van Acker, B. (2004). Remote e-voting and coersion: A risk assessment model and solutions. In Prosser, A., & Krimmer, R. (Eds.), *Electronic voting in Europe - Technology, law, politics and society* (pp. 53–62). Bregenz, Austria: GI-Editions.

Venkatesh, V., Morris, M. G., Davis, G. B., & Davis, F. D. (2003). User acceptance of Information Technology: Toward a unified view. *Management Information Systems Quarterly*, *27*(3), 425–478.

Virili, F., & Sorrentino, M. (2009). Value generation in e-government from service-based IT integration. *Transforming Government: People, Process and Policy*, *3*(3), 227–247.

VoIP and ENUM. (2006). *FTTH in Vienna to all households*. Retrieved July 2, 2010, from http:// voipandenum.blogspot.com/ 2006/ 01/ ftth-in-vienna-to-all-households.html

Wade, R. H. (2001). US hegemony and the World Bank: The fight over people and ideas. *Review of International Political Economy*, *9*(2), 215–243. doi:10.1080/09692290110126092

Wade, R. H. (2004). Bridging the digital divide: New route to development or new form of dependency? In Avgerou, C., Ciborra, C., & Land, F. (Eds.), *The social study of information and communication technology: Innovation, actors and contexts* (pp. 185–206). Oxford University Press.

Wagner, C., Karen, S. K., Cheung, R. K. F., & Ip, S. B. (2006). Building Semantic Webs for e-government with Wiki technology. *Electronic Government, an International Journal, 3*(1), 36-55. Inderscience Publishers.

Wagner, W., & Antonucci, Y. L. (2004). An analysis of the Imagine PA Public Sector ERP Project. *Proceedings of the 37th Hawaii International Conference on Systems Sciences*, Hawaii, (pp. 1-10).

Waisanen, B. (2002). The future of e-government: Technology-fueled management tools. *Public Management*, *84*(5), 6–9.

Wallerstein, I. M. (1991). *Unthinking social science: The limits of nineteenth-century paradigms*. Cambridge, MA: Polity Press.

Wallerstein, I. M. (2004, October). *After developmentalism and globalization, what?* Paper presented at the Keynote address at conference, Development Challenges for the 21st Century, Cornell University, Ithaca, NY.

Walsham, G. (2005). Development, global futures and IS research: A polemic. *The Journal of Strategic Information Systems*, *14*, 5–15. doi:10.1016/j.jsis.2004.11.009

Walsham, G., Robey, D., & Sahay, S. (2007). Foreward: Special issue on Information Systems in developing countries. *Management Information Systems Quarterly*, *31*(2), 317–326.

Walsham, G. (2005). Development, global futures and IS research: A polemic. *The Journal of Strategic Information Systems*, *14*(1), 5–15. doi:10.1016/j.jsis.2004.11.009

Walsham, G. (2009). *Interpreting Information Systems in organizations*. Global Text.

Walsham, G. (1993). *Interpreting Information Systems in organizations*. Chichester, UK: John Wiley.

Wang, B. Wei, Q., Tan, Q., Yang, S., & Cai, B. (2004). *Integration of GIS, GPS and GSM for the Qinghai-Tibet railway information management planning*. Retrieved February 27, 2010, from http:// citeseerx.ist.psu.edu.tr

Ward, M. A., & Mitchell, S. (2004). A comparison of the strategic priorities of public and private sector information resource management executives. *Government Information Quarterly*, *21*(3), 284–304. doi:10.1016/j.giq.2004.04.003

Warkentin, M., Gefen, D., Pavlou, P., & Rose, G. (2002). Encouraging citizen adoption of e-government by building trust. *Electronic Markets*, *12*(3), 157–162. doi:10.1080/101967802320245929

Warner, J., & Chun, S. A. (2009). Privacy protection in government mashups. *Information Polity*, *14*, 75–90.

Washington State Digital Government Plan. (2001), *National Association of State Information Resource Executives. Nomination for 2001 recognition awards for outstanding achievement in the field of Information Technology,* Retrieved February 10, 2010, from http:// www.nascio.org/ awards/ nominations/ 2001Washington9.doc

Weate, J. (2003). Achille Mbembe and the postcolony: Going beyond the text. *Research in African Literature*, *34*(4), 27–41. doi:10.2979/RAL.2003.34.4.27

Weber, R. (2004). The rhetoric of positivism versus interpretivism: A personal view. *Management Information Systems Quarterly*, *28*(1), iii–xii.

Weber, M. (1946). *The theory of social and economic organization. Translated from the German*. Glencoe, Ill.: Free Press & The Falcon's Wing Press.

Weber, E., & Khademian, A. (2008). Wicked problems, knowledge challenges and collaborative capacity builders in network settings. *Public Administration Review*, *68*(2), 334–349. doi:10.1111/j.1540-6210.2007.00866.x

Welch, E. W., Hinnant, C. C., & Moon, M. J. (2004). Linking citizen satisfaction with e-government and trust in government. *Journal of Public Administration: Research and Theory*, *15*(3), 371–391. doi:10.1093/jopart/mui021

Wenger, E. (1998). *Communities of practice: Learning, meaning, and identity*. Cambridge, UK / New York, NY: Cambridge University Press.

Wenger, E. (2000). Communities of practice and social learning systems. *Organization*, *7*(2), 225–246. doi:10.1177/135050840072002

Wenger, E., McDermott, R. A., & Snyder, W. (2002). *Cultivating communities of practice*. USA: Harvard Business School Press.

Wenger, E. C., & Snyder, W. M. (2000). Communities of practice: The organizational frontier. *Harvard Business Review*, *78*(1), 139–145. Retrieved from http:// search.epnet.com/login.aspx?direct=true&db=buh&an=2628915./ 2/22/2000 and http://hbswk.hbs.edu/ archive/ 1317.html.

Wenger, E., McDermott, R., & Snyder, W. (2002). *Cultivating communities of practice: A guide to managing knowledge*. Boston, MA: Harvard Business School Press.

Wenger, E. (2001). *Supporting communities of practice a survey of community-oriented technologies*. Retrieved from http:// www.ewenger.com/ tech

Wenger, E., White, N., Smith, J. D., & Rowe, K. (2005). *Technology for communities*. In CEFRIO. Retrieved from http:// technologyforcommunities.com/ CEFRIO_Book_Chapter_v_5.2.pdf

Werner, M. (1996). *Empowering socio-economic development in Africa utilizing Information Technology: Case study of Mozambique*. Retrieved October 11, 2008, from www.bellanet.org/ partners/ aisi/ policy

West, D. (2005). *Digital government: Technology and public sector performance*. Princeton, NJ: Princeton University Press.

West, D. M. (2004). E-government and the transformation of service delivery and citizen attitudes. *Public Administration Review*, *64*(1). doi:10.1111/j.1540-6210.2004.00343.x

West, D. M. (2001). *State and federal e-government in the United States*. Providence, RI: Brown University Press.

West, P., Sebatane, L., Setsabi, A. M., Abdo, T., & Howard, L. (2000). *DaimlerChrysler distance learning support centre, Maseru, Lesotho*. The Information Communications Technology (ICT) Centre, The Technology Enhance Learning Initiative of Southern Africa (TELISA Initiative).

Western, J. L., & Ran, B. (2009). *Information Technology in transportation, key issues and a look forward*. Committee on Information Systems and Technology. Retrieved February 21, 2010, from www.trb.org/ publications/ millennium/00054.pdf

Westin, A. F. (1967). *Privacy and freedom*. New York, NY: Atheneum.

Whitmore, A., & Choi, N. (2010). Reducing the perceived risk of e-government implementations: The importance of risk communication. *International Journal of Electronic Government Research*, *6*(1), 1–8. doi:10.4018/jegr.2010102001

WHO. (1978). *Alma Alta Declaration*. Geneva, Switzerland: World Health Organisation.

WHO/Africa. (1994). *Halting the decline in vaccine coverage. EPI Bulletin 001, June 1994*. Brazzaville, Congo: World Health Organisation, Regional Office for Africa. ADDITIONAL READING SECTION.

Whyte, A., & Macintosh, A. (2002). Analysis and evaluation of e-consultations. *e-Service Journal, 2*(1), 9-34.

Wiebe, J., Wilson, T., Bruce, R., Bell, M., & Martin, M. (2002). *Learning subjective language. Technical Report TR – 02-100*. Pittsburgh, Pennsylvania: Department of Computer Science, University of Pittsburgh.

Wiebe, J. (2000). Learning subjective adjectives from corpora. In Proceedings *of the 17th National Conference on Artificial Intelligence* (AAAI -2000).

Wiebe, J., Bruce, R., & O'Hara, T. (1999). Development and use of a gold standard data set for subjectivity classifications. In *Proceedings of the 37th Annual Meeting of the Association for Computational Linguistics* (ACL-99), (pp. 246-253).

Wiig, K. M. (2002). Knowledge management in public administration. *Journal of Knowledge Management*, *6*(3), 224–239. doi:10.1108/13673270210434331

Wijkman, A., & Afifi, M. (2002). Technology leapfrogging and the digital divide [Electronic Version]. *ICT Regulation Toolkit*, 124-143. Retrieved May 15, 2007, from http:// www.ictregulationtoolkit.org/ en/ Document.1996.html

Williams, C. B., & Fedorowicz, J. (2005). A framework for analysing cross-boundary e-government projects: The CapWin example. *Proceedings of the 2005 National Conference on Digital Government Research*, May 15-18, 2005, Atlanta, Georgia.

Willmott, H. (1994). Business process re-engineering and human resource management, *Emerald publishing, Journal for Personnel Review*, *23*(3). doi:10.1108/00483489410064559

Wong, W., & Welch, E. (2004). Does e-government promote accountability? A comparative analysis of website openness and government accountability. *An International Journal of Policy, Administration, and Institutions*, *17*(2), 275–297.

World Bank Group. (2003). *Definition of e-government*. Retrieved from http:// go.worldbank.org/ M1JHE0Z280

World Bank. (2004). *E-government: A definition of e-government*. Retrieved February 3, 2005 from www. worldbank.org

World Commission on Environment and Development (WCED). (1987). *Our common future*. Oxford, UK: Oxford University Press.

World-Bank. (2004). *Supporting development programs effectively - Applying the comprehensive development framework principles: A staff guide*. Washington, DC: World Bank.

World-Bank. (2005). *E-government* (vol. 8/9). Washington, DC: World Bank Group.

Worrall, L. (1994). Justifying investment in GIS: A local government perspective. *International Journal of Geographical Information Science*, *8*(6), 545–565. doi:10.1080/02693799408902021

WSBPEL 2.0. (2007). *OASIS Web services business process execution language,* version 2.0. Advancing Open Standards for the Information Society, OASIS Standard.

Wyld, D. C. (2004). The 3 Ps: The essential elements of a definition of e-government. *Journal of E-Government*, *1*(1), 17–22. doi:10.1300/J399v01n01_03

X.509. (2005). *Information Technology - Open systems interconnection – The directory: Public-key and attribute certificate frameworks*. Retrieved from http:// www.itu. int/ rec/ T-REC-X.509/ en

Xu, Z., & Ramnath, R. (2009). *Mining opinion from poll results in Web pages*. WWW2009, April 20-24, 2009, Madrid Spain.

Yardley, D. (2002). *Successful IT project delivery: Learning the lessons of project failure*. London, UK: Addison-Wesley.

Yildiz, M. (2007). E-government research: Reviewing the literature, limitations, and ways forward. *Government Information Quarterly*, *24*, 646–665. doi:10.1016/j. giq.2007.01.002

Yildiz, M., Sadioglu, U., & Altinok, R. (2008). *Managing e-government innovation In Turkey: The case of e-government advisory group in the office of the Prime Minister*. Rotterdam European Group of Public Administration e-Government Study Group. September 3, 2008.

Yin, R. K. (1994). *Case study research design and methods*. London, UK: Sage.

YME. (2008). *Strategy for electronic communications and new technologies 2008 – 2013*. Retrieved March 1, 2010, from http:// www.yme.gr/ index.php?tid=21&aid=1532 (in Greek)

Yoshida, M., Kubo, S., & Shimada, T. (2003). Information sharing with citizens through the website of the local government. *Proceedings of the 31st Conference on Japan Association for Management Systems (in Japanese)*, (pp. 165-168).

Young, R. (2001). *Postcolonialism: An historical introduction*. Oxford, UK: Blackwell.

Younis, R. A. (2005). Integral reality, digital cultures, digital divides. *Postcolonial Studies*, *8*(2), 219–226. doi:10.1080/13688790500196744

Yousafzai, S, Y., Foxall, G. R., & Pallister, J. G. (2007). Technology acceptance: a meta-analysis of the TAM: Part 2. *Journal of Modeling in Management*, *2*(3), 281. doi:10.1108/17465660710834462

Yu, H., & Hatzivassiloglou, V. (2003). Towards answering opinion questions: Separating facts from opinions and identifying the polarity of opinion sentences. In *Proceedings of the Conference on empirical Methods in Natural language Processing* (EMNLP-03).

Zabin, J., & Jefferies, A. (2008). *Social media monitoring and analysis: Generating consumer insights from online conversation.* Aberdeen group Benchmark Report.

Zahavi, R. (1999). *Enterprise application integration with CORBA*. New York, NY: John Wiley and Sons Inc.

Zeithaml, V., Parasuraman, A., & Berry, L. L. (1990). *Delivering quality service*. New York, NY: The Free Press.

Ziai, A. (2004). The ambivalence of post-development: Between reactionary populism and radical democracy. *Third World Quarterly*, *25*(6), 1045–1060. doi:10.1080/0143659042000256887

Zornada, L., & Velkavrh, T. (2005). Implementing ERP systems in higher education institutions. In: *27th Int. Conf. Information Technology Interfaces (ITI 2005)*, June 20-25, 2005, Cavtat, Croatia

Zuboff, S. (1988). *In the age of the smart machine: The future of work and power*. New York, NY: Basic Books.

About the Contributors

Thanos Papadopoulos is a lecturer in Knowledge and Information Systems Management, at the School of Management, University of Southampton, UK. He obtained his PhD from Warwick Business School, University of Warwick, UK. He also obtained his diploma (Dipl-Eng – Equivalent to MEng) in computer engineering and informatics from the School of Engineering of Patras University, Greece, and his MSc in Information Systems from the Department of Informatics of the Athens University of Economics and Business, Greece. His research interests include innovation and change in public services, business transformation and networks, and Information Systems' assessment strategies. He has been awarded the Best Paper Award in the 2007 International Conference on the Management of Healthcare and Medical Technology. He has published more than 20 papers in peer-reviewed journals and international conferences.

Panagiotis Kanellis is currently an Executive Director with Ernst & Young in Athens, Greece. Previous to that he held senior positions both in the private and public sectors where he led large transformational programmes. He was educated at Western International University in Business Administration (BSc), at the University of Ulster in Computing and Information Systems (Post-Graduate Diploma) and at Brunel University in Data Communication Systems (MSc) and Information Systems (PhD). He has taught at the Athens University of Economics and Business and is a Research Associate in the Department of Informatics and Telecommunications at the University of Athens. He has published more than 60 papers in peer-reviewed journals and international conferences. He is Fellow of the British Computer Society and a Chartered Information Technology Professional (FBCS CITP), a Chartered Engineer (CEng), a Chartered Scientist (CSci) and a Certified Information Systems Auditor (CISA).

* * *

Gülgün Afacan has BSc degree from Department of Computer Education and Instructional Technology at Middle East Technical University in 2006. After undergraduation, she was accepted to Master's Program of Information Systems in Informatics Institute of the same university. Research focus of MSc was measurement of e-goverment and the title of MSc dissertation was E-performance of Turkey and a new e-transformation metric system. She has received MSc degree in 2009. She is currently conducting her PhD studies at the same department.

Niv Ahituv is the Academic Director of the Institute of Internet Studies and the Marko and Lucie Chaoul Chair for Research in Information Evaluation at Tel Aviv University. From 1989 to 1994 he served as the Dean of Graduate School of Business Administration and from 1999 to 2002 he served as Vice President and Director General (CEO) of Tel Aviv University. In 2005 he was awarded a Life Time Achievement Award by The Israeli Association for Information Technology. Ahituv represents the Israeli Government in UNESCO in issues related to Information Technology. His main areas of interest are: information economics, IT strategy and management, and social and business implications of the Internet. On the latter issue he published a book (in Hebrew) in 2001 titled "A World without Secrets: on the Open Information Society." He holds degrees of B.Sc. in Mathematics, MBA, and M.Sc. and Ph.D. in Information Systems Management.

Tomohide Akebe is a graduate student at Setsunan University, Graduate School of Business Administration and Information, Neyagawa City, Osaka, Japan. His research interests lie in local government personnel training in Japan, and IT vendors contributing to regional development. His research is focused on the effect of personnel training at collaboration with organizations and citizens in region, and ability of leadership of regional development. Presently he is involved in regional development projects in Neyagawa City and the empirical survey of e-governments and management levels of local governments in Japan. He has undertaken the responsibility of the development of Web applications in empirical surveys in the laboratory. His efforts in this area are useful in the conduct of questionnaire surveys.

Spyros Angelopoulos is currently a Doctoral researcher at Warwick Business School, UK. He holds a Diploma (Dipl-Eng, equivalent to MEng) in Production Engineering and Management as well as an MSc in Management Engineering from the Technical University of Crete, Greece. His current research is on the emergence and evolution of social networks within public-private partnerships and his research interests include social networks, e-government, Information Systems management and implementation in public services, business transformation, and networks, as well as complexity and transformation of organizations and socio-economic contexts. His publications include book chapters in handbooks, papers in journals, as well as presentations in conferences and workshop.

Ali Arifoglu graduated from Mathematics Department of Hacettepe University in 1978. Then, he was admitted to MSc program in Computer Engineering Department of Middle East Technical University. After MSc, he continued studies in the same department and received PhD degree. Currently, he takes roles in the e-government process of Turkey by conducting various studies and research projects. He has been working as lecturer in METU Informatics Institute since 2004. At the same time, he is the director of the e-Government Research and Development Center since 2006. He has published two books, "Software Engineering" and "e-Transformation: Roadmap, Turkey, World."

Asim Balci holds the position of Associate Professor in the Department of Public Administration, Selçuk University, Turkey. Prof. Balci assumed advisory and managerial roles in Turkish Ministries of Health and Transportation (Turksat) between 2003 and 2010. He received his Doctorate degree from the Department of Political Science and Public Administration, Middle East Technical University, Turkey. Professor Balci has published numerous books and contributed to various journal publications and conference proceedings in the fields of public administration, as well as TQM and e-government. He has also recently been involved in EU projects on e-government maturity model development based on citizen evaluation, and development of ubiquitous platform for citizens' involvement in local policy-making.

Roberta Bernardi is about to complete her PhD in the Information System and Management Group of the Warwick Business School at the University of Warwick. Her research interests are in IT innovation of healthcare, health Information Systems, ICT for development, institution theory, and IT-enabled organisational change. Before her PhD she worked in Kenya on a Parliamentary Information System project sponsored by the United Nations.

Jeries Besharat is an M.Sc. candidate at the Computer Engineering and Informatics Department of Patras University. His area of expertise is Web metrics, data mining, and natural language processing. He received his diploma from the Department of Information and Communication Systems Engineering of the Aegean University.

Sandford Borins is Professor of Strategic Management at the Joseph L. Rotman School of Management at the University of Toronto. He is also a Research Fellow at the Ash Institute for Democratic Governance and Innovation at the Harvard Kennedy School. His interests include management narrative, Information Technology, innovation, and public management. He is the lead author of *Digital State at the Leading Edge* (University of Toronto Press, 2007), a comprehensive study of the impact of Information Technology on both politics and service delivery, based on case studies of two arguably leading edge jurisdictions, the governments of Canada and the Canadian province of Ontario. Prof. Borins writes a weekly blog at www.sandfordborins.com.

Christos J. Bouras obtained his Diploma and PhD from the Computer Engineering and Informatics Department, University of Patras (Greece). He is currently a Professor in the above department. Also he is a scientific advisor of Research Unit 6 in Research Academic Computer Technology Institute (CTI), Patras, Greece. His research interests include analysis of performance of networking and computer systems, computer networks and protocols, telematics and new services, QoS and pricing for networks and services, e–learning, networked virtual environments, and WWW issues. He has extended professional experience in design and analysis of networks, protocols, telematics, and new services. He has published more than 350 papers in various well-known refereed conferences and journals. He is a co-author of 8 books in Greek. He has been a PC member and referee in various international journals and conferences. He has participated in numerous R&D projects.

Dimitris Christodoulakis was born in Samos. He received the B.Sc. degree in Mathematics from the University of Athens (1975) and the PhD degree in Informatics from the University of Bonn (1980). From 1980 to 1983 he was a researcher at the National Informatics Centre of Germany (GMD, Bonn). Assistant and Associate Professor in Computer Engineering Dept. of Patras University (1984-1995). From 1995 until now he is a Professor in the same Dept. scientific coordinator in many research and development projects in the followings sections: knowledge and data base systems, very large volume information storage, hypertext, and natural language technology for Modern Greek. Author and co-author in many articles published in international conferences. Editor in proceedings of conventions. Responsible for proofing tools development for Microsoft Corp. From September 1997 until 2001 he was Chairman of Computer Engineering and Informatics Dept. of Patras University and from 2001 until 2008 he was Vice President of the Department.

Phillip Ein-Dor received his Ph.D. in Systems and Communications Sciences from Carnegie-Mellon University in 1971. He is Professor Emeritus at Tel-Aviv University since 2003 and is now Professor at The Academic College of Tel-Aviv-Yaffo. As a founding member of the Association of Information Systems, Ein-Dor has held various positions in the organization including President (2002-2003). In 2005 he founded the Israel Chapter of AIS. He was inducted as a Fellow of AIS in 2000 and received the LEO Award in 2006. Ein-Dor was appointed founding editor of the Journal of AIS, which began publication in March 2000, and served in that role until 2002. He serves on the editorial and/or advisory boards of ten journals. Dr. Ein-Dor's research interests have included MIS, Information System theory, artificial intelligence, economics of computers and Information Systems, technology diffusion, and the digital divide. He has published four books and some 50 papers on various aspects of Information Systems and their management.

Deniz Türsel Eliiyi is an Assistant Professor in the Department of Industrial Systems Engineering at Izmir University of Economics. She received her B.S., M.S., and PhD degrees in Industrial Engineering all from Middle East Technical University. She has worked as a research and teaching assistant in the Department of Industrial Engineering in Middle East Technical University, and as an instructor in the Department of Statistics in Dokuz Eylül University. Her research interests include production planning and scheduling, port operations analysis, management Information Systems, and combinatorial optimization.

Erkan Er graduated from Department of Computer Education and Instructional Technology at Middle East Technical University in 2006. After undergraduate education, he started his Master's studies in Information Systems Department of Informatics. The primary research focus was enhancement of distance education to enable better learning process. His dissertation was developing a learning management system to support synchronous distance education. He has completed MSc program in 2009. Currently, he is a PhD student in the Information Systems department and working as a research assistant.

Dimitra Florou is a teacher and a researcher in the New Technologies Laboratory in Communication, Education and the Mass Media in University of Athens. She is graduate of the Faculty of Political Science and Public Administration of the National and Kapodistrian University of Athens (1983), the school of Pedagogical Science (1985) and has a Master's in "Technologies of the Information and the Communication for the Education." She was a member of the pedagogical team of Argyroupoli Centre for Environmental Education (1998-2000) and was also in charge of the administration of the Environmental Education of the 4th District of Primary Education in Athens (2003-2008). She has collaborated with the University of Aegean (2004-2006) and the National Technical University of Athens (2007-2008) in educational programs for the teachers regarding the sustainability. She is member of the authors' team of the school book of Social and Political Science for the 5th grade. Her research interests include education for citizenship, sustainability, and the use of social media in education.

Marc Fudge is a PhD student in the School of Public Affairs and Administration at Rutgers University, Newark. His research focuses on e-governance, the factors that impact public sector information and communication technology adoption and implementation, performance measurement and improvement, and organizational theory. He is an Associate Director at the E-Governance Institute and the Associate Editor of the Journal of Public Management and Social Policy. He teaches Technology and Public Administration, Leadership and Diversity, E-Governance, The Urban Experience in the United States, and he lectures at the New Jersey Institute of Technology (NJIT).

Petros Ganos obtained his Electrical Engineering diploma from the Electrical Engineering Department, School of Engineering, University of Patras, Greece. He obtained his Ph.D. from the same department. He has worked as an R&D engineer at the Networking Technologies Sector of Research Academic Computer Technology Institute (RACTI), Greece. He is currently an employee of the Municipality of Patras at the Telecommunications and Networks Sector of the Informatics Department, and an external associate of RACTI. His research interests include network administration, broadband networks, and green ICT. He has participated in more than 20 R&D projects, and he has published 3 articles in scientific journals, and 9 research papers, 1 chapter in a book, and 1 book in Greek.

John Garofalakis is Associate Professor at the Department of Computer Engineering and Informatics, University of Patras, Greece, and Director of the applied research department "Telematics Center," of the Research Academic Computer Technology Institute (RACTI). He is responsible and scientific coordinator of several recent European and national IT and Telematics Projects (ICT, INTERREG, etc.). His publications include more than 120 articles in refereed international journals and conferences. His research interests include Web and mobile technologies, performance analysis of computer systems, computer networks and telematics, distributed computer systems, and queuing theory.

J. Ramon Gil-Garcia is an Assistant Professor in the Department of Public Administration and the Director of the Data Center for Applied Research in Social Sciences at *Centro de Investigación y Docencia Económicas (CIDE)* in Mexico City. Currently, he is also a Research Fellow at the Center for Technology in Government, University at Albany, State University of New York (SUNY) and a Faculty Affiliate at the National Center for Digital Government, University of Massachusetts Amherst. His research interests include collaborative electronic government, inter-organizational information integration, adoption and implementation of emergent technologies, digital divide policies, new public management, and multi-method research approaches.

Dimitris Gouscos is a Lecturer with the Department of Communication and Media Studies of the University of Athens and a research fellow of the Laboratory of New Technologies in Communication, Education, and the Mass Media. He has graduated (1990) and has a PhD (1998) in the department of Informatics of the National and Kapodisrian University of Athens. He has participated in European (ESPRIT, IST) and national research and development projects for informational systems, electronic services and digital learning games, while he has published over 40 papers in international scientific conferences and magazines. He has taught in the University of Aegean (2000-2002) and the University of Peloponnese (2002-2006), while he has also collaborated as a Special Consultant with the General Secretariat of Public Administration and Electronic Administration of the Ministry of Interior (2003-2004) and the General Secretariat for Information Systems of the Ministry of National Economy (1997-2002) as well, where he participated in the development of the electronic service TAXISnet. His research interests include digital communication, electronic governance, social media, and digital games

Muhammad Mustafa Kamal is a Research Fellow at the Brunel Business School, Brunel University, UK. He received his PhD from Brunel University in the area of Information Systems (specifically focusing on Enterprise Application Integration Adoption in the Local Government Authorities), in addition, he holds two MSc degrees – Distributed Computing Systems (Greenwich University, London) and Computer Sciences (Punjab Institute of Computer Science, Lahore, Pakistan). His current research interest includes investigating and evaluating factors influencing the decision making process for EAI adoption in public sector, and e-Government/t-Government. In his recent appointment, Dr. Kamal worked as a Post-Doctoral Research Assistant on a European funded research project (Ref: proposal n° 2006/VP021/30137) namely – the REFOCUS (snio**R** **E**mployees training on in**FO**rmation and **C**omm**U**nication technologie**S**) Project. Currently, he is an active editorial review board member for International Journal of Electronic Government Research (IJEGR) and Transforming Government: People, Process and Policy (TG:PPP). He has published in several leading journals such as GIQ, IJIM, JEIM, TG:PPP, IJEGR, and several leading international conferences such as AMCIS, EMCIS, and HICSS.

Vaggelis Kapoulas obtained his Computer Engineering diploma from the Computer Engineering and Informatics Department, School of Engineering, University of Patras, Greece. He obtained his Ph.D. from the same department. He is currently an R&D engineer, and Head of Research Unit 6: Networks Telematics and New Services at Research Academic Computer Technology Institute (RACTI), Greece. His research interests include Networks, Telematics and Algorithms for Distributed Systems. He has extended professional experience in the analysis and design of networks, applications of networks and advanced network services, telematic applications, open & distance learning, and tele-working. He has participated in numerous (more than 50) R&D projects in several national and EU (co-) funded programmes. He has published more than 10 articles in scientific journals and more than 50 research papers in various well-known refereed conferences.

Athanasios Karantjias has obtained the Degree of Electrical and Computer Engineering from University of Patras in 2000 and a PhD in Computer Science from National Technical University of Athens in 2005. He is currently Assistant Professor at the Department of Computer Science of University of Piraeus. His current research interests include identification, design and evaluation of synchronous security and interoperability issues on enterprise architectures, and advanced wireless Information Systems

Fotis Kitsios is Lecturer at University of Macedonia, Department of Technology Management. He has graduated from the Technical University of Crete with a diploma in Production and Management Engineering Department, he went on with a Master's degree on organization and management and he did a PhD on innovation management with a specialization in services. He has worked as a consultant in several SME's in the field of marketing, management, in adopting innovation techniques, and financing. He is also a certified auditor in quality management systems. He has been involved in the implementation and coordination of national and European research projects including: RKMnet, ISTOS, Meta-Foresight, Innoregio, Leonardo da Vinci, Ecos Ouverture, Adapt, Youthstart, and Fair. He has lectured on marketing, management, market research, strategic planning, total quality management, production management, design technologies, data analysis, and technological forecasting at Technical University of Crete, University of Macedonia, and University of Central Greece, as Adjunct Professor, and he has jointly supervised numerous Master's and diploma theses. He also teaches in various public and private vocational training centers and institutions. His scientific research interests mainly focus on new service and product development, innovation measurement, marketing management, and decision making.

Antreas Koskeris has a degree on Computer Engineering and Informatics (University of Patras - 1993). He is now Vice Director of Research Academic Computer Technology Institute's Telematics Centre department, from its establishment, with the task to act as technical coordinator of all Department R&D projects. His previous experience includes: i) He employed in the Research Academic Computer Technology Institute (RACTI) and worked in several projects concerning computer integrated manufacturing, simulation, telematics applications and other research projects. ii) He occupied as a researcher in computer network applications for the University of Patras working in several projects (computer supported cooperative work applications, educational multimedia, electronic commerce applications). His research interests include: actions to deal with rural digital divide, regional development through ICT penetration, risk-crisis management systems, e-government, Web technologies and applications, and simulation.

Ioannis Kotrotsos is an M.Sc. candidate at the Computer Engineering and Informatics Department of Patras University. His area of expertise is Web metrics, data mining, and natural language processing. He received his diploma from the Computer Engineering and Informatics Department Greece.

Athanasia Koumpouri is an M.Sc. candidate at the Computer Engineering and Informatics Department of Patras University. Her area of expertise is text mining, data management and organization, and natural language analysis. She received her diploma from the Computer Engineering and Informatics Department Greece.

Sadaya Kubo is an Associate Professor at Setsunan University, Faculty of Business Administration, Neyagawa City, Osaka, Japan. He received his PhD in industrial engineering from the Osaka Institute of Technology (1999). He is the information policy and the general plan adviser and a personnel training coordinator at Several Cities. His research interests lie in industrial engineering, information management, e-governments, regional development (focusing on regional brands or personnel training, etc.), and management of local governments. He is one of the pioneers of the empirical survey using the Web technology in Japan. Presently, his research is focused on the interaction between residents and the public sector through information and communication technologies (ICT) and the essence of regional development. His publications include "Local E-Governments in Japan: IT Utilization Status and Directions" (with Tatsumi Shimada) in Global E-Government: Theory, Applications and Benchmarking (edited by Latif Al-Hakim, IGI Global, 2007).

Nick Letch is a Senior Lecturer in the Business School at the University of Western Australia where he teaches both undergraduate and postgraduate students and researches in the field of Business Information Systems. His PhD thesis investigated public sector Information Systems and in particular their support for citizen-administration relationships. His key research areas in e-government and knowledge management have been published and presented in a range of national and international forums. Prior to entering academia Nick held positions in data operations and administration with a multinational IT firm as well as general management position in the in the retail sector. He continues to provide consultancy services to government and private sector organisations in areas such as Information Systems evaluation and Information Systems management and governance.

Euripidis Loukis is Assistant Professor of Information Systems & Decision Support Systems at the Department of Information & Communication Systems Engineering, University of the Aegean. He is also Professor at the postgraduate program of the National Academy of Public Administration, in the area of e-Government, and at the Postgraduate Program 'Athens MBA' of the National Technical University of Athens and the Athens University of Economics and Business, in the area of Information Systems and decision support systems. He has been member of the Strategic Planning Unit and ICTs Advisor of the Ministry to the Presidency of Government (1991-2002), Scientific Director (1994-1996) of the Operational Program for the Modernization of Public Administration (with a total budget 300.000.000 Euro) and Information Systems Advisor at the Ministry of Culture and Sport (1995-2000).

Luis Felipe Luna-Reyes is a Professor of Business at the Universidad de las Américas Puebla in México. He holds a Ph.D. in Information Science from the University at Albany. Luna-Reyes is also a member of the Mexican National Research System. His research focuses on electronic government and on modeling collaboration processes in the development of Information Technologies across functional and organizational boundaries.

Aroon Manoharan is an Assistant Professor of Public Administration at Kent State University. His research focuses on e-governance, performance measurement and reporting, organization management, public opinion research, and comparative administration. He holds an MPA from Kansas State University and a Ph.D. from Rutgers University - Newark.

Christos D. Manolopoulos graduated from the School of Law Economics and Political Sciences of the University of Athens (1983) and holds a PhD from the Psychology Department of the Panteion University. He is currently director of the e-Government Sector of the Research Academic Computer Technology Institute (RACTI). His research interests include virtual communities & social networks and agent-based social simulation. He has various publications in international journals and conferences and a long professional record through his participation in various e-government projects.

Drakoulis Martakos is an Associate Professor at the Department of Informatics and Telecommunications at the National and Kapodistrian University of Athens. He received his B.Sc. in Physics, MSc in Electronics and Radio Communications, and Ph.D. in Real-Time Computing from the same university. Professor Martakos is a consultant to public and private organizations and a project leader in numerous national and international projects. He is author or co-author of more than 100 scientific publications and a number of technical reports and studies.

Tunc D. Medeni is a full-time researcher in Turksat and also affiliated to various academic institutions as a part-time staff. He was awarded a PhD degree from the Japan Advanced Institute of Science and Technology (JAIST), Japan, his MS degree from Lancaster University in the UK, and his BS degree from Bilkent University, Turkey. He has contributed to various conference presentations, book chapters, and journal articles in his interest areas such as knowledge management, cross-cultural learning, and e-government. He has been awarded funding and scholarships from Nakayama Hayao Foundation, JAIST, Japanese State in Japan, Lancaster University in UK, and Turkish State and Bilkent University in Turkey, and European Union for his education and research activities as distinguished individual, group and institutional works.

Theofanis-Aristofanis Michail was born in Trikala on 25/11/1978. He graduated from Department of Computer Engineering and Informatics (University of Patras) in 2002. Now he is doing his Master's thesis in P2P Load Balancing. Since 2002 he is working in Telematics Center of the Research Academic Computer Technology Institute (RACTI), participating in many projects concerning computer integrated manufacturing, telematics, databases, computer supported collaboration environments, et cetera. His interests include load balancing, e-commerce, e-learning, e-government, data mining, and information extraction from the Web.

Vasilis Moustakis is a Professor in Operations Management at the Technical University of Crete (TUC), Department of Production Engineering and Management and a Principal Research Investigator at the Institute of Computer Science, Foundation for Research and Technology – Hellas (FORTH) – Biomedical Informatics Laboratory. He has managed numerous R&D projects co-funded via the European Commission and the Greek Secretariat for Research and Technology and has consulted numerous companies and government agencies in Europe and the USA in his areas of expertise (Information Systems, management, economic analysis). He is the Director of the Management Systems Laboratory (http://www.logistics.tuc.gr/). He has supervised numerous PhD and MSc students at the Technical University of Crete and other Academic Institutions in Greece and abroad. He holds a Diploma in Mechanical Engineering (University of Patras, Greece, 1978), a Master's in Engineering Administration and a Doctor of Science (both from the George Washington University, USA, 1980 and 1984, respectively.)

Keiko Nakagawa is a graduate student at Setsunan University, Graduate School of Business Administration and Information, Neyagawa City, Osaka, Japan. She is involved in an empirical survey on e-government and the management levels in the local governments of Japan. Her research interests lie in the regional brands of Japan. She studies the combination of the regional resources and activities through empirical surveys. In addition, she participates in project of building the indicator of the regional vitality in Neyagawa city and designs the street investigation. Furthermore, she is involved in the "Wagaya-Neyagawa" project, which is the practical activities constituting the cooperation between local governments and universities.

James M. Njihia is a Lecturer in Information Systems and Project Management at the School of Business, University of Nairobi, and Chairman of the Department of Management Science. He obtained his PhD from Warwick Business School in 2009 from a study on complex postcolonial contexts for Information Systems projects in developing countries, and MBA and BSc. Eng. from the University of Nairobi in 1995 and 1989, respectively. His research interests include IT project development and evaluation, strategy and Information Systems, postcolonial theory, ICT for development, philosophy of science, critical realism, and complexity theory in management. Before joining academia in 1998, he worked on large scale infrastructure projects as a Civil Engineer, and later as a manager in an export oriented industrial investment promotion programme. He consults in project and Information Systems management for international development agencies, government, and private firms in the southern Africa region.

Flora Oikonomou was born in Megara, Greece, in 1984. She received the Diploma Degree in Computer Engineering and Informatics from the University of Patras, in 2007 and the Postgraduate degree in Computer Science and Engineering in the aforementioned department, in 2010. In her Master's thesis she dealt with personalized Web search by creating semantic clusters of user profiles. Now she is doing her PhD thesis in personalized Web search. Flora Oikonomou has published 4 research works in international conferences in research fields concerning mobile Web technologies, data mining, personalization, and e-government. She is working in Research Academic Computer Technology Institute as researcher and developer. Her research interests include Semantic Web analysis, information retrieval, and mobile Web technologies.

Elpida Prasopoulou holds a PhD in Information Systems from the Department of Management Science and Technology of the Athens University of Economics & Business (2009), a MBA jointly awarded by the National Technical University of Athens and Athens University of Economics and Business (2001) and a BSc (Hons) in Public Administration from the Panteion University of Political and Social Sciences (1999). She worked in many research projects on e-government, identity management, and inter-organizational networks. She has also worked as an external collaborator to the General Secretariat of Research and Development (eBusiness Forum) and N.C.S.R. Demokritos. She has published in academic journals and peer reviewed conferences in Information Systems (e.g., European Journal of Information Systems, Management Science, IFIP 8.2, Bled eConference, Ethicomp, Mediterranean Conference on Information Systems). Her main research interests focus on ICT innovation in late-development countries, e-government, and the interplay of ICTs with a state's administrative tradition.

Ronit Purian has successfully completed her doctoral dissertation under the guidance of Ahituv and Ein-Dor. She applied multiple research methods to profile the technophile individuals in organizations and society, including an evaluative study that yielded the Local E-government Index, and built a new theory of technology adoption and innovation, termed Technophilia. The impact of Information Technology on government and governance is a main research interest as well as transparency levels in business models. Dr. Purian holds BA and MA degrees in Psychology from Tel Aviv University (TAU). Research experience: Policy studies carried out with decision-makers in government, Knesset, academia and the third sector; Research director for the KMI Fellows Program (2007-9); Research fellow at the Institute of Technology and Society, TAU (2008-9); Research consultant for Henry Crown Institute of Business Research, TAU (2009-present). Work experience: Professional writer and editor for leading newspapers in Israel (1985-2005); Consultant for the national e-government unit (2005-present).

Dicle Yurdakul Şahin is a PhD candidate in Business Administration/Marketing and working as a research assistant in the Department of Business Administration at Izmir University of Economics. She received her B.S. and MBA degrees in Business Administration from Dokuz Eylul University. As of June 2010, she completed the course stage of the Ph.D programme and she is currently in the thesis stage. Her research interests include consumer behavior, city branding, and services marketing.

Dimitrios P. Sofotassios received a B.E. degree in Computer Engineering and Informatics from University of Patras in 1989 and a PhD in 2007. He is currently Deputy Director of e-government sector of the Research Academic Computer Technology Institute (RA CTI). His research interests include data structures and algorithms, production management systems, e-government architectures, standards & services, and IS security. He has published over 25 research articles in peer reviewed international journals and conferences, and he is co-author of a book on production management and a book chapter on privacy protection on electronic voting. Since 1990, he supports various teaching activities in the Computer Engineering and Informatics Department of University of Patras and was involved in a number of R&TD projects funded by the European Union, the General Secretariat for Research & Technology of Greece, and private contracts.

Pedro Soto-Acosta holds a PhD in MIS (with European Ph.D mention) and a Master's in Technology Management from University of Murcia. He received his BA in Business Administration from University of Murcia and his BA in Accounting & Finance in Europe from Manchester Metropolitan University (UK). He attended Postgraduate Courses in Management at Harvard University (USA) and participated in the Leonardo da Vinci Programme in Bradford (UK). Pedro Soto has published in prestigious International Journals such as the European Journal of Information Systems, the International Journal of Information Management and the Information Systems Management, among others. His work has won research awards such as the ABG Award to Research and Business Spirit, the Best Research Paper Award at Information Systems One World 2007 (ISoneWorld 2007), held in Las Vegas (USA), and the Best Conference Paper Award at BITMED 2009, held in Beijing (China).

Paul Spirakis, born in 1955, obtained his Ph.D. from Harvard University, in 1982. He is currently the Director of the RACTI and a Full Professor in the Patras University, Greece. He was acknowledged among the top 50 scientists worldwide in Computer Science with respect to "The best Nurturers in Computer Science Research," published by B. Kumar and Y.N. Srikant, ACM Data Mining, 2005. His research interests are algorithms and complexity and interaction of complexity and game theory. Paul Spirakis has extensively published in most of the important computer science journals and most of the significant refereed conferences contributing to over 200 scientific publications. He was elected unanimously as one of the two Vice Presidents of the Council of the EATCS.

Teta Stamati has obtained a Degree in Computer Science from National and Kapodistrian University of Athens (Greece) in 1998. She also holds an MPhil Degree in Enterprise Modelling Techniques from University of Manchester Institute of Science and Technology (UMIST) (UK), an MBA Degree from Lancaster University Business School (UK) and a PhD in Information Systems from Informatics and Telecommunication Department from National and Kapodistrian University of Athens (Greece). She has extensive experience in top management positions in leading IT companies of the Greek and European private sector. She is currently Research Fellow at the Department of Informatics and Telecommunications of National and Kapodistrian University of Athens. Her current research interests include Information Systems, electronic and mobile government, systems migration, and IT security.

Yannis C. Stamatiou was born in 1968 at Volos, Greece. He is currently Assistant Professor at the Department of Mathematics at the University of Ioannina and Consultant on Cryptography and Security at the Research and Academic Computer Technology Institute, both in Greece. His interests lie in cryptography and ICT security with a focus in e-voting and e-government related security protocols and systems. He is acting as a Program Committee member in several security/cryptography related conferences as well as a reviewer for several peer reviewed scientific journals. He has published over 50 research articles in peer reviewed international journals and conferences. He has also participated as a reviewing expert three times in EU calls for proposals in security related areas.

Sofia Stamou is a Lecturer at the Department of Archives and Library Science of the Ionian University. Her area of expertise is text analysis and language processing with an emphasis on semantic analysis of textual data. Her research interests include Web searching, personalization, ontologies, text mining, and data organization. She received her Ph.D. and M.Sc. degrees from the Computer Engineering and Informatics Department of Patras University in 2002 and 2006 respectively and her B.A. in Philosophy from the University of Ioannina in 1999.

George Stylios holds a diploma in Physics from the Aristotle University of Thessaloniki (1994) and a MSc. degree at Information System and Technology (IS&T) from Department of Information Science, at City University of London, UK (2002). He is a PhD student at the department of Computer Engineering and Informatics of the Patras University in Greece. Since June 2006 he is a lecturer at the Technological Educational Institute of Ionian Islands in Greece at the department titled as: "Information Technology Applications in Management and Economics." His research interests are focused at the area of e-government, e-participation, e-culture, e-citizen, data mining, log analysis, and algorithms related to Web analysis.

Maria-Alexandra Vonitsanou is an M.Sc. candidate at the Computer Engineering and Informatics Department of Patras University. Her area of expertise is text mining, data management and organization, and natural language analysis. She received her diploma from the Computer Engineering and Informatics Department Greece.

Alexandros Xenakis belongs to the new academic interdisciplinary field that results from the applications of the information society. He is an Economist, Political Scientist and his Doctoral thesis "Electronic voting in the United Kingdom" was supervised by Professor Ann Macintosh (Professor of E-governance) at Edinburgh Napier University. He teaches in the Postgraduate program "Virtual Communities" of the Department of Psychology of Panteion University. He has taken part in European research projects in the area of e-participation, he has been a Reviewer for FP7 in SSH programme and an expert Consultant for the Hellenic Ministry of Electronic Governance.

Index

D

E

F

G

H

I

J

K

L

M

N

O

P

Q

Y

CPSIA information can be obtained at www.ICGtesting.com
Printed in the USA
269236BV00003B/1/P

9 781609 608392